Politics of Compromise

Politics of Compromise

Coalition Government in Colombia

Edited by
R. Albert Berry
Ronald G. Hellman
Mauricio Solaún

Transaction Books
New Brunswick, New Jersey

This is one of a series of publications sponsored by the Center for Inter-American Relations. All statements of fact and expressions of opinion contained in this publication are solely those of the authors and do not necessarily represent the views of the Center's membership, officers or staff.

Library of Congress Catalog Number: 78-64478
ISBN: 0-87855-301-0 (cloth); 0-87855-723-7 (paper)
Printed in the United States of America

Library of Congress Cataloging in Publication Data

Main entry under title:

Politics of compromise.

1. Colombia—Politics and government—1946-
—Addresses, essays, lectures. 2. Coalition governments
—Colombia—Addresses, essays, lectures. 3. Partido
Conservador (Colombia)—Addresses, essays, lectures.
4. Partido Liberal (Colombia)—Addresses, essays,
lectures. I. Berry, R. Albert. II. Hellman, Ronald G.
III. Solaún, Mauricio.
JL2831.P64 320.9'861'063 78-64478
ISBN 0-87855-301-0
ISBN 0-87855-723-7 pbk.

Politics of Compromise
A Center for Inter-American Relations Book

The Center for Inter-American Relations has worked, since it began operations in 1967, to build in the United States an understanding of the other nations in the Western hemisphere. Through its Literature, Visual, and Performing Arts programs, the Center promotes a broader awareness in the U.S. of the cultural achievements of the Americas. In numerous meetings scheduled each year by the Center's Public Affairs program, political, social, and economic subjects of inter-American interest are discussed and debated. The Center offers an unofficial platform from which public and private leaders, scholars, and social critics can make their thoughts known to diverse international audiences.

The purpose of this publication is to expand the Center's efforts by reaching those interested in inter-American affairs who are not able to participate personally in the Center's activities. We hope that this work, along with previous and forthcoming volumes sponsored by the Public Affairs program, will contribute significantly to the permanent body of research and commentary.

Ronald G. Hellman

Contents

Preface

The essays in this volume focus on the Colombian National Front as a coalition political system; they examine its origins, characteristics, and especially its implications for the social, political, and economic development of Colombia. The National Front is of general interest as an apparently successful political arrangement, which returned civilian rule to Colombia after the massive *Violencia* of the 1940s and 1950s and the resulting military government of General Rojas Pinilla. A sixteen-year coalition regime, the Front began in 1958 when the two traditional parties—Conservative and Liberal—agreed to alternate the presidency and share the government equally. It was formally terminated on schedule in 1974, but certain coalition features were retained for the future. This continuation, along with the relative control of civilian violence and the liberalization experienced by the polity, suggest the political successes of the National Front. The objective of this volume is to evaluate the Front in terms of the goals of its founders and of other relevant criteria of political, social, and economic development.

The book results from four meetings during the first half of 1974, under the aegis of the Center for Inter-American Relations. These meetings, which were supported by grants from the Ford Foundation and the Tinker Foundation, were part of the Center's ongoing series of "country studies" seminars. Our seminar brought together for sustained discussion a group of individuals with considerable expertise on Colombia from a variety of professional, disciplinary and political perspectives: including Colombians, North Americans, political scientists, historians, sociologists, economists, journalists, and businessmen. The diversity of our group contributed significantly to the lively and exhaustive debates during the duration of the seminar. We have sought to include the most constructive aspects of those debates in the expectation that the readers of this book will be able to share our findings.

Part I of this volume discusses the National Front in historical perspective.

As Solaún and Kline emphasize in the first two chapters, that history has been dramatically characterized by a system of two powerful traditional parties between which the so-called "hereditary hatreds" have grown up. The military, meanwhile, has played an unusually small and dependent role in Colombian history. The National Front is one of a series of compromises between the Conservative and Liberal parties in Colombia's history; it had many partial precedents. Solaún develops a theory of compromise and violence in Colombian interparty relationships. The intensity of the pre-Front violence is explained partly by the relatively long period since the previous bouts of major political violence, and partly by the type of political objects that tend to serve as "issues" in the interparty competition. The incentive to coalition is, in turn, a reflection of the imminence of violence (in retrospect or in prospect) and of the existence of an arbitrary executive, especially one which is antiparty. Kline notes that the Front had many points in common with the previous coalitions; it differed in having constitutional force and legitimacy over a fixed period, in the complete political control the two traditional parties wielded under it, and in the focus on economic development as an objective of the coalition per se.

Part II reviews some of the developments in political institutions and processes during the National Front period, including such related areas as the military and the church. Losada discusses electoral institutions, especially the degree of electoral participation. He concludes that the low levels of participation, particularly toward the middle of the period, were consistent with the historical pattern in Colombia; high turnouts have tended to be limited to elections in which the two major parties seriously contested the victory. Electoral abstention did not necessarily suggest a high degree of public disaffection with the administrations. In some ways, political competition during the Front era was greater than in the past. Hoskin discusses the restoration and the character of the Colombian Congress under the Front—no sessions had been held between 1949 and the fall of Rojas Pinilla in 1957. While formally restored, Congress did not regain its previous power: the initial need for more than a simple majority to enact legislation and the parity provisions dampened its dynamism, and the Constitutional Reform of 1968 undercut its powers, especially in economic matters; the technocratic trend in government—a strong current during the Front era—detracted from traditional political inputs.

The major threats to the smooth passage of the Front included the challenge from Rojas Pinilla, which centered on the electoral process, and the challenge from General Ruiz Novoa, which drew strength from the armed forces. Dix discusses the nature of the political opposition, from López Michelsen's dissidence within the Liberal party to Rojas' almost victorious popular campaign of 1970. Ruhl explains the generally correct relations between the military and the National Front governments—interrupted briefly by Ruiz Novoa's maverick challenge—as the result of several factors: a tradition of nonintervention, the absence or weakness of major precipitants for coup d'état activity, and a military ideological stance close to that of the civilian governments.

As discussed by Wilde, the Front period was an eventful one for the church. The constitutional arrangement eased the disengagement of the church from its traditional involvement in partisan conflict. Freed from that conflict, the church was able to devote new energies to its own structures and try to create the basis for an active pastoral involvement in social change. However, this new aspiration, which reflected international Catholic currents, created considerable internal dissension. Conflict was constrained by the essentially "institutional" conception the church had of itself, with a resultant emphasis on its own survival, by accommodation when necessary. In the later years of the Front, the church drew back from some of its earlier social initiatives.

The chapters by Cepeda and Michell, and Bagley and Edel reflect two aspects of the political character of the National Front. Cepeda and Mitchell probe the implications of the evident trend toward technocracy during these years, in particular the push given to that trend by certain international agencies and the heightened influence that they gained in Colombian economic affairs. Bagley and Edel review the inconsistent attitudes of Front governments toward local grass-roots organization. While formally and, to a certain point, actually sponsoring community action groups and selective lower-class interest group development, the Front (especially the more conservative administrations) came to see some of these activities as a threat and felt bound to control them.

Part III studies the policies adopted by National Front governments in certain key economic and social areas. Reviewing overall economic policy and development, Berry concludes that considerable economic structural change and growth characterized these years, especially during the last two administrations. Nevertheless, consistent with the political constraints posed by the maintenance of a coalition regime, no major policy was implemented to reduce extreme economic inequalities. Economic policy was, however, relatively innovative and sophisticated in comparison with that of many other countries. Industrial development, discussed by Thoumi, was induced by a fairly typical protectionist apparatus, which favored capital intensive industries and largely benefited the privileged economic sectors. While an agrarian reform law was passed in 1961, Havens, Flinn, and Lastarría find that it had little redistributive impact on the agrarian structure. The overall agricultural sector policy of the Front governments continued to be directed mainly to the benefit of the large agriculturalists. Educational levels advanced considerably during the Front, though Arnove finds that, once again, the gap between the rich and the poor subsisted. In the area of population policy, however, the

National Front governments were particularly innovative. McGreevey describes how they moved quietly toward modern policies. Here, perhaps, more than in other areas, the bipartisan character of the government prevented any successful fundamentalist overreaction from blocking progress.

In Part IV, Berry and Solaún summarize the Front experiment as having largely succeeded in the political objectives of the founders. These were to design a workable coalition between the two traditional parties, in order to establish the basis for interparty cooperation and compromise, while maintaining the reins of power in the hands of the civilian elite. While the administrations maintained themselves close to the center of the Colombian political spectrum—the coalition character of the regime assured this—they were also increasingly professional in their policy making, and as the period went on, this professionalism contributed to an improving record of economic growth. The fruits of that growth did not go exclusively to the wealthy, although the large socioeconomic disparities continued to be evident. Despite the efforts toward an "education in compromise" implied by the National Front, there remained sufficient indications of the persistence of some of the endemic political problems. Therefore, the need for continued efforts in combining political institution building with economic development seem warranted, lest Colombia return to periods of violence or repression commensurate to the past.

We wish to express our collective appreciation to many people who helped us to organize and to conduct the seminar series. Special mention goes to those who participated in the seminars and to those who, although unable to attend, contributed their time to respond to our inquiries and requests. Finally, we express our appreciation to the Center for Inter-American Relations for making this series possible, as well as to the Ford Foundation and the Tinker Foundation for their support to this project.

The Editors

Politics of Compromise

Part I
Historical Perspective

Chapter 1

Colombian Politics: Historical Characteristics and Problems

Mauricio Solaún

This chapter surveys some general characteristics and problems of Colombian twentieth-century politics prior to the National Front, the Frente Nacional, in order to throw light on the origins of this coalition regime and help to place it in perspective. Colombian politics is of particular interest as a case in which a two-party system did not result in the long-run institutionalization of a representative democracy; the salutary impact of a small number of parties for successful democratization is well recognized.[1] The recurrent but sparse attempts to organize competitive third parties have so far been unsuccessful in Colombia.[2] Traceable to the early postindependence period in the nineteenth century, the two traditional parties showed their resilience by their survival and even reactivation during the period of New Dealish sociopolitical changes that Colombia experienced starting in the early 1930s. This contrasts sharply with the emergence in many Latin American countries during the 1930s and 1940s of new reformist parties eventually known as the Aprista parties. In Colombia as in the United States, the Depression social reform phenomenon led to a realignment of political forces within the existing two-party system, transforming the previous majority party into the minority.[3] However, in Colombia, the end result of such changes was not democratic reform but escalated political violence of civil war proportions—La Violencia[4]—political breakdown via coup d'état (1953), and an authoritarian military regime (1953-1957). The subsequent attempts to restore civilian party-system rule and end the lingering *violencia*, the concern of this book, took the form of a coalition between the traditional parties.

Despite the existence of a democratic competitive constitution during a large part of the twentieth century, Colombia prior to the National Front had failed to go beyond the institutionalization of *protodemocratic* regimes, a form of partial democracy whose characteristics will be discussed. Neither a mass democracy nor an elitist competitive aristocracy had emerged.[5] Even before universal suffrage was granted (in 1936 literacy and property qualifications for voting were removed; not until 1954 were women formally authorized to vote), electoral competition between Liberals and Conservatives for the control of government was associated with electoral illegalities and escalated violence. Consequently, interparty competition was exceptional and brought with it the threat of civil war. Rather than compete, the opposition party frequently abstained from electoral participation, especially in presidential contests. Between the turn of the century and the initiation of the National Front in 1958, bipartisan competition for the presidency occurred only in 1922, 1930, and 1946. The typical mode for changing the president was by competition within the ruling party. Cleavages along party lines were too disruptive to be contained even by a representative democracy with limited participation.[6] It was impossible to maintain competitive elections proper—those in which party majority status or government control was at stake—for any length of time without escalated violence. The only time sustained interparty electoral competition occurred (1946-49), the result was La Violencia and regime breakdown.[7]

That a truly competitive aristocracy or oligarchy involving the open competition for power between the elites of the two parties did not materialize is noteworthy in light of the argument that the culture, rules, and practices of competitive politics develop more easily in a system with such limited participation. It is assumed that among a small elite the severity of conflict can be kept within bounds, because they have family and friendship ties and common interests and ideology. If public opposition to government and interparty competition cannot be institutionalized in this more homogeneous oligarchical context, the probability of successful passage to the conflictive complexities of a modern mass democracy would appear to be small.[8] The origins of the National Front can be traced precisely to an unsuccessful evolution from a noncompetitive oligarchy toward a mass participatory system, i.e., to an unsuccessful democratization of the polity. We must explore the problems that impeded this evolution.

The *traditional political system* was characterized by the hegemony of one of the parties.[9] This reflected the doubts, especially by the opposition party (including its elite), that it could win power through nonfraudulent elections.

But (employing Dahl's terminology) the system was not a "closed hegemony" or dictatorship.[10] First, the constitutional and other formal-legal texts were democratic. Second, the ruling party did not generally enjoy a total monopoly over governmental positions; there was a recurrent tendency to seek minority representation in the cabinet, partly because full-blown party dictatorship tended to lead to escalated violence.[11] The system was a *partially* democratic party hegemony. For instance, freedom of opposition through the press was (and has been) fairly respected. Office was held on a temporary basis, the executive normally changing according to schedule through periodic ruling party elections; and the opposition often participated in the lesser, nonpresidential elections in which ruling party hegemony was not at stake. Thus, while interparty electoral competition for the control of government or the executive was a pattern seldom carried to the point of its democratic constitutional authorization, the system allowed selective manifestations of public opposition and opposition participation. In short, some democratic constitutional norms were respected in some situations but not in others. There was enough democratic normative compliance and ambiguity so that some Colombians could proclaim, and take pride in, the nation's civilian, democratic institutions in what were in fact only protodemocratic conditions.

The traditional system consisted then of an executive-rotating, partially democratic, two-party system. While the party system failed as a national integrative mechanism in the long run—periods of peace were interrupted by dramatically high levels of mass interparty violence—the Colombian polity was, nevertheless, characterized by relatively institutionalized civilian control. Substantial civilian violence was not frequent,[12] and since 1901 there was no successful political revolution and only two military coups d'état (in 1953 and 1957). In contrast to the more erratic patterns characteristic of other coup-ridden Latin American nations, the dominant party in Colombia typically changed the executive through legally scheduled, and hence regularized and predictable elections. The direct relationship between the party system and the Colombian type of electoral institutionalization or civilian control need not be entirely definitional or tautological. General Reyes (1904-09) and General Rojas Pinilla (1953-57) were the only two leaders who sought to remain in power beyond their legal term in office—what the Latin American literature calls *continuismo*. They did so in conjunction with their attempts to displace the two-party system.[13] Electoral manipulations and illegalities were not usually associated with the maintenance in power of a specific *leader*, but of the ruling party oligarchy. *Party*, as opposed to personal, *continuismo* was the Colombian mode. A measure of party strength—the parties transcend a leader, such party *continuismo* finds a parallel in post-Calles Mexico. However, the Colombian phenomenon was earlier, and ruling party mechanisms were (and continue to be) more decentralized and less bureaucratic than in Mexico, as reflected in the enduring Colombian tradition of open candidacy of several presidential aspirants, and open competition among hegemonic party factions. In Colombia there has been no tradition like the Mexican *tapado* (the hidden one), where the official candidate of the ruling party is selected privately by the government.

The nature and maintenance of the traditional system rested on the strength of both parties. Prior to the initiation of the National Front, the minority party was itself a relatively strong political force.[14] Consequently, when it occurred, partisan violence was very substantial and costly, a fact which inhibited violence. Civilian violence did not result in successful takeover of the government by the opposite party; the opposition was incapable of replacing the party in power because the ruling party, particularly under conditions of polarization, could count upon sufficient rank-and-file support willing to employ counterviolence. Progovernment civilian gangs would form and help to block a successful takeover. On the other hand, it was difficult for the military to intervene effectively to displace civilian elite control, because even under conditions of interparty strife, effective support was not easy to obtain or maintain.[15] In effect, winning the support of one party by ousting the other one could imply the short run loss of support from a relatively strong minority. And of course, any actual intervention to displace the two-party system could be and was eventually challenged by successful interparty coalition, as in the cases of General Reyes and General Rojas.

Typically, the experience of extreme violence in a situation of relative equilibrium of forces would eventually prompt the urge for compromise and lead to coalition government. In other words, violence itself was conducive in the aftermath to the development of ''civic'' restraint. It was not a case of legal participation contributing to the efficient development of civic virtues; rather the opposite. The historical recurrence of civil war, such costly violence, produced a mutual ''socialization through violence'' which resulted in a relatively lasting, though not permanent, spirit of compromise.[16] After Mil Días, more than four decades passed before comparable massive violence emerged, and the subsequent coalition governments lasted approximately two decades. La Violencia resulted in the National Front coalition regime, which is still partly in effect. In my opinion, this strength of the two parties was the relatively enduring or endemic structural variable that led to the periodic search for coalition governments, while actual coalitions were precipitated by specific situational factors.[17] In sum, in Colombia the minority party counted upon sufficient support to make it very costly to govern with extreme disregard for its interest. As evidenced by La Violencia, party dictatorship further escalated violence, and prolonged escalated violence eventually endangered the vested economic and political interests of the elites of both parties. Thus, full-blown dictatorships have been rare in Colombian history, and paradoxically, prolonged violence itself has led to coalition governments, since neither party was capable of really vanquishing the other.[18] Despite the recurrent need to employ the state of siege to quell civil disruptions, Colombia's traditional patterns stand in contrast to that widespread Latin American historical mode of political control: the coup-prone, military based, "authoritarian" regime, with its nonrotating personalistic leadership, a weak or nonexistent party system, and relative reliance on corporate interest-group participation.[19]

Little is known about the historical sources of party system strength. Colombian parties have long been national in scope and have commanded a multiclass following—in fact the belief that sectors of illiterate peasants were often among the most partisan adherents has been part of the local political folklore.[20] The parties have also been ideologically heterogeneous. Indeed, party identification has tended to be inherited rather than the product of a thoughtful or ideological decision. One can find in Colombia the equivalents of a U.S. liberal Republican and a conservative Democrat; in both societies the parties have contained more and less ideologically-oriented and radical subgroups. In addition, Colombia has experienced periods of greater and lesser ideologization of politics.

However, any meaningful discussion of party identification in Colombia prior to the National Front must start from two propositions. First, for various groups, party identification was linked to a personal or family experience involving violence, creating a basis for more or less ingrained partisan hostility—the so-called "hereditary hatreds."[21] Secondly, the Conservative party was historically closely linked to the Catholic church. The *successful* involvement of the Colombian church in the party system, clearly apparent well into the 1950s, was unusual for Latin America.[22] Conservatives considered themselves the laymen most loyal to or sympathizing with the spiritual and material concerns of the church. No Conservative administration would propose what a Liberal did: the elimination in the 1936 constitution of any reference to the Catholic church as the official church of the nation. Such a theocratic link provided a basis for conceptualizing and "ideologizing" party differences. Moreover, given Catholic historical claims to doctrinal and moral truth and certainty, it was a source of partisanship.[23] Surely, both factors strengthened the tendency to "moralize" interparty conflict, providing elements for a Manichean definition of interparty conflict—e.g., a total confrontation between "all good" and "all evil" forces—that conflictive definition that has been related in the contemporary social science literature to escalated conflict and violence. Specifically, the traditional political culture of party identification with its nonsecular elements constituted a more or less latent, endemic factor that could foster extreme partisanship (*sectarismo*) when interparty competition was precipitated.

One indication of the relative positions of the parties can be obtained by observing their radical wings. Liberal extremism was "socialistic"; Conservative, a "clericalism with a theocratic vision of society."[24] While Liberal radicalism was mainly concerned with class "exploitation" and the "redemption" of the working class from capitalism, themes well known to the reader, Conservative radicals were mostly preoccupied with the struggle between "orthodoxy" and "heresy," God and Lucifer, not necessarily in a figurative or metaphorical sense. The flavor of *one* of the styles of politics present in the traditional system can be obtained from the comments made on the election of Liberal President Olaya Herrera in 1930 by the presbyter of the Cathedral of Santa Rosa de Osos, when he publicly asked who could believe in the promises of tolerance that came from this "refined Liberal who on various occasions has made frank professions of atheism. . . . What ignominy! The emblem of the Fatherland which has been consecrated to the Divine Heart of Jesus Christ, illuminating the body of a persecutor of Christ."[25]

Liberalism was a relatively more urban and cosmopolitan phenomenon.[26] The Liberal elites were more likely to mirror themselves in Paris or London, while Conservatives sought the Hispanic traditions. The Conservative elite was not only more exposed to Catholic education: it was significantly more provincial in origin and less active in Bogotá's social circles.[27] Some Conservatives stereotyped the Liberals as somewhat frivolous urbanite followers of "fashions in international ideology for lack of any securely anchored convictions comparable to those of Conservatism."[28] Conversely, some Liberals perceived Conservatives as "traditional" or "static" oriented. There were alleged differences in "temperament" associated to party identification.[29] Liberals were viewed by some as being somewhat anarchical, Jacobinical, or libertarian; Conservatives as being preoccupied more with order and reaction than with progress.

Still, Liberal mainstream solutions were more "welfarist" than socially radical or socialist. Similar to the New Deal American experience of the Democratic party, the Liberal achievement of majority party status after 1933 was partly the product of its relatively greater linkage to the more modern and "class conscious" urban areas in an urbanizing society, and partly of its maintenance of traditional rural ties. Nevertheless, Conservative social thought did not espouse the "laissez-faire" doctrines of American conservatives but rather reflected, significantly through Jesuit educational influence, papal preoccupations with the increased "individualism," "anarchic equalitarianism," and "materialism" that seemed to accompany post-French Revolution developments.[30] The stress was on moral responsibility as opposed to individualistic, materialistic profiteering. Catholicism favored a third theoretical alternative between capitalism and communism: a class collaborationist organic model that would restore and expand medieval urban corporativist guild structures.[31]

The above differences define the framework for pre-Frente interparty distinctions and, hence, for analyzing political conflict in Colombia. A few further clarifications are in order. We are faced with multivariate phenomena; no single factor explains the nature of interparty differences; the effects of some factors are "suppressed" by the presence of other factors. For instance, despite the noted sociological differences in party leadership and support, the multiclass, national coalition nature of both parties clearly reduces the validity of a class or urban-rural conflict interpretation.[32] Further, Liberals, as well as Conservatives, could have a Catholic self-identification. Most Liberals were at least nominally Catholic; any disavowal of this inherited religious identity was cumbersome in a religiously (almost) unitary society. In accordance with Catholic tradition, the church's theocratism was only partial: the fusion between the church and Conservative party structures was not total. While segments of the lower clergy often went to the extreme of campaigning for Conservative candidates, the highest religious authority did not as a general rule condemn the Liberal party as incompatible with Catholicism but rather acted out the ecumenical, paternalistic role of the "Mother Church." That is, the church viewed with disappointment the somewhat inadequate behavior of some of her (Liberal) children while not closing the door to receiving them warmly. (On occasion, particularly during periods of intense interparty strife as in the late 1940s, some bishops did openly condemn Liberalism on ideological or doctrinaire grounds.)[33] The anticlericalism of the Liberal elite, on the other hand, had more bark than bite during this century.[34] At the same time, the injection of the religious issue into interparty competition reinforced any existing tendency toward moralizing and ideologizing political competition, thereby contributing toward escalation of conflict. In Colombia the religious element, more than any other factor, served to differentiate the parties and provide the basis for their ideological differences.

Another dimension of the pre-National Front party system deserves comment: the substantially upper-class character and the resilience of the traditional elites of both parties. Colombia's ruling group was fully renovated by the early 1930s through the cooptation of new elements socialized into the two parties. The bulk of this new generation were young individuals fairly well integrated with "society" circles, their private values and norms. In contrast to many Latin American countries, the Colombian traditional system was characterized by "parties of notables," not middle-class-led parties. Such upper-class presence surely lent weight to them and facilitated this class' political control in what remained a preindustrial society. Party leadership was highly resilient. Despite recurrent rumors that the political system was on the verge of total collapse,[35] the party elites were not much displaced, either by the strain of La Violencia or by the 1953 military coup d'état. In 1958, five years after the coup, the same small group of civilians that had been ruling or controlling the opposition since the early 1930s returned to power with the restoration of civilian rule under the National Front. (Colombia is currently experiencing the second generational change of this century. It is still too early to determine when the total demise of the old guard will occur and whether or not its protégés will remain in power.) It can be argued that to a large extent these elites "anticipated" demands for reforms, articulating the interests of unorganized or weakly organized strata. Reform movements tended not to be the product of "undetainable" participatory demands on the part of the masses.[36] Instead, they largely resulted from the political will of groups fully integrated with the nation's exclusivist social circles, following the pattern of modernization by a dominant elite. Since Colombia has been characterized more by a "rhetorical" than "real" reformism, it is difficult to assess the full impact of these policies.[37] Nor is it clear that "reform" contributed to political system maintenance. The banner of reform could threaten vested interests and lead to elite divisiveness. This appears to have been the case during the 1940s when division among the traditional political elite caused a temporary increase in the strength of middle-class counterelites, violence, and political breakdown. During the National Front, Lleras Restrepo's "reformism" was also followed by elite divisiveness, as measured by the plurality of presidential candidates in 1970, and by the maximization of the Rojista counterelite threat. As I will attempt to show, under system-stress the elite code of sociability and etiquette, or "aristocratic" good manners and propriety, more than the constitution or the law itself, was a critical normative safeguard in restraining tendencies toward tyranny and in reintegrating the polity. Such was the nature of the equilibrium in the traditional protodemocratic two-party system.

As noted earlier, and in contrast to the weak attachment to political parties found in many Latin American countries, "significant" elements from all segments of Colombian society identified traditionally with both parties.[38] Party vigor was characterized by leadership plurality and decentralization or factionalism. The party system was flexible. Factionalism counteracted any propensity to form new movements or parties, since dissident elements could compete for power without a need to abandon the parties, simply by presenting their own lists of candidates in elections. Decentralized factionalism allowed dissidents to capture control of political office at the legislative, departmental, or local level without having to challenge the top national party oligarchies directly. There was an informal tradition of coopting or incorporating electorally successful "dissidents" into the mainstream of the party "structures," final elections often serving the function of the United States primary election.

Perhaps Colombia's middle level socioeconomic development within the Latin American spectrum also favored party system continuity. The absence of any large proportion of unassimilated Amerindian populations permitted an early filtering down of party identification to the local level, thus providing a measure of rank-and-file anchorage to the parties. As urbanization and industrialization came to Colombia slowly and in small doses, the party system was not even faced with any major working-class challenge before the National Front.

But of the various historical features affecting the Colombian party system, the role of the church was most important. In this relatively religious and unurbanized land, the consolidation of the two-party system itself was facilitated by church support of one of the parties. Given these conditions, anticlerical forces had to be relatively united under a single party label or succumb to great political weakness. And Colombia was still sufficiently developed and a far too complex regional mosaic for the control of any one party by a single leader or family from any one region; hence, the oligarchic, as opposed to monocratic, party structures.

To summarize, Colombia exemplifies the historical inability of a Third World two-party system to evolve even as far as a representative democracy with limited participation or an interparty competitive oligarchy. Attempts to go beyond protodemocracy by engaging in competitive interparty electoral politics led to escalated violence; so did full-blown party dictatorship. The National Front was the latest attempt to cure this "pathology" of Colombian democracy. To better understand this pathology we must pursue a bit more our historical sociological analysis.

EQUILIBRIUM AND STRESS IN THE TRADITIONAL SYSTEM

From the end of the Mil Días civil war until 1930, Colombia had relatively little interparty conflict. The contrast with La Violencia suggests that this period, characterized mainly by an executive rotating protodemocratic Conservative regime, deserves analysis. The first source of system strain is traceable to the Civil War itself and took the form of a short-run erosion of support for the two-party system at the center of the polity. Just as La Violencia resulted in Rojas' attempt to displace the two-party system, Mil Días was followed by an attempt to supplant traditional party rule, first by General Reyes in 1904-09, then by the Republican Party in 1910-14. Reyes sought to develop national unity by creating nonpartisan institutions, such as a professional army, and bringing both Conservatives and Liberals into his administration. He tried to constitute an authoritarian regime to provide his continuance in power; as is often the case with this type of Latin American regime, he justified his personal *continuismo* as necessary to minimize interparty conflict. The Republican party crystalized with the Conservative-led interparty coalition to unseat Reyes. It attempted later to acquire an independence of its own and to break the two-party tradition; Republicans saw identification with the traditional parties as conducive to violence.[39] The Republican party was overwhelmingly defeated in its attempt to reelect a president for the 1914-18 term by a Conservative-Liberal coalition, which took a Conservative to the presidency with 90 percent of the vote. It became apparent that the success of third-party movements would not easily be achieved.

The dislocating impact of the Civil War on the two-party system was temporary. However, the violence had more lasting effects. Just as La Violencia ultimately led to the National Front coalition, Mil Días resulted in minority representation in cabinets—albeit less formalized—until 1920. With the exception of the violent election of 1922, Liberals abstained from mobilizing their masses and performed as a fairly loyal opposition during the entire period until 1930. It was this relative interparty equilibrium and the absence of any sustained competitive mass political mobilization to demonstrate majority status that minimized violence during the period. As the 1946-49 experience illustrated, interparty coalitions have not typically eliminated violence unless one of the parties was willing to accept, at least tacitly, a minority role.[40] That the Liberals engaged in a politics of restrained opposition and did not present a presidential candidate except in 1922, actually supporting some of the Conservative candidates, indicates that they generally accepted or adapted to a minority role during the period.

The tranquility of this period appears to have been a reaction to the Mil Días civil war, and its alleged consequences. The war had ended with the defeat of the Liberal attempt to overthrow Conservative rule; yet it was not interpreted as a clear Conservative victory. The war had been long and deliberate. In contrast to future interparty violence, the party leaders themselves led the armies; at the end an estimated one hundred thousand were dead.[41] Above all there was a general feeling at the time that had Colombia not been divided and exhausted by the war, Panama would not have been lost. A strong consensus, reflected in the press of both parties, arose on the need to prevent civil wars at practically any cost in order to safeguard the national territory. Not even under maximum pressure for civil war, such as was provided by the 1922 presidential campaign, did the specter of Panama disappear. It is perhaps significant of the style of politics that emerged from the ashes of the war—somewhat aristocratic in orientation, purely civilian, and largely adaptive—that the president of the Bogotá Jockey Club, when it reopened its doors, was a man who later was to become president on two critical occasions (when presidents Reyes and Suárez resigned, 1909 and 1921), a gentleman of high social prestige also known for his ability to compromise.

Politics of Restrained Refinement

In order to understand the nature of the equilibrium found in the traditional political system it is necessary to take a closer look at the opposition style that prevailed until 1930. Opposition activity was concentrated in the press under the leadership of *El Tiempo* and *El Espectador*. Briefly Republican—in this lies the direct link between Mil Días and the opposition style—these two newspapers became the platform for the Liberal leadership and intelligentsia. As they grew into Colombia's "big press" they created the climate of public opinion that permitted the Liberal victory in the 1930 presidential election. Because of its origins I shall refer to this Liberal political style as Republicanism.[42] Republicanism sought a nonviolent, somewhat aristocratic (rule by courteous, well-bred citizens), but pluralistic political system. Rather than an abrupt displacement of the political or social elites, the goal was gradual "penetration" and "cooptation." Republicanism intended to promote political tolerance, *tolerancia racional* and mutual respect, *respeto mutuo*.[43] It attacked violence as "barbarism" and saw its mission as one of "civilizing" Colombia by bringing foreign culture to the country and thus integrating the nation into the "universal culture." As children of the Enlightenment, a firm belief in the "inevitability of progress" gave Republicans hope for Colombian progress and their civilizing mission.

Three key aspects of Republicanism warrant attention. First, there was a desire to further the secularization of politics by eliminating the divine or sacred sources of Conservative power; a total structural differentiation between the church and the party system was sought. At the same time, as gradualists, an open or total split with the church was avoided. The need to emphasize the fact that they were Catholics was felt at times. These "modernizing" efforts were carried out in other institutions as well but not without difficulties.[44]

Secondly, moderation was sought by espousing an elegant orientation that was antipopulistic and condemned emotionalism and personal or moral insult. Republicanism equated intellectual pursuits with *cultura*, that is, not only knowledge but more importantly etiquette or good manners as well. Criticisms were meant to be "impersonal" in nature; differences of opinion should not involve lack of courtesy. The ideals were *discusión culta* (enlightened discussion) and *serenidad* (tranquility). In short, by opposing the "personification" or "moralization" of conflict, expressions which are of the essence of political extremism, Republicanism adopted a moderate antiradical position.[45] Both were considered to be manifestations of populism or demagoguery made to please the uncultivated and unsophisticated peripheral segments. Yet their orientations were not extremist or "oligarchical"; while socialism was considered "premature," Republicanism favored the growth of the labor movement.[46] The ideal was to spread the ethos of *cultura* to the lower segments of the population through educational expansion in a pluralistic system.

A third objective was to build trust among the different elites and sectors, in order to combat tendencies toward conspiratorial conceptions of politics. In 1912, for example, General Uribe, leader of the Liberal party, accused the government of planning "civil war and criminal acts." *El Tiempo* demanded factual evidence to support the accusation.[47] And nothing conspiratorial or sinister was seen in the progress of workers. The editorial of May 1, 1920—Labor Day—is revealing: "This holiday is celebrated with happiness and solemn serenity, free of any dangers or threats, and should not disturb anyone who knows just how absurd it would be to close the door to those universal currents that carry on their swirling waves elements of good and equality.'' In attempting to override the distrustful tendencies so apparent in Iberian-American political culture, Republicanism was seeking to overcome a trait inimical to a democratic or civic culture.

In sum, after Mil Días, a politics of ''restrained refinement'' materialized on the part of the opposition, oriented toward facilitating the development of democratic politics. Yet any inference that such style only prevailed among the principal center of opposition is unwarranted. It appears that the emphasis on the ethos of *cultura* became fairly generalized within the more urban and centric segments of the society.[48] Such ideas as that Colombia should take pride in its culture, in the ''cultivated'' capital city of Bogotá (called the ''Athens of South America''),[49] and in its legalistic governments were common. In contrast to the neighboring Latin American countries, ''historians, statesmen and poets, not the military''[50] were the pride of Colombia, a country where presidential candidates took newspaper columns to further their cause, rather than resorting to more forceful methods. Equilibrium and a sense of ''democracy'' and legalism were brought to the traditional system by elites who publicly upheld both a democratic creed and private norms of sociability or etiquette that were conducive to civility. Nevertheless, as indicated by the events surrounding the 1922 election, the first interparty presidential competition since the end of Mil Días, the polity was incapable of going beyond its protodemocratic characteristics. It is important to analyze this election.

The 1922 Violence

Factionalism was an important dynamic factor in the traditional system, and consequently, a source of stress. Encouraged by and miscalculating Conservative divisiveness, Liberals unsuccessfully competed for the presidency in the 1922 election. A look at that election indicates that the Liberal elite conducted a short, restrained electoral mobilization.[51] The election took place in February 1922; Liberals did not decide to participate with their own candidate until December 1921. During the campaign, Conservatives sought Liberal participation in the cabinet. Both the Liberal and Conservative candidates and directorates made public statements seeking moderation. Liberal candidate Herrera stated that Liberals ''should not forget that Conservatives, too, are patriots''[52] and sent personal greetings to his opponent, Ospina. As the electoral debate continued, it became more heated. Ospina and Herrera cosigned a manifesto asking for peace. Other efforts to alleviate the increasing interparty suspicion and mutual distrust included personal visits to the president by opposition leaders, and the refutation of rumors that there would be electoral fraud on the part of the government and that the Liberals would drag the country into civil war if defeated at the polls. An attempt was made by the elites to define the parties as legitimate and trustworthy competitors, orientations supportive of democratic, competitive politics. Despite efforts on both sides to alleviate interparty conflict, it escalated, particularly on the periphery, where violence coexisted with mutual accusations of *illegality*: ''electoral fraud,'' ''government persecution,'' ''opposition violence,'' etc. In sum, despite these elite efforts, a syndrome of *normlessness*, technically a form of alienation[53] materialized in the periphery. Ultimately the elite itself was drawn into this syndrome. The Liberal elite declared that Herrera had been defeated because electoral norms had been broken, i.e., there had been electoral fraud. While unwilling to organize revolutionary violence, the Liberals proclaimed electoral abstention for the future, thereby tacitly defining the government as illegitimate. Abstention orders reduced political participation, subsequently ending the violence.

A closer look at the patterns of *violencia* is warranted. First, they were not associated with a class uprising nor lower-class vindicatory violence. It was not characterized by executions of landlords by peasants, peasant refusals to pay rents, or the like. Payne describes the Colombian violence as a strictly political conflict[54] or political partisanship proper. The conflict was along party lines between Conservative and Liberal town and rural folk, over an election, i.e., over political power. In stable democracies, political conflict proper, as a polar ideal-type, would be over ''personnel,'' e.g., the ''best man or team,'' or over the optimal implementation of commonly agreed upon policies. In Colombia, however, political conflict tended to escalate. When it escalated, the political issues went beyond ''personnel'' or even discrete policy preferences, to involve the alleged *criminal* behavior or normative breakdown produced by the countergroup. The conflict thus moved beyond the realm of ''consensus'' politics.[55] Although the described ideological background differences between the two parties exacerbated the partisan conflict, much of the reported overt conflict at the local level took, as its paramount issue, this *collective criminality* dimension.

The patterns of escalated conflict at the local level indicated the presence of two outstanding and eventually quite generalized factors: (1) the belief that the opposition was not law abiding, i.e., that opponents were conspiring to or engaging in criminal acts; and (2) the belief that governmental authorities were not neutral, i.e., that governmental formal organizations were making illegal, highly partisan decisions. These two beliefs denote the weakness of the rule of law or formal-legal integration in the polity. They led to escalated conflict and violence via two key processes: the ''diffusion of illegality'' and the ''diffusion of deformalization.'' For instance, rumors would spread in a politically nearly-homogeneous Liberal *vereda* (an outlying settlement of a town) that the inhabitants from a nearby Conservative *vereda* were arming themselves, and the Liberals would execute a preventive attack. The alleged (or real) illegality of the countergroup led to another illegality in "self-defense," e.g., to a diffusion of illegality. Alternatively, a mayor would prohibit a rally or order its early dissolution; accusations spread that he was applying the law in a partisan fashion, not universalistically. As a reaction, the countergroup might conspire to arm itself in revenge or self-defense. In anticipation of this eventuality, some mayors or governors went beyond their legal authority, forming or reactivating progovernment gangs to help them keep order. By these processes of "diffusion of deformalization," government organizations and offices lost their formal-legal character, and were perceived as being partisan, e.g., a judge was seen as a *Conservative* judge, not really a *judge* but an individual who applied the law "only against the Liberals." Similar perceptions involved other offices as well.

This labeling of the formal-legal governmental structure as sectarian or "privatized" (i.e., defined as the property of the rulers) is nothing new, nor is the fact that in the absence of neutral or nonpartisan government agencies there is a tendency toward the "privatization" of violence for self-defense and atonement or revenge.[56] The problem in Colombia was that the state—the basic formal organizations of government—lacked sufficient autonomy or development to withstand party competition. As suggested by Laserna,[57] the state was relatively weak to begin with. Therefore, its mediating-control function tended to disappear under party competition. Government agencies and their agents were seen as partisan agents of a political party. In stable democracies with a greater *semblance* of government legality or neutrality, administrative or judicial review serves to correct problems of electoral illegalities, thus integrating the polity through formal-legal means. In Colombia, however, the lack of faith in such formal mechanisms led to perceptions of normlessness and government illegitimacy, with the associated need to privatize violence.

Control of such violence was made difficult by the tendency to exaggerate the "criminality" on both sides, by scapegoating, misrepresentation, and guilt by association. Moreover, the few available law-enforcement agents were poorly trained.[58] The tendency in some areas for residential settlements to be politically homogeneous meant that the violence could involve intercommunity conflict; the difficulty of breaking communal solidarity to single out the culprits under these conditions is evident. (There was a regional aspect to the political violence that cannot be dealt with in this chapter.) In short, communal violence tended to lead to gang formation, with the problems that this implied for demobilization, once the process spread and the gangs became institutionalized. Fortunately, in contrast to La Violencia, party competition in 1922 was brief enough to prevent the full fruition of this tendency toward gang rule, the ultimate expression of the "withering away" of a weak state under conditions of interparty competition.

Another feature of the violence was that relatively little of it was directed toward the creation of impersonal, legal mechanisms of control that would assure an end to the problem that was causing it—the perceptions of electoral fraud.[59] Apparently a cultural paradox was present, perhaps traceable to the traditional Hispanic low regard for impersonal organizations. While there was a propensity toward distrust, there was a parallel propensity against openly institutionalizing this distrust by adopting formal mechanisms that could control irregularities. Since the cause of the violence remained unsolved, communities were both highly vulnerable to external sources of conflict and unduly dependent for equilibrium on personal contacts and friendships between locals.

To summarize, the 1922 experience indicated the Colombian inability to institutionalize a democratic, competitive regime, even under the theoretically favorable conditions of limited participation. Despite the discussed preelectoral commitment of maintaining trust and avoiding the personification or moralization of conflict, the election resulted in escalated moralization and mutual accusations of criminality. For wide sectors, government was perceived as "dictatorial" and illegitimate; for other sectors, the opposition were illegitimate "revolutionaries." Only a strong pacifist commitment at the elite level restored a semblance of *legality*, truncating the full fruition of the patterns of violence that were to prevail later during La Violencia. The politics of "restrained refinement" served to counter the tendencies toward tyranny and reintegrate the protodemocracy. Indeed, the Liberals, who triumphed in practically all the larger cities but were defeated in the overall vote by the rural returns, cited "coercion and fraud at the hands of the rural *caciques* [bosses]," an interpretation seeking to maintain a measure of elite solidarity by using lesser politicians as scapegoats.[60] The Liberal press emphasized that the president himself was not responsible for the bulk of the violence and other illegalities. The Liberal elite evinced "constructive" feelings. The post-Mil Días motto—*la patria sobre los partidos* (the nation above the parties)—continued to be used. It was felt that moral coercion should be limited to electoral abstention and refusal to participate in the cabinet. The evolutionary technique of "liberalizing" the country, largely through journalistic campaigns, was maintained as the main element of strategy.

Liberals would abstain from participating in presidential elections and in the cabinets for the remainder of the pre-1930 period, but although they would at times severely criticize the government (as for instance, during the bloody labor strikes against the United Fruit Company in the late 1920s), ideologizing interparty relations a bit with their recurrent anticlerical themes, on the whole they maintained their policy of "loyal opposition." By 1925 they engaged in electoral participation for a tacitly accepted minority role in congress. In 1930 their policies paid off; an intraparty Conservative split gave them the presidency in a three candidate contest. However, before analyzing the future escalation of interparty conflict that unfolded into La Violencia-political breakdown-National Front, it is important to take a closer look at the nature of the normlessness associated with the 1922 violence.

Character of the Traditional Normlessness

The main political problem of the traditional system was its propensity to fall into more or less acute states of normlessness associated with escalated conflict and violence. Specifically, interparty competition resulted in a strong and widespread belief in law breaking, e.g., electoral fraud; it included formal declarations to that effect by the losing party *elite*; it was related to a diffusion of illegalities justified in self-defense and revenge. Moreover, perceptions of normlessness—e.g., the criminality charges—were associated by many Colombians with a questioning of the opposition's democratic intentions, even commitment; conflict tended to escalate to involve perceptions that a state of alienation or "estrangement" in fundamental values and norms existed among the parties. As I will illustrate in the following section, this syndrome of norm breaking and normative ambiguity could eventually terminate support for the regime and reinforce authoritarian tendencies, producing the breakdown of the political system; it impeded the evolutionary democratization of the polity.

There are several probable contributing factors to this normlessness. Most generally, there is empirical evidence that Colombians are distrustful; they do not usually perceive others as law-abiding citizens.[61] Secondly, there was present in Colombia something of what Fallers observed in his analysis of protobureaucracy in Africa: while individuals expected government functionaries to act "impartially," they in turn activated all sorts of particularistic networks in order to influence officials, even in nonpolitical areas of decision making.[62] The *palanca* (literally, lever; e.g., "pull"), the pattern of calling friends, relatives, or patrons to intercede for one's case with government authorities, is readily observable and widely legitimate in Colombia. How can a population accustomed to the fairly uninhibited exercise of particularistic influence believe in governmental neutrality in a highly competitive election? The traditional system did not develop a modern governmental formal organization approximating Weber's ideal type of the modern bureaucracy under legal domination,[63] as opposed to a patrimonial organization, so that government would be perceived to act within *workable* standards of universalism and neutrality, e.g., legality.

Colombia's incapacity to go beyond a protodemocracy was directly related to the underdevelopment of formal-legal integration in the polity, e.g., the rule of law, formal-legal organizations included. This type of organization contrasts sharply to patrimonial organization.[64] Under the latter type, government organizations are largely defined as being above the law, as the property of or at the service of the ruling party, friends, and clients. In contrast, modern formal-legal organizations are *intended* to be: (1) subject to

Figure 1
The Traditional Political System

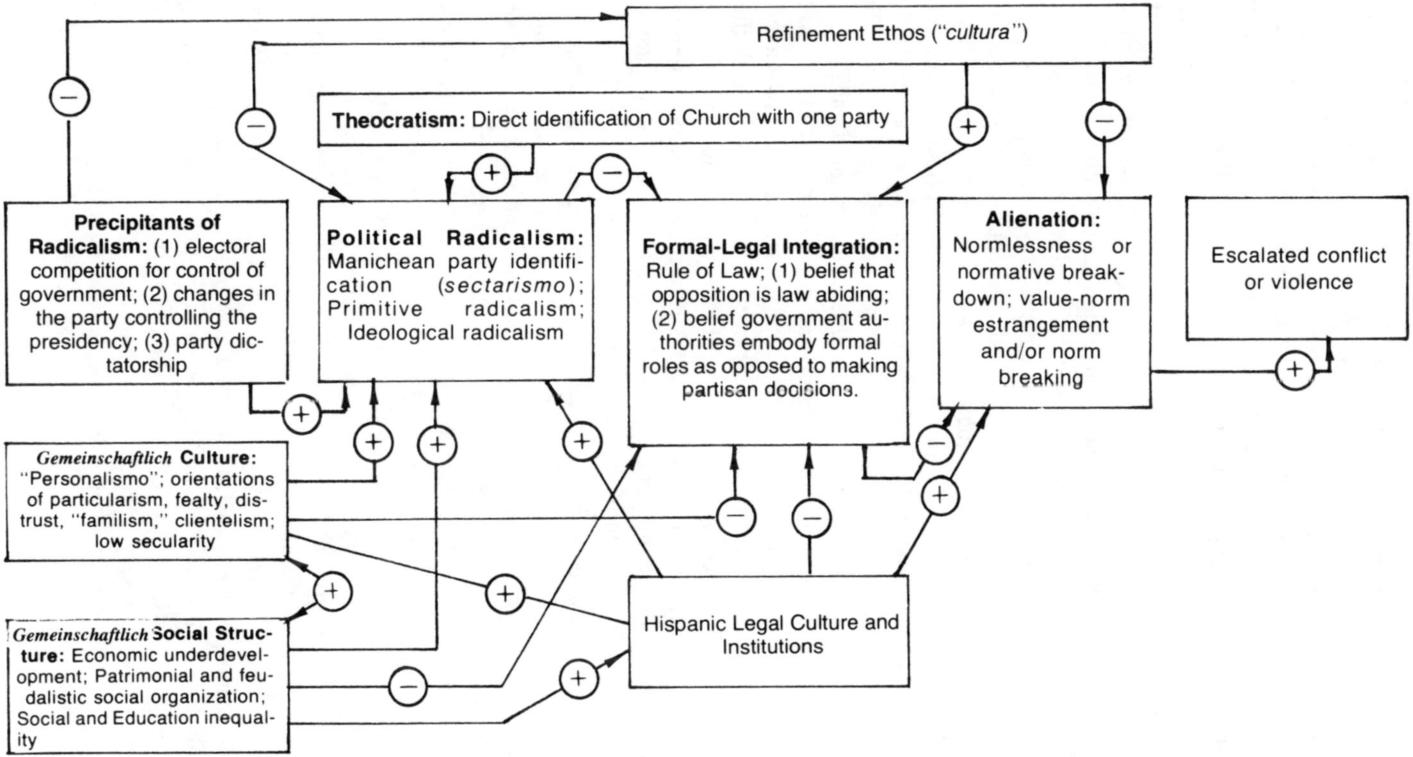

Note: The lines predict positive (contributing) or negative (reducing) effects. In interpreting effects the reader should backtrack the analysis. For instance, the Refinement Ethos is seen as reducing Alienation but this effect is conditioned by the reduction of the Refinement Ethos itself produced by the Precipitants of Radicalism.

and limited in scope by universalistic rules (the "law"); (2) neutral (*impersonal*) appliers of these rules; (3) constituted by a set of "offices" autonomous from their staff; (4) characterized by competitive staffing. Surely these absolute standards are never fully implemented in any polity.[65] Yet Colombian patterns would certainly indicate that their formal "impersonal" organizations were not sufficiently developed or autonomous enough to permit effectively regulated or peaceful electoral competition.[66] We have observed how, particularly under the stress of competition, government organizations and offices lost their formal-legal character, becoming perceived as fully appropriated by their incumbents and consequently employed for partisan purposes. Clearly, democracy requires an identification with and support for, and hence the relative *autonomy* of, the constituted regime (the basic formal-legal organizations and offices of government). The superimposition of formal democratic institutions on a social system supportive of traditional patrimonial organization led to a structural *fusion* between the regime and the ruling group in Colombia. The implicit motto was too often: *l 'état c'est le parti* (evidenced by the noted tendency toward party *continuismo*, the illegalities associated with the continuation in power of the ruling party). This lack of *structural differentiation* between the state or regime and the party system impeded the effective institutionalization of democratic elections; fusion led to perceptions of normlessness and illegitimacy.[67] In Colombia, democratic ideology was sufficiently developed so that competitive elections were not entirely stifled; no party had the traditional right to govern. At the same time, the democratic culture was not sufficiently developed to prevent fusion between the regime and the ruling party. This was a fundamental characteristic and problem of the traditional system.

Normlessness was not a simple consequence of this weakness in formal-legal integration; it was also conditioned by a syndrome of political radicalism linked to the nature of the party identification. (The interested reader may refer to Figure 1 as a guide to the discussion.) We know the charges of criminality were concentrated on interparty, not intraparty, relations. A likely factor for this was the ingrained partisan prejudices or *sectarismo* (the "hereditary hatreds"); the sectarian views the opposition party as "evil" thus expecting it to *break norms*. "Universalism," the effectiveness of common norms, a necessary condition to avoid perceptions of fraud, is thus eroded. The ideological dimension was always implicit in partisan conflict, ultimately linked to the role of the church in the party system. Definition by some radical clerical sectors of the philosophies of the countergroup as "evil," promoted alienation in the form of "value" estrangement. This type of conflict tends to be nonnegotiable because it produces a dogmatic ideologization and moralization of conflict, precluding the notion that the adversary is working within a common normative framework. Indeed, one expects fraud from individuals who are evil or uphold totally unacceptable views. Further, the church had an ambiguous position toward the principle of democratic sovereignty. Although not formally against elections, Pope Leo XIII had declared that the moral order emanating from God was more binding than the will of the majority.[68] This surely did not increase confidence in the electoral process. In sum, as noted in Figure 1, the weakness in formal-legal integration that led to normlessness was related to two other factors that were in turn interrelated: political radicalism and theocratism. More will be said on these variables later.

The factors contributing to normlessness can be related to Colombia's traditional culture and socioeconomic underdevelopment; in sociological terms, to its *gemeinschaftlich* cultural orientations and social patterns.[69] As these characteristics have been dealt with extensively in the literature, I will be brief in noting their relationships to the weakness in formal-legal integration, i.e., the problems of electoral fraud and mutual accusations of collective criminality. This cultural configuration has been characterized by an emphasis on expressive orientations that are supportive of "affective release, rhetoric and verbalism." The emphasis is on *personalismo*: personal status (*dignidad*), interpersonal loyalty or fealty, and the favoritism characteristic of "friendism" (*amiguismo*), "familism" and clientelism—the *palanca*. Impersonal relations and organizations are distrusted. There is a "personalistic" religious orientation in the culture with a "saints vs. devils" dramatic interpretation of everyday reality. When expected, redemption is to be "externally" obtained through the favors or grace of external (often charismatic) figures or forces. Such general orientations when applied to the political arena undermined the impersonalities of formal-legal integration, nurturing the Manichean conception of politics that, as I will document, was directly linked to the breakdown of the traditional political system.

Some of these cultural characteristics are rather general in non-Catholic, premodern social systems; consequently, they seem to be correlated to Colombia's economic underdevelopment—its patrimonial-feudalistic socioeconomic structure.[70] The feasibility of a Marxist interpretation of democracy is underlined by Parsons's pattern variables as they relate it to formal-legal organization, modernity, and economic development.[71] Sufficient socioeconomic development is necessary to provide the cultural secularization and the development of impersonal organization patterns, the "structural differentiation," supportive of formal-legal integration.

Finally, there must be taken into account the role that Colombia's Hispanic legal tradition played in undermining the legal integration of the polity. Hispanic legal culture and institutions have been associated with a tradition in which laws are largely viewed as moral ideals not to be enforced if their enforcement is, for some reason, too harsh, impractical, or unjust.[72] The fundamental law is not conceived as a social compact that establishes relatively fixed universalistic ground rules within which the boundaries of social action are defined. The strong "idealistic" theme of the Hispanic legal tradition makes the constitution a political program, a national platform for political action. Not infrequently, the constitution includes articles or clauses whose implementation is not intended for many years, their impracticality rendering them inapplicable. More or less acute states of normlessness follow from this tradition; it is associated with a "constitutional fetishism" by which the writing of new constitutional texts is a substitute for actual norm implementation. The Hispanic legal tradition favors "natural law" and "casuistry" over the impersonal application of the law. Paradoxically, its emphasis on "justice" is paralleled by a relatively casual attitude toward the implementation of man-made law. The linkages between this legal configuration and the problems of radicalism and formal-legal integration in the Colombian traditional system will be subsequently described. Given the logical relationships between the *gemeinschaftlich* culture and social structure and the legal tradition, the latter must be partly determined by the former factors.

Figure 1 summarizes my interpretation of escalated political conflict in Colombia as the result of a situation of alienation or normlessness, produced in turn by a weakness in formal-legal integration. Both of these sets of variables are determined by (1) a political variable—radicalism, (2) Colombia's Hispanic legal cultural and institutional tradition, and, more generally by (3) the *gemeinschaftlich* traditional culture and socioeconomic underdevelopment. The latter are treated as exogenous factors.[73] The system found itself in equilibrium under the counteracting effects of the *cultura* ethos of restrained refinement. As documented earlier, this ethos fostered trust, political restraint, and moderation, and supported "legalistic" formality. Nevertheless, as shown by the incapacity to institutionalize electoral competition, its impact was limited and not sufficient to permit the operation of either a competitive oligarchy or a representative democracy with limited participation. It was no substitute for the rule of law. The integrative effects of *cultura* were neutralized in the presence of the precipitants of radicalism treated here as exogenous, though in fact partly related to party factionalism. For simplicity we have also excluded from the diagram the effects of the recency of massive violence or civil war, though it was a factor for equilibrium inversely related to time.

UNSTABLE EQUILIBRIUM AND POLITICAL BREAKDOWN

The Conditioning Period (1930-46)

With the advent of Liberal party rule in 1930 a new political era began, ushering in sixteen years of Liberal-led sociopolitical change. Increases in rural violence would be linked to the redistribution of local political power accompanying the change in the party controlling the presidency, as witnessed by the electoral majorities which the Liberals registered by 1933, when they became the effective majority party. (Liberals won in 1930 with only 44.9 percent of the votes against two Conservative candidates; in the congressional elections of 1933 they obtained 61.5 percent of the vote). The violence would soon disappear, however, since Conservatives did not again engage in electoral competition for the presidency until 1946, an event that initiated La Violencia.[74] The Liberal victory brought attempts to modernize the society. Typically, these included steps designed to increase the secularization of the state and policies to enlarge or popularize the polity—universal male suffrage was established and governments encouraged the development of urban labor unions. Initially, this increased political "inclusion" was in some aspects relatively successful. In contrast with most Latin American countries, Liberal-led Colombia was able to ride over the Depression, grafting onto the polity some welfare-state institutions without political breakdown. In Colombia there were no coups d 'état nor successful civilian revolts in the 1930s.

It is noteworthy that Conservatives would give up power in 1930. The divided, aging, and demoralized Conservative elite, besieged by economic problems and Liberal-steered social unrest—two phenomena that were at least partly foreign induced and mirrored, respectively—allowed the opposition to win the 1930 electoral contest under promises of a coalition government. The young progressive Liberal opposition, with a virtual monopoly over "new" ideas, had extensively penetrated the centers of Colombian society, where there was considerable support for the need for socioeconomic changes. The Liberal presidential candidate had been the Conservative government's envoy to Washington. Out of the fifteen provincial (departmental) capitals—the index of urbanization readily available to me—in 1930 Liberals won majorities in eleven. The party formed a powerful upper-class-led coalition that included urban-middle and working-class elements, and traditional rural sectors—in terms of the literature, a party of "representation" or "aggregation" of multiple interests.[75] The plural, multifaceted Liberal elite appeared to have a leader for every occasion. For instance, López was available to push reforms and Santos to consolidate. In sum, consistent with extant comparative theory, the aging of the ruling group, its divisiveness and demoralization, and economic crisis were all conducive to political changes. These changes were absorbed without breakdown because of the unusual stabilizing effects of a modernizing, significantly upper-class leadership that provided an alternative to the ruling group, while giving guarantees to the rulers (as demonstrated by the preceding years of civil political opposition and social conviviality between both groups), and operating within a multiclass, "aggregating" party. The coincidence between the generational change in the ruling group and the achievement of power by a new cohort with new views produced a relatively enduring Liberal majority in the country.[76]

Some rural violence was caused by the change in party control. However, its brief duration, as well as the government-controlled, urban social mobilization of the 1930s, signaled the consolidation of a new, more modern protodemocratic regime with some of the old problems and some new ones. Once again the opposition was reluctant to compete in presidential elections, partly because of the disbelief that they would be honest. But new styles of opposition materialized, consonant with the increased political popularization.

With the advent to power of the new generation of Liberal politicians in 1930, a parallel process unfolded in Conservative ranks. Conservatives, led by Laureano Gómez, initially engaged in a populistic type of agitational opposition defined elsewhere as "primitive radicalism"[77] that cannot be handled easily by the regime. When the Liberal *cultura* oriented elite had been the opposition, it had tended to exonerate the president and the ruling elite for the electoral illegalities and the related violence. Under the new mode of opposition, the Conservatives accused the president himself of being the principal part of the collectivity of criminals. Gómez emerged as the definite leader of the opposition by accusing President Olaya Herrera (1930-34) of the illegalities associated with the consolidation of Liberal rule. In his words:

> A general impunity, without exception, and irritating to the highest degree, has protected all of the thousands of assassinations, fires, acts of violence, rapes and assaults committed against the Conservatives by agents of the government and of Liberalism. When sections of the national and departmental police forces went into provinces of indisputable Conservative majority spreading terror by murder, burning of homes and robberies of the scanty belongings of the Conservative peasants, if complaints were filed because of these many abuses, it was the officers of these very same [police] forces who were in charge of hearing the indictment, the immediate result being imprisonment and torture of the claimant and his witnesses . . . .
>
> There have been incorporated into the ranks of the police known criminals [who were] found running from justice under the Conservative administration.
>
> Unfortunately for his [good] name, in his rage against Conservatism President Olaya did not limit himself to being a corrupter. He has been a bloody and unjust persecutor as well.
>
> His is a cruel, impious soul. He is literally soaked with the honest blood of his brothers. And he smiles.[78]

While some progress toward political inclusion was being made through the growth of a labor movement, no parallel advances were occurring in real or stable ''liberalization''—a nonrancorous public contestation that would result in greater participation and choice with order. The elites were starting to argue ruinously; an *unbalanced* democratization was unfolding that would eventually result in political breakdown. Clearly, when increases in participation and liberalization are tied to such Manichean expressions of political radicalism, they are likely to end in authoritarian reaction, as witnessed by its recurrence in Latin American history.

It could be argued that the emergence of this style of opposition was conditioned by Gómez's inclinations, for the older Conservative guard was supporting participation in the Olaya Herrera cabinet. Gómez was a maverick who had a history of opposition within the party itself and of collaboration with Liberals; he had proved himself a gifted orator and agitator.[79] His talent and political experience enabled him to consolidate party leadership during this process of generational change; Conservatives did not achieve such a plural leadership at the top as the Liberals. Personality factors are most important when new groups are crystallizing, and Gómez's impact should not be underestimated. However, this mode of opposition was not an isolated event; it would be employed recurrently and become the most prominent form. Further, its success, as measured by Gómez's continued prominence, can be traced to the outlined sociological background of normlessness. In Colombia's political culture, Gómez had credibility. Formal-legal mechanisms were not strong enough to legally resolve the public criminality charges within the existing judicial procedures of the regime. The fact that other important Latin American opposition leaders have used this same style—e.g., Chibás in Cuba, Lacerda in Brazil, etc.,—is suggestive that it should not be treated as an isolated event, as opposed to a protodemocratic propensity.

Primitive radicalism is an elite manifestation of populism that tends to produce alienation in the previously described form of ''norm breaking.'' Whether primitive radicals become ideological ones or not, their expression is not ideological. The contention is not over different philosophical views, but over the alleged breaking of moral and legal norms. However, such conflict, if successful, has ideological implications, eroding support for the *regime* itself, defined in this chapter as the basic principles, laws, and formal organizations of government or the state, not as a specific government.[80] The process by which primitive radicalism erodes support for the regime is straightforward enough. For those who believe that the president and his backers are ''criminals,'' distrust in government increases. Unless the president is removed, alienation grows, and some politically aware citizens perceive important parts of the regime itself (the basic government normative order) as breaking down. If the leader of the opposition is prosecuted, the government will be perceived by this group as not upholding the democratic regime values or principles.[81] If, as occurred in Colombia during the 1930-46 period under consideration, not only is the president not legally removed but another president is also defined as a "criminal," then citizens are likely to start questioning the *type* of regime (normative structure or organization) that results in the selection of "criminals." In sum, primitive radicalism leads to a complex set of perceptions such as regime ineffectiveness; its "melting down"; the emergence of normative "breakdown"; the illegitimacy of the ruling group, as it appropriates or fuses with the regime; that democracy is not working and should be transitionally suspended—the well-known Latin American "pathology of democracy" syndrome. As populistic interpreter of the people, the elite agitator (the primitive radical) sooner or later, and with more or less ambiguity, depending on circumstances, inexorably suggests the employment of illegal means to rid the nation of the prevailing conditions of alienation and restore a viable regime. The Conservative elite talked of *acción intrépida* (intrepid action) and of making *la república invivible* (an intolerable republic) by their political agitation, thus escalating conflict by introducing the noted "diffusion of illegality" syndrome into the very center of the polity.

The weakening of the regime was by no means the exclusive result of the actions of Conservatism. As Colombians of all stripes saw it, particularly after 1934, *la República Liberal* (the "*Liberal* Republic") had been established. Colombians knew that the state now belonged to the Liberal party. To confirm the fact that it *was* Liberal, even though the moderates were then in control, in 1936 the ruling party unilaterally changed the constitution to separate state and church, and to establish the principle of government intervention in the economy and the social function of property, all in accordance with Liberal secular ideology. This was of course unacceptable to the Conservatives. Colombians, thus, lacked a common constitution upheld by both Liberals and Conservatives. Sociopolitical change, "modernization," was leading to alienation or normlessness in two of its forms: norm breaking and value-norm estrangement, all centered in the regime itself. Generalized perceptions that fundamental norms were being broken, and the absence of a commonly-held normative system, all at the very center of the polity, inexorably led to the collapse of the traditional political system.

Opposition to the "*Liberal* Republic" was mostly carried out by Conservative laymen mainly from Gómez's populistic, sensationalist newspaper, *El Siglo*. Founded in 1936, its "yellow press" aspects contrasted sharply with the described pre-1930 "restrained refinement" of the Liberal opposition press. Conservatives used other public forums as well, including the radio and parliament, the latter when they decided in 1939 to stop boycotting electoral participation, tacitly accepting for a while a minority role in Congress. However, clerics could flex muscles. The anticlerical aspects of the constitutional change—"the Revolution on the March," as the 1934-38 Liberal program was known—led to church mobilization, which reached a peak in the Bolivarian Congress of 1935. Conservatives claimed that 400,000 of the faithful "pros-

Figure 2
Protodemocratic Unstable Equilibrium

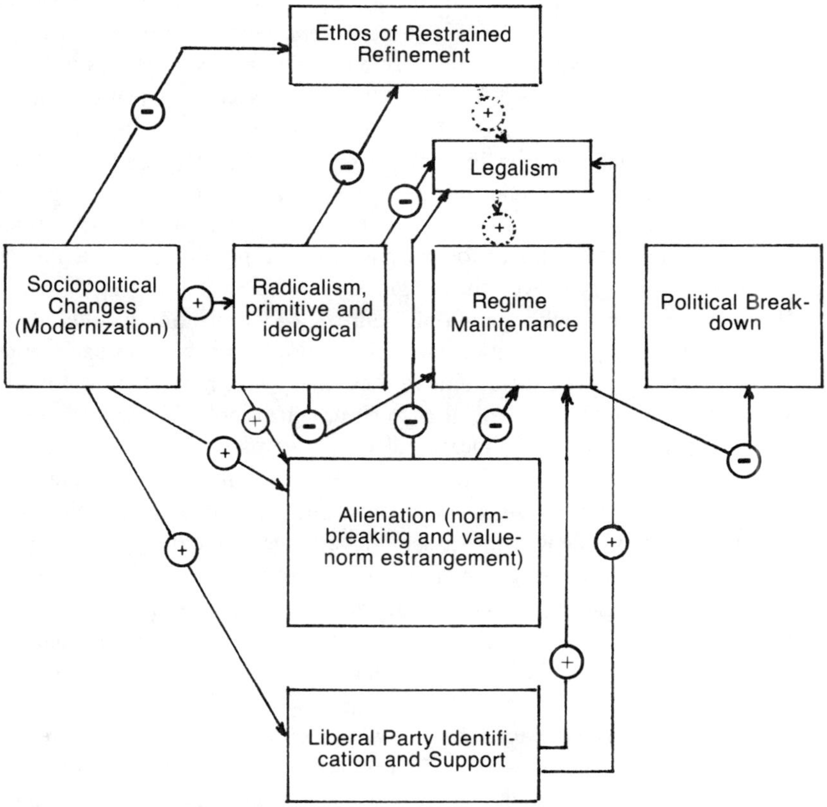

Note: The dotted lines signify that under prevailing conditions the predicted positive (contributing) or negative (reducing) effect is inoperative or minimally so.

trated themselves before the Holy Sacrament . . . as a warning against a local repetition of the Mexican or Russian Revolution. The theme of the Congress [was] 'to be or not to be! Catholics or nothing! A *Christian* Republic, or nothing!'"[82] (my emphasis). The struggle between two hegemonies was unfolding.

European development of the 1930s and early 1940s, particularly the Spanish Civil War, also added ideological images to the partisan conflict in Colombia. The leadership of both parties was too conservative to allow either party to develop into a modern totalitarian mass party with a heavy emphasis on ideology and indoctrination of the masses. Communist and Falangist groups, especially the latter, were small and remained on the fringes. However, the manipulation of symbols provided fuel for the conflict between the "right" and "left." Implicit in the confrontation was Conservative pursuit of their solution for Colombia—*their* regime or *república*. Conservatives were, however, *ambiguous*; ambiguity in these matters often accompanies political breakdown in Latin America. For instance, while periodically using Catholic doctrine to question the democratic "rule of numbers," they did not come outright against majority rule in their programs. But, as noted in 1946 by Lozano y Lozano,[83] the end result of the strategy of ideologizing and deideologizing conflict caused many Liberals to believe that Conservatives had lost faith in the traditional formally democratic political system. As we shall soon see, history proved them right.

We may summarize with the aid of Figure 2. Modernization resulted in an initial period of unstable equilibrium. Sociopolitical changes, an exogenous factor, consisting of the Liberal innovations (that were, nevertheless, foreign influenced and reinforced by social change: urbanization)[84] led to an increase in political popularization and increased conflictive participation. Modernization somewhat eroded the *cultura* ethos of restrained refinement, increasing radicalism and alienation. Accusations of criminality (primitive radicalism, norm breaking) and ideological dissent (ideological radicalism, value-norm estrangement) reduced regime support. The formal-legal integration of the polity was under assault. The cost of maintaining an appearance of legalism required the periodic prosecution of Gómez and-or the president. Further instability was added as the inhibiting after effects of the Mil Días civil war gradually waned.

The posited historical relationship between sociopolitical change, increases in radicalism and alienation, and a reduction of regime support is of course not unique to Colombia. More stable democracies have been similarly affected by *transitional periods*, which are characterized by observable political pressures for bringing about qualitative changes in power relations among social groups—classes, races or ethnic groups. Often fundamental norms and values are questioned during these periods, and the regime's legitimacy is weakened because it is to some extent perceived as patrimonially appropriated by (or fused to) the ruling group. There is no enduring "end of ideology" in stable democracies. Radicalism often results from the emergence of differentiated politicized groups whose demands and/or attacks cannot be readily satisfied by government.[85] Whether or not breakdown occurs depends on the nature of the demands and on regime strength and flexibility.[86] Indeed, the propensity of the Colombian traditional system to convert *normlessness* (criminality) into a *key issue* of interparty competition rendered it less capable of absorbing the increased participation and redistributions in power associated with transitional politics.[87] The fusion between the regime and a political party, a basic Colombian historical propensity, substantially weakened the regime and reduced its long-run flexibility; the rule of each party was associated with a "Liberal" or "Conservative" hegemony, constitution, or republic. In stable democracies, by contrast, sociopolitical change is frequently justified by reference to the principles of the existing constitution, a normative structure that is relatively more *differentiated* from and above the party system. These polities are characterized by regimes that are internally effectively differentiated.[88] Hence, they institutionalize change mainly by making normative adjustments at the middle and lower regime normative levels of statutory law and contract, not at the top or constitutional level. For example, the comparable period of the New Deal in the United States witnessed labor unrest and contestation over constitutional issues and the fundamental ideologies that legitimized the regime, all in accordance with the predictions of "transitional" politics. Yet during the New Deal, evolutionary change was obtained mostly through statutory and contractual adjustments, not by proclaiming unilaterally a new "Democratic party" constitution or the "Democratic Republic." These changes *within* the regime led to the deideologization of the interclass conflict and to its "institutionalization" to the point that strikes today are not interpreted in the United States as challenging the regime; they mainly challenge a lower normative level—e.g., contracts.

Colombia's protodemocratic regime did not, however, withstand the winds of sociopolitical change. The traditional weakness of formal-legal integration traceable to the low cultural secularization, the patrimonial-feudalistic social organization, and the Hispanic legal tradition did not support the regime differentiation required to absorb change under competitive conditions. The turning point toward breakdown was a leftist Liberal dissidence that permitted the Conservative minority to win the 1946 presidential election in a three-candidate race. Its arrival was delayed by several factors. First, much of the early agitation was restricted to selected urban centers.[89] After the consolidation of Liberal local power structures, there was small *actual* political participation on the part of the opposition, particularly in the periphery. Second, while the described processes were undermining support for the regime, this picture is only partial. Liberal-led sociopolitical changes resulted in majority support for this party, and in turn for the Liberal regime, the ruling group upholding a political democratic philosophy relatively consonant with the theory and practice of the traditional system. (See the bottom part of Figure 2.) The moderate Liberals in control of the party attempted to maintain the semblance of legal continuity, and to curtail unsettling religious and labor disputes. The situation was one of unstable equilibrium in that changes in ruling party support would affect the regime itself. However, protodemocratic party regime-fusion can last relatively long periods (as with the Mexican PRI) provided that the ruling group maneuvers effectively to maintain its cohesiveness and power. This factor was particularly important in Colombia's two-party system, given the historical electoral strength of the minority party.

The Conservative victory of 1946 can be attributed to Gómez's populistic campaigns. In 1942 López was returned to the presidency in what Gómez considered a fraudulent election.[90] There followed a period of almost perpetual regime crises. Gómez threatened armed revolution. He accused the president of complicity in the assassination of a boxer, and of personal involvement in family financial scandals. Gómez was briefly encarcerated for libel after he accused the minister of government, the most important cabinet official, of personal complicity in the murder. Mobs formed outside the prison to free Gómez. In 1944 there was an unsuccessful military coup, quelled partly with pro-Liberal labor union intervention. Gómez was exiled for precautionary reasons as the (Liberal) public saw his masterful hand behind the military plot. Unfulfilled Liberal reform caused labor union unrest. In 1945 the president resigned, and a Liberal leftist dissident presidential electoral attempt, initially backed by Gómez, gave Conservatives the presidential plurality and victory.

As noted, many Liberals distrusted Conservative commitment to majority rule. However, they were unable to heal their internal divisiveness and feared that civil disorders would occur if fraud impeded a Conservative electoral victory, so the Liberals gave up the presidency in 1946 to the victorious Conservative candidate.

La Violencia (1946-53)

With the advent of Conservative party rule, La Violencia began. The inability to regularize interparty relations became even more dramatic after the initiation of the Conservative government, in conjunction with a further "democratization" of the polity. An important feature of this new period was that, in contrast to the past, the opposition did *not* abstain from electorally contesting the party in power. Liberals and Conservatives competed in the presidential election of 1946, and again in the congressional elections of 1947 and 1949. Between the two latter elections, political rallies continued into 1948. The fraud and violence associated with interparty elections in the past reappeared.[91] But, given the sustained nature of the mobilization of the 1940s, more gangs formed and they became institutionalized. Conservatives, of course, wanted to rule Colombia for longer than the 1946-50 presidential term, while the Liberals considered themselves the majority power and wanted a quick return to power. Every election served to test the extent of Conservative electoral fraud and Liberal capacity to avoid it, with the associated violence; this was the main "issue." As early as the 1947 campaign, explicit reference was made to the implications of a Liberal victory in that election for a return to power in 1950.[92] Congressional electoral participation was now a test of whether a Conservative *hegemonía* or *regime* would or would not prevail. The crucial historical question about La Violencia is which factors contributed to the sustained electoral competition for power (from 1946-49) and the subsequent establishment of the Conservative party dictatorship (in 1949), for these appear to have been the key precipitants of La Violencia.

The first twenty months of Conservative government experienced a further increase in regime instability as a new, more virulent, and disloyal opposition resulted in increased *actual* participation. Gaitán's leftist Liberal dissidence took the form of a populistic mass mobilization, designed both to capture control of the Liberal party—which he achieved—and to block the establishment of a Conservative regime—which he failed to do. Support for the regime was further eroded by the fact that the minority party was in power, and by the nature of Gaitán's radicalism. Like some other Latin American populist "reformers," Gaitán did not wholeheartedly support formal-legal integration; his strategy included political revolutionary threats (and some actions) to unseat government. And his leadership further eroded the ethos of "refined restraint." He opposed the moderate Liberal architects of the 1930 victory and of the Liberal Republic. This group, previously villified by Gómez, was now trying to conduct a more loyal and adaptive opposition than Gaitán's, following their pre-1930 pattern. Led by Santos, *El Tiempo*'s owner, the moderate Liberals were collaborating with the government in the cabinet and seeking to provide continuity. In Gaitán's eyes they were oligarchs, and their adaptive, *cultura* styles oligarchical—"we call anti-Liberal those men that feel revulsion for the multitudes; those that have divided the people in two categories: a thinking minority that should rule over the people; the other, the illiterate rabble with no right to think . . . ."[93] Gaitán was against "salon politics" and its private dinner parties. As the self-proclaimed "captain of Colombian multitudes," he argued that there was only evil in gentlemen's political agreements, which he called "*contubernios*"—i.e., a base or infamous alliance—made against the people. He focused on Colombia's "deep moral putrefaction"—"*honda putrefacción moral*"; his group and the people would "never submit themselves to the dominion of crime"—"*nunca nos someteremos al imperio del delito*." He was a "preacher" of redemption—"we are the Colombian reaction against that Phoenician attitude that has been forced upon us, that the worth of men is not found in their conscience, their virtue, nor intelligence, but in their capacity to yield."[94] Like Gómez, Gaitán emphasized "normlessness" rather than "policy issues," but his populism was emotionally more intense and was linked to actual participation in mass rallies. The

1947 rural violence related to the *gaitanista* electoral victory became a crucial political issue. Gaitán personally made accusations of "collective criminality" in highly threatening rallies that often ended with calls to direct action, such as: "Comrades of battle: on your graves we swear vengeance, reestablishing statutes of peace and justice in Colombia with the victory of the Liberal party. You have physically departed but are imposingly alive among us! Comrades: your silence is a scream. Your death is the life of our final destiny. Charge!"[95]

According to Gaitán, there were two estranged countries or communities in Colombia: the political country (*el país político*), led by the "oligarchy," and the national or human country (*el país nacional*). Collective alienation was largely a result of the perversity of successful politicians: *el país político*. A key issue in his campaigns was "the true liberation of Colombian man [whose] rightful place has been treacherously usurped by *el país político*, which unleashes its grudges, its hypocrisies, its corrupt passions as though the other great human country did not exist. For *el país político* politics is a game, a tool, a winning of elections . . . [by the] repugnant electoral hero."[96] While not entirely abandoning the electoral road, Gaitán expressed doubts about it, opening the door to political revolutionary action.

The polity had traveled a long way from the ethos of self-restraint to a highly messianic-millenarian style of politics resulting in escalated alienation.[97] Sociopolitical changes had helped to generate a rebellion against authority, and this was strengthened by Gaitán's antioligarchical leadership. Under the new conditions of sustained mobilization, a cultural dynamic occurred; messianic elements prevailed over the *cultura* orientations and the stage was set for intensification of conflict.

Gaitán was more a political radical than a social radical—more a source of political than class alienation.[98] His social democracy consisted of a mixed economy in which the various factors of production would have a fair share of the economic results. This vision was, of course, consonant with basic regime legal institutions. Indeed, his success was largely based on his capacity to mobilize traditional loyalties and obtain the support from the provincial elites. However, he falls within a type of Latin American populistic "reformer" that tends to be more threatening than its counterpart in stable democracies, for they often ideologize conflict, increasing estrangement by emphasizing the "evil" values of the opposition—the "reaction" or the "right." Often vague as to the specific socioeconomic institutional adjustments that they intend to make, they also suggest the plausibility of employing illegal (political revolutionary) means to achieve their goals. This disregard for the formal-legal trappings of the regime makes them disproportionately menacing.

To summarize, the following elements of the 1946-48 patterns of conflict, amidst the successive participation in and withdrawal from the cabinet by Liberals, signaled the acute regime crisis.

1. There were frequent rumors of military and congressional "conspiracies" to overthrow or impeach the president, and of unilateral attempts by the Liberal-controlled Congress to alter the regime and strip the president of his constitutional powers as commander in chief.
2. Gaitán's mixed strategy of legality-illegality kept open the option of overthrowing the government. The largely Liberal labor confederation (the CTC) employed first the "solidarity" strike and ultimately, despite a Gaitanista minister of labor, the revolutionary general strike against "the government's dictatorship and Falangism."[99] The general strike failed; the government dissolved the CTC by declaring it an illegal organization, and thereby ended Liberal revolutionary labor; meanwhile it sponsored the growth of Catholic unions. Consistent with the interpretation that reformism in Colombia was more the product of elite articulation of working-class interests than of lower-class initiatives, labor proved to be the "paper tiger" of La Violencia; the proletariat was still small and the peasantry was unorganized along class lines.
3. Highly threatening mass rallies maintained an ambiguous revolutionary climate. February 1948 saw Gaitán's final major show of force, a rally in Bogotá, where he delivered his famed "Prayer for Peace." In it he blamed the president for the assassination of the Liberals, particularly in the provinces, and threatened to take the "diffusion of illegality" to the top of the regime itself—government overthrow. A pro-Gaitán source interpreted the event as a notification "to the President to prevent violence to avoid the civil war . . . . [Gaitán] proved that Bogotá could be taken . . . . Humble dead were the government's answer."[100] A putschist situation was developing.
4. The culmination of these processes was the Bogotazo, the April 9 revolutionary mass uprising that was triggered in Bogotá and a few other urban centers by Gaitán's assassination (attributed to a still unsolved plot). Much of the populace blamed Gómez and his Conservatives, and consonant with the political climate, the mobs attacked the Presidential Palace itself. The regime almost collapsed with the Bogotá rebellion of the National Police—that same police than had been villified as "criminal Conservative" agents—an event that coincided with Liberal elite demands that the president resign. The "Liberal" mobs blemished sacred Conservative symbols: the Cardinal's Palace and some churches were attacked. Gómez was seen as a destabilizing element in the fluid situation and had to go once more into exile. The Conservative government finally survived, bringing Liberals into a coalition government of national unity and reconstruction. But the weaknesses in the legal integration of the polity evidenced by the illegalities associated with partisan conflict resulted in escalated violence, precisely at a time of increased popular political participation and competition. The traditional protodemocracy was incapable of absorbing an increased democratization.

The following year of 1949 was decisive for the fate of the traditional regime. With Gaitán's death, the moderate Liberals regained control of the party, an event indicating the long-term political weakness of the leftist, more middle-class leadership that had clustered around the charismatic dissident leader. Time was running short. A decision had to be made between returning power to the Liberal party, which no longer posed any significant economic or status threat to the establishment, thus recognizing the continuing Liberal electoral majorities, or formally altering the regime itself at the risk of expanding government coercion and dictatorship. True, the Liberals had conducted a disloyal opposition; but there had been understandable suspicions about Conservative intentions to establish their *hegemonía* or ''republic.'' Despite the more moderate post-Gaitán techniques of the opposition, violence accompanied the June 1949 congressional elections. Shots were fired in Congress. In the eyes of many Conservatives, the traditional two-party ''democracy'' had become associated with mob rule. To some, a Liberal return to power implied a vengeful bloodbath. Gómez returned from his exile in Spain in late June, declaring that civil war was inevitable and making a falangist salute in the airport. The Liberals, with their electoral majority, wished a continuation of the traditional protodemocracy; President Ospina proposed a new regime—an interparty coalition constitutional system in the spirit of the future National Front. But both parties rejected this innovation, and Gómez's formula prevailed: continuation of Conservative rule, achieved through the total suspension of parliamentary bodies and his fraudulent election to the presidency in November 1949 (with 99.9 percent of the vote). With these events signaling the initiation of Conservative dictatorship, the traditional system broke down. Conservatives sought a new, Catholic-inspired, theocratic oriented, corporativist regime with limited suffrage that would depoliticize Colombia and save it from ''Marxists'' and ''crypto-communists.''[101]

The remainder of this case study involves Conservative inability to establish a stable regime in a situation of deadlocked escalated *violencia*; the end to maximum political violence—La Violencia proper—with the 1953-57 interlude of a coup-emergent military regime; that regime's inability to survive as it evolved from an interparty mediating regime to one dominated by a continuistic leader, after the typical historical authoritarian pattern; and the successful formation of the intertraditional party coalition—the National Front—which reactivated traditional forces to restore rule by the civilian ''establishment,'' overcome General Rojas' social class populistic challenge, and fully pacify the country.

Before concluding, a brief reference to the actual patterns of violence is in order. The *violencia* was a multifaceted phenomenon that underwent several stages. Largely rural, although very present in some provincial urban centers (e.g., in Caldas and Valle), from 1946 to mid-1949, it was highly dependent on the discussed electoral processes and problems. Secondary sources reveal similarities between La Violencia and the patterns of violence during the presidential election of 1922. This time, however, the electoral competition was sustained; more Liberal and Conservative gangs crystallized for ''self-defense vengeance,'' and became institutionalized, thus developing a dynamic of their own. Despite recurrent Liberal representation in the cabinet, the regime ''withered away'' throughout vast areas of the periphery, where it was unable to contain the ''illegalities'' and ''deformalization'' associated with the competition.[102]

Electoral results show the strength of Liberal resistance to Conservative gains and the central role of the rural sector in the overall Conservative political strategy, both in contrast to what had occurred in the past. From 1930 to 1933, the Liberal share of the total vote rose from 44.9 to 61.5 percent. From 1946 until the congressional election of 1949, Conservatives advanced only from 43.5 percent in 1946, to 44.8 percent in 1947, and to 46.5 percent in 1949. These gains were larger in rural areas. The proportion of the urban vote going to the Liberals increased from 61.5 percent in 1946 to 64.2 percent in 1949.[103]

An additional element in the struggle was introduced with the reorganization of the National Police after its 1948 rebellion. The government used new recruits to transform this allegedly "Liberal" organization into a loyal, partisan "Conservative" police. The *chulavitas*, as these agents were called, achieved notoriety as instruments of Conservative violence and objects of Liberal hatred and counterviolence. Their assignment by the central government to areas they did not come from constituted an "external" source for violence and gang formation.

Between 1949 and 1953, *violencia* escalated further in response to the attempts to impose a *pax Conservadora* and Liberal resistance to any Conservative hegemony. After the Liberal elite had unsuccessfully tried to impeach President Ospina in 1949 and declared that Gómez had been illegally elected, new Liberal gangs were formed to organize government overthrow. Other Liberal gangs were formed in "self-defense" vis-à-vis the political homogenization of regime formal organizations; progovernment gangs continued to crystallize in support of a militarily weak central government. Two crucial types of gangs materialized: the *guerrillas* and *cuadrillas*. The *guerrillas*, quite scarce, had more of a middle-class and intellectual leadership—small merchants and landowners, ex-army and police officers, and students. They were politically revolutionary, articulating government overthrow as their main objective. In contrast, the more numerous *cuadrillas* were mostly led by uneducated peasants, and their goals were less sophisticated; they were more "communally" oriented toward "self-defense" and "revenge" actions. Their organization appears to have been less complex and their activities more predatory.[104] In the struggle, entire displaced communities developed, as attempts were made to homogenize the party colors of some territories.

Several other characteristics of this violence deserve comment. First, it did not have a high and explicit social revolutionary content. The ultimate political objective was to defeat the other party, but much of the violence had the more private objective of self-defense and revenge. As both parties had a mass basis, the mobilization of either led to a countermobilization by the other party. Thus violence tended to become "communal" in scope, making it difficult to overthrow the government.[105] Second, in contrast to the Mil Días civil war, the party leaders of this more urbanized polity with its more bureaucratic and professional armed forces did not lead the armies themselves. They, therefore, had less control over the violence and the *violentos*. While the Liberal leaders had some operational contacts with some *guerrillas*, their efforts to sustain a political revolutionary movement were not substantial. As early as 1951, Liberal expresident López was participating in a Crusade for Peace with presidential and church support, visiting with *guerrilla* leaders in an unsuccessful attempt to lay down the bases for peace. Third, although the stalemated violence finally led to the 1953 military coup d'état welcomed by both parties, little recognition came to the *guerrillas* for their role in the termination of Conservative rule; this was partly a consequence of the low social and political revolutionary content of the violence. No *guerrillero* became a political leader of national scope. Political power fully returned to the "establishment" of both parties with the founding of the National Front in 1958.

With the 1953 military coup, La Violencia proper ended. The emergent military regime was widely viewed as one of mediation, the final consequence of minority party inability to govern. At the center of the polity, it was considered that the time for reconciliation had come, and the subsequent demobilization indicated that such sentiments had spread to the periphery.[106] Probably the bulk of the demobilization was by the politically more articulate and responsive *guerrillas*, rather than the *cuadrillas*. But despite a lull in the political violence, Colombia was not easily pacified this time. In a situation which had been increasingly characterized by "banditry"—the employment of violence for economic profit—not all the gangs demobilized; and new groups of *bandoleros* were formed up to and through the National Front. *Bandolero* activity continued, especially in the relatively wealthier, socioeconomically more developed provinces (e.g., the famed *pájaros* in coffee rich territory). As it became more difficult at the local level to disguise economic motives under traditional partisan banners, there was a progressive transformation of political gangs into bandits.[107]

Several factors blocked total demobilization: personal risk of being murdered by enemies in underpoliced areas; profitability of the rackets, in many instances carried out with the protection of government officials; psychological problems; and unwillingness of government to incorporate many of the *violentos* into the armed forces (as is often done in successful revolutions). In addition, there remained Marxist rural activities which had developed during the pre-1953 period. These, despite the Conservative government's propensity to call the *violentos* communists or crypto-communists, were of secondary importance. Until the initiation of the National Front and the post-Cuban Revolution period, Marxist activities took mostly the form of relatively self-contained territorial enclaves. Even post-Castro social revolutionary guerrilla and terroristic activities never achieved sustained momentum, notwithstanding the spectacular character of some of the actions. All in all, the *violencia* was a costly phenomenon for the rural population, not only in lives but in business losses. The post-1953 concentration of *violento* activities in the relatively modernized and prosperous provincial areas revealed that the disorganization of La Violencia proper had interacted with the socioeconomic deprivation of the relatively more active segments to induce and facilitate the search for economic gains via illegal means. This pattern, which spread to major urban areas, was not entirely reversed during the National Front.

SUMMARY INTERPRETATION AND IMPLICATIONS

The National Front was a regime innovation designed to cope with the historical incapacity of a two-party system to institutionalize competitive, democratic politics. We have seen that political changes and socioeconomic modernization were tied in Colombia to a ''democratization'' of the polity as indicated by increases in political participation and in open interparty competition. The result was an unsuccessful groping toward democratic welfarism, which led to La Violencia, political breakdown and dictatorship; the effects of these events are still felt today.[108] Endemic political problems related to cultural and socioeconomic realities of the society impeded the successful completion of this ''transition.'' We have noted that the combination of sustained *open* political competition and evolutionary political development requires the prevalence of formal-legal integration in the polity. The belief or myth that the government and the governed are maintaining themselves within workable boundaries of legality is a necessary condition for continued open competition.[109] In Colombia's traditional protodemocracy, under competitive conditions the elites tended to accuse each other of ''collective criminality,'' normlessness becoming a key political issue. This included perceptions that government organizations and offices had lost their formal-legal pretensions to become entirely ''appropriated'' by their incumbents and consequently employed for partisan purposes. When either party disputed the right of the other to remain in power, there was a strong tendency toward a diffusion of illegalities or escalated violence; therefore, more complete or developed forms of democracy could not be institutionalized. I have related these patterns to the prevalence of patrimonial, as opposed to formal-legal, governmental organization. Patrimonial organizations are not constituted by a set of ''offices'' autonomous from the rulers, nor are they characterized by competitive staffing according to general or universalistic rules. In Colombia's traditional system, patrimoniality took the special form of party hegemonies (*hegemonías*) and the illegalities associated with the continuing rule of one of the parties. Patrimonial patterns were, of course, illegal in Colombia, where the basic laws established periodic competitive elections as the mode of changing the executive. Colombia's ''unbalanced-dependent'' development resulted in the importation of political-legal forms incongruent with its sociopolitical realities.

My analysis stresses that in order to maintain the semblance of legality required to combine political development with democratic continuity, the regime itself—the basic formal-legal organization of the state—must integrate the polity. Regime breakdown—the unilateral alteration of this basic formal-legal organization—is a fundamental component of protodemocratic (and, of course, democratic) political breakdown.[110] Regime weakness is a most fundamental characteristic and problem of protodemocracies. Clearly, in stable democracies the semblance of legality amid sustained political competition is maintained through the *structural differentiation* between the regime and the party system. This differentiation permits the carrying out of electoral competition without widespread illegalities, as government officials maintain workable levels of impartiality. Differentiation also permits changes in government without implying changes in the regime itself. Typical of stable democracies is the fact that elections occur while the basic regime formal-legal structure remains unchanged—this is at the essence of their political stability. In these polities, as a general rule, elections produce only changes in government personnel and in ''policies.'' The latter, carried out according to regime formal-legal procedures, consist of changes *within* the existing regime—i.e., changes in legislation, as opposed to the constitutional order itself. Indeed, stable democracies are also characterized by regimes that are internally differentiated, so as to usually permit lower-level normative changes (e.g., changes in statutes), without a need to alter the basic regime normative structure (e.g., the constitution itself). We have observed how in Colombia political competition escalated to involve the advocacy of different regime types. As groups with perceived significantly different regime preferences compete, the regime itself becomes a political issue, and there is an absence of common basic norms; hence, the propensity toward the diffusion of illegalities, violence, and political breakdown.

What was the nature of Colombia's regime weakness? Despite the formal existence of a differentiated regime, there was a propensity toward a *structural fusion* between the regime and the ruling party. It found two basic expressions. First, there were beliefs that the rulers might break key regime norms (particularly, though not exclusively, electoral laws) in order to remain in power; the state was largely defined as a ruling party fiefdom.[111] Second, there was a tendency to alter regime symbols, values, and norms so that the regime would conform to ruling-party ideology (changes deemed highly undesirable by strong sectors of the opposition). Fusion meant that the structure and principles of the regime itself varied according to which party was in power. This absence of a commonly upheld political-legal structure reinforced the normlessness and illegalities in the system and was conducive to recurrent political breakdown.

How much did ideology matter in weakening regime support? Ideological conflict was a variable—there were periods when the parties' constitutional positions were not a key issue, others in which strategic ambiguity prevailed in the question, and others in which the illegality or criminality of the opposition (primitive radicalism), not party ideological positions, appeared to be of paramount importance. Still, the parties did in fact propose quite different regime configurations consonant with their philosophical traditions (Catholic, Aristotelian based, organicism versus the Enlightenment's liberalism turned "welfarism"). Regime preference was not a simple matter of political expediency (e.g., regardless of electoral outcomes, in contrast to Conservatives, Liberals never proposed a Christian corporatist system with limited suffrage). The greater exposure to Catholic educational indoctrination on the part of the Conservative political elite underlines the role of ideology in differentiating the parties. There was another difference: the greater urbanism of the Liberal party, a social difference consistent with party ideologies. Yet there was considerable *overlap* in the sociodemographic (including social class) profile of the two parties.[112] It is in this light that the relative importance of ideology proper—the nature of systems of beliefs, as opposed to economic or class interests—comes to bear. The theocratic element injected into the traditional party system by the near fusion of the church with the Conservative party was conducive to conflict over regime values in any sustained interparty competition. The transformation of religious ideas or sentiment into a public issue is unsettling in any situation. The church's historical emphasis on dogma and heresy contributed toward giving an "ideological," nonsecular character to the traditional political culture. Church historical reservations about democracy heightened the long-run potential for dissension over the regime, particularly during those periods of stress and change that necessarily confront all societies.

A source and a reflection of regime ineffectiveness was the Colombian Hispanic legal tradition traceable to the structure and culture of the preindependence patrimonial state.[113] It has three salient, not entirely harmonious themes: (1) the notion that laws are government orders, as opposed to an outgrowth of a fundamental social *compact* that protects all the citizens, and, consequently, must be respected and implemented by all; (2) the concept that the *real* law is an ideal that transcends executive, legislative, and judicial actions; and (3) the belief that laws reflect ideals whose enforcement is to be avoided, if at all possible, when they are too harsh, unjust, or impractical. The lightness with which public legal matters were dealt in the traditional system can be inferred from the described patterns of conflict. Colombia was characterized by a history of frequent constitutional changes, partly the result of the belief that the legal system itself, not only its implementation, was inadequate. The reading of Colombian legal treatises supports the existence of the second theme. A substantial part of legal training consisted of the study of definitions and other conceptualizations unrelated to Colombian statutes, executive decrees, or case law. Colombian constitutions have had numerous articles with detailed provisions, some of them inapplicable because of their impracticality.[114] Partly as a consequence of this lack of constitutional implementation, there were recurrent perceptions of normlessness and illegalities among jurists and leaders of both parties. Yet remedial action often entailed the proclamation of other ''ideal'' constitutional norms that were again deficiently implemented, if at all. The legal tradition weakened any belief in a solid edifice of legality. Moreover, it was also linked to the ideological expression of radicalism, according to which, ''salvation'' or the ''new order'' would be possible only with substantial formal innovations in the regime itself.

Were there socioeconomic determinants to the traditional system's incapacity to evolve beyond its protodemocratic nature? Briefly, with due reservations for any notion of linear evolution and ultimate convergence, static considerations (relationships between relatively constant socioeconomic traits—e.g., whether a society is ''developed'' or not, ''industrialized'' or not—and political patterns) suggest that there was a connection between Colombia's low levels of ''modernity'' and the weaknesses in formal-legal integration. Modernity has been associated with a secularized culture and strong impersonal organizations. The issues that proved so destabilizing to the traditional system under competitive conditions were an extension to the political realm of the Manicheanism, ''particularism'' or favoritism, and low ''differentiation'' characteristic of traditional societies. No premodern society ever developed the rule of law.[115] In Latin America, only the polities of the socioeconomically more developed societies have maintained for any length of time the semblance of electoral neutrality to be characterized as democratic.[116] The short-run cost of redistributing economic resources in poorly developed, stratified societies is exceedingly high and detrimental to the success of evolutionary social changes during ''transitional'' periods. In my view, the traditional regime weakness can be traced not only to the specifically Colombian syndrome of political radicalism that was tied to the theocratic aspects of the party system, but also to the incompatibilities between the requirements of a formal democratic regime and the traditional, *gemeinschaftlich* social system in which it was embedded.

Beyond socioeconomic development per se, social and economic changes were associated with the breakdown of the traditional system. However, there is no simple relationship between economic crises and breakdown in Colombia. From the end of the Mil Días civil war until the mid-1940s, the economic problems created by international wars and the international capitalist business cycles did not result in breakdown. The undetermined effects of economic crises are readily exemplified: the economic dislocations of World War I did not dislodge Conservatives from power, yet the 1930 Depression was associated with the origins of Liberal rule. Clearly, it is the interaction between economic crisis and political dynamics (the latter having an independence of its own) that determines the political results.[117] In the traditional system "development pressures," i.e., demands for political changes that would result in socioeconomic changes, were largely articulated by an elite sector influenced by foreign developments. (Note the historical coincidences between the New Deal and the Liberal Republic.) Therefore, any hypothesized relationship between such pressures for sociopolitical change and previous social change occurring in Colombia might be spurious. My own interpretation is that social change (i.e., urbanization) was one of the factors related to the breakdown of the traditional system, in that it reinforced political structural changes—a Liberal majority. This in turn contributed to ideological changes. Conservatives, now in the minority, reactivated those antidemocratic Catholic tenets that had been latent in their philosophy while they were the working majority. These ideological changes served to justify the breakdown and demise of the traditional regime to establish a new corporatist regime limiting majority rule.

The traditional system survived into the late 1940s. While it was never integrated by formal-legal institutions in the same fashion as stable democracies, there was a measure of legal continuity in it. The absence of successful revolution and the rarity of coups d'état evidence such continuity. The periodic changes in the executive according to schedule, usually carried out by the ruling party, suggest a degree of political institutionalization far above politically less developed Latin American states. The traditional system was effectively integrated over the middle run by ruling party oligarchies. Support for the ruling party and the cohesiveness of its elite were two basic instruments of integration in the traditional system.

However, the traditional system of *two* strong parties implied special problems for long-term political integration and regime continuity. Given the strength of the minority party, ruling party factionalism increased the likelihood of an opposition electoral victory, thus encouraging interparty competition. In contrast to one-party systems, where the fusion between the regime and the ruling party can produce long run monopolistic stability, Colombia's traditional system was relatively more prone toward competition and, therefore, to illegitimacy and *violencia*. It would appear that in a strong two-party system context there is no substitute for the integrative role of the regime itself in order to avoid the recurrence of civil war. Nevertheless, although the party system failed as a supportive integrative mechanism in the long run, its nature inhibited some forms of violence. First, its multiclass character reduced interclass conflict—we have observed that this type of violence was relatively controlled. Second, the absence of stable one-party dictatorships (i.e., the system's propensity toward coalition) owes itself partly to the system of two strong parties. The historical rarity of coups d'état and military-based "authoritarian" regimes may be similarly explained. These latter effects operated as predicted by extant comparative political theory.

The level of interparty competition was by no means a constant in the traditional system. Not all groups had the same propensity to moralize or ideologize conflict. An important inhibiting factor was the volume and recency of previous violence; massive violence increased the tendency to coalition government, with transitory but still relatively lasting "postwar adaptive" legitimacy. In addition, the ethos of "restrained refinement" or *cultura* fostered self-restraint and trust. While it did not produce the developed formal-legal integration necessary for stable democracy, it contributed to give a semblance of legality and normative integration to the polity, and redress tendencies toward tyranny and normlessness; by helping to overcome political crises, it contributed to periods of protodemocratic equilibrium. During the span of our study, it was the moderate Liberals (whether in opposition or in power) who adapted most to the trappings of the protodemocracy and had the highest score in upper-class, foreign-oriented, liberal "cosmopolitanism." The breakdown of the traditional system resulted from the waning power of this group in the face of maneuvering by the populistic "right" and "left." Observing that the paths away from dictatorship crystalized with elite successful responses to extreme and direct challenges to its solidarity and rule, (e.g., the government fostered attacks on the private residences of the top Liberal leaders in the early 1950s and the economic and status threat posed by General Rojas in the mid-1950s), illustrates the central role of the oligarchy in Colombian politics. That the combination of restrictive modes of political participation and significant freedom of expression at the elite level did not result in an interparty competitive oligarchy nor in democratic evolutionary development casts doubt on those interpretations that stress the historical role of oligarchies in long-run successful democratization. The secularization of the political culture and the development of a relatively autonomous state appears to be a necessary condition for this outcome.

To summarize, the traditional Colombian proto- or partially democratic system involving rotation of the executive within the ruling party proved incapable of developing sufficient regime autonomy and internal regime differentiation to evolve into competitive democracy. Interparty competition implied not a change in government but a struggle for "hegemony," with its associated normlessness and potential for breakdown. However, in the absence of interparty competition, the system experienced an equilibrium largely sustained by "post-violence adaptive" legitimacy, ruling party support, and the *cultura* ethos. Because these latter variables, rather than the regime itself, provided the empirical basis for system maintenance, competitive democracy could not be institutionalized.

This chapter has dealt with historical details that appear to be related to La Violencia and the associated breakdown of the traditional system; how the inhibiting specter of the distant Mil Días civil war waned; how various modernization efforts were undertaken, partly under the influence of ideas from abroad; how a new Liberal generation anticipated other groups in introducing sociopolitical innovations which, aided by the increased urbanization, resulted in an enduring Liberal majority; that this structural change in the polity reactivated within Conservative ideology an interest in the undemocratic tenets of their philosophical tradition; how the mobilization to modernize generated political heroism in the form of populistic and threatening *caudillos*; how "reformism" succumbed to the factionalism common to "transitional" politics; the destabilizing efforts of a majority party fearful of the hegemonic intentions of a minority government; how recently established working-class organizations, undisciplined and threatened, lent themselves to an unsuccessful mobilization to overthrow minority-party rule; how the messianic-millenarian orientations of a deprived population, previously contained by oligarchical structures, were unleashed by a more middle-class opposition leadership reflecting little of the previously dominant *cultura* ethos of self-restraint; how the violent ochlocracy associated with this period of competitive "democratization" reinforced any tendency to impose dictatorially a nontraditional regime structure; in sum, the backdrop to the combination of cultural and structural interactions which precipitated the escalated violence. In exploring the power struggles, the toying with (making and unmaking of) the constitution, and extensive violence itself, it is difficult to avoid paraphrasing Comte. Colombia's traditional system appeared to be in a "metaphysical" stage, with lingering theocratic elements; symbols and ethical and legal abstractions dominated the competition, rather than pragmatic considerations of discrete "issues" and the problems of articulation and implementation of specific policies. In Colombia dissent tended to involve illegalities and the regime itself, as opposed to middle- and lower-level regime norms. It is interesting that even under escalated violence, the political hyperactivity was accompanied by little change in the basic social fabric.[118]

The National Front was the culmination of the analyzed regime problems. It was the most formal and detailed attempt to circumvent them in Colombia's twentieth-century history. Rather than a Liberal or a Conservative *república*, the state was equally divided between the two traditional parties; a bipartisan, as opposed to partisan, hegemony or fusion materialized. This hegemony was not through extra-legal or illegal manipulations, but by constitutional mandate. In giving a formal-legal dimension to the coalition, its founders departed from Colombia's tradition of informal coalition; as a result, a truly consociational regime materialized. Interestingly, despite the existence of Western European democratic coalition arrangements, no acknowledgement was given to these foreign patterns to reinforce the Front's legitimacy. It was quite successful in restoring civilian rule and minimizing interparty competition and strife. The Front was a national institutional adaptation to endemic national problems. However, it was a transitory arrangement. The elites hesitated to make such a constitutional structure permanent, and inserted provisions to dismantle it. The latest constitutional amendment only establishes that after 1978 the executive should be staffed to give an "adequate and equitable participation" to the largest party other than the president's. Implicit in the transitional nature of the Front and in such modifications is a belief that Colombia is capable of evolving toward a fully competitive, democratic system.

The implications of the National Front for Colombia's future and especially the extent to which it has altered the nature of Colombia's society and polity to promote political stability along with social and economic progress are the questions to which this volume is addressed. I have only attempted here to trace its origins to certain Colombian historical characteristics and problems in order to establish grounds for its evaluation. The political and economic developments that occurred during the Frente must be understood against the political dilemma that it was designed to resolve. To some extent, of course, only the experience of future developments will prove the contribution of this institution. Still, a careful analysis of what happened during the years of the National Front provides clues.

Not surprisingly, many of the characteristics of Colombia's political history were visible during the years of the National Front; the question is whether they were altered in nature or degree. The historical pattern of regime weakness continued, or appeared to. Party factions and interparty coalitions used elections to challenge the constitutional structure itself; in fact, these electoral challenges were more open and frequent than in the past. The National Front itself was a key object of political contestation. It cannot be automatically assumed, however, that such electoral challenges implied the same degree of unacceptance of regime as did earlier ones. Some were not explicitly directed toward the right of Conservatives or Liberals to govern the country, but to their right to do so without open competition with other parties. Such challenges would, in principle, disappear with the end of the Front. At another level, although there was nothing like the verbal virulence and participatory "activism" of La Violencia, the Front still witnessed a lower keyed Manicheanism and ideologization by politically radical opposition, including one led by an expresident. These styles were linked to electoral normlessness—e.g., the 1970 charges of electoral fraud in favor of the "official" presidential candidate.[119] Governments recurrently employed the state of siege. The continued thinness of formal-legal integration is also indicated by the necessity felt by some leading pro-Front factions to periodically alter the constitution, processes culminating in the major changes of 1968. These patterns have remained beyond 1974.

Some events of the years of the Front suggest a continued propensity toward "hegemonies." It might be speculated that constitutional continuity during the National Front was partly due to forces similar to those of the post-Mil Días period, especially a "postwar adaptive" legitimacy. This was not only the case among the leadership. Fragmentary survey data suggest a sense of "adaptation" in *violencia* areas.

Two major developments of these years constituted breaks with the past. The Colombian church largely withdrew from identification with a specific party, partly in response to international currents. And there was a significant technological input within the ruling coalition. Whether the secularizing effects of the former development will affect the survival of the two-party system is still an open question; as discussed in this volume, the assessment of the impact of the new, recent clerical radicalism also falls in this same category. Technological developments within the Front appear to have widened the bases and channels for more pragmatic, issue-oriented, modernizing, styles of poltics.

Yet there has been a lag in the scientific development of political analyses, which could be used as a basis for developing those other than authoritarian, "apolitical," technocratic forms of government. The encouragement, channeling, and development of a broad interdisciplinary knowledge of our societies cannot only give us satisfaction but also make us better at the task of institution building. Given the substantial urbanization and population growth that occurred during the Frente years—by the end of the Front, Colombia was no longer a predominantly rural, small-scale society—more than the tradition of *cultura* these scientific paths might be increasingly necessary to provide stability and growth to the system; they seem necessary for the future development of democratic, competitive political forms consistent with Colombian realities. There can be no doubt that during the National Front there was both change and stagnation. The remaining chapters of this volume are designed to assess the changes in Colombia's polity and economy, and to judge to what degree they were related to the regime innovation of the National Front.

NOTES

1. See Robert A. Dahl, *Polyarchy, Participation and Opposition* (New Haven, 1973), pp. 225-26. Of course, few developing nations have a tradition of a two-party system, making the Colombian case even more interesting.

2. The most recent case is ANAPO. Its electoral strength rose sharply from 1962 to 1970, when it received 25 and 39 percent of the congressional and presidential votes, respectively, under the cover of a bipartisan coalition. However, in 1974 its support was reduced to 9 percent of the total vote. The electoral strength of other third-party movements has been less significant.
3. The change was from a Conservative to a Liberal majority. A rapid erosion of party identification has been associated elsewhere with periods of social and economic crises. See A. Campbell, P.E. Converse, W.E. Miller, and D.E. Stokes, *The American Voter* (New York, 1960).
4. This phenomenon, analyzed later in this chapter, is considered by most sources to have started in 1948 with the assassination of Liberal leader Gaitán. However, interparty violence began to escalate in 1946, making this a more accurate date for its beginning. The interested reader can consult the Colombian press in support of this contention. The end of La Violencia is a more debatable problem to be dealt with later. Estimates on the number of casualties oscillate widely and have probably been overestimated. The most quoted source considers that the total number killed between 1949 and 1962 was about 200,000; Germán Guzmán Campos, Orlando Fals Borda, and Eduardo Umaña Luna, *La Violencia en Colombia* (Bogotá, 1963), p. 292. A more recent study applies statistical analysis to a total of 84,114 deaths from 1949 to 1958; John C. Pollock, "Violence, Politics and Elite Performance: The Political Sociology of La Violencia in Colombia," *Studies in Comparative International Development*, 10 (Summer 1975): 22-50.
5. Dix refers to the latter system as an "Athenian" democracy; Robert H. Dix, *Colombia: The Political Dimensions of Change* (New Haven, 1967), p. 78. Such a competitive aristocracy might draw from Solonic ideological orientations, where a clearly defined and firmly founded governing class would exist to restrain tendencies toward extreme populism and anarchy, while the well born and wealthy would be restrained by law from exploiting the underprivileged. A pertinent discussion is found in A. Andrewes, *The Greek Tyrants* (New York, 1963), pp. 89-91.
6. The term is borrowed from Gino Germani and Kalman Silvert, "Politics, Social Structure and Military Intervention in Latin America," *European Journal of Sociology*, 2 (1961): 62-81.
7. The rate of electoral participation rose sharply during the 1946-49 period: 1943, 41 percent of the potential vote (congressional); 1945, 39 percent (congressional); 1946, 60 percent (presidential); 1947, 64 percent (congressional); 1949, 73 percent (congressional); Departamento Administrativo Nacional de Estadística (DANE), *Colombia Política* (Bogotá, 1972), p. 152.
8. See Dahl, *Polyarchy, Participation and Opposition*, pp. 36-38.
9. For our purposes here, the traditional system can be considered in operation since the end of the Mil Días civil war at the beginning of this century until 1946, although 1914 is a more accurate date because of the consolidation of Conservative party rule that occurred then. The 1946 cutoff date is adequate, because during this year the unusual subperiod of sustained interparty electoral competition and violence started. These processes resulted not in the traditional partially democratic type of party hegemony, but in the closedown of parliament and the initiation of the Conservative party dictatorship that lasted until the 1953 military coup d'état. The National Front was the institutional mechanism devised to restore civilian rule.
10. Dahl, *Polyarchy, Participation and Opposition*, presents a useful regime typology along two axes: (1) public opposition or open contestation and (2) inclusiveness or

participation. Regimes high in (1) and (2) are defined as "polyarchies" (modern mass democracies); regimes low in both as "closed hegemonies" (traditional dictatorships or authoritarian regimes); regimes high in (1) but low in (2) as "competitive oligarchies"; those low in (1) and high in (2) are "inclusive hegemonies" (modern totalitarian regimes).

11. Pollock, "Violence, Politics and Elite Performance." Most sources agree that during La Violencia, violence was further escalated by the Conservative dictatorship initiated in 1949. Such a system was characterized by the closing of Congress and practically no representation of the opposition in any institutional segment of the regime.
12. There were only two episodes of widespread mass violence: the Mil Días civil war at the turn of the century and La Violencia. However, both processes were costly. Of approximately 1,000 days duration, Mil Días resulted in about 100,000 deaths. See Jesús María Henao and Gerardo Arrubla, *Historia de Colombia* (Bogotá, 1967), p. 815. The loss of Panama through its independence from Colombia was attributed to this civil war. For a monographic treatment of the civil war see Charles W. Bergquist, *Coffee and Conflict in Colombia, 1886-1904: Origins and Outcome of the War of the Thousand Days* (unpublished Ph.D. dissertation, 1973). For the death toll of La Violencia, see note 4. Between these two highly tragic episodes there were other less costly and shorter events of partisan violence and some eruptions of social class violence.
13. *Continuismo*, an indicator of weak electoral mechanisms and a trigger of Latin American military coups, refers to a number of techniques that Latin American presidents resort to in an attempt to remain in power beyond their formal or legal term in office. Examples of this are the unilateral abrogation of the usual constitutional prohibition of reelection for successive terms or the extension by decree of the presidential term to avoid an electoral contest. For the role of *continuismo* in Latin American military coups, see Mauricio Solaún and Michael A. Quinn, *Sinners and Heretics: The Politics of Military Intervention in Latin America* (Urbana, 1973), pp. 60-61.
14. In the three competitive elections that occurred, the minority obtained the following proportions of the total vote: 38 percent (1922), 44.9 pecent (1930), and 43.5 percent (1946). Henao and Arrubla, *Historia de Colombia*, pp. 860, 885, and 916. The first two percentages corresponded to the Liberal party, the last one to the Conservative.
15. James L. Payne, *Patterns of Conflict in Colombia* (New Haven, 1968), pp. 143 ff.
16. I am arguing that the inhibiting effect of "civil war recency" was inversely related to time. The evolutionary conception of the democratization of the polity through participation is a recurrent theme in the literature. For instance, Bagehot considered that tolerance "is learned in discussion and, as history shows, is only so learned" in *Physics and Politics* (Boston, 1956), p. 119.
17. Examples of these factors are: (1) escalated violence, e.g., post-Mil Días and post-La Violencia governments, and the post-Bogotazo (1948) government; (2) antiparty system threats by emergent third forces, e.g., interparty coalitions versus General Reyes (1909), the Republican party (1914), and General Rojas (1957); (3) when the opposition successfully attempted to gain power through a presidential election, in order to reduce the dislocations brought about by changes in the party in power, e.g., following the 1930 and 1946 elections.
18. Mil Días resulted in less of a tie than La Violencia in that the Conservatives did not then alternate the presidency with the Liberals. At the turn of the century, the

opposition warring the government was probably the minority party and the military was then a very small unprofessional organization. After La Violencia, it took a more formalized coalition, a coalition regime as opposed to governments, to restore party system control away from military rule.

19. Departures from this "average" historical model can, of course, be found. On the one hand, there is the Latin American *version* of patrimonial hereditary monarchies found in some of the lesser developed societies, e.g., Trujillo's Dominican Republic, and Duvalier's Haiti, with their emphasis on family rule. On the other hand, there is a more modern pattern exemplified by post-1964 Brazilian developments. Brazil could be viewed as hesitantly evolving toward a leadership-rotating, protodemocratic, military hegemonic regime. Indeed, Juan Linz, a pioneer in typifying authoritarian regimes does not define this innovative regime as "authoritarian," possibly because of its leadership rotation and electoral features. See Juan J. Linz, "The Future of an Authoritarian Situation or the Institutionalization of an Authoritarian Regime: The Case of Brazil," in Alfred Stepan, ed., *Authoritarian Brazil, Origin, Policies and Future* (New Haven, 1973), pp. 233-54.
20. Orlando Fals Borda, *Peasant Society in the Colombian Andes* (Gainesville, Fla., 1957) and Eduardo Santa, *Sociología Política de Colombia* (Bogotá, 1964). There is a tradition in Western thought relating rural areas to political intolerance. For the inverse relationship between socioeconomic status and the strength of party identification in the United States and India as well, see S. Verba and N.H. Nie, *Participation in America* (New York, 1972), pp. 220-24 and S.J. Eldersveld, "Party Identification in India in Comparative Perspective," *Comparative Political Studies* 6 (1973): 271-95.
21. Particularly Colombian Marxists have complained bitterly about what they consider to be an unreflective and intolerant traditional party identification. See, for instance, Antonio García's "Prologue" in Daniel Caicedo, *Viento Seco* (Buenos Aires, 1954), pp. 16-17. Interestingly, a majority of a sample of Bogotá high school freshmen and seniors still considered in a survey taken during the National Front that "political discussions easily can cause the loss of friendship." See J.P. Heggen, *Political Socialization in Colombia's Schools: The Impact of Three Secondary Institutions on Student Political Attitudes and Behavior* (unpublished Ph.D. dissertation, 1969), pp. 114-17.
22. The church has often taken pride in Colombia for its Catholicism. See Wilde's chapter in this book.
23. By "ideologization" I mean a tendency to view the opposition as upholding beliefs that are *wrong* and *evil*. Analytically speaking it is possible to distinguish an ideological syndrome—a tendency to relate politics to a coherent set of ideas—from a syndrome of partisan hostility characterized by perceptions that the countergroup is "immoral" or "evil." See the discussion central to Robert D. Putnam, *The Beliefs of Politicians: Ideology, Conflict and Democracy in Britain and Italy* (New Haven, 1973). While the tendency to employ an ideational political style need not be highly correlated with partisanship, to the extent that the content of the ideology is dogmatic, it calls for intense conflict. As Putnam notes, intense conflict "calls" for ideology; pp. 44, 82, and 88.
24. See the most useful discussion in Christopher Abel, "Conservative Politics in Twentieth-Century Antioquia (1910-1935)," Occasional Paper III, Latin American Centre, St. Antony's College, Oxford, 1973.
25. Ibid., p. 27. The ideologization could involve doctrinal conflict with individuals not willing to declare themselves anti-Catholic or agnostic. For instance, accord-

ing to Abel (p. 16) ''lawyers in the 1910's whose teachings rested in relativist and not Catholic absolutist concepts of law were severely rebuked by the Archbishop of Medellín . . . . Archbishop Manuel José Cayzedo accused Restrepo of omissions and truncations of Church doctrine in his writings on constitutional law. In answer to Cayzedo's allegation that he had denied absolute truth and preached principles of 'materialistic evolution' and 'determinism,' Restrepo replied that he was merely following [Pope] Leo XIII.''

26. See Richard Weinert, ''Violence in Pre-Modern Socities: Rural Colombia,'' *American Political Science Review* 60 (1966): 340-47. Even Payne, whose central thesis is that ideology has no explanatory value in Colombian politics, considers that Liberals had greater urban support, and were more receptive to Marxist influence; *Patterns of Conflict in Colombia*; pp.85; 89; and 234.
27. For details see Mauricio Solaún, *Political Violence in Colombia* (unpublished Ph.D. dissertation, 1971), pp. 386-94.
28. Abel, ''Conservative Politics,'' p. 34.
29. See *Las Mejores Oraciones de Jorge Eliécer Gaitán 1919-1948* (Bogotá, 1958), p. 391, and the excellent discussion in John D. Martz, *Colombia: A Contemporary Political Survey* (Chapel Hill, 1962), p. 19.
30. The main Catholic texts are two papal encyclicals, Leo XIII's *Rerum Novarum* (1891) and Pius XI's *Quadragesimo Anno* (1931). Of course, while the church took upon itself a leadership role in attacking liberal and socialist developments, other European conservatives were concerned by post-French Revolution developments as well. The similarities in some points between church doctrine and de Tocqueville and Burckhardt's preoccupations with social change, for instance, are apparent.
31. Reference is made here to an ideological corporativism held in the past as a political constitutional *ideal* by the church, not usually followed by a sustained clerical action to accomplish it. This should be distinguished from the empirical ''corporativist'' tendency that some social scientists observe in Latin America. Partly because of the weakness of voluntary associations and lack of governmental resources, Latin American governments have often induced the formation of trade associations and followed the old tradition of granting some ''public'' policy-making authority to these ''corporate'' groups. Governments with chronic problems of legitimacy have also been prone to ''officialize'' potentially threatening mass organizations by granting them some public functions in order to control them more effectively. See the Bagley and Edel chapter in this book for one such case. Pertinent discussions on the origins and practices of these ''private'' governments are Kenneth L. Karst and Keith S. Rosenn, *Law and Development in Latin America, A Case Book* (Berkeley, 1975), pp. 48-51, and Robert E. Scott, ''Political Elites and Political Modernizations: The Crisis of Transition,'' in Seymour Martin Lipset and Aldo Solari, *Elites in Latin America* (New York, 1967), pp. 117-45. Howard Wiarda, an expert on the Dominican Republic, has emphasized the absolutist monarchical aspects of corporativism in ''Toward a Framework for the Study of Political Change in the Iberic-Latin Tradition: The Corporative Model,'' *World Politics* 25 (1973): 210-12. However, as noted by Linz, ''The Future of an Authoritarian Situation,'' ideological corporativism has lost much of its appeal even in Catholic circles. For an incisive statement on the limited nature of the corporativist solution see Linz's article.
32. Charles Bergquist has recently argued for a ''political economy'' interpretation of party differences during an earlier period but also finds difficulty in reducing the observable party ideological differences to a unicausal interpretation; ''The

Political Economy of the Colombian Presidential Election of 1897," *The Hispanic American Historical Review* 56 (1976): 1-30. In his words: "[s]ome Liberal and Historical Conservative political leaders also considered the possibility of a bipartisan electoral alliance . . . .[H]owever attractive in terms of elite economic interests and world views, such an alliance across traditional party lines was not given serious attention. Given the polarization of Colombian society into rival Liberal and Conservative patron-client groups, realistic politicians recognized the ineffectiveness of bipartisan political coalitions"; p. 28.

33. While Monsignor Perdomo, the primate of Colombia, declared in the politically crucial and violent year of 1949 that the church condemned "philosophical liberalism but was not necessarily opposed to parties referring to themselves as 'liberal' " (Martz, *Colombia*, p. 83), an opposite stance was taken by some other bishops. See, for instance, Monsignor Miguel Angel Builes, *Cartas Pastorales, 1949-1957* (Bogotá, 1957). Naturally, political issues were also divisive among the church hierarchy. This is why former militant Conservative party leader, Laureano Gómez, talked about "his" bishops.
34. Liberal religious political changes were, in fact, more symbolic than real. According to an approved Catholic source, the 1936 constitutional changes, made without Conservative participation, in the direction of a more secular state did not touch family law (divorce), and a subsequent concordat with the Vatican left the position of the church "virtually unchanged"; Hermano Justo Ramón, F.S.C., *Historia de Colombia* (Bogotá, 1963), pp. 371-72. Nevertheless, such changes were perceived as threatening by the church (Dix, *The Political Dimensions of Change*, p. 92). According to Martz, after the restoration of Conservative party rule in 1946, Protestant activities were restricted (*Colombia*, pp. 139-40); and during the 1948 Bogotazo uprising, the Episcopal Palace and some churches were desecrated.
35. See Ruhl's comments on the continuation of this pattern during the Frente Nacional in his chapter in this volume. Although a high proportion of the pre-Frente, post-1930 elite had an upper-class background, prior to an appointment as a cabinet minister, an individual would typically hold a number of minor political posts; Solaún, *Political Violence in Colombia*, pp. 391-92. Despite the large bias favoring privileged individuals in Colombian politics, there was still a need for familiarity with the lesser political posts and public administrative jobs. This experience may have contributed toward political expertise, invigorating the political system, and contributing to oligarchical resilience.
36. The case that this is not an uncommon phenomenon in Latin America is recently made in Henry A. Landsberger, ed., *Rural Protest* (New York, 1973), pp. 12-13.
37. Miguel Urrutia, for example, argues that the pre-National Front reformism of the Liberals had little impact on real wages. See Miguel Urrutia Montoya, "El Impacto de los Sindicatos Sobre el Salario Industrial," *Razón y Fábula*, No. 3, 1967, pp. 85-92.
38. Party identification was apparently less stable in the nineteenth century, as indicated by President Mosquera's change in party identification and the long experiment with the Núñez regime. This weakness is reflected by William Paul McGreevey, *An Economic History of Colombia 1845-1930* (London, 1971). Paradoxically, the civil wars may have served to solidify party identification. For pertinent comments on the recent extent of party identification see Richard Maullin, *Soldiers, Guerrillas and Politics in Colombia* (Lexington, 1973), pp. 10-14.

39. See the first editorial of *El Tiempo*, when it started as a Republican newspaper on January 30, 1911.
40. During these three years there was a cycle of interparty coalitions that ended only to be formed again. The details are summarized by Martz, *Colombia*.
41. If inaccurate, this figure was widely publicized in the country. See, for instance, *El Tiempo*, April 28, 1911, p. 1.
42. The following clarification is pertinent for the reader knowledgeable about post-1930 Colombian politics. Around these two newspapers developed the bulk of the younger members of the Liberal party leadership who took power in 1930 and whose ranks are being thinned by old age. Of the two papers, Santos' *El Tiempo* was the leader. Much more weight should be given to the long-run impact of President Santos in the 1930 victory and in the Liberal party itself than most sources give. While López's bold leadership should not be underestimated, the background for reform was established by the press. Santos surely provided much continuity and consistency to Liberal politics up to the initiation of the National Front.
43. *El Tiempo*, January 30, 1911, p. 1. All following quotations from this newspaper are taken from the editorial page.
44. Such was the case, for instance, in the establishment of the Gimnasio Moderno, the still prestigious elite private high school. Church opposition was neutralized by attempting to co-opt the hierarchy into appointing a chaplain, while gearing the curriculum away from philosophical disciplines most closely related to theology, which would have made it subject to greater church resistance. See Tomás Rueda Vargas, *El Gimnasio Moderno* (Usaquén, 1945).
45. Quinn and I have explored elsewhere the nature of these processes as applied to Latin Ameica; Solaún and Quinn, *Sinners and Heretics*, pp. 72-83.
46. With respect to labor there were two goals: progress and nonviolence. They gave their support to isolated strikes which exhibited qualities of "discipline, decorum, and prudence . . . Strikes are fair [*El Tiempo* editorialized] as long as they are not violent" (December 21, 1917). Conversely, in 1919, a labor rally was criticized on the grounds that "there was too much propaganda and too little restraint" (March 17, 1919). The aim was gradual progress without "excessive" militancy and mobilization. When nonviolence arrested progress, then the former was preferable. Actually, in some instances they held a naive position, as when attacking the closed shop. For instance, in 1918, *El Tiempo* defended the freedom of workers to continue working after a strike had been declared (January 11, 1918). Yet the underlying approach was to compromise. When an "excessive" number of strikes occurred in 1920, *El Tiempo* considered a law for compulsory arbitration preferable to a complete abolition of the right to strike (May 8, 1920). And rather than abolish the constitutional right of workers to form associations, it was considered preferable to bar foreign agitators from gaining entrance to the country (October 18, 1920).
47. *El Tiempo*, January 23, 1912.
48. A most perceptive statement on this ethos, *one* of Colombia's cultural themes, is José Gutiérrez, *De la Pseudo-Aristocracia a la Autenticidad* (Mexico, 1961). However, I disagree with him as to its extent and consequences. In support of its continuation during the Frente Nactional, Heggen found among Bogotá high school students that they tend to view a breach of politeness on the part of a politician as being far more serious than the illegal appropriation of public funds; Heggen, *Political Socialization in Colombia's Schools*, pp. 226-31.
49. Despite early manifestations of regionalism, this major source of nineteenth-

century political disturbances progressively became less of an issue. Even radical Liberals disclaimed any interest in their traditional federalist solutions, given their desire to create a strong, interventionist state. For a discussion of the nineteenth-century Liberal combination of federalism with laissez-faire economic liberalism (the so-called *liberalismo manchesteriano*), see Jaime Jaramillo Uribe, *El Pensamiento Colombiano En El Siglo XIX* (Bogotá, 1964). Also pertinent is Bergquist, "The Presidential Election of 1897."

50. *El Tiempo*, January 6, 1917.
51. The best readily available source on the election is the compilation of press reports in Partido Liberal, *El Partido Liberal en Colombia* (Bogotá, 1922). I depend heavily on it.
52. *El Tiempo*, January 4, 1922.
53. I cannot enter here into a discussion of the concept of alienation. I am basically following Melvin Seeman's conception that it has several meanings or dimensions, one of which is normlessness. See his "Alienation and Engagement," in *The Human Meaning of Social Change*, Angus Campbell and Philip E. Converse, eds., (New York, 1972), pp. 467-527.
54. Payne, *Patterns of Conflict*.
55. Some of the relationships of these processes to political breakdown in Latin America are discussed in Solaún and Quinn, *Sinners and Heretics*.
56. Of course, the materialistic conception of history essentially views the state as being appropriated or by fused to the ruling class, and consequently, as illegitimate. See, for instance, Friedrich Engel's discussion in *Socialism: Utopian and Scientific* in *Ten Classics of Marxism* (New York, 1930), pp. 67-70. In the Colombian traditional system, however, such a definition was given along party lines. The "privatization" of violence for self-defense and revenge is the norm of stateless societies; Lucy Mair, *Primitive Government* (Baltimore, 1962).
57. Mario Laserna, *Estado Fuerte o Caudillo* (Bogotá, 1968).
58. An idea about the historically small size of Colombia's armed forces can be obtained from Ruhl's chapter in this book. I am confident that a similar inference can be made on the judicial system.
59. The relative absence of this type of instrumental electoral violence on the part of the opposition can be placed within perspective by observations from my own field work in the mid1960s. Some rural community development programs experienced internal distrust. Treasurers, in particular, were frequently suspected of misappropriation of funds. Surprisingly, the locals themselves were not inclined to resolve their distrust by creation of impersonal mechanisms such as the counting of the moneys by persons other than the treasurer himself.
60. *El Tiempo*, February 18, 1922.
61. My own preliminary survey data collected in conjunction with a 1969 racial study in Colombia indicate that over 80 percent of each class category considered that one had to "beware of others." Such distrust impedes democratization through its impact on the legal system.
62. Lloyd A. Fallers, *Bantu Bureaucracy* (Cambridge, 1956). Fallers foresaw the inimical nature to democracy of these institutional patterns in preindependence Uganda at a time when many scholars were optimistic about the future of democracy in "British educated" Africa.
63. See this conditional formulation in Max Weber, *Law in Economy and Society*, Max Rheinstein, ed. (Cambridge, Mass., 1954), p. 351.
64. Richard M. Morse has referred to this problem in his important work, "The Heritage of Latin America," in L. Hartz, ed., *The Founding of New Societies*

(New York, 1964), pp. 123-77. I am simply elaborating on Morse and on Weber's classic categories.

65. The relationship between democracy and formal-legal organization has been underestimated in the contemporary literature for other reasons as well. Part of the problem is that formal organizations are often equated with "bureaucracies," which are defined as a centralized, hierarchical, self-recruited, nonparliamentary type of formal-legal organization. The main formal organizations of a democratic regime cannot, of course, be "bureaucratic" in this sense. Others have questioned the problems of participation even posed by "democratic" decentralized formal-legal organizations. Marxists are famous in this regard. As noted by Lenin there is the danger that the state will become "a force standing *above* society and "increasingly separating itself from it' "; V.I. Lenin, *State and Revolution*, in *Ten Classics of Marxism*, p. 9. While concern with the problems of representation and participation posed by the various types of formal-legal organizations is warranted, the Colombian traditional system involved a challenge to democracy different from that posed by "overbureaucratization" or "overformalization" in stable democracies.

66. None other than Blau and Scott, who have expressed reservations about the role of formal organizations in modern democracy, consider that "the essence of [formal-legal organizations] is circumscribed [limited] authority"; Peter M. Blau and W. Richard Scott, *Formal Organizations: A Comparative Approach* (San Francisco, 1962), p. 61. The same authors stress the impact of impersonal mechanisms of control in reducing conflict (pp. 176-83). It is not a coincidence that Parsons' pattern variables, inferred from Weber's analysis, describe both orientations supportive of democracy and formal-legal organization. See Seymour Martin Lipset, "Democracy and the Social System," in Harry Eckstein, ed., *Internal War, Problems and Approaches* (New York, 1964), pp. 267-334, and Blau and Scott, pp. 60-62.

67. Marxists are also puzzled by this converse problem characteristic of patrimonial organization that is created by the appropriation of the state by a particularistic (class) group, their theoretical conception of democracy largely being the classical direct form, coming from antiquity via Rousseau. Engels recognized the possibility that the state acquire sufficient autonomy [or development] during "exceptional periods" to become an "apparent mediator"; Frederich Engels, *The Origins of the Family, Private Property and the State*, cited in Immanuel Wallerstein, *The Modern World-System* (New York, 1974), p. 159. It is not clear, however, how the problem of representation inherent in large-scale societies would be solved beyond the "withering away" of the state, with the constitution of one social class, affluence and successful socialization into communist values and rules. Engels is "optimistic" or "cautious," considering at one point that the state ends when "at last it becomes the real representative of the whole society. The first act by which the state really constitutes itself the representative of the whole of society—the taking of possession of the means of production in the name of society—this is, at the same time, its last independent act as a state . . . the government of persons is replaced by the administration of things . . . . The state is not 'abolished.' It dies out . . . ."; Engels, *Socialism*, pp. 69-70. It is intriguing that Americans refer to their government as the administration and to their political system as a government of laws, not persons.

68. See Leo XIII's encyclical *Libertas*.

69. The term *gemeinschaftlich* connotes in the sociological literature a traditional social system characterized by close personal relations and a weak penetration of

the impersonalities of commercial-industrial civilization. I use it here to denote a series of Latin American cultural traits associated with economic underdevelopment that have been amply discussed in the area literature. The reader can find a still relevant discussion in Morse, "The Heritage of Latin America." My own interpretation as to the relationship between Latin American culture, socioeconomic development, and politics is detailed in Solaún and Quinn, *Sinners and Heretics*, pp. 190-205.

70. I cannot enter here into the question as to the penetrability of "capitalism" in Colombia. It is well known that not even in Spain was "feudalism" a full-blown reality; Marc Bloch, *Feudal Society* I (Chicago, 1961), pp. 187, 266. I find it helpful to use a neo-Marxist perspective relating the syndrome of *personalismo* with its described patrimonial-feudalistic elements to the economic underdevelopment of Colombia's traditional system.
71. Contrast Lipset, "Democracy and the Social System," with Bert F. Hoselitz, "Noneconomic Factors in Economic Development," *American Economic Review* 47 (1957): 28-41, and Blau and Scott, *Formal Organizations*, pp. 60-62. I might note that the most recent research on modernity suggests that two orientations particularly inimical to democracy—familism and distrust—appear to be less amenable to eradication in modernizing societies than other "traditional" orientations. This has led Inkeles and Smith to question the "modernity" status of these two orientations; Alex Inkeles and David H. Smith, *Becoming Modern, Individual Change in Six Developing Countries* (Cambridge, Mass., 1974), p. 104. This finding underscores the difficulties of developing a democratic culture in developing societies.
72. For details of Hispanic legal culture and institutions, see Morse "The Heritage of Latin America," and Karst and Rosenn, *Law and Development in Latin America*, especially chapter 1.
73. Lack of space precludes any approach to the foreign and domestic impediments to sociocultural modernization in countries such as Colombia, and to the related issue of whether revolution is required to obtain modernization. I must deal with underdevelopment as an unexplained given.
74. I cannot provide an accurate estimate of the extent and duration of the violence, a topic that has not yet received monographic treatment. In all probability it ended by 1932 with the consolidation in power of Liberal local bosses and the call to national unity to cope with a border dispute with Peru.
75. As observed earlier there is some evidence that, paradoxically, the reformist Liberal elite had a greater upper-class representation than its Conservative counterpart. President Alfonso López Pumarejo (1934-38 and 1942-45), considered by some as Colombia's equivalent to Franklin Delano Roosevelt, was also a member of the upper class.
76. The importance of this coincidence is underlined by Dahl, *Polyarchy, Participation and Opposition*, pp. 184-85. The stabilizing role of multiclass parties has been emphasized in Gabriel Almond's work.
77. See Solaún and Quinn, *Sinners and Heretics*, especially chapter 4. I can only concentrate on the main characteristics of this type of radicalism as manifested in Colombia. Surely, Gómez's populism had elements of the George Wallace type of populism: protest against the centers of political power referred to as the "oligarchy"; an underlying provincial orientation; a "backwoods" radicalism against the corruption of urban culture and mismanagement in the capital city; the purity of the folk; etc.

78. See Laureano Gómez, *Comentarios a un Régimen* (Bogotá, 1935), pp. 5, 6, 8, 9, 14, 198, 199, 255. Also see the later attacks against President López in Laureano Gómez and José de la Vega, *El Crimen de la Magdalena* (Bogotá, 1944).
79. The interested reader can consult some background details in Solaún, *Political Violence in Colombia*, pp. 274-84. Gómez's early friendship and collaboration with López is part of the local political folklore, as well as his abstention in challenging López's successful candidacy for the 1934-38 presidential term. Apparently he overestimated his influence over López—who appointed Gómez's enemy, Olaya Herrera, as his foreign secretary to negotiate a settlement with Peru—and underestimated Liberal strength. Gómez's phrase "López tricked me" referred to the post-1934 consolidation of Liberal hegemonic rule. Gómez's overall importance in the Conservative party can be appreciated from Augusto Ramírez Moreno, *La Crisis del Partido Conservador en Colombia* (Bogotá, 1937). It was not until the 1948 Bogotazo that a truly plural leadership started to emerge in the Conservative party with Ospina Pérez's increased prestige.
80. In defining regime not as a "government" or "administration," as in the "Ford regime," but as a complex political object formed by the constitutional system, its values, principles, and symbols, and the basic government formal-legal organizations that are constitutionally defined, I am basically following David Easton, *A System Analysis of Political Life* (New York, 1965).
81. These perceptions occurred in Colombia. For instance, in 1939 the Conservative convention stated that "a collective despotism prevents one half of all Colombians [the alleged percentage of Conservative followers] from exerting their political privileges; the rule of law does not exist, it does not protect the exercise of civil liberties; the agents of the government are the product of partisan sectarianism, and direct the persecution and political warfare from within the government"; Directorio Nacional Conservador, *Los Programas Conservadores de 1839 a 1949* (Bogotá, 1952), p. 70.
82. Abel, "Conservative Politics," p. 26.
83. The article in question was given to me by this most important journalist of the period, and was reproduced immediately after Gómez's death in 1965 in *El Espectador*.
84. Weinert, "Violence in Pre-modern Societies," shows for the later period of early *Violencia* (1946-49) how Liberals successfully mobilized the urban population, e.g., that their majorities were disproportionately produced by urban gains. The issue is still open as to the role of urbanization as an independent determinant of the political changes under consideration. As the innovations were dependent on developments in foreign countries, it is difficult to assess the impact of Colombian social change on them The analytical problem posed by this fact of external dependency, common to many developing nations, is discussed by Reinhard Bendix, *Nation-Building and Citizenship* (New York, 1946). In my opinion, urbanization was a variable, cumulatively reducing the likelihood of traditional Conservative majorities—i.e., majorities with the old platforms and styles—and, hence, affecting Liberal and Conservative behavior mainly in an indirect fashion.
85. I employ "attacks" because of the need to transcend an ethnocentric, highly adaptive input-output scheme viewing demands as being mostly negotiable by government and evolutionarily absorbable by the regime.
86. These two qualities have been stressed by S.N. Eisenstadt, *Modernization: Protest and Change* (Englewood Cliffs, 1966).

87. We could construct a scale of political conflict from (1) conflict over "personnel" (e.g., the best man or team) passing through, (2) conflict over the optimal way to implement commonly agreed upon policy preferences, continuing to (3) conflict caused by different preferences over discrete, specific policy issues, to (4) conflict over the collective criminality of groups, and ending with (5) ideological conflict, over ultimate, contradictory philosophies, their symbols and the derived fundamental norms, i.e., the regime. As we ascend in the scale we move from a condition of stable equilibrium to one of dynamic equilibrium arriving with (4) and (5) to situations of probable political breakdown with smaller and larger political changes, respectively. The Colombian traditional system was only capable of maintaining intraparty conflict at the lower levels; interparty conflict escalated rapidly toward levels (4) and (5).
88. The interested reader can refer to a more detailed treatment of these regime characteristics and problems in Solaún and Quinn, *Sinners and Heretics*, pp. 184-90. We argue there that the evolution, as opposed to breakdown, of openly competitive systems is contingent upon the strength of formal-legal integration in the polity, which in turn requires the structural differentiation between the regime and the party system, and the existence of an internally structurally differentiated regime. In doing so I attempt to make more explicit and specific the relationship between structural differentiation and political integration suggested in the literature, e.g., Parsons, Eisenstadt, Almond.
89. Abel, "Conservative Politics," considers that during the early 1930s, interest in Conservative party politics declined, surely because of the initial attractiveness of Liberal innovations.
90. López ran against a Conservative-backed Liberal presidential candidate. It may be indicative of the political culture of the times that years later the losing candidate would interpret the result to me personally as the product of President Santos' preferences, not the voters'. Similarly, personal correspondence available to me of another Liberal presidential candidate, defeated in 1946, blamed the president's prejudices for the result.
91. For a discussion of the violence around the heated 1946 race, see Alberto Lleras Camargo, *Sus Mejores Páginas* (Bogotá, n.d.); for 1947, see Gaitán, *Las Mejores Oraciones*; for 1949, see Guzmán, *La Violencia en Colombia*, p. 50. Those who consider the 1948 Bogotazo, the date of the assassination of the head of the Liberal party, Gaitán, as the initiation of La Violencia forget that the most famous of his speeches—*Oración de la Paz*—was a condemnation of preexisting violence; Gaitán, *Las Mejores Oraciones*, pp. 434-36. The Bogotazo did prove to be a point of no return in La Violencia.
92. Reference to this new pattern, in which congressional elections are not a contest to fill in discrete positions in the regime, appears in Gaitán, *Las Mejores Oraciones*, p. 420.
93. Ibid., p. 380.
94. Ibid., pp. 355, 371, 393.
95. Ibid., pp. 380, 438.
96. Ibid., pp. 345, 353, 376.
97. The presence of both messianic-millenarian and *cultura* orientations in Colombian culture is described by Gutiérrez, *De la Pseudo-Aristocracia*. As with other cultural systems, Colombia's lacked perfect integration, experiencing tension, and, consequently, being capable of change.
98. The socioeconomic aspect of Gaitán's rebellion was consonant with some other

Latin American expressions of populistic "reform." He was neither a Marxist nor a social revolutionary; he did not seek to eliminate any social class nor proletarianize the society. Change meant the emergence of a somewhat romantic, moralistic, Christian, or charitable order. His "left," the *fuerzas de avanzada* (the progressive social forces), was battling only against the concentration of wealth, the lust for money, and moral chaos; Gaitán, *Las Mejores Oraciones*, pp. 353, 382, 394, 404 and 405.

99. *Semana*, May 17, 1947, p. 6. Liberal *Semana* reported that Gaitán awaited the result of the general strike in silence, though the public saw his hand behind the revolutionary conspiracy. According to *Semana*, Gaitán considered that "the members of the oligarchy had set a trap for him so that he would become 'ensnared by his own triumph' and discredit himself. Wary of this trap . . . he authorized cooperation [Liberal participation in the cabinet] without any obligation or responsibility, against his 'private conviction,' and kept silent with respect to the general strike"; *Semana*, May 24, 1947, p. 4.
100. Gaitán, *Las Mejores Oraciones*, p. 437.
101. A thoughtful presentation of the Conservative major constitutional transformation is made by the highly respected Félix Restrepo S.J., *Colombia en la Encrucijada* (Bogotá, 1951).
102. These processes are defined in the section on the 1922 election. Electoral irregularities were again present. Cases were reported of campaign violence; assassinations of leaders; intertown and inter*vereda* attacks; intratown violence; the arming of civilians by government officials. "Political" intraregime conflict escalated, as each group gave a patrimonial definition or reconstitution to the formal offices that they held, i.e., conflict between the *Liberal* mayor and the *Conservative* judge, etc. Liberal journalistic protests of Conservative fraud and violence were matched by Conservative counterprotests, and, of course, each group accused the other of being "criminals," while referring to the need for violence in "self-defense." See Guzmán, *La Violencia en Colombia*.
103. See Solaún, *Political Violence in Colombia*, pp. 347-49.
104. This impression one gets from Guzmán, *La Violencia en Colombia*, and from the *guerrillero* memoirs of Eduardo Franco, *Las Guerrillas del Llano* (Bogotá, 1959). The clearest statement in these matters is an unpublished manuscript by James M. Daniels, prepared for the Center for International Studies, Princeton University, 1964.
105. Franco, in *Las Guerrillas del Llano*, for example, describes the problem of maintaining political revolutionary momentum by concentrating the employment of violence against the government as opposed to Conservative civilians.
106. According to Guzmán, 3,953 men surrendered in an undefined period after the coup, and during five days of September 1953, an additional 6,500 did so; *La Violencia en Colombia*, pp. 99-100.
107. I cannot deal adequately here with this not unusual phenomenon. Much confusion comes from the propensity of some sources to view acts against property as by definition "social": manifestations of discontent which are a precursor of social revolutionary movements. But such illegal actions can be following quite "capitalistic" orientations. For example, American gangsters generally challenge some rules of the game, not capitalism itself. An opposite bias to interpret violence as economically motivated is reinforced by the tendency of governments to define the illegal acts of political opponents as "banditry," in order to underplay their political significance and diminish support for them. Then again, some partici-

pants, under propitious circumstances, tend to give a noneconomic definition to their illegal actions in order to legitimize them. There are also the eclectic motivations of some patterns of violence, and the linkage between revolutionaries and some bandits. The importance given by social revolutionaries themselves to avoid the designation of bandits is documented in James Kohl and John Litt, *Urban Guerrilla Warfare in Latin America* (Cambridge, Mass., 1974).

108. This linkage between democratization, a movement toward both "inclusiveness" and "contestation" (see note 10), and political breakdown and retrogression is not unusual. For instance, Huntington has suggested the need for a positive relationship between social participation and "institutionalization" to avoid breakdown, and Stepan has stressed that democratization preceded political breakdown in Brazil in 1964. See Samuel P. Huntington, "Political Development and Political Decay," *World Politics* 17 (1965): 386-430 and Alfred C. Stepan, *The Military in Politics: Changing Patterns in Brazil* (Princeton, 1971).

109. Under a dictatorship, recognition of the existence of competition for power consists of defining the opposition as law-breakers or criminals, with the subsequent repression.

110. This lack of constitutional continuity, and the corresponding illegalities, are widespread phenomena in Latin America. They are manifested under both democratic (e.g., Chile 1973) and authoritarian regimes. For a well-documented discussion applied to Argentina and Brazil, see Karst and Rosenn, *Law and Development in Latin America*, especially chapter 2. The skeptic might consult this text for an illustration of the intimate relationship between political breakdown, moves toward democratization and dictatorship, and formal changes in regime structure in these countries. Also see Solaún and Quinn, *Sinners and Heretics*, pp. 6-8.

111. This relative lack of autonomy (differentiation) of the state or regime from the ruling group is pervasive throughout Latin America, where the recurrent tendency is for such groups to define themselves as "lords" over the state. There are variations in the types of political "appropriations," from the more personalistic ones (e.g., the monocratic dictatorships characterized by the perpetuation of a leader in power) and their familistic derivations (e.g., the "hereditary" systems such as the Somozas in Nicaragua and Duvaliers in Haiti), to the more developed forms characterized by party or military hegemonies with rotating executives (e.g., post-Calles Mexico and post-1964 Brazil). The reader will note that I am departing from Philippe C. Schmitter's conceptualization of Brazilian realities in "The 'Portugalization' of Brazil?," Stepan, ed., *Authoritarian Brazil*. Crucial to the fusion is the presence of *continuismo*, the willingness to use force if necessary to remain in power. (Since 1964, military *continuismo* has been the norm in Brazil; witness the 1969 coup that broke the regime's formal-legal structure of presidential succession so that a civilian would not become president.) There are also the *social* interpretations of fusion, such as the Marxist one, which despite the turnover of "bourgeois" parties in power, still consider that the state "belongs" to a social class. In the Colombian case, we are concerned with a situation unable to develop into this latter type of fusion, in the sense that not even a "bourgeois" democracy became effectively institutionalized because of the prevalent *political* fusion between the state and the ruling party.

112. As observed for an earlier period by Bergquist in "The Presidential Election of 1897," members of the Colombian upper class are rarely involved in only one occupation. Thus, there was considerable overlap in economic interests at least at this level of the system.

113. The following brief comments reflect my ongoing research on Colombian legal development. The parameters for the research and their historical background are established by Karst and Rosenn in *Law and Development in Latin America*, the fundamental treatise on the subject. Some key relationships between the legal tradition and the colonial political structure and Catholicism are well treated by Morse, "The Heritage of Latin America."
114. These have ranged from provisions regulating civil wars (e.g., the Constitution of 1863) to the area of congressional authorization of extraordinary legislative powers to the executive. Despite a judicially sanctioned congressional-executive liberal tradition in this latter area, some Colombian constitutions have prohibited to no avail the "delegations" of authority that these authorizations entailed. As late as 1945, the Liberal-sponsored constitutional changes of that year included such a prohibition in the sphere of government economic intervention (article 4). Yet economic legislation often continued to be enacted by presidential decree under the state of siege, unilaterally declared by the president himself; Carlos Restrepo Piedrahita, *Las Facultades Extraordinarias, Pequeña Historia De Una Transfiguración* (Bogotá, 1973), p. 8.
115. A recent statement on the reasons for this is found in Roberto Mangabeira Unger, *Law in Modern Society* (New York, 1976).
116. As recent events in Chile and Uruguay indicate, such democratic institutionalizations have been cyclical, not going beyond several decades. Argentina exemplifies dramatically that socioeconomic development has been a necessary but not sufficient condition for middle-run democratic institutionalization in the area.
117. Examples of these independent political variables in Colombia were the recency of civil war, and, possibly, the class background of the pre-1930 Liberal opposition.
118. Charles W. Anderson has stressed how in Latin America, political changes are seldom matched by substantial social change, *Politics and Economic Change in Latin America: The Governing of Restless Nations* (Princeton, 1967). Marx made a comparable statement about the "unchangeableness" of Asiatic societies in "striking contrast with the constant dissolution and refounding of Asiatic States"; Karl Marx, *Capital* I (New York, 1967), pp. 357-58.
119. Here again, it could be argued that there is change with continuity. The visible evidence of fraud was less than on other occasions but the razor-thin margin of victory provided a greater incentive for charges of fraud than in some previous instances. This time, however, extensive violence did not follow the charges.

Chapter 2

The National Front: Historical Perspective and Overview

Harvey F. Kline

While it is certain that the tendency to form coalitions with other parties is a general characteristic of party politics, this phenomenon has been particularly important in Colombian history. Colombian politics departs sharply from the experiences of other Latin American nations. In contrast to most of these Latin American countries, the Colombian polity has been characterized by the prevalence of civilian or party politics. Since the turn of the century, Colombia has experienced only two coups d'état (1953 and 1957) and only four years of military rule (1953-57). The prevalence of civilian regimes has not meant, however, the institutionalization of democratic regimes. Full-blown competition for power among the two traditional, elite-controlled parties—the Liberals and the Conservatives—has led to civil wars with dramatic death tolls.[1] Because the civil wars have not resulted in total partisan victory, interparty competition has been countered by the formation of coalitions.

In this chapter, after a discussion of some general characteristics of Colombian politics, I will make a brief survey of pre-National Front coalitions, to describe and analyze later the basic characteristics of the Frente Nacional. In so doing, I hope to provide a general framework for the more specialized chapters which follow.

CHARACTERISTICS OF COLOMBIAN PARTY POLITICS

At the outset, it is important to place coalition formation in Colombia within the context of the political party system. This may be done through a number of "tendency statements," which describe what generally has been the case in Colombian politics.

Colombian parties started as elitist instruments, a characteristic which they have maintained to this day. In structure, they have more in common with European "parties of notables"[2]—parties with minimal permanent organization, control by the top leaders, and few dues-paying members—than they do with "mass parties." The exact date for the beginning of Colombian political parties depends on the definition used for "party." A convenient date for my analysis is 1849, when for the first time there were two parties, one calling itself the "Liberal," and the other the "Conservative," each with public pronouncements of programs. These parties did not originate from a series of mass demands; rather, they developed among well-to-do groups, for their purposes of obtaining the benefits of governing. During no time in Colombian history has one of the traditional parties tried to form a "mass party." These parties, based on dues-paying memberships, regular meetings, extensive party organization, and the theoretical upward flow of power and decision making, originated in Europe. However, this does not mean that there has been no party organization in Colombia. Both parties have typically had national, regional, and local directorates, as well as youth groups. Yet the desire to get people directly involved in political participation other than voting does not exist as much as it does in the classical "mass party" cases. For instance, in the past decade, a new party, ANAPO (Alianza Nacional Popular, National Popular Alliance) of Gustavo Rojas Pinilla, has attempted to form such a mass party, without any major result.[3] As will be argued below, there never was a reason to organize parties in a mass fashion since the masses could be tied successfully to the parties by patron-clientele relationships and, especially in this century, through appeals to tradition.

During the nineteenth century, the elite sectors of the two parties developed ideological differences that still exist to some extent. At the beginning, the two party elites were very similar in ideology, as evidenced in their first programs.[4] However, as the nineteenth century continued, their positions diverged. The Liberals were for federalism, free trade, and anticlericalism. The Conservatives, on the other hand, favored centralism, protectionism, and policies generally favorable to the church. There were notable exceptions to this generalization,[5] but most often these were the positions of the respective parties. Furthermore, the parties changed the constitutions and policies of the country when they came to power, so there were shifts from extreme federalism to centralism, and the Jesuits came and went.

The nineteenth-century ideological split began to break down in the 1920s, largely due to the influence of Rafael Uribe Uribe.[6] A significant faction of the Liberal party demanded that the state take a direct role in social reform. This faction was especially active during Alfonso López Pumarejo's "Revolution on the March" (1934-38), and their demands were later symbolized by Jorge Gaitán. In answer to this new thrust in Liberalism, one part of the Conservative party, led by Laureano Gómez, took a reactionary stance, evoking as model the Spain of Ferdinand and Isabella, that is, of Spanish corporativism. This model was one of a highly centralized state, with corporate representation, especially for the military, the landowners, and the church, and with those groups having their own areas of domain and control, called fueros.

Today the ideological differences of the three congressional party elites (Liberals, Conservatives, and ANAPO) are about as great as those of the Democratic and Republican parties in the United States.[7] The Liberals are more welfare-state oriented, more anticlerical, and less private-property-oriented than the Conservatives, who tend to take opposite positions on these ideological dimensions. ANAPO is—despite the official positions of the party given in the declarations of the leaders—a middle-of-the-road party, with a greater orientation to the middle and lower classes than the other parties. In short, cynicism and motive analysis notwithstanding,[8] there are and have been ideological differences between the parties. Whether these differences are sufficient for Colombian development depends basically on normative considerations.

Historically, the elites of the parties were very effective mobilizing segments of the masses behind their respective parties. This support was probably not because of socioeconomic programs, but through the use of the patron-clientele relationships. At the beginning of party history, the voters for the parties were the clientele of the elites. Dependent *campesinos* voted for the party of the landowner, whatever it was. The clientele of economic elites other than the large landowners went along because of similar dependency. This situation was not unlike the patron-clientele politics in other countries and at other times. In Colombia, however, many families had martyrs who had died for a party in one of the frequent civil wars. As a result, the masses developed intense loyalities, which reinforced the initial patrimonial reason for choosing a political party and in some sectors outlived it.[9] Over time, the masses became the cannon fodder for the party elites in the wars between the two parties (six in the last century and two in this). The appearance of a strict and intense political socialization which transcended patron-client relationships among the Colombian lower classes seems to be a product of having relatives who had been killed by the other political party. The socialization was strict in the sense that most Colombians were "born with a party carnet attached to the umbilical cord''.[10] It was intense because it was built on hatred. This, combined with the religious nature of the conflicts—the Conservatives used the Catholic religion to mobilize their followers—led to a division of the Colombian population in two closed worlds, one Liberal and one Conservative.[11] Thus, peasant and small town communities tended, and still tend, to be associated with one of the parties, and even in the large cities the main difference between *barrios* can be partisan loyalties. Even among the highly educated, the author has encountered this extreme hatred of the other party. In brief, the masses of Colombia were ''organized,'' not in the sense of a European mass political party, but in an emotional sense. The effect of the emotional organization was similar to that of the European mass-party organization: the masses were obedient followers of the party leaders.

The results of this intense socialization have been many, three of which seem particularly noteworthy. First, other cleavages, such as social class or economic considerations, have been placed in a secondary position to overwhelming importance of political party. This is evident today in the relationships of interest groups with the political parties. Because party cleavages emerged before those economic considerations led to interest groups, economic interests tend to be organized into several groups (as in the case of labor) along party lines, or to have equal access to the memberships of all parties, (as in the case of the upper status groups such as the Coffee Growers Federation).[12] This party cleavage has been observed with dismay and disbelief by various observers, who deem it ''irrational.'' What is clear is that many socioeconomic issues have not historically been as important in Colombian politics as perhaps they should have been. Second and relatedly, third-party movements have been notably unsuccessful. This was true of Jorge Gaitán's UNIR in the 1920s and now seems also to have been the case of Rojas Pinilla's ANAPO. It is difficult to begin a new political party if a substantial proportion of the electorate has an ascribed, intense identification with political parties in existence. Third, the masses seem to take these party differences more seriously than do the elite elements, although research does show a remarkably high percentage of congressmen and other party leaders who come from the same party as their fathers and paternal grandfathers.[13] The difference can probably be related to the *intensity* of the political socialization process among the lower classes. Indeed, the party coalitions which are the subject of this chapter would not have been possible if the elites had taken the party differences as seriously as have the masses, or at least had done so as constantly.

There is yet another important characteristic of the Colombian polity: the tendency toward party hegemony. This consists of relatively long periods of time, during which one party controls the presidency and the majority of the national Congress and is dominant in national government. Party hegemony is a common theme in two party systems in general; in Colombia, the three most notable periods of such hegemony have been the Liberal hegemony of 1861-86, the Conservative hegemony of 1886-1930, and the Liberal dominance of 1930-46. Some observers would add a final hegemony of the Conservatives from 1946-53, but this period differed from the other three cases because of the relatively short duration and the majority status of the Liberals in the Congress during part of the period. As will be shown below, coalitions between the two parties form an important part of such hegemonies.

During these periods of hegemony, the dominant party has tended to split, while the minority party (which might also be split) has tended not to participate in presidential elections at all. This splitting of the dominant party is in keeping with what William Riker has called the "size principle."[14] The factions within Colombian parties have had great importance since the beginning of party politics and, generally speaking, they are the basis of party coalitions. Periods of hegemony have usually ended with the dominant party presenting two presidential candidates and losing to the one presidential candidate of the minority party (for instance in 1930 and 1946).

In summary, Colombian parties have always been instigated and controlled by the elite. The ideological differences of the elites have varied over time, at best being called moderate today. Probably, most Colombians have followed parties not for ideas (although they might learn the party ideology in the same way as they learn the party loyalty), but for reasons of family tradition. These elite-controlled parties have tended to exercise power during periods of hegemony, and the socioeconomic cleavages which have appeared with the modernization of Colombia have had secondary roles. Thus, coalition formation, the corollary of hegemony, is also an elite activity, resulting from the decision of a few party leaders—although there might be various mass pressures which cause party leaders to look for coalitions. The leaders plan such coalitions with a fairly strong assurance that the party members will follow them. Parties, in short, have generally been instruments of elite politics and control, with few "linkages" from the masses upward.

BIPARTISAN COALITIONS BEFORE THE NATIONAL FRONT

Nineteenth Century

If we place the start of Colombian two-party competition in 1849, it was only five years later that the first bipartisan coalition was formed. This was a coalition of the Conservatives and a faction of the Liberals called Gólgotas or Radicals against the dictatorship of Melo. The government of Obaldía, rightful designate, formed in Ibagué, included two secretaries of state: one was Liberal and one Conservative.[15] It was the first indication of "parity" (the equal sharing of posts) in Colombian history. Later in the same year, the Conservatives and the Radical Liberals joined once again, in this case to elect Mallarino vice-president of the republic.[16] This was the first case of a joint candidate of the two political parties, albeit part of the Liberal party (the Draconianos, later called Independents) did not participate. These two methods of coalition—*parity* and *support of a joint candidate*—have been common in Colombian history, culminating in the National Front.

The presidential election of 1857 also saw party cooperation of a kind. In addition to one Liberal and one Conservative candidate, there was a candidate of a "National party," which was made up of individuals from both parties. This candidate was Tomás Cipriano de Mosquera, who lost the election to the Conservative Ospina Rodríguez.[17] This National party coalition of 1857 is unlike most of the other coalitions of Colombian partisan history, because it was in addition to the two traditional parties. Ten years later, the tables were turned on Mosquera, by then President of the Republic. In 1867, it was the Radical Liberals and the Conservatives, working in conjunction, who opposed Don Tomás and caused his downfall,[18] when they felt that Mosquera was becoming too dictatorial.

Two years later, in 1869, the Radical Liberals and the entire Conservative party agreed to share public posts equally, in order to assure peace, republican institutions, and reconciliation.[19] This agreement was notable in being more extensive and formalized than the previous ones. Other points of agreement included: support of the candidacy of Mosquera; equal representation of both parties in the Congress, departmental legislatures, and other public corporations; and mutual agreement of both parties in the face of "all other political questions."[20]

There was then a hiatus of some fifteen years, during which there were no coalitions. This was at the height of the Liberal hegemony. In 1884, Rafael Núñez was inaugurated for his second term of office, declaring himself an "irrevocable member of Colombian Liberalism."[21] The Conservatives had been defeated in a civil war in 1877, and by 1879 the leading chiefs of that party had concluded that revolution would not work; the most feasible route to power, they thought, would be through cooperation with the Liberals. Hence, the Conservative party supported Núñez to a significant extent in 1879 and gave him their official support in the election of 1883.[22] Núñez reciprocated by naming a bipartisan cabinet, including not only Conservatives but also his Radical Liberal opponents along with his Independent Liberal supporters.[23] Despite this effort at conciliation, the Radical Liberals nonetheless mounted a revolution against Núñez, albeit unsuccessfully.

What followed was the most significant shift of party labels during the nineteenth century. In an effort to destroy those old partisan labels, supporters of the "regeneration"—as the Núñez government was called—formed a new political organization called the "National party."[24] This was basically composed of Conservatives and Independent Liberals. Although the term "National party" was used as late as 1892, by mid-1888 the preponderance of Conservatives within that group had been assured. The Independent Liberals either drifted back to the Liberal party or remained in the Conservative party as members of the "Nationalist" wing.[25] In brief, what started as a bipartisan coalition intended as the basis for a new political party changed back into the Conservative party and the hegemony of that party.

Twentieth Century

The turn of the century coincided with the War of the Thousand Days[26] (1899-1902), another civil war over party hegemony. In this three-year-long war, some 100,000 Colombians were killed in the name of political party. Although the Conservative party was not overthrown, the tragedy of the loss of Panama occurred the year after the struggle ended and was attributed to the civil war. Thereafter, a spirit of interparty collaboration materialized, crystalizing in the administration of Rafael Reyes (1904-09). With themes like "peace and brotherhood" and "less politics and more administration," Reyes formed a government in which two of the six ministers were Liberals, the other four coming from his Conservative party.[27] In addition, President Reyes, in 1905, instituted an "incomplete list" system of voting for the Congress.[28] According to this system, two-thirds of the congressional seats within an electoral district would go to the party receiving the most votes, the other one-third would be given to the second party. President Reyes hoped that his actions would give the minority Liberals some representation in government at the national level, hence reducing their revolutionary desires and bringing peace.

In 1909, yet another coalition, the "Republican Union," was formed. It was composed of individuals from both parties who reacted to the heavy-handed government of Reyes.[29] He soon resigned, but his successor, Conservative González Valencia, included Liberals in his cabinet. Carlos Restrepo, also a Conservative, continued the coalition and its label during his presidential term of 1910-14.[30] (One individual who helped organize this coalition was Enrique Olaya Herrera, who was later to be a protagonist in another coalition.)[31] Similar Conservative-Liberal coalitions in the cabinets were maintained during the Conservative administrations of José Vicente Concha (1914-18) and Marco Fidel Suárez (1918-22).[32] During the period before 1918, the Liberals supported the moderate Conservative presidential candidate. In 1918, some of the Liberals banded with dissident Conservatives in offering a presidential candidate against both the Conservative and Liberal party candidates.[33] Four years later, however, there were again only two candidates: one Liberal and one Conservative. The victorious Conservative, Pedro Nel Ospina, (1922-26) attempted in vain to get Liberal collaboration in his cabinet, as did his successor, Miguel Abadía, (1926-30).[34] By the 1920s, however, the Liberals had decided to go their own way. The changing party ideology mentioned earlier was increasing in importance, and it widened the difference between the two parties.

Toward the end of the 1920s, the Conservative party ran into difficulties, caused in part by the Great Depression, in part by apparent bankruptcy of the party itself, and in part by the scandal of the massacre of the banana workers in Santa Marta.[35] The hegemony was not ended by a clear victory of the Liberal party, but by a coalition, the "National Concentration." The new president, Liberal Enrique Olaya Herrera, invited members of the Conservative party to form part of his cabinet, which they did for several years.[36] The two parties were, however, unable to maintain the coalition after violence broke out between their followers in 1930. This conflict, it has been suggested, might have been as widespread and intense as the one that started sixteen years later, if it had not been for the international conflict with Peru over Leticia.[37] The National Concentration government of Olaya was followed by the purely Liberal "Revolution on the March" of Alfonso López Pumarejo, initiating the period of Liberal hegemony known as the "Liberal Republic."

The closest predecessors in time of the recent National Front were also the closest spiritually. They were the "National Union" coalitions under, first, Liberal President Alberto Lleras Camargo (1945-46) and, then, Conservative President Mariano Ospina Pérez (1946-50). The National Union began in 1945 when President López resigned during his second term amid personal and political difficulties. The personal difficulties had to do with scandals about the alleged involvement of his family in all sorts of sordid events, most notably the death of a prize fighter. Politically, his reformist policies of social mobilization were encountering extreme opposition from party elites, both from the Conservatives and from the moderate wing of his own party. Included in those difficulties was the attempted coup d'état of Pasto (1944). López resigned and Alberto Lleras became the president for the remaining year of the term. During that time, "National Union" meant that three Moderate Conservatives held cabinet posts,[38] although the Historical Conservatives and particularly Laureano Gómez denounced the coalition government.[39] Not much was accomplished during the year of Lleras rule, but civil war was avoided despite growing labor and partisan agitation and strife. At the end of his term in 1946, Lleras Camargo stated: "In the moment that I assumed the presidency, my political perspective had to be conditioned strictly to the necessity of preserving national political stability, above all other considerations."[40] Throughout Lleras Camargo's speeches, the theme clearly emerges that Colombia was not ready for a democracy with a loyal opposition. Democratic competition for power, Lleras thought, would lead to violence. The only way to avoid this was through a coalition government of both parties.[41] It is not coincidental that ten years later one of the major architects of the National Front was Alberto Lleras Camargo.

During the presidential campaign of 1946, Conservative candidate Mariano Ospina Pérez promised a continuation of the National Union.[42] Ospina was clearly not the most important leader in the Conservative party; that was Laureano Gómez. The position of Gómez vis-à-vis the National Union during the electoral campaign remains a point of controversy. Some argue that he was quiet and did not want the continuation of the coalition.[43] Others see Ospina's use of the slogan of ''National Union'' as a stroke of the brilliant Gómez; hence it posed a bipartisan candidate—or at least one who promised bipartisan government—against two partisan Liberal candidates, Jorge Gaitán and Gabriel Turbay.[44] Two things are clear. First, Gómez did come out against the National Union soon after the Conservative Ospina became president. Second, Ospina not only continued the coalition government, but extended it beyond what it had been under Alberto Lleras. The cabinet was divided equally between the two parties, six Liberals and six Conservatives.[45] In addition, Ospina inaugurated a ''cross-over'' system in the *departamentos* or provinces. The governor (appointed by the president) and the secretary of government were named from different parties within each *departamento*. Toward the end of his term, Ospina proposed that the next presidential term be of four presidents, two Liberals and two Conservatives, each serving for one year. Nothing came of this proposal.[46]

The Ospina National Union had difficulties from the very beginning. First, it was challenged by both Gómez and Gaitán—representing the extremes of their perspective parties—in a struggle to establish party hegemony. Second, the rural violence—La Violencia—was beginning, although it had not reached the intensity that resulted from the assassination of Gaitán on April 9, 1948. Perhaps the National Union was also doomed from the start because it did not meet the fundamental problems of the society.[47] At the elite level, there were constant shifts of cabinets and increasing hostilities between the politicians themselves. Finally, in March 1948, Gaitán denounced the National Union and the Liberals withdrew, leaving a list of demands.[48]

The following month, Gaitán was assassinated, and Ospina requested a new National Union to save the system from this social upheaval. The Liberal leaders, led by Darío Echandía, preferred the resignation of Ospina, but since it was not forthcoming, they accepted the new coalition.[49] Given the difficult times, it is somewhat surprising that the second Ospina National Union lasted thirteen months. Violence was raging in the countryside; the extreme Conservatives led by Gómez were against the coalition (Gómez had his eyes on the

Table 1
Basic Characteristics of Coalition Governments in Colombia before the National Front

Years	Name	Participants	Purpose and Stipulations
1854	———	Conservatives Radical Liberals	Against dictatorship of Melo; two secretaries of state, one from each party.
1854	———	Conservatives Radical Liberals	To elect Mallarino vice president.
1857	National Party	Parts of both parties	To support candidacy of Mosquera.
1867	———	Conservatives Radical Liberals	Against strong government of Mosquera.
1869	———	Conservatives Radical Liberals	To elect Mosquera; equal representation in Congress and other public corporations; mutual assent on all political problems.
1883-1888	National Party	Conservatives, Independent Liberals	In support of Núñez and his "regeneration." Began as an attempt to get all factions into the cabinet, which failed. An attempt to do away with old parties, which failed.
1904-1909	———	Parts of both parties	As part of reconciliation after War of the Thousand Days; two Liberals in cabinet of six.
1909-1914	Republican Union	Parts of both parties	Against strong government of Reyes; after his fall, continued through sharing of cabinet posts.
1914-1922	———	Parts of both parties	A continuation of the Republican Union, without using name. Minority representation of Liberals in cabinet; support of Moderate Conservative presidential candidate through 1918.

Table 1 (cont'd)

Years	Name	Participants	Purpose and Stipulations
1930-1932	National Concentration	Parts of both parties	In support of candidacy of Olaya. Bipartisan cabinet.
1946	National Union —Lleras C.	Liberals, Moderate Conservatives	Political conflict over López; general instability; three Moderate Conservatives in cabinet.
1946-1948; 1948-1949	National Union —Ospina	Liberals, Moderate Conservatives	In support of candidacy of Ospina; after election, in response to being a minority president and to the violence, especially after the death of Gaitán. Cabinet divided equally, with six from each party; "cross-over" system in *departamentos*, with governors and secretaries of government from different parties.

presidency for the following 1950-54 term); Liberal demands on the president increased.[50] It should be remembered that the Liberals were a majority party. In none of the cases discussed above had the entire majority party entered into a coalition with a minority president. Finally, in May 1949, Ospina Pérez fired several Liberal governors. This led to the resignation of the six Liberals in the cabinet,[51] the dissolution of Congress, and the virtual dictatorship of the Conservative party. Coalition government ended for the next decade.

In conclusion, it is evident that during the twentieth century, coalitions between the two traditional parties were almost as common as straight party government (see Table 1). If one examines the years of civilian government in this century prior to the military government of 1953, one finds that fully twenty-three years were of coalition between the Liberals and the Conservatives. These coalitions, as shown, often consisted of mutual support of the same presidential candidate and, even more frequently, coparticipation in the president's cabinet.

THE NATIONAL FRONT REGIME

In discussing the National Front coalition, three aspects are important. First, the conditions which led to formation of the coalition must be described. Second, the motives of the founders should be considered. Finally, the Front must be evaluated by the perspective of whether it was able to meet its objectives, and its effects on the polity, i.e., government, political parties, interest groups, and political participation.

Conditions Leading to the National Front

The decade that followed the end of the National Union government (1949) was a traumatic one in Colombian political history. At least 200,000 Colombians were killed in the name of party loyalty, even after the party leaders asked their followers to stop the bloodshed.[52] The only military dictatorship of this century was established in 1953, with the support of all groups within the parties, except the Historical Conservatives led by Laureano Gómez. The dictatorship was only partially successful in ending the violence. Although it talked of social reform and carried out a great deal of economic infrastructure improvements, the government became corrupt, showed signs of perpetuating itself, and grew increasingly repressive.[53] While the Rojas Pinilla dictatorship was probably not so reformist as some would have us believe,[54] it did have the advantages of not being bound by the traditional party hatreds and of having the highest coffee prices of the century. It is not the purpose here to evaluate the Rojas government; the point is that several things were not "normal" for Colombian politics during the dictatorship. First, there was the continuing bloodletting in the countryside, which was out of control of the party leaders. Second, and perhaps more important for the party elites,[55] the "rules of the elite political game" were being violated. The traditional parties and civilian politicians were not in power. Both of these factors helped motivate the founders of the National Front to form a coalition to replace the Rojas government.

Although it might have been inspired by the ideas of the expresident Alfonso López Pumarejo, the concrete plan of coalition government which came to fruition in the National Front grew out of two meetings of former presidents Laureano Gómez and Alberto Lleras Camargo, and from two agreements signed in Bogotá. At the first meeting in Benidorm in 1956, while Rojas was still in power, the two political leaders agreed on five points: (1) that common action by the Liberal and Conservative parties was needed to insure the quickest possible return to civilian, democratic government; (2) that both parties must share the blame for the violence and the breakdown of political order that had occurred; (3) that the role of the military should be returned to that of protecting Colombia from external aggression and internal disturbances; (4) that a coalition government or a series of coalition governments would have to be established; and (5) that "Colombia is unfertile land for dictatorship."[56] While the rhetoric implied that both parties were united behind this agreement, such was not the case. Gómez definitely represented only one wing of the Conservative party; the other wing, headed by Mariano Ospina Pérez, was still cooperating with the government of Rojas. This split of the Conservative party later impeded the implementation of the original agreements, and proved to be a disturbing factor for policy making during most of the National Front.

The followers of expresident Ospina were pushed toward agreement with the Liberals by the events of late 1956 and early 1957. The National Constituent Assembly (ANAC) was closed in the wake of Rojas's proclaimed candidacy for another presidential term (1958-62), and the *ospinistas* were excluded from the military government for the first time.[57] This led to the "Pact of March" between the Liberals and the Ospina Conservatives; it differed in language, but not in substance, from the earlier Pact of Benidorm. However, even though the Laureanista Conservatives wrote the Pact of March, they refused to sign it since it appeared to them that the *ospinistas* were asserting themselves too strongly.[58] Conservative party divisions between the factions of the two former presidents prevented agreement.

After Rojas was overthrown by a military coup in 1957, Conservative factional conflict increased. This was evident in the third pact of the series, signed by Laureano Gómez and Alberto Lleras, this time in Sitges, Spain. While the original goal of ridding Colombia of the military government had become unnecessary after the coup, as the military leaders sought a return to civilian rule, the Sitges agreement made more explicit the conditions of the interparty coalition. But once again this was basically an agreement between the Liberals and the Gómez Conservatives, with the Ospina Conservatives relegated to a secondary role.[59]

The pact, later to be incorporated into the formal-legal National Front pact, agreed that the first president under the coalition would be a Conservative. The question then became, which Conservative? Internal conflicts over this question finally led to the fourth, and final, pact of the negotiation for the National Front, the "Pact of San Carlos," signed by members of all the major factions of the two traditional parties. The main stipulation added by the Pact of San Carlos was that the Conservative candidate would be chosen by the National Congress, which would be elected before the president.[60]

The results of these agreements were submitted to the people of Colombia, who overwhelmingly approved them as constitutional amendments in a plebiscite, held in December 1957. Soon afterward, congressional elections were held. The Laureanista Conservatives emerged from the election as the largest Conservative faction in Congress, and hence effectively vetoed the candidacy of Guillermo León Valencia, until then the strongest Conservative candidate for the presidency. After negotiation, the top party leaders then agreed that the first president would be a Liberal and that the coalition would be extended from twelve to sixteen years. The final accord, as amended after the plebiscite, was ratified by the Colombian Congress as a constitutional amendment in 1958.

The basic stipulations of the National Front amendments for the 1958-74 period follow:[61]

1. The presidency would alternate every four years between the two traditional parties (*alternación*).
2. All legislative bodies (national congress, departmental assemblies, municipal councils) would be divided equally between the Liberals and Conservatives regardless of the electoral results within a district (*paridad* or parity). Within each of the traditional parties, seats would be assigned by a list form of proportional representation.
3. This same rule of parity would apply to all high administrative appointments, such as the president's cabinet, governors' cabinets, governors, and mayors.
4. No new political parties could take part in elections during the sixteen-year period; only the Liberal and Conservative parties could participate. However, as will be seen below, this stipulation was interpreted loosely.
5. The lower level, nonappointive bureaucrats would not be chosen on the basis of partisan affiliation, but rather on the basis of merit in a proposed civil service system. This was to end the pre-National Front practice of complete changes of bureaucrats with changes of the party in power.
6. All legislation had to be passed by a two-third majority in the National Congress.
7. A minimum of ten percent of the national budget had to go to education.
8. Women were given equal political rights.

In sum, the National Front was a legal mechanism designed to divide political power equally among the two traditional parties. In doing so, it established a limited or partial democracy. Political competition was legally restricted to the two traditional parties, and indeed they would not compete with each other in elections.

The 1968 Constitutional Reform changed parts of the National Front for the rest of the period, and extended other parts beyond 1974. While the reform was long, complicated, and often misunderstood, the following are its central points in terms of interparty coalition government:

1. Cabinet ministries, governors, mayors, and other administrative positions which are not part of the civil service will be divided equally between Liberals and Conservatives until August 7, 1978—four years after the termination of the National Front. After that date, the same offices will be divided among the parties "in such a way that gives adequate and equitable participation to the major party distinct from that of the president." However, if that party decides not to participate in the executive, the president is free to name the officials in any way he chooses.[62]
2. The elective legislative bodies will not be divided equally, however. Departmental assemblies and municipal councils became completely competitive in 1970 and Congress in 1974.
3. Beginning in 1970, new political parties could participate in elections where the rule of parity did not exist, and in all elections from 1974 on.
4. The two-thirds vote was no longer necessary to pass legislation in the Congress after 1968.

Thus, the reform sought a gradual return to a fully democratic constitutional government.

Motives of the Founders of the National Front

The study of the motives of politicians is fraught with difficulties. In the first place, interview responses and/or memoirs present only what the politicians say their motives were. In the second place, brief, pseudo-psychological analysis is unsatisfying. And in the third place, assigning motives on the basis of other factors (such as socioeconomic ones) tends to be excessively deterministic and one-sided. Nevertheless, in this section I shall (1) consider the purposes of the National Front as seen by its two basic architects, Alberto Lleras Camargo and Laureano Gómez, and (2) discuss the common secondary analysis of the "real" motives, as seen by Marxist critics.

We have seen that in 1946, Alberto Lleras deemed Colombia unready for full, competitive democracy. This was leading, he stated, to instability and an escalation of conflict between the two political parties. When the National Front was being formed, Lleras Camargo held to his earlier opinion. After the fall of Rojas, the future president clearly credited Rojas's sudden "abdication" to the agreement of the two parties through the Pact of Benidorm.[63] In a New Year's speech to the nation on January 1, 1959, the first president of the Front cited five purposes of the Front other than the overthrow of Rojas: (1) to pacify the country; (2) to restore the economy; (3) to implement serious development plans for the future of the country; (4) to restore external credit and use wasted resources; and (5) to give all Colombians basic human rights, such as education, property, and personal material and spiritual development. All of this would result if the *clase dirigente* (the ruling class) would dedicate itself for sixteen years to a gigantic effort of progress and justice, without pulling itself apart. The parties would then become instruments of "democratic action" and stop being arms of destruction; national institutions would be consolidated and respected. Lleras Camargo concluded by saying: "In other words: to do everything that the two parties had said should be done, but that each had not allowed the other to do; and not to do in sixteen years what one of the parties might want to do, against the will of the other."[64] The publically stated motives of Laureano Gómez were quite similar: (1) combat Rojas' dictatorship; (2) restore civilian political institutions; (3) pacify the country; (4) bring order to collective life; (5) give the government all the possible dynamic qualities; and (6) search for progress and justice.[65]

Several things are apparent from the foregoing. First, the goals mentioned by both political leaders were of the "valence" kind; that is, goals that few could be against, at least within the civilian elite sectors of the polity. Second, although Lleras Camargo did mention the "ruling class," neither of the two mentioned the consolidation of that class as a primary objective. However, Marxist analysts, such as Diego Montaña Cuéllar, do see such motives. Basically, such an analysis posits that the National Front was the political expression of the economic phenomenon of "upper bourgeoisie" dominance. Before the Frente, the upper bourgeoisie had used the two political parties in competition. This method had not proved successful, but instead had led to the Violencia and military rule. Hence, the traditional party elites had come together to form a "*clase dirigente*," the same term used by Lleras Camargo. Montaña argues that the National Front should be interpreted in the following way: "This constitutional two-party system is the recognition that they cannot continue existing separately because nothing differentiates them, everything unifies them, except for the fight for bureaucratic positions that now are divided equally."[66]

One can question whether the founders of the National Front were thinking in precisely those terms. But to analysts like Montaña the results of an agreement such as the Front are more important than the verbalized motives, simply because one does not have to think in class terms to behave in a classist way. In any case, it is a fact that the traditional parties are elite-controlled and that the Front gave those parties a monopoly. Furthermore, the requirement of a two-thirds majority on legislation built a conservative, status-quo bias into the system, inhibiting the formulation and implementation of policies which lacked bipartisan support.

Effects of the National Front

This section is not intended to evaluate completely the National Front; that is the goal of the chapters which follow. I will only look at the National Front in relation to the above described goals of its founders and consider the impact on government, political parties, interest groups, and electoral behavior.

The initial pact of the two parties signed in Benidorm probably did have some effect in the fall of Rojas Pinilla. Also important, however, were other factors, such as the growing opposition of the church and student groups, the deterioration of the economy, the increasing repressiveness of the regime, the decision of Rojas to extend his presidency for another four-year period, and finally, the opposition of the military. Hence the initial steps toward the formation of the National Front can be seen as only a partial cause for the fall of the dictator.

Perhaps the greatest accomplishment of the Front was the end of the party-oriented violence in the countryside, though it was a long process that took about six years to complete.[67] This does not mean that all violence ended. Pockets of banditry remained, and after 1964, there was a resurgence of leftist guerrilla activities. However, it is clear from our previous discussion that the pacification of the countryside was extremely important to the founders of the Frente. In this the Front was successful, although there were some unanticipated effects, such as political "disengagement" in the form of electoral abstention.

The planning machinery of the Colombian government increased greatly during the National Front years, not only because of the expressed intentions of the founders, but also because of the emphasis placed on planning by the Alliance for Progress, as a prerequisite for aid. Whether the elaborate planning apparatus and the growth of the technocracy that occurred during the Frente led to a more rational allocation of resources and increased development is beyond the scope of this discussion. But it is clear that Colombia's external credit was extensive during the period, and the National Front appears to have had something to do with it. Indeed one reason Colombia became a showcase of the Alliance for Progress was because of the perception of United States policy-makers that the National Front was an experiment in "democracy" worthy of their support.[68] In the long run, one should question whether this external credit was to the benefit of Colombia. In fact, the staff of the United States Senate Committee on Foreign Affairs concluded that the Alliance for Progress aid made it possible for Colombian political leaders to put off needed reforms.[69]

No one can seriously argue that all Colombians have the rights of education, property, and material and spiritual development proclaimed by the Frente's founders. Given the social and economic difficulties of 1958,[70] these goals were overly ambitious. More pertinent would be to question whether Colombians have more of such things than they did in 1958 (government figures, for example, indicate that per capita income and education have increased),[71] and if there is any reason to think that progress in such areas has been more rapid because of the political arrangements of the National Front. Although some of these matters are considered in later chapters, one should realize that these "counterfactual conditional"[72] arguments can never be answered empirically. In short, some of the goals proclaimed by the founders of the National Front have been realized, others have been partially realized, and yet others seem to be no closer to realization than in 1958. But the effects of the National Front have been important in areas not mentioned by its founders, and it is to the consideration of several of these aspects that we now turn.

One of the most dramatic political results of the National Front was the increased factionalization of the two traditional parties. This phenomenon of factions within the parties was hardly new in Colombia; indeed, we have seen factions throughout Colombian party history. It has also been noted that the conflict between the factions within the Conservative party caused difficulties in the negotiation of the National Front and that the necessity of having a Liberal as the first president led to a four-year extension of the Front. Nevertheless, factionalism during the Front years was even more pronounced, because of a combination of two factors.[73] First, the National Front, as was the intention, eliminated all competition between the two traditional parties; this gave groups and factions within the parties the freedom to fight among themselves. The real political competition during the period was *within* the two parties. Secondly, the Frente's proportional representation system accentuated this factionalism, probably more than a single-member district plurality system would have. One characteristic of the proportional representation system led to even further fragmentation. This was the stipulation that, if a list did not receive one half of the electoral quotient (total number of votes for a party divided by the total number of seats assigned to that party), then the votes of that list went to the list *with the same label* that received the most votes within the same party. Thus, a group (as, for example, the Unionist Conservatives) could offer more than one list, with the security that any "wasted" votes would revert to the list with the most votes.

During the National Front, the Conservative party was the more factionalized of the traditional political parties. The major factions were those associated with Ospina, later called the Unionistas, and with Gómez, earlier called the Historicals or Doctrinaires and later, the Independents, while a third important group, for a short period at the beginning of the Front, was headed by Gilberto Alzate. The Liberal party was less divided although during part of the period there was competition between the "Official Liberals" and the MRL (Movimiento Revolucionario Liberal, Revolutionary Liberal Movement), as well as other less important groups. This situation was complicated by the emergence of a "movement" led by Gustavo Rojas Pinilla, ANAPO (Alianza Nacional Popular, National Popular Alliance). Until 1971, when ANAPO officially proclaimed itself a political party, it claimed to be a movement of both parties (a suitable strategy, since before the Constitutional Reform of 1968, it could have entered no elections if it had been considered a new party). ANAPO presented both Liberal and Conservative candidates for legislative bodies and for the presidency, but was much more successful with its Conservative candidates. In short, while there was no big competition between the two traditional parties, the electorate did have a choice between factions of the various parties, usually operating under four or five major labels.

Furthermore, these factions often offered more than one list in a given electoral district (corresponding to the *departamentos*). While the process of negotiation between the national and regional leaders of the parties was complex and varied from case to case, it can be summarized as follows.[74] An individual at the local level could obtain a *renglón* (or position on the party list) in various ways. First, he could work within the official party at the departmental level, seeking the support of the influential members of the party. These influentials included national party leaders and the regional party leaders, who maintained a reciprocal power relationship, the exact amounts of power varying from region to region and party to party. For example, national party leaders appear to have had the most power within ANAPO, and regional party leaders seem to have been particularly strong in the areas that have traditions of independence, such as the Antioquia region. An individual's success with these party influentials no doubt varied according to his own social and political status as well as depending on the desire of the influentials to attract the individual. If someone was successful in this first strategy, for whatever reasons, he became a member of the "official" party list. In some cases, a party named two or more official lists (this reached its high point in 1966 in Nariño when there were ten official Liberal party lists in the lower house elections). If an individual could not get this official status through the influentials of the party, he could launch his own list. Sometimes such a list even obtained the blessing of the party (in which case it was an "official" list). Without that blessing, the individual became a party dissident.

As a result, the electorate had a multiciplicity of choices among the various factions, and usually various lists within the factions, both official and dissident. During the period, ANAPO tended to offer the fewest lists per electoral district, while the Liberals tended to offer the most.[75] Some observers have maintained that such an arrangement, as might have been anticipated, led to undisciplined factions in the National Congress,[76] and no doubt this was the case some of the time. There was, however, some discipline—including on major pieces of legislation such as budget proposals and the Constitutional Reform of 1968. One reason for this discipline was that almost all congressmen were elected from the "official" lists of their factions—indicating that the national leaders approved of the list at least tacitly—and very few from the "dissident" lists. A second reason was a number of "rewards and punishments" that the national leaders of the factions could use with the congressmen, apparently with great success.[77]

The major importance of the existence of different factions within the parties was the difficulties they caused in governing. The National Front stipulated that all legislation had to be passed by a two-thirds vote, so the party (or faction thereof) of the president had to form coalitions with at least part of the other party. This was relatively simple during the administration of Alberto Lleras Camargo, who had almost all the Liberal congressmen in his coalition. Alberto Lleras could increase the size of his support through coalition with one of the two major Conservative factions. For the first two years (1958-60), the coalition was with the Gómez Conservatives, the largest of the Conservative factions. After the congressional elections of 1960, from which the Ospina Conservatives emerged as the largest group of that party, the Lleras coalition included them. In both cases, a two-thirds vote was usually possible.

This coalition between the Official Liberals and the Unionist (or Ospina) Conservatives continued through much of the National Front, except for the occasions when the entire Conservative party was united. However, after the Alberto Lleras administration, the two-thirds coalition became more and more difficult, due to the rise of other factions within the two parties and the ensuing numerical difficulties. Perhaps the gravest, unanticipated consequence of the National Front was the inability of the presidents to pass legislation because of the lack of a coalition of two-thirds of the Congress. In many cases this delayed or impeded legislation and gave a conservative bias to the entire policy-making process.[78]

A related development during the National Front was the increasing electoral abstention, which was a source of constant worry for the leaders of the government. From the very high participation in the 1957 plebiscite, the percentages of Colombians voting decreased almost continuously until the presidential election of 1970.[79] This was not surprising, although the strong reactions of the leaders to it was. The intent, as stated above, of the Frente was to eliminate political violence (a form of political participation), and in so doing, the National Front also decreased voting (another form of political participation). One might ask, why vote, if constitutionally the presidency is going to alternate and all legislative bodies are divided equally? There seem to be only two possible reasons: (1) because of a sense of civic responsibility or (2) because of a preference for one of the various factions within a party. Hence, the marginal utility of voting was decreased by the National Front with the decrease in partisanship, and, when the marginal costs were not proportionally reduced, many Colombians apparently did not take the trouble of voting. The other possible reason for electoral abstention is alienation, a feeling that one's vote does not count. This seems to have been the case often during the National Front, and perhaps it was reasonable in light of the limited options offered by the electoral system. This does not mean, however, that the "alienated" voter was a "revolutionary," as several parties have concluded.[80]

In the realm of interest-group behavior, the effect of the National Front was to consolidate the "multiclass" nature of the political parties. Colombian parties, as has been mentioned, were never based on specific social groups. Hence, either interest groups from differing social strata were indiscriminate in their contacts with political parties—unlike similar groups in European democracies, or separate groups of the same social strata were formed in the two traditional parties. An example of the latter was the apparently contradictory existence of labor federations formed by both the Liberal party (the CTC) and the Conservative party (the UTC). However, the traditional attachments of groups to particular parties tended to break down with the necessary bipartisan governments of the National Front.[81] The result was to reinforce the formation of different interest groups from different social strata; these groups had relations with both parties, and with most factions within the parties. It is questionable whether this is an efficient way for a political system to express the demands of the people, since such a system means duplication of organization at the interest-group level and duplication of work with the national political leaders.

In conclusion, while the National Front was successful in some of the original goals as stated by its founders, it produced outcomes which had not been anticipated. Some of these results were plainly neither approved by the founders nor very beneficial for the Colombian political system.

CONCLUSIONS

It is apparent from the discussion that Colombian politicians have a "cyclical fascination" with coalitions across party lines. It is thus interesting and important to ask if certain conditions cause these interparty coalitions. While it is somewhat hazardous to generalize from a very small number of cases, the following are tendency statements about coalition formation in Colombia (and, as such, of course, do not apply to every case).

1. Political party leaders tend to form coalitions when there is an arbitrary and powerful executive, especially if that executive is antiparty. In most cases, factions of the executive's party will join in the coalition against him. If the executive is nonpartisan, both parties will join the coalition.
2. Political party leaders tend to form coalitions when civil war between their followers has just concluded or seems to be imminent. This is true whether civil war is purely partisan or if it has socioeconomic content. However, political party leaders will not form coalitions if they think their party can win the civil war.
3. The masses in Colombia influence the formation of a bipartisan coalition only when there are certain mass pressures on the elites. Beyond that, the elite sectors of the parties decide whether or not there will be a coalition. If the elite sectors form a coalition, the masses can do only one of two things if they do not agree with the coalition: they vote for the candidates who oppose it or don't vote at all.
4. While elite party coalitions tended to be of short duration during the last century, those of this century have tended to be long (especially 1904-22 and 1958-74). Both generalization 1 and 2 apply to these two long coalitions, although in the case of the first one, the executive who formed the coalition as a result of the War of the Thousand Days was later the arbitrary executive against whom the Republican Union was founded.
5. Elite party coalitions have tended to end when the elites have decided that the coalitions no longer suit the purposes for which they were constructed. Elite groups would rationally make such a decision only if (1) they feel that they can win more power alone than in a coalition; (2) they feel that the conditions which made the coalition necessary no longer pertain; or (3) they are not constitutionally proscribed from ending the coalition.
6. Elite party coalitions tend to occur at the end of a party "hegemony" and can therefore be viewed as a method of transition from one party hegemony to another.
7. To the extent that generalization 1 and 2 are more important, the coalition will be more formalized, more encompassing, and last longer. The inverse also seems to be true.

There is no doubt that the National Front is *sui generis*, but all of the coalitions considered above are somewhat different. The points which distinguish the Frente Nacional most sharply from its predecessors are the following:

1. It had constitutional force and legitimacy, with a fixed starting and ending point. Those who said that it would not last the full sixteen years were in the end proven wrong.
2. Absolutely *all* political power was shared by the two traditional political parties. If a branch was plural in membership, it was divided equally (*paridad*). If a branch was formed by one man, it was divided equally over time by alternating the party of the incumbent (*alternación*). In none of the previous cases in Colombia was all political power divided equally; hence, the Frente was a more extensive coalition.
3. The Frente not only had elements of "political education in compromise"; economic development was definitely sought in its stipulations.[82] This is clear from the statements of the two principal founders.

The National Front was able to run its course, not only because there was nothing effective that the masses could do to end it, if they wanted to, but also because the great majority of the party elites believed in the coalition. Evidently, they held this belief because they feared a return to violence and/or rapid social change. While we cannot discount completely the effect of the constitutional restriction on ending the Front prior to 1974, except by another constitutional amendment, it seems even more important for its continuation that the elites saw the National Front as something which "worked."[83] The Front was formed under extreme conditions of civil war and strongman dictatorship; hence, its longer and more formalized life.

NOTES

In addition to the editors of this book and the other participants of the Center for Inter-American Relations Conference, I would like to thank my colleagues at the University of Massachusetts who were extremely generous in their aid—Jerome Mileur, Jane Loy, and Howard Wiarda. I take full responsibility, however, for the content of this chapter.

1. See German Guzmán, Orlando Fals Borda, and Eduardo Umaña Luna, *La Violencia en Colombia: Estudio de un Proceso Social* (Bogotá, 2 volumes, 1963, 1964), especially volume 1, chapters 1-2 and volume 2, part 3, chapter 3.
2. Maurice Durverger, *Political Parties* (London, 1967).
3. Gary Hoskin, Francisco Leal, Magdalena León de Leal, and Harvey F. Kline, *Los Partidos Políticos en Colombia* (in preparation).
4. Eduardo Santa, *Sociología Política de Colombia* (Bogotá, 1964), pp. 44-48.
5. Germán Colmenares, *Partidos Políticos y Clases Sociales* (Bogotá, 1968), p. 11.
6. Orlando Fals Borda, *Subversión y Cambio Social* (Bogotá, 1968), pp. 121-30.
7. Harvey F. Kline, "Las Ideologías en la Política Colombiana," *Razón y Fábula* 31 (January-March 1973): pp. 46-58.
8. Vernon Lee Fluharty, *Dance of the Millions* (Pittsburgh, 1966). James L. Payne, *Patterns of Conflict in Colombia* (New Haven, 1968).
9. For a case study of this, see Orlando Fals Borda, *Campesinos de los Andes: Estudio Sociológico de Saucío* (Bogotá, 1961).

10. Santa, *Sociología Política*, pp. 55, 74-75.
11. Fals Borda, *Subversión*, pp. 101-02.
12. Harvey F. Kline, "Interest Groups in the Colombian Congress: Group Behavior in a Centralized, Patrimonial Political System," *Journal of Inter-American Studies and World Affairs*, 16 (August 1974): pp. 274-300.
13. Gary Hoskin, Francisco Leal, Dora Rothlisberger, and Harvey F. Kline, *El Comportamiento Legislativo en Colombia* (Bogotá, 1974), chapter 5. See also Kline on recruitment in Hoskin et al., *Los Partidos Políticos en Colombia*.
14. William Riker, *A Theory of Political Coalitions* (New Haven, 1962).
15. José María Henao and Geraldo Arrubla, *Historia de Colombia* (Bogotá, 1967), p. 685.
16. Ibid., p. 689.
17. Ibid., p. 693.
18. H. Delpar, "Aspects of Liberal Factionalism in Colombia, 1875-1885," *Hispanic American Historical Review* 51 (May 1971): 254.
19. Robert H. Dix, *Colombia: The Political Dimensions of Change* (New Haven, 1967), p. 129.
20. Miles Wendell Williams, "El Frente Nacional: Colombia's Experiment in Controlled Democracy," (unpublished Ph.D. dissertation, Vanderbilt University, 1972) p. 47, quoting from Guillermo Hernández Rodríguez, *La Alternación ante el Pueblo como Constituyente Primario* (Bogotá, 1962), pp. 162-63.
21. Delpar, "Aspects of Liberal Factionalism," p. 270.
22. Ibid., p. 271.
23. Henao and Arrubla, *Historia de Colombia*, p. 763.
24. Delpar, p. 272; Henao and Arrubla, p. 770.
25. Delpar, p. 273.
26. Henao and Arrubla, p. 813-15.
27. Justo Ramón, S.C. *Historia de Colombia: Significado de la Obra Colonial, Independencia y República* (Bogotá, 1962), p. 357.
28. Dix, *The Political Dimensions of Change*, p. 130.
29. Henao and Arrubla, p. 824.
30. Williams, "El Frente Nacional," p. 50.
31. Fluharty, *Dance of the Millions*, p. 43.
32. Ramón, *Significado de la Obra Colonial*, p. 361-65.
33. Ibid., p. 362.
34. Ibid., p. 366-68.
35. Miguel Urrutia, *The Development of the Colombian Labor Movement* (New Haven, 1969), pp. 99-109.
36. Fluharty, p. 41.
37. Fluharty, p. 45.
38. John D. Martz, *Colombia: A Contemporary Political Survey* (Chapel Hill, N.C., 1962), p. 42.
39. Fluharty, p. 78.
40. Alberto Lleras Camargo, *Sus Mejores Páginas* (Bogotá, n.d.), p. 104.
41. Ibid., p. 54, pp. 106-07, p. 111.
42. Martz, *A Contemporary Political Survey*, p. 47.
43. Ibid., p. 47.
44. Fluharty, p. 82.
45. Martz, p. 47.
46. Dix, p. 131.
47. Fluharty, pp. 84-85.

48. Martz, p. 52.
49. Ibid., p. 61.
50. Ibid., p. 73.
51. Ibid., p. 81.
52. The best description of La Violencia is in the two volumes of Guzmán, Fals and Umaña, cited in footnote 1.
53. For various views of the Rojas dictatorship, see Fluharty, chapters 7 through 17; Martz, chapters 11-14; and Dix, chapter 5.
54. Fluharty makes a very positive evaluation of the Rojas regime.
55. Hoskin, et al., *El Comportamiento*, V, chapter 5.
56. Williams, p. 78, quoting Hernández Rodríguez, p. 12-16.
57. Williams, p. 83.
58. Ibid., pp. 84-85.
59. Ibid., p. 94.
60. Ibid., p. 95-96.
61. As will be seen below, the Constitutional Reform of 1968 changed some of these provisions.
62. Williams.
63. Lleras, p. 148.
64. Lleras, p. 266.
65. Alonso Donado (pseudonym for Laureano Gómez), *Charlas con el Presbítero Jerónimo* (Bogotá, 1963), pp. 143, 147, 244.
66. Diego Montaña Cuéllar, *Colombia: País Formal y País Real* (Buenos Aires, 1963), p. 222.
67. Dix, p. 378.
68. Subcommittee on American Republics Affairs, Committee on Foreign Relations, United States Senate, *Survey of the Alliance for Progress, Colombia—A Case History of U.S. Aid*. (Washington, 1969), pp. 7-8.
69. Subcommittee on American Republics Affairs, p. 5.
70. For a discussion of economic policy of the National Front, see the chapter by Albert Berry in this volume.
71. For a discussion of government successes and failures in such policies during the first half of the Frente Nacional, see Dix, pp. 147-58.
72. The counterfactual conditional kind of argument has to do with questions such as, "what would have happened if things had been different," or in this specific case, "what would have happened if there had been no National Front." While these questions are intriguing and stimulating to think about, there is no way in the social sciences to replicate history, changing only one thing, in order to arrive at definite conclusions.
73. For a discussion of this factionalism and the effects that it had in the national congress, see Harvey F. Kline, "The Cohesion of Parties in the Colombian Congress: A Case Study of the 1968 Session," (unpublished Ph.D. dissertation, University of Texas, 1970), and Hoskin et al., *El Comportamiento Legislativo*, especially chapters 8 and 11.
74. Hoskin et al., *El Comportamiento Legislativo*, chapter 5.
75. Ibid.
76. Those who emphasize the lack of factional discipline are Hoskin et al., *El Comportamiento Legislativo* chapter 11, and Mario Latorre, *Elecciones y Partidos Políticos en Colombia* (Bogotá, 1974), especially part 2.
77. Hoskin et al., *El Comportamiento Legislativo*, chapter 5.

78. See the chapter of Gary Hoskin in this volume and Mauricio Solaún, Fernando Cepeda, and Bruce Bagley, "Urban Reform in Colombia: The Impact of the 'Politics of Games' on Public Policy," in F. Rabinovitz and Felicity M. Trueblood, eds., *Latin American Urban Research* (Beverly Hills, California, 1973), pp. 97-130. Both of these discuss the effects of factionalism on policy making.
79. See the chapter by Rodrigo Losada in this volume.
80. Many Colombian parties, especially of the extreme left and ANAPO, but even sometimes the traditional parties, have used this argument. See Dix, p. 161, and Kenneth Johnson, "Political Radicalism in Colombia: Electoral Dynamics of 1962 and 1964," *Journal of Inter-American Studies and World Affairs*, (January 1965), pp. 15-26.
81. Kline, "Interest Groups."
82. Dix, pp. 130-31.
83. Hoskin et al., *El Comportamiento,* chapter 7.

Part II
Institutional Dimensions

Chapter 3

Electoral Participation

Rodrigo Losada

The concept of political participation embraces a wide range of behavior in any political system. It may refer to "active" behavior such as campaigning or voting, and to "passive" behavior such as obeying laws and benefiting from public services. "Every person participates at least passively in the political system in which he lives."[1] Political participation also refers to system inputs (for instance, the support or opposition one may manifest to his government or to the system's political creed, or demands for government works and regulations), as well as to outputs such as the actual provision of any public goods or services by government.

Out of this wide spectrum, this chapter will concentrate on one aspect of active political participation—electoral participation—while leaving aside any detailed analysis of the direction of the voting act, that is, the candidates, issues, or parties who are the beneficiaries (or victims!) of the votes. Further, only elections for the presidency, the national congress, and the departmental assemblies will be considered; elections to municipal councils will be omitted.[2]

POLITICAL CONTEXT

The National Front in Colombia meant a return to civilian and electoral politics after the period of La Violencia and the military government of General Rojas.

The Front, as is well known, was an experiment carefully designed to lead Colombia from the bloodshed of partisan violence to the eventual resumption of free democratic competition. During the sixteen-year transit period of "controlled democracy,"[3] elections for the presidency, congress, departmental assemblies, and municipal councils were to be held regularly, but only the Liberals and Conservatives, the parties that have traditionally dominated Colombian politics, would be allowed to participate. Further, the two traditional parties would alternate in the presidency and share equally the seats in congress and lesser elective bodies. I might note, however, that anyone was free to declare without contest an identification with either of the two parties, a factor that contributed to a certain degree of openness in the system.

It has been argued that this experiment, designed to eliminate unacceptable forms of political conflict, would lead to a general decline in most political participation. If this argument is valid, we should observe decreasing rates of electoral participation throughout the National Front period.[4] The following data, however, does not support any such simple proposition. There was also during the National Front a recurrent feeling that the electorate was increasingly discontented with the traditional parties and their leaders. The rates of electoral abstention were interpreted by some—without much historical perspective—as clear signs of lack of support either for the two parties and/or for the National Front system itself. This proposition, too, lacks any firm basis. Any inference that the electorate had no political options at all during the Front is unwarranted. In fact, in every presidential election that took place, there was an unsuccessful candidate challenging the ruling coalition or the coalition regime itself. On two occasions (in 1958 and 1962), despite constitutional regulations, candidates of the two parties actually competed for the presidency; in the other two presidential elections (in 1966 and 1970), interparty coalition candidates, under the legally appropriate party banner, challenged the continuation of the regime. These electoral patterns were unusual for Colombia; prior to the National Front, more than one party contested the presidency in only three elections during this century. The historical norm in Colombia has been intra-ruling-party competition.

The expectation that the absence of free partisan electoral competition would cause a decline in voting participation seems quite plausible; indeed, it is worth asking why people voted during the National Front. There is no empirical evidence on the subject. I hypothesize three main reasons for such participation:

1. The party carries great emotional appeal. Party attachment seems to have been particularly widespread and strong in Colombian politics prior to the Front. Two indicators of this phenomenon are worth underlining. First, the initial years (roughly 1949 through 1953) of La Violencia; the 1922, 1930, 1946, and 1947 violence outbreaks; the One Thousand Days civil war (1899-1902); and most

nineteenth-century civil wars were fought on overt grounds of, or heavily mixed with, partisan attachments. Second, and deeply related to the violence, the party socialization process in Colombia has traditionally started so early in life and so effectively that expressions such as "Colombians are born with a party label attached to their umbilical cords" are frequently used to describe that process. Given such a background, when the party leaders call to the polls, one can assume that those who identify strongly with their party will most probably comply and carry with them some of the less strongly attached.

2. In the National Front elections, the two traditional parties usually split into several national factions. These factions seem to have principally originated either on programmatic grounds or on the personal ambitions of the national leaders, and an interest on the part of lesser leaders in obtaining a share of the political "spoils" (a seat in congress or in a municipal council, a coveted position in the administration, etc.). According to the National Front formula, a specified number of these "belonged" to their party no matter how many votes it obtained. Since some party spoils were divided by "quotas" among party factions, the struggle for them could have given elections a limited sense of democratic competition among the participants. Moreover, some national factions (especially the Leyva Conservative faction in 1958, the Movimiento Revolucionario Liberal, MRL, in 1962, and the coalition of factions, Alianza Nacional Popular, ANAPO, in 1970) emphasized their claim of programmatic differences in such a way that they became genuine opposition movements, at least in some regions.[5]
3. The *patrón*-client relationship that has prevailed in Colombian politics—chiefly though not exclusively in the rural areas—makes it possible to mobilize the electorate behind national and regional factions and to exploit the emotional attachment to the traditional parties. Thus, the three factors cited reinforce one another and help explain electoral participation during the National Front.

A final background comment is in order. Female electoral participation began with the first election of the Front in 1958.[6] For that reason, and when electoral data by sex are available, I will analyze male and female voting behavior separately.

PERSPECTIVES FOR EVALUATION

In addressing the general question of how the National Front affected political behavior in general and voting participation in particular, the most relevant point of comparison would seem to be the years prior to the Front. The pre-National Front electoral data help to place the period in historical perspective. The problem is which elections to consider. In 1936, universal male suffrage was established in Colombia. Between that time and 1958, the two traditional parties competed at the polls only from 1939 to 1949.[7] The 1949 congressional election, however, is surrounded by such exceptional circumstances that it is not really a valid point of comparison. At that time, partisan fighting had broken out in so many places that little semblance of free democratic competition seems to have existed. Thus, only two presidential elections (1942 and 1946) and five congressional elections (1939, 1941,

Table 1
Electoral Participation in Presidential Elections

Election Year	Votes as percentage of voting-age population: Males	Election Year	Votes as percentage of voting-age population: Males	Males & Females
1938	26	1958	61	50
1942	55	1962	48	38
1946	60	1966	42	34
		1970	56	47
		1974	63	54

Source: For 1942-62 population estimates, DANE, *Colombia política*, pp. 152, 216. For 1966-74, my estimates. Here as elsewhere, the 1958-74 electoral returns have been taken from the official records published by *Registraduria Nacional del Estado Civil.*

1943, 1945, and 1947) can plausibly be compared to the National Front elections because the two parties participated.[8] However, I also use the uncontested 1938 presidential election as a means to contrast historical fluctuations in participation.

A historical characteristic of the Colombian polity has been the difficulty in institutionalizing interparty competitive elections.[9] Prior to the Front, interparty electoral competition for control of the presidency and/or of congress led to escalated violence. Such was the case, for example, in 1930 and 1946. Between the turn of the century and the initiation of the National Front in 1958, the presidency was contested by both parties only three times—in the 1922, 1930, and 1946 elections. The congressional elections associated with a competition for party hegemony were also violent, not only in 1949 but (less seriously) in 1947 as well. In these highly contested elections, mutual accusations of electoral fraud were the norm. Such considerations emphasize the analytical difficulties of comparing electoral participation in Colombia. In the following pages, presidential and congressional elections will be considered separately. Since they are quite different arenas of electoral competition, indiscriminate comparisons across these two types of elections are not possible, particularly prior to 1970 when they were held on different dates.[10]

Unless otherwise indicated, the percentages on electoral turnout used in this paper were calculated on the total number of persons twenty-one years old and over, not on the number of persons possessing *cédula* (identification card), a document required for voting. The latter number (or *potencial de sufragantes*, that is, the population eligible to vote) is the only one mentioned in the official electoral records published by Registraduría Nacional del Estado Civil. The difference between the two sets of data is worth noting; during the National Front, people with *cédula*, therefore qualified to vote, were on the average 84 percent of the population that was of voting age.[11]

Figure 1
Male and Female Electoral Participation
(1942-46, 1958-74)
Presidential Elections Only

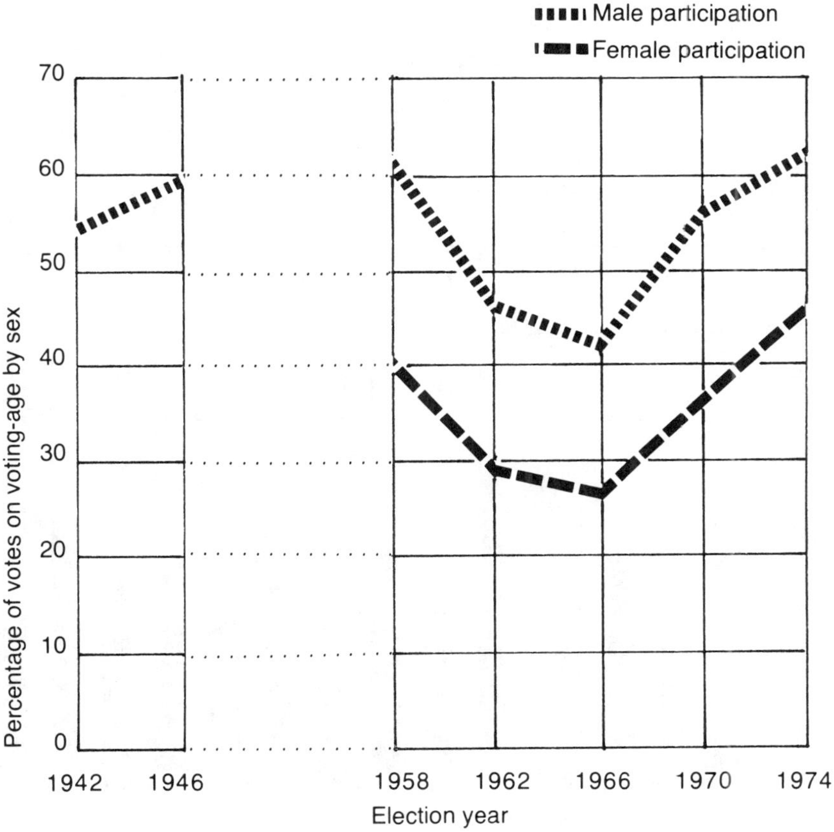

Source: For 1942-46 population estimate: same as Table 1. For 1958-74, my estimate.

TRENDS IN GROSS ELECTORAL PARTICIPATION

Presidential Elections

During the National Front, the overall level of participation in presidential elections (and in congressional elections, as will be seen shortly) roughly followed the movement of a pendulum: from 50 percent in 1958 to 34 percent in 1966 (the midpoint of the National Front years) and up again to 54 percent

Figure 2
Male Electoral Participation of Traditional Parties, Congressional Elections, 1941-1974
(Only House Elections Immediately Previous to Presidential Elections)

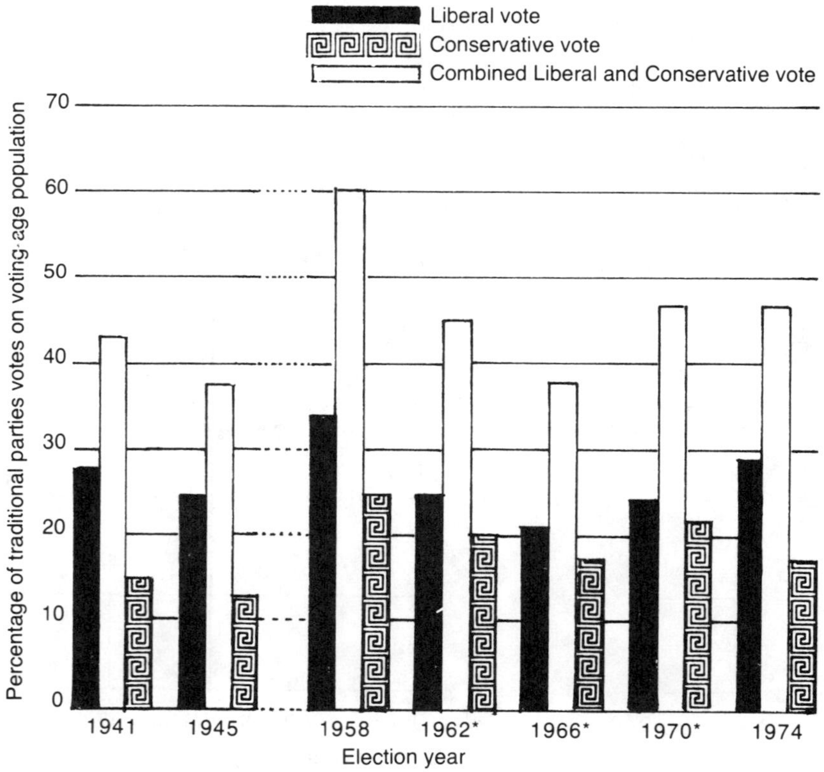

Sources: For 1941-62 Population Estimate, see Dane, *Colombia Política*, op. cit., pp. 152, 216. For 1966-74, my estimate.

*ANAPO vote has been included in the traditional parties.

in 1974 (see Table 1). Since men were the only participants in the elections prior to 1958, comparisons must focus on them. As national data by sex are available, the pertinent information can be differentiated by sex (see Figure 1).

Comparing the pre-National Front rates of *male* electoral participation with those of the National Front reveals no sustained increase in electoral absten-

Figure 3
Male and Female Congressional Electoral Participation (1939-47, 1958-74)
House Elections Only

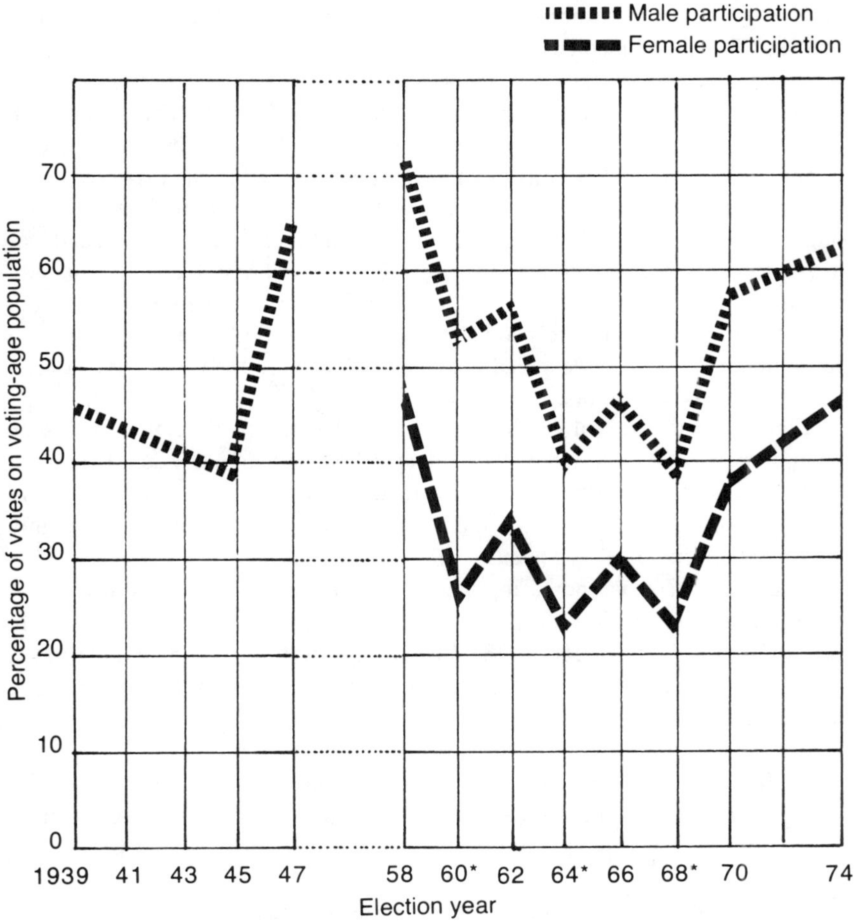

Source: For 1939-47 population: same as Table 1. For 1958-74, my estimates.

*This is a mid-term election

tion. The electoral participation rates did decrease toward the Front midpoint, but had resumed the 1942-46 levels by 1970. The lack of interparty competition was largely responsible for the progressive decrease until 1966, and the renewal of competition (first by an anti-Front opposition coalition led in the polls by an expresident in 1970, and later by the legal renewal of interparty presidential competition in 1974) explains part of the subsequent increase. The same pendulumlike movement is observable for both men and women. Any withdrawal from the polls was temporary; certainly there was no lasting depoliticization of the electorate. Further, Table 1 shows that there is a pre-Front precedent in substantial fluctuation in the rates of participation.

Nor did the Front witness a diminishing percentage of votes for the national parties. Their combined electoral backing at the end of the Front was about the same or slightly higher than in the 1942 and 1946 presidential contests. The data of Figure 2 point to the exceptional character of the 1958 elections; both parties exceeded their own past and future (up to 1974) records of electoral mobilization. Most likely this phenomenon was related to the extremely sour experience of La Violencia. Probably the National Front nourished exhilarating expectations of an end to the bloodshed, and these were a strong inducement for adherents of both parties to support the Front formula, not only during the 1957 plebiscite but in the two elections immediately following it.[12] One other factor that is likely to have influenced this high rate of participation was the presumably widespread desire to return to civilian government after General Rojas's dictatorship.

Figures 1 and 3 reveal the distinctly lower electoral participation of women than of men. In the relation between electoral participation and sex, Colombia follows what seems to be a universal trend: "The finding that men are more likely to participate in politics than women is one of the most thoroughly substantiated in social science."[13]

The hypothesis that increasing modernization tends to erode sex differences in electoral participation receives some preliminary support from the data. In the 1974 presidential election, the ratio of male to female participation in the five largest urban areas[14] is closer than the ratio for the rest of the country. The evidence follows:[15]

> Ratio of male votes/male population to female votes/female population in five largest urban areas: 1.24:1.00. Ratio of male votes/male population to female population in the rest of the country: 1.33:1.00

If the hypothesis holds—and if other political variables remain constant—then electoral participation rates should increase in the measure the country modernizes.

Congressional Elections

In what follows, only elections to the House of Representatives will be discussed. Direct popular elections of senators every four years was adopted in 1945 and exercised with bipartisan participation only once (1947) before

Table 2
Electoral Participation in Congressional Elections
House Results Only

Election Year	Percentage of votes on voting-age population	
1958	60	
1960*		39
1962	45	
1964*		31
1966	38	
1968*		31
1970	46	
1974	53	

*This is a *mitaca* (that is, a mid-term) election. Sources: For population estimates, same as in Table 1.

the National Front. Hence, Senate elections supply the Front analyst with a very short historical perspective. House elections, on the contrary, were held every two years between 1936 and 1968, and after a 1968 constitutional amendment, every four years.

During the National Front, the rate of electoral participation in House elections (henceforth, simply congressional elections) roughly follows a pendulumlike pattern similar to that observed in the presidential elections (see Table 2). It is also characterized by a regular short-term fluctuation: it is lower in every midterm election (that is, one held in the middle of a presidential term) than in the other elections. (See Figure 3, where the data are disaggregated by sex and compared with the pre-National Front competitive elections). The lower participation levels in midterm elections are probably due to the lower political stakes at issue. With neither the presidency nor the Senate in contest, the campaign is less intensive and the electorate harder to mobilize. Midterm elections are, nonetheless, quite important in intraparty competition, because they test electoral strength of future presidential candidates and/or of party factions that aspire to control the presidential nomination process.

Our chief concern is the comparison between *male* participation figures before and during the National Front. Male participation during the National Front was on average higher (53 percent) than it was during the 1939-47 pre-Front period (47 percent).[16] From 1939 to 1945, there was a mild downward tendency, which was suddenly and strongly reversed in 1947. The 1946 presidential election ushered in a period of high tension between the two parties, largely due to their exacerbated ideological differences and to the triumph of the minority Conservative party in that contest—a result of the

Figure 4
Electoral Participation in Presidential and Congressional (House) Elections

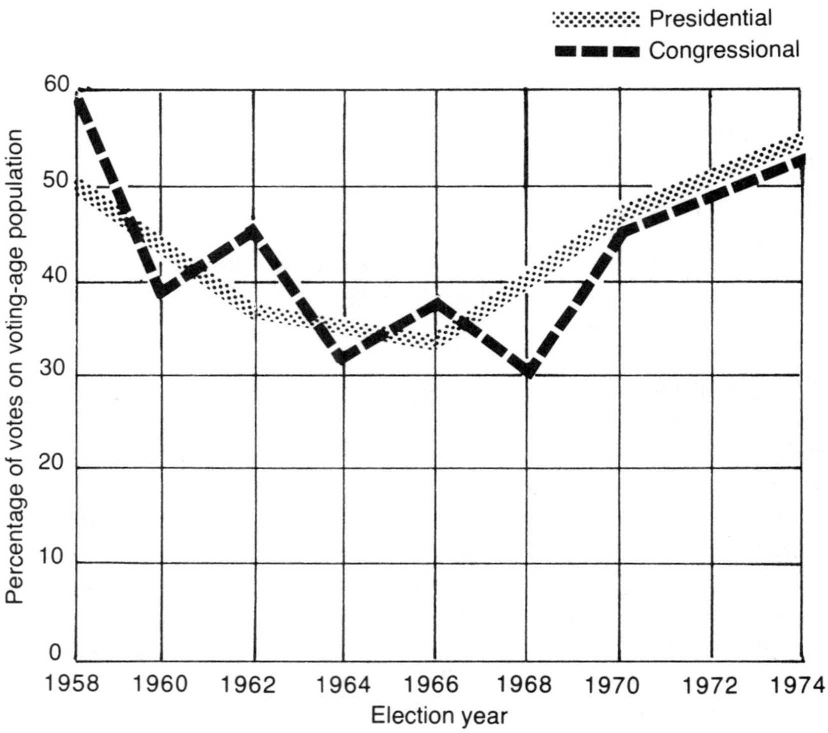

Source: Tables 1 and 2

Liberal split into two factions. This victory was apparently strongly opposed by many Liberals, and their response led in turn to a violent Conservative reaction, the prelude to La Violencia. That the electoral victory of a minority party was so fiercely contested suggests that Colombia was not then ripe for Western-type democracy.

The high participation level in the 1958 elections once again stands out, even in comparison with the presidential elections of the same year (see Figure 4). As previously suggested, it seems to be related to the heightened expectations about the new era that had been inaugurated by the 1957 plebiscite, and also to the intense activity of national, regional, and local political leaders of both parties. These men were anxious to demonstrate their electoral strength to the other party or to other factions within their own party (particularly within the Conservative ranks).

Interestingly enough, the participation levels in congressional elections exceeded those of presidential elections held the same year during the first half of the National Front. This was probably due to the lack of meaningful competition for the presidency in 1958-66, and to a coincident vigorous factional contest for seats in other elective bodies. On the other hand, when competition for the presidency was sharp, presidential participation rates were higher than congressional ones. This happened in 1970 when two interparty coalitions faced each other in the presidential arena and, of course, in 1974, when the two traditional parties competed at the polls in uninhibited fashion. Thus electoral contests which are perceived as really competitive, whether they be congressional or presidential, are likely to raise participation levels (see Figure 4).

FACTORS UNDERLYING ELECTORAL PARTICIPATION

The aggregate data on electoral participation presented in the previous section provided no support for the proposition that the National Front period led to abnormally high levels of abstention, although it is true that abstention did gradually increase until 1970 when the trend was reversed. To better understand the tendencies just described, it is necessary to consider factors that may underlie participation, such as sex, age, stage of the urbanization process, educational levels, social class, and strength of partisan identification. Unfortunately, except for data by sex and by level of urbanization, the evidence must be taken from a few isolated surveys. I have dealt already with the first variable and will proceed with the other ones.

Urbanization Process

The available evidence for the National Front period does not support the contention of certain analysts that electoral abstention is systematically higher in urban, modern areas, than it is in rural, traditional ones.[17] The picture painted by the data is more complicated. For the midterm elections to the departmental assemblies, there is a definite trend for fewer people to vote in larger cities than in smaller ones in rural areas.[18] But from 1960 to 1972, the available data show this tendency becoming less pronounced and more ambiguous.[19] See Figure 5.[20] For the years of presidential elections (bearing in mind that I use data on departmental assembly elections as a reasonable approximation to presidential election data) no clear correlation emerges between town size and electoral participation rate.[21] In three out of four election years (with the exception of 1962), the data show a wavy line, with two or

Figure 5
Mid-Term Electoral Participation and Urbanization Levels (1960-72)
Departmental Assemblies Elections Only

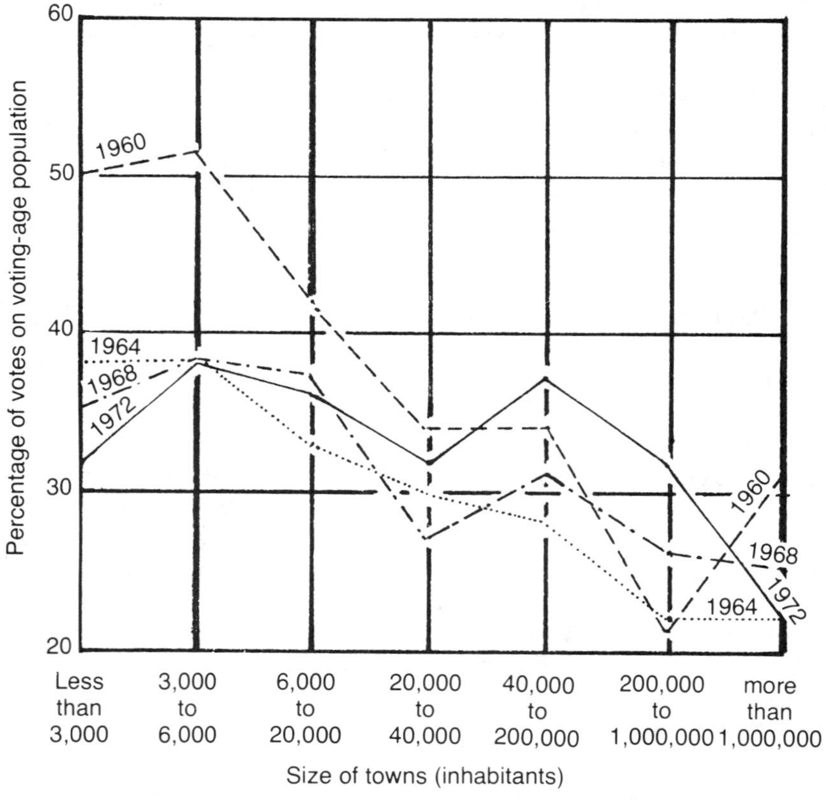

Source: My estimates.

three crests at quite different levels of urbanization (see Figure 6). These participation rates are, again, notably higher for the presidential years. While the National Front data reveal no firm relationship between degree of urbanization and electoral participation rates,[22] they are, nevertheless, consistent with the hypothesis that the larger centers are more affected by the perceived significance of an election than are smaller and rural areas.[23]

I suspect that any relationship that may exist between urbanization (in the way it has been measured) and electoral participation is either small or spurious, in the sense that whatever the size of the urban center, certain variables remain the same and are more directly or causally linked to electoral participa-

Figure 6
Electoral Participation and Urbanization Levels (1962-74)*
Departmental Assemblies Elections Held in Presidential Election Years

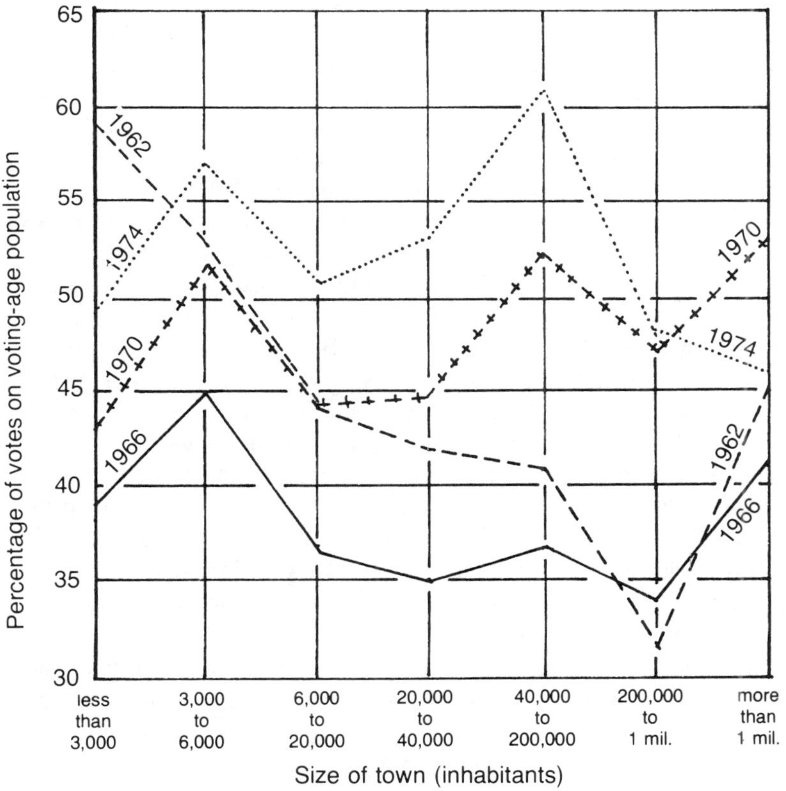

tion rates. For instance, we earlier noted the lower participation of women than of men. Since we know also that the female/male ratio is higher in larger centers, this would lead to a tendency, *ceteris paribus*, for overall participation to be lower in such centers. I now turn to other variables which may explain more about voting rates, but on which the Colombian evidence is extremely incomplete—it comes from surveys in one or two cities and in one or two electoral years only.

Urban Surveys

Two postelectoral surveys have been carried out in Bogotá (1970 and 1972) and two in Cali (1968 and 1970 plus one preelectoral in 1970), which provide information on nonvoters' sociodemographic characteristics and opinions.[24]

Although the survey questions sometimes differ, they underline some tendencies.

All five surveys support the proposition that older citizens are more likely to vote than younger ones.[25] The relationship was unilinear in the midterm elections (Cali, 1968, and Bogotá, 1972),[26] but in the 1970 presidential election, fewer aged of both cities voted than middle-aged. Possibly the middle-aged withdraw more from the polls in midterm elections than other age groups do, a phenomenon which could be attributed to the lesser stakes of those elections.

Electoral participation bears a close positive relation to the individual's educational level. This finding is common to many different countries.[27] People are presumably more interested in what they understand—or believe they understand—and politics is a matter of no easy understanding. To nourish this sort of thoughtful interest in politics,[28] the citizen needs a good deal of information on current issues and a minimum of general education to be able to interpret that information. The Bogotá 1972 survey revealed another common tendency for the level of interest in the electoral campaign to be positively related to the level of education.[29] Finally, interest in the electoral campaign was closely associated with electoral turnouts.[30]

Closely related to educational level is social class or socioeconomic status. No wonder, therefore, the Bogotá and Cali surveys found a fairly neat positive relationship between socioeconomic strata and electoral turnout.[31] Another interesting variable is the strength of party identification; the Bogotá 1972 survey showed that persons who strongly identify with any of the traditional parties are more likely to vote.[32]

It will be noted that all the above-mentioned evidence refers to individuals in urban, relatively modern contexts. Survey evidence on electoral behavior in small urban centers and rural areas is, unfortunately, next to nothing. Any quantitative conclusions about the impact of, for instance, the *patrón*-client relationship on voting turnout must await future research.

In summary, the individual characteristics contributing to participation are the levels of education, social class, and interest in the campaign. A person with a low level in these closely correlated factors is likely to seldom vote. Women, the young, and persons with a weak political party identification have below average participation levels. Studies from other countries suggest that education is likely to exert a stronger impact on electoral participation than are individual socioeconomic factors such as occupation and income, or demographic variables such as age and sex.[33] If this is so, then the increasing educational attainments of the population should be accompanied by higher electoral turnouts.

Pending a more detailed multivariate analysis, any conclusions as to the impact of various possible determinants of electoral participation must remain very tentative. We have considered the simple relationship (i.e., without allowing for the possible effect of other variables) between electoral participation and (1) factors that are inherent to the person who participates in electoral contests (for instance, his sex, age, level of education, etc.) and (2) factors that determine the environment within which he acts (for instance, the degree of competitiveness between parties or candidates, the elective offices at stake, the impact of voting legal regulations, the modernization degree of the socio-economic milieu where the person lives, etc.) Each such factor presumably exerts its own influence on a given electoral participation pattern and possibly interacts in a complicated way with other factors. Problems in organizing the data and manipulating them using multivariate-analysis have prevented me from reaching more definitive conclusions.

CONCLUSIONS

Based on the data referred to above, I am inclined to think that the National Front did not cause any major lowering of Colombian electoral participation rates. There was a U-shaped, parabolic pattern of participation. Nevertheless, in the past wide fluctuations in participation also occurred, often because the opposition party deliberately abstained. The Frente phenomenon must be viewed in terms of Colombian historical experience, not according to our ideological ideals. Prior to the Front, the presidency was electorally contested by two parties on only three occasions in this century, and all three were associated with partisan violence. The Frente does not seem to have closed electoral political options more than any other regime. In fact, it witnessed a more regular electoral competition for the presidency on the part of party factions and interparty coalitions, and this without escalated violence. Whether this is a "good" outcome is another question. Given that the Front was designed to mitigate and control electoral competition so as to inhibit partisan passions, it would perhaps have been surprising if the bipartisan regime had led to increased voter turnout.

NOTES

I am pleased to acknowledge the research assistance of Gladys Delgado in the preparation of this paper.

1. Lester W. Milbrath, *Political Participation* (Chicago, 1965), p. 9.
2. I rely chiefly on official aggregate data because they are the only ones available for drawing a national characterization. But use will also be made of some survey data available on urban electoral behavior. Even aggregate data are often difficult to find and at times not very reliable.
3. See Miles W. Williams, "El Frente Nacional: Colombia's Experiment in Control-

led Democracy'' (unpublished Ph.D. dissertation, 1972) and H. Kline's chapter in this book.

4. Based on the evidence of the first four to eight years of the National Front, see the diverse interpretations of electoral returns given by Robert H. Dix, *Colombia: The Political Dimensions of Change* (New Haven, 1967), especially chapters 6 and 7; Kenneth Johnson, ''Political Radicalism in Colombia: Electoral Dynamics, 1962 and 1964,'' *Journal of Inter-American Studies* 7 (1965):15-26; Mario Latorre-Rueda, ''Radiografía de dos elecciones,'' *Acción Liberal* 2 (October-November 1965):84-115, and his ''20 de marzo — 1 de mayo: Las elecciones de 1966,'' *Acción Liberal* 4 (May-June 1966):52-60; Robert H. McDonald, ''Political Protest and Alienation in Voting: The Case of Colombia,'' *Inter-American Economic Affairs* 21 (Autumn 1967):3-22; Richard S. Weinert, ''Political Modernization in Colombia'' (unpublished Ph.D. dissertation, 1967); and Anita Weiss, *Tendencias de la participación electoral en Colombia, 1935-1966* (Bogotá, 1968).
5. See Dix's discussion in this volume.
6. The first time women went to the polls was in December 1957, on the occasion of the national plebiscite to sanction the National Front constitutional formula. Plebiscite returns do not seem to be comparable to electoral returns because they reflect quite different political issues and contexts.
7. In the latter year, only for the congressional elections. In the periods 1936-38, and 1949 (presidential election) to 1953, only one party accepted to go to the polls; the other party usually argued that it had no fair chance to win because of government partiality.
8. In 1942, the two presidential candidates were Liberal, but one of them had the official backing of the Conservative party.
9. See Solaún's chapter in this volume.
10. From 1970 onward, presidential and congressional elections have been held on the same date.
11. My estimate. See also Departamento Administrativo Nacional de Estadística (henceforth, DANE), *Colombia política—Estadísticas 1935-1970* (Bogotá, 1972), pp. 153, 218. Most voting-age population estimates used here were made especially for this paper from the 1964 and 1973 census data. At times, however, I have used some population estimates obtained by DANE, particularly for the years prior to 1964. Unfortunately, DANE's population estimates are not always reliable.
12. The plebiscite was held in December 1957, the next congressional elections in March 1958, and the presidential election in May of the same year. The percentage of the voting-age population who participated in the plebiscite was close to 73 percent.
13. L.W. Milbrath, *Political Participation*, p. 135.
14. That is, Bogotá, Medellín, Cali, Barranquilla, and Bucaramanga, and nearby towns.
15. The following ratios should, in principle, relate votes to persons of voting age rather than to all persons of a given sex. It appears, however, that the results would not be significantly different.
16. This percentage is still higher if we consider only the House elections held in presidential election years—that is, 1958, 1962, 1966, 1970, and 1974. It then becomes 59 percent.
17. Lars Schoultz has a good summary in ''Urbanization and Changing Voting Patterns: Colombia, 1946-1970,'' *Political Science Quarterly* 87 (1972):22-45.
18. Although I could only use the returns on the biennial elections to Departmental Assemblies, they closely match the urban-rural electoral participation distribution

of the congressional and presidential elections which take place simultaneously or shortly after in the same year. Thus, we may confidently infer broad national patterns from those returns.

19. The coefficients of the corresponding linear regression equations are: −4.39 (for the 1960 data), −2.96 (1964), −2.14 (1968), and −1.54 (1972). The Pearson linear correlation coefficients for the same years are: −.90, −.98, −.85, and −.61.
20. For Figure 5 and 6, all capitals (*cabeceras*) of *municipios* (those small territorial, administrative units which are similar to the U.S. counties) were ranked by size of population and classified in seven categories, roughly equivalent in population numbers. When the number of capitals in any category was too large to be handled, a random sample was drawn. For the analysis, however, the population taken into account was that of the entire *municipio*, not that of the capital only.
21. The Pearson linear correlation coefficients between size of town and electoral participation percentages are: −.77 (1962), −.33 (1966), +.50 (1970), and −.25 (1974).
22. Similar conclusions, using data up to 1966, were reached by A. Weiss, *Tendencias de la participación electoral en Colombia*, pp. 110-12, and by R.S. Weinert, ''Political Modernization in Colombia,'' pp. 174-76.
23. I also observed that the percentage in voting turnout within each urbanization category varies much more in rural areas than in urban ones. That is, it is much more likely to find *municipios* with participation rates of 95 percent or, the opposite case, 4 percent, in smaller town categories than in large city ones. However, those seem to be exceptional cases, for most of the *municipios* in each category do show participation percentages fairly close to the category mean.
24. The pertinent reports have been published: Rodrigo Losada and Miles W. Williams, ''El voto presidencial en Bogotá, ''*Boletín Mensual de Estadística* (DANE) 229 (August 1970):xv-xviii; and, ''Análisis de la votación presidencial en Bogotá, 1970,'' in DANE, *Colombia política*, pp. 1-56 (this is an enlarged version of the first report); Rodrigo Losada and Gabriel Murillo, *Análisis de las elecciones de 1972 en Bogotá* (Bogotá, 1973); Pedro Pablo Morcillo, Judith Talbot de Campos, John McCamant, Harold Rizo-Otero, ''Estudio sobre abstención electoral en las elecciones de Marzo de 1968 en Cali,'' *Boletín Mensual de Estadística* 221 (December, 1969):x-xxix (reprinted in *Colombia politíca*, pp. 57-80); Judith Talbot Campos and John F. McCamant, ''Colombia política 1971,'' *Boletín Mensual de Estadística* 242 (September 1971):69-128 (reprinted in *Colombia política*, pp. 81-146); and *Cleavage Shift in Colombia: Analysis of the 1970 Elections* (Beverly Hills, 1972).
25. See Campos and McCamant (1972), p. 56; and Losada and Murillo, p. 46.
26. See Campos and McCamant, p. 55; and Losada and Murillo, pp. 41-43.
27. L.W. Milbrath, *Political Participation*, p. 122.
28. This should be distinguished from the partisan interest of the person branded from birth as an unquestioning Liberal or Conservative.
29. Losada and Murillo, pp. 68-74. See also Angus Campbell et al., *The American Voter* (New York, 1960), pp. 102 ff.
30. Losada and Murillo, p. 66.
31. Losada and Williams, p. 20; Campos and McCamant, pp. 55-56; Losada and Murillo, pp. 30-38.
32. Losada and Murillo, pp. 117-29.
33. See, for instance, A. Campbell et al., *The American Voter*, pp. 485-87; and Gabriel Almond and Sidney Verba, *The Civic Culture* (Princeton, 1963), pp. 121, 400.

Chapter 4

The Impact of The National Front on Congressional Behavior: The Attempted Restoration of El País Político

Gary Hoskin

I

As a consequence of the prolonged violence in the 1940s and early 1950s, and the subsequent military government led by General Gustavo Rojas Pinilla, the role of traditional civilian party elites in Colombia had become precarious by 1957. The military regime (1953-57) had displaced and reduced their influence in the political system. The National Front was designed primarily to remedy this situation through the restoration of the political hegemony formerly discharged by the two traditional political parties. In addition, the provisions of the National Front were directed toward reducing the previously intolerable level of interparty competition, a major factor contributing to La Violencia and the military government. Thus the two parties agreed to share equally all legislative and appointed bureaucratic posts until 1968. This was later extended to 1974 for legislative posts, and to 1978 for bureaucratic positions.[1] Moreover, the constitutional reforms of 1959 provided for the two parties to alternate the presidency until 1974.[2] Bipartisan support for governmental programs was incorporated into the National Front coalition through the requirement of a two-thirds vote for passing laws in legislative bodies.[3] The National Front represented, therefore, a mutual endeavor on the part of the Liberal and Conservative elites to restore the democratic process in Colombia through sharing all governmental posts, alternation in the presidency, and a mandated joint support for governmental programs.

Congress' anticipated role within the National Front coalition was a formidable one for a variety of reasons. The Frente restored to power what had been labeled El País Político—"the political country or domain"—which referred to those politicians dominating departmental (provincial) and local political arenas, who were often elected to the National Congress. During Rojas's military government, not only the National Congress but departmental assemblies and municipal councils as well had been closed. They had been replaced at each level by constituent assemblies whose memberships were restricted and often dominated by the national executive.[4] With the Frente, this largely dispossessed group of *políticos* returned to their arena of power in the National Congress, where they supposedly were to discharge their legislative tasks within the context of the bipartisan agreement. If the democratic process was to operate as effectively as envisioned, congressmen necessarily would contribute forcefully to the return of political stability by performing their representational roles. It was hoped that this would reduce dependence upon the military for political pacification. Moreover, Congress was to constitute a key arena in the governmental decision-making process, as reflected by the constitutional provision that all laws were to be approved by a two-thirds vote. Congress was to become a full-fledged partner, if not the core, of the National Front coalition.

The exalted role projected for Congress failed to materialize fully. Paradoxically, this failure was due to the impossibility of implementing the constitutional provisions created by the National Front. More specifically, the two-thirds voting rule became a stumbling block to effective legislative action because the coalition partners were unable to mobilize sufficient votes in Congress. This situation resulted from indiscipline within party ranks and from the formation of multiple dissident factions, each faction utilizing one or both traditional party labels to gain entry into legislative bodies. The principal factions opposed to the National Front governments—Independent Conservative (after their electoral defeat in 1960), the Movimiento Revolucionario Liberal (MRL), and Rojas's Alianza Nacional Popular (ANAPO)—expressed their opposition through their voting patterns in Congress, though not always as forcefully as their militant rhetoric suggested. Legislative conflict did not revolve so much around specific governmental policies related to economic and social matters. Rather, it centered on legislative action directly affecting El País Político—that is, politically strategic measures impinging upon the perceived growth or survival of political parties or factions thereof.

As a consequence of the legislative paralysis stemming from the two-thirds rule, National Front presidents felt obligated to devise methods of minimizing congressional opposition and/or inaction. Therefore, they increasingly invoked article 121 of the constitution, which provided for a state of siege. During the National Front period, from 1958 to 1974, Colombia was governed under a partial or total state of siege approximately 75 percent of the time.[5] The constitutional reforms of 1960 provided for the automatic convocation of Congress when a state of siege was in effect and authorized Congress (by a majority vote of both houses) to send presidential decrees to the Supreme Court for constitutional rulings. Nevertheless, the net effect of governing under the terms of article 121 was to reduce dramatically congressional powers, because Congress' role was to react to policies already implemented by the executive.[6] The constitutional reforms of 1968 abolished the two-thirds rule in all but a few areas of legislation, thus diminishing congressional veto powers.[7] These reforms, supposedly designed to "modernize" legislative activity, also drastically curtailed congressional powers, particularly in budgetary matters, where the initiative formally belonged to the executive.

Although the National Front legacies associated with governing under article 121 and the 1968 constitutional reforms combined to reduce Congress' decision-making powers, this should not be interpreted as a blanket condemnation of the Colombian Congress because, as one author notes, "the principal function of most of the world's legislatures is not a decisional function."[8] Whether legislatures in any part of the world are equipped to handle contemporary political and economic problems is an unresolved matter at best.[9] Before dismissing the Colombian Congress as an irrelevant, anachronistic body, critics should inquire into the additional functions that it performed during the National Front period. The impact that the abolition of Congress would have had within the wider political system must also be weighed. If these considerations are taken into account, the role of the Colombian Congress during the Frente Nacional appears greater in the sense that the legislature constituted a formidable pillar of the political system.

The National Front coalition directly affected the role of political parties in Congress, as well as in the wider political system, providing elements of both continuity and discontinuity with the past. Turning first to the similarities, the pact perpetuated the influence of the Conservative party in governmental decision making, despite the fact that the Conservatives had not won a majority vote in a contested national election since 1930. Since Mariano Ospina Pérez's victory in 1946—arising from a division within the Liberal party—the Conservatives have occupied the presidency for fifteen years in comparison to eight years for the Liberal party. Considering its minority electoral status, the Conservative party has a penchant for power that exceeds the wildest expectations. A second link with the past consisted of the restoration of the power of the traditional parties and the concentration of power in the hands of a few politicians within the two traditional parties. Among the National Front presidents, only Misael Pastrana Borrero was not an important political party leader before the Frente, and he was imposed by Ospina Pérez and Carlos Lleras Restrepo.

Departing from the past, the National Front envisioned the curtailment of pronounced interparty competition and, in this respect, was eminently successful. Frente presidents were selected in a bipartisan manner and each governed accordingly. The exception, to some extent, was Carlos Lleras, whose relatively independent approach almost destroyed the National Front—a peril that was reflected in the political crisis surrounding the 1968 constitutional reforms and in the 1970 electoral upset. Liberal President Alberto Lleras Camargo was accused of favoring the Conservatives and President Misael Pastrana was reprimanded by Conservative-party stalwarts for not utilizing governmental machinery in favor of his party in the 1974 elections. Thus the bipartisan Frente governments seemingly reduced the power of any specific political party in governmental decision making. In doing so, it favored an increased reliance upon technocrats and on proliferating interest groups.

Constitutional restrictions placed upon interparty competition in the electoral arena contributed to reduced participation levels in 1964, 1966, and 1968 (the abstention rate surpassed fifty percent in each), yet both the 1970 and 1974 electoral returns suggest that the traditional parties had not lost their mobilization capacity. In this respect, the post-Front period may well display considerable continuity with the past. Moreover, sharing governmental posts and alternating control of the presidency did not signify the end of electoral competition during the National Front. Electoral lists within each party multiplied, and dissident groups challenged the very legitimacy of the National Front itself. Rojas Pinilla's electoral success in 1970 almost toppled the National Front. Despite his association with Lleras Restrepo's government, the winner of the 1974 presidential election, Alfonso López Michelsen, established his political credentials as an avid foe of the National Front.

This article now turns to an examination of Congress' role in the Colombian political system, with particular emphasis upon the impact of the National Front. The next section focuses upon selected patterns of congressional activity between 1930 and 1974. Section III interprets aspects of legislative behavior as reflected through interviews conducted with national congressmen in the 1968-69 session. The data for both are drawn from studies executed in the political science department of Los Andes University in Bogotá.[10] Parts IV and V synthesize my interpretation of the role of Congress in the political system.

To anticipate, Congress is the cornerstone of what has been called El País Político in Colombia: the domain of the traditional *políticos* or politicians. We shall argue that the País Político defies traditional notions of legislative behavior and can be characterized by a series of paradoxes that prevent facile categorization. On the one hand, congressmen monopolize power in the spheres of political activity within the domain of El País Político—such as electoral politics and legislative recruitment. On the other hand, political decision making is held firmly by the executive branch and, in certain crisis situations, by key political party leaders, usually former presidents. In other words, while Congress exercises considerable autonomy in the political system, at the same time, it is often relegated to a supportive (sometimes opposition) role in governmental decision making. Whether it supports or opposes depends upon the issues involved. Relationships between Congress, the presidency, and political party *jefes* represent complex, subtle exchanges around which the dynamics of the Colombian political system unfold.

II

The Colombian Congress represents a viable, ongoing institution within the political system; it is buttressed by the weight of tradition and the norms, both formal and informal, that orient and sustain legislative behavior. The legal powers invested in Congress by the constitution clearly signify that Congress is not intended to be an impotent political actor. Nonetheless, Congress generally fails to utilize its constitutional powers to the fullest.[11] Its approbation of legislation initiated by the executive branch is often ritualisic, and it frequently delegates law-making responsibilities to the president. Such delegations of authority enable the president to "legislate" in specific issue areas through the promulgation of executive decrees. Such *decreto-leyes* constitute one of the most pervasive legal bases of governmental policy making, particularly in economic matters. These trends were noticeably reinforced during the National Front, as power drifted toward the executive branch, and Congress became less and less involved in government decisions.[12] Congress, however, continues to wield a marked autonomy in the electoral arena, as indicated above.

In his analysis of patterns of political development in Colombia since the 1930s, Francisco Leal demonstrates clearly that congressional behavior reflects societal trends not endemic to the legislature. Perhaps Leal's most significant conclusion was that legislative behavior usually represents a reaction to political and economic events outside the legislature itself, while the parameters of congressional decision making are firmly embedded in power relationships prevailing in the political system. One prominent example is the "crisis of oligarchical hegemony" and the subsequent restructuring of societal power. These events were followed by alterations in the composition and activities of Congress—new groups were admitted, the limits of accept-

Table 1
Comparison of Pre-Frente and Frente Periods in Relation to Number of Sessions, Absenteeism, Legislative Efficiency, and Initiation of Laws in the Colombian Congress*

	Pre-Frente		Frente	
Number of Sessions (Yearly Averages)	**Regular**	**Special**	**Regular**	**Special**
House	86.4	30.8	58.1	24.9
Senate	88.3	30.6	56.3	27.3
Absenteeism†				
House	12.7	20.0	16.4	25.5
Senate	20.4	26.0	18.3	27.0
Legislative Efficiency‡				
Absolute	.52	.10	.73	.14
A. Lleras Camargo			.59	
G. Valencia			.85	
C. Lleras Restrepo			1.08	
M. Pastrana			.38	
Relative	.16	.06	.29	.18
A. Lleras Camargo			.26	
G. Valencia			.19	
C. Lleras Restrepo			.40	
M. Pastrana			.31	

*Data for this table are drawn mainly from Francisco Leal's chapter in Hoskin, except those for the portion on legislative initiative, which come from Leal, part II, chapter 4. The time periods involved are from 1930 to 1953 for the pre-Frente span, and 1958 to 1974 for the National Front period; the data on legislative initiative is an exception and terminates in 1966 for the second period.

†The abstention index is calculated as follows: the number of Congressmen attending sessions divided by the total possible attendances, times 100.

‡Absolute legislative efficiency is based upon the total number of laws passed in both houses divided by the total number of sessions. The relative efficiency index is computed similarly, allowing for discrimination between laws based upon their economic and social impact.

able behavior established, and Congress became a staunch defender of the status quo.[13]

Leal examines three aspects of congressional behavior since the 1930s: legislative absenteeism, legislative efficiency, and the political influence of Congress. Congressional critics often berate congressmen for not attending sessions more regularly, but this analysis reveals that absenteeism has little

Table 1 (cont'd)

	Pre-Frente		Frente	
Number of Sessions	**Regular**	**Special**	**Regular**	**Special**
Legislative Initiative§				
Absolute				
Congress	79.2		77.0	
President	20.8		23.0	
Relative				
Congress	52.2		61.4	
President	48.8		38.3	

§This index consists merely of the percentage of all laws approved according to the source of initiative in both ordinary and special sessions. Absolute and relative are defined as for efficiency.

impact upon legislative efficiency (defined as the ability of Congress to draft and pass laws). In fact, Congress tends to become more ''efficient'' when it has a high rate of absent congressmen.[15] Finally, absenteeism, legislative efficiency, and Congress' political powers seem to be molded more by the wider political system than by factors internal to the legislature.

Table 1 summarizes selected aspects of congressional behavior, comparing the 1930-53 period with that of the National Front. Generally speaking, these indicators suggest that, at least at a formal level, the Colombian Congress has not entirely abandoned the functions associated with the congressional institution. The data indicate a reduction in both ordinary and special sessions during the Frente period. This tendency stems, in part, from the formation of permanent committees in Congress after 1945; supposedly fewer plenary sessions of both houses would then be required to conduct legislative business. Considering that around 75 percent of the National Front period was conducted under a state of siege, and that the constitution stipulates that Congress hold sessions when article 121 is in effect, the reduced number of special sessions during the Frente is unanticipated. It suggests that Congress did not take advantage of its constitutional prerogatives. Both houses held approximately the same number of sessions during both periods.

During the National Front, member absenteeism increased in the lower house and decreased slightly in the Senate. Nevertheless, senators attended sessions less regularly than their house colleagues. (Note the increase in absenteeism during special sessions.) Despite these tendencies, legislative efficiency, in both absolute and relative terms, increased during the National Front as a result of the bipartisan support that existed during the initial phases of the coalition, and of the constitutional reforms of 1968, which curbed legislative bottlenecks. Once again, the data for special sessions reveal a lack of congressional initiative during these sessions called by the president; Congress tends to be much less productive then than during regular sessions. Carlos Lleras Restrepo's administration enjoyed more success in the legislature than did that of other National Front presidents. Congressional productivity was due to his forceful leadership which included threats to resign and restructure the governing coalition if he did not obtain political support in Congress. During Misael Pastrana's government, absolute efficiency was at its lowest but this administration ranked second on the index of relative efficiency. This undoubtedly represents an indication of the extent to which Pastrana's government reacted to the threat posed to the National Front in the 1970 elections, which ANAPO claims to have won. Pastrana sought to strengthen the governmental coalition by creating a climate of cordiality between the two branches of government, by curbing political conflict between and within the traditional parties, and by channeling increased governmental resources into urban areas where ANAPO successfully mobilized discontented voters.

There are limitations in evaluating the power relationships between Congress and the presidency, but the data indicate that Congress is not characterized by inertia in terms of initiating legislation. As Table 1 reveals, the absolute number of laws passed under legislative initiative exceeds by a factor of three those sponsored initially by the presidency, both prior to and during the National Front. The situation changes, however, when laws are weighted according to their social impact. Before the National Front, the weighted average showed a relative balance between the legislature and the presidency, but in the Frente period, Congress surpassed the executive in initiating significant legislation. These data should, nonetheless, be interpreted cautiously as a measure of assessing power relationships between the two branches of government.[16]

III

Having presented the above global indicators of legislative behavior both preceding and during the National Front, we now turn to selected aspects of congressional activity during one session of the national legislature—1968-1969—as derived from interviews with congressmen. The overwhelming conclusion regarding the socioeconomic backgrounds of congressmen revolves around their privileged status vis-à-vis society as a whole.[17] Approximately 80 percent of those interviewed have completed a university education (74 percent are lawyers) and display high socioeconomic status. Almost 90 percent of the respondents enjoy either upper- or middle-class status; the social composition of Congress is preponderantly middle class. Colombian

Table 2
Comparison of Congressmen's Birthplaces with Location of Secondary and University Education

Site	**Birthplace** (%)	**Secondary Education** (%)	**University Education** (%)
Bogotá	7.4	19.0	64.9
Departmental Capital	30.6	51.2	31.4
Other Colombian Cities	61.6	29.3	0.0
Abroad	.5	.5	3.7
Totals	100.1	100.0	100.0
N=	(216)	(203)	(188)

congressmen, moreover, tend to be fairly young when they arrive for the first time in Congress (over 50 percent were less than forty-five). They also tend to be highly mobile in a geographical sense. The roots of congressmen run deep into the various regions of the country; 27 percent of them originate in areas with populations of fewer than 20,000 inhabitants, 37 percent in areas whose populations range between 20,000 and 100,000, and the remaining 36 percent come from areas where the population is over 100,000. Congressmen are local notables. As Table 2 suggests, the process of obtaining an education and ultimately becoming a congressman tends to undercut the rural and departmental origins of congressmen. However, regional ties are evidently not obliterated by this socialization process, for regionalism is often manifested in the halls of Congress. Perhaps as significant as the elite status of Colombian congressmen is their tendency to resemble one another across political party lines; that is, variations in socioeconomic background characteristics can be explained satisfactorily neither in terms of their party affiliations nor in terms of their regional political bases.

Legislative recruitment is characterized by two striking phenomena: its autonomy vis-à-vis the executive branch of government, and its departmental basis.[18] The common route to Congress passes through lesser legislative posts such as municipal councils and departmental assemblies (77 percent of those interviewed held such posts), along with political party positions at the same local level (76 percent of the respondents). Only 3.2 percent had never discharged either a political party or a governmental post before becoming a congressman (six of the seven enjoy high socioeconomic status). At least 80 percent of the respondents had no executive experience at either the national or regional level when they arrived in Congress. These dual recruitment routes prevail not only at the national level (less than 10 percent had discharged jobs in the national executive) but at the regional level as well where only 20 percent had held such positions. In sum, Colombian congressmen are the politicians or the *políticos*, not the administrators.

Congressional recruitment reflects the departmental basis of El País Político: campaign funds for congressional races are raised primarily within the departments; congressmen believe that support of departmental party directorates is tantamount to election; and, with only occasional exceptions, the formation of electoral lists for Congress reflects departmental rather than national politics. Departmental fiefdoms are more highly represented in the Senate than in the House—42 percent of the senators interviewed in 1968 had spent more than ten years in that august body while only 9.2 percent of the representatives could make an equal claim. Legislative turnover in the Cámara is particularly high; some two-thirds of the representatives had not served more than four years in Congress. Finally, recruitment to the pinnacle of El País Político is not undercut by the fact that approximately a third of those interviewed reported having relatives with high political and governmental posts.

The decision-making powers of the Colombian Congress are restricted and often intermittent. Therefore, the representational roles of its members necessarily deviate from the traditional ones which generally relate directly to the decisional functions of a legislature. Nevertheless, congressmen still perceive their representational roles according to the formal model characteristic of legislative behavior in Western democracies, and this perception provides them with a rationalization for their activities, however removed from reality. Unfortunately, leading critics of Congress predicate their attacks precisely upon the "inability-unwillingness" of Congress to act in accordance with the formal-legal norms. Yet, for Congress to do so is an impossible dream in light of the constraints placed upon the legislature by the prevailing structure of power in the society.

Discrepancies between representational norms and actual behavior do not, however, negate the significance of the Colombian Congress as a representational institution. Thus congressmen report that along with committee work and law making in the halls of Congress, they perform a series of services for their electors: they provide services in ministries and decentralized institutes; they identify regional problems; they perform brokerage services between constituents and institutions in Bogotá; and they seek to diminish unemployment in their departments through public works.[19] In their perceptions of purposive roles, congressmen recognize that they should emphasize representational functions to a greater extent. Principal model activities revolve around committee work and drafting legislation, while normative beliefs underscore the need for greater representation of various constituencies.

Table 3
National-Regional Orientation
and Perceived Representational Style

Roles	**Regional** (%)	**National-Regional** (%)	**National** (%)	**N**
Delegate	17	18	31	(45)
Político	51	56	47	(111)
Trustee	32	26	22	(58)
Totals	100	100	100	
N=	(81)	(82)	(51)	(214)

$X^2=5.35$

For a variety of reasons—including the elite character of the political system, decentralized electorates, and weak party discipline—Colombian congressmen should perceive themselves as following a trustee or Burkean role in legislative decision making. That is, they should take the position that ultimate decisions reside with them rather than they follow instructions from selected constituencies (delegate role).[20] As Table 3 shows, such a tendency does exist, although it is not pronounced, and it corresponds with an orientation toward the regions rather than the nation. This contrasts to similar role orientations in other parts of the world.[21] In addition, the lesser cosmopolitan-oriented congressmen—those inclined toward the regions in a nation-region continuum—tend to be more conservative and antagonistic toward economic associations and the executive branch of government. These orientations reflect a Colombian brand of conservative populism that has a parallel in other Latin American countries. Finally, the core of legislative representation in Colombia, underpinned by a strong sense of regionalism, involves mostly relationships with clientele groups rather than with individual electors. (The latter is a prominent feature of the traditional model of representation.)

Traditionally, the Colombian Congress has not been far removed from the center of political conflict, recognizing, however, that such conflict frequently is tangential to social conflict.[22] Three dimensions of political conflict, varying in intensity from one period to another, have historically underpinned the dynamics of congressional behavior: (1) the struggle to gain control of government, (2) regional cleavages, and (3) ideological differences. Such disputes involve the distribution of political power in the society and, as such, are manifested fully within Congress. Many of the legislators interviewed agreed on the major conflicts confronting Congress. These conflicts were in part a consequence of the democratic norms that legitimize and rule

Table 4
Relationship between Congressmen's Political Party Affiliation and Economic Ideology

Economic Ideology	Liberal (%)	Union Conservative (%)	ANAPO (%)	Independent Conservative (%)	(N)
Conservative	17.5	44.2	30.0	54.5	(67)
Medium	43.7	32.6	45.0	36.4	(89)
Radical	38.8	23.3	25.0	9.1	(63)
Totals	100.0	100.0	100.0	100.0	
N=	(103)	(43)	(40)	(33)	(219)

$X^2=24.57$

legislative activity, in part a result of the shared perceptions of the role the legislature discharges in the political system. More specifically, during the 1968 session, four categories of conflicts were reported by our respondents to predominate—political party and faction behavior (36 percent of the conflicts mentioned); congressional-executive relations (20 percent); *técnico-político* (technicians versus politicians) conflict (12 percent); and nation-region cleavages (11 percent). Over half of all respondents mentioned each of the foregoing conflicts, which represent 79 percent of the total conflicts listed by congressmen.[23] Such responses emphasize the continuity of political conflict in Congress over time, along with the sometimes tense interface between Congress and the presidency.

During the Frente two main conflicts permeated congressional behavior. Opposition to the government and ideological cleavage were reflected in a multidimensional scale analysis of congressmen's perceptions of political leaders and groups.[24] The basis of ideological conflict emerged in a series of attitudinal scales based upon interview responses of congressmen. Three general attitudinal syndromes, identified by factor analysis, are present: (1) social class orientations, (2) economic and political ideology, and (3) religious and nation-region orientations. These attitudes tend to hang together in the sense that, for example, those congressmen oriented toward the upper class also relate positively to economic associations, to the executive branch of the government, and to the United States. They fall on the conservative side of both ideological scales, are more inclined toward the regions than the nation, and score highly on the religiosity scale. In addition, political party affiliation facilitates predicting attitudinal orientations. As Tables 4, 5, and 6 indicate, Colombian political parties differ considerably in terms of economic and political ideology, as well as religiosity.

Although the beliefs of Colombian congressmen are characterized by ideological constraints, and ideological differences separate the political par-

Table 5
Relationship Between Congressmen's Political Party Affiliation and Political Ideology

Political Ideology	**Liberal** (%)	**Union Conservative** (%)	**ANAPO** (%)	**Independent Conservative** (%)	**(N)**
Conservative	16.5	58.1	47.5	45.5	(76)
Medium	35.0	27.9	32.5	42.4	(75)
Radical	48.5	14.0	20.0	12.1	(68)
Totals	100.0	100.0	100.0	100.0	
N=	(103)	(43)	(40)	(33)	(219)

$X^2 = 40.4$

ties, this should not be interpreted to signify that Congress is rampant with ideological conflict. Ideological differences, along with the struggle for governmental hegemony and regional cleavages, become significant only within the context of the overall dynamics of political conflict. Thus, ideological differences among congressmen may well not affect legislative decisions in all situations.

While Congress represents the cornerstone of El País Político, political parties necessarily discharge a similar function within Congress; to disassociate congressional from political party behavior constitutes a hazardous, if not impossible, enterprise. Political parties, like Congress, are not without their paradoxical bases. Many congressmen report discontent with the role of parties in Congress. This discontent ranges from 87.2 percent of the *anapistas* to 55.5 percent of the Conservative *unionistas*. Forty-two percent of the respondents indicated that they would continue with another party with similar ideas should their own party disappear from the political scene.[25] Such manifestations of discontent and superficial attachments to the parties are deceptive, however, since a party label has been essential to pursue a congressional career. This appears to be the case despite the weak party discipline that generally prevails in Congress. When asked to name outstanding congressmen, friends in the legislature, and members known for their speaking talents, congressmen's preferences revealed that party affiliation played a prominent role in the assessments, although legislative norms that are unrelated to political party membership also are important. Finally, the polyclass basis of Colombian parties, with slight modifications in the case of General Rojas's ANAPO, clearly emerges in analyzing the interviews with congressmen.

Interest groups usually direct their efforts toward influencing key decisionmakers. The discovery that Congress falls within the realm of pressure-group activity is somewhat unanticipated, considering the asymetrical power rela-

Table 6
Relationship between Congressmen's Political Party Affiliation and Religiosity

Religiosity	Liberal (%)	Union Conservative (%)	ANAPO (%)	Independent Conservative (%)	(N)
Low	49.5	4.7	35.0	12.1	(71)
Medium	37.9	30.2	47.5	15.2	(76)
High	12.6	65.1	17.5	72.7	(72)
Totals	100.0	100.0	100.0	100.0	
N=	(103)	(43)	(40)	(33)	(219)

$X^2=75.1$

tionship between Congress and the executive branch of government. It suggests that Congress is not completely removed from the policy-making process. More than half of the Congressmen interviewed had been visited by representatives from six of the following interest groups: community action groups, peasants, municipal governments, the clergy, labor unions, departmental governments, school teachers, and economic associations.[26] However, congressmen reported fewer links with economic associations than with other categorical groups, and 40 percent of the respondents indicated that no organized economic groups had contacted them. The reduced contact with powerful economic associations reflects the more extensive and closer relationships of such groups with the executive, where they wield considerable power. During the National Front, organized economic associations multiplied in number and influence. By taking their claims directly to the executive and decentralized institutes, these associations undermined the traditional aggregation role of the political parties.[27] The contacts of the political parties with interest groups vary only slightly—ANAPO has more extensive contacts with the Asociación Colombiana de Pequeños Industriales (ACOPI), and the Independent Conservatives are well connected with agricultural groups.

Finally, congressmen are well aware of the preponderance of the executive in policy making; 85 percent believed that Congress had lost powers during the past thirty years. A similar number would like to see it recuperate those powers, although the possibility seems remote. Indeed, the president can wield a heavy hand in Congress. He can send his ministers to testify, transmit urgent messages, and meet with political party leaders, not to mention his extraordinary powers when a state of siege or an economic emergency is in effect. Note, however, that only 7.7 percent of the respondents maintain that the president exercises influence in Congress through the process of presenting legislative proposals and studies. The reverse also holds—only 4.9 percent suggested that Congress exercises control over the president by passing laws.[28] More common forms of control practiced by Congress are citation of ministers, committee investigations, parliamentary debates, and to a lesser extent, budgetary supervision.

IV

The functions of the Colombian Congress have been shaped significantly not only by Western democratic theory and the role of the legislature therein, but also by the structural characteristics of Colombian society, particularly the power structure and the party system. Most congressmen justify their activity largely in accordance with normative postulates of democratic theory. Nevertheless, facile acceptance of such explanations leads to erroneous conclusions in as much as legislative activity in Colombia deviates significantly from the formal model. The boundaries of legislative behavior have become limited.

The growing heterogeneity of interests represented in Congress, and the conflict resulting from that, has caused political power to be transferred increasingly to the executive branch of government. (Although the trend toward executive power seems to be universal, the degree to which it has risen in Colombia surpasses that of some other countries.) As noted, the 1968 constitutional reforms represent a culmination in the shift of power from Congress to the executive—congressional power and initiative were drastically curtailed, particularly in budgetary and fiscal matters. In terms of recruitment patterns and policy orientations, the executive remains a more faithful spokesman for the traditional power structure or the "establishment" than the legislature. As one congressman puts it,[29]

> With the populist movements that have arisen in the country, people such as myself who identify with the popular classes have become congressmen. It is important to the governing class that the popular classes not be elected to parliament and if they are elected, their actions are not taken into consideration. In this manner, the oligarchy, through many means at its disposal, sees to it that parliament does not function, because if it does work well it is a weapon against the elite or governing class of the country.

During the Frente, the function of law making has been usurped, to some extent, by the presidency, and Congress is left with the task of legitimizing those actions. This does not imply, however, that Congress is a rubber stamp for the president; sustained congressional opposition to the president can be formidable and effective.[30] Such opposition generally crystallizes around conflicts between the president and the political parties (mostly factions) rather than being struggles for power between the two branches of government.[31] As discussed below, the activity of parties and factions in the legislature can be viewed partly in terms of tactics designed to maximize the power of a group. If the president advocates policies that do not coincide with the goals of a particular group, then that group may oppose them forcefully. As a consequence of the two-thirds rule that existed during most of the National Front, opposition groups frequently succeeded in paralyzing legislative action.

Thus the Colombian Congress does not constitute a strategic institutional locus of decision making in the political system, and this is largely because of the concentration of power in the executive branch. Congress has not, however, abandoned its law-making tasks entirely;[32] congressmen define their actions in accordance with norms emanating from democratic theory; constituents are represented within the legislative process; congressional activity serves to legitimate decisions taken elsewhere in the political system;[33] parliament constitutes a forum for the discussion, sometimes the resolution, of political conflict. Frequent criticisms are launched at Congress by the press and legislators themselves, often stressing the irresponsibility of congressmen. These criticisms are influenced forcefully by the "inability" of the institution to fulfill its legislative duties, but these duties are defined within the context of formal democratic theory norms—ample testimony to the ideological salience of those norms. Thus in calling for the modernization of Congress, former president Alberto Lleras Camargo stated: "in comparison with other State organs, especially the executive branch, the Colombian Congress not only has failed to modernize itself but is one of the most archaic and obsolete working bodies, in whatever sense of the term that one wants to employ."[34] Such pleas form an integral part of discussions about Congress, but they contribute little toward bridging the gap between legislative norms and practices. Calls for modernization of Congress probably are counterproductive, in the sense that politicians and the press focus their energies upon this issue rather than discussions of more significant socioeconomic problems of the society.

As previously noted, Congress has performed a key role in the integration of new groups into the political system, along with delimiting and legitimating the activity of those groups. Similarly, the legislature has served as a key political institution in the territorial and political integration of the country by providing a forum where regional politicians interact and relate to political party and governmental activity. The importance of the legislature as a forum for the institutionalization of political party relationships should not be minimized, even though Congress as an institution figures only intermittently in the exercise of political power. Moreover, congressional approval of executive actions cloak them in an aura of legitimacy, although the gap between theory and practice makes Congress increasingly vulnerable to criticism, particularly in its legislative and supervisory roles.

Congress constitutes the scenario of what has been labeled El País Político; it is here that the politicians from the various regions coalesce into what some have called *la clase política colombiana*.[35] Such a group is composed primarily of party notables, who can be characterized by the following features: they have departmental and, to a lesser extent, national power bases, a high degree of individual autonomy in Congress on most matters, and political independence vis-à-vis the executive branch of governmment. As Mario Latorre notes,[36]

> generally speaking, there exist two isolated, distinct compartments in the system; the government proper and the political parties. Each is staffed by different people. Consequently, there are several recruitment channels to government and politics, one of these being the political parties. However, access to government posts through the party channel tends to be quite restricted. In contrast, recruitment to the parties and their legislative arenas revolves primarily around the political party route, but this alternative does not constitute the only possibility. Often those associated with government may move into the party and legislative arenas. Furthermore, it can be argued that those who reach the Congress via the political parties usually remain in this compartment, and are unable to gain access to the government unless they develop new sets of relationships and different sources of support.

These two distinct political segments are composed of disparate people. They have different socioeconomic backgrounds, political recruitment patterns, political behavior, and more often than not, there is not a high degree of interaction or integration between the two groups. Comparing social background features of congressmen with upper-echelon bureaucrats, the following pattern emerges: bureaucrats enjoy higher socioeconomic status than congressmen, are more highly educated, receive their education in more urbanized areas (especially Bogotá and abroad), and are not so exclusively composed of lawyers.[37] In addition, upper-level bureaucrats usually begin their careers at the national level—80 percent in comparison with 36 percent of the legislators.[38]

As discussed earlier, the channels for becoming a congressman are unique and predictable. Sixty-eight percent of the legislators interviewed for this study held lower-level political and legislative posts before arriving in Congress; 63 percent reported no executive experience at either the national or regional level; and only 3 percent never discharged any political posts. Congressional recruitment, therefore, draws primarily upon those individuals who start their political careers at the local and regional levels and work their way upward to the National Congress; those coming directly from the government bureaucracy represent a miniscule proportion of the total. Although the accumulated data on the subject are sparse, the number of congressmen who later enter the government is probably not pronounced, particularly for those who are not well connected with major national politicians.[39]

The problem of foreign credits is a good illustration of the compartmentalization between Congress and the executive branch, and the reluctance of the former to exercise its constitutional, legal, administrative, and supervisory powers.[40] The constitutional reforms of 1968 gave Congress the right to participate actively in economic and social planning, but it did not exercise these powers during the Pastrana administration; internal congressional strife prevented the formation of the Comisión del Plan (planning commission). Moreover, Congress has the authority to veto all foreign loans and credits if (1) their projected impact is unduly inflationary,[41] or (2) such credits are not distributed equitably to the various regions of the country.[42] Despite the ease with which either provision could be invoked by congressmen, neither power has ever been utilized, or even debated. Consequently, the planning process and the acquisition and distribution of foreign credits have become an executive prerogative, and Congress has been isolated almost entirely. As Cepeda suggests, development planning and its relation to foreign credit have been oriented more toward the foreign and international lending agencies than toward domestic political affairs, and the lending agencies have represented "the functional equivalents of a ruling class."[43]

Within the arena of El País Político, congressmen display considerable autonomy in voting patterns and political positions assumed, which makes it difficult to impose party discipline and authority in Congress. The traditional decentralized nature of the party system rests upon easy access to the formation of dissident lists and factions, and heightens the problems associated with maintaining party discipline.[44] This decentralization and indiscipline is predicated upon what has been called "the wheel of fortune":[45] "departmental party directorates designate municipal directorates; members of municipal directorates serve as delegates, or name them, to state conventions; the conventions select the candidates; the candidates also are named to departmental directorates. In this way, the circle is completed internally with no external influences or outside challenges. This closed system precludes any type of competition."

In view of the "wheel of fortune," departmental party directorates generally are free to draft congressional lists, often in a highly competitive atmosphere as a consequence of the political infighting characteristic of regional politics. This is manifested clearly in the widespread practice of forming many dissident lists for public corporations. National party directorates, with the exception of ANAPO which is more highly centralized than the traditional parties, frequently are unable or unwilling to participate in the drafting of such lists. Much to his subsequent dismay, the head of the national Liberal party directorate, Julio César Turbay Ayala, intervened, by and large unsuccessfully, in a few departmental squabbles during the 1974 elections. In addition, members of the government who have not ascended the ladder of El País Político, and who seek a position in congressional lists are often thwarted, in some cases because of the opposition of *jefes naturales*—the "natural leaders" or key departmental politicians.[46] Thus, what political competition there was in Colombia during the Frente existed at the departmental rather than the national level; electoral competition was keen both within and between political parties in the departments.

Members of parliament, even those with long tenure, can lose in the *juego* or "bet" of the lists and, consequently, not be reelected to Congress, although most of our sample expressed a desire to retain their seats. The relatively high turnover in Congress, particularly in the House, offers ample testimony to the fierceness of electoral politics at the departmental level, both in terms of intra- and interparty competition.[47] The high legislative turnover in Congress disguises, and at the same time, perpetuates the pronounced leadership stability within departments. The departmental bosses, *jefes naturales*, most of whom are elected to Congress, promote legislative turnover as a means of maintaining their power; for example, they often name congressmen or aspiring politicians from their departments to governmental posts where they are not permitted to campaign for public office.

Formation of party lists from the municipal to the national level falls within the exclusive domain of El País Político. The lists represent perhaps the principal raison d'être of congressional and party activity in the political system. Colombian parties are, for all practical purposes, congressional parties that thrive upon electoral politics, obviously including the nomination and election of a president. In the process of selecting a presidential candidate, relations between the politicians' world and that of the government are most intimately linked, for congressmen participate fully in presidential nominations, generally, but not always, following cues from the *jefes naturales*. In 1969, the nominal aspirant of the congressional party bosses, Evaristo Sourdís, was vetoed by the leader of the Conservative party, Mariano Ospina Pérez, and with the consent of the Liberal party, Misael Pastrana was selected. In 1973, the Liberal party nominated Alfonso López Michelsen for the presidency rather than Carlos Lleras, largely because the traditional Liberal party leaders, once again mainly congressmen, preferred López Michelsen. In short, El País Político has the potential for selecting a president, and even if it does not do so, it forms the core of the electoral campaign for the presidency.

Once a president assumes office, however, Congress becomes rather introverted; legislators divide their time between Congress and departmental politics, while the president directs his energies toward governing the country.

Congressional politics revolve around faction and party behavior, often by jockeying with the presidency about legislative proposals. Formal aspects of legislative behavior, such as law making, assume an aura of unreality; congressmen frequently do not display a keen interest in such matters, and members of the executive branch sometimes reciprocate. Thus, coordination between the two branches is less than ideal in the sense that congressmen are usually unaware of presidential initiatives in Congress and vice versa. One would expect a dominant executive to coordinate legislative activities through his various ministers, yet this often is not the case. Individual congressmen, to complicate even further the legislative process, sometimes launch their pet projects with neither the knowledge nor the backing of their party.[48]

This lack of policy coordination between Congress and the executive may stem in part, though not entirely, from the curtailment of interparty competition during the National Front. More important is the difference in the background chartacteristics, and political recruitment and behavior of the two groups. The executive branch's dominance of policy making is an indication of the inability of the "establishment" groups to control congressional politics effectively.[49] Paradoxically, the executive branch more nearly reflects the oligarchical interests in the society while at the same time being the locus of reform in the system. Congress, in contrast, tends to be more conservative than the executive and not a major source of reform in the system.

Where then does policy making reside in the system and what role does Congress play therein? The answer can be traced to the interactions between the presidency, Congress and the national *jefes naturales*, or "Club de ex-presidentes."[50] While both the president and Congress are characterized by considerable political autonomy in their respective activities, each may become totally paralyzed as a result of political crises. These are subsequently resolved by the club. However, such crises, seemingly ever present in Colombian politics, cannot be resolved until conciliation has run its course;[51] only then do these *jefes naturales* mediate the crisis.

Interestingly enough, congressional conflict is related intimately not only to strictly political cleavages but to economic and social conflict as well, although to a much lesser extent.[52] The two sectors tend to be compartmentalized; economic and social disputes fall principally within the domain of the executive branch. The strictly political debate is almost totally devoid of substantive concerns, centering instead upon personal matters and problems of personnel: a *disneylandia* not connected with the economic and social realities of the country. Congress and political parties, relegated to an inferior position in policy formulation, were increasingly replaced during the National Front by powerful economic associations that negotiated directly with the presidency.

Considering that policy making in Colombia often depends upon the conflict-laden relations between the president, Congress, and the "Club de ex-presidentes," the most striking aspect of the process is why it works at all. The end result, however, is policies that are necessarily piecemeal, erratic, unpredictable, and conservatively oriented.[53] As Pecaut observes, when political conflict centers on economic and social matters, the state encounters much difficulty in formulating coherent and rational policies.[54] In addition, the political factionalism represented in Congress "makes action almost impossible without top leadership participation."[55] Consequently, policy making that deviates from the status quo almost inevitably encounters opposition from Congress and from the influential economic groups in the society, and the process of conciliation produces a policy that accommodates nearly everyone involved. Of course, these problems were exacerbated by the bipartisan requirements of the Frente.

The frequency of political conflict and the movement from one crisis to another does not, I think, mean that an autonomous *clase política* prevails in the country. Political decisions capable of altering structural relations in the society are blocked in the policy-making process or, if passed, are frequently not implemented. Political autonomy in either the executive or congressional branch does not go so far as to permit the enactment and implementation of measures that alter, in any fundamental way, power relationships in the society. Within the day-to-day activities of El País Político, considerable autonomy prevails but it is limited. The presence of undisciplined, political mavericks in either branch of government does not imply that their predispositions will ultimately prevail.

The instability of the relationship between formal institutional norms and political behavior has traditionally been a feature of politics throughout Latin America as well as in Colombia. In Colombia, however, social mobilization, political participation, and the expectations surrounding governmental performance widened the breach between formal norms and behavior. Congress was not the only formal-legal institution in Colombia to depart significantly from its formal role. Societal tensions associated with the process of developing a country are undermining the representational process, in both the legislative and executive branches of government. Sometimes the tensions overwhelm both, but the legislature appears more vulnerable to such pressures than the executive.

It is difficult to isolate the changes that are attributable to generalized processes of development occurring throughout Latin America during the 1958-74 period from those which reflect provisions of the National Front coalition itself. However, we can speculate along these lines in relation to congressional behavior. Prior to the Frente, Congress served as a forum for the "great" political debates associated with interparty conflict, La Violencia. The principal agitators (Laureano Gómez and Jorge Eliécer Gaitán) made spectacular speeches in Congress about moral scandals, social issues, and partisan differences. Congress was the principal arena of escalated political party conflict. The polyclass, conservatively-oriented, and elite-dominated party system was overcome by pressures for economic, political, and social change. President Ospina Pérez closed Congress in 1949, and no sessions were held again until after the Rojas military government fell in 1957. Adoption of the National Front coalition was accompanied by a restoration of Congress and El País Político. Because of the bipartisan constitutional rules, Congress received great potential power, but it "failed" to perform its formal roles. Explanations for this unanticipated "nonrestoration" of El País Político can be traced directly to provisions of the National Front and to factors related to political traditions and the development process.

Turning first to the coalition agreement: the parity provisions of the Frente had the effect of dampening the dynamism of congressional behavior. The role of a forceful opposition in Congress became less pronounced, despite intermittent opposition on the part of dissident groups. Moreover, the National Front facilitated the return of traditional politicians to power and contributed to the consolidation of their hegemony by removing the necessity for interparty competition in the electoral arena. Unexpectedly, the internal divisions within the traditional parties and the formation of dissident factions did not entirely eliminate electoral battles. Because the National Front was designed to placate a variety of interests, policy formulation and implementation during this period was almost predestined to be conservative, piecemeal, and erratic. This situation was aggravated considerably by political stalemates in Congress which resulted from a combination of the two-thirds rule for passage of legislation (until 1968), party factionalism, and sporadic interparty competition between the traditional parties. Finally, the constitutional reforms of 1968 significantly undercut congressional powers, especially in economic matters. Presidential authority increased dramatically with the inclusion of article 122, which enabled the president to dictate emergency economic measures, and the retention of article 121, which provides for a state of siege.

The constitutional features of the National Front coalition are not solely responsible for the unsuccessful restoration of El País Político. Political traditions and development patterns also contributed to the widening chasm between the "Political Country" and the "National Country." The return of *la clase política* to the congressional arena carried with it pre-Frente traditions that were probably not much affected by the coalition agreement itself. While by no means unique to Colombia, legislative traditions seemingly adapt more slowly than executive ones to the exigencies of technocratic government. The general trend toward increased reliance upon technocrats in governmental operations has reinforced the tradition of a strong executive. In addition, funding policies of the international agencies and the foreign policy of the United States have greatly strengthened technocratic influences in government. Despite frequent complaints of leading Colombian *políticos* about the magnified role of *técnicos*, including incumbent President López Michelsen, the fact remains that the drift away from El País Político as a source of governmental recruitment seems irreversible.

The trends established for congressional behavior during the National Front are not likely to be modified significantly. Disappearance of parity provisions in Congress will probably have little effect in the immediate future. Despite the overwhelming Liberal party victory in the 1974 elections, Congress remains a relatively docile body: Conservative as well as Liberal congressmen generally support governmental programs enthusiastically. By mid-1975, an atmosphere prevailed in which governmental criticism bordered on heresy; only Carlos Lleras and a few Liberal congressmen offered any sustained opposition. This situation may change in so far as the issues relate to electoral behavior, but probably government policy making will not change. As the 1978 elections approach and the bureaucratic parity nears an end, the Conservative party could well offer more vehement opposition—though its effect will be limited in light of the party's tenuous electoral base. Similarly, dissent within the Liberal party may mount, and criticism may be directed toward the government as Liberal politicians jockey for power. However, those who believe that upon the termination of the National Front Congress will assume a greater role in the political system are likely to be disillusioned. Political realities dictate otherwise.

NOTES

For their helpful comments on an earlier draft of this paper, I want to thank my Los Andes colleagues, Fernando Cepeda, Dora Rothlisberger, Francisco Leal, along with Harvey Kline of the University of Massachusetts.

1. The constitutional reform approved by the plebiscite held on December 1, 1957 provided for parity in all legislative and appointed bureaucratic posts until 1968. See article 2 in *Constitución Política de Colombia*, Presidencia de la República, Secretaría Jurídica (Bogotá, 1973), pp. 389-91. As reformed by the Legislative Act Number 1 of 1959, parity in legislative posts was extended until 1974 (article 6 in ibid., p. 394). The constitutional reform of 1968 terminated parity in elections for departmental assemblies and municipal councils after January 1, 1970, and in the National Congress after January 1, 1974 (transitory paragraph of article 50 in ibid., p. 422). In addition, these reforms extended the parity provisions in appointed bureaucratic posts until August 7, 1978 (article 1, in ibid., p. 410).
2. Acto Legislativo Número 1 de 1959, in ibid., pp. 393-94.
3. The two-thirds rule was amenable to modification in the sense that Congress, by a two-thirds vote of each house, was authorized to designate which legislative materials could be approved by a simple majority vote, but only for a period not to exceed two years. (Ibid., pp. 390, 394). The two-thirds rule was abolished by the 1968 constitutional reform for all materials other than those related to the alternation in the presidency and parity in Congress—through 1974—reforms of bureau-

cratic parity—through 1978—and modification of electoral laws—no time limit specified.

4. Acto Legislativo Número 2 de 1954, in ibid., pp. 381-84.
5. Dora Rothlisberger et al., "Esbozo de la Realidad Colombiana con Referencia al Pacto Andino" (Bogotá, 1974), p. 38.
6. For details see *Constitución Política*, Acto Legislativo Número 1, 1960, p. 399.
7. See note 3.
8. Robert Packenham, "Functions of the Brazilian National Congress," in Weston Agor, ed., *Latin American Legislatures: Their Role and Influence* (New York, 1971), p. 260.
9. Gerhard Loewenberg, ed., *Modern Parliaments: Change or Decline*? (Chicago, 1971), particularly chapter 1, pp. 1-20. Also see Hernando Agudelo Villa, *Antioquia Liberal: De la Resistencia a la Libertad Democrática* (Bogotá, 1974), p. 85.
10. Field work for the Legislative Behavior Project was conducted in the political science department of the Universidad de Los Andes from 1968 to 1970, with financial assistance from the Rockefeller Foundation. The study has been published in two volumes: Francisco Leal Buitrago, *Estudio del Comportamiento Legislativo en Colombia. Tomo I, Análisis Histórico del Desarrollo Político Nacional, 1930-1970* (Bogotá, 1973); and Gary Hoskin, Francisco Leal, Harvey Kline, Dora Rothlisberger, and Armando Borrero, *El Comportamiento Legislativo en Colombia, Tomo II* (Bogotá 1974).
11. For a similar analysis in respect to the former Peruvian Congress, see Terry L. McCoy, "Congress, the President, and Political Instability in Peru," in Agor, *Latin American Legislatures*, p. 334.
12. This tendency for power to gravitate toward the executive branch is likely to continue. An indication is that President López invoked a state of economic emergency in September 1974 for a period of forty-five days, based upon article 122 of the revised 1968 constitution. This article enables the executive to issue emergency economic decrees that are subsequently amenable to congressional revision, although such revision is unlikely. A meeting of Liberal congressmen voted overwhelmingly to uphold the president's right to invoke article 122—one negative vote and four abstentions.
13. See Leal, *Estudio del Comportamiento*.
14. Ibid., p. 274.
15. Ibid., pp. 275-76.
16. Ibid., pp. 297-301.
17. Davidson offers a similar observation regarding the lower house in the United States: "perhaps the strongest conclusion to be drawn from a study of background characteristics is that the recruitment process yields a remarkably homogeneous collectivity of men and women." Roger Davidson, *The Role of the Congressman* (New York, 1969), p. 37.
18. See Kline, "Candidate Selection," in Hoskin et al, *El Comportamiento Legislativo*.
19. Gary Hoskin, "Dimensions of Representation in the Colombian National Legislature," in Agor, *Latin American Legislatures*, p. 424.
20. Ibid., pp. 426-38.
21. Davidson, *The Role of the Congressman*, pp. 125-26; John Wahlke et al., *The Legislative System: Explorations in Legislative Behavior* (New York, 1962), pp. 755-56; Allan Kornberg, *Canadian Legislative Behavior: A Study of the 25th Parliament* (New York, 1967), p. 107.

22. Daniel Pecaut, *Política y Sindicalismo en Colombia* (Bogotá, 1973), translation by Bernardo García, p. 38.
23. Gary Hoskin, "Dimensions of Conflict in the Colombian National Legislature," in Chong Lim Kim and G. Robert Boynton, eds., *Legislative Systems in Developing Countries* (Durham, 1975).
24. Ibid.
25. Kline, "Political Parties," in Hoskin et al. *El Comportamiento Legislativo*.
26. Kline, "Pressure Groups," in ibid.
27. Rafael Rivas, "Los Partidos y los Grupos de Interés," in *El Espectador*, Bogotá, October 29, 1974, p. 3.
28. Kline, "The Executive," in Hoskin et al., *El Comportamiento Legislativo*.
29. Jorge Sedano, "Por qué no opera el parlamento?," *Flash*, Bogotá, September 8, 1971, p. 23.
30. Robert Dix, *Colombia: The Political Dimensions of Change* (New Haven, 1967), p. 172.
31. James Payne, *Patterns of Conflict in Colombia* (New Haven, 1968), p. 249.
32. Leal, *Estudio del Comportamiento*, p. 295.
33. For a rather exhaustive list of legislative functions discussed in relation to the Brazilian Congress, see Packenham, "Functions of the Brazilian National Congress," pp. 267-78.
34. Alberto Lleras Camargo, *El Espectador*, May 20, 1974. Also see Héctor Charry Samper, *El Tiempo*, April 18, 1974; and Abelardo Forero Benavides, *El Siglo*, May 20, 1974.
35. Mauricio Solaún, Fernando Cepeda, and Bruce Bagley, "Urban Reform in Colombia: The Impact of the 'Politics of Games' on Public Policy," in F. Rabinovitz and F. Trueblood, eds., *Latin American Urban Research III* (Beverly Hills, 1974) Mario Latorre Rueda, *Elecciones y Partidos Políticos en Colombia* (Bogotá, 1974), p. 289; Pecaut, *Política y Sindicalismo*, p. 38.
36. Latorre, *Elecciones y Partidos Políticos* pp. 268-69.
37. Rodrigo Losada, *Perfil Socio-Político del Congresista Colombiano* (Bogotá, 1972), pp. 22, 45, 51, 56.
38. Rodrigo Losada, *Incidencia de Factores Sociales-Personales en las Opiniones Políticas del Congresista Colombiano* (Bogotá, 1972), p. 24.
39. Latorre, *Elecciones y Partidos Políticos* p. 269.
40. See Fernando Cepeda, "The Political and Legal Impact of International Lending Agencies in Colombia," unpublished manuscript, 1974.
41. See article 3, Ley 18 de 1970.
42. See Ley 12 de 1965.
43. Cepeda, "International Lending Agencies." p. 33.
44. Gary Hoskin and Gerald Swanson, "Political Party Elites in Colombia: A Spatial Analysis," *Comparative Politics* (April 1974).
45. Latorre, *Elecciones y Partidos Políticos*, p. 155.
46. In the 1974 elections, former minister of development in the Lleras Restrepo government, Hernando Gómez Otálora, and the editor of *La República*, Mario Laserna, were not included in departmental lists for Congress as a result of stiff opposition from leaders of El País Político.
47. In reference to the viciousness of the 1974 electoral competition among Liberal party members in Norte de Santander, the National Director of the Liberal party, Turbay Ayala, referred to his cohorts there as *caníbales humanos* (human cannibals).
48. Solaún et al., "Urban Reform in Colombia."

49. Latorre, *Elecciones y Partidos Políticos*, p. 269.
50. Solaún et al., "Urban Reform in Colombia."
51. Latorre, *Elecciones y Partidos Políticos*, p. 289.
52. Pecaut, *Política y Sindicalismo*, p. 38.
53. For a theoretical discussion of why legislative bodies tend to be more conservative than the executive branch, consult Samuel Huntington, *Political Order in Changing Societies* (New Haven, 1968), p. 388.
54. Pecaut, *Política y Sindicalismo*, p. 39.
55. Solaún et al., "Urban Reform in Colombia."

Chapter 5

Political Oppositions under the National Front

Robert H. Dix

Organized politics in Colombia has been run mainly by the Conservatives and the Liberals, since at least the midnineteenth century. Occasionally factions from the two dominant parties have joined to form a new party as with Rafael Nuñez's National party of the 1880s or the Republican party of the early twentieth century. But these have been short-lived. Apart from the small Communist party of Colombia (PCC) founded in 1930, and the more recently founded (1959) and even smaller Christian Social Democratic Party (PSDC), no third party in Colombian history has endured for much over a decade.[1] Moreover, in contrast to British, and even American, political history, where factional defection from one of the major parties has often been a transitional step, prefatory to entry into the opposite party, the invariable Colombian pattern has been for the defecting faction to be reabsorbed into its party of origin.

In a society where clientelistic dependency of the many on the few has been the norm,[2] the competing parties and factions have tended to be multiclass (*policlasista*), with landowners and peasants, for example, on both sides of the political battlelines. Years of partisan combat, including several civil wars, and an attendant process of family and communal defensive socialization, have ingrained in many Colombians an identification with either the "blues" (Conservatives) or the "reds" (Liberals).[3]

These party loyalties have become so intense that they have been referred to as "hereditary hatreds." During the sixteen years of the National Front, interparty competition was prohibited altogether. All legislative seats were by law distributed evenly between the parties (and *only* between the traditional two), while the presidency alternated between them. Electoral competition was thereby reduced to contests among competing factions with the same partisan label. Potential new oppositions who wished to compete electorally had to do so, nominally at least, as either Liberals or as Conservatives.

Prospective new oppositions also had some peculiar opportunities, however. For simply by presenting themselves as Conservative or Liberal, they might acquire a certain factional legitimacy. Of more profound and potentially long-range significance was the fact that, with the coalescence in the National Front of the leaders of the two traditional partisan enemies, other, heretofore latent, dimensions of conflict were potentially laid bare.

Organized oppositions may of course take forms other than that of the political party or faction. The military, student associations, labor unions, churches, national associations of manufacturers or merchants, even foreign governments, have on occasion played leading oppositional roles, in Colombia as they have elsewhere.[4] This discussion, however, will be limited to those oppositions that did assume the guise of a political party, movement, or faction during the era of the National Front. We begin by delineating several types of opposition to the National Front, then go on to discuss in detail the Alianza Nacional Popular (ANAPO)—which is in several respects the most significant of the oppositions. Three related sets of questions are raised:

1. To what extent did oppositions under the National Front resemble, or differ from, both each other and the traditional pre-National Front patterns of opposition.
2. Why did oppositions under the National Front take the form they did, and what does this indicate about the nature of Colombian politics and the nature of the National Front?
3. What is the significance and long-run impact of the patterns of opposition that characterized the National Front, both for the Colombian party system and Colombian political development? What is their broader, comparative significance?

In short, we are interested in the impact of the unique coalitional arrangement of the National Front on Colombian patterns of opposition, and particularly the long-run significance of certain substantially new types of opposition (notably ANAPO) which emerged during the years between 1958 and 1974.

TYPES OF OPPOSITIONS

Factional Oppositions

The principal early oppositions to the National Front took the form of factions of one or the other of the coalition partners. Some sought primarily

Figure 1
Electoral Strength of Political Groups During the National Front*

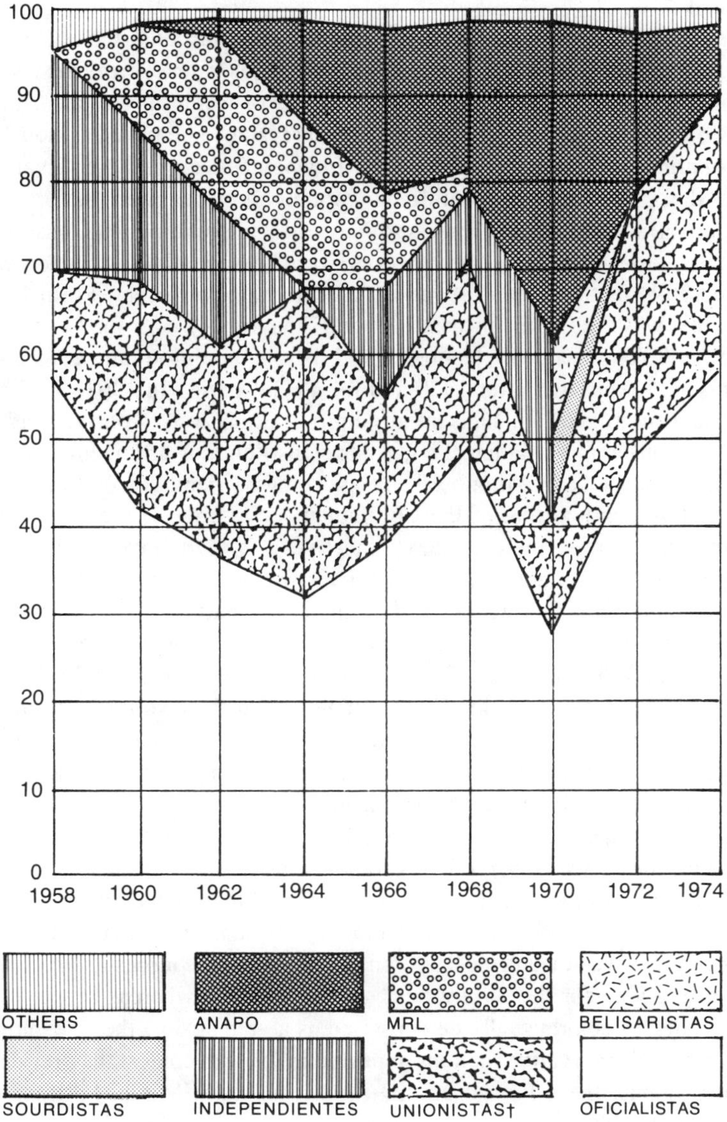

Source: DANE, *Colombia Política, p. 155. 1970, 1972, and 1974 data from the* Registraduría Nacional del Estado Civil.

*Elections are those for the Chamber of Representatives, except in 1972 (departmental assemblies) and 1974 (president).
†Includes the *Independientes* in 1964.

changes in the leadership of the Front and a share in the perquisites of office; others sought significant policy changes as well; while still others opposed the National Front system itself.[5]

The Conservative party had been divided since at least the early 1950s between the followers of former president Mariano Ospina Pérez (the Ospinistas; later to be called the Unionistas) and those of former president Laureano Gómez and his son, Alvaro (the Laureanistas; later to be called variously the Doctrinarios, the Lauro-Alvaristas, the Independientes, and the Alvaristas). Since the pragmatics of coalitional collaboration required the dominant (Oficialista) faction of the Liberals to join with the predominant Conservative faction in order to govern, the election returns essentially determined which Conservative faction would be represented in the government. From 1958 to 1960, this was the Laureanistas; following their victory over the Laureanistas in the 1960 congressional elections, the Liberals' coalition partners were the Ospinistas, except that after 1970 and for a brief period in 1963-64, the two factions were joined in a substantially unified Conservative party. Neither of these factions really challenged the basic institutional arrangements of the National Front, let alone proposed any sweeping reorientation of policy or any fundamental restructuring of the Colombian social order. Like most historic Colombian factions, their primary objective was to replace the incumbent personnel of government (or a segment of them) with their own, while simultaneously gaining the ascendancy within their own party.

True, some small differences existed in the compositions of these two major Conservative factions. There were distinctions in rural and urban support and in regional strength. Class differences in their voting support were apparently minimal, although the requisite survey evidence on this point is sparse.[6] Variations in social status between the congressmen representing the two factions were, in any case, practically nil.[7]

The Unionistas did appear more ready than the Independents to go along with such measures as the 1961 Agrarian Reform Law, which was pushed primarily by the Liberals, but the Unionistas and the Independientes differed little on a Left-Right ideological continuum.[8] Perhaps the principal distinction between them was that, from 1960 on, a vote for the Unionistas was at least implicitly a vote for the government and its policies, whereas a vote for the Independientes could usually be construed as a vote against the government.

Two new Conservative factions appeared in 1970 to contest the presidential election against the official National Front candidate, Misael Pastrana Borrero, a Unionista who had the backing of the Liberal party. They were the Belisaristas, led by Belisario Betancur and supported by some erstwhile Independientes; and the Sourdistas, led by former Unionista Evaristo Sourdís.

Two things distinguished these factions (both of which faded from sight long before the next presidential election)[9] from the other Conservative factions. One was that their appeals were made to constituencies that were somewhat different from those of the long-standing Conservative factions. The Belisaristas called for "reform," made a particular appeal to Colombia's middle class, and did in fact receive disproportionate support from sectors of that social station.[10] Betancur also received the official backing of Colombia's two major labor confederations, the Union of Colombian Workers (UTC) and the Confederation of Colombian Workers (CTC). Sourdís, for his part, proved to be essentially a regional candidate of the Atlantic coastal departments.[11] To the extent that they sought revisions in government policy in favor of particular groups or regions, these factions might be termed policy oppositions.

The second distinctive mark of these short-lived factions was that, in contrast to the Unionistas and the Independientes, they ran congressional slates under both Conservative and Liberal labels. Although their presidential candidates were both Conservatives, a number of their Liberal-list candidates for lesser offices were elected.

Other factions of the traditional parties opposed aspects of the institutional arrangements of the National Front. Most prominent of these was the Revolutionary Liberal Movement (MRL), which was especially opposed to the alternation of the presidency between the parties every four years (particularly since it believed—correctly—that the Liberals had a national majority and would normally win that office). The Conservative presidential candidacy of Jorge Leyva in 1958 (despite the parties' agreement that a Liberal, Alberto Lleras Camargo, should be the initial president under the National Front) was another example of a factional candidate opposed to the bipartisan arrangement.

The MRL was in addition a severe critic of government policies in the social and economic fields, putting forward its Plan de SET (for the Spanish words Salud [health], Educación, and Techo [roof, housing]), and calling for an independent and nationalistic foreign policy. Despite its name, and a tacit alliance at one point with the Communist party (PCC), the MRL was clearly reformist rather than revolutionary in intent, as evidenced above all by its rather innocuous program of agrarian reform.[12]

Its support, moreover, came not primarily from the masses of the large cities nor—as far as can be surmised in the virtual absence of appropriate survey data—from the "proletariat," but from intensely Liberal partisans in certain small- and medium-sized towns and in rural areas that had been particularly afflicted by strife during the years of quasi-civil war (La Violencia) that preceded the formation of the National Front.[13]

The leader of the MRL, Alfonso López Michelsen, was the son of a former president of Colombia and a member of the upper class. The leadership as a whole, however, was more pronouncedly middle class than the main body of the Liberals or any other important faction during the National Front years.[14]

The MRL held its first convention early in 1960, and by 1963, it too had split—between a "soft line" and a "hard line." By mid-1967, the "soft line," led by López, had reentered the main body of the Liberal party;[15] López became a departmental governor, then foreign minister, and in 1974 the successful Liberal candidate for the presidency. Soon after the 1968 elections, the "hard line" faction of the MRL also disappeared.

A number of other Conservative and Liberal factions emerged during the National Front years, many of them of local or departmental significance only, and most lasting no more than one or two elections. The primary goals of the great majority of these factions were, like those of the Unionistas and the Independientes, to place their leaders in high office and to capture for their followers a greater share of bureaucratic positions.

Policy objectives were a bit more explicit for the Belisaristas and the Sourdistas in 1970, and much more so for the MRL, which opposed at least certain facets of the National Front institutions themselves. Yet only the Unionistas and the Independientes, whose rivalry dated from the 1950s, endured for more than a decade, and even they were sporadically joined in a more-or-less united Conservative party, as they have been since 1970.

Implications of Factionalism

Factionalism had always been a salient feature of Colombia's traditional two-party system. But the National Front, which eliminated interparty competition by constitutional fiat, thus diverting electoral competition into strictly intraparty channels, measurably increased that factionalism, as James Payne's tabulations show. Payne argues that, in a political system like the Colombian where leaders are largely motivated by status incentives, the dispersion of administrative resources between the parties under a political arrangement such as the National Front is inherently conducive to an increase in factionalism—a factionalism that will presumably revert to the somewhat lower pre-1958 levels now that the institutionalized coalition has come to an end.[16]

Although the threats posed by factionalism to basic political and social structures proved minimal, it did nonetheless create problems for the National Front.[17] First was the constant threat that a factional candidate opposed to the continuation of bipartisanship, or to certain of its constitutional artifacts, such as presidential alternation, might win the presidency. This never occurred, but there was a close call in 1970, as we shall see. Nevertheless, each election, besides choosing the president, was perforce also a plebiscite on the continuation of the Front.

Secondly, since a coalition between the parties meant essentially coalition between the dominant factions of the two parties, congressional elections

Table 1
Composition of Colombian Chamber of Representatives, 1958-70

	1958	1960	1962	1964	1966	1968	1970*
Pro-Government							
Seats	123	95	109	124	105	126	87
%	83.1	62.5	59.2	67.4	55.3	61.8	41.4
Anti-Government							
Seats	19	38	36	—	26	37	52
%	12.9	25.0	19.6	—	13.7	18.1	24.8
Anti-National Front							
Seats	6	19	39	60	59	41	71
%	4.1	12.5	21.2	33.6	31.1	20.1	33.8
Total Seats	148	152	184	184	190	204	210

Source: Based on data in *Registraduría Nacional del Estado Civil, Estadísticas Electorales*, April 19, 1970 (Bogotá: 1970), p. 392.

*No congressional elections were held in 1972. According to the constitutional reform of 1968, after 1970 such elections were to be held only every four years. The 1974 elections, which returned the country to unrestricted partisan competition, came only months before the termination of the original National Front agreement and were essentially irrelevant to its functioning.

might give the opposition (antigovernment and/or anti-National Front) enough seats to frustrate the government's legislative program. This was especially the case in the years prior to the constitutional reform of 1968, when under the terms of the original coalitional agreement a two-thirds majority was required to pass legislation. Anti-National Front forces never attained more than a third of the votes in a congressional election or of the seats in either House. At the same time these groups, notably the MRL and ANAPO, when aligned with antigovernment factions such as the Independientes, did at times win sufficient votes (and seats) to hamper the government's program. Following the 1970 elections in fact, ANAPO, together with the Belisaristas, controlled at least eight of the twenty-two departmental assemblies.[18]

In short, the enforced bipartisanship of the National Front increased political factionalism, but this never reached the point of disrupting the two-party coalition. The growth of anti-Front (as distinct from merely antigovernment) factions over the years (see Table 1) seemed indicative, however, of a growing dissatisfaction among Colombians not merely, or even perhaps primarily, with the institutions of bipartisanship, but with the leadership of the coalition in the area of social and economic policy.[19] Several other kinds of opposition, not quite possible to delineate by the term factionalism, were, in part at least, further indicative of this rather new basis of opposition.

Nonfactional Oppositions

There are three kinds of exceptions to the generalization that oppositions to the National Front took essentially factional form, though each was of a quite different order. In the first place, there were during the years of the National Front—as there have been at least since the formation of the Communist party in 1930—a number of "third" parties and political movements which were not factional splits from the traditional parties. Some, like the Christian Social Democratic party (PSDC), and the National Democratic Movement (MDN), led by a former general, Alberto Ruiz Novoa, were essentially reformist; that is, they sought changes in the personnel, policies, and institutions of the Front without fundamentally challenging the basic features of the social system (even while some in their youth movements might be inclined in a more revolutionary direction). Most, however, did seek radical change. They included the PCC, the United Front of Revolutionary Action (FUAR), the Peasant-Student-Worker Movement (MOEC), the Independent Revolutionary Workers' Movement (MOIR), the Peoples United Front (FUP) of the late revolutionary priest, Camilo Torres, and several Marxist-oriented guerrilla movements that sprung up during the 1960s. These "third" parties or movements occasionally operated in the electoral arena under a Liberal or Conservative guise, since they could not compete under their own names. More often, they eschewed elections (sometimes campaigning for "belligerent" abstention, which might include voting in blank, as the vehicle of conscious protest), preferring to confine their tactics to mass organization and/or violence. Their ideology was for the most part Marxist, whether orthodox or not, as well as virulent nationalistic, especially against "Yankee imperialism." Most of their leaders came from class- or generation-based counterelites although, as was the case with Father Torres, a few were of considerable social status.

The PCC was the largest among these "third parties," and in 1970, when contests became open again for seats in departmental assemblies and on municipal councils, it won 6 (of 406) seats.[20] All these parties were, however, distinctly minor and some, like the FUAR and the FUP, were also exceedingly short-lived. Abstention may also be deemed another kind of electoral opposition, even though it does not take party or factional form. The percentage of eligible voters who failed to go to the polls increased markedly after 1958, and voting remained below the 50 percent level throughout most of the National Front period. Figure 2 indicates the trends. In the case of the Frente, however, the evidence indicates that abstention was more the product of apathy, brought on at least in part by the suspension of traditional partisan conflict, than it was a sign of conscious protest against the National Front. There are, however, some ambiguities in the data, and "lack of interest," as a

Figure 2
Electoral Participation 1939-68*

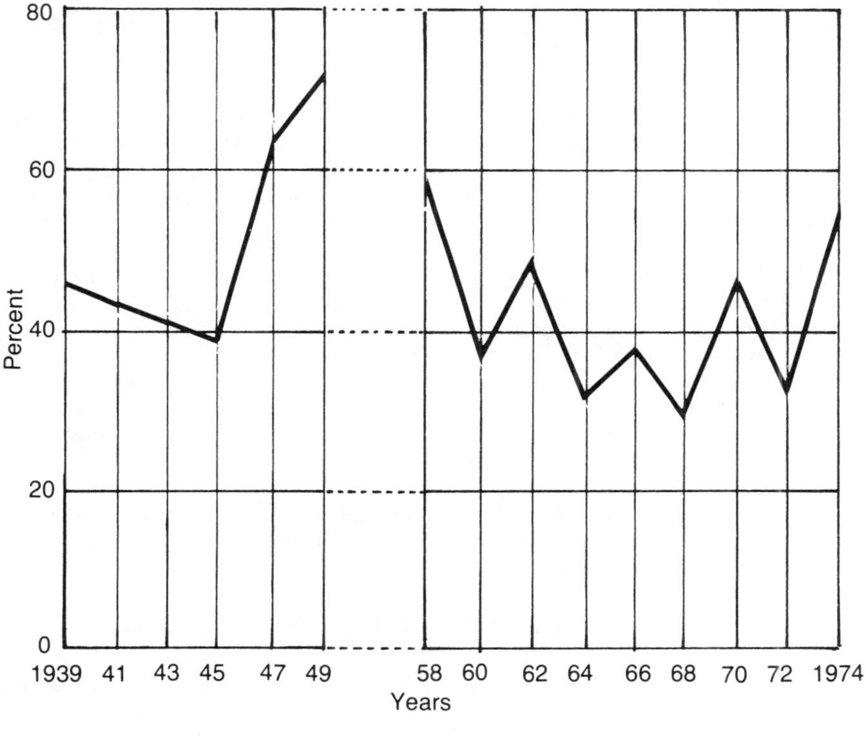

Source: Adapted from Morcillo et al., op. cit., p. 58, and from data published by the Registraduría Nacional del Estado Civil.

*Percentages are based on the estimated population over twenty-one years of age and on the vote for the Chamber of Representatives (except for 1972, when departmental assembly data were used, and 1974, when presidential data were employed).

reason for not voting is not necessarily synonymous with the respondent's satisfaction with his own situation or with the government.

The high rates of abstention during the National Front years were in one sense healthy for the bipartisan arrangement. Since nonvoters tended to have social characteristics that would incline them toward the principal opposition movement[21]—General Rojas's Alianza Nacional Popular (ANAPO)—high rates of abstention presumably meant fewer votes for the opposition. Abstention also had positive implications for the coalition in that it manifested a lower level of polarization than prevailed, for example, in Colombia in the 1940s, when levels of voting were higher in a situation of open political competition that produced violence and dictatorship.[22] On the other hand, abstention also undermined the National Front's claims to legitimacy and led to agonizing appraisals of the causes by politicians and pundits alike.

A third type of opposition to the National Front that could not strictly be included in the factional oppositions discussed above was ANAPO. It merits our extended attention for several reasons:

1. First, because of its importance, since in its electoral support and consistent duration it was the most important of the oppositions during the years of the National Front. In fact, it was the only one of the oppositions to come really close (in 1970) to destroying the National Front before its constitutionally-mandated term of sixteen years.
2. Secondly, especially in the nature of the electoral support it was able to mobilize, but to some extent as well in the composition of its leadership and in the nature of its program and organization, it came closest to challenging the norms and alignments of Colombia's traditional politics.
3. Thirdly, it was one of the few opposition groups to recruit from both traditional parties, to run candidates under both labels, and to seek expressly to supersede the long-standing party system.
4. Fourth, ANAPO has remained the most paradoxical, the most difficult to interpret, and the most misunderstood of Colombian political phenomena.
5. Finally, because it is rooted in changes characteristic of many other Latin American nations, and has interesting parallels as a political movement in other Latin American countries (e.g., Argentina's Peronism), an analysis carries implications for political development beyond the borders of one country.

THE NATIONAL POPULAR ALLIANCE (ANAPO)

The former dictator (1953-57), General Gustavo Rojas Pinilla, and a handful of close associates founded ANAPO as a political movement in 1961.[23] It first presented candidates in an election (almost exclusively under the Conservative label) in 1962. Running candidates on both Conservative and Liberal lists, ANAPO subsequently gained in strength until in 1970 its presidential candidate, General Rojas (albeit running nominally as a Conservative), won 39 percent of the vote nationwide and with it, in a four-way race, almost won the presidency. Anapistas in fact claimed that they had been fraudulently denied victory over the government's candidate. Nevertheless, a movement which had originated essentially as a factional challenge to the National Front, seeking vindication for the deposed Rojas and doutless a restoration of perquisites for his followers, had become within a few short years the major opposition to the two-party coalition.

In the process ANAPO proved innovative in at least three related respects. It had quite successfully built an organization and cast its appeal on a basis that crossed traditional Conservative-Liberal lines, culminating in the founding of a separate party in 1971 and the running of a "third party" candidate,

Table 2
Official Election Results in Stratified Barrios, Bogotá (1970)
(in percentages)

Class	Pastrana	Rojas	Betancur	Sourdís	Blancos	Total
Upper	75.8	8.3	11.9	3.5	.4	100
Upper-middle	67.0	11.9	17.6	3.0	.5	100
Middle	56.4	19.5	20.9	2.4	.8	100
Lower-middle	35.5	50.0	13.0	.8	.7	100
Lower	27.8	62.7	8.3	.3	.8	100
Slum	11.8	84.0	3.0	0.0	1.2	100
Total	40.8	44.6	12.6	1.2	.8	100

C=.495

Source: Adapted from Campos and McCamant, *Cleavage Shift,* p. 60. For comparable survey data see Losada and Williams, p. 19.

(Rojas's daughter, María Eugenia) for the presidency in 1974. Further, the nature of its support among the electorate had come to pose a strong, albeit perhaps temporary, challenge to the hold of the traditional multiclass parties on Colombian political life. At the same time, and finally, the nature of ANAPO's support, its leadership, its appeals, and its organization strongly suggested that a new kind of heterogeneous political movement—not a genuinely class-oriented movement, but one which joined popular malaise to some of the forces of Colombian traditionalism and united them around a leader—had made its appearance in Colombia as it had in many other Latin American countries. To delineate the type we have used the term populism, by which we mean a political movement characterized by the mobilization by (usually marginal) elites of a heterogeneous mass base, beyond or "above" existing attachments, and offering a new cross-sectional identity focusing on a leader, the nation, social justice or, typically, all three.

ANAPO's bipartisan structure, the class-based alignment of its vote, and its populist nature were all in a real sense the product of the coalition of the country's two multiclass parties. Yet in all of these respects the rise of ANAPO had potential implications as well, which extend beyond the duration of the National Front.

Urban Bases of Support

ANAPO, and political movements like ANAPO, pose an initial paradox. While much of their support depends on class alignments within the electorate that were previously largely unfamiliar to the country's partisan politics, they also receive important backing from some of the country's most tradition-minded elements. In Colombia's case, this heterogeneity becomes clear from an analysis of the Anapista vote and its group support.

Thus there is no question that in the country's largest cities the vote for president in 1970 was rather strongly polarized along class lines, with the have-nots voting substantially for ANAPO's candidate, General Rojas. Both surveys and ecological data show that the vote for ANAPO consistently increases as one descends the social scale (see Table 2). The percentage of the lower-class vote accruing to ANAPO in 1970 apparently exceeded that of other Latin American countries which have had significant class voting, like Chile and Argentina, and was not too far behind the percentage of the working-class vote going to working-class parties in such European countries as Sweden and Italy.[24]

This was a startling development for Colombia, with its two historic multi-class parties.[25] It appeared that ANAPO had brought about a substantial shift, from a "vertical" to a "horizontal" axis of politics, at least in the large cities in the 1970 election. In this it differed sharply from the other important oppositions to the National Front.

However, available surveys and *barrio*-level ecological studies[26] reflect only the vote in Colombia's three largest cities, which contain only about a fifth of the nation's population. Whether the class divisions were similar in other localities is therefore largely unknown.[27] Moreover, even in the large cities the real dividing line among the classes in their support for Rojas in 1970 came not between the lower two classes and the others, but between the middle and lower-middle class, at least in the *barrio* analysis.

It is also important to note the distinction between the lower class in most Latin American countries, including Colombia, and the classic European working class. Rather than an industrial working class, the lower strata of urban Latin America tend to comprise an impoverished mass, only marginally related to the central productive processes of their societies. For Latin America, the rate of urbanization far outpaces any concomitant availability of industrial employment and, hence, the formation of a class-conscious proletariat in the European sense. Such a proletariat is not the major component of the urban lower strata in a country like Colombia, nor therefore of the ANAPO vote.

Evidence from elsewhere in Latin America indicates that newcomers to the city tend to see themselves in terms of individual, rather than group or class, mobility.[28] Relatedly, surveys show a tendency of ANAPO's urban supporters to view its program in terms of direct and immediate benefits, rather than in terms of longer-range structural reforms or changes.[29]

Though ANAPO did receive some support from manual workers in 1970 according to the sample surveys, workers were not very numerous in the samples, while those workers who were also union members tended to favor other candidates. In terms of the proportion supporting ANAPO, shopkeepers, petty tradesmen, and door-to-door salesmen, as well as domestic servants stood out. ANAPO also showed relative strength among the unemployed.[30]

Age, length of residence in the city, and even gender, likewise had some cross-cutting impact on the large-city vote in 1970, although occupation and socioeconomic position were apparently much stronger influences.[31] Thus it is worth noting that ANAPO received disproportionate support in some large cities in 1970 from the 21-30 age group, a support that nearly doubled between 1968 and 1970.[32] Furthermore, at least in Cali, there was a tendency for the Rojista vote to correlate with the brevity of residence in the city.[33] Analysis of the actual vote by sex in 1970 also showed a slightly greater tendency for men than for women to support Rojas. Moreover, men voted in appreciably greater numbers than women, making women the one group of previous abstainers which ANAPO failed to mobilize to a notable degree.[34] There is much about the ANAPO vote in the cities, especially in 1970, to suggest that, whatever its correlation with socioeconomic variables, it was in the first instance a massive expression of protest against the policies of the National Front, and especially against the inflation, unemployment, and other economic hardships perceived as having been brought about by the "developmentalist" programs of the outgoing president, Carlos Lleras Restrepo.[35] Though correlated in significant degree with variables such as social class, the vote for Rojas in 1970 was above all else a vote against the National Front and its works,[36] and at the same time an expression of hope (confidence?) that the erstwhile dictator would bring immediate relief to those in economic distress.

In short, even while in the largest cities the 1970 vote for ANAPO polarized the electorate along class lines to a degree probably unprecedented in Colombia, there was much to suggest that a classic Marxian class struggle was not necessarily implied. For, at least at its peak in 1970, ANAPO's urban supporters ranged from the middle class (whom Eldon Kenworthy has depicted as objectively lower class, but subjectively not, in the Latin American context)[37] to many among the lower strata who were by occupation and outlook hardly proletarian. They included those left behind by development even more than they embraced those expolited by industrialization.[38] Many ANAPO supporters were urban dwellers and some of them *campesinos* and small-town dwellers displaced to the larger cities—not really integrated into the productive processes of an industrializing society, and with but minimum political consciousness. They were therefore ripe for manipulation by a caudillo,[39] tending to confirm William Kornhauser's point that differences in receptivity to mass symbols and leaders is more the consequence of the *strength* of social ties rather than of the influence of class or social status itself.[40]

Table 3
ANAPO'S Percentage of the Liberal, Conservative, and Total Popular Vote from Municipios Ranked by Size: House Elections, 1962-70
(% of Vote in Municipios Ranked by Size*)

Election Date		I	II	III	IV	V	VI	National Average
1962	%C	23.6	13.8	11.0	18.1	6.1	5.9	8.2
	%T	6.5	4.7	3.4	6.2	2.7	3.2	3.7
	%L	0.5‡	9.4	15.2	8.0	1.8	0.2	1.4
1964	%C	61.6	31.4	38.8	35.6	23.1	21.4	26.8
	%T	25.7	15.8	18.3	16.3	10.8	11.6	13.6
	%L	19.2	18.2	9.4	10.2	3.5	1.3	6.2
1966	%C	61.0	34.7	36.3	41.4	25.9	28.1	32.5
	%T	31.7	20.4	16.2	24.9	12.2	15.1	17.8
	%L	9.2	15.4	11.1	8.2	6.6	2.1	6.2
1968	%C	52.6	28.2	41.9	40.2	29.0	28.8	32.3‡
	%T	22.9	20.2	22.1	19.6	15.6	16.8	18.3‡
	%L	33.9	41.3	31.5	29.8	24.6	18.9	27.7
1970	%T	43.5	41.3	42.1	41.1	33.2	29.3	35.3
	%C	61.1	41.3	54.2	53.3	41.5	37.6	43.9

Notes:
%C - Per cent in relation to total Conservative vote
%T - Per cent in relation to total popular vote
%L - Per cent in relation to total Liberal vote

*Based on 1964 census. Group I corresponds to the municipio of Bogotá, which includes the Federal District and represents 9.8 per cent of the national population. Group II contains the municipios of Medellín, Cali, and Barranquilla, which in 1964 fell within a population range of 500,000-775,000. Combined they represented 10.9 per cent of the population. Group III contains all municipios between 100,000-250,000, which accounted for 11.2 per cent of the population. Group IV covers the range of municipios between 50,000-100,000, totaling 9.1 per cent of the population. Group V considers all municipios between 25,000-50,000, representing 14.3 per cent of the total population. Group VI contains the vote for all municipios of fewer than 25,000.

†This percentage is suspect. There is evidence that the Registrar's figure of 401 votes for ANAPO's Liberal House vote in Bogotá in 1964 is inaccurate.

‡Includes ANAPO-Alvarista coalition vote.

Source: Premo, op. cit., pp. 266-67.

Nonurban Bases of Support

The data make abundantly clear that ANAPO has, relatively, been an urban phenomenon.[41] Taking the 1970 elections for the Chamber of Representatives as typical, 40.1 percent of the total departmental vote came from the urban capitals of the twenty-two departments, whereas 46.7 percent of the Anapista vote came from the same capital cities. In only four such cities did the percentage vote for ANAPO fail to exceed the percentage of the total de-

Table 4
Election Results by Departments (1970)

Department	Pastrana %	Rojas %	Betancur %	Sourdís %	Voters n	Voting %
Atlantic Coast						
More developed						
Magdalena	26.6	31.3	1.2	40.8	124,096	48
Atlántico	16.3	31.5	1.3	50.8	200,211	52
Bolívar	28.1	26.6	2.8	42.5	157,483	48
Less developed						
Guajira	30.3	35.3	1.8	32.5	46,630	53
Sucre	43.8	21.3	.7	34.1	83,052	48
Córdoba	46.3	36.3	4.3	13.2	136,691	49
Urbanized						
More developed						
Antioquia	41.7	41.9	16.0	0.4	457,397	38
Cundinamarca	42.8	42.4	13.8	1.0	775,744	51
Valle	38.9	48.0	12.1	1.0	405,787	46
Extractive						
High tenancy						
Cesar	21.0	45.1	0.9	33.1	71,249	38
Norte de Santander	47.1	44.1	8.4	0.3	135,674	57
Santander	36.5	52.2	10.6	0.9	242,452	54
Boyacá	36.1	55.8	7.7	0.3	198,148	42
Meta	31.7	50.5	17.6	0.3	45,177	39
Central						
More developed						
Caldas	38.6	29.3	31.9	0.2	138,735	46
Risaralda	46.0	31.3	22.5	0.2	89,945	44
Quindío	40.4	35.9	23.4	0.2	58,698	32
Southwest						
Less developed						
Tolima	47.2	39.8	12.8	0.1	156,908	45
Huila	63.9	26.1	9.9	.0	105,987	55
Cauca	59.1	22.4	18.4	0.2	119,112	38
Chocó	52.4	10.8	35.6	1.1	36,403	46
Nariño	56.7	23.1	12.3	7.9	151,878	42

Source: Campos and McCamant, op. cit., p. 53.

partmental vote cast in those same cities.[42] Yet what evidence it is possible to muster concerning voting patterns outside the large cities points up that ANAPO's electoral roots are by no means entirely a product of urban disaffection. The partisan derivation of Anapista voters, as well as the support ANAPO has received (or has failed to receive) from organized groups, are further indications both of ANAPO's heterogeneous composition and its deep roots in traditional Colombia.

When the *municipios* of the country are ranked by size into six categories, ANAPO's vote proves to be consistently greater in the largest cities, and there is a noticeable tendency for the average Anapista vote to decline with the size of the community. But, as Table 3 shows, the latter tendency is not very consistent. Only when one compares the vote in "very rural" *caseríos* and *corregimientos* with the corresponding departmentwide vote does the disparity in Anapista strength become truly striking.[43]

Fully a third of ANAPO's votes in the presidential elections of 1966 and 1970 (and almost a half in 1962) came from *municipios* defined as rural.[44] Moreover, many of the "provincial" cities are as Anapista as the country's burgeoning metropoli; indeed the truly large proportional vote for Rojas in 1970 (over 50 percent) came not from the largest cities but from those of secondary rank in terms of size.[45] Finally, it should be noted that more than half of the population of such major cities as Bogotá and Cali comes from rural or small-town origins,[46] while the 1970 Bogotá survey (though not the Cali surveys) showed that those who were born in towns of less than 20,000 persons had a much greater tendency to vote for ANAPO than did those born in larger communities.[47]

Taken together, the foregoing data clearly demonstrate that ANAPO, as the major opposition to the National Front both in dimension and portent, was very far from being merely a product of discontent in Colombia's largest cities, and that even those who were urban in residence were not necessarily urban in their orientations toward politics.

Regional voting patterns further point up the fact that ANAPO's strongholds have included parts of the country that are not particularly urban or "modern." Of the eight (of twenty-two) departments giving 40 percent or more of their vote to Rojas in 1970, three did indeed contain Colombia's three largest cities (Bogotá, Medellín, and Cali). The other five strong Anapista departments, however, including the only three to give Rojas more than 50 percent of their votes in 1970, were mainly agricultural (see Table 4).

Furthermore, in one of the three "most developed" departments (Valle del Cauca), the 1970 vote for Rojas outside of Cali was slightly greater than his vote from the city itself. Rank-order correlations at the departmental level, while they show a mildly positive correlation between the vote for ANAPO and such indicators of development as literacy (.42), show an even higher correlation with an indicator of traditional rural patterns such as land tenancy (.65).[48] The correlation between religiosity (as measured by religious vocations per capita) is a modest .41; nevertheless, the strong ANAPO departments do tend to be high in religiosity (even while others that are high in religiosity are not strongly Anapista).[49]

Partisan Bases of Support

There is a final relevant question concerning the derivation of the ANAPO vote; namely, where in partisan terms did that vote go prior to the rise of the new party? First of all, in 1970 when eligible Colombians voted at a higher rate than at any time since 1958 (see Figure 2) and when the ANAPO vote simultaneously reached its peak, previous abstainers voted disproportionately for General Rojas. Indeed, surveys show that the 1970 ANAPO campaign mobilized many new voters, not only the young but also many others who had seldom or never before cast a ballot.[50]

The rise in ANAPO's electoral fortunes roughly parallels the decline of the MRL, and for the 1968 elections Rojas made a concerted attempt to strengthen ANAPO's Liberal wing in the wake of the MRL's merger with the main body of the Liberal party the previous year. Nevertheless, circumstantial evidence at least suggests that on the whole the consequences for ANAPO were modest. The 1970 vote for ANAPO at the departmental level does correlate positively (.45) with the 1962 MRL vote. However, ANAPO's percentage of the total Liberal vote did not increase in 1968, while that of the Oficialistas did.[51] Moreover, the MRL vote was inversely correlated with size of place, centering in towns and rural areas rather than in the large cities where ANAPO has been relatively strongest. In the virtual absence of germane survey data,[52] one cannot, of course, be certain where the erstwhile electorate of the MRL did go. However, the presumption must be that, while many former adherents of the MRL did back ANAPO, the majority either turned to other Liberal lists, primarily Oficialista, or joined millions of other Colombians in abstention once they were deprived of what they regarded as a genuine Liberal list for which to vote.

Electoral data, as well as surveys in both Bogotá and Cali, in fact confirm that, despite its strength in the (predominantly Liberal) large cities, erstwhile Conservative voters have supported Anapista candidates proportionately more often than have Liberals. Conversely, with the principal exception of some of the larger cities in 1970, an ANAPO voter has been more likely to view himself as a Conservative than as a Liberal.[53]

To begin with, there have always been more Anapista Conservative lists than Anapista Liberal lists in the elections, while at ANAPO's peak in 1970 the Anapista Liberals garnered only 39.9 percent of the total ANAPO vote. Again, in those departments (seventeen of twenty-two in 1970) where both the Conservative and Liberal wings of ANAPO have run candidates, the Conservative lists have usually captured more votes. The exceptions have been relatively few and occurred mainly in 1970.[54]

Outside the largest cities, the *Rojista* vote has tended to come from certain departments in eastern Colombia where initial opposition to the National

Front on the part of some Conservatives was quite high,[55] (even while there are Conservative departments, such as Nariño in southwestern Colombia, where ANAPO has proved to be rather weak).

The ANAPO vote has thus generally been more Conservative than Liberal. It is, however, definitely bipartisan in nature, tending to be Liberal in large cities, Conservative in small communities, and of mixed partisan origin in towns and cities of intermediate size.[56] ANAPO therefore confronted the National Front with a kind of bipartisan coalition of its own.

Bases of Support—Organized Groups

The heterogeneous elements of Anapista support are further illustrated by facts not discernible from the data on voting. Thus one of the most vociferous (among the few) organizations backing General Rojas in 1970 was PATRIANAL, a reserve officers association founded by Rojistas in order to combat the influence of the pro-National Front Reservist Union. Its claim of 100,000 members was undoubtedly exaggerated, but a rally and parade on March 6, 1970 particularly impressed observers.[57] Organized reservists (under a different name) were also active on ANAPO's behalf in the 1974 presidential campaign.[58] Evidence of another level of support is that priests have occasionaly been active in electoral campaigns on behalf of ANAPO, while ANAPO's congressmen have evinced a relatively high level of contact with the clergy.[59] ANAPO has also received some support from the radical Golconda group within the Colombian clergy.[60] These indications do not mean that the majority of either group could at any time be counted in ANAPO's favor. What is apparent, however, is that substantial numbers of persons associated with two of Colombia's principal institutions have been supportive of the ANAPO cause.

In addition, Anapista congressmen ranked highest among the political factions in the number of visits they received from representatives of peasant groups.[61] However, while ANAPO congressmen report extensive contact with labor union leaders, such contacts do not often include the leaders of the major labor confederations, the UTC and the CTC.[62] Neither confederation has supported ANAPO in a presidential campaign, nor have individual unions.[63] By 1974 organized groups supporting ANAPO electorally included a women's committee apparently organized for the campaign, and a group of actors and intellectuals.[64] In general, however, support for ANAPO from established interest associations was minimal.

In summary, then, we have in ANAPO a political movement which in terms of its support was, at least at its peak in 1970, more nearly class-based than any in Colombian history, and more nearly so than most in Latin America, but which has at the same time constituted a diverse coalition

Table 5
Socioeconomic Status of Party Leaders by Party and Party Level

Socioeconomic Status	Liberal			Unionist			Party ANAPO			Independent		
	B	*C*	*N*	*B*	*C*	*N*	*B*	*C*	*N*	*B*	*C*	*N*
Low	22	0	0	32	0	0	50	0	0	35	0	0
Lower-Middle	47	42	5	39	9	0	30	20	0	26	50	0
Upper-Middle	24	8	15	20	48	25	20	20	50	13	28	18
Upper	6	50	80	8	42	75	0	60	50	26	22	82
Total	99	100	100	99	99	100	100	100	100	100	100	100
Number	95	12	20	71	33	8	95	5	18	23	18	11

Source: Kline, "Recruitment," p. 40.
Notes: B denotes barrio-level leaders; *C* city-level leaders, and *N* national leaders.

including support from some of the more traditionalist redoubts of Colombian political life.

Leadership

If ANAPO has differed from other parties and factions in its combination of support, its leadership has more nearly resembled that of the Liberals and Conservatives, with some subtle, but significant, distinctions. The data show that leaders of ANAPO at the national level, as well as ANAPO congressmen, are like the leaders and congressmen of other major parties and factions, generally high in social status. Their social standing, however, is slightly lower on the average than that of other factions of the traditional parties.

In a composite index of socioeconomic status—combining education, income, and nature of employment, and based on a sample of leaders of all major factions in Bogotá—just 50 percent of Anapistas were rated high, whereas at least 75 percent of the national-level leaders of the other factions were so rated (see Table 5). The differential in education alone was even more notable; only 42 percent of ANAPO's national leaders graduated from a university (another 21 percent attended but did not finish) compared to between 85 and 100 percent for the other factions.[65] Similar status gradations are discernible at the level of *barrio* and city-wide leadership.[66] Data on congressmen, broken down by party, manifest a similar pattern. Of those rated "low" on a summary index of social status, ANAPO has more than double the percentage (22.5) of any other faction; similarly it has fewer (25 percent) rated "high" in status.[67]

The differences between ANAPO and the other parties/factions are not always great, and do not invariably place ANAPO leaders lowest in status among the political leaderships. But the tendency is clear and consistent. Although in the larger sense Anapista leaders at the national level are members of the Colombian elite, they are relatively marginal members of that elite. They are also less likely to be listed in *Quién es Quién* (Who's Who),[68] although many of them are listed there and, it appears, they are less likely to be members of such elite associations as Bogotá's Jockey Club or Country Club.[69]

In line with this pattern, ANAPO's representatives in Congress report somewhat fewer contacts with the major economic associations than do the representatives of other parties—except with ACOPI, the Association of Small Industrialists.[70] The members of ACOPI, while of course having high status relative to Colombian society as a whole, nonetheless tend to be marginal in power and prestige compared, say, to the industrialists who are members of the National Association of Manufacturers (ANDI).

Rojas himself confirms the picture: he grew up in a family of small landowners in the department of Boyacá and obtained an engineering degree from a small college in Indiana. The military officers' corps—made up largely of men of middle-class (rural and urban) and provincial elite origin who are not of the highest social prestige in Colombia—had been his career.

The roles of three specific groups in the ranks of ANAPO leadership are worth mentioning briefly. Former military men, many with ties to the former Rojas regime, have played an important role in ANAPO, especially in its early years. Twenty-six people attended the first organizational meeting, and nine of them, including Rojas, were retired military or national police officers. Of ANAPO's first "national command," named by Rojas in late 1961, twenty-four of the seventy-nine members were retired military officers.[72] Such military influence at the upper level of Anapista leadership was unique in Colombian party life, even though it faded considerably in subsequent years.

A survey of a sample of Colombian elites carried out in 1966 found that none among the category "intellectuals" identified themselves as supporters of ANAPO.[73] Some intellectuals later associated themselves with the party, but they were relatively few and such support is significant in a country where intellectuals have considerable prestige. Particularly notable was the general failure of ANAPO to appeal to *técnicos* (technical experts in economics, engineering, public administration and the like) who have become increasingly important to the Colombian developmental process in recent years.

Lastly, despite the large role played in ANAPO by Rojas's daughter, María Eugenia Rojas de Moreno, women have not been especially prominent in the party. Prior to 1970, ANAPO elected only 3 women to Congress as *principales*, plus three alternates (*suplentes*).[74] In 1970, ANAPO's high point, 5 women (out of 109 elected on its lists) were elected as *principales* and 9 (109) as *suplentes*. ANAPO did not differ appreciably from the other parties/ factions, then, in providing relatively few places on its electoral lists to women, nor in the tendency to assign them the inferior position of *suplente* on those lists.[75]

Together such traits point up the differences as well as the similarities between the social backgrounds of Anapista leaders and the leaders of other parties/factions. Politically, too, there were both analogies and distinctions. Politically, the backgrounds of ANAPO leaders were in the main Conservative. A survey of Colombian congressmen carried out in 1967 found that the fathers of virtually 90 percent of the Anapistas were Conservatives.[76] Indeed, the *perceptions* of Anapista leaders were that the ideological distance between Anapistas and Conservatives was narrower than that between Anapistas and Liberals (or, for that matter, between Liberals and Conservatives).[77]

In fact, it initially appeared that Rojas seriously considered restricting ANAPO's scope to that of a dissident Conservative faction, and no Liberals were present at its first organizational meeting. Protests from Liberals present at the second ANAPO organizational meeting, plus arguments from some of the reservists present that support from the military was more likely to be forthcoming for a bipartisan group, convinced Rojas that the new movement should be bipartisan.[78] Nonetheless, beginning in 1966, the Liberal wing of ANAPO was accorded equal representation on the national command; ANAPO's candidate in 1966 was a Liberal (José Jaramillo Giraldo) in order to comply with the conditions of alternation; a number of erstwhile Liberal leaders joined ANAPO during the late 1960s; and the congressional, departmental, and municipal electoral lists of ANAPO's Liberal wing were considerably expanded.

Most of the Liberals who joined ANAPO were themselves rather marginal Liberals as far as the main body of Liberalism was concerned. Many were former members of the defunct MRL. Others were Rojistas of longer standing, mainly "Popular Liberals," as the rump of the formerly much larger Gaitanista wing of the Liberal party had once been called. Some had served in the Rojas-appointed National Constituent Assembly (ANAC) during his years in power. A few had socialist or other Marxist backgrounds and connections.

The incorporation of Liberals into the upper echelons of the movement helped make ANAPO a bipartisan movement to a degree, at least recently, rare for Colombia. At the same time, this dual partisanship never overrode the basically Conservative origins and orientations of the bulk of ANAPO's leadership cadres. Indeed there were a number of indications that Rojas himself acted to keep the Liberal wing subordinate to the Conservatives in the movement.[79]

Overall, those who were attracted to the movement and took an active part in the leadership appeared to include a relatively high proportion of individuals whose status was marginally elite. Some of these marginal elites were undoubtedly seeking fuller access to the material and status rewards of the system. Perhaps, too, many of them were seeking to resist the changes being instituted by the "bourgeois developmentalists" and technocrats of the National Front.[80] Such an interpretation seems to be supported by the fact that the core of Anapista leadership was clearly Conservative and quite traditionalist. That such a group should seek to lead a movement so largely comprised of the urban lower classes gave ANAPO its unique character.

Organization

Prior to the founding of ANAPO in 1961, Rojas and a knot of loyal supporters from the years of his late regime were implicated in several abortive coups attempting to restore the general to power. Even after the creation of the new movement, there remained a distinct undercurrent of implication that ANAPO was less a mass movement for electoral purposes than a vehicle for conspiracy, or perhaps for popular insurrection. The prominence of former military officers in ANAPO's early organizational life gave added credence to such an interpretation, as did the legacy of the Rojas regime itself: while in power the general had attempted to found a Third Force whose axis was to be an alliance between the armed forces and the people.[81]

Beginning about 1964, when ANAPO's electoral gains appeared to indicate that the ballot box might prove a more feasible means for a return to power, this aspect of ANAPO faded into the background. It was some time, however, before all suspicions regarding a conspiracy disappeared, reinforced as they were by periodic pronouncements by Rojas saying in effect that the people would acquire power before new elections, or that he and his followers would not accept defeat at the polls.[82] This aspect of ANAPO gave to it, especially in its early years, a nonelectoral dimension not shared by other significant oppositions to the National Front. Indeed, at first, ANAPO was organizationally little more than Rojas' personal vehicle. It had little formal structure and was dependent on the *gira* (personal campaign tour) for its recruitment of mass support. Only sixteen *barrio*-level commands existed in the country at the time of the 1962 elections, while initial attempts to mobilize lower-class support in urban centers were met with indifference and in some cases with hostility.[83]

Yet by 1970, in the large urban areas especially, ANAPO had come to resemble a modern mass party, complete with myriad ward (*barrio*) level organizations, regular dues, membership cards, mass rallies, party training schools, more or less regular party media, a centralized command structure, and strict party discipline.[84] By the time of the 1970 election, several hundred thousand party cards had avowedly been issued to ANAPO adherents,[85] clearly surpassing anything ever effectively achieved by the traditional parties. More than 3,000 "commands" purportedly functioned throughout the country during the campaign, with some 200 of them in Bogotá itself.[86] A higher proportion of Rojista voters (in the Cali area) reported that they had attended political rallies during the 1970 campaign than did the supporters of other candidates,[87] and more Rojistas in Bogotá reported being contacted by a party worker during that campaign.[88] In a survey of *barrio*, district, and national party leaders carried out in Bogotá in 1969, Anapista leaders reported significantly more attention to *barrio*-level organization, more involvement in "social work," and more frequent visits by national leaders to the *barrios* than did Liberal or Conservative leaders.[89]

In the absence of virtually any positive coverage in the regular press, ANAPO began its own newspaper, *Alianza Popular*, as early as 1961. Published only sporadically, it was succeeded in 1969 by *Alerta*, which appeared somewhat more regularly. *Alerta* attained a distributional peak of perhaps 40,000 copies just prior to the 1970 election.[90] The movement also had its own radio outlet in Bogotá, as well as sporadically functioning outlets (and newspapers) in other parts of the country. Its media were not central for ANAPO, however. *Alerta* could not compete effectively with the daily press, which was largely controlled by politicians of the established parties, while the radio station had only a low kilowattage.

Like most mass parties, ANAPO made some effort to develop affiliates among women, youth, labor, and military reservists. Unlike most mass parties, however, ANAPO's group linkages of this kind, especially those with organized labor, have been weak.[91] More important than ties to other mass organizations, and more important than the media, has been ANAPO's grassroots organization, often connected with such social service projects as the distribution of food and clothing to the poor, and free medical services. Personal contact with the urban masses *between* elections on the part of party leaders was one of the keys to ANAPO's urban success—something seldom undertaken in Colombia's political past.

ANAPO has also been highly structured and tightly disciplined in the formal sense. Rojas himself was from the beginning chief of the party, with María Eugenia assuming the role of campaign manager for the 1970 election and subsequently that of "national director." In effect, beginning in the late 1960s, she became codirector of the movement and the principal impetus behind its urban organizational expansion. Below the positions of chief and national director, the particulars of ANAPO's command structure have varied somewhat over time. During much of its life there has been a national command appointed by Rojas, along with a hierarchy of departmental, municipal, and *barrio* commands. The power to appoint and to remove leaders at any given level has formally rested with the next higher command level and has been frequently exercised. In sum, as Campos and McCamant note, "The ANAPO organization gave the party greater control from the center and greater work participation at the bottom than has been the case with the traditional parties."[92]

In certain other respects, however, ANAPO does not much resemble the modern mass party. In the first place, it continues to bear some of the traits of a traditional Colombian political faction. Thus, in many departments and *municipios*, the relationship of party leaders to party followers appears to reflect the traditional roles of patron and client. Some Anapista leaders had developed personal or regional followings prior to associating themselves with the movement.[93] Those who defected or were expelled from ANAPO were often able to carry their followers with them.[94] A study of Colombian congressmen, broken down by party, revealed that, while a higher proportion of Anapistas could be categorized as more highly disciplined and nationally-oriented than congressmen of other parties, more Anapistas also had a strictly regional focus.[95]

Party financing manifests a similar pattern. ANAPO raises money from party dues and the issuance of special bonds to an extent undoubtedly beyond that of other parties, and, as is common with mass parties, it exacts a portion of its legislators' salaries to support the party.[96] But it has also relied heavily on more traditional modes of fund raising. Hence, the study of Congress indicated that for campaign financing ANAPO candidates relied primarily on their own funds and those of friends, rather than on the party.[97] Asked what factors led to their becoming congressmen, more Anapistas (10.6 percent) replied "personal economic resources" than did other congressmen.[98]

ANAPO differs further from the modern, mass party in having a relatively personalistic as opposed to an ideological orientation. The party's media, including both press and radio, contain constant references to both General Rojas and his daughter. With the exception of 1966, either one or the other was the ANAPO candidate each time the party contested the presidency, and even in 1966 it was clear to all that the candidate was little more than a surrogate for Rojas and was imposed by the circumstances of the National Front.

All command decisions, including the appointment and expulsion of party officers at the departmental level, and often at the municipal level, emanate from the circle of Rojas, his daughter, and María Eugenia's husband, Samuel Moreno Díaz, who is also a senator. The "family" has usually selected ANAPO's congressional candidates as well. For the most part, the party's national command has played only a rubber-stamp role in such matters. Rojas has taken personal loyalty to himself very seriously indeed, and the family triumvirate has been intolerant of any initiative within the party that has not had their authorization.

Claims are sometimes made by ANAPO adherents (and affirmed in party documents) that ANAPO leaders, at the local level at least, are popularly elected, but there is little evidence that this is the case.[99] In a real sense, both the party itself and the party's campaigns have been run along militaristic lines, with total obediance demanded by the supreme commanders and those to whom they delegate authority. Thus, there is little real collective decision making in the party, and even little pretense of it, as distinct from most European mass parties, for example. There is also little of the kind of elite collegiality which tends to govern the Liberal and Conservative parties, and little of their decentralization and diffuseness of organization. The role of the leaders is paramount.

That leadership has had something of the charismatic, although it was hardly that of a Fidel Castro or a Juan Perón. Rojas's image was that of the strongman who would resolve the pressing problems of the poor. The election of 1970 thus conjoined a situation characterized by economic deprivation, social stress, and political alienation with the availability of an appropriate leader. Subsequently, with Rojas ill and growing old (he was seventy in 1970), María Eugenia took on something of the same aura.[100]

Surveys show that Rojas's appeal to voters far surpassed any loyalty to ANAPO. This is hardly surprising, given the recentness of ANAPO's birth. The surveys also point up a problem that ANAPO would carry with it as an openly declared separate party, namely that, even while voting for Rojas or ANAPO, many still considered themselves to be Conservatives or Liberals in terms of party identification.[101]

The closed, hierarchical structure of ANAPO has not, of course, precluded competition to gain the "ear" of the top leadership. Nor has it precluded factionalism that has on occasion led to violence among Anapistas,[102] nor frequent defections from the ranks. A number of those who have left ANAPO have, in fact, placed much of the blame for their disaffection on the unwanted influence of the Rojas family in directing the party.[103]

ANAPO has been organizationally vulnerable in another sense as well. Most of its leaders and congressional candidates have been recruited from among old Rojas loyalists or from defectors from other political factions such as the MRL. There has been little attempt to promote a new generation of leaders from within its own ranks. This in turn may be responsible for the relatively high rate of turnover which characterized the lower levels of leadership, at least prior to 1970.[104]

In summary, ANAPO has more closely resembled the modern mass party than any other Colombian party, especially in the large cities. It nonetheless continues to bear a number of the organizational traits of Colombia's traditional parties. In the last analysis, it is also very much the product of mobilization "from above" by a party leadership centered in a *caudillo* and his family and close associates.

Of course, ANAPO has been *sui generis* to Colombia not only in the nature and extent of its mass-based, hierarchically-structured organization, but also in the fact that it has encompassed wings from both traditional parties. In this ANAPO clearly differed from such factions as the MRL, the Unionistas, and the Independientes, none of which sought seriously to recruit followings from both traditional parties.

Ideology and Program

Ideology has never played the same central role for ANAPO that it has for most of Europe's mass parties; nor does ANAPO's program have the kind of philosophical foundation afforded by Marxism or Christian Socialism, for example. A survey of party leaders confirms that the motivations of Anapistas are neither particularly ideological nor programmatic, despite the party's claim to represent real ideological distinctiveness in contrast to the traditional parties.[105] And Daniel Premo stresses the extent to which "loyalty to Rojas and the inducement of personal gain were substitutes for ideological conviction in maintaining ANAPO's unity at the leadership level."[106]

At the same time, Rojas had claimed, "I consider that the important thing is not to look for unity around a person, but around a set of principles . . . ."[107] Over the years, ANAPO has come forth with several formal statements of its program, including the so-called Decalogue (1970) and the Ideological and Political Platform (1971). Beginning in 1966, the party has also made an effort to complement Rojas's personal appeal by forming an institute in Bogotá to conduct political orientation sessions for party cadres and militants.[108] Voters in 1970 more frequently cited aspects of ANAPO's programmatic appeal, such as "aid to the poor," as reasons for choosing Rojas than "personal values of the candidate."[109] It is therefore important to examine ANAPO's ideology through its programmatic statements, the party press, and its campaign rhetoric,[110] to gain a sense of what it claims its objectives to be. What emerges rather clearly is the essentially populist (rather than Marxist or otherwise revolutionary) nature of the movement.

Rojas' initial conception of ANAPO appears to have been a reincarnation of the so-called Third Force of his earlier administration, stressing the union of "the people" and the armed forces apart from the oligarchies that purportedly controlled the Conservative and Liberal parties. Vitriolic attacks on the personnel, policies, and institutions of the two-party coalition—which had been largely responsible for the demise of the Rojas regime in 1957—along with a tendency for Rojas to assume the role of the wronged martyr, have constituted a very important "negative" side of ANAPO's campaign appeals. As late as 1974, the party organ, *Alerta*, devoted 85 percent of its space to such attacks and vindications, and to ANAPO organizational matters, compared to only about nine percent devoted to such "positive" aspects of ANAPO's program as social and economic policy.[111] Verbal assaults on Colombia's system of privilege abound, replete with assertions such as, "ANAPO is the revolution."

There has, however, been another side to ANAPO, which is summed up in the phrase "*socialism a la Colombiana*." The socialist side of ANAPO harked back to the very last days of the Rojas regime when, grasping at straws that might win him the support to survive politically and heeding the advice of Antonio García, head of the then-Colombian Popular Socialist party (PPSC), Rojas proposed such measures as the nationalization of the Bank of the Republic. ANAPO's "socialist" proposals have included the nationalization of education, of imports, of private banks, and of oil and other natural resources, as well as profit sharing for workers and the liberalization of credit.[112]

Although such proposals became more prominent during the latter years of the National Front, they have, for the most part, played a secondary role in ANAPO's appeals to the electorate. Surveys confirm that for the Anapista electorate, the attraction of ANAPO has been the promised relief from economic distress and other material benefits. Reduction of the cost of living and tax relief have been stressed in ANAPO campaigns. Rather than specific proposals for structural change, the immediate easing of economic hardship and the distribution of largesse, along with attacks on the "oligarchs," the "plutocrats," and the "official corruption" alleged to characterize the National Front, have constituted the core of ANAPO's appeal. Income redistribution was not really the issue; rather, the demand was for "aid to the poor" and entry into ranks of a consumer society. As one voter for Rojas in 1970 phrased it, "He will reduce the cost of everything to the point of giving it away, [also] he promised to provide scholarships for all children and I have seven . . . ."[113]

Despite ANAPO's professed concern for the poor, and despite its proposals for nationalization in some areas, it has shown little inclination to view society explicitly in terms of class divisions or the need for deep-seated structural change. Thus, Rojas has spoken of being "a father to both the poor and the rich" and of "full guarantees to both capital and labor."[114] The ANAPO "revolution" was not to be one of class against class, but rather a revolution of the outcasts against the privileged. There was indeed much to suggest that Rojas had not fundamentally changed his 1953 view that "the class struggle has been the product of the greed of the powerful or the excessive ambitions of the weak. In opposition to the class struggle, which has no meaning in democracies, we must provide a Christian application of social justice."[115]

ANAPO has tended to make its appeals to "the people" and to "the popular classes" rather than to the proletariat or to other specifically delineated groups. When such appeals are made, they are as often to such status groups such as teachers and retired army officers as they are to workers or peasants. ANAPO's programmatic statements are seldom concerned with the organization of labor.[116] Similarly, ANAPO has been quite emphatic about its respect for private property, including the encouragement and protection of medium-sized and small industries and landholdings. Thus "neither the urban reform nor the agrarian reform ought to be carried out contrary to the right of property."[117] The approach to agrarian reform is especially indicative, as it so often is with Latin American political parties and governments. There is virtually no mention of land redistribution. Instead, the focus is on the mistakes and maladministration of the governments of the National Front in carrying out the current agrarian reform program, and on the need to form cooperatives and to increase agricultural productivity. Interviewed along with the other candidates during the 1970 campaign, Rojas gave a more negative response than did the National Front candidate to the question, "Should adequately cultivated lands be expropriated and distributed among the landless?"[118]

Again, although rhetorically nationalistic, Rojas in the same interview made clear that he saw foreign participation in development of the oil industry as beneficial for the country, and was most forthright of all the candidates in his praise of the United States: "We cannot deny that the contribution of the United States to the development of Colombia has been and always will be positive."[119]

It has of course been impossible to avoid certain overtones of class struggle in a program that directs its appeal primarily to "the popular classes" and "the outcasts," and which casts that appeal in terms of social justice. Some within ANAPO have made explicitly class-oriented appeals, especially during the 1970 and 1974 presidential campaigns. Rojas himself has done so on occasion in his efforts to expand his following among the urban lower classes.

On the whole, however, the approach is consensual—stressing the unity of classes and of erstwhile political enemies—rather than conflictive. As Daniel Premo put it, "Rojas and ANAPO's conservative leadership have been willing to promote the essence of class struggle in their quest to gain power, without embracing its attendant ideology."[120]

ANAPO's media occasionally invoke in a positive light such names from the Latin American revolutionary tradition as Ché Guevara, Salvador Allende, and the Colombian priest, Father Camilo Torres. More frequently mentioned, and closer to an ideological mentor, especially for the former Liberals in the ANAPO camp, is Jorge Eliécer Gaitán, who aroused the urban masses during the 1940s and was assasinated in 1948.[121] Simón Bolívar, and several of Colombia's "strong" presidents or dictators, such as Rafael Reyes and Rafael Núñez, are also regarded favorably. Outside Colombia, Argentina's Perón and Peronismo are sometimes considered to be the inspiration for

ANAPO, just as they were something of an influence on the Rojas regime.[122] Authoritarian and populist strains clearly predominate, although one Anapista official insisted in an interview that the party had come more closely to resemble Acción Democrática, the center-left party of Venezuela, than it did Peronismo.[123]

In Congress, Anapista representatives tended to oscillate between "absolute and emphatic opposition," and occasional accord with the government. They frequently tried to obstruct the legislative process, by boycotting congressional sessions, and even at times using disruptive violence, as well as blocking legislation in committee and on the floor. On at least one occasion, Anapistas voted against a bill (providing for obligatory social service for women) which they had not long before proposed.[124]

Such opposition for opposition's sake was held in abeyance, however, when temporary collaboration with the government could be used to bargain for executive posts or, as in 1968 when the proposed constitutional reforms promised to lead to the partial dismantling of the institutions of the National Front—not to mention providing a tactical opportunity to throw the bipartisan coalition into disarray.[125]

The point is that ANAPO's congressional delegation made very little attempt either to put forward a concrete legislative program of its own or to confront the government's proposals on an essentially programmatic basis.[126] ANAPO's disinterest in promoting a program in Congress has had its parallels elsewhere. Despite claims to be a party of the people, ANAPO can seldom be found supporting such mass struggles as strikes or land invasions. Aside from prosyletizing and organizing, its activities among the masses have been limited largely to the dispensation of food and medicine.[127]

Finally, the party's programmatic statements contain important traditionalist elements. Military terms and references recur. Thus *Alerta* refers to members of ANAPO as "worthy soldiers of the glorious army" of General Rojas,[128] and María Eugenia appeared (in December 1970) in a military-style uniform to unveil a plaque of her father (pictured in full military regalia). There are also occasional allusions to the military's "moral duty" not to continue to absent itself from the political scene, and wistful allusions to the days when Rojas and the armed forces were supposedly united, shoulder to shoulder, with the people of Colombia.[129]

Furthermore, besides being "socialist," ANAPO was said to be "national" and "Christian" as well. It was to be national, not only in the sense of calling for nationalization in certain areas of the economy controlled by foreigners, but also in the sense of rejecting foreign doctrines and foreign interpretations of the national reality.

It was to be Christian both in rooting its social policies in the Catholic conception of social justice, and in defending the application of divine law in the secular sphere.[130] Thus Rojas, of all the candidates in 1970, affirmed most strongly his opposition to divorce and to birth control.[131] Rojas frequently invokes God in his speeches, at one point during the 1970 campaign declaring that he was "God's candidate." Particularly when campaigning among the peasants of eastern Colombia, religious symbolism has often been employed. Considered blasphemous by the church, such appeals nevertheless "constituted a major element in Rojas' regional appeal to the rural masses in those departments."[132] Anapista spokesmen also stress the compatibility between socialism (*a la Colombiana*) and Christianity.[133] Both the church and the military are to be represented in the corporate National Constituent Assembly which, according to some ANAPO proposals, is to replace Congress.[134]

The traditionalist strain running through the ideology and program of ANAPO, and especially of Rojas himself, is evident in other ways as well. It surfaces in Rojas's view of women ("motherhood is the most sublime role in the world"), in spite of a seemingly contradictory stress on women's rights. It is evident, too, in the lesser hostility shown to the landed than to the industrial elite during the years when Rojas was president-dictator of Colombia.[135] The aversion to *técnicos* may also be in part related to a suspicion of the more technical, rationalized aspects of modern society.

Somewhat vague to begin with, and not always consistent internally or over time, ANAPO's program and ideology are yet another indication of its ambivalent populistic-traditionalist nature. Its efforts to appeal both to the peasant of traditional Boyacá and the slumdweller of Bogotá have lent it at times the guise of a traditional conservative faction and at others, that of a modern mass party. On balance, however, the program is centrist, and is so perceived by at least the upper-level leaders of the various parties.[136]

Conclusion

The nature of its program, of its organization, of the composition of its leadership, and of its electoral support depict ANAPO as a heterogeneous combination of populist and traditionalist elements which, despite its substantial electoral base among the lower social strata of Colombia's cities, strongly suggest that ANAPO does not at bottom constitute a genuine counterelite. Rather, it seems more nearly to comprise a movement of dissident or marginal members of the elite who have sought to mobilize the marginalized masses in the name of social justice, in good part to promote their own political and economic ends.[137] ANAPO has not been, then, really structural in its opposition, not really a revolutionary party. From the perspective of the existing system it has constituted an effort to conciliate popular dissatisfaction by promising certain benefits, rather than to promote class struggle. Yet through its appeals to "the people," against the "oligarchs" and across traditional party lines, as well as in its political loyalty to an erstwhile military dictator, it carried at least an implicit threat, not just to the personnel, policies, or institutions of the National Front, but to many of the fundamental political and social assumptions of the Colombian system. Even if it should in short order disappear, it will have proved a significant, albeit short-lived, challenge to Colombian developmentalism and to the reigning political elites. In that sense, it may well leave an important legacy.

ANAPO did not remain entirely what it was at its inception or in its years of early growth. Such changes do not negate what has already been said about ANAPO in the years of its electoral rise and organizational maturing, but they do introduce certain qualifications. Ideologically, ANAPO has in recent years moved noticeably leftward. Comparing ANAPO's Decalogue of the 1970 campaign, for example, with María Eugenia's twelve-point platform of 1974, one sees a definite shift of emphasis, both in content and phraseology. Whereas three of the ten points of the Decalogue concerned governmental mechanisms and relations with the church, these matters are not mentioned in the 1974 platform. Instead, there is talk of "the progressive nationalization of basic industries," and of "profound, drastic, and massive agrarian reform," language that does not appear in 1970.[138] Also, "classist" terms, such as "the proletariat" were now used on occasion. Antonio García, a socialist author and professor, became the party's principal ideologue, replacing the late Hernando Olano Cruz, whose background was Conservative.[139]

The transfer of effective party leadership from General Rojas to his daughter—who was always closer to the urban mass base of the Anapista electorate than was her father—partly accounts for such changes, as does the increased membership of intellectuals seeking in ANAPO a viable alternative to the traditional parties. Partly, though, the apparent change seems to have been a matter of tactics, with ANAPO leaders interpreting the 1972 fall-off in their vote as an indication that ANAPO should take a stronger class-oriented line in order to make up for the partisan factional vote that had once accrued to it under the restricted competitive conditions of the National Front.[140]

This latter-day ideological shift should not be exaggerated. During the 1974 campaign, *Alerta* still devoted relatively little space to programmatic issues in general, and to proposals for structural change in particular. Moreover, the speeches that Rojas made during the 1974 campaign still sounded more like the populist trying to vindicate himself than like a socialist (even *a la Colombiana*).[141]

The change was evident enough, however, to be at least the purported cause of the defection of some old-time ANAPO loyalists, including the president of the party's command in Boyacá,[142] as well as one of Rojas's own sons (Gustavo). The latter charged that the party was not what it was in 1970, and that it had fallen under the ideological tutelage of "persons of Marxist ideas," thus contradicting what General Rojas had tried to do for the Colombian people.[143]

As for ANAPO's leadership and organization, María Eugenia increasingly became the real leader of the party, with Rojas by 1974 playing a largely symbolic role, and seldom in direct contact with the party organization. While ANAPO had lost some earlier adherents (although by no means all), it had acquired some new acolytes among leftist youth and intellectuals. By the accounts of most observers, both its membership and grassroots organization had fallen well below the peak of 1970.[144]

Most notably, the party experienced a marked decline in its electoral fortunes. However, the decline was not abrupt. Its percentage of the 1972 vote was in fact slightly *larger* than its vote in the previous nonpresidential election (1968). The absolute number of votes accruing to ANAPO also increased, while the Liberals and Conservatives (excluding the ANAPO votes under both rubrics) showed a slight decline. Nevertheless, compared to the high hopes and prospects of 1970, the results were disappointing; 1974 then confirmed the downward trend.[145] What accounts for the fall-off in the Anapista vote? The reasons are in the main speculative but surely include:

1. The approaching end of the National Front's enforced bipartisanship, heralded by the open competition for departmental legislatures and municipal councils in 1972, led many erstwhile Liberals and Conservatives to return from ANAPO to their ancestral parties. Some doubt is cast on this explanation, at least for 1972, by the fact that, though ANAPO lost heavily in comparison to 1970, the traditional parties also lost votes. Abstention, rather than a switch in electoral allegiances, therefore seems a more probable explanation.[146] This does not hold for 1974, however, when the Anapista vote dropped precipitately (to 7.4 percent of the vote) while the vote for the traditional parties in a freely competitive election climbed substantially.
2. The tendency toward radicalization of the party, the more explicitly socialist proposals and class-oriented rhetoric of the 1974 campaign, may have alienated voters,[147] just as it drove from the party some of its long-standing leaders. By becoming better defined programmatically, ANAPO may well have lost some of its ability to be all things to all men. Moreover, in choosing to make ANAPO somewhat more explicitly class-oriented, the party's leadership may have misinterpreted the new competitive situation and underestimated the historic pulls on Colombia's voters of the country's traditional multiclass parties.[148]
3. The disappointing performance of the Anapistas elected in 1970, not only in Congress but also in departmental assemblies and municipal councils, where they often held a majority, should also be noted.[149] Anapistas seldom put forward specific programs for the alleviation of the immediate concerns of their constituents. Political bickering, sometimes among Anapistas themselves, and an alleged unseemly appetite for positions and perquisites, may have discouraged the party's followers who expected instant redress for grievances—something no party could accomplish in short order.
4. The denial of victory legitimately won in the 1970 presidential election—at least as Rojas's supporters saw it—may also have played an important role in the downturn in ANAPO's subsequent electoral fortunes. In a postelectoral survey conducted in 1974 in Bogotá, former ANAPO voters gave the expectation that their candidate

would be denied office even if victorious, as the principal reason for not voting for María Eugenia.[150]

5. In 1974, the fact that the Anapista candidate was a woman may also have hurt the party. It was the second most common rationale for their failure to vote for ANAPO given by former ANAPO supporters in the 1974 Bogotá survey.[151] María Eugenia's role may also have played a part in the disaffection of some of the party's more traditionalist leaders.
6. Finally, it seems probable that the peak attained by ANAPO in 1970 was itself a product of some exceptional circumstances. The vote for Rojas was in considerable part a protest against the National Front and its works, which had had their quintessential embodiment in the outgoing administration of Carlos Lleras Restrepo. The purported emphasis by the Lleras Restrepo government on "development" at the expense of "social justice," on "technical" as opposed to "human" solutions and on technocrats as distinct from politicians fueled the protest, as did scandals in some government agencies. During the course of the campaign, moreover, ANAPO—assisted by the denunciations of spokesmen for the National Front[152]—became identified as the principal focus of opposition to the Front. Perhaps even more important, Liberal voters had no Liberal for whom to cast their ballots in 1970. Many apparently turned to the "populist" Rojas, returning to the fold to vote for a Liberal president in 1974.

In sum, during the last year or two of the National Front, ANAPO became somewhat more structured in an ideological sense, and more socialist-oriented, and to that extent less vaguely populist. There was also some change in its leadership and organization. At the same time, and most strikingly, it lost much of its earlier support, although as noted this may have been as much the cause of ideological change as vice versa.

Immediately following its 1974 debacle, ANAPO announced long-range plans for improving and expanding its radio outlets, for making *Alerta* into a daily paper, and for the more effective participation of workers, peasants, and other groups in the life of the party. It claimed that it had attained the important goal of establishing itself as a viable third party in free competition with Conservatives and Liberals.[153] Yet ANAPO was clearly badly demoralized, at least momentarily, with deep-seated fissures showing between traditionalist and leftist elements in the party.[154] Its future remained highly uncertain.

In the past, the very existence and nature of the National Front had enabled ANAPO to flourish. By permitting ANAPO to win both Conservatives and Liberals to its banner, the coalitonal arrangement helped to make of it the heterogeneous party that it became.[155] Moreover, the developmental emphasis of the National Front, which tended to relegate distributional concerns to second place, served to enhance the attractions of a populist party. ANAPO's success, therefore, very much depended on the Front's perceived lack of success in the area of economic and social reform.[156]

Meanwhile, by serving as an electoral outlet for mass dissatisfaction, ANAPO may in a sense have served as something of a legitimizing device for the National Front, even while calling it into question.

The existence of ANAPO also served as somethng of a catalyst for coalitional behavior on the parts of Liberal and Conservative leaders. Thus upper-level leaders of the two parties (precisely those responsible for coalition) perceived the ideological distance between themselves and ANAPO to be greater than that between each other.[157] For a time following the fright of Rojas's near victory in 1970, the parties talked of running a joint candidate in 1974, and even of extending alternation through two more presidential terms, though they were no longer constitutionally obliged to do so. Thus "ANAPO's presence in the party system may have served the function of throttling ideological conflict among the traditional political elite, in view of the preoccupation with the threat of an ANAPO victory."[158]

ANAPO was in a real sense a product of the National Front; paradoxically, it may well at the same time have helped to sustain it.

SUMMARY AND IMPLICATIONS

Legacy of the National Front

Most oppositions under the National Front conformed to the traditional pattern of Colombian oppositions in their essentially factional nature and in their tendency to reintegrate—usually fairly soon with the main body of their party of origin. This was true of the Independientes (Laureanistas), the Belisaristas, the Sourdistas, the Leyvistas, and even the MRL. It has been true to a degree even of ANAPO. Virtually the only full-fledged exceptions were the myriad small parties and movements of the revolutionary Left and the tiny Christian Democratic Party (PSDC).

By the end of the National Front period, however, oppositions taken as a whole did manifest several new attributes. Perhaps most important for Colombia's developmental future has been the tilt in the axis of sociopolitical conflict from an essentially vertical one, between multiclass parties, in the direction of a horizontal, class-defined axis. The tilt has, overall, been very modest, reaching significant dimensions only in the election of 1970. Moreover, such polarization has yet to carry over appreciably to party elites or to the realm of party loyalties, and so far it primarily concerns voting behavior. Nevertheless, the recent changes in ANAPO and its continued, though tenuous, viability suggest that 1970 cannot simply be dismissed as a phenomenon wholly without precedent or sequel. The formation of the MRL, with its reformist content, as well as the middle-class appeal of the Belisaristas in 1970, hinted at change in the same direction.

Meanwhile another political movement which sought to appeal to class as opposed to traditional attachments—the Unión Nacional de Oposición (UNO)—was formed in 1973. Together, ANAPO and UNO won 13 percent of the nationwide vote in the presidential race the following year. UNO was the product of an alliance between the Movimiento Amplio Colombiano (MAC), a spinoff from ANAPO, and the Colombian Communist party, along with certain other leftist groups. UNO (and the Communist party) clearly view it as the potential nucleus of a broader coalition of "popular unity" which will win power and wield it "with a socialist criterion in the service of the people."[159] Although ANAPO and UNO have occasionally cooperated in particular tactical situations, the two remain rivals for much the same mass constituency.

Even should ANAPO and UNO fade as political movements in the latter years of the 1970s, it seems unlikely that over the long term, partisan competition in Colombia will wholly revert to its previous nonclass nature. As Hoskin and Swanson note, political conflict in Colombia has heretofore centered more around the control of the government than it has around ideology. But "the National Front, in de-escalating traditional party rivalries has created a situation that no longer makes traditional inter-party competition viable."[160] Some of this may well carry into the postcoalitional period, not only because of any lasting impact made by sixteen years of partisan truce, but also because Colombia is a much more urbanized and less traditional society than it was in 1958. Members of the growing middle class, for example, who tend to complain most about lack of a voice in the selection of candidates,[161] may increasingly express their demands in terms of *policies* rather than merely invoking the old partisan loyalties.

The continual high abstention in 1974, when the parties again competed against each other for the presidency, further suggested that it might no longer be the mere absence of partisan conflict that was keeping millions of Colombians from the polls, but perhaps also a frustration with the perceived inability of any politician—or at least any currently on the scene—to solve the country's fundamental social and economic problems. Even the country's traditional rural violence has changed in nature: where once it centered on the "hereditary hatreds," since the early 1960s it has primarily taken the form of guerrilla warfare waged by small bands of would-be social revolutionaries.

The period of the National Front also witnessed the mobilization of new voters, at least in the 1970 election, on behalf of Rojas and to that degree against the traditional parties. For in spite of markedly increased levels of social mobilization during the years of the National Front, political mobilization lagged badly. During the entire period of the National Front, the percentage of those eligible who voted never reached the level of 1958 (see Figure 2). Furthermore, until 1974 neither traditional party was able to increase its total number of votes (exclusive of the ANAPO votes under their respective labels).

Quite clearly, the institutionalized coalition had a demobilizing effect by dampening the partisan incentive to vote. Yet the extent of absention, and ANAPO's at least temporary appeal to the previously unmobilized, including youth, may be harbingers of an erosion of support for the traditional parties and of a gradually increasing willingness to vote on grounds of attachment to social class, interest group, or candidate personality in place of the traditional partisan loyalties. True, both the total vote, as well as the vote for the traditional parties, showed a marked upward surge in 1974 under the conditions of renewed unrestricted competition, finally surpassing the totals of 1958. But it at least seems possible that this vote is now more volatile, and more dependent on government and party performance, than it was in earlier decades. It further seems possible that, should large numbers of new or former voters enter, or reenter, the electoral arena in the post-National Front period, it might have destabilizing effects on the system.[162]

Whether the National Front will prove to have had enduring effects on the shape of the party system is problematical. Based on their study of the "spatial distribution" of the perceptions of party leaders, Hoskin and Swanson judge that "the bases for a multi-party system now prevail in Colombia."[163] The persistence of ANAPO (and UNO) into the era of open competition may also be indicative.

Nevertheless, the results of the 1974 election, when the major parties captured almost 90 percent of the vote, suggest that it may be a long time before "third parties" compete effectively with the established parties. More likely, future channels for the expression of discontent will be factions of the traditional parties which, like the MRL or for that matter ANAPO in its initial stages, adopt a reformist posture and seek to appeal to those of various groups and classes who feel excluded from the prevailing pattern of power and benefits.[164]

Despite historic animosities some crossing of traditional party lines was not entirely new to Colombian politics. Temporary coalitions of one party with a faction of another had occurred before, while Gaitán made an attempt in the late 1940s to appeal to the masses of the two traditional parties against the "oligarchs" of both. But the joint selection of presidential candidates, the attendant campaigning of party leaders for the candidate of the other party, and the frequency of negotiation for congressional and administrative support across party lines was quite new, certainly in its magnitude.

The oppositions followed suit. ANAPO in particular recruited support from both Conservatives and Liberals to an unprecedented degree at both the leadership and electoral levels. Gaitán, the principal earlier analogy, had throughout his political career remained much more identifiably a Liberal than Rojas had been a Conservative. Moreover, Rojas's charge that an oligarchy controlled both parties was rather more credible when the two parties were in coalition than when they were "warring figuratively at a national level and literally at local levels."[165] In the 1970 elections, both Belisaristas and Sourdistas presented candidates for Congress and other legislative bodies on Liberal as well as Conservative lists. These tendencies to transcend traditional party lines may not survive the National Front, but at any rate precedents may have been set, and habits formed, which may make the crossing of party lines easier to accomplish in the future.

Lastly, the truce of 1958-74 appears to have helped to habituate Colombians to tolerate their political adversaries. As Dankwart Rustow has put it, "A distasteful decision, once made, is likely to seem more palatable as one is forced to live with it."[166] In this case the "distasteful decision" was of course the agreement on the part of the leaders of the two "hereditary hatreds" to act in coalition for a period of sixteen years.

Hard evidence that the toleration of oppositions has really taken deep root among Colombians is difficult to come by. However, La Violencia in its traditional form has apparently come to an end, which in itself is a signal achievement.[167] The 1974 election is perhaps another indication of a new political tolerance. It was the first fully competitive election since 1949. In 1949, political tensions were high and La Violencia was already under way. In 1974, there was almost no violence, and there was full acceptance of the opposition's victory by the losing side. True, some artificial circumstances attended the election, in particular the fact that parity in administrative posts would continue for another few years. But the leaders of both parties seemed to feel that the coalition period had led to "a nation politically much more civilized and with a solid civic conscience."[168]

How deep all this goes, particularly since the coalescent attitudes of the National Front period were always more prevalent among the national leaders of the parties than they were at the intermediate or *barrio* levels,[169] is difficult to say. Moreover, should future political conflict become more ideological in nature, the survival of the spirit of toleration would be even more dubious. Probably the habits of tolerance fostered by the National Front would assuage the intensity of any such conflict in its early stages, but it is doubtful that such habits go deep enough, especially among nonelites, to enable system survival under conditions of intense class conflict. At any rate, the example of Chile—where tolerance was much more deeply rooted than in Colombia—argues against it.

Significance of ANAPO

The most significant among the specific oppositions to the National Front has of course been ANAPO. What has it meant, both to Colombia and in comparative terms, and what is its likely future? Although factional in some of its attributes, ANAPO has clearly been more than just another faction, or even coalition of factions, of the traditional parties. Certain aspects of its program and organizational behavior, together with its evident strength among the uprooted and the lower-middle class, as well as among the tradition-oriented, suggest parallels with European fascism. But ANAPO's lower-class electoral base, the Conservative and even elite origins of much of its leadership, let alone the relative absence of paramilitary trappings, suggest that the term fascist is also inappropriate.[170]

Its mass, lower-class dimension has perhaps been ANAPO's most striking feature, but to characterize it as a genuine class-oriented or revolutionary party omits or distorts significant aspects of its life as a political movement. Rather, we have in ANAPO what we have called populism, or what Gino Germani has referred to as a "national popular" movement which seems "to represent the peculiar form of intervention of the traditional strata in the national political process in the course of rapid mobilization in countries of delayed industrialization."[171] Ambivalence and ambiguity is inevitable in such movements, seeking as they do immediate benefits, including upward economic, social, and political mobility for their leaders, and welfare, public works, and entry into the consumer society for their followers, without paying the presumed costs of genuine development in terms of real structural or attitudinal change. A desire for the rewards of development often coincides with a kind of resistance to it, or to certain of its aspects or consequences.

Populist movements tend to be short-lived, because of their own internal contradictions and their frequent dependence on a certain leader or given set of circumstances.[172] In line with this generalization, ANAPO itself has already undergone a marked decline. But this *type* of movement can be expected to recur in Colombia and in many other parts of Latin America as long as the fundamental conditions that foster them persist. It could be argued, in fact, that populism is the most "natural" type of mass movement for the sort of corporatist societies depicted by Philippe Schmitter, Howard Wiarda, and others, that are characteristic of contemporary Latin America. Such societies are rooted in late or delayed development, in which rapid urbanization far outpaces the growth of industrialization and of an industrial proletariat, and where mass mobilization is controlled "from above" by governments, parties, and elites. Certain of these aspects of late development are in turn reinforced by Hispanic political culture (e.g., in their corporatist aspects) and by external dependency.[173] In Colombia, the long heritage of popular loyalty to vertically-structured parties may enhance susceptibility to mass mobilization by elites, marginal or otherwise.

The kind of Latin American political system depicted by Charles Anderson would also appear propitious for populism.[174] For Anderson, Latin American politics tend to incorporate a variety of power contenders such as the military, the church, mass political movements, and student organizations, none of which is eliminated from the system when another comes to the fore. As long as a contender proves it has some power, and as long as it does not unduly threaten the existence of other contenders, it is admitted to the system. Socially heterogeneous parties with objectives that do not at bottom seek structural change—such as ANAPO—are a case in point, whatever initial discomfiture may attend their full acceptance as legitimate political actors.

Thus in Colombia, and in countries like Colombia, especially in Latin America, populistic parties and movements like ANAPO tend to be more significant than strictly class-oriented, Marxist, and/or revolutionary parties as political responses to the advent of the mass suffrage amid the strains and prospects of the early-to-middle stages of the industrial revolution. More often than revolutionary change under the aegis of a counterelite, populism, in the guise of marginal elites mobilizing a heterogeneous mass and unified around a leader, is a typical Latin American reaction to developmentalism.

Codicil

To date, ANAPO has been the most notable challenge to Colombia's traditional—albeit factionalized—bipartisanship, and its emergence was one of the signal developments of the National Front years. There were other legacies of the sixteen years of formalized coalition, although like ANAPO their permanence and significance remain to be tested. They included some signs that Colombian politics might be developing political cleavages along class lines in supplement to (though hardly in replacement of) the traditional partisan loyalties; a concomitant decline in the rate of political mobilization combined with an increase in the volatility of party allegiances, especially among the more recently mobilized; a rise in the propensity of political leaders to seek alliances and electoral support among the partisans of their traditional adversaries; and the enhancement of a "civic culture" of political tolerance.

The National Front may have a lasting impact, in the ways suggested, on the patterns of opposition in Colombia. But what stands out even more is the tenaciousness of time-honored patterns and the ways in which the years of coalition have seemingly served the purpose of their maintenance. The fact that in 1974 the three major candidates for the presidency were all progeny of former presidents seemed symbolic in this sense. The very duration of the National Front for its intended lifespan—despite initial doubt by many both in Colombia and abroad—was in itself testimony to the determination of the country's elites to forestall a return to violence and dictatorship, and above all to prevent the capture of the government by a mass-based movement that might irreparably rend the established system of power. The coalition's survival was also testimony to the cooperative abilities of the leadership of the dominant parties, as well as, no doubt, to a growing convergence of those leaderships concerning a developmental process whose goals and rewards they increasingly shared. It is largely for reasons such as these that oppositions in Colombia, other than the essentially factional, have had such a difficult time sustaining themselves, even under such "artificial" conditions as those of the National Front which quite unintentionally seemed to foster them.

NOTES

1. The Alianza Nacional Popular (ANAPO), the political vehicle of the former dictator, General Gustavo Rojas Pinilla, to be discussed at length below, was organized in 1961 but did not formally become a party distinct from at least nominal status as a faction (or factions) until 1971.
2. Gary Hoskin and Gerald Swanson demonstrate the empirical basis for such clientelism within the Colombian parties in their "Inter-Party Competition in Colombia: Return to *La Violencia*?," *American Journal of Political Science* 6, (April 1974): 316-50. See also Gabriel Murillo and Israel Rivera Ortiz, *Actividades y Estructura de Poder en Los Partidos Políticos Colombianos* (Bogotá, 1973) for an empirically-based argument that the structure of Colombian politics is essentially oligarchical. For a contrary view see James Payne, *Patterns of Conflict in Colombia* (New Haven, 1968).
3. This meant that there was very little of an independent or "swing" vote and that the parties could only alternate in power when the majority party split, thus, as in 1930 and 1946, permitting the minority party to win the presidency.
4. Cf. Robert H. Dix, "Latin America: Oppositions and Development," in Robert A. Dahl, ed., *Regimes and Oppositions* (New Haven, 1973), pp. 278-84.
5. This typology follows, albeit incompletely, that to be found in Robert A. Dahl, ed., *Political Oppositions in Western Democracies* (New Haven, 1966), pp. 341-44.
6. A survey conducted in Cali, Colombia's third largest city, in 1968, showed the Unionistas to be easily the stronger of the two factions, with their strength proportionately greatest in the upper, working, and lower social categories. The Independientes were strongest among middle-class voters. Pedro P. Morcillo, Judith Talbot de Campos, John McCamant, and Harold Rizo Otero, "Estudio sobre Abstención Electoral en las Elecciones de Marzo de 1968 en Cali," in Departamento Administrativo Nacional de Estadística (DANE), *Colombia Polí tica* (Bogotá, 1972), p. 72.
7. Harvey Kline, "Candidate Selection in the Colombian Congress"(draft consulted courtesy of the author), p. 12. See also Rodrigo Losada, *Perfil Socio-Polí tico del Congresista Colombiano* (Bogotá, 1972), p. 97, for comparable data on political elites more broadly defined.
8. Hoskin and Swanson, "Inter-Party Competition," p. 333. As Joan Garcés points out, it is precisely this characteristic lack of substantial ideological distance among the factions, as well as their similar bases of recruitment, that permits them so readily to rejoin their original parties when circumstances warrant. See his "La continuidad del sistema a través del cambio: el sistema bipartidista de Colombia," *Revista Latinoamericana de Sociología* 6 (March 1970):27-29.
9. The Sourdistas disappeared soon after the 1970 elections. The Belisaristas retained some identity until late 1972, when most of their remaining congressmen rejoined official Conservative ranks. During their brief life, they even published a (supposedly biweekly) newspaper, *Galán*, and at one point sought to form an opposition coalition with ANAPO.

10. Rodrigo Losada and Miles Williams, "Análisis de la votación presidencial en Bogotá, 1970," in DANE, *Colombia Política*, pp. 17-21.
11. See the regional breakdown of the 1970 vote in Judith Talbot Campos and John F. McCamant, *Cleavage Shift in Colombia: Analysis of the 1970 Elections* (Beverly Hills, Calif., 1972), p. 53. This study also appears, in a somewhat different version, in the *Colombia Política* volume. Where the two duplicate, the later, English, version is cited. Juan Pablo Martínez and María Isabel Izquierdo argue in their *ANAPO: Oposición o Revolución* (Bogotá, 1972), p. 40, that Sourdismo is best viewed as an alliance of landowners against the developmentalist policies of the National Front, rather than as a regional phenomenon.
12. For a fuller appraisal of the growth of the MRL, and its program, see Robert H. Dix, *Colombia: The Political Dimensions of Change* (New Haven, 1967), pp. 257-69.
13. See Payne, *Patterns of Conflict*, pp. 234-37; Richard S. Weinert, *Political Modernization in Colombia* (unpublished Ph.D. dissertation, 1968) pp. 160-62; and Dix, *Colombia*, pp. 262-64. The correlation between the MRL and urban size is generally inverse.
14. Losada, *Perfil Socio-Político*, p. 97.
15. López Michelsen had earlier argued that the existence of the MRL had deterred dissident Liberals from leaving the party to join the ANAPO, the PCC, and other opposition parties. "In the MRL I have not embarked on a personalistic dissent in order to harm the Liberal Party, but on an ideological dissent in order to save it." Quoted in Garcés, "La Continuidad," p. 40.
16. Payne, *Patterns of Conflict*, pp. 201-2.
17. For a more extensive discussion, see Dix, *Colombia*, pp. 136-47.
18. Registraduría Nacional del Estado Civil, *Estadísticas Electorales: 19 de Abril de 1970* (Bogotá, 1970), p. 326. Opposition lists together won well over half (58.5 percent) of the total vote for the Chamber of Representatives in 1970.
19. Miles Williams suggests that, once the National Front had accomplished its primary initial task of greatly diminishing the endemic political violence of the post-World War II years—circa 1964—support for the coalitional arrangement accordingly declined. His evidence shows that those areas most prone to La Violencia tended to be more supportive of the National Front than those areas less affected. Cf. his *El Frente Nacional: Colombia's Experiment in Controlled Democracy* (unpublished Ph.D. dissertation, 1972), pp. 133-36. At the same time, the correlation between a departmental rank ordering of levels of La Violencia (according to Campos and McCamant, *Cleavage Shift*, p. 22) and the vote for ANAPO (based on the author's composite ranking of the 1966, 1968, and 1970 vote for the Chamber) was .51.
20. According to Partido Comunista de Colombia, *A la Batalla Popular contra la Oligarquía y el Imperialismo* (Bogotá, 1971), p. 41. This claim jibes with official figures (Registraduría Nacional del Estado Civil, *Estadísticas Electorales: 1970*, p. 327) if one assumes that those elected under the designations of various small leftist parties were in fact Communists.
21. Losada and Williams, "Análisis de la votación presidencial," pp. 11-12, 20.
22. Cf. Morcillo et al., "Estudio sobre Abstencíon Electoral," p. 78. See also Figure 2.
23. Almost immediately after taking office in August 1958, the first government of the National Front (that of President Alberto Lleras Camargo) announced that Rojas was free to return to the country, apparently with the expectation that his presence (and attendant trial before the Senate) would help to rally support for

the new administration. Rojas did return in October 1958 and was subsequently convicted of malfeasance in office, stripped of his military titles and pension, and deprived of his political rights (which he subsequently regained). The government obviously miscalculated the longer-term effects of his presence in the country, however. For a fuller discussion see Daniel Premo, *Alianza Nacional Popular: Populism and the Politics of Social Class in Colombia, 1961-1970* (unpublished Ph.D. dissertation, 1972), pp. 27.32.

24. Campos and McCamant, *Cleavage Shift*, pp. 8-9.
25. The election of 1946, when Jorge Eliécer Gaitán ran for president as an "antioligarchical" candidate in a three-way race, was the one Colombian precedent. Most of the Gaitanista vote evidently derived from the urban lower strata, although hard data are lacking to confirm this.
26. The relevant surveys and other data may be found in DANE, *Colombia Política*. They included a postelectoral survey undertaken in Cali in 1968, pre- and postelectoral surveys carried out in Cali in 1970, a postelectoral survey conducted in Bogotá in 1970, and a *barrio*-level study of the vote in Medellín and Bogotá in 1970.
27. Campos and McCamant did find similar, although slightly lower, correlations in the towns and rural areas in the immediate vicinity of Cali. *Cleavage Shift*, p. 61.
28. Alejandro Portes, "Urbanization and Politics in Latin America," *Social Science Quarterly*, 52 (December 1971): 697-720.
29. Losada and Williams, "Análisis de la votación presidencial," pp. 28-29.
30. Ibid., pp. 16-17, 20-22.
31. For a ranking of variables, according to the 1970 Bogotá survey, see Losada and Williams, "Análisis de la votación presidencial," p. 39.
32. The 1970 postelectoral survey in Cali found a statistically significant relationship, while the Bogotá survey did not. Campos and McCamant, *Cleavage Shift*, pp. 56-57; see also Losada and Williams, "Análisis de la votación presidencial," pp. 11-12.
33. There was a negative correlation of −.36 at the departmental level between the Rojista vote in 1970 and the percentage of the population born in the department; ibid., p. 51. According to Gabriel Murillo, reporting on preliminary results of a 1974 postelectoral survey carried out in Bogotá, there was no correlation in that year between migrant status and the vote. Interview, Bogotá, July 24, 1974.
34. DANE, *Colombia Política*, pp. 296, 383; Campos and McCamant, *Cleavage Shift*, p. 59. Men and women voted at separate *mesas*, thus making such distinctions readily apparent.
35. By "developmentalist," we mean policies that stress economic growth at the expense of the broad distribution of economic and social rewards,
36. Campos and McCamant, *Cleavage Shift*, pp. 63-67 and 72-74; see also Losada and Williams, "Análisis de la votación presidencial," pp. 22-23, 34, 39.
37. Eldon Kenworthy, Cornell University. Remarks at Workshop on "Income Distribution and Its Role in Development," Rice University, April 25, 1974.
38. The result is a very different set of life experiences for the two groups. Ibid.
39. Martínez and Izquierdo, *ANAPO*, stress this point. A parallel interpretation is that of Rodrigo Escobar Novoa, who argues that many such persons embody traditional rural values in an urban society that has rejected them. *Revista Javeriana* 73 (Bogotá, June 9 1970): 579-80.
40. *The Politics of Mass Society* (New York, 1959), pp. 180-81, 237. Philip Converse and George Dupeux note that "flash" parties in France such as the various Gaullist parties and the Poujadists seem to reflect spasms of political excitement

in unusually hard times on the part of citizens whose involvement in politics is, as a rule, abnormally weak. ''Politicization in France and the United States,'' in Roy Macridis and Bernard Brown, eds., *Comparative Politics*, 3rd ed. (Homewood, Illinois, 1968), pp. 370-71.

41. This corresponds with Samuel Huntington's observation that oppositions in modernizing societies are predominantly urban. See his *Political Order in Changing Societies* (New Haven, 1968), pp. 435 ff.
42. Cf. the tables in Premo, *Alianza Nacional Popular*, pp. 256, 259.
43. Lars Schoultz, ''Urbanization and Changing Voting Patterns: Colombia, 1946-1970,'' *Political Science Quarterly* 87 (March 1972): 40.
44. See Table 5, p. 39, in ibid.
45. Ibid., pp. 38, 41-42.
46. Ibid., p. 30.
47. Campos and McCamant, *Cleavage Shift*, p. 59.
48. Campos and McCamant, *Cleavage Shift*, p. 51. Most such correlations, of somewhat dubious value at a level such as the departmental, tend in any case to be weak due to the diversity of ANAPO's support, thus tending to confirm one of our central points.
49. For data on religiosity (as measured by priestly vocation per capita), see Gustavo Pérez, *El Problema Sacerdotal en Colombia* (Bogotá, 1962), p. 66. Four of the five departments which are highest in religiosity are among those most strongly Anapista.
50. Campos and McCamant, *Cleavage Shift*, pp. 55-7, 72.
51. See Ibid., Table 17, p. 51, and Premo, *Alianza Nacional Popular*, pp. 155-59, 165-66; also DANE, *Colombia Política*, p. 230. It should be noted in this connection that a small rump of the MRL, the MRL del Pueblo, continued to function for a time.
52. Of the seven persons in the 1970 Bogotá survey who still claimed affiliation to the MRL, and with no Liberal among the candidates, only one claimed to have voted for Rojas. Losada and Williams, ''Análisis de la votación presidencial,''p. 32.
53. For characteristics of Conservatives as more clerically-oriented and rural in background than other Colombians see Dix, *Colombia*, ch. 9; and Payne, *Patterns of Conflict*, pp. 231-34.
54. See the tables in Premo, *Alianza Nacional Popular*, pp. 86, 112, 156, 239.
55. Such opposition was indicated by a relatively high negative vote in these departments in the plebiscite of December 1957 which approved the National Front, as well as strong support for the anticoalition Conservative candidate, Jorge Leyva, in the presidential election of 1958. The correlation between the vote for Leyva and the 1964 vote for ANAPO at the departmental level was .82.
56. Weinert, *Political Modernization*, p. 165-70; see also the table in DANE, *Colombia Política*, p. 234. As noted above, however, the *percentage* of large city Conservatives who vote for ANAPO tends to be higher.
57. Premo, *Alianza Nacional Popular*, pp. 209-11.
58. *Alerta*, April 5, 1974, p. 9; and April 18, 1974, p. 8.
59. See, respectively, Premo, *Alianza Nacional Popular,* pp. 48, 117, n.30; and Harvey Kline, ''Interest Groups in the Colombian Congress; Group Behavior in a Centralized, Patrimonial System'' (draft consulted by courtesy of the author), p. 7.
60. Golconda advocated abstention in the 1970 election, but one of its leaders wrote a column in *Alerta* for a time and shortly before the election the group made a

qualified public endorsement of ANAPO. Campos and McCamant, *Cleavage Shift*, p. 40.

61. Kline, "Interest Groups," p. 7.
62. Ibid., pp. 7, 10, 18.
63. Premo, *Alianza Nacional Popular*, p. 211. Exceptions include the *Unión Nacional de Choferes* in 1970, and the *Sociedad de Loteros Inválidos* (invalid lottery-ticket salesmen) in 1974.
64. *Alerta*, April 5, 1974, p. 11.
65. Harvey F. Kline, "Recruitment to Colombian Political Cadres" (draft consulted by courtesy of the author), p. 35.
66. Ibid., pp. 34-44. The data on citywide leadership do not show a consistent pattern in this respect, however. City, and especially *barrio*-level leaders of all factions ranked markedly lower in social status, it should be noted, than did national-level leaders.
67. Kline, "Candidate Selection," p. 12.
68. Based on the author's examination of *Quién es Quién en Colombia*, 4th ed. (Bogotá, 1970).
69. A *New York Times* correspondent once described the Rojistas as "short, swarthy men in ill-fitting suits." Quoted in Campos and McCamant, *Cleavage Shift*, p. 41.
70. Kline, "Interest Groups," p. 18.
71. Premo, *Alianza Nacional Popular*, p. 39.
72. Ibid., p. 56n.
73. Losada, *Perfil Socio-Político*, pp. 94-5.
74. Premo, *Alianza Nacional Popular*, p. 148n.
75. The author's calculations, based on data in Registraduría Nacional, *Estadísticas Electorales 1970*.
76. Kline, "Candidate Selection," p. 8.
77. Gary Hoskin and Gerald Swanson, "Political Party Leadership in Colombia," *Comparative Politics* 6 (April 1974): 412, 419.
78. Premo, *Alianza Nacional Popular*, pp. 38n., 43. Most Conservatives associated with ANAPO in its early years had also been associated with the military government of 1953-57.
79. Ibid., pp. 177, 329.
80. This tends to be the interpretation of Martínez and Izquierdo, *ANAPO*.
81. Daniel Premo, the most thorough student of ANAPO's early development, affirms (*Alianza Nacional Popular*, p. 88n.) that "the results of our research lend support to the thesis that the underlying motivation behind ANAPO's organization prior to August, 1963, was essentially conspiratorial in design."
82. Ibid., pp. 137 and 266, respectively.
83. Cf. ibid., pp. 48-49, 58-59, 323-25.
84. The closest thing to party statutes is contained in the last few pages of the *Plataforma Ideológica y Política de Alianza Nacional Popular* (Villa de Leyva, 1971), pp. 62-64.
85. Alvaro Monroy Sotomayor, *Alianza Nacional Popular* (unpubl. thesis, Universidad de los Andes, Departamento de Ciencia Política, Bogotá, 1971), p. 96. Similar claims were made by an ANAPO official in an interview, Bogotá, July 24, 1972.
86. Saturnino Sepúlveda Niño, *Las Elites Colombianas en Crisis* (Bogotá, 1970), p. 79.

87. Campos and McCamant, *Cleavage Shift*, pp. 43-44.
88. Losada and Williams, "Análisis de la votación presidencial," pp. 29-30.
89. The data are reported in Murillo and Rivera, *Actividades y Estructura*, pp. 23-24, 26-30, 70-75, 111-14.
90. Of these only about 4,000 were distributed outside the Bogotá area, thus making *Alerta* a national publication only in a very limited sense. See Premo, *Alianza Nacional Popular*, pp. 44n, 182.
91. Interview with ANAPO official, Bogotá, July 23, 1974.
92. Campos and McCamant, *Cleavage Shift*, p. 41.
93. One example was Carlos Luis Turriago of the department of Meta who was the erstwhile military governor of the eastern plains region; another was José Ignacio Vives, a Liberal whose stronghold was the Atlantic coast.
94. This was the case, for example, with Manuel Bayona Carrascal, senator from the department of Cesar. See *El Tiempo* (Bogotá), August 29, 1972, p. 2B.
95. ANAPO was relatively weak in the intermediate national-regional category; Gary Hoskin, "Dimensions of Representation in the Colombian National Legislature," in Weston Agor, ed., *Latin American Legislatures: Their Role and Influence* (New York, 1971), pp. 448-50.
96. According to a high ANAPO official, the latter was the principal means of support for the party organization; interview, Bogotá, July 23, 1974.
97. Kline, "Candidate Selection," p. 32-33; see also Murillo and Rivera, *Actividades y Estructura*, pp. 115-16.
98. Kline, "Candidate Selection," p. 37.
99. Examples of this control from above abound in *Alerta*; see also Premo, *Alianza Nacional Popular*, pp. 164-65, 306, 327.
100. María Eugenia had directed SENDAS, a social welfare agency, during the Rojas government. Not a particularly effective speaker, she made up for it through "her political acumen, indefatigable energy, organizational ability, and her willingness to associate with the lower class urban and rural masses." Premo, *Alianza Nacional Popular*, p. 82n. See also Campos and McCamant, *Cleavage Shift*, pp. 36-37. The result was an ability to "turn on" the masses.
101. Losada and Williams, "Análisis de la votación presidencial," p. 32; Campos and McCamant, *Cleavage Shift*, p. 23.
102. Cf., *El Tiempo*, January 15, 1972, pp. 1A, 6A.
103. Cf. Premo, *Alianza Nacional Popular*, pp. 138, 146. Cf. also Roberto Harker Valdivieso, *La Rebelión de las Curules* (Bogotá, 1968); Harker, a former Anapista congressman, placed much of the blame for his own disaffection on Rojas's son-in-law, Samuel Moreno Díaz. Again, one of ANAPO's founders, Carlos Monroy Reyes, charged subsequently that the national command of the movement functioned in name only; *El Siglo* (Bogotá), Sept. 20, 1973, pp. 1, 11.
104. Cf. Premo, *Alianza Nacional Popular*, p. 338.
105. Kline, "Recruitment," p. 19.
106. Premo, *Alianza Nacional Popular*, p. 126.
107. Quoted in Alan Angell, "Populism and Political Change: The Case of Colombia," *The Sociological Review, Monograph No. 11* (Keele University, England), February 1967, p. 87.
108. Premo, *Alianza Nacional Popular*, p. 140.
109. Losada and Williams, "Análisis de la votación presidencial," pp. 27-29; Campos and McCamant, *Cleavage Shift*, p. 48.

110. The principal sources for the following discussion include selected issues of *Alerta* (1969-74), the *Plataforma Ideológica y Política* of 1971, and Premo, *Alianza Nacional Popular*, ch. 9.
111. The remaining 6 percent was classified as "miscellaneous." Based on a column-inch count by the author of randomly available 1974 issues.
112. Guillermo Hernández Rodríguez, a senatorial spokesman for ANAPO, contrasted ANAPO's program to that of Salvador Allende of Chile by noting that the latter's goal was a full-scale socialist society, while ANAPO's objective was the coexistence of capitalist and socialist sectors and the strengthening of both for the ends of development. See his *Análisis del Programa Anapista* (Bogotá, 1970), p. 71.
113. Morcillo et al., "Estudio sobre Abstención Electoral," p. 74. At one point during the 1970 campaign, Rojas promised that "my government will be in a position to assure every Colombian his own automobile;" from a speech published in *Alerta*, March 12, 1970, p. 10.
114. *El Tiempo*, March 15, 1967, p. 6; as quoted in Premo, *Alianza Nacional Popular*, p. 179.
115. *Economía Colombiana* (n.d.), p. 258; quoted in Premo, *Alianza Nacional Popular*, p. 303.
116. What there is suggests the prospect of a single labor entity under state auspices in line with the abortive efforts of the Rojas government; see Premo, *Alianza Nacional Popular*, pp. 314-16.
117. Interview with Rojas published in *Revista Javeriana* 73 (April 1970): p. 278.
118. Ibid., p. 275.
119. Ibid., p. 292; see also pp. 286-88.
120. Premo, *Alianza Nacional Popular*, p. 348.
121. As Premo suggests (*Alianza Nacional Popular*, p. 34n), aspects of ANAPO's program had considerable affinity to the proposals presented to Congress by Gaitán in 1947. As *Alerta* put it in its issue of April 9, 1970, p. 3, "Yesterday Gaitán and today Rojas; they continue to represent the maximum hope of the majority of the Colombian people;" quoted in Premo, *Alianza Nacional Popular*, p. 308.
122. See Dix, *Colombia*, p. 119.
123. Interview, Bogotá, July 23, 1974.
124. Premo, *Alianza Nacional Popular*, p. 291.
125. See ibid., pp. 169-75. According to Kline's tabulation of five key congressional votes during 1968-69, ANAPO voted more frequently with the government than did the Independientes; see his "Political Parties in the Colombian Congress" (draft consulted courtesy of the author), p. 43.
126. For further discussion of ANAPO and antisystem groups, see Mauricio Solaún, Fernando Cepeda, and Bruce Bagley, "Urban Reform in Colombia: the Impact of the 'Politics of Games' on Public Policy," in Francis F. Rabinovitz and Felicity M. Trueblood, eds., *Latin American Urban Research*, III (Beverly Hills, Calif., 1973), p. 122.
127. Martínez and Izquierdo make this point, *ANAPO*, pp. 45-54.
128. *Alerta*, December 1970, p. 14.
129. A lower-level Anapista official stated in an interview (Bogotá, July 24, 1972) that all governments were corrupt, including military ones, but that at least the latter did something for the people; he went on to praise the regimes of Perón, Franco, and Mussolini.

130. According to *Alianza Popular*, February 21, 1966, p. 4, "ANAPO has manifested its submission to the Catholic faith in the structural content of its programs;" cited in Premo, *Alianza Nacional Popular*, p. 299; see also pp. 310-11.
131. *Revista Javeriana*, 73 (April 1970): 265-97.
132. Premo, *Alianza Nacional Popular*, p. 58n.
133. Hernández Rodríguez, *Análisis del Programa Anapista*, pp. 98-99.
134. *Alianza Popular*, February 12, 1966, p. 3; cited in Premo, *Alianza Nacional Popular*, p. 317.
135. Albert O. Hirschman, *Journeys Toward Progress* (New York, 1965), p. 124.
136. At least this was the case in 1969; Hoskin and Swanson, "Political Party Leadership," pp. 409, 411.
137. In Marxist terms, ANAPO reflects an alliance of the petit bourgeoisie with certain great landowners, these groups in turn manipulate the masses as a device for confronting the parties of the National Front dominated by the bourgeoisie; see Martínez and Izquierdo, *ANAPO*, especially pp. 7-8, 69-72.
138. For the text of the Decalogue see Sepúlveda Niño, *Las Elites*, pp. 74-77; the 1974 platform was published in a pamphlet entitled *Bases de una Nueva Colombia*.
139. For their respective ideas see Hernando Olano Cruz, *Su Obra* (Bogotá, 1972); Antonio García, *Dialéctica de la Democracia* (Bogotá, 1971); and García, *Una Vía Socialista para Colombia* (Bogotá, 1973). García reputedly was the author of María Eugenia's principal progammatic statements during the 1974 campaign.
140. See *El Espectador* (Bogotá), April 24, 1972, p. 2A.
141. Cf. *Alerta*, April 5, 1974, pp. 6, 7, 12.
142. *Revista Javeriana* 81 (May 1974): 416.
143. It should be noted, however, that Gustavo Rojas had never been particularly active in politics. *Revista Javeriana* 81 (Jan.-Feb. 1974): 91; for Rojas's reply, as well as the statement of another "defector," see p. 92.
144. An ANAPO official admitted a 25 percent diminution in an interview, Bogotá, July 23, 1974.
145. The above calculations were based on data from Registraduría Nacional del Estado Civil, *Estadísticas Electorales: 1972* (Bogotá, 1972) and from preliminary 1974 figures provided the author by the Registraduría.
146. For a discussion of ANAPO's 1972 "decline," see Rodrigo Losada and Gabriel Murillo, *Análisis de las Elecciones de 1972 en Bogotá* (Bogotá, 1973).
147. The only real clue that this might be the case, aside from the party's overall decline, is the disproportionate decline of the vote (in 1974) in rural Boyacá and Norte de Santander compared to the vote in the capital cities of the same departments. Elsewhere in the country, however, the decline was proportionate in urban and rural areas.
148. Thus Rojas's son-in-law saw the 1970 elections as portending a class struggle, despite what he claimed were ANAPO's efforts to prevent it; *Revista Javeriana*, 73 (June 1970): 529-38.
149. For María Eugenia's reply to such charges ("we are being slandered") see *El Siglo* (Bogotá), February 21, 1972, p. 6.
150. Gabriel Murillo, interview, Bogotá, July 24, 1974. This coincides with the attitudes of Anapistas expressed in the wake of the 1970 election that they had been denied their rightful victory. See Campos and McCamant, *Cleavage Shift*, pp. 68-69.
151. Gabriel Murillo, interview, July 24, 1974. On the other hand, 73 percent of the

respondents in the 1972 Bogotá survey indicated that being a woman was no obstacle to becoming president of Colombia; Losada and Murillo, *Análisis de las Elecciones*, p. 217.

152. The Bogotá newspaper, *El Tiempo*, led in this respect; cf. Premo, *Alianza Nacional Popular*, p. 344.
153. *Alerta*, April 24, 1974, pp. 3, 4, 5.
154. A high ANAPO official asserted following the 1974 election that María Eugenia was at the center of the party ideologically, and a political pragmatist who would move ANAPO in whichever direction political survival seemed to indicate; interview, Bogotá, July 23, 1974.
155. The difference between the two wings of the party have not only been political, but show up in social background as well. Thus Conservative Anapistas in Bogotá tended to have more education than Liberals and were more likely to have been educated in religious schools; Losada and Williams, "Análisis de la votación presidencial," pp. 14-15.
156. Premo, *Alianza Nacional Popular*, makes this point, p. 119.
157. Hoskin and Swanson, "Political Party Leadership," p. 417.
158. Hoskin and Swanson, "Inter-Party Competition," p. 337.
159. Hernando Echeverri, 1974 candidate of UNO, quoted in *El Espectador* (Bogotá), July 21, 1974, p. 7C.
160. Hoskin and Swanson, "Inter-Party Competition," p. 348.
161. Morcillo, et al., "Estudio sobre Abstención Electoral," p. 79.
162. Cf. Morcillo et al., "Estudio sobre Abstención Electoral," p. 79.
163. Hoskin and Swanson, "Inter-Party Competition," p. 337; see also p. 350. The original study, done in 1969, seems to have overestimated the staying power of ANAPO.
164. One would surmise, for example that a Christian Democratic party would make a viable third party in Colombia. But the PSDC got less than 1 percent of the vote in 1974 and the party has always been miniscule. Its presumed potential has apparently been absorbed over the years by dissident factions of the Conservative party and by ANAPO.
165. Weinert makes this point, *Political Modernization*, p. 227.
166. "Transitions to Democracy: Toward a Dynamic Model," *Comparative Politics* 2 (April 1970), p. 385.
167. Cf. the argument of Hoskin and Swanson, "Inter-Party Competition," pp. 348-50, which is based on a survey of the perceptions of party leaders.
168. From a speech by Roberto Arenas, then minister of government; *La República* (Bogotá), July 21, 1974, p. 11.
169. Hoskin and Swanson, "Inter-Party Competition," pp. 345-46.
170. For the pros and cons of ANAPO as fascist see respectively Ivan E. Rodríguez Escobar, *El 19 de Abril; un Estudio de la Pasada Campaña Electoral* (Medellín, 1972); and Hernández Rodríguez, *Análisis del Programa Anapista*, pp. 9-16.
171. Gino Germani, *Política y Sociedad en una Epoca de Transición* (Buenos Aires, 1965), p. 157. Rather than the "traditional strata" only, we would prefer to use the more inclusive term "marginal elites."
172. The movement headed by Carlos Ibáñez del Campo in Chile (1952-58) is a classic example of the frequently ephemeral nature of such movements; that of Getulio Vargas in Brazil is more ambiguously so. Gaitanismo is an obvious Colombian example; another is the would-be populist movement, the Movimiento Democrático Nacional (MDN), led by former General Alberto Ruiz

Novoa, which had a brief life during 1965; for Gaitanismo, see Dix, *Colombia*, pp. 99-107; for the MDN see, Dix, pp. 284-85 and Premo, pp. 98-100. The Peronist movement in Argentina has of course been something of an exception.

173. Philippe Schmitter, "Paths to Political Development in Latin America," in Douglas A. Chalmers, ed., *Changing Latin America* (New York, 1972), pp. 83-105. Cf. also Howard Wiarda, ed., *Politics and Social Change in Latin America* (Amherst, Mass., 1974).

174. Charles Anderson, *Politics and Economic Change in Latin America* (Princeton, N.J., 1967), ch. 4.

Chapter 6

The Military

J. Mark Ruhl

The institution of the first National Front government in 1958 brought an end to an atypical five-year period of direct military rule, first by Lt. General Gustavo Rojas Pinilla (1953-57) and then by the military junta that replaced him. The military never regained the formal reins of power during the National Front era but it did retain a major political role. The governments required its support in their frequent use of emergency powers. The institutional capabilities of the armed forces were expanded so that they might better maintain domestic order. Despite military interference in the initial civilian attempts to regain control of the government, civil-military relations became smooth during the National Front.[1] However, these "obedient" armed forces did not become entirely apolitical. In fact, the military's experiences in this period, particularly in internal warfare training and the antiguerrilla campaign, apparently sharpened and clarified its ideological stance.

The existence of a relatively cohesive, effective civilian elite, able to manage executive succession according to scheduled elections and the absence of a serious counterelite threat of social revolutionary proportions precluded the possibility of a military coup d'état. Contrary to a current of thought found in the literature, the National Front experience shows that the new military professionalism, which emphasizes internal national security and social development, need not result in overt intervention and military regimes.[2] Nonetheless, the new professionalism and ideological sophistication of the armed forces may have raised their future potential to intervene in an overt and cohesive fashion should conditions change. This chapter will survey pre-Front military developments, then discuss the expansion of the military and its patterns of behavior under the National Front. The chapter will conclude by examining the effects of the military's recent experiences on its institutional ideology and future political role.

HISTORICAL PERSPECTIVE

Colombia has traditionally been ruled by civilians. The nineteenth-century Colombian military was distinctive in Latin America for its low prestige and weakness. Colombian leaders never had much affection for Simón Bolívar's predominantly Venezuelan army of liberation. They regarded it as threatening, uncouth, and expensive.[3] The antagonistic wartime relationship between that army's largely Venezuelan officer corps and the Colombian leadership was one of the principal causes behind the breakdown of the Gran Colombia federation in 1830.

After the Venezuelans departed to form a separate nation, the Colombian elite was able to accelerate its efforts to reduce military influence. Previously demobilized from its wartime level of almost 30,000 to a force of 12,000 men in 1826, the army consisted of only 3,000 men by the early 1830s.[4] A new constitution further restricted the role of the military by prohibiting civil and military functions to be unified under any single government office. Most importantly, a truly professional corps of specialized military personnel did not develop in the nineteenth century.

The armed forces' influence was further diminished during the 1850s after the small army failed to sustain its overthrow of the civilian government. The government of General José María Melo, despite support from a dissident faction of the Liberal party, was soon deposed by an armed coalition of Liberals and Conservatives. Civilian politicians proceeded to reduce the army further. Through the 1880s, the military ranged between 109 and 1,200 men.[5]

During the nineteenth century, the national military played little role in Colombia's civil wars. León Helguera argues that these struggles between makeshift armies were especially savage precisely because of the lack of a developed military organization led by trained military officers.[6] The regular army only began to reemerge as the Liberal-Conservative conflicts subsided early in the twentieth century. Several early attempts at its reconstruction and professionalization under Rafael Núñez were obliterated by the highly costly Mil Días Civil War, or War of the Thousand Days (1899-1902). The lengthy peace that followed the conclusion of this war finally permitted a basis for a professional military.

The birth of the modern Colombian military dates from the post-Mil Días reforms of Conservative President Rafael Reyes (1904-09). Reyes sought to avoid another civil war by developing bureaucratic institutions capable of mediating or withstanding partisan conflict. He considered a professional army to be one of the tools that could neutralize partisan civilian strife. The president founded the major institutions of the military educational system—the Military Cadet School and the Superior War School. The new army was instructed in the latest European concepts of military technology and professional discipline by Prussian-trained Chilean officers who were invited to Colombia in 1907 and 1909.[7] The professionalization of the small 1,500-man armed forces continued under the direction of French, British, Swiss, and German instructors during the 1920s and 1930s.[8]

The early twentieth century was a period of unbroken military obedience to civilian authority. At times, the civilian elite used the emergent professional army to maintain internal security, as when it quelled worker and peasant unrest in the bloody United Fruit strike of 1928. Later, in 1932, the army proved itself in an external conflict in Peru. Not only did the military gain importance from this brief encounter; its officers were able to press successfully for institutional expansion and better pay in preparation for any further international involvement. Specialized infantry, cavalry, and artillery schools opened in 1936. A corps of engineers was founded in 1940 as the military expanded to more than 6,000 men.[9] Nonetheless, the Colombian military was still the smallest armed force relative to population in the Western Hemisphere.

Civil-military relations experienced some tensions during the Liberal Republic (1930-46), so called for the party in power. Some of the social reforms carried out during this period caused interparty conflict.[10] Because the Conservative party had ruled Colombia prior to 1930, the army was predominantly Conservative, and it played no part in the election of the first twentieth-century Liberal president, Enrique Olaya Herrera, in 1930. However, Olaya's successor Alfonso López Pumarejo (1934-38), a more partisan and dynamic social reformer, feared that the armed forces could be used as a Conservative tool to arrest his reforms and even challenge Liberal party rule.[11]Consequently, he interfered with promotions in order to favor Liberal officers and transferred personnel he distrusted to isolated or noncritical areas. López nationalized the departmental police forces in an attempt to construct a Liberal counterweight to the military and tried to keep the armed forces occupied with the national development task of jungle colonization. The army's dissatisfaction with the president surfaced in 1936 with the discovery of a minor anti-López conspiracy involving several officers.

Eduardo Santos, who followed López (1938-42), was much more a consolidator of Liberal gains and social reform than a controversial initiator of innovative policies. More of a conciliator than his predecessor, Santos succeeded in lowering the tensions in the polity, including civil-military relations. He demonstrated a genuine concern for the armed forces' professional capabilities.[12] The reelection of López in 1942, however, soon dissipated the tranquility that had characterized the Santos administration. The new government faced substantial social mobilization, labor union unrest, political strife, and scandal. The partisan and social tensions ultimately resulted in López's resignation from the presidency in 1945 in favor of Liberal Alberto Lleras Camargo.

The general climate of crisis throughout the second López administration affected the armed forces as well. This was reflected in the unsuccessful coup of July 1944. While on maneuvers near the Ecuadorian border, a group of officers led by Colonel Diógenes Gil took President López prisoner in the city of Pasto. Although the coup had some support within the army, it failed, partly because of poor coordination with the Bogotá garrison. Also important was the decisive action of acting President Darío Echandía, who rallied military forces to the government side by appealing to their traditional sense of "professional discipline."[13] Once freed, López dismissed many Conservative officers, some of whom had had no connection whatsoever with the attempted coup.

The military was drawn much deeper into politics during the administration of Conservative Mariano Ospina Pérez (1946-50). Elected over a divided Liberal opposition, Ospina attempted to govern in coalition with representatives of the Liberal majority. However, his term was characterized by a culmination of the earlier social and partisan unrest in what was to become La Violencia. Ospina's administration experienced a sustained and highly conflictive competition between the two traditional parties. As early as 1947, interparty violence, which intensified as the congressional elections approached, was too great for the police to control, particularly in some provinces and rural areas.[14] The regular army was therefore increasingly called upon to maintain public order as the Liberal-Conservative conflict intensified. Military officers became the temporary mayors of over 25 percent of Colombia's troubled municipal districts.[15]

In April of 1948, this volatile situation of growing interparty antagonism exploded into mob violence with the assassination of Liberal party chief Jorge Eliécer Gaitán in Bogotá. The army had to be used to quell the Bogotazo, the mass revolutionary riot named after the city where the rebellion was concentrated. During the uprising the Bogotá police deserted. (It should be recalled that the national police had been established by Liberal President López as a possible counterweight to Conservative influence in the army.) The army's political role expanded considerably after this successful defense of the Ospina minority government. The national police, for instance, were placed under the leadership of a military commander. Military officers also assumed departmental governorships in "unstable" areas where Liberal guerrilla bands had organized to resist the Conservative repression. When Liberals left the

Ospina cabinet in disgust, they were often replaced by military representatives.[16] Finally in 1949, when the Liberal Congress threatened impeachment, Ospina used the army to close it, declared martial law, and enforced the unilateral electoral victory of Conservative party leader, Laureano Gómez, as president for the 1950-54 term. A brief period of Conservative party dictatorship was initiated.

It is clear that throughout the Ospina administration, as conflict escalated and La Violencia became an inescapable fact, the military was increasingly brought into the conflict by the civilian politicians. Liberals wished to regard the military as somewhat of a buffer that could ultimately restore free elections and thus enable the Liberals to regain power. On the other hand, Ospina and his successors, Laureano Gómez and Roberto Urdaneta Arbeláez,[17] increasingly employed the army (in combination with Conservative irregulars) to maintain Conservative party rule. As it became critical to the survival of Conservative governments, the military was enlarged in terms of size and budget (see Table 1). Significantly, the partisan conflict led to a much more deferential treatment of the armed forces by civilians as the latter grew more dependent on them.[18] These developments produced wounds. Some Liberal officers were purged; a few deserted to the Liberal guerrillas or collaborated with them; others, including possibly some potentially troublesome officers, accepted assignment to the Colombian battalion which was fighting in Korea from mid-1951. Interestingly, about 3,000 soldiers, or 20 percent of the active army, participated in the Korean War.[19] That this was the case even though there was substantial rural violence in Colombia at that time suggests the desire of a hard-pressed government to obtain United States approval in what it was attempting to define internally and externally as a struggle of Christianity against Communism.

By 1952, the military had become uneasy with the difficult and blatantly partisan role thrust upon it by the Conservatives. The rural violence had frustrated military attempts to control it. Civilian support for the government was dwindling too, as the Conservative party itself fractionalized between the moderates led by former President Ospina and the extremists loyal to Laureano Gómez.[20] Gómez, who still retained power while Urdaneta was acting-president, opposed any compromise with the Liberals, and in 1953 began to intimidate his Conservative opposition as well. Moderate Conservatives now joined in urging the military to take power. It had become clear that there could not be a partisan solution to the deadlocked violence.

The military, however, intervened only after a series of events that exemplify the dramatic, passionate, and chaotic nature of the politics of the period. The coup was executed against Gómez after serious frictions and an eventual test of wills between him and General Gustavo Rojas Pinilla, the head of the armed forces. Gómez, who seems to have suspected Rojas's independent power and alleged connections with his Conservative opposition, first attempted to send the general abroad as a military representative. Rojas refused to leave, and in May 1953 he publicly intimated the army's dissatisfaction with Gómez, at the same time pledging full support for acting president Urdaneta.[21] Shortly thereafter, Gómez seized upon the army's handling of a suspected assassin, prominent industrialist Felipe Echavarría, as a pretext for ordering Urdaneta to remove Rojas as military commander and to reassert control over the armed forces. (Echavarría had supposedly been involved in a plot to kill Rojas and other top officers. Alleging that the military had tortured Echavarría, Alvaro Gómez, Laureano's son, tried to have the investigation taken out of the hands of the military.) When Urdaneta refused to fire General Rojas, Gómez reassumed the presidency. On the evening of the same day, June 13, 1953, the military under Rojas executed a bloodless coup d'état, ending half century of military obedience to civilian authority.

The coup was almost universally praised by Liberals and Conservatives alike. Rojas' amnesty program convinced thousands of guerrillas to lay down their arms, and the general climate was of approval of military mediation in the partisan conflict. Nonetheless, the longer Rojas was in office, the less acceptable his authoritarian regime became. Initially he was politically clumsy, in that he soon began to identify his administration with the Conservative party more closely than was warranted to retain the role of a mediating regime. Second, his government gradually became associated with military privilege and authoritarianism. Thirdly, when toward the end of his government Rojas attempted to initiate a permanent political solution away from the party system, it was linked to his *continuismo*—his personal continuation in power without any resort to electoral process[22]—and to a proto-Peronist formula that antagonized not only the elites and key segments of the two traditional parties but clerical sectors as well.[23] Undeniably Rojas showed concern for Colombia's disadvantaged poor. Whatever his motives, he was responsible for the first major governmental effort at social welfare by creating the National Secretariat of Social Assistance (SENDAS). However, General Rojas's attempts to play the populist messiah probably had little effect on the lower class; the high coffee prices, rather than Rojas's economic policies, kept his treasury full. When the coffee bonanza ended, Colombia's precarious international payments situation became obvious.[24] Rural violence had once again increased as well. All these factors contributed to the success of the anti-Rojas intertraditional party coalition that precipitated his removal and ultimately led to the constitution of the National Front. When Rojas attempted to interfere illegally with the electoral process in 1957, he was deposed by a military junta.[25] He had been in power only four years. Clearly, the military was not able or inclined to provide a lasting political solution other than a return to civilian rule.

Table 1
Colombian Military Statistics
1950-70

Years	a. Size of Forces	b. Military Expenditures in Millions of U.S. Dollars*	c. Military Expenditures as Percent of G.D.P.	d. Military Expenditure as Percent of Budget
1950	14,660	27	1.1	15.7
1951	14,660	32	1.2	15.5
1952	15,660	43	1.6	19.8
1953	15,660	62	2.1	22.5
1954	15,660	65	2.0	24.4
1955	16,589	61	1.9	19.9
1956	16,589	62	1.8	21.1
1957	20,800	50	1.4	20.5
1958	20,800	48	1.4	23.0
1959	20,800	47	1.3	19.8
1960	20,800	52	1.4	22.7
1961	20,800	54	1.3	17.7
1962	22,800	56	1.3	15.9
1963	22,800	61	1.4	23.0
1964	22,800	62	1.3	23.3
1965	37,000	62	1.3	20.5
1966	53,500	65	1.3	23.9
1967	52,000	65	1.2	22.0
1968	64,000	86	1.5	21.8
1969	64,000	78	1.3	20.0
1970	64,000	96	1.5	17.6

Sources: (a) *The Statesman's Yearbook* 1953-1970, except for 1965-1967, found in Richard Maullin, *Soldiers, Guerrillas and Politics in Colombia* (Lexington, Mass., 1973), p. 82; (b, c) Gertrude E. Heare, *Trends in Latin American Military Expenditures 1940-1970*, U.S. Dept. of State publication 8618 (Washington, 1971), p. 14; (d) Jorge Villegas, "Presupuestos Nacionales de Ingresos y Gastos 1871-1970," *DANE, Boletín Mensual de Estadística* #257-258 (Dec.-Jan. 1972-1973), pp. 187, 189, except for 1950-1957 found in Maullin, pp. 83-84. Figures listed combine Dept. of Defense with National Police.

*Converted at 15.82 pesos to the U.S. dollar, the principal selling rate at the end of 1967.

It was this junta, nominally headed by provisional president Gabriel París, which worked with Liberal and Conservative leaders to carry out the transition to the National Front. The generals remained in office as a caretaker government for fifteen months, although civilians handled most governmental duties. After monitoring the 1957 elections, the army formally returned to the barracks, although, as discussed below, some elements later made an unsuccessful attempt to interfere in the early stages of the National Front.

Table 2
Major Latin American Military Establishments
Circa 1965-70

Country	a. 1969 Size Per 100,000	b. 1970 Milt. Exp. as %GDP	c. 1964 Milt. Exp. % Govt. Bud.	d. Milt. Exp./ Soldier
Argentina	557.8	2.0	17.3	2,114
Brazil	205.9	2.0	15.2	1,363
Chile	667.7	3.3	10.1	2,144
Colombia	332.6	1.5	16.0	2,126
Peru	434.8	3.3	16.3	811
Venezuela	363.3	1.6	10.2	5,911
Colombia Rank in Latin America (mid-1960s, of 19-20 countries)	11th	9th*	6th	——

Sources: (a, c, d, and ranks) Maullin, pp. 85-87, 91, 95; (b) Heare, p. 8
Notes: *GNP

In summary, the Colombian military has been most remarkable in Latin America for its tradition of nonintervention in civilian politics. The armed forces have generally been content to stay on the political sidelines or to act as disciplined tools of the civilian elite in power. The atypical 1953 military coup and regime occurred only after the party system had drawn them into the political process by failing to maintain even minimal public order.

INSTITUTIONAL EXPANSION

During the National Front, the armed forces tripled in size and doubled its budget in real terms (Table 1).[26] Although the military is still neither one of the largest nor best financed in Latin America (Table 2), it did become a much more imposing force. Paradoxically, the military establishment experienced this dramatic growth during a period when civilian political control was restored in an environment of reduced partisan mobilization and civilian political violence.[27]

Apparently the government of Guillermo León Valencia (1962-66) was especially willing to devote a large share of governmental resources to the military in an attempt to eradicate the remnants of the Violencia and respond to the growing threats of the Marxist guerrillas. This response to a potential revolutionary danger was, of course, encouraged and partly financed by the United States as part of the military aspect of its Alliance for Progress program.[28] One can observe in Table 1 an obvious incongruence between the rapid growth of the armed forces and the modest increase in military expeditures, so that the portion of Colombia's gross domestic product and budget allotted to the military decreased or held constant. This is probably explained by the fact that substantial U.S. financial assistance for military expenditures did not appear in the published budget data. A secondary reason for military expansion may also have been the crystallization during the Lleras Restrepo administration (1966-70) of the dispute with Venezuela over the oil-rich northern border areas.

In this period of rapid growth, the Colombian military also raised its level of professional sophistication. Educational capacities had to be greatly enlarged to meet the new influx of soldiers, and the curriculum was modernized to emphasize problems of internal subversion and war. Currently, all recruits receive a basic primary education along with their military training, while officers have the benefit of a widening range of specialized and advanced schools. Courses at the impressive Superior War School now range from the latest weapons technology to development economics and sociology, two subjects of particular value in antiguerrilla operations. Training is also available from the United States military mission in Colombia or from American installations abroad. Results of this professional educational innovation can be seen in any of the armed forces' publications. The *Revista del Ejército*, the army's official publication, is especially full of intelligent, knowledgeable articles by Colombian officers covering a wide range of topics such as new weaponry, counterguerrilla strategy, and even general public policy.[29] These developments in increased military intellectual sophistication and political awareness have also been related to the educational modernization of the profession in other Latin American countries as well.[30]

The armed forces have also become increasingly well equipped for their role of keeping internal order,[31] drawing upon the U.S. and domestically produced weapons and munitions. The Colombian military has been relatively better supplied in counterguerrilla material, such as small arms, helicopters, and jet trainers; in less immediately useful tanks and supersonic jets its stock is lower than that of other Latin American militaries. Colombian officers agreed with U.S. advisors on the need to emphasize their counterguerrilla capabilities. However, this attitude has changed recently when the guerrillas proved unable to pose a sustained revolutionary challenge to the National Front governments and as the Venezuelan border dispute became more important. In 1973, the armed forces began to purchase some more expensive, ''externally useful'' weapons, notably a number of French Mirage M-5's.[32]

The armed forces are also well provided for in terms of salary, career stability, and fringe benefits. Although they were underpaid during the early National Front years, the military usually receives salary advances regularly and are able, at least, to keep pace with Colombia's rampant inflation.[33]

Conscripts, in particular, find basic military living conditions preferable to their previous circumstances. Officers and enlisted men also can draw on many additional benefits such as subsidized housing, military hospitals, pensions, and family security plans. In short, by the conclusion of the National Front, the Colombian military had become an increasingly professionalized force, well educated, well equipped, and occupationally secure.

CIVIL-MILITARY RELATIONS

While its professional capabilities were improving, the Colombian military remained subordinate to civilian authority throughout the National Front era. With the exception of a few incidents, civil-military relations have been quite smooth. The armed forces, in fact, became a major support of the National Front, acting to quell any disorder. By 1974, they constituted one of the very few Latin American militaries remaining under civilian control.

Earlier, lingering pro-Rojas sentiment in the army had interfered with the beginning of the National Front. In 1958, two days before the May 4 elections, elements of the military and national police had arrested National Front candidate Lleras Camargo and four of the five-member military junta. The bulk of the armed forces, however, did not support the coup, and its leader, Lieutenant Colonel Hernando Forero, the head of the military police, was himself arrested. Rumors of higher officers' implication circulated widely. Later in 1961, a provocative speech by General Rojas encouraged two army lieutenants to lead another unsuccessful mutiny, in an attempt to create a rebel movement in the eastern plains.[34] Soon crushed, this marked the last armed effort of military personnel to end the National Front experiment.

The most significant civil-military confrontation of the National Front began to take form shortly thereafter and culminated in 1965 in the dismissal of General Alberto Ruiz Novoa, minister of war under President Guillermo León Valencia. Discussing the Ruiz affair in some detail is useful because of the light it sheds on the rise and decline of overt military influence during this period, its professionalization, and the ultimate reluctance of the military to displace the civilian political elite and to take a larger role in public decision making.

Several studies conducted by individuals associated with the Rand Corporation group have suggested a positive relationship between increased professionalization and military politicization in Latin America.[35] Specifically, they argue that during the Cold War a "new," United States-sponsored professionalism developed which emphasized internal, as opposed to conventional, warfare. While the old professionalism defined the role of the military as "apolitical," its new, antiinsurrectionist role involved the military in the internal social and economic factors that had fostered disloyalty and rebellion in the first place. Thus, proper military training had to be broadened to include analysis of sociopolitical factors that were conducive to social revolutionary situations. Consequently, the new professional military became politically more articulate and developed ideologies justifying a broader military institutional role to "correct" the social pathologies that cause insurgency. The result is military organizations with a broader scope, which are more prone to intervene in the political process and establish military authoritarian regimes.

General Ruiz had won early recognition for leading Colombian troops in Korea and for his efforts as an economic administrator under the military junta. He was named war minister in 1962 and he immediately became the spokesman for those who thought the military should play a greater role in Colombian development and policy making. Initially, he stressed only the need to combine military action with civilian efforts to improve rural living conditions as part of the antiguerrilla campaign, a theory highly popular with United States counterinsurgency experts. Americans advising the Colombian armed forces felt that the military had to be increasingly involved in community public relations and development in order to wage successful counterguerrilla operations. Soon, however, General Ruiz began to criticize Colombian society and government more generally, emphasizing that inequality and poverty were the principal ills behind the guerrilla movement. In his 1964 report to the Congress, he referred to "the need to eliminate the social and economic differences which Colombian society today suffers . . . the injustice in which a vast section of the population is buried, living in very difficult conditions, constituting an undeniable cauldron for disorder."[36]

Ruiz placed the blame for rural misery clearly with the Colombian ruling class. He charged them with impeding Colombia's progress and development. Specifically, he advocated "structural changes" and criticized the Valencia government of which he was a cabinet member for its lack of national purpose. After a visit to Israel, Ruiz became even more insistent on an increased and autonomous role for the armed forces in the socioeconomic development process. He argued that the government must "open the road to the necessary integration of the armed institutions and their members into the society, as an urgent evolution and in contrast to the traditional isolation of the military."[37]

While sponsoring a larger role for the armed forces, Ruiz Novoa was employing the military and the mass media to enhance his own political position. Other military leaders resented his maneuvering and found an opportunity to effect his removal in early 1965. In late December and early January, when a major labor strike threatened, rumors of Ruiz's plans to take "crisis" powers circulated widely, although Ruiz publicly proclaimed the "illegality" of such action. He met privately with civilian and labor leaders, and four days before he was dismissed, leaflets appeared in the capital proclaiming: "The country demands order, progress, development. Ruiz Novoa is the solution."[38]

Ruiz later disavowed both the leaflets and any intentions of seizing power, but his previous actions had convinced the head of the services to urge President Valencia to dismiss him. On January 27, after a lengthy conference in the Presidential Palace, Ruiz resigned at Valencia's insistence and was replaced by General Gabriel Rebéiz Pizarro, the head of the army.

President Valencia explained that he had acted "to remove the tense situation that had been created in the breast of the armed forces."[39] New war minister Rebéiz Pizarro justified Ruiz's removal because of the need to maintain professional discipline and military internal cohesion. He elaborated on the nature of the institutional tensions, noting that "the presentation of theories about economic, political and social themes that General Ruiz Novoa was making could not continue in that way, because considering that the statements come from the mouth of an army officer and minister of war . . . puts in danger the unity of the institution."[40] Once deposed, Ruiz Novoa passed into relative obscurity. Many army officers disliked him for the rigid discipline he had imposed on the institution in attempting to increase its efficiency and professionalism,[41] and he appears to have had as little support among civilians as he had among army officers. (Ruiz has reappeared only recently as the head of a minor organization of retired officers identified with the Liberal party.)

Under Ruiz Novoa, the Colombian armed forces implemented programs of modernization which resulted in the already noted increases in their size and intellectual sophistication. Simultaneously, the Colombian armed forces assumed, especially through General Ruiz, a critical, in his own words *deliberante* (deliberative), political role because of an increased awareness of the relationship between socioeconomic preconditions for revolt and military effectiveness. According to Ruiz, force alone could not prevent revolutionary pressures. Therefore, the armed forces had to contribute directly to the resolution of development problems. General Ruiz was at least toying with a military reformist authoritarian solution of the Peruvian style.[42] Clearly, in agreement with the predictions of the "Rand Corporation" interpretation, key actors in Colombia employed the reformist logic of the "new professionalism" to justify actions that appeared to be leading to coup d'état—military authoritarian regime. However, insubordination did not occur, the balance of the officer corps refusing to follow General Ruiz into politics.

What were the arguments employed to remove Ruiz? This is an important question to elucidate the impact of professional training on military intervention. In essence, the argument against politicization was its negative impact on professional discipline and institutional unity or cohesion.[43] Thus it appears that while, on the one hand, the "sociological" or social reform elements in the "new professional" training increases the political awareness of the military and justifies a broader role on their part, the "professional discipline" and "unity or cohesion" aspects of any military professional training serve to justify nonintervention when this course is decided upon.[44] In Colombia "professionalism" has been the ideology of nonintervention. One must recall that Colombia had recently emerged from an exceptional period of military rule that had resulted in widespread military unpopularity, alleged economic mismanagement,[45] and internal military division—the internal problems that characterized the transition from the Rojas to the Frente regime. Therefore, a "historical" variable supported General Rebéiz's position for nonintervention in the interest of organization cohesion and professional corporate interest. His stance was particularly appropriate during this period when the levels of political violence were declining, and no major political group was posing a social revolutionary threat to military class or professional interests. Thus "situational" variables also inhibited overt military intervention. In sum, whether or not a military regime materializes obviously depends on factors other than the level of counterinsurgency training.

Since the Ruiz dismissal, the military has been content simply to maintain order and has avoided statements of broader significance. The only other civil-military conflict of note occurred in February 1969 when President Carlos Lleras Restrepo removed Army Chief General Pinzón Caicedo for his article in a military journal criticizing civilian interference with the military budget.[46] Colombia's civilian leadership seemed to be much more certain of the military's reaction in this case. In contrast to Valencia's vacillation in the Ruiz case, Carlos Lleras dismissed Pinzón almost immediately and nearly without consultation. Once again, civilian control prevailed.

Prior to the 1970 elections, rumors of a preemptive coup directed against General Rojas Pinilla's ANAPO political movement were widespread. Later, in mid-1971, the respected British news journal *Latin America* noted that at a time of cabinet resignations and ANAPO's legislative harassment of the National Front "there have been constant murmurs of an army takeover. Of late these rumors have increased to such an extent that there would be few surprised if this actually happened."[47] However, in neither case did armed intervention actually materialize. Indeed, Colombia has experienced only two coups d'état since 1901, yet there has been a recurrent propensity in the country to perceive the political situation as crisis-laden and on the verge of military takeover. No one has yet explained Colombia's attraction to the "politics of rumor." In any event, ANAPO's decline in the 1972 and 1974 elections and Rojas Pinilla's death in 1975 undercut interest in an anti-ANAPO coup scenario.

DEFENSE OF THE NATIONAL FRONT

Despite the recurrent rumors of military takeover and with the exception of some remaining Rojista sentiment (1958-61) and Ruiz Novoa's unsupported ambitions, civil-military relations have been quite correct. Instead of interfering with often-beleaguered National Front governments, the armed forces have become their defenders. A frequent pattern has been for governments to respond to crises by resorting to emergency powers or announcing a state of siege, rallying compliance from the military and thus threatening repression of the discontented groups while pressuring for "negotiated" solutions within the existing legal framework.[48]

One can only speculate on the military's motivations for assuming this role of compliance and support. During the National Front, the armed forces have obviously gained the material rewards of larger size, increased budget, and greater professional sophistication in return for their protection and subordination. However, a more important underlying reason for their loyalty would seem to be the fact that the National Front's mildly reformist policies offer the military the most credible hope of national development without threatening either their professional institution or the middle class from which they are largely recruited.[49] The most significant pockets of violence in the period have been in the rural area. Antiguerrilla military operations have been successful enough in containing and then dispersing this threat to the political system. Judging from Latin American, and specifically Colombian, experience, escalated violence precipitates successful military rebellions.[50] Hence, the control of violence should also have contributed to the survival of the National Front. However, it is possible to make puzzling comparisons. For instance, in Peru the military, which appears to have a class background similar to that of the Colombian armed forces, also confronted and controlled a guerrilla movement during this period. Yet, the Peruvian military still chose to overthrow the moderate reformist government of Belaunde in 1968.

Comparisons of this nature suggest that the traditional, historical characteristics of political institutions can be decisive in explaining military loyalty.[51] Military governments are the exception in Colombia, whereas Peru has experienced countless military takeovers. The Colombian pattern both historically and during the National Front has been a party system supported by significant levels of traditional party identification. This party system has usually resulted in electorally rotating executive power within a plural party leadership.[52] The main line of cleavage in the society has been interparty in nature, the military intervening, as I have shown, to mediate this conflict. In Peru, on the other hand, APRA, historically the most important party, has been traditionally defined as threatening to the symbolic or material corporate interests of the military. In Peru "traditional hatreds" involve the military directly rather than being mainly interparty, as they are in Colombia. Consequently, a different pattern of more frequent military intervention has materialized in Peru. Because the Colombian political civilian elite has succeeded better in managing the development process without challenging military interests, the Colombian military is more motivated to trust civilian rule than their Peruvian counterparts.[53]

During the Frente, the armed forces were most directly involved in defending the civilian political elite in rural Colombia, where the bulk of actual violence (as opposed to unrest) occurred. This rural violence has gone through distinct phases. In the earlier years of the Front, prior to the consolidation of the Cuban Revolution as a Marxist-Leninist phenomenon, the violence was mostly a residue of the older interparty conflict of La Violencia combined with increasing banditry.[54] After the traditional parties reduced their militancy and signed the bipartisan accords, the violence began to lose its original political justification in the rural communities, and gradually became regarded as self-seeking robbery and murder. Some of the still active *violentos* probably had somewhat mixed motives, but most sources agree that by 1965 they had degenerated almost completely into banditry. About 3,000 guerrillas were active at this time, roughly 10 to 15 percent of the earlier (1946-53) level. Fighting concentrated in the departments of Tolima, Valle, and Cauca.[55]

The military under Ruiz Novoa's Plan Lazo (initiated in 1962) successfully combined civic action and repression to reduce the violence. American counterguerrilla training and equipment obviously helped in this respect. United States' aid specifically underwrote the civic action program, a wide variety of rural improvement projects designed to win peasant support away from the *violentos*. School and road construction as well as health care and sanitation figured prominently in the program. The success of the military is suggested by the decline of civilian victims in rural violence from 1959 to 1965. Between 1959 and 1962, 200 people lost their lives every month, but by 1963 this rate had been cut in half. In 1965, only 544 were reported killed during the whole year.[56]

The most significant political success of the pre-1966 period, however, was the virtual elimination of the "independent republics." During the mostly traditional party conflict of La Violencia, a number of relatively self-contained, Marxist-controlled areas had been established.[57] After failures in 1962, the army in 1964 employed roughly a third of its force in taking control of the most important enclave, Marquetalia in Tolima. El Pato, Río Chiquito, and Guayabero fell to the army in 1965. Contact with these Marxist areas helped give the military a different view of the nature of guerrilla warfare. Their encounters with ideologically motivated guerrillas reinforced their professional training and helped prepare them for the transition to the more ideological post-1965 violence.[58]

After 1965, the character of the violence changed considerably. The *violentos* were fewer, but they had become more clearly political and were intent on attacking and overthrowing the National Front establishment. The Marxist "independent republics" had been defensive, relatively inactive enclaves available for sustained guerrilla activity in the future when conditions permitted. However, the Cuban Revolution fostered a new kind of Marxist revolutionary who concurred with Ché Guevara that "objective conditions" need not be present in order to begin the armed struggle; guerrilla violence itself could create the necessary revolutionary environment.[59] As epitomized by former priest Camilo Torres, the new revolutionaries were young, well-educated individuals without any previous contact with the Communist party. To counter the new type of adversary, the armed forces relied increasingly on armed repression while the civic action program decreased proportionally.[60]

Between 1965 and 1974, two major guerrilla groups were active. The first organization appeared in 1964-65 when the Vásquez Castaño brothers organized a group of students from the Industrial University of Santander into the ELN, the Army of National Liberation. This band, in which Camilo Torres became active, drew its ideological inspiration from Cuba's Fidel Castro and had little, if any, connection with earlier interparty violence. The ELN, which was estimated to consist of up to 300 active guerrillas, concentrated its operations in the difficult terrain of rural Antioquia and Bolívar as well as in its native department of Santander.[61] The other major guerrilla organization was the FARC, the Colombian Revolutionary Armed Forces, which officially came into being in mid-1966. The FARC represented a coalition of older guerrilla bands that had been organized into the Southern Guerrilla Bloc, an organization which the regular Colombian Communist party had aided financially for some time. Politically committed to social revolution, the movement had fewer urban intellectuals than the ELN and so was less ideologically sophisticated. The FARC controlled an estimated 350 to 500 men who operated in traditionally violent South Central Colombia, especially Tolima. Its head was Manuel Marulanda, alias "Sure-Shot," himself a relic from La Violencia.[62]

By the early 1970s, the army had reduced the guerrillas to more of a nuisance than a serious concern. Fragmentary figures suggest that casualties were rather higher again in 1973 but this was largely due to the military's intensified efforts to destroy the guerrillas completely.[63] For some years after the attacks on the "independent republics" and the early contacts with the ELN and FARC, the armed forces had been content to contain the guerrillas in their isolated rural zones of operation, but in 1973 they decided to enter these areas in force.[64] The greatest military success was the virtual destruction of the ELN in Northeastern Antioquia and Medio Magdalena. Two of the three Vásquez Castaño brothers were killed in one operation, and sometime later, Lara Parada, characterized as the movement's ideologue, was captured. With the ELN dispersed by the end of October 1973, the military turned its attention to the FARC. By early 1974, three of the army's ten brigades were already deeply involved in Southern Tolima and Huila.[65] As a result of these efforts, most Colombian newspapers were praising the armed forces' "final" eradication of the guerrillas, although successful kidnappings continued, particularly in the countryside.

The armed forces' role of keeping order, of course, extended beyond the rural guerrilla conflict. It frustrated ELN attempts to initiate an urban guerrilla movement and contained recurrent student rioting in the late 1960s and early 1970s, especially in Bogotá and Cali. Various violent striking groups were also held in check, e.g., oil workers, teachers, bus drivers. Under the state-of-siege laws operative during most of the era, military courts were used to try most public order violations. Perhaps most importantly, however, military compliance was obtained by President Lleras Restrepo to ensure the acceptance of the questionable 1970 election returns against the ANAPO opposition, which claimed electoral fraud.

Finally, the armed forces have continually assisted the National Front governments in a variety of more peaceful ways. Military officers have served on the board of directors of government development agencies such as INCORA, the Colombian Agrarian Reform Institute. With the reduction in urban and rural violence in the 1970s, the armed forces concentrated much effort on the government's colonization programs. Its engineers directed land clearing activities and constructed roads and airfields.

THE MILITARY'S POLITICS

While acting as the National Front's protector, the Colombian military has remained subordinate to civilian authority since 1958. Nevertheless, it has not become an "apolitical" institution. The military's political preferences have simply led it to prefer the current ruling elite to the Marxist and populist counterelites that lie outside the traditional parties. Beneath a thin façade of political neutrality, the ideological consciousness of the armed forces has probably increased because of their National Front experiences.

Colombian military spokesmen, such as Defense Minister General Hernando Currea Cubides, never tired of asserting the military's unwavering "impartiality" and aversion to politics. In return, the Liberal and Conservative press missed few opportunities to praise the armed forces for their self-sacrifice and obedience to civilian direction.[66] Opposition politicians, on the other hand, were much more critical of the military and skeptical of its protestations of political disinterest. ANAPO, created by General Rojas, tended to criticize only the higher leadership of the armed forces which had, at least, a symbolic complicity in ousting the general from the presidency in 1957 and supporting the anti-Rojas electoral result of 1970. The National Union of Opposition (UNO), the small Marxist coalition based on the Colombian Communist party, condemned the armed forces, without exception, as the conservative, atrocity-committing "gorillas" who kept the National Front in power by unprovoked murder of workers and peasants.[67]

The initial phases of the antiguerrilla campaign under General Ruiz Novoa had some trends toward ideological social reform and genuine concern for lower class miseries within the military, as discussed above. In addition to Ruiz Novoa, General Alvaro Valencia Tovar was a particularly strong voice in favor of socioeconomic reform. His novel, *Uisheda*, reveals an almost sympathetic view of guerrilla motives. However, such thinking became increasingly rare in the in-service publications after 1965, when General Ruiz was retired.[68]

The Ruiz crisis in civil-military relations had been immediately followed by a revitalization of Marxist revolutionary activities brought about by Camilo Torres's defection to the ELN. The actions of Torres, a popular, upper-class priest, increased psychologically the short-run credibility of the Marxist threat to the military's institutional and class interests. Faced with a more believable, purely Marxist guerrilla threat of social revolution, and perhaps uneasy over the effects on the institution of Ruiz Novoa's social reformism, military thinking, as represented by the professional publications, became dominated by rabid anticommunism. In *Armed Forces*, Vice Admiral Rubén Piedrahita Arango noted in 1972 that the armed forces remained apolitical "in spite of the daily struggle they have to maintain, disadvantageously, with the strong influence of pernicious, underhanded foreign doctrines, that with abundant money and profuse Marxist and Communist propaganda are poisoning the people."[69]

By far the most hostile anticommunist of the military writers was former minister of defense, General Gerardo Ayerbe Chaux (1967-70), later the overseer of Colombian elections. As early as 1965, he noted a communist threat that encompassed far more than just the usual guerrillas.

> It [communism] is a palpitating reality which has for some years been manifesting itself by means of intense, copious and well-directed propaganda, by the methodical agitation of different social sectors, by various front organizations, by the infiltration into the university, the high schools and into different state and private organizations, and finally by the guerrilla movements in the country which have taken different names according to the circumstances.[70]

An overview of the military periodicals, particularly the *Army Review*, reveals that the Colombian armed forces also increasingly perceived its solidarity with the United States and with numerous "conservative" military regimes, particularly those of Argentina, Brazil, and even prerevolutionary Portugal. Guest authors from each of these nations often appeared to stress the monolithic nature of their common adversary and the need for closer international military coordination, while Colombian officers went to great lengths to distinguish themselves from the social-reformist Peruvian officers.[71]

In short, it is not difficult to imagine how the Colombian military would behave in the face of a tangible Marxist or Marxist-populist threat if these orientations continue to prevail. Ayerbe Chaux put it succinctly: "To believe . . . that Communism can coexist within Democracy is like thinking water and oil can mix. . . . In Brazil the military was forced to intervene before the country was dominated by the Communist masses."[72]

An additional factor that contributed to the military's rising ideological conservatism and to its reduced interest in social reform may have been the role played during the National Front by General Rojas Pinilla's ANAPO movement. Persisting pro-Rojas, anticivilian feelings had, as discussed above, resulted in military dissension and some aborted military rebellions during the early years of the National Front. In his efforts to vindicate himself, Rojas established the populist, anti-National Front ANAPO vehicle.[73] Some noncommissioned and retired officers were attracted to ANAPO as the movement stressed its intent to increase military salaries and benefits, particularly for the common soldier. Rojistas, however, resented the "betrayal" of the top military leaders who restored civilian control in 1957 at the expense of their "brother officers." Therefore, the military leadership was fearful of any attempt by Rojas to settle old scores after an ANAPO victory. (Similar motives fueled the Argentine military's opposition to Peronismo.[74]) As ANAPO gained strength prior to the 1970 elections, the armed forces quietly dismissed a number of supposedly pro-ANAPO junior officers. Many editorial writers, such as Conservative party leader Berta de Ospina, came to regard the military as the ultimate check against ANAPO.[75] Rumors of an anti-ANAPO coup persisted well into 1971 as ANAPO proved incapable of winning the support of the well-fed military institution that had earlier been embarrassed by General Rojas's governmental mismanagement.

Military leadership essentially followed a defensive strategy with respect to General Rojas and ANAPO. Rather than fuel Rojas's Bonapartist appeals to the lower military ranks by toying with ideas of overt military intervention and social reform themselves, the military elite opted for an easier, safer alternative: define itself as professionally neutral upholder of the constitutional system and the defender of public order against a weak Marxist movement.[76]

CONCLUSIONS

The initiation of the National Front marked the end of an unusual period of military rule in Colombia. This period of overt intervention (1953-57) resulted from the incapacity of the polarized and fractionalized civilian elite to rule in a violence-torn society. Nonetheless, the military itself soon felt compromised by what it came to view as the mismanagement of the Rojas regime, and finally chose to remove Rojas in 1957 and return to the barracks in 1958.

The military had not, however, abjured politics. During the early years of the National Front, United States counterinsurgency theories encouraged a preoccupation with social reformism within the Colombian military that fueled General Ruiz Novoa's aborted "proto-coup" of 1965. As a result of Ruiz's dismissal and the increased saliency of the Marxist guerrilla threat, the armed forces deemphasized social reform as well as their pleas for a greater political role. The military opted, instead, for an "apolitical" professionalism devoted to the defense of the constitutional order and civilian rule while espousing an ideologically militant anticommunism.

How does one account for the Colombian military's distinctive political role? Will the Colombian armed forces continue to avoid overt intervention in civilian politics? It would appear that Latin American militaries often resort to direct rule for two reasons: (1) in order to replace a hopelessly divided or incompetent civilian leadership that endangers basic public order and national development, or (2) to counteract a Marxist or populist movement that they perceive as threatening to their institution or class. Both factors are often present in specific cases, although the Colombian military intervention of 1953 seems largely attributable to civilian elite failures, while the Brazilian military intervention of 1964 and the Chilean one of 1973 appear to have been more the result of the armed forces' fears of social revolution.[77]

The climate of hostility that had precipitated the 1953 coup was reduced during the National Front. Although some political differences persisted, the majority of both traditional parties agreed on the need to cooperate on programs of defensive reform in order to avert social revolution.[78] The very existence of the coalitional regime that produced regular electoral presidential succession without major violence worked to inhibit overt military intervention. Given the ability of the traditional civilian elite to maintain a workable ideological consensus and to direct the economy without major failures, one would expect the military to be content to keep these civilians in power. The military's own embarrassment about the Rojas government's record of economic management (1953-57) certainly did not encourage it to replace the civilian political elite. Nonetheless, memories of the Rojas interlude will not last forever. Thus, should the civilian political elite's disunity or its economic incompetence become major problems in the future, the military may be inclined to consider trying its own hand again.

Colombia never faced a serious threat of social revolution during the National Front. Marxist groups were always electorally weak and the guerrillas never placed the established elite's survival in real doubt. On the other hand ANAPO's populist threat was not excessive. When it was most powerful in

1970 the movement did not command an electoral majority and it was still ideologically confused and heavily populated with traditional politicians. The 1974 electoral returns, which gave over 85 percent of the vote to the traditional parties and resulted in ANAPO's demise, demonstrate just how remote the possibility of counterelite success is in contemporary Colombia. In the absence of such threats, the armed forces have had no need to risk internal divisions and follow their Brazilian or Chilean counterparts into a policy of overt intervention and military rule.

What type of program would the Colombian military pursue if altered conditions ever did bring about direct military rule? Given the armed forces' growing conservatism under the National Front, could the military still contemplate a Peruvian model of social reform? The Peruvian experience suggests that military social reformism is more plausible in the absence of a serious leftist danger to the armed forces.[79] The Peruvian guerrilla movement was even weaker than that of Colombia; also, the APRA, the army's traditional rival, had mellowed considerably, reducing its threat to established institutions. Thus, when the military took power, it did not need to build a defensive coalition of conservative elements in order to forestall a threat to its class and institution. In the absence of an organized, dangerous, leftist movement, such as that faced by the military forces of Brazil and Chile, the Peruvian armed forces felt safe enough to build a popular coalition around social reform.[80]

The Peruvian case suggests, therefore, that although the Colombian military became increasingly conservative under the National Front, the institution's future politics may become more flexible. Neither Marxist guerrillas nor ANAPO pose viable threats to the military now; thus, if civilian elite disunity or incompetence alone should cause the armed forces to take power, a Peruvian-style policy of social reform is still a possibility. On the other hand, if the armed forces are drawn to oust the civilian political elite because of a future threat of social revolution, they will be almost certain to play a conservative role in defense of class and institution.

Overt military rule, thus, has not, and for the time being will not, occur in Colombia because the conditions that encourage it are simply not present nor are they likely in the near future.[81] Once confronted with the unlikely prospects of another breakdown in civil order as in 1953 or with a durable, threatening coalition such as Allende headed in Chile, the armed forces would undoubtedly take control of the government. How long the Colombian soldiers would hesitate in such a situation, agonizing over the rupture of their tradition of a noninterventionist professionalism, as the Chilean officers claim to have done, is unknown. Nonetheless, if either condition ever crystallizes, Colombia would soon be found to possess no special immunity to military rule, in spite of its history of correct civil-military relations. In this case, their increased professional sophistication may contribute to a more effective military regime than the one of the 1950s.

NOTES

The author wishes to express his great appreciation to Mauricio Solaún for his many helpful suggestions on an earlier draft of this paper. The manuscript has also benefited from the comments of Robert Kramer, Ronald McDonald, and Shirley Hall.

1. For a discussion of the initial, mostly pre-Front civil-military strife which included an aborted coup in 1958, see John D. Martz, *Colombia: A Contemporary Political Survey* (Chapel Hill, 1962), pp. 270-71. Martz shows the difficulties that were found in the transition from military to civilian rule at the initiation of the National Front.
2. The importance of other regime and societal variables in military coups is stressed in Mauricio Solaún and Michael A. Quinn, *Sinners and Heretics: The Politics of Military Intervention in Latin America* (Urbana, Ill., 1973). The role of the new professionalism in the constitution of military regimes is stressed in Alfred Stepan, "The New Professionalism of Internal Warfare and Military Role Expansion," in Alfred Stepan, ed., *Authoritarian Brazil* (New Haven, 1973), pp. 47-65. See also Luigi Einaudi, *Peruvian Military Relations with the United States* (Santa Monica, 1970).
3. The original Independence Army led by upper-class Creole Colombians had been destroyed by the Spanish in the early phases of the conflict and had to be replaced by an army full of lower-class, mixed-blood elements that upper-class Colombians found distasteful. See David Bushnell, *The Santander Regime in Gran Colombia* (Newark, Del., 1954), p. 251.
4. Bushnell, *Santander*, pp. 249-50, 258.
5. Anthony P. Maingot, "Social Structure, Social Status and Civil-Military Conflict in Urban Colombia, 1810-1858," in Stephen Therustrom and Richard Sennett, eds., *Nineteenth Century Cities: Essays in a New Urban History* (New Haven, 1969), p. 328.
6. J. León Helguera, "The Changing Role of the Military in Colombia," *Journal of Inter-American Studies* 3 (July 1961): 352.
7. Richard Maullin, *Soldiers, Guerrillas and Politics in Colombia* (Lexington, Mass., 1973), p. 55.
8. Helguera, "Changing Role," p. 353.
9. Ibid.
10. For details see the excellent treatment in Robert H. Dix, *Colombia: The Political Dimensions of Change* (New Haven, 1967).
11. Dix, *Political Dimensions*, p. 297 notes that López was fond of calling the soldiers "parasites." Conservative party strength within the military is discussed in Tomás Rueda Vargas, *El Ejército Nacional (Bogotá*, 1944), pp. 257-61.
12. Maullin, *Soldiers*, pp. 57-58.
13. The events of the Pasto coup are discussed in Francisco Leal Buitrago, "Política e Intervención Militar en Colombia," in Rodrigo Parra Sandoval, ed., *Dependencia Externa y Desarrollo Político en Colombia* (Bogotá, 1970), pp. 173-77.
14. See Richard Weinert, "Violence in Pre-Modern Societies: Rural Colombia," *American Political Science Review* 60 (June 1966): 341.
15. Maullin, *Soldiers*, p. 58.

16. Given its political weakness, Ospina's government periodically sought Liberal party collaboration in coalition cabinets. Such cabinets were formed to be dissolved following a pattern of recurrent political crises. This period is well covered in Martz, *Contemporary Survey*, and Dix, *Political Dimensions*.
17. Gómez suffered a heart attack in 1951 and was replaced by Urdaneta. However, Gómez was really in semiretirement as he could still direct government action through Urdaneta.
18. This crucial period of rising military "politicization" is very well discussed in Lee M. Simpson, "The Role of the Military in Colombian Politics" (Princeton, N.J., B.A. thesis, 1968).
19. Maullin, *Soldiers*, p. 59.
20. Other factions existed, as well, such as that led by Gilberto Alzate Avendaño, but the Ospina opposition posed the most serious threat. Ospina, however, did not openly denounce the government until January 1953 and did not offer himself as a presidential candidate until April 1953. See Simpson, "Role of the Military," p. 62.
21. Dix, *Political Dimensions*, p. 113.
22. *Continuismo* is a process that often triggers political unrest and even coups in Latin America. See Solaún and Quinn, *Sinners*.
23. For details see Dix, *Political Dimensions*. Dix's negative evaluation of the Rojas government is summarized in pp. 122-25.
24. The existence of strong international financial pressures to change his economic policy is revealed by David E. Lilienthal in his *Journal*, vol. 4, pp. 6-15.
25. Rojas claimed that he "stepped down" and actually was not deposed at all. See Martz, *Contemporary Survey*, pp. 240-41.
26. The army constitutes the largest of the three regular services (50,000). It is organized into ten brigades, each quartered in one of Colombia's major cities. The navy and air force together encompass an additional 10,000-12,000 effectives. The National Police (35,000) are also considered to be part of the military although these forces are not included in Table 1.
27. For an analysis of the decline in political participation, see the chapter by Rodrigo Losada in this volume.
28. The military's share of governmental expenditures would have been even higher had the United States Military Assistance Program not provided 10 to 15 percent of the Defense budget in the mid-1960s. See Maullin, *Soldiers*, p. 103. However, except between 1964 and 1967, disclosed U.S. military aid has never been especially high. Colombia received $106.2 million in aid from 1946 to 1969; this was less than the amount received by either Chile or Peru, both of which are smaller in population. See John M. Baines, "U.S. Military Assistance to Latin America: An Assessment," *Journal of Inter-American Studies and World Affairs* 14 (November 1972), pp. 477-81. None of these official figures are highly reliable, however, Many Colombian scholars assume both U.S. aid and the military budget to be much greater than officially disclosed.
29. See for example: Colonel Hermes de Araujo O., "Las Fuerzas Armadas ante la Subversión," *Revista del Ejército* 9 (February 1969), pp. 47-52 and Captain Gustavo Medina P., "Planeación en Colombia," *Revista del Ejército* 5 (September 1965), pp. 173-80.
30. See Stepan, "New Professionalism."
31. The armed forces obtain most of their ammunition and some weapons domestically, although most sophisticated equipment must be purchased abroad. See the discussion in Thomas E. Weil et al., *Area Handbook for Colombia* (Washington,

D.C., 1970), p. 531. The military owns some of its own munitions and weapons industries. See *Revista de las Fuerzas Armadas* (March 1972), p. 16.

32. See *El Siglo* (October 16, 1973), p. 4, and *El Tiempo* (December 17, 1973), p. 1-D.
33. Note the 1973 wage increase of 30 percent discussed in *El Espectador* (December 28, 1973), p. 1. This increase roughly corresponds to the prevalent rate of inflation as described in *El Tiempo* (December 29, 1973), p. 8.
34. Dix, *Political Dimensions*, p. 380.
35. See Einaudi, *Peruvian Military*; Maullin, *Soldiers*, pp. 111-18; and Stepan, "New Professionalism."
36. General Alberto Ruiz Novoa in *Memoria del Ministro de Guerra* (1964), pp. 5-6.
37. General Alberto Ruiz Novoa, "El Derecho de Opinión," *Revista del Ejército* 4 (September 1964), p. 3.
38. *El Tiempo* (January 24, 1965), p. 1.
39. Ibid., (January 28, 1965), p. 1.
40. Ibid., p. 27.
41. Leal Buitrago, "Política," p. 193.
42. Reference is made here to the social reformist military regime that crystallized in Peru after the 1968 coup d'état. For details on this Latin American version of "Nasserism," see Julio Cotler, "Political Crisis and Military Populism in Peru," *Studies in Comparative International Development* 6 (1970-71), pp. 96-113.
43. The negative impact of military politicization on discipline in the Brazilian army is discussed in Alfred Stepan, *The Military in Politics: Changing Patterns in Brazil* (Princeton, N.J. 1971).
44. Of course, these were the arguments also employed by the military leaders in Chile until they finally decided to intervene against Allende.
45. While some of the charges of economic mismanagement against the Rojas government are probably best interpreted as political in origin, there seems little doubt that crisp administration and well-thought-out economic strategy were not among the regime's strong points.
46. The crisis evolved out of the 1968 constitutional reforms which had given the executive more direct budgetary control. See *El Tiempo* (January 28, 1969), pp. 1, 6.
47. See *Latin America* (London, June 4, 1971), p. 1. As ANAPO seems to have had some support in lower echelons of the military, a movement against ANAPO might have reinforced internal divisions.
48. See the discussion in Fernando Cepeda Ulloa and Mauricio Solaún, "Direct Private Foreign Investment in Colombia: A Socio-Political Perspective," *Sonderdruck Aus Viertelijahres Berichte* (Bonn, W. Germany, 1972), pp. 285-305.
49. Most commissioned and even noncommissioned officers are recruited from the middle class; however, a number of elite and upper-middle-class officers still populate the armed forces' higher ranks. On social background and military motivation, see Dix, *Political Dimensions*, pp. 56, 303; and Leal Buitrago, "Política," pp. 199-200. Personal interviews with active and retired officers were also helpful in this respect. A recent article on the tendency of military service to inculcate middle-class values is "Los Militares: de Troperos a Pensantes," *Alternativa* 8 (May 17-June 9, 1974), pp. 16-17.
50. This was clearly the case of the 1953 Colombian coup d'état. See the discussion in James L. Payne, *Patterns of Conflict in Colombia* (New Haven, 1968), pp. 150-51. For Latin America in general see Solaún and Quinn, *Sinners*, pp. 112-18.

51. Military traditions of intervention or nonintervention are usually caused by the historical viability or weakness of civilian political institutions according to Samuel Huntington, *Political Order in Changing Societies* (New Haven, 1969) pp. 194-96.
52. In Colombia, attempts by a leader to continue in the presidency beyond the fixed legal term (*continuismo*), a frequent precipitator of Latin American coups, have been made by only two executives, General Reyes (1904-9) and General Rojas (1953-57), both of whom sought to destroy the traditional party system. See Solaún and Quinn, *Sinners*, pp. 137-38.
53. Of course, the Brazilian case of military intervention in 1964 falls into the easier category explainable by the social revolutionary threat of the Goulart regime and several corollaries. For details see Stepan, *The Military*. A similar classification applies to Chile in 1973.
54. See Germán Guzmán et al., *La Violencia en Colombia* (Bogotá, 1962, 1964). Note also a recent study by Steffen W. Schmidt, "La Violencia Revisited: The Clientelist Bases of Political Violence in Colombia," *Journal of Latin American Studies* 6 (May 1974): 97-111.
55. Maullin, *Soldiers*, p. 28.
56. Dix, *Political Dimensions*, pp. 378-79.
57. Such areas would currently be defined by Marxists as *focos* or nuclei for the spread of revolutionary guerrilla activity. See James Kohl and John Litt, *Urban Guerrillas in Latin America* (Cambridge, Mass., 1974).
58. See Leal Buitrago, "Política," p. 193.
59. See Kohl and Litt, *Urban Guerrillas*, p. 391.
60. The civic action budget particularly decreased after 1968-69 although various programs continued to provide benefits to rural areas. *Plan Andes*, which in 1968 sent many community development units into the country to teach basic reading and other skills, was the most significant of these. See General Gerardo Ayerbe Chaux, *Memoria del Ministerio de Defensa Nacional* (1968), p. 9.
61. Estimate from *El Tiempo* (September 11, 1973), p. 9.
62. A third guerrilla group, the Maoist EPL or Army of Popular Liberation, began operations in Antioquia and Córdoba in early 1967. However, since it is so small (estimates range as low as twenty effectives), it is not considered very significant. See *El Tiempo*, September 11, 1973, p. 9.
63. Roughly seventy guerrillas were killed in the first eight and one-half months of 1973; *El Tiempo*, September 16, 1973, p. 1. See *Memoria del Ministro de Defensa Nacional*, 1962-73, for incomplete figures on earlier soldier and guerrilla deaths.
64. A frequent pattern of army-guerrilla relations throughout Latin America is for long periods of relative inactivity to alternate with cycles of escalating conflict. See Kohl and Litt, *Urban Guerrillas*.
65. On recent army-guerrilla conflict, see *El Espectador*, October 18, 1973, p. 1, and *El Espectador*, December 16, 1973, p. 1.
66. See military claims in *El Espectador*, December 27, 1973, p. 1; and the response of the traditional parties in *El Tiempo*, October 25, 1973, p. 4, or *El Siglo*, December 16, 1973, p. 1.
67. See the whole issue of *Voz Proletaria* (October 23-31, 1973).
68. The official military periodicals obviously best represent the thinking of the military leaders. The degree to which Peruvian-style social reformism persists among lower-ranking officers is unknown since no attitudinal surveys or independent

publications exist. As an example of the new ideological coloration of the highest leadership, see Major General Gerardo Ayerbe Chaux, "La Amenaza Comunista," *Revista del Ejército* 5 (December 1965): 237-40. Interestingly enough, General Valencia Tovar himself was in charge of the military operations that resulted in Camilo Torres's death in 1966 and was later the target of revengeful revolutionary assassins.

69. Letter to *Revista de las Fuerzas Armadas* (June 1972), p. 2.
70. Ayerbe Chaux (1965), p. 238.
71. See the Argentine contribution of Lieutenant General Juan Carlos Onganía, "El Gobierno, las Fuerzas Militares y la Comunidad Nacional," *Revista del Ejército* 4 (September 1964), pp. 517-25. Note also the criticism of the Peruvian military in Major General Jaime Durán P., "Las Fuerzas Armadas Respetan las Instituciones Democráticas," *Revista del Ejército* 12 (1971): 13-14.
72. Ayerbe Chaux, p. 238.
73. For details, see the chapter by Robert Dix in this volume.
74. For the lingering effects of similar processes in Brazil, see Stepan, "New Professionalism."
75. *El Siglo*, October 16, 1973, p. 5.
76. In Colombia, both communism and socialism have been politically weak movements. See Dix, *Political Dimensions*, pp. 269-81.
77. See the discussion of the conservative role of the Chilean middle class and its institutions in Peter A. Goldberg, "The Politics of the Allende Overthrow in Chile," *Political Science Quarterly* 90 (Spring 1975): 93-116. For Brazil see Stepan, *The Military*, pp. 153-71. He shows that the precoup climate of 1964 included an aborted rebellion of enlisted men.
78. The new climate of Liberal-Conservative compromise and cooperation is obvious in the Alvaro Gómez interview cited in *El Tiempo*, May 9, 1974, p. 1, and in the Liberal attitudes expressed in *El Tiempo,* May 7, 1974, p. 4.
79. Huntington, *Political Order*, pp. 220-21, makes exactly this point. The military and the middle class from which it springs can act as reformist forces until the disadvantaged classes are mobilized to the point of posing a credible threat. See also José Nun, *Latin America: The Hegemonic Crisis and the Military Coup* (Berkeley, 1969).
80. See Cotler, "Political Crisis," pp. 96-113.
81. In May 1975, General Alvaro Valencia Tovar was removed from his post in what may have been a programmatic dispute within the armed forces. Valencia Tovar, like Ruiz Novoa, had spoken and written on the social ills of the country. His demise seems to demonstrate again the dominance of the conservative elements within the military. Other sources attribute his dismissal to his support of two insubordinate officers, General Puyana García and Lieutenant Colonel Valentín Jiménez Carvajal, in a dispute with the minister of defense over assignments. On these issues, see "El Golpe Que No Existió," *Visión* (June 15, 1975): 18; "Chafarotismo Contra Illustración," *Alternativa del Pueblo* (June 9-22, 1975), pp. 6-7; and Valencia Tovar's own statement in *El Tiempo* (May 18, 1975), p. 1.

Chapter 7

The Contemporary Church: The Political and the Pastoral

Alexander Wilde

If the Catholic church has a distinctive importance in the development of Latin America,[1] then the church of Colombia is particularly worthy of study. It has long stood out among churches of the region as the most orthodox, conservative, and in some sense, powerful. It is certainly the most successful in terms of its traditional aspirations. "The Catholic Church," wrote the leading historian on the subject, "has been more tenacious in its hold upon national and civil life in Colombia than in any other Latin-American country."[2] This ability to endure through the considerable conflict and upheavals of Colombian history is traceable to the capacity of the church—a capacity possessed by some other traditional institutions, such as the parties—to resist change and yet adapt to it.

The National Front provides abundant evidence about both the success and the limits of the distinctively conservative response of Colombian institutions to change; among these institutions, the church is an especially interesting case. In terms of its own past, it changed perhaps more than any other traditional institution. With perfect consensus, its hierarchy consciously foreswore any participation in partisan politics, burying historical associations with the Liberal-Conservative conflict. It replaced its former loose confederation with a new, more centralized structure of organization. An attempt was made to rethink the fundamental relationship of the church to society; new forms and structures of social action were begun. These initiatives resulted in unprecedented internal conflict, of which the cases of Camilo Torres and the other "rebel priests" were only the most public indications. Yet, for all this, the changes in the church are less striking than its continuity.

This essay is an interpretation of the institutional church (the hierarchy and clergy) during the period of the National Front. To a lesser extent, it is also a study of the National Front, of the ways that Colombia's experiment in grand coalition and the developments in the church affected one another. The National Front represented for the church what seemed like fruitful solutions to several historical problems. These concerned its involvement in partisan politics, its relationship to state and society, and its organizational capacities. We consider these problems in the next two sections, first how they were posed in the traditional church, and the ways in which the church attempted to resolve them during the National Front.

The case of Camilo Torres, the priest-sociologist who became a guerrilla-revolutionary, occupies the central section of the essay. His actions frame many of the fundamental questions about church social action, particularly whether "pastoral" concern can be distinguished from "political" commitment. The succeeding section considers two other forms of church social initiative—a national institute of teaching and research, and grassroots activities of individual priests—that have created conflict over lay autonomy and hierarchical authority. The manner in which these conflicts have been handled suggests some of the directions that the institutional church may take in the future. A concluding section summarizes the problems and suggests an overall interpretation of the church and the National Front.

THE TRADITIONAL CHURCH BEFORE THE NATIONAL FRONT[3]

As an institution, the Catholic church always has a conception of its relationship to society. In any given country, that conception is formed from the general ideas received from the universal church combined with the more particular national experience. The relationship toward which the universal church aspired in modern times was "triumphalist."[4] According to this conception, the purposes of the church were realized when Catholic doctrines were supported by public authority and embodied in public structures. The church assumed a broad tutelage of society in association with the state, and the two were interdependent. The institutional church was part of a regime.

In the view of the traditional Colombian church, these triumphalist aspirations happily coincided with the conditions of its national reality. In Colombia, unlike most of Latin America, it was the proclerical forces that finally triumphed at the end of the civil wars of the nineteenth century. In the long hegemony (1886-1930) of the Conservative party, the church had a privileged place. It was given a kind of corporatist public authority by the constitution (1886) and the concordat with the Vatican (1887).[5] Its moral teachings shaped the curriculum of all public schools and were translated into family law and *rites de passage*. Vocations to the priesthood were the highest in all Latin America.[6] Other religions were virtually absent. The Colombian church did not find it difficult to think itself one with this "Catholic society"—and with the "Christian Republic" that reigned over it.

The traditional church was well suited to such a situation as long as the regime remained stable. If it was threatened by political or social change—as it was after 1930—the traditional institution was in difficulty. It felt threatened indeed by the renascence of the Liberals, the historical anticlerical party, and by the rising level of conflict in society. The Revolución en Marcha government of Alfonso López Pumarejo (1934-38) introduced secularizing reforms in the constitution and in education, thus undermining the public authority previously delegated to the church. Eduardo Santos (1938-42) negotiated a reform in the Concordat in 1942 which, though subsequently left unratified by the Vatican, created serious conflict within the institution. Most seriously of all, the Liberals encouraged the organization of labor unions (CTC) and the mobilization of what the church considered revolutionary rabble, the populist movement led by Jorge Eliécer Gaitán. When Gaitán's death led to an intensification of the Violencia, the breakdown of oligarchical democracy,[7] and the irregular military government of Gustavo Rojas Pinilla (1953-57), the church was far indeed from the conditions which had underlaid its traditional operations.

The church was unsure where to turn when it no longer felt secure in its public authority, and as in past political crises, it was divided on strategy and tactics. From 1930 until the mid-1950s, the larger group allied itself with the Conservative party and stood ready for direct confrontation. This group saw the situation as a crisis of regime and urged militant mobilization. Its members found little difficulty in continuing the habits practiced during the previous Conservative hegemony, when bishops routinely participated in selecting candidates, and parish priests turned out flocks of the faithful at voting urns. In the elections of 1949, there were bishops who called it "mortal sin" to vote for the Liberals; parish priests in some zones of the violence certified Conservatives for safe-conduct passes.[8]

A more moderate group, led by the primate archbishop of Bogotá (Ismael Perdomo, 1928-50), believed that bargaining and conciliation would best protect the institution. The Catholic church was, after all, a public religion—the religion of the whole Colombian people. Some accommodation with a particular government might be necessary, but to identify the interests of the church with one political party brought many dangers. Such a step risked alienation from half the population, to say nothing of the anticlerical persecution that would follow Conservative defeat. It also threatened the central principle of ecclesiastical authority. Priests would grow accustomed to listening more closely to Conservative *gamonales* (local party leaders) than to their own bishops. The politics of partisan mobilization—as the Violencia made increasingly clear—was ultimately uncontrollable: it put the fate of the church in hands other than its own.

But the crisis after 1930 was not merely political; it involved society as a whole. Colombia was undergoing those sweeping, interrelated transformations that are collectively called, rather euphemistically, "modernization": urbanization, industrialization, agricultural commercialization, communications integration, social mobilization. As the bounds of traditional society were broken down, the changes became the underlying causes of the convulsive violence of the 1940s and 1950s.

They had also forced the Colombian church to begin to rethink its relationship to society. Armed with the responses then prevalent in Rome and the European church, the Colombian church began to reach out toward "the world" with structures different from the canonical, hierarchical ones of parish and diocese. The Jesuits in particular were active in creating new bodies of Catholic Action and, more broadly, of "Catholic inspiration." These structures were functional rather than territorial in conception. Meant to perform a new role in or for the church, by linking it to new groups in society that parish organization could not reach, they ranged from university youth groups to the National Union of Colombian Workers (UTC).

These organisms were meant to provide "Catholic" answers for the problems of the modern world. They were conceived as initiatives of "the church" as it was then understood. Although they mobilized lay people,[9] they were intended to remain under clerical supervision, connected to the hierarchical structures of the institutional church. The organization of the traditional church, however, made this a difficult task. Formally hierarchical and national, in reality it was flat and decentralized. At best, authority lay at the level of individual bishops, in their separate diocesan principalities. The church as a whole lacked the mechanisms necessary for sustained, nationwide activities. Most of the new kinds of social action were the result of the entrepreneurship of individual priests (such as Vicente Andrade, S.J., with the UTC). They still awaited the conditions that would enable the church to integrate them into its organization—and through them itself into "developing" society.

The National Front and, almost simultaneously, *aggiornamento* in the church universal brought the necessary conditions. The first finally gave the church new public guarantees, which would remove it (it thought) from partisan politics; the second brought new ideas and resources from abroad to support its social initiatives. However, the new conditions also made manifest the ambiguities—perhaps even contradictions—inherent in the new ways the church was trying to reach out to "the world."

THE CHURCH OF THE NATIONAL FRONT

The National Front, with its stable arrangement of grand coalition, broke the temptation of the church to depend on the Conservative party and therefore erased the historic cause of division within the institution. The Front did this by making the church secure in its public authority, making it part of the regime itself. Catholicism, in the words of the preamble to the 1957 agreement, was indeed the "Religion . . . of the Nation" and an "essential element of the social order." This gesture by the politicians was matched by an equally important event within the church itself: the ascension to the chair of archbishop of Bogotá in 1958 (upon the fortuitous death of Cardinal Luque) of Luis Concha Córdoba. Concha, secretary in his early years to Archbishop Perdomo, had been known throughout his episcopal career as a political moderate (for which he had been excoriated by Laureano Gómez and other Conservative leaders). He was the ideal person to preside over the extrication of the church from "politics," a term that had historically meant partisan conflict.

Despite the challenge of "rebel priests," the hierarchy maintained remarkable unity about the wisdom of such a disengagement throughout the period of the National Front.[10] Overt pro-Conservative electioneering ceased. The head-on clashes of church and state that had been prominent in the political past did not reappear. Where there were issues of vital concern to the church institution—birth control, education, missions, divorce—there was public controversy, but no political confrontation. Instead, party politicians sat down with ecclesiastical elites to work out mutually acceptable solutions (often, as on birth control, involving some facesaving formula for the church).[11] It was a prudent, diplomatic approach to differences within a broader consensus.

Having found what seemed like solutions to old problems, the church turned with unprecedented energies to its own organization. The church of the National Front had, in a sense, greater ambitions than the traditional institution. Profoundly shaken by the Violencia, it could no longer celebrate (in the phrase of Pope Pius XII) Colombia's "four centuries of irreproachable Christianity." Instead, it had to consider itself in a "mission territory." The "task of re-evangelization is urgent among us," said the hierarchy in *La Iglesia ante el cambio* (1969).[12] The organization of the traditional church was attuned to a conception of the "social order," to a certain *state* of society; the new church needed organization appropriate to its *transformation* (or, in the words of the 1973 concordat, its "integral development.")[13]

If the organizational innovation of the church was a response to needs indigenously felt, it was also significantly shaped by conceptions and resources coming from abroad. New programs of social action were encouraged by the larger *aggiornamento* throughout Catholicism in the time of John XXIII. In his directions to the Second Vatican Council, John was particularly concerned that the church come to terms with the secular, the "modern world" against which his predecessors had spoken so shrilly. His encyclicals *Pacem in Terris* (1961) and *Mater et Magistra* (1963), and the council's *Gaudium et Spes*, all suggested a positive view of human society as a place where man could come to know God by helping Him to perfect His creation. If the Christian should not be of the world, he should still live in it, sharing with his fellow men their burdens and joys. It was a vision which suggested a changed conception of the church institution: a saving leaven rather than an embattled fortress.

These ideas took on concrete form in the context of the "developmental decade" of the 1960s. Developmentalism represented a survival of the international "competition" of the Cold War, although the terms were redefined. Urged on by the Cuban Revolution of 1959, the United States and the rest of the so-called West resolved to prove the viability of their "model" in Latin America. They were confident of their ability to understand and manage complex social processes, and they were willing to commit resources to those efforts in underdeveloped countries which reflected their conception of appropriate "infrastructure."

The Vatican shared a similar mentality. It mobilized its resources for what it perceived as the key testing ground for the church international. The Pope issued a call for volunteers to Latin America that drew thousands of priests, nuns, and lay people from Europe and North America. Increasing numbers of Latin American priests were sent abroad for education, not only in the new theology but equally in the techniques of "development" and "modernization" in vogue in the advanced countries. The richer national churches—Germany, Holland, the United States—gave material support to these Latin American priests when they returned home and tried to apply their ideas to their own churches.

The Colombian church underwent two kinds of organizational modernization during the National Front: a strengthening of its central institutional structures and the creation of new forms of social research and action. The Second Vatican Council had given new emphasis to the "collegial" ties of bishops. Within the Colombian Conferencia Episcopal, bishops were assigned to different specialized commissions (some fourteen in number by 1968)[14] in charge of ongoing church concerns such as missions and social assistance. Primed with information and advice from their national Permanent Secretariat (thirty full-time employees, seventy half-time by 1972),[15] they endeavored to direct and manage an extensive enterprise.

A symbol of the process of centralization was the new six-story headquarters for the Permanent Secretariat in Bogotá, which, with the help of financing from the international church, was completed in 1971. Although such an entity was new in the Colombian institution, it was essentially an extension of traditional ecclesiastical conceptions—one very much in keeping with Rome's ideas of the proper sort of *aggiornamento*. It was assigned by canon law, to the bishops, and derived its authority from them. The new central bureaucracy was a kind of national version of the traditional diocesan curia.

The new structures of social action and research, which were much more innovative in terms of traditional organization, also received important international support. Several new research centers were founded to help the church assess both its own resources and its changing environment. The Center of Social Research (CIS, later ICODES), founded by Father Gustavo Pérez Ramírez in 1959, and the Jesuit Center of Social Action and Research (CIAS), founded in 1962, were separate (and sometimes competing) examples of this impulse.[16] A large new building was erected for ICODES with special loans from the Dutch Catholic church, and the institute supported many of its activities with work done on contract for agencies such as USAID.

Both ICODES and CIAS produced research on the church itself and, increasingly, on the society in which it existed.[17] The two centers shared the assumption that social science could be put at the service of the church, that it could modernize church organization and help it be more effective in a new world. (The same assumption initially sent almost all of the men involved in these bodies abroad for training—among them, Camilo Torres.) This concept represented an important break from the suspicion and hostility of the traditional church toward the categories and methods of "positivistic" science.

International resources were also important in expanding social action focused through the parish and *párroco* (parish priest), key elements in the traditional territorial conception of the church. Cáritas Colombia grew into a very large bureaucratic operation because it was an agency of the U.S. Catholic Relief Services (and Food For Peace); it was nevertheless essentially an extension at the national level of the traditional welfare activities of a parish. By the mid-1960s it was coordinating an enormous program distributing food and medicine through parish priests across the country.[18] During the same period, Radio Sutatenza, originally a local undertaking by a single priest, had grown into the national Acción Cultural Popular (ACPO). Monsignor José Joaquín Salcedo (as he had then become) presided over a program of basic education in literacy, religion, and agriculture which reached several million peasants through a nationwide radio network.[19]

Individual parishes founded various social services on their own or with support from their dioceses. The "Minuto de Dios" in Bogotá was founded in 1958 as a model Christian community, the members of which shared more than Mass together on Sundays. Under Father Rafael García Herreros, it grew by the 1970s to a community of some 10,000, which controlled its own stores, banks, schools, and art and recreation centers. In Cali, Colombia's third city, Archbishop Alberto Uribe led in the creation of a series of parish centers which combined cooperatives with schools and health centers in about twenty of the city's poorest *barrios* by the 1970s.[20] These *centros parroquiales* and other initiatives, reflected a greater interest within the church for the material conditions of the faithful. The church was concerned with the development of the whole man and believed that much of it should revolve around the parish unit.

In all, the new structures of the church during the National Front were meant to make it a more effective, active presence in changing society. They were intended to transform the church from the essentially defensive capabilities developed by the traditional institution to resist challenges and protect itself from change[21]—into a more positive power to transform society. It is difficult to conclude that the Church was successful in this undertaking. It did achieve a more modern organization with more systematic information gathering, and orderly decision making, but the new structures had been overlaid upon more traditional ecclesiastical conceptions which emphasized executive control, that is, hierarchical authority. The hierarchy found it hard to tolerate the autonomy necessary at lower levels for creative innovation and tried consistently to circumscribe it. As a result the church lost many who, under less fearful and traditional leadership, might have been a more dynamic force for change.

The church of the National Front remained conservative compared to those elsewhere in Latin America. It stayed strikingly clericalist; it failed utterly to excite the laity energy that produced significant social Christian movements in other countries. Although it acted as host to the 1968 conference of CELAM at Medellín,[22] it clearly disagreed with the progressive conclusions of the conference, particularly the implied need for the church to take active ("political" as the Colombian church saw it) stands against the "violence" of existing society.[23] It consistently supported conservative positions within the Church Universal, as in the 1972 Synod in Rome and its statement on *Justice in the World*.[24]

The organizational modernization of the church did not, in itself, accomplish the more vital involvement in the "integral development" of the nation for which the church had hoped. This was partly due to internal conflict. Such a fundamental transformation of its tasks could not be accomplished smoothly and painlessly simply with better information processing and more informed elite direction as many writers during the period seemed to suggest.[25] Inevitably, men fought about what and how the church should contribute to social change. These issues, ultimately involving the most profound and personal moral concerns, led back to questions about the institution itself—to who made up "the church" and to whom it should be speaking. The normative bases of conflict were paralleled by others of position within the institution—the inescapable clash of interests which accompanied the creation of the organization.[26] Internal conflict absorbed many energies that might otherwise have been directed outward, and partly accounts for the failure of the church of the National Front to change greatly in its social role.

THE CASE OF CAMILO: THE "POLITICAL" AND THE "PASTORAL"

The case of Camilo Torres was a turning point in the complex turmoil within the church. His career, which placed him in many of the structures most involved in social innovation, illustrates many of the options open to the church at the time. Torres's experience clarified his principles, and his efforts to carry out these principles helped his thinking to evolve. The sequence of his choices among Christian alternatives, down to a radical end, had a powerful logic which the institutional church could not accept. In its reaction to him, and to his successors, the church made certain "choices" of its own, foreclosing some possibilities but transforming others.[27]

From the beginning of his clerical career, Camilo Torres was part of the contemporary church effort to reinterpret its broad purposes. He was initially attracted to the priesthood by a socially-conscious interpretation of Christianity which he learned from French Dominicans (and later added to his standard curriculum in the Conciliar Seminary in Bogotá). After his ordination in 1954, he was sent with the special patronage of the cardinal to Louvain, Belgium, for further studies in sociology. In the years following his return to Colombia in 1959, he filled a series of posts in keeping with his dual role as a priest who was also a professional in a worldly sense. He became professor and chaplain at the National University, member of the board of the national agency of agrarian reform (INCORA), dean of a training institute within the government's Higher School of Public Administration (ESAP), restless organizer of pilot projects of social reform (both urban and rural), inveterate participant in seminars and conferences, public lecturer, and teacher.

In this stage of his career, Torres was part of the cutting edge of the church, interpreter to it of the secular, its representative in "the world." His purpose then and after (and presumably that of the church) was to make human society more Christian, just, and loving. The focus of his efforts (and historically that of the church) was the elite, or ruling class. He was deeply concerned about the condition of ordinary people, but at first his strategy for helping them was to change the values of the elite. This he tried to do both in the university and, significantly, the government itself. It was not from an ignorance of his country's politics that he turned away from this strategy. Rather, it was because he did understand something of politics—the ways it reflected not just values but interests—that he came to believe that even if changing the values of the elite were possible, it was not the answer.

In 1965 he went into more direct action. He played a leading role in formulating a "platform" of socioeconomic reforms which became a basis for the United Front. This broad political movement tried to bring together various existing groups of the Left with the "nonaligned" masses.[28] Torres devoted months of effort to addressing large public rallies, editing a newspaper, and attempting to create grassroots organization across the country. Nonvoting was widespread, the masses increasingly disenchanted with the National Front. Conditions seemed ripe for a radicalizing movement. However, government hostility and divisions within the United Front ended its power as an effective political force by September 1965. For Torres, the next logical step was open insurrection.[29] He joined the guerrillas in October 1965 and was shot in an encounter with the army in February 1966.

With this course Camilo Torres repudiated not only the government but also the institutional church. He had stood on the boundary between the church and secular society, his sympathies in the latter frequently in tension with his responsibilities to the former. As early as 1962, during a controversy in which he sided with student rebels at the national university, the basic dilemma was clear. In this case he acceded to Archbishop Concha and resigned his university post, speaking of "the obedience to which I committed myself when I decided to become a priest and which I would not accept now if it were not an integral part of what I consider my mission to the world." At this stage he was still willing to accept that actions dictated by his "conscience" might have to be curtailed to protect "the reputation of the church," for which "responsibility belong[ed] to the bishop."[30]

By early 1965 Torres could no longer take such an attitude. His work in a secular role, in "the world," had given him a new perspective on the institution, a "more objective vision" of it, he wrote. As a sociologist as well as a priest, he could not shut his eyes to the grievous effects of the "economic power of the church and the political power of the church" on its mission. The issue came to a head in April 1965 when the Archbishop tried to bring him under closer supervision, as director of research for the pastoral program of the archdiocese. Torres's "innermost reaction," as he wrote the auxiliary bishop, was "a profound repugnance at the thought of working within the ecclesiastical structure of the church" (i.e., the institutional church, governed by hierarchical authority).[31] In two months he was reduced to the lay state, at his own request. In his opinion, he had to leave the institution to realize the "Christian imperative" of revolution;[32] in the view of the hierarchy, he had left "the church."

There were here, obviously, profoundly divergent ideas about what Christianity should mean for Colombia under the National Front. Torres felt himself forced along his path by his very commitment as a Christian, and by his vision as a sociologist. He was driven by a concern to make Christian love *effective*, which implied to him increasingly a "structural" kind of perspective. Men's social relations should reflect love of their neighbor. All that stood in the way had to be removed. To change elite values was inadequate. Noblesse oblige would never be enough; structures had to be changed. Power had to be met with power, peacefully if possible, violently if necessary.

In the first of his "messages" to various groups published when he was aiding the United Front (significantly, these messages were addressed not to "the church" but simply to "Christians"), Torres put his position in direct terms:

> In Catholicism the main thing is love for one's fellow man: ". . . he who loves his fellow man has fulfilled the Law" (Romans 13.8). For this love to be genuine, it must seek to be effective. If beneficence, alms, the few tuition-free schools, the few housing projects—in general, what is known as "charity"—do not succeed in feeding the hungry majority, clothing the naked, or teaching the unschooled masses, we must seek effective means to achieve the well-being of these majorities. These means will not be sought by the privileged minorities who hold power, because such effective means generally force the minorities to sacrifice their privileges . . . . Thus, power must be taken from the privileged minorities and given to the poor majorities. If this is done rapidly, it constitutes the essential characteristic of revolution. The revolution can be a peaceful one if the minorities refrain from violent resistance.[33]

Characteristically, Torres made no reference to papal encyclicals or to the social teachings of "the church." He started from a central aspect of the Gospel in the New Testament and drew out its implications as he saw them.

The Colombian hierarchy emphatically rejected Torres's argument that the Christian must accept conflict and violence. It did so on the basis of doctrine drawn from the Church Universal and reinforced by its own national experience. The social encyclicals of the Popes had always stressed the natural harmony of the different orders of men. Their concept of social change was a peaceful one in which the separate classes of society could be persuaded to work together for the common good. For Torres this was simply unrealistic. To ignore the way change really came about was for him not simply irrelevant, but indeed un-Christian: the Christian imperative of love of neighbor entailed the acceptance of conflict in order to destroy unjust structures. His ideas centered around this belief, which implied a radical acceptance of "the world'' the church could not endorse. Although his position shared some elements of papal social thinking (e.g., its antiliberalism and anticapitalism), the Colombian bishops were right in thinking that its fundamental thrust and implications broke sharply with established social doctrine. The Pope himself made that clear in his visit to Bogotá in 1968.[34]

The Papal repudiation of violence had particular resonance in Colombia with its memories of the Violencia. Few nations could offer so stark an example of unrevolutionary bloodshed as Colombia, where Torres called Christians to revolution. As Archbishop Concha asked in 1965:

> Isn't the havoc produced through many years of violence enough to force Colombians into a position of prudence? What would be accomplished with the sacrifice of more lives and with the accumulation of more wreckage? Will it be necessary to destroy what our fathers constructed with extraordinary efforts and sacrifices in order to build afterwards on the ruins? Would not this be a program of madmen? No one denies that there is much to do, that there are many things to correct and many injustices to repair; but the remedy is certainly not to destroy everything that exists and to create chaos in order to begin anew and to arrive at who knows where.[35]

The spectre of La Violencia was a continuing presence for the hierarchy into the 1970s.[36] The parties had mobilized for conflict in the past, and some in the church had been involved in it. Now, just when the church had finally extricated itself from an historic problem, the bishops thought, Camilo Torres would begin the devastating dialectic anew, in reckless disregard of the lessons of Colombian history.

It was ultimately for ''politics'' that the hierarchy—and many National Front politicians—condemned Torres and those who followed him. Clerical activation of conflict and hatred could involve the whole institution in contention with secular power all over again and thereby threaten hierarchical authority. For Camilo Torres and his successors, such an attitude was sheer hypocrisy. The church had not ceased, in their eyes, to be ''political.'' It no longer took sides between the traditional parties, but it denied legitimacy to any who challenged them. There was no salvation, politically, outside the National Front.[37] The church was still political because it endorsed and was part of a particular regime. The hierarchy did not consider this ''political'' because it believed the church was part of society as a whole, not merely associated with particular groups—and because it preached conciliation rather than conflict.[38]

The hierarchy consciously tried to lead the church away from ''political'' involvement to ''pastoral'' action.[39] The distinction depended on separating activities proper to priests from those appropriate to lay people. Because ''the world'' must be considered to have a legitimate autonomy, it is the appropriate arena for ''lay'' action. The role of the ecclesiastical institution should be restricted to awakening the consciences of the faithful (*concientización*) by ''counsel,'' ''exhortation,'' and ''promotion.'' ''The creation of new structures,'' wrote the hierarchy, ''is not in our hands'': the salvation of the church is not that of an earthly power.[40] As the Colombian bishops said in 1965, in effect replying to Camilo Torres:

> [T]he activity of priests is . . . necessary, not to substitute for the lay person in tasks and decisions that belong to him, but to form the Christian conscience according to social principles that are derived from Revelation; in order to clarify problems in light of these principles and to stimulate activities necessary. The noble function of the priest in the social field is precisely to sacrifice all personal political interest in order, guided by the Magisterium, to interpret faithfully the demands of the Word of God in social life.[41]

Concientización must be properly understood. The true dignity of man cannot be merely ''temporal'' but must be linked to his salvation through Christ.[42] The church has, to be sure, a ''prophetic office'' to ''denounce structures that impede the process of personalization,'' ''a situation of injustice that can be called institutionalized violence.''[43] But this must not mean taking sides. The ''formation of conscience'' implies:

> a call to the generous collaboration of *all* really to work together in the tasks of an integral development. This call should be directed especially to those who have greater possibilities of shaping decisions in the socio-economic field. ''To you, men of the ruling classes, what can we say? . . . of you we ask generosity. That is, the capacity to . . . serve those who need your wealth, your culture, your authority . . . that your ears and your heart be sensitive to the voices of those who ask for bread, concern, justice . . . .''[44]

Above all the church must not fall prey to the ''temptation of violence.'' The ''so-called'' theologies of liberation and of revolution must be rejected, because they would commit the institution to a violent class struggle.[45]

In practice the ''pastoral'' proved almost as difficult to define and restrict as the ''political.'' Conflict over both arose continually in the years after Camilo Torres's death: with his fellow priest-sociologist Gustavo Pérez Ramírez,[46] with the ''Golconda'' group[47] and ''Sal,'' and with a substantial number of parish priests both in cities and the countryside. The response of the Colombian church, which was consistent with that of Rome, crystalized with the Torres case and grew stronger with every succeeding controversy. Clerical rebels were isolated and, with few exceptions, they left the priesthood. Challenges to hierarchical authority, real or perceived, were not tolerated. Priests might be advisers (*asesores*) but not activists, and "pastoral" action was to remain under the control of those with institutional responsibilities.

The preceding assessment of the church position on clerical involvement in social conflict is fair but gross. A finer judgement is made difficult by the wide range of social activism within the church, whose particularities challenge easy classification as "political" or "pastoral." Moreover, the assessment's emphasis on the conservatism of hierarchical authority—which is surely right in a comparative context—neglects some of the ambiguities inherent in the relationship between hierarchy and clergy. We do not have the scope here to consider such questions systematically, but we can at least illustrate in the next section some of the nuances which should be added and which have, indeed, important implications for the future.

A "PASTORAL" CHURCH?

The Institute of Doctrine and Social Studies (IDES) was established by the Colombian bishops in 1967. Its purpose, like that of the earlier ILADES in Chile, was to relate the social teaching of the church to Latin American development. Intended as an institute of teaching and research, not a political organization in any sense, it was entrusted to the Jesuits (through CIAS), who had long proven their orthodoxy and loyalty in administering the official social action of the hierarchy. However, within a few years, conflicts arose which manifested many of the same characteristics as the earlier problems over politics. That was not surprising, since the underlying questions, the relations of the church with the world, had not disappeared.

IDES performed various functions in discharging its goal "to teach and diffuse social Christian doctrine in order to inspire, stimulate, and orient a coherent and efficacious action relating to the integral development of the countries of the region."[48] Probably its central function was to deepen the social understanding and Christian consciences of people who had (or would have) positions of responsibility in society. The chief vehicle was a nine-month course, which included a section on theology and doctrine along with others on economics, sociology, politics, and other secular subjects. Between 1968 and 1970, this course was attended by some 100 students, about one-third priests and religious, the others lay professionals, university students, and "popular" leaders. The institute also organized shorter courses and conferences, prepared reports, and issued various publications. Groups receiving their services ranged from CELAM, the Franciscans, the Colombian Conference of Bishops, and Acción Cultural Popular, to grammar school principals and professionals studying industrial sociology.[49]

In 1972, direction of IDES was taken from the Jesuits, and the institute was integrated into the National Secretariat of Pastoral Activities (SNPS), part of the new central bureaucracy of the Bishops' Conference. This move was more than a simple attempt to gain greater organizational efficiency. It was the culmination of a series of theological and organizational conflicts over the operation of the institute.

The controversy took concrete form in a critique of IDES sent in September 1971 by Bishop Raúl Zambrano, of the Episcopal Commission on Social Pastoral Activities, to Father Gustavo Jiménez, vice-provincial of the Society of Jesus. Jiménez and the directors of CIAS replied, defending their actions and understanding of the institute. Three interrelated areas of disagreement can be inferred from the letters exchanged:[50] the character of "social Christian doctrine," the appropriate audience for the institute, and its relationship to the institutional church.

The Jesuit-directed IDES understood church social doctrine within the developmental perspective suggested by Pope Paul's *Populorum Progressio*. It saw its object as "elaborating, teaching, and diffusing an overall [global] Doctrine of Latin American Development within a Christian perspective, with solid scientific bases, to the end of inspiring, stimulating, and orienting coherent and efficacious action."[51] Such an interpretation represented a subtle but significant shift of emphasis within the purposes laid down for the institute, away from "social doctrine" per se toward "development." It implied that the secular world was not just a receptacle for Catholic wisdom but something from which Christians might learn. That meant concretely, in the operation of the Jesuit IDES, taking seriously secular interpretations of social change—considering in its courses non-Catholic theories and ideas about, for example, class struggle or international dependency.

After 1972, when the IDES was taken over by the SNPS, it reflected a different orientation. The teaching of theology and the social encyclicals, as the Church's special answers for the problems of the world, was central. The competitive secular ideas about these problems were not so much a source of greater understanding for the church as one of confusion and even danger. Students should learn about such ideas, if at all, from those who possessed the ecclesiastical authority to interpret them. The change of direction in IDES implied a retreat to a more defensive, Catholic-Action kind of mentality in the church.

The second area of controversy over the character of IDES concerned the nature of its audience. The Jesuit IDES had included in its courses and other activities a large proportion of people from secular roles and organizations. That followed naturally enough from its belief that development was "in great part a responsibility of the temporal order." It also implied a genuine independence of lay people within the church itself: "[W]e think that IDES should form its students in such a way that they decide for themselves, in their own conscience, where and how they are going to exercise their vocation of agents of social change: . . . linked to a trade union movement, to a political party or if they prefer 'a closer hierarchical connection to fit themselves into plans of social pastoral action in the diocese to which they belong.'''[52] Within such a conception of its audience the Jesuit IDES had, in 1970, received requests for courses and seminars from secular bodies such as the Agrarian Reform Agency (INCORA), the government's Community Action program, the Division of Indian Affairs of the Interior Ministry, the largest national peasant organization (ANUC, the "Usuarios"), and the government's vocational training institute (SENA).

The conception of Monsignor Zambrano and the other bishops, embodied in the later SNPS-directed IDES, was different. They saw IDES as primarily a servant of the institutional church. That meant training above all priests and religious from Colombia (one-third of the previous students had been from other countries). Lay people were to be included, but, in the manner of Catholic Action, from among those who worked in diocesan pastoral programs under episcopal authority.

This was related to the third area of disagreement over IDES, the extent to which it should be controlled by the hierarchy. It became placed essentially within the national curia structure, that is, presumably under the direct authority and supervision of the bishops. IDES was to be the handmaiden of the hierarchy.[53] The Jesuits had conceived of it as a much more autonomous body, which took responsibility for its own actions under the more diffuse, general commitment of the Society of Jesus to the ecclesiastical institution. During the years the Jesuits had operated IDES, there had been much concern about the need for openness, dialogue, and more generally democratic kinds of relationships within the organization. Again innovation in the external purposes of IDES (over, for example, whether *concientización* of a relative handful of elites was an effective contribution to change) developed more questions about its internal structure. To the extent that the hierarchy was unwilling to consider such challenges in the institution as a whole, they were right to end the experiment and to restrict the autonomy of IDES.

The resolution of this particular church controversy over the control of the definition of "pastoral" was just one stage in a continuing dilemma. What is a "pastoral" church? Clearly, it differs from the traditional church, which exercised its functions primarily through political influence and public authority. "Pastoral" evokes the image of the shepherd and his flock, the priest and his parish. Pastoral theology deals above all with "the care of souls." But in the modern world, after the Second Vatican Council, such concerns are no longer as simple as they once seemed: what is needed to "care for souls"? Indeed, who even is "the flock"?

The Colombian church has tried to pull back from clerical "politics," mobilization of conflict, but it cannot avoid these questions. Its central religious message, the ideas contained in church documents, and the convictions they engender raise the same question again and again. Centralization had made bishops and priests throughout the country aware of (the most orthodox) contemporary social thinking within the church. The national hierarchy collectively was given a month-long course on current theology in Bogotá in 1972, an unprecedented event in the Colombian church. In the mid-1970s, the reformed IDES sent out teams to most of the dioceses of the country to present similar courses at a lower level. The implications of the ideas taught and discussed are difficult to predict, but it is already clear that they are not confining the church to some new other-worldly spirituality.

The most significant signs of this, perhaps, are the continuing cases of socially-active *párrocos*. At the grassroots, more priests than ever before understand their "pastoral" responsibilities to include making their flock aware of their full human dignity through activity in this world (*concientización*). For some this has included innovation in liturgy and parish organization; for others, it has meant solidarity with the causes and interests of the people in their parish.

The action of these parish priests, many of whom have actively sought the support of their bishops, is slowly broadening the conception of what is legitimate "social-pastoral" activity. In 1965, the hierarchy found it easy to call Camilo Torres "political" for his platform and United Front. It found itself compelled, on the other hand, to consider Padre Jaime Santander "pastoral" in 1972, when he was jailed for publically defending the rights of his parishioners against government officials who had seized peasant land in Manatí. The Jesuit provincial, Fernando Londoño, who made a personal investigation of the case, wrote in his report:

> The facts known, my position is of total solidarity with Father Santander's attitude. I do not think that that of the Province can be different. . . . It is a difficult task, not to fall into injustice in the name of justice. But it is a really courageous position, in conformity with commitment to the Gospel, to defend justice even at the risk of suffering persecution. What impressed me most is his *clearly priestly attitude*, the absence of any cheap populism. He is a brother of ours who fights sincerely for ideals that must be very dear to us. Perhaps we are not accustomed to *these challenges of the apostolate in our time*. Let us recall today, the 31st of July, that San Ignacio [founder of the Society of Jesus], victim of outrages and prisons, demanded that the justice of his cause be made clear.[54]

Let us consider, briefly, some of the range of social action at the local level in a single region. The Cauca Valley was an area of general rural change and intense peasant violence during the 1950s and 1960s. By the latter half of the National Front, the church was engaged in three different kinds of social action in the valley: the Jesuit-sponsored FANAL peasant federation, the parish-based programs of Cáritas in the archdiocese, and the work of individual parish priests.

FANAL was active principally through the organizing efforts of Jesuit Padre Célico Caicedo. Caicedo's approach was eminently religious and "pastoral." He tried to build study groups around parish priests throughout the region, in order to form lay leaders who would then promote and participate in Christian forms of social change. His message was social Christian doctrine, his method that of consciousness raising. *Concientización* tried to begin with the experiences of the participants and then to induce from them Christian perspectives on ideas such as the dignity of the individual and the nature of work. As in the message of Camilo Torres, the stress was on the love of neighbor, an ethical conception of Christianity. Caicedo proceeded from the assumption that social change was inevitable; if it were not made by the church, it would surely be made against it. The church should participate in the process primarily through ideas and values.

The second group of programs, Cáritas-Cali, used one of the most traditional functions of the church, social assistance, for much broader purposes. On the foundation of the distribution of food and medicines, the program stimulated various kinds of change in rural parishes in the archdiocese. One was liturgical reform, with more "community Masses" and lay homilies. The Mass was frequently linked to social-action meetings on community concerns (much in the manner of César Chávez in his farmworker organizaton in the U.S.). Cáritas-Cali also stimulated *concientización* and new kinds of adult catechetical instruction (virtually nonexistent in the traditional church). Finally, it helped broaden parish activities to include organizing cooperatives and community stores. Like FANAL, it operated within the hierarchical structure of the church in ways that enlarged the social content of "religious" and "pastoral."

In addition to these more organized efforts, individual priests, such as Padre Santander in Manatí, defended what they considered the just interests of their peasant flocks. Concretely, this meant cooperating with various land invasions in the area and attempting to use the church (e.g., the archbishop of Cali) to intervene on behalf of the peasants.[55] Sometimes priests tried explicitly to justify their actions in terms of Catholic social values; at other times they seem to have acted out a kind of mute priestly witness.[56]

These efforts did make a visible immediate impact, although their capacity to affect the overall direction of change is not clear. Father Caicedo had more than 700 meetings with FANAL leaders and gave some eighty courses to several thousand people over a five-year period.[57] Cáritas-Cali had some effect on parishes in about thirty *municipios* over about eight years. ANUC and FANAL in the valley had priests among their organizers and frequently justified their public actions by referring to Catholic ideas about property and the human person.[58] Landowner complaints made it clear that the clergy was no longer a reliable protector of the "sacred right" of private property.[59]

Such social action in the rural districts was reflected in the pronouncements of the hierarchy, which had historically defended landed interests.[60] Bishops began to speak more often of the social functions of property, its necessary relation to the common good, rather than of private rights.[61] They collectively endorsed peasant organization as the only way for the rural poor to improve their lot.[62] The peasant movement clearly enjoyed strong sympathies among the Colombian Jesuits, who gave it extensive coverage in their various publications.[63]

Even more important than such indicators were the changes in the behavior of ecclesiastical elites in the face of the conflicts that continuously arose at the local level, as individual priests pursued what they took to be the demands of social justice. Each case confronted elites with choices—whether to support such initiatives as the work of "the church," whether to disavow them as disruptive betrayals of its institutional mission, or simply to be silent. In the early 1970s, notable cases occurred in which elites were willing to back their priests if they were convinced that the priests' actions fit within a broadening conception of the "pastoral." The support of Padre Santander at Manatí by all the superiors of the Jesuit order in Colombia was significant:

> Faithful to the orientations of the Church and urged by the situation of our peasantry, we feel obligated to denounce injustices wherever they are found.... In accord with the line of conduct laid down by the Provincial Superiors of Latin America, ... we propose to give the social problem "an absolute priority in our apostolate as a function of this problem." ... We feel solidarity with priests, religious, and lay people that, following the norms of the Hierarchy and with an authentically evangelical spirit, have committed themselves to the defense of the weak and given a voice to those who had none. We are profoundly troubled therefore that forces exist in Colombia that try to gag evangelical freedom with tactics that range from the subtle labeling as "subversive" or "rebel" every priest committed to a social apostolate all the way to putting them in prison.[64]

In other cases of agrarian conflict, bishops took no public position regarding the activities of their priests. Even such tacit tolerance marked an important change from earlier times, when episcopal support for the powerful was almost automatic.

The church's proper "pastoral" relationship with society, however, will continue to be controversial. It involves a fundamental conflict between the authority of the church and the autonomy of "the world" (and the questions of who represents each). The church risks irrelevance if it does not, in some sense, "accept" the secular, with rules of its own (e.g. the positive purposes of social conflict). But it risks the very core of its identity, its transcendental mission, if it does not remain distinct from the secular and hold up to society standards other than those of the world. The church wants to "accept" the world, and at the same time, make it (in some sense that Christians profoundly believe) "better." A "pastoral" definition of the church assumes it has a special responsibility to edify the world; those in the institution can all share this assumption even while they continue to disagree over how to go about it.

CONCLUSION

For the church, the National Front seemed to solve certain important problems of long standing. The constitutional agreement between the two major political parties give the religious institution secure public authority, allowing it to disengage from traditional partisan conflict. It was then able, with support from the international church, to devote new energies to its own organization and to try to create the basis for an active, "pastoral" involvement in social change. These new aspirations, however, created considerable internal conflict, which prevented the church from achieving the unified impact on "development" it desired. Internal dissent may have been the reason for this frustration, which it shared with other churches in Latin America, but it does not explain the conservatism of the Colombian case. For that we must consider the national environment in which the church existed.

The National Front was a negative formation, meant to *prevent* rather than create. The regime (and the church within it) was addressed to "old problems," particularly partisan violence, and the solutions adopted did not go beyond institutionalizing traditional, more informal exchanges. The National Front governments, formed to avoid a problem, did not legitimate any positive change. The conditions surrounding the birth of the regime limited what was possible within it.[65]

The social initiatives of the church during this period, like the programs of the National Front governments, attempted to pour new wine from old skins. The traditional structures of the church had historically possessed substantial *defensive* capabilities—the clerical mobilization of its lay "reserves of loyalty" to defend the institution from external threat. Those structures of parish and diocese were in fact considerably strengthened by the organizational modernization that took place during the National Front, but such change did not institute a shift from defensive to innovative involvement. In particular the church failed to gain any clear and creative new way to deal with internal conflict, which it tried to resolve by extending hierarchical authority. Since the church had neither a strong positive vision nor the sort of inspired leadership which could greater appreciate the creative possibilities of conflict, the insistence that the change should be directed by the existing elite meant that no transformation was really possible.

Beyond its lack of *mística*, the National Front did not face the kind of coherent, organized political challenge that might have forced more significant change. During the period there were, certainly, feelings of malaise and disorientation. The electoral abstention, the rural insurgencies, the various "rebel priests" were all perhaps signs of an incipient crisis, but not of a felt emergency. No person, no group was able to channel these forces and shake the regime. The transitoriness of the threat of ANAPO, the only possible exception, confirms the generalization. The simplest fact about the National Front is that it persisted. Colombia did not experience a crisis (and in most cases change) of regime in the same way as did Cuba, Brazil, Peru, Chile, Uruguay, or Argentina.

Such a setting meant that the deepest questions were not imposed so powerfully upon the Colombian church as on its counterparts elsewhere. Even after the Violencia it maintained recruitment to the priesthood at high aggregate levels;[66] it could afford to remain a clericalist institution.[67] It did not face a strong Marxist movement or an ambitious military. Most relevantly, it did not have to deal with a significant social Christian movement, under autonomous lay leadership. The small Social Christian Democratic party (PSDC) never constituted a viable political alternative. Perhaps the Conservatives, the traditional proclerical party, in some sense preempted its potential by their long-term survival and relative success. In any case the absence of a strong social Christian party meant that any link to politics almost necessarily had negative connotations for the institutional church, and therefore priests such as Camilo Torres were impelled to more radical alternatives.[68] (Whether such a "middle way" would have been a viable basis for change—in light of the fate of the church and the Christian Democrats in Chile since the late 1960s—is another question.)

The ultimate reason, however, for the basic conservatism of the church under the National Front is that those in it continued to conceive of the church above all in institutional terms; it was, therefore, identified primarily with its ecclesiastical structures, which were in turn associated with a larger regime of authority. The central tenet of such a self-definition is survival; it implies accommodation. But it also implies acceptance of a certain internal pluralism around several purposes.

In defining the adaptation of the institution to "the world," the most broadly accepted relationship was "pastoral." Although the emphasis on "pastoral" was intended to keep the clergy out of "political" conflict, its practice over time became more political. During the last years of the National Front, "pastoral" action came to include not only the "formation of Christian conscience" in lay people, but also acts of clerical solidarity with the poor, and "prophetic" denunciation of injustice. These "pastoral" functions are embraced by even the moderate middle group of the hierarchy: "[The church] must go beyond the clear exposition of the principles that regulate economic and sociopolitical relationships to the frank and brave denunciation of situations which violate the ethical order, although that endanger the mere established order."[69] What is perhaps even more germane, they are the basis for concrete actions by individual priests at the local level. Every time a *párroco* accompanies peasants who have "invaded" lands, bishops are confronted with a choice between supporting their priest or backing secular power.

What is most significant about new forms of this "social apostolate" is that it commits even those holding an institutional conception of the church to direct involvement in social conflict. For the hierarchy to become involved in this way does not depend in the first instance on their own commitment to clerical activism. It simply depends on their desire to preserve unity within their institution[70] in the face of "pastoral" initiatives by their clergy at the grassroots. Naturally they attempt to exercise their episcopal authority, but they must also adapt to pressures from below. Their leadership implies finding the position which will unite the largest number within the institution. At a time when they have self-consciously tried to deepen their religious mission, it becomes increasingly hard to disavow "pastoral" actions of "their" people who are in conflict with secular interests.

This is, admittedly, an optimistic interpretation of recent trends (from the point of view of those who, like myself, hope that the church can help to create a more just society). But a "pastoral" church is not a "prophetic" church. The former is possible within an institutional conception; the latter is not. A "pastoral" redefinition marks a break from the political and cultural Catholicism of the traditional church while trying to keep the institution away from the commitments that have been so divisive in the past. A more active, partisan kind of commitment, the bishops would say, would be sociological suicide—even if it could be justified theologically. Even if the church could be effectively united around such a position, what of the rest of society? The church would not be strong enough to carry the day alone. And when it lost, what then? Who would protect and carry on the message of salvation? The church must not lag very far behind the consciousness of its society, but it cannot go very far in advance of it. The church always needs its prophets, but it cannot itself be one.

The Colombian church still has its prophets, and it will continue to have them. It will also have an elite determined to protect the institution. The two will continue to exist in a kind of dialectical tension. The hierarchy will attempt to restrain lower-level initiatives and to organize more integrated efforts. However, if they are to succeed in these efforts, they must listen as well as command.[71] Thus, a kind of contradiction will continue, within the church, despite its monolithic pretensions.

This is inherent in its institutional character, and it is what maximizes its capacity for survival. Colombia during the National Front was shot through with emotive symbols, but social reality proved complex and contradictory. In such a setting, the preservation of the church as an institution has special importance. Its institutional character is ambiguous: while it hinders innovation, it can protect dissent. This latter quality may become critical if future change in Colombia resembles that of the past—confused, halting, and frequently violent. Then the institutional church, if it is secure in its central religious concerns, can again take on its medieval function as a place of refuge. The recent history of Latin America demonstrates that this may be the greatest contribution of the church to the dignity of the human individual.

NOTES

Research for this study was completed in September 1975.

1. The pathbreaking analysis by Ivan Vallier, *Catholicism, Social Control, and Modernization in Latin America* (Englewood Cliffs, N.J., 1970) is essentially concerned with this question. Like other students of the contemporary Latin American church, my debt to Vallier is great and will be evident throughout this study.
2. J. Lloyd Mecham, *Church and State in Latin America*, 2nd ed. (Chapel Hill, N.C., 1966), p. 115.
3. This section in particular is drawn freely from my book, *Politics and the Church* (Durham, N.C., forthcoming), which deals at length with the development of the traditional church in Colombia.
4. The culmination of such a conception in the pontificate of Eugenio Pacelli, Pope Pius XII, is brilliantly discussed in Malachi Martin, *Three Popes and the Cardinal* (New York, 1972).
5. The concordat, which is printed in full in English in Mecham, *Church and State*, pp. 126-31, was regarded by the Vatican as a model of its kind.
6. A comprehensive survey done in the 1960s grouped the Colombian church with those of Chile and Ecuador as the strongest in Latin America. See Ivan Labelle and Adriana Estrada, *Latin America in Maps, Charts, Tables*; No. 2, *Socio-Religious Data (Catholicism)* (Cuernavaca, Mexico, 1964), pp. 270ff. Colombia produced proportionately the largest number of native diocesan priests in the region and, in comparison to Chile, was much less dependent on foreign priests. See pp. 85-192, passim.
7. For a general characterization of this regime and an analysis of the processes of breakdown, see my *Conversaciones de caballeros: quiebra de la democracia oligárquica en Colombia* (Bogotá, 1979).

8. See *El Colombiano* (Medellín), June 4, 1949, "Los Obispos Colombianos hablan sobre elecciones: claras instrucciones se imparten a los Católicos," and John D. Martz, *Colombia: A Contemporary Political Survey* (Chapel Hill, N.C., 1962) pp. 84, 92. Most of the priests in novels about the Violencia are partisan militants. See Gerardo Suárez Rondón, *La novela sobre la Violencia* (Bogotá: Ed. Luis F. Serrano A., 1966) pp. 61-80, for a discussion of various perspectives.
9. The Spanish word *seglares*, or "secular people," is used interchangeably with *laicos*, or "laity." This lack of distinction between a social term and a religious one is natural enough in a society which is conceived in its entirety as somehow "Catholic." But in historical context it implies that the laity were not really considered *part* of "the church"; rather, they were its clients.
10. The deaths of the only two bishops considered at all "progressive" in the hierarchy—Gerardo Valencia Cano (1972) and Raúl Zambrano Camader (1974)—strengthened the conservative consensus. Although it has had ample opportunities, Rome has apparently not felt called to give the hierarchy a more progressive cast through new appointments (as it did earlier in Brazil, Chile, and Peru).
11. Colombia had one of the most extensive birth control programs in Latin America in the 1960s, at the same time that the Colombian hierarchy fully endorsed the Pope's prohibitions. The government's major concession was to operate through formally autonomous university faculties of medicine, rather than administer the program directly. See Thomas Sanders, "Family Planning in Colombia," American Universities Field Staff Reports, West Coast South American Series, Vol. 17, No. 3 (1970); and the useful undergraduate thesis (at the Universidad de los Andes, Departamento de Ciencia Política) on the topic by Rafael Piñeros Pardo, "La Iglesia y la política demográfica del país," 1970.
12. The whole second part (pp. 87-117) of this document, the most important systematic statement of the contemporary hierarchy, (Bogotá, 1969), departs from this premise (p. 89).
13. Article I. The concordat is reprinted in full in Andrés Holguín, *Análisis del nuevo concordato* (Bogotá, 1973), pp. 67-76. Holguín urged that the Colombian Congress refuse to ratify the agreement negotiated by the executive.
14. *Directorio Católico Latino-Americano, 1968* (Bogotá), pp. 184-85.
15. "La Iglesia Colombiana: su evolución, sus problemas, sus perspectivas: entrevista con Mons. Muñoz Duque," *El Catolicismo* (Bogotá), July 30, 1972, p. 8.
16. Such research was also undertaken by individual dioceses, sometimes also with support from abroad. The province of Medellín (including the archdiocese and four neighboring dioceses) undertook an extensive survey of its own in 1968. It was originally intended to make studies of a wide variety of aspects of the provincial Church and its environment, including demography, economic conditions, education, religious attitudes, and practice. Despite some funding from the Latin American Bureau of the U.S. Catholic church, not all the studies were finished. A similar local undertaking was made in the archdiocese of Manizales somewhat later.
17. Examples of the first kind would be Zuluaga, *Estructuras eclesiásticas;* Gustavo Pérez, *Anuario de la Iglesia Católica* (Bogotá, 1961); Gustavo Pérez, *El problema sacerdotal en Colombia* (Bogotá, 1962); and Gustavo Pérez et al., *Población, Iglesia y cultura: sistemas en conflicto* (México, 1970); and a large number of more restricted studies, done on contract. Studies of society were even larger in number, including books by Gustavo Pérez such as *El campesinado Colombiano*

(Bogotá, 1959) and (with Juan Luis de Lannoy), *Estructuras demográficas y sociales de Colombia* (Bogotá, 1961), and a long list of titles published by CIAS, such as Hermann J. Mohr et al., *La revolución demográfica* (1966), *Impuestos y desarrollo económico de Colombia* (1969), and *Hacia una reforma agraria masiva* (1971).

18. Cáritas-Colombia in 1968 reached 1,019 of the 1,622 parishes in the thirty-two dioceses and archdioceses and three mission territories. See Departamento de Promoción y Coordinación, *Estudio institucional de Cáritas* (Bogotá, 1969), Table 3.
19. Among the many studies of ACPO are: Camilo Torres and Berta Corredor, *Las escuelas radiofónicas de Sutatenza-Colombia* (Bogotá, 1961); Stefan A. Musto et al., *Los medios de comunicación social al servicio del desarrollo rural* (Bogotá, 1971); and Hernando Bernal Alarcón, *Educación fundamental integral y medios de comunicación social* (Bogotá, 1971). The basic literacy method was much copied in the rest of Latin America, notably by the Basic Education Movement of Brazil (MEB), which gave it a more radical content.
20. An extensive study of the operation of the centers was made by Drs. Rodrigo Guerrero V. and Humberto Lores G., for the Fundación Hernando Carvajal, which funded some of their operation.
21. Eldon Kenworthy has seen this essentially defensive kind of power as characteristic of Latin American politics. See "Coalitions in the Political Development of Latin America," in Sven Groennings et al., eds. *The Study of Coalition Behavior* (New York, 1970), esp. pp. 115-24.
22. The conference was held at Medellín, according to CELAM staff, because the seminary outside the city there was the only place in Latin America both isolated enough to protect the proceedings from a prying press and large enough to house all the Latin American bishops and their entourage.
23. The conclusions of the Medellín conference are available, CELAM, *La Iglesia en la actual transformación de América Latina a la luz del Concilio*, vol. 2: "Conclusiones" 2nd ed. (Bogotá, 1969). A useful brief discussion in English, which reflected the widely-held view that the meeting charged a whole new direction for the Latin American church, is David Abalos, "The Medellín Conference," *Cross Currents*, vol. 19, no. 2 (Spring 1969), pp. 113-32.
24. The volume *La justicia en el mundo* (Bogotá, 1972) documents the process of consideration of the bishops from the first draft for discussion through the final document. The Colombian hierarchy intervened primarily to criticize the "structural" analysis of the draft and any implied legitimation accorded to violent opposition—a position much more reflected in the ultimate synodal document.
25. Vallier, in *Catholicism*, was very optimistic about organizational modernization.
26. David Mutchler, a former Jesuit, emphasised competing bureaucratic interests as the major basis for intrachurch conflict in Colombia and Chile, *The Church as a Political Factor in Latin America* (New York, 1971). Though a useful corrective to prevailing ideological explanations, Mutchler's perspective was ultimately reductionist because it neglected the *operative* significance of normative conflict.
27. The biography *Camilo Torres*, by Walter J. Broderick (New York, 1975) is highly personal, thorough, and indispensible. The best collection of Camilo's writings is the very complete and extensively annotated *Cristianismo y revolución*, ed. Oscar Maldonado, Guitemie Olivieri, and Germán Zabala (México, 1970). The other full-length biography of Torres, Germán Guzmán, *Camilo Torres*, trans. John D. Ring (New York, 1969) reprints some useful documents but does not distinguish

clearly between Torres's ideas and the author's own. Other collections of Torres's extensive published works are *Revolutionary Writings*, ed with an introduction by Maurice Zeitlin (New York, 1972) and *Revolutionary Priest*, ed. with an introduction by John Gerassi (New York, 1971). A good realistic overview is John Womack, "Priest of the Revolution," *New York Review of Books*, October 23, 1969, pp. 13-16.

28. The group members of the Frente Unido were the Communist party (both lines); the hard-line and youth movement (Vanguardia) of the Movimiento Revolucionario Liberal (MRL); the youth organization, trade unions (CLASC), and some party elements (PSDC) of the Christian Democratic movement; the *Movimiento Obrero-Estudiantil-Campesino*, and the *Vanguardia Nacional Popular*.
29. Broderick is original in dating Camilo's decision to join the guerrillas *before* the launching of the United Front. In this light the movement does not represent a more conventional political strategy—from the failure from which Camilo learned and was radicalized—but rather the preliminary phase of urban organizing, of a revolutionary commitment he had already made. See Broderick, *Camilo Torres*, chs. 9-10.
30. See Gerassi, ed., *Revolutionary Priest*, pp. 163-65.
31. Quotations are from Gerassi, ed., *Revolutionary Priest*, pp. 302, 303, 305.
32. *La revolución: imperativo cristiano* was the title of a study (at that stage rather theoretical) published for Camilo in 1965 by the Christian Democrat Ediciones del Caribe (Bogotá).
33. Gerassi, ed., *Revolutionary Priest*, pp. 367-68.
34. See his homily printed in full in *El Tiempo* (Bogotá), August 24, 1968, p. 20.
35. Cited by Guzmán, *Camilo Torres*, p. 136.
36. Daniel Levine, who systematically interviewed virtually all the Colombian bishops in 1972-1973 found that many of them spontaneously raised the relationship between political activism and violence. See Alexander Wilde and Daniel Levine, "The Catholic Church, 'Politics,' and Violence: The Colombian Case," paper prepared for the conference of the Rocky Mountain Council of Latin American Studies, Glendale, Arizona, April 24-26, 1975, pp. 17-18. The theme was echoed in innumerable documents of the hierarchy after 1965, its tone set by the statement issued at the height of the United Front, "On the Social Moment of the Country," printed in *Revolución violenta*? (Bogotá, August 1965).
37. The hierarchy more or less explicitly tended to endorse candidates of the National Front by warning Catholics against voting for those who advocated violence or the destruction of the existing social order. See, for example, the passages quoted from their statement before the 1966 election, in Oscar Maldonado, "Las elecciones del 20 de Marzo en Colombia," *CIDOC Informa*, vol. 3, no. 8 (April 15, 1966), pp. 137-41. Cf. those quoted briefly in *Anali-CIAS*, no. 21 (February 1974), pp. 44-45, covering the final election of the National Front in 1974.
38. A deeper exploration of the different conceptions of "politics" of the hierarchy on one hand and of Camilo and his successors on the other (particularly following the theology of liberation), is found in Wilde and Levine, "The Catholic Church, 'Politics,' and Violence."
39. See the lecture given by Msgr. Darío Castrillón, coadjutant bishop of Pereira, at the Higher War College in April 1973, "Política y pastoral," *Tierra Nueva* (Bogotá), vol. 2 (July 1973), and the influential article by Msgr. Alfonso López Trujillo, the most important defender of the "nonpolitical" position (and now

head of CELAM, the regional conference of Latin American bishops), "El Cristiano ante la política, "*El Catolicismo* (Bogotá), February 22, 1972.

40. *La Iglesia ante el cambio*, p. 43; *La justicia en el mundo*, p. 62. The distinction of appropriate spheres of action is invoked repeatedly throughout the former.
41. *Revolución violenta*?, p. 8.
42. See especially the overview of Archbishop (later Cardinal) Aníbal Muñoz Duque, upon leaving the presidency of Bishops' Conference, "Panorama pastoral del país," *Documentación* (IDES), no. 17, July 1972.
43. *La Iglesia ante el cambio*, pp. 43. 42.
44. Ibid., p. 44 (emphasis in original). The quoted passage is from Pope Paul VI, "Discurso en el día del Desarrollo," (Bogotá, August 23, 1968).
45. See *La Iglesia ante el cambio*, esp. pp. 44-46; and Muñoz Duque, "Panorama pastoral," esp. pp. 12-14. Two collections from a conference held in Colombia on the newer theological currents are *Liberación: opción de la Iglesia Latinoamericana en la década del 70* (Bogotá, 1970), and *Liberación en América Latina; Encuentro teológico* (Bogotá, 1971). A very sophisticated critique by the (at that time) auxiliary bishop of Bogotá, Alfonso López Trujillo, is "La Liberación y las liberaciones," *Documentación* (IDES), no. 13 (Bogotá, Febrary 1972).
46. It would be interesting to compare the careers of Torres and Pérez. They were students together at Louvain and cooperated in various ways up to Torres' political last phase. Pérez was a strong sympathizer with Torres to the end but tried to stay within the institutional church. For years he directed the ICODES center for sociological research. As his own thinking evolved, he encountered increasing hostility from the hierarchy. He tried alternatives within the church which Torres had not—various leaves abroad, a parish ministry within the slums—but eventually he was also forced out of the priesthood. Mutchler's treatment of him, *Church as a Political Factor*, is a cruel careerist caricature. This is unfair not only to Pérez personally but to the many other priests caught painfully between their social beliefs and their ecclesiastical vows.
47. There is no study of the rise and fall of the Golconda group as a movement. Among available sources are: *Golconda: el libro rojo de los "curas rebeldes,"* ed. Anita Weiss and Octavio Belalcázar (Bogotá, 1969); "Social-Activist Priests: Colombia, Argentina" (Washington D.C., 1974); and Rick Edwards, "Religion in the Revolution? A Look at Golconda," *NACLA Newsletter*, vol. 3, no. 10 (February 1970).
48. Article 13 of its statutes. The "region" mentioned is the northern part of South America.
49. This case study of IDES is based in addition to sources cited below, on interviews carried out in Bogotá and Bucaramanga in July and August of 1972, on prospectuses issued by IDES in 1969 and 1972, on a mimographed report of its activities (August 1970), and on its monthly publication, *Documentación* (in its fifth year in 1975).
50. The three letters involved were mimeographed and circulated by CIAS—an important break from traditional patterns of reserve and an indication of the depth of feeling on the issues.
51. IDES prospectus, 1969, p. 1.
52. Father Gustavo Jiménez C., S.J. letter of October 18, 1971 to Bishop Raúl Zambrano Camader. The phrase he quotes is from the earlier letter of Bishop Zambrano.
53. An effort was made to bring ACOP— another autonomous national structure of

social action—more closely under central curial control about the same time. The move seems to have been based primarily on the desire to make clear its subordination to hierarchial authority, rather than any "dangerous" practices on its part. With its outside resources (e.g., from the U.S.) and more personalistic character (under Msgr. Salcedo), it was more successful than IDES resisting.

54. *Anali-CIAS*, No. 5 (August 1972), p. 4; a monthly publication of the CIAS center, Bogotá.
55. In the case of Bitaco in 1972-73, the archbishop played a role in attempting to free peasants who had been jailed. Indians invaded lands of the archdiocese of Popayán in 1973. After negotiations and with some bad grace, the archbishop donated the lands. See *Anali-CIAS*, no. 14 (June 1973), pp. 13-14; and no. 20 (January 1974), p. 44.
56. They seem to embody the conception that Camilo Torres had in mind when he wrote: "The priest . . . should weep with those who weep and rejoice with those who rejoice. He should carry out the Incarnation of the Lord by taking full responsibility for the human adventure of his flock." (Gerassi, *Revolutionary Priest*, pp. 162-63).
57. *Documentación* (IDES), no. 14 (March 1972), Annex 3. The bulletin reproduces the whole "Manual of Peasant Social Formation" used by Padre Caicedo.
58. "We have recognized that we are human persons and that we have the same rights as the exploiting class as children of God," read a manifesto from ANUC of the Valle del Cauca. "We seek land, that according to God belongs to him who works it," begins another, of the peasant movement of Bitaco.
59. See, for example, the interesting study of a Cauca Valley case by Gustavo I. DeRoux. *Jamundí: realidad social y análisis* (Bogotá, 1971), p. 5. DeRoux was an extremely helpful informant, beyond the contributions of his written research.
60. *Sacerdote y cambio social* (Bogotá, 1967), by Gustavo Jiménez Cadena, S.J., is a very useful study of the influence of the rural priest and gives some historical background on the positions of the national church. A good history of peasant movements is Pierre Gilhodes, "Agrarian Struggles in Colombia," in Rodolfo Stavenhagen, ed., *Agrarian Problems and Peasant Movements in Latin America* (Garden City, N.Y., 1970), pp. 407-51.
61. There was an evolution of hierarchial pronouncements after the mid-1960s. The 1965 declaration on the "Momento Social" spoke of the "essential social function" of property but then went on to discuss various "errors" about the right of property, including the assumption that land should belong to those who worked it (*Revolución violenta*?, pp. 10-13). The 1967 statement pointed to the continuing seriousness of the agrarian problem but dismissed redistribution of land as an adequate reform. It endorsed the stated ends of the governmental program, while excusing its failures in implementation."Declaración de la Conferencia Episcopal sobre la Iglesia y desarrollo" in *Conferencia Episcopal de Colombia: XXIII Asamblea Plenaria* (Bogotá, 1967), pp. 17-19. By 1972 the bishops were simply pointing to the social function and omitting lengthy qualifications. See "La justicia social en el magisterio del Episcopado Colombiano," in *La justicia en el mundo*, p. 66.
62. "Conclusiones del seminario episcopal sobre reforma agraria" in *XXIII Asamblea Plenaria* (1967), pp. 23-24. Their 1968 statement went even further and explicitly praised the government-sponsored ANUC. See *La Iglesia ante el cambio*, pp. 51-52.
63. The summary analysis of the events of 1972 in Colombia by *Anali-CIAS*, no. 10, gave strong emphasis to peasant organizations (February 1973, pp. 5-11).

64. *Anali-CIAS*, no. 6 (September 1972), p. 10.
65. Cf. the very suggestive analysis of the "revolutionary" military government in Brazil by Juan Linz, "The Future of an Authoritarian Situation or the Institutionalization of an Authoritarian Regime," in Alfred Stepan, ed., *Authoritarian Brazil* (New Haven, Conn., 1973), pp. 233-54.
66. The third part of *La Iglesia ante el cambio* deals with the "crisis" of the clergy. There were certainly problems in comparison to its own past, but they were of a different order of magnitude from those of many other places in Latin America.
67. Priestly ordinations, and the numbers of those studying in major and minor seminaries, were higher in 1970 than at any time in the previous twenty years. See Francisco Zuluaga, S.J., *Estructuras eclesiásticas de Colombia*, 2nd ed., (Bogotá, 1971), p. 37. Figures for the church—for the number of priests, of ordinations, or even of parishes—are only approximate. Sources differ among one another. Zuluaga, for example, lists the number of priests in 1969 as 4,864 (*Estructuras eclesiásticas*, p. 35). Hubert Schwan, on the other hand, lists a national total of only 4,236. *Directorio de la Iglesia Católica en Colombia, 1969* (Bogotá, 1969), p. 288. Though Zuluaga's figures are derived from other secondary sources and Schwan's are original, the latter's are not necessarily more accurate. The many obstacles Schwan ran into in gathering his data may account for his lower total. Similar discrepancies exist between the numbers of priestly ordinations recorded in the *Annuario pontificio* published by the Vatican and those given by Zuluaga. Out of all this it is clear only that, if there has been a decline in clerical recruitment (as some figures seem to show), it has not been dramatic enough to move ecclesiastical elites out of their clericalist conceptions.
68. As it was, the Christian Democrats were the first group to leave the United Front in 1965. In the 1970 elections, some priests are known to have worked for ANAPO.
69. Castrillón, "Política y pastoral," p. 90.
70. In his interviewing in 1972-73, Levine found a strong concern among the bishops to preserve unity. See Wilde and Levine, "The Catholic Church, 'Politics,' and Violence," pp. 239-40.
71. The hierarchy has demonstrated some sensitivity to this problem. See Muñoz Duque, "Panorama pastoral," pp. 9-12; *La Iglesia ante el cambio*, part 3; and the whole message of the 24th Bishops' Assembly, "Mensaje a los Presbíteros" (Bogotá, 1968).

Chapter 8

The Trend towards Technocracy: The World Bank and the International Labor Organization in Colombian Politics

Fernando Cepeda Ulloa
Christopher Mitchell

The National Front system in Colombia tended, among other effects, to depoliticize the governmental structure. The establishment-sponsored, legal coalition form of government (1958-74) guaranteed equal distribution of power between the traditional parties regardless of electoral outcomes. Thus political conflict—at least within traditional boundaries—became less meaningful, and political modernization in the form of a more technocratic state materialized. This technocratic trend increased and strengthened the influence of two international agencies: the World Bank and the International Labor Organization (ILO). In this chapter, we will examine the sources and direction, and also some of the possible limits of these two organizations' political influence in Colombia.

It is important to recognize that the World Bank and the ILO are not primarily political organizations, but are mainly concerned, respectively, with economic development and worker's rights. We are not arguing that these agencies had hidden or, still less, unworthy political objectives. At the same

Table 1
World Bank's Loans to Colombia (1949-72)
(thousands of dollars)

Sector	Number	Original Amount
Power	18	294,130
Transport	11	210,650
Industry (Steel)	6	192,500
Water Supply	4	122,500
Agriculture (Irrigation & Land Colonization)	8	84,100
Telecommunications	2	31,000
Education	2	14,000
Total	51	$948,880

time, the actions and choices of even functionally-focused agencies do have long-term political influence—which it is worthwhile to understand clearly.

Both the World Bank and the ILO relied for a good part of their influence on what might be called a transnational technocratic elite: a group of respected technicians who shuttled back and forth between posts in Colombia and in the multilateral agencies. Both agencies also promoted autonomous public institutions in Colombia; relatively free from political pressures, these ''institutes'' and ''services'' came to dominate many specific subsectors of public policy. Both agencies also sought to influence macroeconomic policies, an effort in which the World Bank, for reasons we will explore, was more successful. Let us first examine the World Bank's role, turning later to that of the ILO.

IMPACT OF THE WORLD BANK

Loans and Leverage

Colombia is a founding member of all the three institutions which comprise the World Bank Group. Colombia has been the fourth largest borrower from the Bank after Brazil, Mexico, and Turkey. Between 1948 and 1972, the Bank made fifty-one loans to Colombia for the total amount of $948.88 million (U.S.). The World Bank's financial resources have been channeled principally toward the building of physical infrastructure. Only recently has it shown interest in contributing to the development of social infrastructure (see Table 1).

Power, transport (roads and railways), industry and agriculture are the sectors where the Bank has traditionally concentrated its resources. Power loans amount to more than a fourth of the total; power and transport together absorbed $504.78 million out of the total of $948.88 million made available through 1972. Water supply, telecommunications, education, and export promotion are the new sectors to which resources are being allocated. In 1971, Colombia obtained from the Bank the first program loan for the implementation of the General Plan of Development, particularly to support one of the "four strategies" of the plan: promotion of exports.[1]

As part of the management of this large financial investment, the World Bank has been willing, at times, to use the blunt threat of cutting off loans in order to change Colombian macroeconomic policy. However, loans were officially suspended only in 1956, during the Rojas Pinilla administration. The relationship between the Bank and the Colombian government had been deteriorating since 1955, the third year of military government. It is difficult to document in detail the ups and downs of the Bank-Colombia dealings. Bank officials have often denied that loans were ever formally suspended. But we have the important testimony left in his *Journals* by David E. Lilienthal, who was frequently a Bank consultant. Through them it is possible to follow, at least in part, the development of the crisis. Lilienthal's version:

> June 21, 1955: Talked on the phone to Gene Black of the World Bank today, at some length. Things not going well in Colombia. Sending Bob Garner down July 1 to "talk cold turkey to them" about proposed large "supplier credits" they are negotiating for from the Germans and French . . . . Another thing that is going badly is the way the military are running things . . . .
>
> July 6, 1955: The place has been full of intrigue. Military men, riding high and liking the emoluments of power, were replacing cultivated civilians all over the place. Rumors of graft, disaffection, and definite reports of reckless handling of the finances of the country had things looking pretty black . . . . To add to the ugly aspect, there were Garner and the World Bank ready to pull out of Colombia because of the military's maladministration.
>
> July 10, 1955: . . . the increased coolness growing into tension between the World Bank and the Minister of Finance and his policies, leading to Garner's trip and virtual ultimatum—put these things all together and the outlook was not good . . . . Garner had laid down the Bank's ultimatum in a session just before lunch; if they continued to borrow, through the device of supplier credits for waterworks, etc. (pushed by a French firm, Degremont, whose international murder mystery type representative picked a seat just behind me in this plane), the Bank would have to withdraw as banker to Colombia. So the subject of those waterworks was very much in his mind. Said the President: "Without health, nothing is good. People must have good water to have

> good health. Everywhere I go in Colombia they ask for water, water plants." Garner was in a lecturing mood, trying to explain that, unless people could afford things, they should spend their money in increasing their productivity, then in time they could afford things that made life better. With his southern drawl, which many New Englanders would have trouble following, and his use of Americanisms as parables, I wonder how much the President got ("first you need to have more pie," he said, "and then there will be more pie to divide"—perhaps El Presidente understood the figure of speech, but I rather doubt it).[2]

It seems that for several months the conflict entered on a period of cooling off. But in 1956, perhaps as a result of the Waterston Mission report on public investment policies (March 1956), the Bank conditioned future loans on several expected government actions. In mid-October 1956, loans were formally suspended. Lilienthal, in his journal for entry October 20, 1956, comments on his own temptations to "feed the fires of dissatisfaction against President Rojas" and refers to the Bank's formal suspension of loans to Colombia: "The World Bank, we learned last week, has formally notified all Colombian projects that no more funds will be loaned by the Bank until they straighten up their financial picture, particularly as to commercial loans."[3] World Bank loans were only renewed in April 1958, one year after the fall of General Rojas Pinilla (May 10, 1957).

Rather than use such direct and unsophisticated persuasion, the World Bank relied much more often, particularly during the National Front period, on instruments such as missions, the multidonor Consultative Group, and a resident Bank representative in Bogotá. The use of these instruments was aided by the existence of a technocratic elite with experience both in national and international positions. In practice, this elite often served as both interpreter and legitimist of World Bank suggestions in Colombian policy debates. One member of this elite was Jorge Mejía Palacio, who served as Colombia's executive director at the World Bank from 1960 to 1968 except for his term as finance minister (1961-62). From 1968 to 1974, the executive director was Virgilio Barco, former senator, former minister of public works, former minister of agriculture, ambassador to London, and mayor of Bogotá.

Also, particularly since 1970, high Colombian officials have shifted to high posts in international agencies. At least twelve very distinguished Colombian technicians have been incorporated in the international bureaucracy. Among them are two former directors of the Planning Department, two former directors of the Agrarian Reform Institute, the former directors of the National Fund for Pre-Investment Studies (FONADE), the former director of the Bogotá Telephone Company, and the former director of the Colombian Power Institute. The highest international jobs occupied by Colombians within the

World Bank and the International Development Bank bureaucracies have been held by two former directors of the Colombian Planning Department. Edgar Gutiérrez was director of the Central America and Caribbean Division at IBRD until 1974, and Jorge Ruiz Lara is technical assistant to the IDB president. Let us look in turn at the important persuasive tools of the World Bank.

Missions

Several times since the World Bank began its intense activity in Colombia, it has sent teams to examine and advise on economic conditions and policy. Made up of roughly a dozen experts from the Bank and other agencies, these missions were designed "to put forward a set of recommendations that were tailored to the area and could be taken to heart by the appropriate political authorities."[4] The recommendations have carried considerable weight; a good example is the second "general survey mission," which visited Colombia in 1962. The Bank's mission evaluated Colombia's Ten-Year Development Plan.[5] The main Bank policy suggestions for future action in Colombia were: (1) tax increases; (2) devaluation; (3) minor-exports promotion; (4) public investment; and (5) the creation of the Private Investment Fund in order to channel foreign capital to the private sector. The future actions of the consultative group (see below) were conditioned by the Bank to "specific action on these matters."[6] The Bank evaluation was also a key requirement for the U.S. decision to support a Bank-led consultative group for Colombia.[7] As a catalyst to desired policy steps, the Bank negotiated with Colombia a series of economic policy memoranda. Through the memoranda, the Bank has promoted policies of public savings and public investment, minor-exports promotion, and public utilities rate reforms. For the Bank negotiations, the memoranda are the equivalent of the IMF letter of intent. The memorandum is a statement of past policy execution and future action. It covers most of the items related to the overall economic activity of the government. (The volume of the memorandum is a good indicator of its broad coverage: 56 double-space pages in 1969, 121 pages in 1970.) Since 1969 the same memorandum has served for joint negotiations with the U.S. Agency for International Development (AID) and the World Bank.

The Consultative Group

At the beginning of the Alliance for Progress, the World Bank already had a long experience of cooperation with the Colombian government. Based on this experience and within the framework of the Alliance, the Bank considered a 1961 Colombian "request" for the arrangement of a "consortium" (eventually a somewhat weaker consultative group was formed). It was to be a mechanism for the coordination of external assistance to Colombian economic development. The consultative group was not prepared to make financial pledges. But it was geared to find ways to avoid duplications, cross purposes, and inconsistencies in the agencies interested in providing help to Colombia.[8] The first meeting of the group was held in Washington from January 22 to 24, 1963, under the sponsorship of the World Bank. The meetings were attended by representatives of Belgium, Canada, Denmark, France, Germany, Italy, Japan, the Netherlands, Switzerland, the United Kingdom, and the United States, as well as representatives from the Interamerican Bank and the International Monetary Fund. (Spain and AID later became members.) Five more consultative group meetings have been held: June 1964, June 1967, December 1969, February 1971, February, 1972.

From its beginning, the consultative group has been linked with the evaluation and execution of Colombia's development plans. Minister Mejía (1961-62) noted in his comments on the history of the group: "The first step that was needed was the preparation of the economic development plan with projections over a ten year period, formulated by the Lleras Camargo Administration [1958-62]. It was my responsibility as Minister of Finance to bring about the approval of said plan by the World Bank as well as the Committee of Nine, predecessor of CIAP. At the same time a Project List was prepared with feasibility studies, a list that was circulated among the countries that accepted the invitation of the World Bank to become members of the Group."[9] Consultations between the Colombian government and the World Bank staff to analyze possible projects and types of financing for them precede meetings of the consultative group. Thus the meeting itself is in some ways a ritual; by the time it convenes, the Bank has usually endorsed, in effect, the final Colombian project list. It is not surprising, therefore, to find that this gathering—more important politically than economically—is generally quite short, lasting only one or two days. Usually the session starts with an opening statement by the Bank representative who presides at the meeting. His statement explains and puts in perspective the Colombian political, economic, and social situation. Then the Colombian minister of finance makes a brief speech that serves as an introduction for the analysis of the project list. This analysis consists of a presentation of each one of the projects by the Bank representative followed by an inquiry as to which of the lenders is interested in the project. After some clarifications are offered by the Colombian delegation, the group continues its deliberations in closed meetings. At the end of the session, the Colombians return and a pre-prepared minute of the session is approved. Joint financing of certain projects may be discussed at an informal group session the next day.

As a mechanism for the presentation, consideration, and financing of Colombia's long-term development plans, the consultative group system in fact has often eclipsed the Colombian Congress. Since 1960, the Colombian executive has presented four general development plans; in every case, they have been presented publicly when Congress was not in session or was about to adjourn. However, all the plans have been published two or three months before the meetings of the consultative group. It seems clear that these plans were intended more to sway potential international lenders than to afford Colombian politicians an opportunity to criticize and control macroeconomic policy.

Resident World Bank Representatives

To affect government policy, aid agencies must often rely on simple persuasion—which tends to work best when the persuader is well-known and thoroughly familiar with local conditions. The World Bank has used such steady face-to-face persuasion effectively in Colombia. In August 1962, almost simultaneously with the creation of the preliminary consultative group in Washington, Peyton Kerr was appointed as the first permanent Bank regional representative in Bogotá. The principal function of the representative was to be the coordinator of the consultative group, which tended to give his advice added weight. The representative's office was shortly to acquire its own dynamic, and to become one of the strongest tools of the Bank in influencing the Colombian development process. The office was located within the Department of Planning, enjoying all of the advantages—in terms of knowledge and communication—offered by such a location.[10] Moreover, long tenure of the individuals who have served as representative of the Bank has been a factor facilitating these contacts. These were: Peyton Kerr, August 1962 to August 1964; Kenneth Iverson, August 1964 to January 1969; José Diego Tegeiro, January 1969 to August 1970; Albert Favilla, August 1970 to 1973.

The World Bank and Autonomous Public Institutions

The power to aid is seldom the power to impose policies on an unwilling government. Much more often, it is the power to choose which groups will execute policies, and to stress some areas or methods of governmental action. David Lilienthal has described the need for an intergovernmental organization to find allies and to "take root" in a host country: "More than making a report is necessary. The strength of any plan or program is no greater than the men who are available in that country to take initiative, fight the battles, devise the policies that will fit that country or region at that time. Find the men. Look for the men. When they appear, encourage them: when they have zeal, enthusiasm, some skills, develop those men."[11] Of course any multilateral agency has certain biases or preferences in choosing which local groups and organizations to encourage and support. The international lenders, and

Table 2
World Bank Loans to Colombia, 1949-72, by Executing Agency

	Nat. Gov.	Autonomous Public Inst.	Total
1949-59 (11 years)	4	14	18
1960-72 (12 years)	11	22	33
Total	15	36	51

specifically the World Bank, have tended to favor highly technical, functionally specific, and politically insulated autonomous agencies. Though nominally under the control of traditionally-organized ministries, these agencies' very numbers, their superior operative and technical skills, and their links with outside donors have often helped them elude political oversight.

Between the fall of Rojas Pinilla and 1974, fully fifty-four "public establishments" (to give these agencies their legal title) were set up in Colombia. They dealt with such basic tasks as preinvestment studies (FONADE), agricultural research (ICA), school construction (ICCE), export promotion (INCOMEX) and port development (Puertos de Colombia). Several Colombian autonomous agencies pioneered new development techniques, and became models for other Third World countries to follow. These models included the regional development corporation (Corporación Autónoma Regional de la Sabana de Bogotá) and the "free zone" for industry and commerce (Zona Franca de Barranquilla). In addition, thirty-six preexisting "establishments" were reorganized or reformed under the National Front, embracing such fields as social security (ICSS), urban housing (ICT), petroleum exploitation (ECOPETROL), and industrial promotion (IFI). As World Bank President George D. Woods wrote to the Colombian president in 1963: "Colombia has organized many efficient autonomous public institutions and the Government has permitted them to function on a strictly technical basis. The existence of these institutions will greatly facilitate the execution of the program. It is important that this freedom to operate as strictly technical organizations be maintained."[12]

A review of the loans granted by the World Bank during the period 1949-72 reveals that thirty-six loans were made to autonomous public institutions, and only fifteen directly to the national government (see Tables 2, 3). As indicated by Table 3, only four projects out of forty presented to the consultative groups were to be executed by the central government. The Bank's motives in thus channeling aid towards autonomous units of the central government included: (1) assuring direct control in the execution of the loan; (2) providing for independent systems of accounting and auditing; (3) establishing procurement policies not related to domestic standards on this matter; (4) escaping political interference and other domestic inconveniences (national legislative criticism and control, domestic recruitment systems for the public service, etc.).

Table 3
Projects List Presented to the Consultative Group for Financing by the World Bank, 1962-71, by Executing Agency

Consultative Group	Central Government	Autonomous Public Institution	Total
First	—	8	8
Second	—	9	9
Third	3	3	6
Fourth	1	4	5
Fifth	—	12	12
Total	4	36	40

What were some of the political consequences in Colombia of this World Bank strategy? In the first place, sectors tended to be selected for special attention according to the preferences of the Bank and according to the existing technical skills in Colombia. The National Planning Department itself remarked on some international agencies' preference for Colombian institutions that were already strong, operatively and financially: "The indecisiveness of some entities concerning reorganization of their structure and system of administration has invalidated their claim on foreign loans or, at the very least, has caused considerable delays in obtaining them."[13] Efforts in transport, power, and industry were favored over other priorities. The World Bank's evaluation criteria also tended to stress particular, ad hoc success or failure in judging Colombian development administration, rather than general economic performance or policy coherence.[14] A Colombian planning process in which outside agencies played a lesser role might well have emphasized different sectors, such as justice or agriculture, whose pressing needs now appear obvious. It is worth pointing out, however, that much of Colombia's current capacity to plan development is a result of its experience in grappling with the proposals of the international lenders.

A second consequence of the World Bank strategy was that popular political initiative and response became less and less relevant to the making of public policy. As technical criteria became more important, development planning went more smoothly, but had less opportunity to recruit firm popular backing. Thus, for example, regional considerations became "barriers to efficiency." Increases in the cost of public services followed one upon another. The gross national product increased. Every indicator rose except those measuring political development. Politicians became more cut off from the opportunity to base a campaign on the government's achievements. The trend towards depoliticization also had a built-in accelerator, as new agencies modified themselves, on their own initiative, in the image of the previous ones. While the World Bank was not solely responsible for this trend, its potential aid tended to make technocracy and political autonomy fashionable.

Only in the early 1970s did the government autonomous agencies come under public criticism, and the controls recently applied to them have been largely administrative, not political.

THE IMPACT OF THE INTERNATIONAL LABOR ORGANIZATION

The International Labor Organization, like the World Bank, has successfully promoted functionally-specific technical organizations within the Colombian government. But it has been markedly less successful in influencing macroeconomic and macroadministrative policies. This failure seems to stem from the ILO's use of more overtly political tactics rather than the familiar World Bank technocratic strategies of influence. Let us first look at one of the ILO's outstanding successes, and then at some of the reverses it met when it put aside technocratic methods.

Development of the National Apprenticeship Service (SENA)

The key agencies of the labor sector in the Colombian government have counted and relied upon ILO inspiration and contributions; the ministry, the two main autonomous public institutions under its direction, ICSS (Instituto Colombiano de Seguros Sociales) and SENA (Servicio Nacional de Aprendizaje); the two main advisory bodies for the ministry, the Councils of Labor and of Salaries, are all institutions that can be easily linked to ILO activities and orientations.

ILO, like the World Bank, has benefited from the key role in Colombian life played by people well acquainted with the agency. It is worth mentioning names such as John Agudelo Ríos and Rodolfo Martínez Tono. Agudelo was ILO "representative"[15] in Colombia and he assisted ILO efforts when he served as secretary general of the presidency and later as minister of labor (1966-70). It is interesting to observe that during this last period a considerable number of ILO conventions were approved by the Colombian Congress. Among the actions favorable to the ILO were the following: an important ILO mission headed by Dudley Seers was invited to Colombia, the social security system was substantially modified, the Ministry of Labor was restructured, and the Council for Rehabilitation was created. Martínez has been the key man in an enormous experiment related to vocational training—he was the director of SENA from its creation up to 1974.

The National Apprenticeship Service (SENA) is an autonomous public agency under the Ministry of Labor and Social Security; SENA's objective is professional training of human resources in Colombia with a view towards increasing national productivity and promoting social and economic development. SENA is responsible for the organization of training programs for workers of the industrial, commercial, agricultural, mining, and catering sectors.

SENA appears to be the most important institutional contribution of the ILO in Colombia. The ILO itself recently prepared a report for the Colombian government outlining the achievements of SENA during the 1960s. This report asserts that without the collaboration of the ILO, Colombia would have been unable to obtain the same results in labor-force training.[16] Such collaboration goes back to 1956, two years before the Frente, when the government requested technical assistance to draw up statistics on skilled manpower.[17] In response, SENA of Brazil loaned the services of an expert, Salas Da Silva, at the request and expense of the ILO. It is generally considered that the contribution of Da Silva was decisive in the creation of the SENA as a public autonomous institution in 1957. As SENA has developed, its planning process has been aided by ILO. The first four years (1958-62) were spent largely in the work of planning, investigating skills and manpower needs, training instructors, constructing centers, acquiring equipment, and pursuit of international cooperation. Thereafter, active work began. By 1969, SENA had a budget of nearly $15 million, sixty-five centers for professional training, and 153,579 trainees. It had produced 486,089 qualified workers over the total period, and had received the cooperation of various countries: Germany, Holland, Switzerland, France, Israel, South Korea, the United Kingdom, and international organizations, for example, the Food and Agriculture Organization. In its turn, SENA has helped other Latin American countries in the promotion of professional training. SENA exhibits a remarkable administrative continuity. Both the director and the national planning adviser served the institution and its precursor, the Worker Training Institute. The ILO, with a minimal outside contribution provided by the United Nations Special Fund, has also maximized the utilization of local resources in this project.

Nominalism in Administration and Legislation

One of the most salient characteristics of the legal system in underdeveloped countries is so-called nominalism: the existence of a set of laws only "on the books." In a number of instances, the ILO has sought to reorganize large Colombian administrative units, or to add broad labor-related clauses to Colombia's written legislation. These quite overtly political efforts—dictated sometimes by tactical decisions, and sometimes by the ILO's basic format as a convention-drafting agency—have not met much practical success. Requiring more resources for execution than were available to the ILO, they have fallen victim to nominalism, achieving much in writing but little in day-to-day practice.

A case in point is the restructuring of the labor ministry. In 1968, the ministry was reorganized by the means of Decrees 3134 and 3136, drafted under the guidance of Giovanni D. Polo, an ILO expert. Under the new rules, the ministry, now termed "of Labor and Social Security," has the responsibility for the adoption, orientation, and execution of the following policies, in harmony with the national development plan: labor, employment, the promotion of professional and technical education, productivity, cooperativism, and social security. Without doubt, this new administrative structure is utopian and can by no means be implemented in the short run. Specific reference to the decree will give an idea of the unattainable functions it suggests for the ministry: "to promote, coordinate and regulate the geographic and professional mobility of the workers," including internal and external migrations, according to the necessities in the labor market.[18] The study of the Colombian migration phenomenon is only now being initiated.[19] It should not be necessary to argue further the futility of trying to implement such a policy.

Yet another example of nominalism would be the norm that proposes that the ministry "stimulate the increase of production and productivity in order to improve the living conditions of workers and their families; accelerate the economic growth of the country; promote decentralized industries, and make them competitive in international markets, and at the same time do everything possible to finance this with national capital, all this in coordination with the respective agencies."[20] Other similar examples from this decree could be cited, allowing us to agree with the conclusion of Minister John Agudelo Ríos, that this is definitely a "reform for the future."[21]

In the field of social security, although there has been important progress in the coverage of several contingencies, in the construction of an efficient administrative machinery, and in the development of a sound financial system, it can be stated that during its twenty-six years of existence, the social security system has not protected a substantial part of the population. Only beginning with the 1971 reform has an attempt been made to extend the benefits to the rural sector and to independent workers. The minister himself recognized this situation when he stated: "Thus it cannot be said that in this country we have a real social security system, but some type of private system restricted to the protection of one sector of the wage earning population".[22] The best example of nominalism is to be found in the situation of the rural sector in respect to labor legislation, job opportunities, social security benefits, and professional formation. A former head of the Planning Department has described the situation in a dramatic way: "Berry's study on the processes of the Colombian rural sector indicates that the income of the rural population utilizing traditional working techniques—more than 65% of the total rural population—has remained practically stationary since 1937. Meanwhile, the average per-capita income in the country during that same period has risen, in real terms, approximately 80%. In other words, rural participation in the total income has been worsening substantially. Different is the case of the industrial worker, whose real income has improved 100% between 1953 and 1969.''[23]

Colombia has ratified fully forty-one ILO conventions, dealing with such varied and basic areas as hours of work, unemployment, child labor, workmen's compensation, and minimum-wage fixing machinery. But the adherence to these ILO ''legislative packages'' seems to have been quite nominal. Colombian delegates have typically agreed in Geneva to ILO standards that cannot be realistically applied in Colombia's present political and socioeconomic situation. That ILO standards are often not appropriate to Colombia's situation was suggested by Minister of Labor Carlos Augusto Noriega in 1968, when he observed that: ''one should consider the influence which legislation [incorporating such standards] succeeds in exercising upon the maintenance of disequilibria among workers and of conditions of underdevelopment in a particular country. Insofar as the advanced legislation only applies to minority groups of workers and constitutes a disincentive to investment, these consequences are inexorable.''[24]

In a second sense, Colombia's adherence to ILO conventions seems nominal, since Colombia's ratification of the ILO standards has typically come several years after their adoption in Geneva, and has occurred in groups. Thus conventions were ratified on only four occassions: twenty-four were ratified in 1931, four in 1962, twelve in 1967, and one in 1968, in several instances long after Colombian delegates to the ILO had approved the conventions in Geneva. This delayed, bunched ratification of the ILO conventions suggests a basic lack of commitment to the Geneva standards, and their ratification at opportune moments for cosmetic purposes.

Out on a Political Limb: The Seers Mission and Report

In 1969-70, an ILO mission led by Dudley Seers of the University of Sussex visited Colombia and presented a report aimed at producing full employment in the Colombian economy. The odyssey of the Seers Report illustrates what can happen when an ILO mission is seen as being too openly political, and particularly as being careless of the technical criteria on which a good part of the ILO's prestige is based. It offers a good example of how such a study, produced by a mission as large as that of the ILO, can be born, grow, fade, and then vanish without trace.

The political profile of the Seers Report, one can say in retrospect, was far too high; it was generally identified with the outgoing administration of President Carlos Lleras Restrepo. The fact that Colombia was chosen for the ILO's first effort in the full-employment field might be related to two factors of a circumstantial nature, namely that the Colombian ambassador to the ILO, Antonio Oviedo, was a close friend of then President Lleras Restrepo, and that the labor minister (Lleras' private secretary for three years in the presidency and therefore also a confidant) had been the ILO's representative in Colombia. The choice might also have been influenced by the Lleras Restrepo government's interest in receiving a report that, it was hoped, would constitute international recognition of its achievements and would, at the same time, link the administration with a world program to combat unemployment. In an inelegant, and worse, unintelligent, gesture, the Seers Report left the incoming Pastrana administration with a series of guidelines that compromised its freedom of action. Once an initial desire to appear in harmony with the departing administration had been exhausted, the new president and his advisers felt little commitment to the Seers recommendations.

Politics contributed to weakness in the report's technical credentials. The pressure exerted by President Lleras to hand over the report at the earliest possible date made it relatively easy to dismiss it as superficial and hurriedly produced. The document was additionally vulnerable because it seemed both self-contradictory and in conflict with fifty years of ILO technical recommendations. On the one hand, the report's preamble states that it does not attempt to deal with problems of development in general. The area of major interest is that of employment and the possibility of restructuring development policies so that they contribute to a reduction in unemployment.[25] But the truth was that it was hard to distinguish between a full employment strategy and a development strategy. The report calls for a "crusade" and an "integral battle" against unemployment. Though ostensibly narrowly focused, it is basically "a development program for the period 1970-1985."[26]

Most controversially, the Seers Report argued that some aspects of labor law (which the ILO had of course sought for years to strengthen) actually prevented the increase of employment, especially in the modern private sector of the economy[27]. It maintained that current labor laws encouraged a system of longer work shifts and fewer hours of use of equipment, in circumstances in which precisely the opposite would be desirable in Colombia. The report criticized a number of points in the Labor Code of 1950, arguing that:

1. Protection against arbitrary dismissal had become an important obstacle to increasing employment.
2. Triple pay on Sundays constituted an obstacle to intermittent/occasional work.
3. Family allowances should not be given in a country with a population explosion.
4. The legal obstacles standing in the way of shift work should be removed. (Requirement of a 35 percent premium for work between 6 P.M. and 6 A.M. and the prohibition of female work between 10 P.M. and 5 A.M.).
5. The concept of "enterprise unity," which means that the same salary is paid throughout the whole "unit" (as in the case of various subsidiaries, both urban and

rural, that had been designated a "unit" by the ministry of labor) constituted an obstacle rather than a stimulus for the strategy of rural development advocated by the report.
6. Finally, the report urged the creation of a commission at presidential level for the drafting of the corresponding legal recommendations.

With these handicaps, the Seers Report had a brief public and political vogue, followed by growing criticism and then virtual oblivion. These were some important stages in this progression:

1. *Presentation of the report.* The head of the group of experts, Doctor Abbas Ammat, had the first Spanish copy of "Towards Full Employment" presented to President Lleras Restrepo at a ceremony in the presidential palace in July 1970. In his speech, President Lleras declared himself totally in agreement with report: "I recommend that the Report's proposals for employment become the basis for a development policy. It is a scheme that I wholeheartedly identify with." He also promised to circulate the report in a simplified version so as to place it within the reach of the greatest number of Colombians possible and announced that he would hand over the report to the incoming president, "who has already expressed in no uncertain terms his preoccupations and plans concerning economic and social policy that coincide with those of the Seers Report."

2. *Speech by the new minister of labor and social security, August 7, 1970.* The new minister, Jorge Mario Eastman, made a short speech in the San Carlos Palace to express his gratitude at having been entrusted with the most important part of the work: the challenge of setting in motion a plan to generate five million new jobs.

3. *The national committee for the evaluation of the report.* By Decree of Law 1507 of August 14, 1970, the president set up a committee of twenty-six persons to evaluate the program presented by the ILO and recommend the necessary measures for its execution. One after the other and for different reasons, both the opposition party (ANAPO, the National Popular Alliance) and the Union of Colombian Workers (UTC) refused to take part in the committee and instead formed their own. ANAPO justified its position on the grounds that it did not recognize the legitimacy of the Pastrana government; the UTC on the grounds that its representative had been appointed without consultation with the union.

4. *Conclusions of the committee.* On October 30, 1970, the committee presented its final document in which it declared itself in agreement with the ILO's diagnosis and advanced the proposal of redistributing incomes and making urban and rural property more accessible to all. The instruments proposed for achieving these goals included: tax policies; industrial, labor,

educational, and incomes policies; cooperatives and organizations for communal action. Finally, the committee recommended that, "the General Development Plan be revised to take into account the government's intention to press for a vigorous decisive employment policy".[28] Eleven members expressed dissenting opinions, generally representing leftist viewpoints (though only some of these comments focused on the real thrust of the Seers recommendations). Among the adverse judgments were these:

> "The suggested solution presupposed the maintaining of the existing system."
>
> "It proposes general policies based on the colonialist type of mentality."
>
> "It is anti-industrialist since it pretends to deny the development of productive forces and the process of industrialization when it poses a false conflict between productivity and employment. It sacrifices productivity for the sake of employment."
>
> "It operates within an ideological framework which believes in Colombia's incapacity for self-development."
>
> "It recommends a devaluation which would have the effect of accelerating the process of denationalization of our industry."
>
> "It does not deal with the fundamental problem of external dependence."[29]
>
> "Errors in and ignorance of Colombian law make the report a document unworthy of any respect. For these reasons its total rejection is recommended."[30]

5. *The new strategy of development.* In December 1971, the government announced a new development plan. It contains a strategy quite different from that of the Seers Report, though the two coincide in some of their recommendations. The new strategy had been devised by Professor Lauchlin Currie, the head of the First World Bank Mission in 1949, whose report, to use a phrase from the Seers Report, "hardly touched on the problem of unemployment." The emphasis of the new plan was on urbanization as a synonym for development. And although it included a strategy for solving the unemployment problem, it conceived of the problem in a very different way. One can say that the ILO's proposition was the redistribution of wealth through wages and full employment, though with low productivity. Currie's strategy was above all one of increased productivity with wealth redistribution by government taxes. In the words of Professor Currie: "The main difference is in diagnosis and strategy. Seers is making work for the sake of making work, and redistributing wealth not as a matter of social policy but as a matter of creating work. Our plan looks upon human resources that should be used as efficiently as possible."[31]

OUTSIDE AGENCIES AS DOMESTIC POLITICAL ACTORS

Colombia's National Front coalition system removed many issues of development policy from direct exposure to political debate. With sixteen years of national power virtually guaranteed to a fairly homogeneous group of traditional party leaders, the probabilities increased that questions of economic strategy could be defined as "technical" and solved accordingly. There was a proliferation of functionally-specific public agencies, designed to operate with efficiency—rather than equity, mass involvement, or other values—as their major goal. At the level of individuals, technical qualifications became a major admission ticket to influence over the making of policy.

As we have seen, both the World Bank and the International Labor Organization participated, sometimes with important influence—within this technocratic trend. Rather than making open demands on the Colombian government, the two agencies relied more often (and more successfully) on good working relations with the newly important Colombian *técnicos*. Through devices including missions, representatives, and the consultative group, the agencies affected such choices as priority sectors for development, some aspects of macroeconomic policy, and the system of job-related education and apprenticeship. Particularly in the case of the World Bank, there were impressive quanitifiable accomplishments, in terms of roads built, kilowatts of hydroelectric capacity installed, and so forth.

At the same time, as we have indicated, the influence of these two international agencies has been subject to certain limits. The Colombian semiautonomous agencies they helped sponsor (SENA for example) have succeeded best when their mandate was sharply focused and functionally limited. When ILO and Bank advice ranged beyond fairly narrow areas of policy, cooperation was necessary from prominent Colombian figures whose credentials were not mainly technocratic. At times, such support was not available, or was not sufficient to provide a buffer against more overtly political forces, such as the public criticism which helped block adoption of the Seers strategy.

In short, the international agencies found Colombia's prolonged "political truce" a congenial environment in which to exercise sometimes significant influence—as long as they stayed within the predominantly technocratic style of policy making. This fact may tell us at least as much about the National Front as it does about the ILO and the World Bank. It underscores the substantial separation between political pressures (voting, congressional competition, public criticism) and key policy choices that was a hallmark of the Colombian two-party coalition system. Whether this prolonged insulation of "technical" decision will ultimately lead to an institutional breakdown—as policy and politics suddenly confront each other once again—is a question we can currently raise but not answer.

NOTES

*This essay includes material from a larger study on the role and impact of the international agencies in the legal and political systems of developing countries. The study covers Colombia, Pakistan and Turkey, and was sponsored by the Carnegie Endowment for International Peace and the International Legal Center. The joint project was directed by Professor Gilbert Verbit of Boston University and was carried out during 1970-72. The author of the Colombian case study was Fernando Cepeda. Both authors of the present essay gladly acknowledge their debt to all the participants in the joint Endowment-Legal Center project.

1. Two-thirds of this program will be directed towards the government's development plans. The other third is going to private enterprises to promote exports. See World Bank, *Informe Anual 1972* (Washington, D.C.), section on the International Development Association, p. 66.
2. David E. Lilienthal, *Journal, vol. 4; The Road to Change, 1955-1959*, pp. 6, 11, 14, 15.
3. Ibid., p. 118.
4. Edward S. Mason and Robert E. Asher, *The World Bank Since Bretton Woods* (Washington, D.C., 1972), p. 303. As these two recent historians of the Bank have also observed (p. 299), Colombia was used as a testing ground in 1949-50 for the basic idea of advisory Bank missions: "In tracing the evolution of IBRD [World Bank] assistance to member countries in development programming, the historian quickly discovers that all roads lead not to Rome but to Bogotá."
5. Banco Internacional de Reconstrucción y Fomento, *Evaluación del Programa General de Desarrollo Económico y Social de Colombia* (Bogotá, 1962).
6. Letter of J. Burke Knapp to President Alberto Lleras, dated June 27, 1962, published in Carlos Sanz de Santamaría, *Una Epoca Difícil* (Bogotá, 1965), p. 91.
7. Staff Study for the Committee on Foreign Relations, U.S. Senate, *Survey of the Alliance for Progress: Colombia, A Case Study* (Washington, D.C., 1969), pp. 68-69.
8. For a discussion of the World Bank's consultative groups, including especially that for Colombia, see Mason and Asher, *The World Bank Since Bretton Woods*, pp. 519-26.
9. Interview with Jorge Mejía Palacio, *La República*, April 3, 1972, p. 3.
10. Only recently did former director Roberto Arenas separate the two entities, at least physically, in an effort to obtain a greater degree of privacy for day to day planning.
11. David E. Lilienthal, *Journal*, vol. 5, p. 283 (entry for December 1, 1961).
12. George D. Woods's letter to the president of Colombia, Guillermo León Valencia, reporting the results of the first consultative group meeting (January 25, 1963). Figures on "public establishments" supplied by Escuela Superior de Administración Pública, Bogotá.
13. Departamento Nacional de Planeación, *Plan de desarrollo económico y social*, 1970-73, Volumen general, Tomo II, p. 8.
14. A limited exception to this statement would be the World Bank's "Willoughby Report," a general evaluation of the Bank's efforts in Colombia, prepared by its own Operations Evaluation Division in 1971. The report is said to have been critical of a number of Bank activities, particularly the relative lack of attention to rural problems. There are somewhat oblique references to the Willoughby Report in Mason and Asher, *The World Bank Since Bretton Woods*, pp. 649-56, but unfortunately the Bank has not made the report publicly available.

15. The ILO used to have *corresponsales*, a type of regional office. John Agudelo was *corresponsal* in Colombia from 1957 to 1963; his role was to provide contacts, information, and coordination. Rafael Caldera, later president of Venezuela, served for a time as ILO *corresponsal* in Caracas.
16. ILO, *Formación profesional en Colombia; Programa de las Naciones Unidas para el Desarrollo*, report to the Colombian government, (Geneva, 1970).
17. C. Vannutelli, *Informe al Gobierno de Colombia sobre estadísticas de trabajo* (Geneva, 1956), vol. 2, p. 71.
18. John Agudelo Ríos, *Informe del Ministro del Trabajo y Seguridad Social al Congreso Nacional* (Bogotá, 1969), pp. 15, 30, 101, 365.
19. See Ramiro Cardona, *Las Migraciones Internas* (Bogotá n.d.).
20. Agudelo Ríos, *Informe, 1969*, p. 366.
21. Agudelo Ríos, interview with Fernando Cepeda.
22. John Agudelo Ríos, *Memoria del Ministro de Trabajo y Seguridad Social, 1970* (Bogotá, 1971), p. 20.
23. Roberto Arenas, from a speech given in 1974, p. 18.
24. Carlos Augusto Noriega, *Memoria del Ministro De Trabajo al Congreso Nacional* (Bogotá, 1968), p. xxi.
25. ILO, *Towards Full Employment: A Programme for Colombia* (Geneva, 1970), p. 10.
26. Interview with a former minister of labor and social security.
27. Seers Report, p. 617.
28. The committee's report was published as *Estategia para una política de Empleo* (Bogotá, 1971). Conclusions are contained in pp. 27-40.
29. The above critical views were expressed by Monsignor Raúl Zambrano Camader, bishop of Facatativá, and Luis Villar Borda, Liberal deputy; see *Estrategia para una Política de Empleo*, pp. 80, 81, 89.
30. Unión de Trabajadores Colombianos, UTC, *Hacia el Cambio Social* (report of the 20th UTC Plenum), p. 30.
31. Lauchlin Currie, interview with Fernando Cepeda.

Chapter 9

Popular Mobilization Programs of the National Front: Cooptation and Radicalization

Bruce Bagley
Matthew Edel

> It may therefore be concluded that the Colombian elite, or rather a significant portion of it, has become a modernizing one with a view to moving the nation through a period of rapid economic growth and social change without further violence or another military dictatorship, and above all without social revolution. The ultimate objective is the preservation of the position of the elite; the method involves a much greater consciousness than in the past of what survival of the Colombian ruling class may require in terms of controlled change. The ultimate political question is whether this will be sufficient. *Failing the development of more effective institutional links between the elite and the masses, and the involvement of a broader segment of the population in both the decisions and rewards of development, the best intentions and the best leadership skills of a modernizing elite might well prove unequal to the tasks of change.*[1]

The above quote points to a fundamental problem that has confronted the National Front leadership: how to preserve the power and status of the ruling class while at the same time accommodating the demands emanating from peasant-, working-, and middle-class groups as a result of capitalist development. The basic objectives of the National Front—social peace and economic development—have generally been supported by all factions of the ruling class. The specific organizational programs, however, have produced significant political conflicts.

The goals of the Frente Nacional required that the government experiment with new forms of administrative decentralization and local participation to provide for regional economic development and to secure governmental control over the population. However, the peasant- and working-class elements organized by the government in these programs have often made demands for participation and distribution of benefits that clashed severely with the interests of important factions of the Frente coalition.

As a result, the various Frente governments have tended to approach local participation in an ambivalent fashion: on the one hand, the Frente leaders have striven to establish institutional links between elites and masses by promoting local organizations. On the other hand, they have taken care to insure that the power and influence of such groups remained channeled and circumscribed. In this paper, we examine the role of local voluntary associations in Colombian politics. Our data are drawn from case studies of two important government-sponsored voluntary associations: Acción Comunal (AC) and La Asociación Nacional de Usuarios Campesinos (ANUC). Our basic line of argument, which is illustrated by the case studies, is summarized in five propositions, which we consider interpretative guides to the actions of the Colombian ruling class during the Frente.

1. The emergence of voluntary associations such as AC and ANUC in Colombia during the Frente Nacional is due to two related sets of factors: (1) the pressures or demands for greater "participation" which emerge as peasant- and working-class groups, involved in a process of rapid capitalist development, become conscious of their group or class interest and organize in order to act upon them politically; and (2) the programs and activities of the ruling class, or fractions of it, in reaction to (or anticipation of) such demands on the part of popular organizations.
2. In order to guarantee continued government control over popular forces and to enlist them in support of national level plans and programs, the various Frente administrations have promoted local participation through voluntary associations such as AC and ANUC. In promoting these associations, the national leadership groups have tended to exclude established local leaders and municipal and regional institutions from direct participation in the budgeting and operation of the voluntary associations. The government hopes in this way to insure that the masses are linked to national rather than local institutions and leadership cadres.
3. National elite control over both local government and local voluntary associations has been exercised through such specific mechanisms as central government domination of local and regional fiscal resources, the extension of the policy-making powers of the executive over other levels of government, and the concentration of

political power in the hands of the national political party leadership at the expense of lower levels of the party hierarchy.

4. Despite the controls exercised by national elites over local-level voluntary associations, the strategy of occasional stimulation of local organizations and leadership has, at times, threatened to establish autonomous bases of power beyond the control of the traditional political parties and leaders.
5. The response of the Frente leaders to a possible loss of control depends on the severity of the threat. Their reaction ranges from governmental recentralization and offers of patronage, through withdrawal of legal recognition and sponsorship of competing organizations, and finally to actual physical repression.

Implicit in these propositions, and in our analysis, is the position that, despite its internal factions and divisions, the National Front did represent the interests of an economic ruling class.[2] In Dix's words:

> Though it by no means has remained wholly closed to new recruits or new ideas, the Colombian upper class has retained in its hands most of the power resources of the society, including economic dominion, highly disproportionate access to education, and control of the mass media and the major political parties. Its approach to change has on the whole been that of palliative, paternalistic reform, designed to alleviate severe stresses in the system and to respond to certain cues (such as anarchic rural violence) or to certain demands on the part of counter-elite groups, without at the same time yielding up any real share of effective control over the major power resources.[3]

ACCIÓN COMUNAL: A CASE OF COOPTATION

The National Front undertook its first experiments with decentralized decision making in direct response to the problems caused by La Violencia. A few months before Liberal Alberto Lleras Camargo took office as president, the interim military junta created a National Commission to Investigate the Violence. This commission recommended a rural development approach to pacification; a solution impelled by the demands presented by rural communities as conditions for signing peace treaties.[4]

After Lleras' inauguration, the Special Rehabilitation Commission adopted the proposals of Father Louis Lebret for the creation of multipurpose teams (*equipos polivalentes*) of technicians and social workers and of rural zone committees of local leaders as vehicles for the delivery of services. Fourteen teams were established, all in violence areas. The teams formed local committees, helped construct and repair schools, gave health courses and agricultural demonstrations, and taught how to build latrines and initiated other practical community projects. The local committees formed in several areas, such as

Chaparral (Tolima), remained in operation thereafter, and some zone-committee leaders became political-party candidates for local *concejos*, or otherwise provided alternative leadership to that of *violentos* or anti-Frente parties.

The initial experience of the rural zone committees was generalized into a national program when the administrative reform (Law 14 of 1958) included a provision for recognition of elected Community Action Boards (Juntas de Acción Comunal). These boards were to be made up of local residents of rural or urban neighborhoods, and could be delegated "functions of control and vigilance and a certain intervention" in the management of various public services. Through these boards the government was to permit popular participation in a number of activities, including school construction and repair; health programs and construction of health centers and public restaurants; construction and administration of irrigation and drainage systems; low-cost housing, roads, and bridges; improvement of agriculture; encouragement of sports as well as recreational and cultural activities; and the organization of cooperatives and labor exchanges. Decree 1791 of 1959 added to this list adult education, reforestation, preparation of residents of overpopulated areas for migration, and the development of animal husbandry for dietary improvement.

These listed activities were not urged on the boards in any systematic way. A National Division of Community Action would certify any board as a Junta de Acción Comunal if it was elected by an assembly of a rural or urban community and it filed certain papers. A few cities imposed political constraints on neighborhood boards, including parity between members of the Liberal and Conservative parties, membership by public officials, or participation in specific city programs. Most rural boards, however, were faced with no prior requirements as to composition or activities. The primary function of Community Action Boards was expected to be organizing construction programs. Government matching funds were made available for some construction programs, including new farm-to-market roads, schoolhouses, and residential water supply and sewage systems.

The initial orientation of the Community Action Program toward pacification is evident in the distribution of promotional efforts and assistance in its early years. Not only were the multipurpose rehabilitation teams directed to areas of violence, but even after the program was extended to a national scale, special provisional efforts were continued in areas of violence. Many of these were directed by private agencies. For a time, the National Federation of Coffee Growers took over support of the multipurpose teams after the rehabilitation commission was disbanded, while in Cundinamarca, a Private Sector Federation for Community Action was formed and directed its activities toward the Sumapaz region where communist activity was strong. An American advisor (paid by a private foundation later alleged to be a CIA conduit) was instrumental in the initial organization of these private efforts, and a team from another CIA-linked organization later attempted to channel student community-action activities. The church, too, promoted community organization as a counter to violence. FANAL (the church-sponsored rural labor union), ELIT (Catholic Action Leadership Training Schools), Radio Sutatenza (a church-founded educational radio network), and local priests all attempted to stimulate community action, often with publicly stated antiviolence or anticommunist motives. Anticommunist organizations such as the Centro de Estudios y Acción Social (CEAS), or "Black Hand," and the Corporación de la Sagrada Familia of Manizales worked in a similar vein.[5]

The distribution of government promotors was less directly tied to zones of violence. Although civil-military action continued to work with Acción Comunal in a number of areas, the National Division of Community Action to some extent avoided violence areas—largely because the Peace Corps was too timid to place its volunteers (who worked with the National Division) in these areas until the late 1960s. Nonetheless, as late as 1964-66, government financial support for community construction projects was greater in Violencia areas than elsewhere, although this may have been the result of a greater volume of requests from these already-organized areas than from a continuation of deliberate policy.[6]

A careful study of the effects of community organization on pacification is lacking. Nonetheless, where the Violencia consisted of control of areas by armed groups with only limited popular support, the community action tactic appears to have had considerable success. An Acción Comunal worker's account of his role in the attack against the guerrilla leader, "Chispas," is a good example. Chispas had been operating in an area of Quindío where different *veredas* (rural communities) had been attacking each other for fifteen years. The promoter began his activities by organizing social festivals in separate *veredas; juntas* were formed and works begun. Next, hitherto warring communities were brought together socially. "Men who had known each other at school at the age of twelve began to remember they had been friends and played in the same patio. They began to ask themselves why they hated each other when they had not done anything." Village collaboration was next secured in the building of roads, health posts, schools, and other community works. After less than half a year of activity, Chispas fell, because "he lost the support that he had in the communities, and he began to wander from one place to another without the confidence of anyone. His group began slipping away from him, and one night, when it was least expected, he ran into the army and was shot."[7]

Areas where more ideological revolutionary groups had some roots among the peasantry were also penetrated, in part, through the use of community action. During the early 1960s, violence areas such as the Alto Sumapaz and Viotá in Cundinamarca were subjected to a barrage of governmental, church,

Cafeteros and Peace Corps organizational activity centered around Acción Comunal. These activities were designed to reestablish central control by bringing peasant groups into closer contact with national agencies. This tactic, accompanied by military and police action in most cases, succeeded in gradually reducing the organizational and ideological coherence of the radical peasant groups which had emerged in these areas during the Violencia.

Even after the immediate threats of violence were contained, community action programs continued to be used periodically as channels for patronage to mobilize the population for political purposes and to compete with leftist organizations. Solaún et al.,[8] for example, describe the use of Acción Comunal programs to compete with the communist-influenced Central Pro-Vivienda, which had organized the land invasion in a Bogotá *barrio* during the 1960s. A more recent case was carried out in the Bogotá newspapers. During 1973 and 1974, the AC *juntas* in several neighborhoods were offered aid and patronage as part of the "Integral Development" Program plan to construct an extremely costly highway around the eastern perimeter of Bogotá. The support of these *juntas* was important for publicity reasons because the highway project had been strongly attacked by a series of more radical *barrio* defense committees that had been formed to oppose the plan.

Even where direct ideological conflict did not arise, the uneven development of *juntas*—which in rural areas became stronger among small farmers than among landless workers, and in urban areas were stronger among middle-status residents than among the poor—deepened local divisions, thus facilitating central control.[9]

Over time, Acción Comunal developed new functions far beyond its initial role as instrument to combat violence. As governmental control over rural areas was extended, the *juntas* came to play an important role in government plans to stimulate economic development. Alberto Lleras spoke of the contribution that self-help activities could make to national development: "If, instead of wasting all their energy in campaigns of sectarian ferocity, the Colombians could unite their forces to construct roads or schools, or for so many other things for municipal or rural progress, and if they, at the same time, exerted themselves to elevate their own levels of living, instruction and nutrition, their agricultural methods, their housing conditions, aiding each other for these purposes, in a short time we would see great changes."[10]

Belisario Betancur, minister of labor during the Valencia administration, maintained that "it is a fact demonstrated by experience that a schoolroom constructed by the residents is more loved by them and better cared for by them, than one built by the action of the state."[11] These themes were not, of course, unique to the Lleras or Valencia governments. They were echoes of the general ideology of development and strategy for political stability that was popularized throughout the Americas as the Alliance for Progress.

From the second year of the Lleras administration through the administration of Guillermo León Valencia, the National Front gave considerable support to Acción Comunal as a development program. In 1959, the National Division of Community Action was created as part of the Ministry of Education. The following year, it was transferred to the Ministry of Government, thus recognizing the fact that the *juntas* were, in effect, a level of local government. A first group of full-time development workers (*promotores*) was hired at this time. The formal launching of the Alliance for Progress led to further initiatives related to Acción Comunal. The Colombia Community Action Program became the first Latin American activity to receive Peace Corps volunteers, and in 1960, the National Division increased its promotional staff to work with the corps. In the same year, Vicente Pizano Restrepo, a strong proponent of Acción Comunal as an independent force for local development, became director of the National Division, a post he held through 1966. In 1962, a new national decree, citing the Charter of Punta del Este, required all secondary and normal school students to contribute seventy-two hours a year of literacy teaching, under the direction of the community action agencies. (This requirement was never systematically enforced.) A 1964 decree, also citing the Alliance charter, elaborated procedures for community action boards to receive allocations under the supervision of the national division. The decree also directed the various levels of government and decentralized institutions to collaborate with the *juntas*. Special national funds for local roads and school construction were also set up in these first years. These funds directed much of their investment through the community boards as did several departmental and municipal governments. Various national ministries and decentralized agencies—including the Instituto Colombiano de Reforma Agraria (INCORA), the Instituto de Crédito Territorial (ICT), and the Federación Nacional de Cafeteros (FEDECAFE)—incorporated community action promotion into their own programs, and a number of private organizations with regional interests outside of the areas of Violencia began to field promotional teams of their own. By the mid-1960s there were more than 500 promoters, including 200 American and Dutch "volunteers" and 57 regional and local promoters who were directly under the National Division of Community Action.

The rural communities of Colombia, and to a lesser extent the urban neighborhoods, responded positively to the opportunities presented by the Acción Comunal program. By 1966, the government estimated that 9,000 boards had been formed. Approximately half were actually functioning. Since 1966, these statistics have doubled, indicating that about half of the identifiable submunicipal communities of Colombia have at least attempted to organize community action boards.

Activities of the boards have varied, but most of them did carry out at least one construction project as their initial activity. Approximately 1,000 schoolrooms per year were constructed by community action throughout the middle and late 1960s while roads, water and sewage systems, and community centers were also frequently constructed. In many cases, *juntas* also took part in organizing community festivals, charitable programs, athletic competitions, and health programs. Agricultural projects, housing construction or improvement programs, artisan workshops, and cooperatives were less common activities generally attempted only by *juntas* that had been successful in previous enterprises.

Within a few years, the community action boards were managing a significant proportion of Colombia's local-level infrastructure investments. In 1966, the national budget included an appropriation of more than 35 million pesos (more than two million dollars) for community action projects and a larger sum for institutional funds which could, in turn, make grants to the community action boards. Investment in projects organized by the boards was estimated at between 100 and 150 million pesos, with approximately 60 percent of the investments consisting of government matching funds. The level of investment was approximately twice what it had been at the beginning of the Valencia administration four years earlier. In 1969, an investment of 300 million pesos was made by the government, and in 1971, direct government grants from the national budget to *juntas* amounted to 140 million pesos—a figure that excludes some of the aid received by indirect channels. Growth in real terms was slower thereafter, for reasons to be discussed below.

From an economic development viewpoint, the community action program was a successful effort. In terms of enlisting local energies and investments as well as the marginal efficiency of the investment, AC proved to be an economical program. A cost-benefit analysis of the construction programs indicated that community construction saved between 40 and 50 percent of the cost of similar construction undertaken directly by the government or other national institutions like the Federación de Cafeteros.[12] The savings involved not only the use of otherwise unemployed labor but also a substantial saving on overhead, design, and supervision costs with no apparent loss in quality on simple construction projects. Despite some difficulties in securing teachers or medical personnel for constructed schools or health facilities, the use made of the works was sufficient to amount to a rate of return on the investment in community action of close to 18 percent (including promotional costs as well as local and national investment costs). This return, which is adequate compared to measured returns on many other development investments, did not include the indirect benefits derived by the community from the organizational experiences in AC projects. Those communities that had experience with community development programs proved, over time, to have somewhat greater receptivity to other development programs—such as agricultural extension efforts—than those that had no experience with Acción Comunal.

The experience with community action also gave many communities the confidence to demand further assistance from the government. The search for matching funds and the experience of managing public monies led the community boards to see themselves as local semigovernments able to represent their communities in matters outside the search for project grants. By the end of the Valencia administration, a large number of community action boards had presented government agencies with petitions for land redistribution, complaints about government services, demands for transportation services, and had made other grievances known. In a 1966 survey, three-quarters of the *juntas* had experience with petitioning for matching funds, and slightly over one-third had presented petitions or demands on other matters.[13]

In a number of municipalities, the *juntas* from different *veredas* or *barrios* had formed municipal or regional federations to coordinate activities and increase their political bargaining power with local and national governments. Federation demands often involved challenges to other government agencies and, at times, to the local power structure itself. The association in Chaparral, Tolima, for example, attacked public officials who favored large landowners over small farmers in the distribution of services. The association in Santander de Quilichao, Cauca, carried out a campaign of letters and telegrams directed at the government demanding that the land reform program for the area be carried out. Another in Viterbo, Caldas, organized a civic strike to protest that town's inclusion in the department of Risaralda. The *juntas* in Buenaventura attempted to form a negotiating committee to represent residents before the Colombian Ports Authority, which was demolishing several *barrios*. In Medellín, the coodinating federation formed by the *juntas* forced a mayor out of office in 1966 when he tried to reorganize the municipal office of community development against their wishes.[14] In Bogotá, an association of *juntas* demanded the nationalization of all educational establishments, the creation of a national cooperative and commerical bank, representation of *juntas* on decentralized agencies' boards of directors, a tax on idle lands, and changes in the municipal structure and zoning codes of Bogotá.[15] In some municipalities, community board associations even put up their own slate of candidates for the municipal councils.

The new activities of the *juntas* were not immediately perceived as a national phenomenon because communication between different areas of the country was limited. But at a national conference on community development held at the National University in 1965, Dr. Pizano, the director of the National Division of Community Action, commented: "The government has received more complaints of dishonesty or failure by public employees through the Community Boards than by direct denunciations by individual citizens. The Minister of Justice told me that the Community Boards gave him more work than all the rest of the country with their petitions.[16]

At the same meeting, Camilo Torres, who had organized student community development activities at the National University and helped National Division promoters, saw in this program the possible origin of a radical trend. Torres stated: "Community organization is not in itself a political party, but it is the school for the formation of a majority political party."[17] What was, for both Pizano and Torres, an encouraging trend was not seen as such by many party and government officials. Local officials were often the first to complain. In 1962, several *juntas* in Neiva were stripped of legal recognition after a meeting at which they had denounced the mayor. In 1970, the novelist Eduardo Caballero Calderón, appointed mayor of the small town he had described in his writings, complained that the *juntas* often obstructed rather than helped government plans. "In Tipacoque, I represent the state as Mayor, but I have the *juntas* to contend with. Any request to the government has to be made through the *juntas*. The *juntas* are useful, as long as the two understand each other the system works. But now there is grave disarticulation. The community action philosophy is good as a mechanism to assure popular participation, but not as co-government."[18]

Complaints by local officials were not necessarily a sign of central government displeasure with Acción Comunal. Where local elites did not support Frente modernization policies, *juntas* were encouraged to oppose them. At times, when *junta* complaints provided evidence of strong popular dissatisfaction with local policies, mayors might be removed at their demand, as in Medellín in 1966. The actions of the national government beginning in 1966, however, indicate that the leadership of the National Front had concluded that the community action boards, despite their usefulness in the antiviolence campaign and in modernization programs, were a potential danger to Frente control. They were in danger of escaping from central influence and had to be brought back under control.

The tightening of control began in 1966, shortly after Camilo Torres had made his bid to form a revolutionary political front and then joined the guerrilla movement. The last educational program in which he had been involved was a course for new local promoters run for the National Division by the Escuela Superior de Administración Pública (ESAP) in 1965. Several dozen students, selected by competitive examination, had taken the course. In 1966, Vicente Pizano's request to increase the number of local promoters, using graduates of the course, was rejected. Only a very few of the graduates received jobs with other promotional agencies, (e.g., INCORA and the Department of Health of Antioquia). Instead of increasing the group of promoters, the Congress moved to bureaucratize the existing promoters by burdening them with new statistical reporting functions with the ostensible purpose of proving that the provisions of Law 19 of 1958 were being observed. The funds that were to have gone for new staff were instead used to reward the *juntas* that had best complied with the 1958 act (Law 4 of August 4, 1966).

In his inaugural address, Carlos Lleras Restrepo presented the familiar developmentalist argument for community action:

> What is needed to transform the country cannot be carried out even in a small part by means of bureaucratic organization. This is now realized, and the flourishing of Community Action, even though it is not yet as widespread as could be is the beginning of this great effort that the Colombian people must make to conquer their well-being and which the government will have to stimulate with well-designed aid and all the means that the modern techniques of motivation and mass communications offer to us.[19]

But he did not entrust the "great effort" he spoke of to the existing, and somewhat independent, Acción Comunal system. First, a new supervisory agency was established—the Consejo Nacional de Integración Popular—to oversee all community development efforts. The new council included the minister of government, two special advisers to the president, and representatives of the Episcopal Conference, the armed forces, the Colombian Association of Medical Faculties, the Colombian Teachers Federation, and the Asociación Colombiana de Voluntariado. Additional members representing the Juntas de Acción Comunal of the country, cooperatives, and private community development agencies were to be selected by the national government (Decree 2263, September 5, 1966). As presidential advisers, Lleras selected José Galat, an expert affiliated with the anticommunist Catholic Action organization, and Emilio Urrea, a Liberal lawyer later to be named mayor of Bogotá. The "community action representatives" selected were Germán Samper, a Bogotá planner and architect from a leading family, and Rodolfo Martínez Tono, a Conservative and Director of SENA (*Servicio Nacional de Aprendizaje*) for more than 10 years. In 1968, decrees 334 and 3159 reorganized the Ministry of Government, combining the Division of Community Action and the Indian Affairs Department into a new bureaucracy entitled Dirección General de Integración y Desarrollo de la Comunidad and imposing formal educational requirements on the position of promoter.

Lleras also attempted to split the community action movement by creating new organizations to compete with or replace the federations of *juntas* as representatives of the communities in their dealings with the government. Through Decree 2263 of 1966, regional Consejos de Integración Popular were set up in nineteen regions and municipalities including the Sumapaz, Puerto Tejada (Cauca), and Pitalito (Huila) where strong federations of community boards already existed. The new councils included not only *junta* representatives, but also representatives of local government, national ministries, decentralized agencies, and private organizations. These councils were supposed to fill an important function in coordinating the activities of hitherto uncoordinated government agencies in the development field. But the inclusion of a large number of institutional representatives (rather than representatives from the preexisting federations of *juntas*) and the failure of the national government to assign any real powers to the councils, suggests that they were created merely to compete with existing organizational structures.

A second set of competing organizations was created by Decree 755 of March 2, 1967, which established a registry of users (*usuarios*) of government agricultural services and credit, and recognized associations of *usuarios* as the groups entitled to represent the state beneficiaries in dealings with national agencies. The history of these usuarios associations is discussed below, but it is important to note that Acción Comunal *juntas* that met certain conditions were encouraged to register as *usuarios* organizations.

The budgetary provisions of the constitutional reform of 1968 and several additional decrees were used to restructure the funding of community action projects in order to create a more centralized patronage structure. Under the 1968 reform, the preparation of the national budget was centralized in the hands of the executive, except for small sums that were made available to individual congressmen to distribute to projects such as Acción Comunal at their own discretion. The practice of distributing funds for specific projects through the budgets of different ministries and decentralized institutes was continued, with the Ministry of Government assigned the supervision of these investments (Decree 3159 of 1968 and 158 of 1970). A Community Development Fund also was to receive some direct budgetary allocations to be distributed as grants or loans to *juntas*, or to be used to acquire equipment for loan to *juntas*, at the discretion of the Dirección General. The control over community action investments by the national Contraloría and by municipal treasurers was also tightened and formalized at this time. The overall result was to reduce the freedom of the *juntas* to seek funds from various agencies and to limit the log rolling among congressmen over the amount of patronage they would have to disperse. Now each congressman has only a fixed amount to give and the *juntas* are forced to compete for that fixed amount. Power to increase the total annual grant available was left in the hands of the national leadership. Under the new system, national allocations to community action projects leveled off, ending the period of rapid growth in Acción Comunal.

Toward the close of the Lleras administration and the beginning of the Pastrana administration, the limits of *junta* independence were more carefully defined through the restructuring of the promotional and subsidy systems. The *juntas* were officially granted the right to form federations and to speak for communities in areas not mentioned in the 1968 Administrative reform (Decree 2070 of December 1969 ; Ministry Regulation 504 of June 1970; and Decree 835 of 1973). As redefined under the 1969 and 1973 decrees, the *juntas* and federations, respectively, were burdened with new bureaucratic requirements. As a result, by 1974 there were fewer functioning municipal federations than there had been informal federations in 1966 or regional Consejos de Integración Popular in 1968. Many of the municipalities in which there had previously been active federations were bogged down in the work of drafting acts and recovering old documents in order to attain legal recognition and be eligible for the limited amounts of patronage theoretically available.

Four National Congresses of Community Action were also organized under government sponsorship (1970, 1971, 1972, 1974). These congresses, attended by both governmental representatives and *junta* delegates, provided a forum for *junta* complaints about lack of government assistance, difficulties in receiving allocated funds because of complex paper work and corruption, lack of taxing powers, and other difficulties. But they have not led to the formation of any real national organization of community action boards or even provided the opportunity for discussion of political issues. Consequently, no national leadership has emerged within the community action movement. Rather, the government has strictly limited any possible "majority pressure group" role for community action, saying that community action has to be an "apolitical, technical program." This argument has been used as a basis for attacking any *juntas* that take dissident or radical stands. The same rationale has been employed to oust any promoters who threaten to revive the concept of community action as a political force. In 1971, Samuel Yohai, the director of Integration and Community Development of the Ministry of Government, who had served for only a few months, was summarily dismissed from his post when he called together a national meeting of promoters. He was accused of having hired graduates of the sociology faculty of the National University and former officials of the peasant federation (ANUC), and of having allowed radical materials at the promoters meetings.[20]

Enrique Santos Calderón, regarded as one of the more radical newspaper columnists in Colombia, called the firing "an indication of the fundamental contradiction of a government that does not cease to preach the urgency of social change, but which periodically blocks the work of those functionaries who have been most consistently conscious of this work of transformation."[21] The Liberal congressmen who defended Yohai did not admit to this counter-reform tendency but rather tried to pass the incident off as one of Liberal-Conservative party maneuvering. Yohai's successor, Guillermo Alberto González, argued that community action had to be political, in a sense, because the political system needed the support and participation of community residents. He went on, however, to criticize politicians who tried to make personal use of community action. He was transferred to another ministry within a year.[22]

During the presidential elections of 1974, Pastrana's Minister of Government, Liberal Roberto Arenas Bonilla, as supervisor of the Acción Comunal bureaucracy, sent out an official letter to all political party directorates in the country emphasizing the neutral, nonpartisan character of the community action boards. However, this communication was ignored massively by both parties in their efforts to mobilize electoral support during the 1974 presidential elections. Indeed, in both urban and rural areas, *juntas* were important vehicles of mobilization.

By 1975, the constriction of Acción Comunal autonomy had apparently been completed. A 1974 thesis written by Ronald Hart based on research done in 1969 and 1970 indicates much less independence from political patronage ties than was found by Edel in 1966. Orlando Fals Borda, one of the original proponents of community action in Colombia has concluded that, while local cooperativism can contribute to the formation of an effective consciousness for change among the peasantry, the process is too slow, and that efforts in this direction provide only palliatives.[23]

ANUC: A CASE OF RADICALIZATION

Carlos Lleras Restrepo, the third Frente president, had been a prime mover of the initial Agrarian Reform Law 135 of 1961. During his 1966 presidential campaign, he repeatedly emphasized his commitment to accelerated social agrarian reform involving active peasant participation at all levels. Lleras was apparently motivated in part by the desire to create a peasant counterweight to the various political forces in Colombia that had resisted the redistribution of land and agricultural modernization. Almost certainly, Lleras was also concerned with providing himself with a strong electoral base among the peasantry for a second presidential bid in 1974 or 1978.

The creation of ANUC should not, however, be seen simply as a product of the actions of a single political figure. Lleras was operating within an historical context particularly propitious for agrarian reform . Elements of the Colombian elite had recognized that the economy required a more rational system of agricultural production in order to supply the rapidly growing urban centers and to provide the economic surpluses needed for industrialization.[24] Externally, the U.S., through the Alliance for Progress, was providing funds for development programs involving land distribution and reform of the agrarian sectors of Latin American economies. Despite the favorable initial circumstances that allowed the Lleras administration to give new impulse to the agrarian reform, Lleras's programs quickly began to generate intense opposition in both the Liberal and Conservative parties.

In June 1966, president-elect Lleras Restrepo appointed an advisory committee (Comité Operativo) to study the possibilities for a governmental program to organize peasants into rural associations of "users" of governmental services (Asociaciones de Usuarios). The committee was composed of nine members, including political leaders, ministerial personnel, private sector representatives, church leaders, and moderate rural labor union figures.[25] The Comité Operativo was, first, to discuss a plan for organizing the users of all national governmental services such as agricultural credit, storage, extension, and marketing. This organization was to promote peasant (*campesino*) participation in the improvement of such services and to help the peasantry to acquire the experience necessary for organizing and operating cooperatives (transportation, production, and consumer), as well as to collaborate in the execution of the agrarian reform. Second, the committee was to study ways in which already existing entities involved in peasant education and organization could contribute their experience to the *usuarios* associations. Third, it was to do the groundwork for organizing the peasants, with emphasis on training local functionaries of state organizations involved in servicing the peasant population as well as the peasant leaders in charge of establishing the *usuario* organizations. Fourth, it was to suggest both direct and indirect methods—written, verbal, or visual—which should be used during the initial phase of organization.[26]

The committee delivered its report in August 1966, the same month in which Lleras officially took office as president. The report reflected a general rhetorical support for some type of government-directed peasant organization, but basic differences surfaced over points such as degrees of democratic or popular participation in decision making, the basic structure and role of the local organizations, specific organizational procedures, and the role of government bodies in the promotion and actual operation of the *usuarios* program. José Elías del Hierro, a committee member representing the Caja Agraria, even went so far as to classify the entire idea of peasant organization as dangerous.[27]

Despite these fundamental divergences within the Comité Operativo, the Lleras administration drew up a series of laws designed to initiate a National Campaign of Peasant Organization (Campaña Nacional de Organización Campesina). The initial law promoting and regulating this new organization was effected by presidential decree (Decree 755 of May 2, 1967) rather than through the normal legislative process. President Lleras based his right to do this on the powers granted to him by Article 22 of Law 19 of 1958 (Acción Comunal) and Article 97 of Law 135 of 1961 (agrarian reform), and on the special powers granted to the executive under the State of Siege Law (Article 121 of the Constitution), which was in force during most of the Frente Nacional.

The goals of the decree paralleled quite closely those that had been put forward by the Comité Operativo. They can be summarized as follows: (1) to incorporate the marginal population of the rural sector into the process of development by greater popular participation in the decision-making process; and (2) to assign to the *usuarios* associations the functions of control and regulation of specific services provided by official or semiofficial agencies, or to allow for their active participation in the management of such services.

The Ministry of Agriculture, headed at that time by Liberal Armando Samper Gnecco, was placed in charge of formulating and implementing the regulations and programs through which the *usuarios* were to be organized and integrated into the decision-making structure of the various governmental agencies operating in the rural areas. One of the first acts of the ministry was to convene a Consejo Superior de Agricultura to clarify how the government might proceed with its organization campaign. This Consejo was composed principally of governmental bureaucrats with only limited private sector and agrarian syndicate representation. The meeting was held in Paipa, Boyacá, on March 17, 1967. From the conclusions of this conference and subsequent work of the ministry flowed a series of executive decrees and resolutions that organized the Campaña Nacional de Organización Campesina. The first of these was Resolution 061 of February 7, 1968 by which the Ministry of Agriculture began to specify the requirements for government recognition of the departmental, municipal, and *veredal* levels of *usuarios* associations. Decree 2420 of 1968 restructured the bureaucratic apparatus of the government in the agricultural sector and extended to the Ministry of Agriculture the authority to create a Division de Organización Campesina (Division of Peasant Organization) with powers to grant legal recognition, to enforce the associations' statutes and to apply sanctions when necessary. Minister Armando Samper Gnecco appointed Dr. Mario Suárez Melo as the first director of this division.

Decree 1817 of 1969 provided more detailed specifications for the registering of the associations, for the application of legal sanctions, and for the utilization of available government resources. A series of resolutions passed during this period by government agencies gave representation (at least formally) to the *usuarios* groups at the local, regional, and national levels. Finally, President Pastrana appointed a Committee for Rural Social Development in order to provide for more effective executive control of the activities within the Division of Peasant Organization and of the *usuarios* as a whole. (Resolution 0316, April 1971).

Early in 1968, the Lleras government began to train a group of seventy-five promoters in order to carry out the organization program at the local level.[28] As of June 15, 1971, the numbers of field personnel had remained roughly constant, while the division personnel had grown to fifty-five positions. Through June 1971, the division staff had managed to recruit 968,490 members into a total of 496 legally recognized municipal *usuarios* groups.

This considerable feat of organization was carried out on an average yearly budget of between 5 and 6 million pesos.[29] Four governmental institutions outside the Ministry of Agriculture—INCORA, IDEMA, ICA, and the Caja Agraria—also financed the peasant organization campaign. The total amount they spent on the program is difficult to determine, but in general their contributions merely represented budgetary transfers rather than new funds. In Delgado's estimation, "the financial cost of organizing the peasantry in Colombia has been very low. In the two most active years (1969-70), the Ministry of Agriculture expended a total of U.S. $605,200, that is, a little less than one dollar for each enrolled member and for the training of a small number of leaders. The budget for 1971 was 233,250 dollars . . ."[30] This is a small sum both in absolute terms and in relation to the official budgetary support given to such organizations as the Federación Nacional de Ganaderos (FEDEGAN). FEDEGAN is the cattlemen's association that directs the public campaign against the Agrarian Reform (and yet it) receives from the Ministry of Agriculture alone, an annual donation of U.S. $300,000 as an official contribution towards its operating and investigatory expenses."[31]

Despite the obvious success of the Lleras administration in increasing the membership of the *usuario* groups, it is necessary to keep official membership figures in perspective. First, not all registered *usuarios* were peasants; any recipient of government services was eligible to be a *usuario*. Second, many of the *usuarios* registered on the roles were not active members due to the fact that many local organizations have become defunct over the years. Third, for bureaucratic and publicity reasons, many of the Lleras administrators tended to inflate the real membership statistics.[32]

The *usuarios* organizations were given a more complex formal structure than Acción Comunal had had. Local-level groups (both *veredal* and municipal) were to be composed of five individuals, who rotated among themselves the five positions of president, vice-president, secretary, treasurer, and *vocal*. In elections each member was allowed to write the name of one individual. No nominations or lists were provided. The ten individuals with the greatest number of mentions were automatically selected with the first five as active representatives and the second five as alternates.[33] Above the *veredal* committees and municipal associations, the next level in the ANUC hierarchy was the Departmental Assembly. There were twenty-two of these assemblies and six National Territorial Assemblies for a total of twenty-eight regional level organizations. Each Departmental Assembly was made up of one member drawn from the Junta Directiva of each of the municipal associations within the given department or territory; the number of departmental delegates, therefore, varied. These departmental associations elected five-man Juntas Directivas organized in the same fashion as the local level associations.

The National Assembly was to be the highest authority within the ANUC. It was made up of a total of 140 delegates composed of all five members of each of the twenty-eight regional associations. These small groups of regional leaders were, in turn, responsible for the election of the National Junta Directiva, made up of one representative from each regional *junta*. The Junta Directiva then appointed a national executive committee made up of five individuals. Departmental and national officers were elected for two-year terms.

From this brief description of the internal structure of the ANUC, it is clear that, at least formally, ANUC was organized in an extremely hierarchical fashion. Delgado, in his comments on ANUC, argued that both the voting procedure and the rigid hierarchy would prevent the emergence of true peasant leadership and that the organization would, as a result, remain dominated and controlled by government bureaucrats and local political bosses, *gamonales*.[34]

From the perspective provided by the First National Congress of ANUC, held on June 7, 8, and 9, 1970, such an assessment appeared reasonably accurate. The Declaration of Principles issued by this first congress was relatively moderate, claiming only that it was necessary to "give impetus to the advancement of the peasants of Colombia and therefore to combat those factors which cause the retardation or the marginalization of poor farmers."[35] The reaction of the Lleras administration to the congress was quite positive; indeed, Carlos Lleras inaugurated the congress in the National Capital Building. He was, however, careful to warn against "the false prophets . . . because many political opportunists will appear with talk of forming a new Agrarian Party."[36] The major newspapers around the country were also highly supportive of the first congress.

Lleras left office on August 7, 1970, firmly believing that he had successfully launched the *usuarios* within the framework which he and the Comité Operativo of 1966 had initially set forth. Conservative President Misael Pastrana Borrero and his first minister of agriculture, J. Emilio Valderrama, soon discovered, however, that the Comité Ejecutivo named during the first congress was composed of a group of radical peasant leaders who rejected the traditional parties and were determined to accelerate the process of agrarian reform through massive land invasions, if necessary. Almost from the very start, the Pastrana administration entered into open confrontation with the *usuarios*. Minister Valderrama, however, who had initially been antagonistic to the *usuarios* gradually became more sympathetic to the peasants demands for land. As a result, he was eased out of office by Pastrana and the president's Ospinista supporters. Pastrana's second minister of agriculture, Hernán Jaramillo Ocampo, adopted a much harsher line with the *usuarios* and the conflict between the government and ANUC intensified rapidly.

Several factors seem to have been involved in the radicalization of ANUC and the resort to confrontation politics. First, the transition from a Liberal to a Conservative administration loosened government control over the organization—new Conservative staff members were appointed while Lleras appointees were shunted aside or dismissed. This political division created considerable tension within the ministry and tended to weaken staff ties with the ANUC organization at all levels. Second, the efforts of the Pastrana administration to establish Conservative control over the organization quickly alienated the national leadership of ANUC. Third, the go-slow attitude of the Pastrana administration toward agrarian reform was apparent from the beginning; the peasants recognized very quickly that they could expect little voluntary help from the Conservative Pastrana administration. Finally, the economic situation of the peasantry was worsening. Traditional systems of exploitation were still in effect in many areas of the country, while at the same time capitalist penetration of the countryside was rapidly accelerating.[37] Such pressures tend to radicalize many sectors of the peasant population, for their very survival as peasants is threatened.

Under such circumstances, ANUC proved uncontrollable by either of the two traditional parties. ANUC's demands for rapid parcelization of the land have clashed with the traditional landholders and their political representatives, as well as with those "modernizing elites," such as Carlos Lleras, who are intent on developing a more rational capitalist system in the countryside. Neither the traditional linkages of patron-client, nor the new "broker" relationships have been able to preserve government dominance over the *usuarios*.

On June 5, 1971, the National Junta Directiva of ANUC was called together for an Encuentro Nacional Campesino, held in Villa del Rosario, Cúcuta, Norte de Santander. During this meeting, the emerging ideological orientation of the ANUC leadership toward more rapid agrarian reform and against the continued dominance of the traditional ruling class was crystallized in a *Plataforma Ideológica*. The essence of the *Plataforma* is summarized in its initial paragraph:

> The National Association of Peasants in Colombia is an autonomous organization of salaried, poor and middle peasants, which is fighting for an integrated and democratic Agrarian Reform; for the revindication of the agricultural worker; for an improvement in the economic, social and cultural aspects of his life; and for the full development of his potential. In order to overcome economic backwardness and to achieve greater levels of well-being for the Colombian people as a whole, it is necessary to break the existing structures of internal and external domination, which have benefited only a small, exploitative class, by means of an organized and permanent battle carried out by the peasantry, the working class and other popular sectors commited to structural change and the total liberation of our country from all forms of domination and colonization.[38]

Seventeen basic demands were put forward in this document. The most significant of these included an appeal to the government to respect the right of the peasantry to organize, a call for expropriation of *latifundio* without indemnization, nationalization of credit, and legal recognition of peasant land invasions of existing *latifundios*.

This Encuentro Campesino was followed by the Fourth National Junta Directiva meeting on August 22, 1971, in Fúquene, Isla del Santuario. At this meeting, ANUC's position regarding the agrarian reform was developed in full detail in a document entitled *El Primer Mandato Campesino*. The principal objectives put forward in the mandate included: (1) elimination of the monopoly over the land; (2) termination of the systems of renters (*arrendatarios*), sharecroppers (*aparceros*), etc.; (3) free distribution of the land; (4) basic changes in the present system of private property; and (5) protection for the small landowners who work their own land. Of particular interest in this document were the provisions for the creation of executive councils on agrarian reform (Consejos Ejecutivos de Reforma Agraria—CERA), paralleling the *veredal*, municipal, departmental, and national level *usuario* organizations. These *consejos* were empowered by the mandate to carry out their own land tenure surveys and then to expropriate, without juridical proceedings or indemnization, lands which did not meet the criteria set up by this document. In reality, this mandate merely formalized a position in favor of land invasions that the ANUC had maintained publicly since December 1970. The official publication and distribution of this document was blocked by Pastrana's minister of government, Abelardo Forero Benavides. The publication of the ANUC newspaper, *Carta Campesina*, had been suppressed by the Pastrana government in April 1971.

With the writing of the *Mandato Campesino*, ANUC's break with the government, which had been gestating for some time, was completed. The Ministry of Agriculture not only continued to block further publication of the *Carta Campesina* (which it had financed through April 1971), but it also reneged on its agreement to provide ANUC with office space and equipment in the Ministry of Agriculture building in Bogotá. Moreover, Minister Jaramillo Ocampo, whose estate in the department of Cesar had been invaded by an ANUC group, began a series of maneuvers designed to divide the ANUC. His key tactic was the creation of an alternate set of peasant leaders (later to be known as the Línea Armenia), closely supervised by the ministry. He also intensified his campaign against the association by firing many of the Lleras trained promoters in the ministry and hiring in their place a number of unprepared, but politically amenable, replacements. These new promoters, using the economic leverage of the government in combination with the right to grant or revoke legal recognition, attempted to coerce local associations to support the Armenia leadership group. Minister Jaramillo Ocampo publicly justified his campaign against the ANUC with the argument that the organization had been captured by Communists.[39].

Throughout late 1971 and early 1972, sizable land invasions were led by ANUC in such areas as Jamundí, the Atlantic Coast, Tolima, and the Valleys of Fúquene and Ubaté. From June 7 to 15, 1972, ANUC sponsored a civic strike in Florencia, Caquetá. This movement was intended as a protest against the abuses and mismanagement of the local agricultural credit programs. The government broke the strike by violently repressing the protesting peasants and by jailing many of the national ANUC leaders who were then meeting in Florencia. Civil strikes were subsequently conducted in the departments of Caldas, Sucre, and Córdoba, and the leaders were repeatedly jailed.

On July 20-24, 1972, in the midst of these confrontations between ANUC and the Pastrana government, ANUC held its Second National Congress in Sincelejo, Sucre. The congress was held under conditions of severe hardship and governmental harassment. During this congress, the government's agricultural policies, as set forth in the *Declaración de Chicoral* of January 9, 1972, were rejected as was the government's Línea Armenia and its leadership.[40]

The two most important measures adopted during this second congress concerned the reorganization of the internal finances of ANUC and the creation of a series of education committees (*Comités de Educación*) to carry out intensive organizational campaigns at the *veredal* and municipal levels. Previously, ANUC had been financed by the Ministry of Agriculture; the withdrawal of support by the Pastrana government, however, forced the organization to impose dues or membership fees of one peso per member per month in order to continue functioning. As subsequent executive committee and national *junta* meetings have emphasized, the collection of these dues has been a slow and difficult process and financial problems continue to severely limit the activity of the organization.[41]

To organize the educational committees, eighty *compañeros* were selected and trained by the Sincelejo executive committee leaders. The principal purpose of the committee was to continue developing new *veredal* committees and municipal associations, to train new leadership cadres, and to combat the counterorganizational efforts of the government controlled Línea Armenia. There are no reliable statistics on the activities of these committees, but in its August 1974 "Summary of Activities," published in the now sporadic *Carta Campesina*, the executive committee claimed that it had been working intensively with these committees and that they have been highly successful in extending the control of the Línea Sincelejo over departmental and municipal associations.

When the second congress at Sincelejo was over, the government intensified its efforts to isolate and discredit the Sincelejo leadership. The limited coverage given by the national press to ANUC was almost universally negative. Under these circumstances, the National Executive Committee concluded that the only way to break the isolation that the government had managed to impose on the organization was through a mass peasant mobilization in all sectors of the country. The marches began in August 1972, and over a period of several weeks were extended throughout the country.

By its own admission, the executive committee failed to organize these marches well, in part because of lack of funds, in part because of the confusion introduced by the Línea Armenia. Consequently, participation was not as high as the ANUC leaders had hoped.[42] Nevertheless, the marches did force the press and the radio to give considerable coverage to the organization for a month. When the regional marches were about to converge on Bogotá, the Pastrana government threatened ANUC with massive jailings of leaders and participants (with the accompanying danger of rioting and violence) if an entry into the city was actually made. In the face of threatened governmental repression, the National Executive Committee decided to suspend the final stage of the march into Bogotá.

Following the Marchas Campesinas, a series of regional seminars were held to consolidate the gains made during the marches, to discuss the concrete problems of each major region in the country, and to stimulate the work of the education committees. The first of these seminars—which included peasants, workers, teachers, students, and intellectuals—was held on September 28, 1972 on the Atlantic Coast. These regional seminars were made permanent through the creation of a series of regional committees. They meet periodically to analyze the situation of the workers and peasants and to make suggestions for strengthening ANUC and coordinating it with other organizations. According to the ANUC , these permanent regional committees are now functioning in the northern and western sections of the country, but not in the east and the south—areas in large part dominated by the Línea Armenia.[43]

Since these first regional conferences, ANUC has continued to hold periodic meetings of the educational committees and of different regional and sectional groups of the peasantry. Indeed, ANUC claims that as of June 1973, in each of the six regions into which it has divided the country for its own administrative purposes, four regional education conferences and one national level education conference had been carried out.[44] In addition, throughout 1972 and 1973, conferences among small coffee and tobacco farmers, *colonos*, women, peasants, and Indians have been held roughly once a year.

Behind these organizational and leadership training activities, ANUC has utilized a range of direct action or civil disobedience techniques in order to make its demands heard. In order to pressure INCORA to move more rapidly on agrarian reform, its offices were occupied for short periods in Bogotá, Cúcuta, Casanare, Pereira, Sincelejo, Montería, Sevilla, Magdalena, Urrao,

Neiva, Pasto, Sibundoy, and elsewhere. On February 21 and 22, 1972, 300 peasant delegates representing thirteen departments occupied the office of the vice-minister of agriculture in order to protest publicly the agrarian counter-reform being carried out by the Pastrana administration. Since 1971, ANUC has carried out over 300 land recuperations (since the *Primer Mandato Campesino*, ANUC has not used the word "invasion") primarily in the departments of Sucre, Magdalena, Bolívar, Cesar, Córdoba, Guajira, Antioquia, Huila, Cauca, and Putumayo. Some areas seized were organized as collective farms. Finally, many of the collective farms organized initially by INCORA were brought together in meetings around the country in 1973. They declared their independence from INCORA domination and control.[45]

ANUC has also attempted to pressure municipal level elites through direct action techniques such as land invasions (throughout the country), civic strikes (e.g. Cunday and San Pablo, Tolima, 1973; Montería, Córdoba, 1974), workers strikes (e.g., *paros tabacaleros* in the departments of Sucre and Magdalena, 1972), and consumer boycotts (e.g., Boyacá and Nariño, 1973). Many of these strikes have been successful, or at least partially successful, in achieving their wage and price demands in negotiations with local landlords and authorities. ANUC also influenced the development of a large and militant movement, the Concejo Regional Indígena del Cauca, among the Cauca Indians.[46]

Pastrana's government consistently opposed these activities. Bureaucratic noncooperation, legal harassment, and jailings have been commonplace for leaders at all levels, and several ANUC leaders (including one member of the National Junta) have been assassinated.[47] These assassinations have generally been attributed to strongmen (*Pájaros*) in the employ of local political bosses and large landowners. Such strongmen are sent to intimidate or murder leaders of organizations such as ANUC that challenge the established order between the peasantry and their landed, bureaucratic, and political patrons.[48]

Despite such repressive tactics, ANUC has continued to flourish at all levels. Accurate estimates of the total membership of ANUC are presently difficult to obtain due to the isolation imposed on ANUC *Línea Sincelejo* and the government's artificial support of *Línea Armenia*. In a personal interview conducted by one of the authors with Conservative exminister of agriculture, Hernán Jaramillo Ocampo, the exminister stated that there were only 5,000 to 6,000 actual militants in the entire ANUC organization.[49] Vargas, in his *El Periódico* report on ANUC just prior to the Third Congress in August 1974, claims that after the 1972 split between Sincelejo and Armenia, Armenia retained 10,000 followers, Sincelejo 300,000 and that 500,000 former members simply dropped out of the organiztion altogether. The Sincelejo leadership claims, to the contrary, that their organization, even after the split, retained roughly 750,000 to 800,000 active members and is still growing, while the Línea Armenia has only a few thousand followers at best and is rapidly declining.[50]

Whatever the precise statistics on ANUC membership may be, it is undeniable that ANUC had emerged as the most powerful and radical peasant organization in Colombia during the period of the Frente Nacional. As a number of studies of peasant life in Colombia demonstrate, the peasantry is experiencing a rapid deterioration in its traditional way of life. Wholesale conversion of peasants into rural salaried workers or marginal urban migrants is taking place at an unprecedented rate. Under these conditions, ANUC, which unlike Acción Comunal, carefully kept itself free from all political entaglements, had managed to seize the leadership of the reemerging peasant struggles in Colombia by the time the Frente period ended in 1974.[51]

CONCLUSIONS

By 1966, the Juntas de Acción Comunal were functioning effectively as channels of local participation in development projects. Indeed, with the creation of regional federations of *juntas*, the community action program had even begun to assert a certain degree of independence from local, regional, and national political elites. In order to strengthen central government control over these *juntas*, the Lleras administration limited and regulated available patronage, replaced the community action federations with Integración Popular, and created a competitive *usuarios* organization paralleling the community action juntas. These maneuvers successfully curtailed virtually all popular pressures for basic societal reforms within Acción Comunal.

By 1970, the Campaña de Organización Campesina, sponsored by the Lleras Administration, had grouped roughly a million peasants into the *usuarios* associations. Like the community action *juntas*, the *usuarios* associations began to pressure for a whole range of services and benefits beyond the initial scope of the organization. After his inauguration in August 1970, President Pastrana and his ministers moved to reassert government control over the *usuarios* apparatus. Unlike Acción Comunal, ANUC was not easily dominated. Despite government harrassment and repression, ANUC remains the most significant and radical peasant organization in Colombia today.

Why is it that ANUC has proven more difficult for the ruling class to control than Acción Comunal? A combination of factors seems to explain this phenomenon. As we mentioned briefly in the section on ANUC, ANUC was radicalized initially (1) because of the efforts of the Pastrana administration to establish Conservative political control over the organization; (2) because the ANUC leadership recognized that the Pastrana administration would not support the agrarian reform voluntarily; and (3) because the conditions of the peasantry were constantly deteriorating in the face of capitalist penetration of the countryside. These radicalizing factors, which were also behind the stirrings in community action, did not find an appropriate organizational vehicle in the AC program. AC *juntas* represent extremely diffuse demands. Conformist behavior has been enforced through patronage often channeled through the traditional political parties. All efforts at politicization have been systematically suppressed and no national leadership cadres have ever been allowed to develop.

In contrast, the demands of the *usuarios* associations are much more specific—they usually revolve around questions of land and agricultural credit. The decreased availability of benefits through established government agencies during the Conservative Pastrana government severely limited the capacity of bureaucratic political brokers to pacify and coopt dissatisfied peasant groups through patronage; and ANUC, through Lleras's Campaña de Organización Campesina, managed to develop skilled regional and national leadership groups capable of providing an alternative to continued governmental party direction.

Whether it is possible for even the most intelligent and capable leaders to mobilize the Colombian peasantry in the face of government indifference and/or repression is doubtful under all but the most drastic of circumstances. To the extent that ANUC truly achieves the mobilization of large segments of the peasant population, government repression will intensify.

NOTES

1. Robert Dix, *Colombia: The Political Dimensions of Change* (New Haven, 1967), p. 168.
2. We do not argue this point here, although the governmental policies we discuss would reinforce the argument on *cui bono* grounds.See, however, S. Kalmanovitz, "Sobre algunas teorías del Imperialismo en Colombia" *Ideología y Sociedad*, 10 (April-June 1973), and "A propósito de Arrubla" (April-June 1974); H. Mohr, *Economía Colombiana: Una estructura en crisis*, (Bogotá, 1972); M. Williams, *The Frente Nacional: Colombia's Experiment in Controlled Democracy*. Ph.D. thesis (Vanderbilt, 1972); and C. Leal, "Social Classes, International Trade and Foreign Capital in Colombia: An Attempt at Historical Interpretation of the Formation of the State, 1819-1935," Ph.D. thesis (Madison, Wisconsin, 1974).
3. Dix, p. 389.
4. Germán Guzmán, *La violencia en Colombia* (Bogotá, 1965). See also CARE, Inc., *Colombia Community Development Survey* (New York, 1960); H. Triana, *Acción Comunal en Colombia* (Bogotá, 1966).
5. G.F. Drake, "Elites and Voluntary Associations: A study of Community Power in Manizales, Colombia" (U. of Wisconsin, 1973). See also *New York Times*, Feb. 14-Feb. 18, 1975 on covert U.S. funding.
6. Matthew Edel, "Determinants of Investments by Colombia Community Action" in *Journal of Developing Areas* 5 (January 1971).
7. From a tape recorded interview done by Matthew Edel with a staff member of the National Division of Community Action, 1966.

8. *El Tiempo*, March 13, 1973; Mauricio Solaún, W.L. Flinn and S. Kronus "Renovation of a Squatter Settlement in Colombia," *Land Economics*, May 1974.
9. Edel, "Investments by Colombia Community Action" and Elizabeth Hegeman, "Community Conflict and the Development of a Worker Elite in a Cali Barrio," in E. Hegeman and L. Kooperman, *Anthropology and Community Action* (Garden City, 1974).
10. Alberto Lleras Camargo, "La Acción Comunal," in Jaime Posada, ed., *Una Política Educativa para Colombia* (Bogotá, 1962).
11. Belisario Betancur, *Colombia Cara a Cara* (Bogotá, 1966).
12. Matthew Edel, "The Colombian Community Action Program: An Economic Evaluation," Ph.D. thesis, (Yale, 1968).
13. Ibid.
14. Ibid.
15. *El Tiempo*, July 25, 1966.
16. SEDEC, *Una Política para el Desarrollo* (Bogotá, 1966).
17. SEDEC, pp. 68-70.
18. *El Tiempo*, June 7, 1970.
19. *El Tiempo*, August 8, 1966.
20. *El Tiempo*, May 8, 1971.
21. *El Tiempo*, May 15, 1971.
22. *El Tiempo*, December 15, 1971, and May 28, 1972.
23. R. Hart, *"The Role of the Local Community in National Political Change"* Ph.D. thesis (Los Angeles, 1924); O. Fals Borda, *El Reformismo por dentro en América Latina* (Mexico, 1972). For information on Fals Borda as the original proponent of Acción Comunal see Fals Borda, *Acción Comunal en una vereda Colombiana* (Bogotá, 1961).
24. Matthew Edel, *Food Supply and Inflation in Latin America* (New York, 1969).
25. The individuals included on this committee were: Ofelia Ocampo de Jaramillo, Rural Reconstruction Movement; Eugenio Colorado, Liberal representative from Cundinamarca and president of FANAL; Otto Morales Benítez, Liberal exsenator from Caldas and exminister of agriculture; Monseñor Jose Joaquín Salcedo, Radio Sutatenza; José Elías del Hierro, manager of the Caja Agraria; Alfonso Moncada, Acción Cultural Popular; José Galat, Integración Popular; Enrique Peñalosa Camargo, manager of INCORA and minister of agriculture.
26. Ministerio de Agricultura, *Informe sobre la Campaña Nacional de Organización Campesina* (1968).
27. Germán Vargas, "Historia de la ANUC ilegal," in *El Periódico*, August 31, 1974.
28. Ibid.
29. Ministerio de Agricultura, *Informe* (1971), p. 19.
30. Oscar Delgado, "La Organización de los Campesinos y el Sistema Político," *Aportes*, July 25, 1972, p. 95.
31. Ibid., p. 96.
32. Ministerio de Agricultura, 1971, p. 6.
33. Delgado, 1972, p. 102.
34. Ibid., p. 82.
35. ANUC, "Declaración de Principios del Primer Congreso de la ANUC," mimeograph (Bogotá, 1970).
36. Carlos Lleras Restrepo, "Discurso de inauguración, Primer Congreso de ANUC," mimeograph (1970).

37. A. Eugene Havens and William Flinn, "Structural Determinants of the Selectivity of Migration in a Declining Economic Area," mimeo. (Madison, Wis., 1974). Gustavo De Roux, "The Social Basis of Peasant Unrest: A Theoretical Framework with Special Reference to the Colombian case," Ph.D. thesis, (Madison, Wis., 1974). Fals Borda, *El Hombre y la Tierra en Boyacá* (Bogotá, 1973).
38. ANUC, *Plataforma Ideológica* (Bogotá, 1971).
39. The *usuarios* have openly rejected Communist party influence. In fact, some Communist leaders actually cooperated with the minister in his maneuvers against ANUC, with the hope of capturing control of the rapidly expanding organization. These efforts failed and the party, at present, has no role at all in the association. (Bagley: Interview with Juan de Dios Torres, Comité Ejecutivo de ANUC, Bogotá, July 10, 1974). Also Vargas, 1974, p. 4.
40. Through the Acuerdo de Chicoral, the Pastrana government signaled its complete abandonment of the notion of a social agrarian reform, as it had been projected by Carlos Lleras. Pastrana's emphasis was placed on increasing agricultural productivity through the stimulation of capital investments in the rural areas. Under such a program, the ultimate fate of the peasantry is liquidation, for they are either forced into the cities (Colombia has one of the highest urbanization rates in the world) or they are converted from peasants into salaried workers on large agroindustries. See De Roux, 1974; Kalmanovitz, "A propósito de Arrubla" in *Ideología y Sociedad*, April-June 1974; and Vargas, 1974.
41. ANUC, 1974, pp. 83, 108.
42. Ibid., pp. 93-94.
43. Ibid., p. 112.
44. Ibid., p. 113.
45. Ibid., pp. 63-75. Along the Atlantic Coast of Colombia, the agricultural population has responded to the growing concentration of land and resulting poverty through land seizures, especially where land titles were obtained illegally or where the land is underutilized. In 1972, in Montería, Córdoba, ANUC helped to organize the first Baluarte de Autogestión Campesina (independent, communally-run peasant communities). The principal attractions of the *baluartes*, in comparison with the INCORA-operated Empresas Comunitarias, are the rapidity with which the land is obtained, the freedom from governmental interference, and the communal nature of the internal organization of the *baluarte*.
46. Bruce M. Bagley and Annette L. Traversie, "Indigenous Peasant Movements in Colombia," mimeo. (Bogotá, 1975).
47. Comité de Solaridad con los presos políticos, *Libro Negro de la Represión en Colombia: El Frente Nacional, 1958-1974* (Bogotá, 1974).
48. Alternativa, May 1-15, 1974.
49. Personal interview with H. Jaramillo Ocampo conducted by Bruce Bagley, July 11, 1974, Bogotá, Colombia.
50. Personal interview with Juan de Dios Torres, Comité Ejecutivo de ANUC conducted by Bruce Bagley, July 18, 1974, Bogotá, Colombia.
51. Throughout 1974, ANUC continued to utilize land invasions, civic strikes, and other direct action techniques in order to pressure the government into more effective action. In the months preceding the Presidential elections of April 1974, land invasions were particularly intense in departments such as Córdoba, Sucre, Cesar, Huila, and Antioquia. (*El Tiempo*, April-May 1974). In addition, a new round of sectoral and regional conferences was held in preparation for the Third

ANUC Congress which was convened in Bogotá from August 31 through September 4, 1974. This Congress was inaugurated with a peasant march through Bogotá which involved between thirty and forty thousand individuals, by far the largest single demonstration ever staged by ANUC. This Congress, held during the first month of Liberal President López's administration, was not treated hostilely, as under Pastrana, but rather was simply ignored by the government.

Part III
Public Policy

Chapter 10

The National Front and Colombia's Economic Development

R. Albert Berry

What did the National Front mean for economic development in Colombia? Any attempt to answer such a question must involve much speculation; one can only guess at the alternative political institutional structure that would have materialized had the Front not been formed. Even if the institutional alternatives were known, detailed, in-depth information would be required to judge which of the economic decisions and events of the National Front years should be attributed to this particular institutional form, and which to other factors. This chapter does not attempt to describe the political alternatives that Colombia had in 1958; rather it will outline the major economic events and the key decisions that occurred during the Frente; make some suggestions about the political decision-making process associated with them; and speculate about the relationship between the existence and goals of the National Front and the decisions taken during it.

We first present some broad economic characteristics of the years immediately preceding the National Front, and note certain features of the country's economic evolution. A brief discussion follows of the economic goals as perceived by the creators of the National Front, and of their relative importance vis-à-vis other goals. The analysis then centers on the most important economic events and policy decisions of the Frente. Finally, a rough assessment of whether and how much the National Front mattered to the economic development of the country is made.

ECONOMIC SETTING FOR THE NATIONAL FRONT

From the point of view of income per capita, and most other commonly accepted indicators of society's welfare or development, Colombia has long been somewhere in the middle of the Latin American countries. Her twentieth-century growth, while not dramatic, has been on the whole quite respectable. Since 1925, gross domestic product has grown at about 4.5 percent per year and output per capita at about 2.0 percent.[1] However, income distribution has always been highly unequal in Colombia and remains so. The most complete study, which uses figures from 1964, suggested that the top 10 percent of income earners received about 48 percent of the income in Colombia, the bottom 50 percent received about 13 percent, and the bottom 20 percent received 2.6 percent.[2] This implies one of the more extreme cases of inequality in Latin America, although cross-country comparisons of this sort are notably hazardous.[3]

As discussed elsewhere, the National Front was the response of Colombia's political elite to the violence which culminated in the presidency of Rojas and to the danger that the independent aspirations of Rojas created for the traditional political elite. Interestingly, the years most characterized by violence and political trauma—the late 1940s to the mid-1950s—were also marked by rapid economic growth. The Colombian economy had performed fairly well during the Depression and the World War II years (growth of 3.3 to 4 percent a year, depending on the precise period chosen). From 1945 to 1957, growth was accelerated on the basis of (1) running down the foreign exchange built up during the war, when imports of many goods were unavailable, and (2) the coffee price, which reached an all-time high during the early 1950s. Gross domestic product (GDP) grew at about 4.8 percent annually, and GDP per capita grew an estimated 2.1 percent over these years, while national income per capita grew at 2.8 percent.[4] Urbanization proceeded apace; possibly the rural violence pushed it a little beyond the fast rate which would have been caused in any case by rapid economic growth.[5] The three largest cities taken together grew at about 6.5 percent,[6] and the share of the population located in urban areas (centers of 1,500 people or more) rose from a little less than a third to about 44 percent. Income distribution appears to have worsened somewhat. A number of factors could have contributed to such a worsening, among them the advance of mechanization in agriculture, and import substituting industrialization in capital intensive industries. Conservative presidents governed from 1946 until Rojas's coup d'état in 1953. Rojas styled himself as the man of the people. However, while a number of his more visible policies and projects could be construed as favoring an improved distribution, it is doubtful that their impact was significant.[7]

The Rojas years (1953-57) were blessed with the buoyancy of such high coffee prices that an increase in average incomes was more or less a foregone conclusion, and output growth was relatively easy to achieve.[8] The collapse of coffee prices in 1957 brought this bonanza to a close, and left the economy in a very vulnerable position—it had a high level of short-run international debt and little in the way of immediate alternatives to coffee as a source of foreign exchange.[9]

Accordingly both the military junta which displaced Rojas in 1957 and later the National Front faced a short term balance-of-payments crisis. This presented a serious growth problem since Colombia was dependent on imports for the great majority of its capital equipment at the time. More important, Colombia faced the permanent challenge of widespread poverty and the possibility that the left leaning stances of Gaitán (assassinated in 1948) and Rojas[10] had fueled the rising expectations of the masses. Poverty, unequal income distribution, and employment difficulties were to receive increasing attention and discussion during the National Front years. Some observers presumed that these were major causes of violence, even though the precise relationship could not easily be traced.

ECONOMIC OBJECTIVES OF THE NATIONAL FRONT

The National Front was conceived by its proponents as a mechanism to obtain political peace (including an end to La Violencia) and to restore the constitutional order under a civilian regime.[11] It was also considered an instrument that would educate Colombians in the arts of political compromise and the acceptance of the legitimacy of opposition, a natural goal both for those whose main concern was the political freedoms of a democratic regime and for those who believed that such a regime was best for the achievement of economic progress. Implicit in these goals was the maintenance of power largely in elite hands. At the same time, economic development was to be advanced, and such changes effected on the social order as were necessary to ward off social revolution. Reform was to be of modest scope and economic growth rather than structural change was to be the focus; dividing the pie more equitably was secondary to enlarging it.[12] Consistent with these goals, Dix describes the economic programs of the first two presidents of the Frente as emphasizing recovery and stability, growth and economic diversification, and balanced regional development;[13] only the last objective could be construed as having much to do with distribution.

To the extent that the National Front was a truce between the traditional parties after both Liberals and Conservatives realized that neither could totally

Table 1
Economic Indicators for the National Front Years

	Population (1)	Labor Force (2)	Gross Domestic Product (at Market Prices) (Millions of 1958 Pesos) (3)	Net National Income (4)	Price Indicators: G.D.P. at Market Prices Deflator [a] (5)	Price Indicators: Blue Collar Cost of Living Index (National) (6)	Gross Output/Person (3)/(1) (7)
1958	15,254	4,629.3	20,683	16,481	100.0	100.0	1,356
1962	17,226	5,071.1	25,615	20,173	133.5	129.3	1,487
1966	19,590	5,625.3	30,658	24,825	240.1	242.1	1,554
1970	22,092	6,244.1	38,492	32,003	339.3	338.2	1,742
1974	24,865 [c]	6,935.6 [d]	49,581 [b]	41,618 [b]	n.a.	660.2 [e]	1,994
Rate of Change:							
1958-66	3.17	2.47	5.05	5.26	11.6	11.7	1.72
1966-74	3.03	2.66	6.19	6.66	n.a.	13.4	3.17
1958-74	3.10	2.57	5.62	5.96	n.a.	12.5	2.44

Gross Output/ Member of Labor Force (3)/(2) (8)	Net Income/ Person (4)/(1) (9)	Net Income/ Member of Labor Force (4)/(2) (10)	Share of Labor Force in Agriculture (11)	Share of Population in Urban Areas[f] (12)	Employment in Manufacturing Factory (13)	Employment in Manufacturing Cottage Shop (14)
4,468	1,080	3,560	50.6	≈47.0	248.4	329.8
5,051	1,171	3,978	48.2	≈50.9	287.5	350.7
5,450	1,259	4,413	45.5	≈53.8	325.	406.4
6,162	1,449	5,123	42.7	55.7	375.0	505.0
7,149	1,674	6,001	<40.0	≈58.0	n.a.	n.a.
2.52	1.94	2.72				
3.45	3.63	3.92				
2.98	2.79	3.32				

Notes:

a. The price index reflecting the prices of all goods and services produced in the country; unlike the cost of living index, it includes investment goods prices.

b. Based on official national accounts figures for 1972, and an assumed growth rate of 7.0% in each of 1973 and 1974. (The 1973 figure is based on Fedesarrollo, *Coyuntura Económica*, Vol. IV, #1, April, 1974, p. 19.)

c. Growth of 3.0% per year assumed over 1970-74. No evidence permitting a good check as to the precision of this assumption is available.

d. Growth of 2.65% per year assumed, as in 1966-70.

e. Assuming the 1974 price index to be 14% above the average of Dec./73 and Jan./74 figures, i.e., a continuation of an annual inflation rate of 30%.

f. Urban areas defined as centers of 1,500 persons or more. Figures based on adjusted census data and DANE, *Encuesta de Hogares, 1970*, with interpolation.

Sources and Methodology: Population and labor force figures are the author's estimates, based on adjustments of census figures. Output and income figures are from the national accounts. (Banco de la República, *Cuentas Nacionales*).

exclude the other from the spoils of managing the government[14] and that continued conflict could open the civilian elite to threats of interlopers such as Rojas, one would not expect dramatic changes of economic policy, at least in relation to the pre-Rojas period. Likewise, a cultural deterministic interpretation such as Payne's, that views Colombian politicians as personalistically inclined participants in the system, acting to maximize their status as opposed to achieving collective and "instrumental" goals, would suggest a weak dedication to development, low technical interest and competence, and certain types of corruption. According to this interpretation, these are constant defining characteristics of the system, so one would not expect the Front to bring any economic change above what was already occurring for structural reasons.[15] And if one views the Front less as a party coalition and more as a class consolidation to defend the privileges of the elite, one would expect palliative steps to calm and control the lower income groups but no significant improvement in income distribution. A comparison of particular interest is between the social content of the latter part of the Rojas presidency and that of the National Front.[16] Several students of the Colombian polity have treated Rojas, since his first administration, as a major new force for positive change on the political scene.[17] In his recent bid for the presidency in 1970, Rojas identified himself with the lower class and sponsored populist policies even more than before. He was viewed by many as a real alternative to the "establishment" National Front-type governments. Others, however, predicted that his policies would not be so "radical." The Frente emphasized economic growth and did not seek any major short run economic redistribution, but its most serious alternative—a General Rojas regime—may not provide too much of a contrast.

During the National Front years, there has been much official attention to growth and development of the economy, leaving little doubt that these are now important formal objectives of the society;[18] how much substantive change in goals has occurred is harder to judge. The increasing prevalence of development rhetoric in the Third World makes it difficult to ascertain how much of the emphasis in Colombian rhetoric was due to the Front. In any case, Colombia's leadership during most of the National Front could, I believe, be broadly characterized as "serious,"[19] in that a fair share of ministers and public officials have taken a professional attitude toward their jobs (rather than using them exclusively as a stepping stone to new political positions, wealth or prestige), and the government (especially the last two Frente administrations) has gradually taken advantage of the increasing stock of technical talents.

While the national plans themselves have probably been of only moderate help to the government in its decision making, Colombia's reputation was bolstered by its presenting the first long run development plan under the

Alliance for Progress (the initiation of the Alliance interestingly, coincided with that of the National Front). Subsequent plans have been relatively meaningful documents.[20]

AN ECONOMIC RECORD OF THE NATIONAL FRONT YEARS[21]

As indicated above, the National Front began under a cloud of economic problems bordering on crisis, just following an abrupt decline in coffee prices. The first half of the period, 1958-1966 was characterized by modest income growth (1.9 percent per capita and 2.7 percent per member of the labor force), as the country struggled to recover from the crisis of the late 1950s. The international terms of trade worsened somewhat and remained considerably less favorable than they had been in the early 1950s (Table 1). While gross output was growing at a creditable 5 percent per year, population growth was around its all-time peak (probably a little over 3 percent per year).

During the first two Front administrations, problems were aggravated by the inability of the governments to control inflation. Averaging about 12 percent a year, it quickly wiped out the potentially positive effects of the devaluation of 1962, and exploded to between 25 and 30 percent the succeeding year. Colombia appeared to be moving into the vicious circle of internal price increases and devaluations which has characterized several Latin countries at various times in this century.[22] In addition, awareness of an unemployment problem was heightened as CEDE, the development research center of the Universidad de Los Andes, took the first survey and estimated unemployment in Bogotá at 9 percent (1962).[23] By 1966-68, unemployment rates above 11 percent were frequent. Meanwhile urbanization continued relatively rapidly and seemed to be a factor in the unemployment. Import substitution remained a keystone of the government's development policy, but industry grew somewhat less rapidly than in the pre-Front period because of the more limited availability of imported capital and intermediate products. Newer industries were more capital intensive, and employment creation in factories slowed.[24] Agricultural policy remained a somewhat neglected area; government expenditures and attention were small in relation to the importance of this sector and to the poverty of the people in it. (See the budgetary figures of Table 2.)

The period of relatively slow growth in average incomes may have been characterized by a slight overall improvement in the income distribution.[25] The improvement was limited to the urban areas, however; within the agricultural sector distribution apparently continued to worsen. One hypothesis in explaining the overall improvement is that distribution tends to worsen during periods of accelerating growth and to improve in subsequent periods of slower growth. Other hypotheses abound, but none convincingly argued to this point.

TABLE 2
Some Fiscal Indicators During the National Front and Earlier
(values in thousands of current pesos except where indicated)

Year	Expenditure of Ministry of Agriculture (1)	Ministry of Agriculture Share of Total Central Government Expenditures[a] (percent) (2)	Tax Revenues and Transfers from Families[b] (3)	Tax Revenues and Transfers from Families as a Share of Gross Domestic Product[b] (4)
1948	9,854	2.39		
1949	9,047	2.20		
1950	12,340	2.37	728.6	9.27
1951	19,224	2.78	913.3	10.21
1952	17,660	2.41	1,018.8	10.56
1953	20,427	2.19	1,165.9	10.86
1954	17,589	1.58	1,478.1	11.58
1955	18,934	0.84	1,625.4	12.27
1956	23,050	1.70	1,702.0	11.45
1957	22,803	1.72	1,860.5	10.45
1958	30,986	1.85	2,282.6	11.04
1959	31,494	1.72	2,631.5	11.13
1960	51,224	2.23	3,000.1	11.22
1961	198,487	5.68	3,145.4	10.34
1962	162,778	4.81	3,259.2	9.53
1963	126,555	3.03	4,277.6	9.83
1964	157,055	3.34	6,138.8	11.42
1965	387,589	6.67	6,841.3	11.25
1966	436,376	5.65	9,590.5	13.03
1967	475,171	5.84	11,314.8	13.62
1968	727,988	6.61	14,009.0	14.53
1969	759,276	5.18	17,621.7	15.88
1970	1,221,114	6.70	20,552.0	15.74
1971	1,261,256	5.66		
1972	1,446,935	5.19		

Source: Cols. (1), (3) and (5) for 1948-67, *Anuario General de Estadística*. For 1968-72, *Revista del Banco de la República*, Dec. 1973, p. 2370. Cols. (4) and (7), the above sources and the National Accounts as well.

Notes:

a. Giros y reservas.

b. Excludes administrative costs falling in the budget category, "Dirección de la Administración Pública," which is very small (less than one percent) of the Ministry expenditures shown here.

TABLE 2 (cont'd)

Expenditures of Ministry of Defense[b] (5)	Military Expenditures / Total Central Government Expenditures (6)	Military Expenditures / National Income (7)	Public Investment (millions of 1958 pesos) (8)	Public Investment / All Investment (9)
83,198	16.0	1.21		
110,921	16.06	1.45		
151,364	20.66	1.83		
221,909	23.84	2.41		
c	——	——		
242,790	10.74[d]	2.15		
266,440	19.64	2.09		
256,408	19.39	1.72		
285,571	17.07	1.73	605.6	16.2
303,299	16.54	1.57	636.7	16.9
365,150	15.92	1.65	622.4	14.7
410,645	11.75	1.61	749.2	18.2
453,510	13.39	1.57	753.3	20.3
605,946	14.51	1.66	647.5	17.7
704,685	14.97	1.55	665.8	16.4
778,908	13.41	1.53	679.9	17.4
933,902	12.10	1.55	975.8	20.3
1,033,553	12.71	1.51	1,290.0	28.3
1,444,691	13.12	1.84	1,472.3	26.3
1,436,641	9.80	1.60	1,047.2	29.2
1,885,227	10.34	1.77	1,767.3	27.5
3,789,308	17.00	3.00	1,884.4	26.3
2,254,782	9.37	1.45	1,971.2	28.5
2,367,096	8.78[e]	1.17[f]	2,024.2	27.1

c. In this year the police force was annexed to the ministry so separate budget figures are not presented in DANE, *Anuario General de Estadística*. The budget was probably similar to that in 1955.

d. Not meaningful; total expenditures included very unusual debt repayment. Excluding these, total expenditures would be about 1275 millions, and this share about 19%.

e. Provisional.

f. Assuming national income rose by about 34% in monetary terms in 1973.

The second two presidencies (1966-74) saw more rapid economic growth and, possibly, the attainment of a sustained rapid growth path; the average annual growth rate of output rose from a creditable 5.0 percent during 1958-66 to approximately 6.2 percent in the 1966-74 period. Since 1970 it has been over 6.5 percent.[26] The acceleration occurred during the presidency of Carlos Lleras and continued throughout that of Pastrana. Many economists feel that the key factor in this sustained rapid growth has been the dramatic expansion of so-called "minor exports" (exports other than coffee and petroleum, in the usual parlance). From constituting only 19.2 percent of all exports in 1966, this category has risen to a predicted 55 percent for 1974. Its growth rate over the last three or four years has been phenomenal, around 20 to 25 percent per year. Along with the rapid overall growth during 1966-74, this boom reflects the economy's release from the shackles which increasingly difficult import substitution were imposing on it. Foreign aid from bilateral and multilateral sources has grown very rapidly during this period, adding further to import capacity.

Controlling the rate of inflation was a goal of Lleras, one that was impressively achieved, as the average annual consumer price increase was cut to 8.7 percent. Under Pastrana, however, price stability was assigned a lower priority,[27] and the average increase was over 18 percent, with incoming President Alfonso López inheriting a rate higher than 25 percent in 1974.

Open urban unemployment[28] in the four largest cities probably fell during the Lleras Restrepo years and remained roughly constant over Pastrana's presidency.[29] More important than unemployment trends, in my view, is the evolution of the income distribution pattern. Information is much less complete for this phenomenon. Several pieces of evidence relating to the years 1966-70 suggest a reversal of the earlier improvement (possibly associated with the rapid growth)[30] but it is premature to do more than speculate loosely. Even less firm evidence is available for 1970-74, but the existing rapid inflation raises at least the possibility of a deterioration in distribution.[31] The labor share of income recorded in the national accounts fell slightly from 1970 to 1972. Real wages in construction in Bogotá, Medellín, and Cali fell markedly (between 10 and 20 percent for most categories) over the 1971-73 period.

MAJOR POLICY STEPS OF THE NATIONAL FRONT PERIOD

What one considers to be major policy steps of the National Front depends on the criteria adopted. A step may be important in the achievement of one economic goal and unimportant for another; it may be important as viewed by the decision maker and/or the public at large, but unimportant in fact, or vice versa. The discussion which follows includes some steps that I believe were important in the attainment of one of the major objectives of economic policy, and some steps that were perceived as such, judging by the attention they received in the political process and in the press. The list is naturally somewhat arbitrary.

Institutionalization of Planning

Under Alberto Lleras (the first president of the Front), Colombia's current Planning Commission was created, along with the National Council of Economic Policy and Planning (Consejo Nacional de Política Económica y Planeación). Earlier bodies had also been assigned responsibility for the overall coordination of economic policy making, but their existence was somewhat discontinous and they were not generally influential. This was partly because their role was advisory in nature and partly because no technical body was created to undertake analysis of the issues under consideration.[32] Creation of the Planning Commission and of the Council was an institutionalization that presumably reflected the government's attitude on how decision making should be undertaken. It also reflected the benefits, in terms of future foreign assistance, implicit in a nicely lined up set of projects suitable for foreign financing and some demonstration of a foreign exchange gap—all of Colombia's plans, going back to that of the Currie mission,[33] have been written with this goal very much in mind.[34]

The results of the new institutions appear to have been substantially positive, especially after the Commission's responsibility for the direction of public investment was strengthened, the Council was reorganized, and the personnel strengthened. The supply of technicians—economists and engineers primarily, but especially economists—expanded very rapidly in the succeeding ten or fifteen years, and under the bipartisan Front governments party labels became less and less significant for entry into the government bureaucracy. Planeación appears to have had little influence on economic policy during its early years, but later its role expanded substantially.

As originally constituted by Law 19 of 1958, the new planning system suffered from organizational defects. On the one hand, two of the four members of the Council were named by Congress (the other two by the President); the congressional nominees were not generally productive members, and the exclusion of important ministers led to a lack of coordination and interaction between those ministries and Planeación.[35] A second problem was the fact that the head of Planeación was Secretary of the Council; this detracted from his influence and led to ambiguity as to whether his authority or that of the four council members was to carry more weight with the Planning Commission.

According to Augusto Cano, the task of writing the first ten-year plan and the strong support from President Lleras Camargo provided an atmosphere of interest and cooperation which kept the council and the commission functioning in harmony.[36] The inherent problems emerged under President Valencia (1962-66). Conflict quickly arose between the two bodies, and in December 1963, Decree 3242 eliminated the four full-time advisors and constituted a council composed of the ministers of finance, development, agriculture, and public works, along with the heads of the Central Bank, the Coffee Growers Federation, and the Planning Commission.

A second organizational problem which required revisions of the 1958 Law related to the planning of the central government budget. Although Planeación had been installed with the authority to study and propose the direction of public investment, the operating mechanism was not spelled out.[37] Decree 1675 of 1964 addressed itself to this question, assigning Planeación the role of verifying consistency, fixing priority among the proposed expenditures of the various entities, and checking execution through trimestral reports submitted to it by the entities. It was an important step along the road to more systematic and technical planning of investment, and naturally met substantial opposition within the Ministry of Finance, although it was supported by the director of the budget.

Planning of current expenditures was (and is) still under the National Budget Office (Dirección Nacional de Presupuesto) and planning of investment was under Planeación. Although the separation implied some new problems of coordination, it was a logical division of responsibility.

However several problems remained. For one, Congress still constituted something of an obstacle in the process. For another, the Planning Commission lost capacity (better personnel) as it lost favor in the Government, so that even tasks clearly within its domain could not be effectively carried out—e.g., coordination of public investment. As a result of this particular failure, the Consultative Group of international agencies lending to Colombia, formed in 1962-63, in effect took on much of the priority setting function. Cano suggests that the failure was at least partly responsible for the decline in real public investment at this time.[38]

The next major change occurred as part of the Constitutional Reform of 1968, which was planned by Carlos Lleras before his elevation to the Presidency. A section of the reform was aimed at clarifying the roles of Congress and the executive branch in planning and carrying out economic policy; the functions and composition of the council and of Planeación were redefined. Broadly, the reform reserved to the executive the initiative for government spending, while Congress' function was that of accepting or rejecting (providing it do so within a reasonable period of time) and overseeing or controlling execution of plans.

Although the Council was reorganized in 1963, it was not operative till 1966. The experiences of 1967 and 1968 were, according to Cano, taken into account in the 1968 reorganization.[39] The 1968 reorganization broadened the membership of the council, defined it as the coordinating and orienting entity for planning economic and social policy, and expanded the power of the Planning Commission by (1) strengthening its role in the national budget, and (2) assigning to it the role of coordinator of foreign technical assistance and the responsibility to approve foreign investments in Colombia.[40]

This structural streamlining was paralleled by a definite strengthening of the Planning Commission's personnel. At least by the technical standards applicable in Colombia today, the personnel included only a few well-trained members until the administration of Carlos Lleras (1966-1970). He assigned to it a much greater importance and prestige than it had received under Valencia,[41] and technical criteria appear to have become more important in recruitment for the Planning Commission. Planeación's contribution during Lleras Restrepo's period was essentially, (1) to improve the process of project selection, evaluation, ranking, and orderly presentation to international agencies for funding (where appropriate), and (2) to advance sectoral planning for electricity and transport.[42] The commission's impact on the broad outline of government policy reached its peak in the administration of Pastrana, whose strategy guidelines and major policy steps were based on Planeación proposals.[43] In considerable measure the new strategies of the Pastrana government are those advocated for some years by Lauchlin Currie, who has been a member of Planeación during the last three years of the Pastrana government. The technical level of the commission remains relatively high.

Agrarian Reform

Colombia's first agrarian reform institute (INCORA) was created in 1961 during the administration of Alberto Lleras, and had its most active period under Carlos Lleras. Neither of the two Conservative administrations were positively disposed to land reform and, overall, INCORA has been a relatively unimportant institution, at least as far as land distribution is concerned. As of 1970, only perhaps 20,000 families, or 1 to 2 percent of all the agricultural families in Colombia had gained access to land through INCORA.[44] Several times this many families have been given title to land on which they were previously squatting, and while the value of INCORA's land titling function should not be underestimated, neither this, nor its land redistribution activities have been enough to leave a real mark on Colombia's rural sector.

The story of INCORA's lack of importance (relative to the task it might have been assigned) is a complicated one, but the main ingredient seems simply to have been the lack of political weight behind it.[45] Large land owners retain substantial (but by no means overwhelming) influence in Colombia; at least as important as their strength is the lack of positive support for land reform. While certain technical groups and reformist politicians have supported it, the political pressure for reform coming from potential recipients has been very limited.[46] Working in the same direction (though its importance is difficult to judge) is the feeling on the part of many serious participants in the discussion that a major land reform program would either have a negative impact on agricultural output or at least make no significant positive contribution. Many INCORA personnel have been doubtful about the productive potential of small farms using fairly traditional technologies. The potential of land redistribution in Colombia is still the subject of rather heated debate at the technical level, and there have been serious issues of administrative and bureaucratic capacity to administer a large land reform. In short, even disinterested specialists placing high priority on income distribution and the welfare of the rural poor can be opposed to land reform in the absence of substantial change in Colombia's political structure. A definitive assessment of what difference INCORA has made can only be undertaken at some future date. It might be tempting to argue that it reflected a certain dedication by the government to the resolution of a serious agrarian problem and although it has achieved relatively little to date, its presence creates some presumption of future activity. It might also be argued that supporters of the status quo prefer to have a weak agency in existence since it discourages creation of alternative routes toward land redistribution and generates exaggerated hopes on the part of some potential "troublemakers." At present there is no indication that land redistribution will become important in Colombia during the foreseeable future.

Monetary Reform

The disastrous devaluation of 1962 helped to crystallize growing dissatisfaction with the management of monetary policy by the essentially private central bank, Banco de la República. In 1963 an important reorganization of the monetary system occurred, with the creation of a Monetary Board (Junta Monetaria) composed of government ministers, and supported by two technical advisors. Prior to 1963 the Bank's responsibility was viewed as essentially the provision of adequate financing for development, with this function not fully subordinate to the needs of overall policy.[47] There were increasing doubts that responsibility for price stability and for a policy consistent with the government's balance of payment and employment strategies should be in the hands of a board of governors dominated by the private banks.[48] A continuing quiet scandal in Colombian political economic life had been the access of the powerful Coffee Growers Federation to whatever credit they seemed to want from the central bank, often at the cost of substantial inflation.[49] The reorganization of 1963 was plausible because it placed the coordination of the responsibility for the country's economic development in the hands of the central government.

It is difficult to judge the effects of this reorganization. Judging from the last four years of the Front, it has certainly not provided a safeguard against inflation.[50] Possibly the transfer of authority has had a greater impact on credit allocation.

Adoption of the Floating Exchange Rate

Perhaps the most important economic policy step in the National Front period was the conversion from a pegged exchange rate system (with inevitable periodic devaluations, given the tendency to internal inflation) to a "floating" rate. The transition was undertaken in 1967 in the wake of balance of payments difficulties and a dispute with the International Monetary Fund about foreign exchange policy. Since that time, the exchange rate has been allowed to depreciate gradually in nominal terms, and during the first few years in real terms as well.[51] The floating exchange rate created an unprecedented stability in terms of the real peso price which exporters could expect. The combination of real devaluation and increased stability of the real exchange rate appears to have contributed substantially to the dramatic minor export boom of these years.[52] In 1972/73, for the first time in recent memory, Colombia found its foreign exchange reserves building up; the inflow exceeded the needs (with the existing pattern of importation). Not only did the switch to the floating rate contribute to the very successful export performance, but it ended the disturbing devaluation-inflation cycle which had been the despair of operatives under the previous system. Because of the acute political controversy that they aroused,[53] devaluations tended to be postponed as long as possible. When the decision was finally taken, the devaluation was usually substantial, and was quickly followed by a round of inflation that before long eroded the positive effect of the devaluation on the relative price of exports.[54] Now the depreciation of the peso is quite gradual and, while it may have a mild inflationary impact, it never creates the concentrated impulse of devaluations like that of 1962. Thus the external forces toward inflation in the Colombian economy have been reduced,[55] as have the political tensions associated with single-step devaluations.

Agricultural Development

The Carlos Lleras presidency marked a new focus on the agricultural sector and a drive to raise agricultural output. Like many other countries in the 1960s, Colombia decided that this sector should receive more attention than it had in the past. Official credit figures indicate that the ratio "loans outstanding from the organized credit system/output''[56] reached a peak of over 22 percent in the late sixties.[57] As indicated in Table 2, the share of central government expenditure handled by the Ministry of Agriculture was markedly higher in the sixties than it had been; it averaged 6.1 percent during Lleras Restrepo's presidency, as compared with 4.7 percent in that of Valencia and 3.6 percent in that of Lleras Camargo. Increased attention to agriculture does not necessarily bring quick results, so it may be partly accidental that the growth rate of agricultural output rose from its 2.9 percent level between 1957-59 and 1965-67 to 4.2 percent between 1965-67 and 1970-72. Lleras Restrepo pushed agrarian reform more than either Valencia or Pastrana, but despite the broader authority to expropriate given by Law 1 of 1968, the absolute level of activity was still very limited in relation to the number of small farmers.

The Andean Development Scheme

Colombia was a charter member of the Andean group, formed in 1966. Earlier Colombia had also joined the Latin American Free Trade Agreement (LAFTA) at its inception. In both cases, especially LAFTA, it is probably safe to say that the impact on the overall pattern of Colombian development has been small. By 1973, 8.7 percent of registered Colombian merchanidse exports went to Andean Group countries and 14.02 percent to LAFTA countries, compared with 3.1 percent and 6.3 percent in 1966; in 1960 only 1.3 percent went to LAFTA countries.[58] The corresponding shares of Colombian imports in 1973 were 2.7 percent (Andean Group)[59] and 8.5 percent (LAFTA); in 1966 2.8 percent and 10.4 percent, and in 1960, 1.0 percent and 1.6 percent.[60] Most of the increases in intragroup trade resulting from the mutual concessions [61] would presumably be trade diversion and would accordingly lower the income of the group as a whole, in the short-run at least.[62] There is the possibility of a more beneficial impact on Colombian development later on, but this seems unlikely in the near future. In the case of industries which would have been protected in the smaller national markets anyway, the broader market may contribute to lower costs and associated benefits. The Andean group appears mainly to be protecting relatively inefficient industries which need a larger market than the individual countries. It may be viewed as a second best policy if the protection would in any case have been given by the individual countries, but especially with the current promise of exporting to the rest of the world, it seems quite doubtful that it is the best alternative. The fact that its creation was in considerable degree a political phenomenon may explain the lack of economic analysis underlying much of the planning and discussion.

Constitutional Reform

The constitutional reform of 1968, whose scope was broad, sought to modify the structure of economic policy making in a number of ways. Some of the items related to the planning process were discussed above. Other important changes were:

1. Extending the use of technical planning procedures and the responsibility for planning to departmental and municipal levels, i.e. decentralizing the planning process by government level, while maintaining mechanisms for integration of the various levels.
2. Decentralizing the planning process by sector so that a given ministry, for example, would be responsible for the planning of that sector, including the overseeing and coordination of the planning in such decentralized institutes as operate within the sector in question.[63]

More generally, the basic objective of the reform was a redistribution of de jure responsibility between the executive and the legislature; de facto this redistribution had already occurred in large part, as National Front presidents increasingly invoked Article 121 of the Constitution which provided for a state of siege.[64] On fiscal matters, the executive was given exclusive right to initiate expenditures and taxes. The legislature's right to decision (essentially veto power) was made conditional on its acting within a reasonable time, and its responsibility to control was emphasized. The impact of the reform was to strengthen the executive.[65]

Urban Development Strategy

Whereas the previously described policies followed orthodox development principles, major steps of the Pastrana administration were related to the attempt to make urban building construction a key motor of economic development and a source of increasing demand for labor, especially low paid blue collar labor. The fuller scheme of which the housing strategy is a major component is presented in the works of Currie, its main architect.[66] To facilitate the flow of funds into the building industry, a fixed real return asset (the UPAC—Unidad de Poder Adquisitivo Constante) was created. This potentially significant innovation in the capital market may have important effects, independent of its introduction as an adjunct of the housing strategy. Too little time has passed to permit a balanced evaluation of the effects that the housing strategy and the associated financial changes have had in Colombia.[67] The already high growth rate remained high under the new strategy, but since its implementation began only in late 1971, the impact on building and on the overall economy could not be expected until the last two years of Pastrana's administration. Moreover, rampant inflation, whose relationship to the plan remains a point of debate, has in any case made it difficult to isolate the plan's effects on blue collar real wage rates.

OTHER ECONOMIC POLICIES OF THE FRONT

The economic policy steps discussed so far, with the exception of those related to agriculture, consisted of discrete changes. Other areas where policy was either altered gradually or not at all deserve commentary as well.

Import Substitution[68]

A major aspect of economic policy during the National Front was import substitution in manufacturing. Production of import substitutes was heavily protected through the whole period, while exports were discouraged by an overvalued exchange rate until the late 1960s, when the floating exchange rate was introduced and other export incentives were strengthened. Most careful analyses of comparable situations have been skeptical of the wisdom of very high protection and critical of the discouragement to exports. The import substitution policy preceded the National Front, of course. Whether the new firms and industries fostered during the Front had less promise of eventual competitiveness than ones fostered earlier is difficult to judge. The artificial discouragement to exports from a usually overvalued exchange rate was, almost certainly, more damaging than before. On the other hand, Colombia, in terms of her relatively early implementation of an export-oriented strategy, compares acceptably, perhaps favorably with other countries that were finding growth more and more difficult under import substitution strategies.

An important and controversial element of industrial policy was the evolution of the Instituto de Fomento Industrial (IFI). Founded in 1941 to develop or support industries considered desirable—especially basic industrial activities calling for relatively high investment and sometimes entailing considerable risks—IFI's assets have risen rapidly; they were 35 million pesos in 1958, 2,157 million in 1969 and 5,935 million in 1972.[69] The capital intensity of many of the supported industries raises serious worries about the impact of IFI on Colombia's industrial development; only an in depth study can reveal whether there have been benefits that warrant the high investment costs of these industries. It seems conservative to presume that the distributional impact has been negative.

Foreign Aid and Private Foreign Investment

Soon after the creation of the National Front, the Alliance for Progess had its beginning in 1961. As one of the few Latin countries characterized jointly by (1) an electoral democracy of sorts, (2) a reputation for relatively stable and serious economic policy making, and (3) a generally pro-U.S. stance, Colombia quickly became a favorite of the Alliance—its so-called "show-case."[70] Before that it had already been the setting for the first World Bank mission (1949) and, with the exception of the Rojas years, for continued high levels of financing by that institution. Relative to her population, Colombia was one of the major foreign aid recipients of the 1960s, with an average of almost 200 million dollars per year between 1961 and 1970.[71] The annual inflow net of repayment of interest and capital averaged 73 million dollars, i.e., about 1.6 percent of the national income over these years.[72] The increased resources available no doubt increased national income over the short run. The longer run impact would depend heavily on (1) the repayment terms, (2) the nature of any impact on domestic resource mobilization (saving),[73] and (3) the nature of any impact on the efficiency of resource allocation and economic policy making in general. The conventional wisdom, of course, is that such aid is beneficial; and except in cases where the impact on domestic policy making was negative or its concession was related to offsetting concessions by the country, this is probably true. Pending careful analysis, such a conclusion would seem warranted for Colombia.[74]

On the private investment front, the Colombian government has been relatively receptive over the whole post World War II period, but Colombia has never had the degree of foreign involvement of Canada, Mexico, or Central America. Prior to the mid-1960s, the petroleum industry accounted for a large share (40-45 percent) of foreign capital in the country.[75] The National Front period, however, saw a great expansion of foreign direct investment in total and in manufacturing.[76] Thus, of the book value of foreign investments in 1970, 30 percent of all investment and perhaps half of that in manufacturing had come since 1960.[77] An unknown but probably substantial share of the recent inflow of investment has been associated with the creation of the Andean Group in that year. In response to the substantial inflows Planeación was, in 1967, assigned the responsibility for overseeing and screening the flow, so that increasing attention was given to the conditions of its entry.[78]

The impact of foreign investment on national income and its distribution is usually hard to gauge, and no comprehensive analysis has yet been carried out in Colombia. Benefits to the nation from past petroleum exploitation by foreigners are hardly at issue. The impact of the more recent developments in manufacturing is less clear cut; while inflow of foreign capital and technology can obviously benefit a country under certain sets of conditions, the opposite is true under other conditions.[79] Grounds for optimism in the Colombian case are provided by the evidence that on average the foreign plants are not more capital intensive than are national plants of comparable size,[80] and that they contribute substantially to exports.[81] On the other hand their relationship to the Andean Market may be a cause for some concern, as is the substantial market power of most foreign firms producing for the domestic market.

Strengthening of the Public Sector

One important shift that crystallized during the administration of Carlos Lleras was the increased importance of government expenditure and government investment in the economy, and the increasing take of the tax system. (See Table 2). Both new legislation and tightened administration contributed to this latter increase. During Pastrana's administration, unfortunately, some ground appears to have been lost;[82] one factor was the introduction of a system of limited time liability for payment of taxes.[83] Meanwhile, the distribution of government expenditures by level of government (unadjusted for transfers since official figures are not consolidated) has reflected increasing urbanization and decentralization of public activity. The shares of the national and departmental levels have fallen since the beginning of the Front (from about 40 percent and 15 percent respectively to less than 38 percent and 10 percent), while that of municipalities (dominated by the big cities) appears to have risen a little, and that of decentralized agencies has risen substantially (from about 30 percent or less to over 40 percent). The gradually decreasing share of the budget spent on the military may be considered healthy; though military expenditures have not fallen as a share of national income (Table 2), they are not unduly high. The National Front years saw also a notable increase in public investment; under the Lleras administration it jumped from 18 percent of total investment (the average for the four years of the Valencia administration) to 28 percent (Table 2).

INCOME DISTRIBUTION AND THE NATIONAL FRONT

Since income distribution is a key determinant of social welfare, it is useful to consider how government policy may have affected it during the Front. As previously discussed, there is evidence that distribution improved during the early Front years and worsened during the last two administrations. It must be remembered that these trends are affected both by government policy and by events outside the government's control.

It is normally assumed that import substitution accompanied by high protective tariffs worsens distribution by holding down labor's share of income. This follows from the fact that in developing countries the industries that cannot compete at world prices and that therefore need protection are industries requiring much capital; and capital is much scarcer than labor. When

Table 3
Characteristics of Colombian Manufacturing Plants Reporting to DANE, by Size

Plant Size (Workers)	Share of Workers	1969[b] Output[c] per worker (thousands of Pesos)	Output[c] per Unit of Physical[d] Capital
5- 9[a]	5.6	24.6	.75
10- 24	11.1	30.7	.68
25- 49	11.6	41.7	.57
50- 99	13.3	51.4	.58
100-199	14.3	84.6	.71
200+	44.1	86.3	.42
Total	100.0	66.6	.50

Notes:
a. Including a few firms and workers in plants of fewer than 5 workers.
b. There is substantial underreporting among the smaller sized plants.
c. Unadjusted DANE statistics, which tend to overestimate output, probably by a greater proportion in larger firms.
d. Physical capital includes fixed capital and inventories.

Sources: Data on the labor force and output are from DANE, *Industria Manufacturera Nacional 1969*. Data on the capital stock are from A. Berry, "A Descriptive History," statistical appendix, Table A-202.

such industries expand under protection from international competition, the demand for capital rises rapidly (since these industries require a lot), while the demand for labor rises only marginally (they require little labor); as a result the share of income going to capital rises.[84] Such protected activities are mainly in the manufacturing sector; among those whose relative incomes suffer through lack of protection are many agricultural activities, already characterized by low incomes. This effect of protectionism would perhaps be strongest during the mid sixties, as investment became concentrated in very capital intensive industries (petrochemicals and chemicals). Export expansion may work in the opposite direction; whether it has done so in Colombia is not clear.[85] In any case, the effect of such expansion on income distribution is almost certainly less negative than that of continued import substitution, so the new emphasis on exports may be presumed to be desirable from this point of view.

Another probably important factor in determining income distribution is the relative stimulus given to productive units of different sizes, whether in agriculture, industry, or elsewhere. Where the unit encouraged is large, the employment generated per unit of capital tends to be small, and the return to capital in the economy as a whole is increased relative to that of labor; the opposite is true with smaller establishments. In most countries the belief prevails that relatively large establishments are, per se, more efficient than

Table 4

Percent Share of Total Output Growth in Manufacturing, by Sector, 1958-1972*

Industry	1958-62		1962-66		1966-70		1970-72†	
20. Food	12.37		21.73		13.50		10.89	
21. Beverages	9.42		10.20		12.38		9.80	23.49
22. Tobacco	2.24		2.69		5.20		2.80	
23. Textiles	14.38		6.38		13.78		20.04	
24. Clothing &								23.97
Footwear	7.01		8.60		6.52		3.93	
25. Wood, except								
furniture	0.05						0.56	
26. Wooden furniture	0.17	0.22		0.03		0.47	0.46	1.02
27. Paper	4.52		5.25		6.37		4.14	
28. Printing	3.91		2.49		2.77		4.51	
29. Leather	0.64		1.31		0.81		1.01	
30. Rubber	2.43		0.60		2.32		2.77	
31. Chemicals	9.63		10.70		10.30		8.96	
32. Petroleum & Coal	3.38		2.56		3.17		6.77	
33. Non-metallic								
minerals	7.40		2.58		5.32		4.65	
34. Basic metals	1.65		2.84		4.16		0.91	
35. Metal products	8.76		5.34		2.59		5.71	
36. Non-electric								
machinery except								
machinery and		19.58		19.44		10.53		15.29
transportation								
equipment	1.94		1.29		0.60		2.18	
37. Electric machinery	6.59		11.33		1.08		1.86	
38. Transport equipment	2.29		1.48		6.26		5.54	
39. Miscellaneous	2.92		2.59		2.40‡		2.34	

Notes:

*Figures may not add to 100 percent because of rounding.

†Provisional and approximate.

‡Very rough estimate

Sources and Methodology. The series on output at the two digit level are from *Banco de la República, Cuentas Nacionales*. Values are compared at 1958 prices except for the 1970–72 period where they are compared at 1970 prices. In some cases original calculations did not add to 100 percent and were scaled up or down to do so. Within the metal-mechanical category (34-38) the *Cuentas Nacionales* does not present separate physical output indices, so DANE figures have been used here.

small ones (an idea to which most large scale capitalists subscribe). While this is true of some industries (e.g., petrochemicals, automobiles) it is less so or not at all in others (e.g. most of agriculture). Labor absorption in Colombia's factory industry would probably have been substantially faster had less of the growth been concentrated in large capital intensive firms.[86] As of 1969, plants of 200 workers and more generated only about 60 percent as many jobs per unit of output as all other plants taken together and about a third as much as small plants with 10 to 24 workers (see Table 3). At the same time their output capital ratio (a relatively good indicator of efficiency when capital is the scarce resource) was only about two thirds as high as for all other plants, and only a little over half as high as for quite small firms (5 to 9 workers). Employment generated per unit of output was quite low in some of the industries such as chemicals, paper, and petrochemicals, that received large shares of new investment and/or contributed importantly to the output expansion during the Front.[87] (See Table 4, which shows the relative contribution of different industries to the growth of the factory sector over this period.)

In addition, during the period of tight exchange rate restrictions (most of 1957 to 1967), there was a natural tendency for import licenses to go to the larger firms, which were more influential and assumed by most decision makers to be more efficient. This artificial disadvantage for small scale firms would tend to worsen income distribution. The government has had programs on behalf of small scale operators in both agriculture and industry, and it is difficult to judge whether the overall policy bias in favor of the large firms rose or fell during the Front. Certainly there is now more awareness of the needs of small farmers than there was twenty years ago; this is reflected for example in a number of "integrated rural development programs" designed to improve the lot of this group.

A development which may have an impact on income distribution and the rural system in general is the organization of Asociaciones de Usarios Campesinos (ANUC) fostered by the Carlos Lleras administration and billed as having the potential to become a progressive small farmer organization.[88] The "users" of such services as agricultural credit, extension and so forth were to be organized under government direction which would encourage them to contribute to improvement of these services, to develop the background needed for a cooperative movement, and to collaborate in the agrarian reform.[89] A National Campaign of Peasant Organization was launched in 1968 and by the end of June 1971 the Ministry of Agriculture's Division of Campesino Organization had recruited almost a million members in 496 legally recognized local *usuario* groups.[90] To the surprise of both Lleras and Pastrana, the latter soon confronted an Executive Committee (named at ANUC's first congress in 1970) composed of radical peasant leaders bent on accelerated agrarian reform through massive land invasions, if necessary. The *usarios* participated in numerous land invasions and despite government attempts to bring the organization to heel or to divide it, it remains the key peasant organization, the one whose future evolution may be quite important from a distributional point of view.

Some of the policies that probably had a major impact on income distribution trends over the National Front period fit in the category of "gradual shifts." Education is an increasingly important factor in distribution[91] as the share of national income going in payment to human capital rises.[92] Wage/salary income is closely associated with one's level of education.[93] Allocation of public funds to higher education normally has a tendency to worsen income distribution since such funds raise the incomes of the better off (very few really poor people reach the university level), and funds allocated to primary, especially rural primary, education tend to improve distribution. As of 1970, Jallade estimated that the overall impact of public education subsidies on distribution was strongly positive, essentially because higher income people tend to enroll their children in private schools, and therefore receive fewer subsidies than would otherwise be the case. His figures suggest that such subsidies varied from over 12 percent of the income of families earning under 6,000 pesos per year[94] to less than 1 percent for those earning over 240,000 pesos.[95] The positive distributional effect is associated with primary education subsidies. The overall distributional impact of public education expenditures in 1958 was also substantially positive. Between 1958 and 1970, the share of public educational subsidies going to the poorest groups increased, as rural primary schools reached a higher share of the population,[96] though at the same time the share going to families in the top quarter may also have increased.[97]

Labor legislation, another area of possible relevance to distribution, did not change significantly during the National Front. Its general outlines were established by Law 90 of 1946, which reflected the interest of then ex-president Alfonso López,[98] and they have been modified only gradually since then. The number of workers covered by social security has, however, expanded quite rapidly, especially during the 1960s. It has been estimated that in 1958, 14 percent of the labor force was covered either by the Colombian Institute of Social Security (ICSS)—about 7.6 percent—or they were covered by state or company plans not affiliated with ICSS—about 6.5 percent.[99] At that time, coverage was limited to the regions of Cundinamarca, Antioquia, Valle and Quindío. In 1970, ICSS reported 926,000 affiliates protected against incapacity, old age, and death; and slightly smaller numbers against sickness and injury.[100] The first figure alone constituted about 15 percent of the labor force. Including other plans might raise the percentage to 20 or 25. Social security reached the better-off workers first (those in the large firms) but has, over the last decade, begun to reach down to levels where its welfare impact should be more substantial. In 1970, 31 percent of the affiliates of ICSS were in establishments with fewer than twenty workers. Very few agricultural workers were covered, however, as of that year.

It appears that few wage rates have been pushed significantly above equilibrium[101] by the minimum-wage, in the medium and large firms to which it is applied. Whether the influence of unions on the wage rate is substantial has been little analyzed in Colombia. Since the impact of either minimum wages or unions on income distribution is theoretically indeterminate,[102] the absence of detailed empirical analysis makes it impossible to infer whether policy has had a positive or negative effect on distribution within the wage and salaried labor force.[103]

Some aspects of public sector activity do have a positive effect on income distribution. The most important such feature is the progressive income tax system.[104] Also of note are government expenditures on certain urban services, especially medicine.[105] Subsidies for bus transport may fit this category. Differential prices for water and electricity (higher prices for the rich) definitely do.[106] And the substantial expenditure on primary education, especially rural, probably has a quite high payoff in welfare terms, so the impact of positively distributive expenditures cannot be discounted.[107] But except for the income tax system, however, the number of policies that clearly improve distribution and the amount of funds involved seem very modest. Rhetoric often differs from reality despite periodic claims to the contrary. The rhetoric of public housing, for example, often implies a positive impact on distribution, but in few countries does this seem to be the case. Colombia, whose Instituto de Crédito Territorial (ICT) has mainly built houses for families in the top half of the income distribution, does not appear to be an exception.[108] The most amusing verbal sleight of hand was the concept of the "popular" car, in a country where not even the top five percent of families owned such a vehicle.

EFFECTS OF THE NATIONAL FRONT ON ECONOMIC POLICY: SOME SPECULATIONS[109]

As indicated earlier, inability to decide except by crude guess work what would have happened in the absence of the National Front makes it difficult to judge what difference the Front made in the various strands of Colombian life. While the economic policies pursued may be compared with those of earlier administrations, much if not most of the difference is probably the result of a normal evolution in societal and government conception of the issues and how they should be handled. There is little doubt, for example, that increasing awareness of income distribution as a problem and the increasing discussion of how to handle it would have been present under most alternative systems—a natural reaction to the worldwide concern with it and to new information as to how bad it is. The increasing use of technicians was certainly due at least in part to their growing availability. Other developments also were affected by exogenous factors and pressures. While it is difficult to measure foreign influence with any precision, the fact that some policies were implemented in several Latin American countries at more or less the same time suggests the impact of extra-national influences. Planning is an example. Virtually all Latin American countries encouraged the development of economic planning agencies in the 1960s, when there was substantial enthusiasm for the Alliance for Progress.

Broadly speaking, economic policy-making under the Front may be characterized as (1) middle of the road (vis-à-vis the Colombian spectrum) in terms of ideology and social content, (2) relatively consistent over time, and (3) increasingly technical. The extent to which these features may have been due to the existence of the Front depends on what alternative systems would have done.

Among the more obvious possible alternatives were continuation of a Rojas type administration, or a nonviolent two-party competition.[110] Differences would be expected in among other things: (1) who is president, (2) the relative influence of the power groups to which the government responds, and (3) the machinery and style of government.

Since much power resides in the presidency, the identity of the incumbent can be significant, independent of the natural relation of the presidency to the structure of power among groups. However, the key determinant of a government's policies is the power structure to which it owes its existence. A continuation of the Rojas government would have been distinguished from the National Front government, one guesses, by (1) a greater focus in rhetoric, and perhaps in fact, on improving the status of the poor vis-à-vis "growth," and (2) less concern with technical efficiency in government. Such guesses are based mainly on Rojas' 1953-57 record. They appear consistent with the nature of ANAPO as it evolved in opposition during the Front.[111] While the rhetoric emphasized help for the poor and the little man, there was no evidence of plans for a serious restructuring of the system.

Under a situation of nonviolent competition between the two traditional parties, Liberal administrations, or administrations heavily weighted toward the Liberals, would have been probable. The underlying power structure would have resembled closely that of the National Front government, although it would probably have been slightly less conservative. The presidency could have been occupied by persons ranging from Carlos Lleras with his technocratic developmentalistic approach, to Julio César Turbay, considered to be in many respects a classic "old-style" Colombian politician; to Alfonso López M., during the early National Front years the leader of the MRL faction of the Liberal party. Only if López had achieved the presidency, could an economic program substantially different from those of the National Front administrations have been expected. Thinking of both Rojas and López as men who could have been president under different sequences of events than that which led to the National Front, and given the low probability of a Conservative reaching that position via an electoral process, it would seem more likely that the Front helped to prevent rather than foster the advent of presidents with a high social content in their programs.

In any case, differences in the mechanisms of government (including the different ways of aggregating or reconciling group interests) would perhaps be more likely as the major source of differences in economic policy between the Front and the alternatives mentioned above. Of particular interest are the implications of the reduced and altered form of political competition under the Front vis-à-vis the two or three party system. Among specific questions of interest are the effects of (1) the bipartisan character of the Front, (2) the presumably weak opposition and/or the greater factionalism within the parties,[112] and (3) the continuity implicit in the arrangement.

The bipartisan nature of the National Front probably impeded the implementation of any major policy designed to produce substantial structural changes in the nature of the economic system or the distribution of property. The shortcomings of the agrarian reform, for example, were outlined earlier. It would appear that in order to maintain the coalition, each government was forced to adopt a position near the center of the political spectrum. Neither a Brazilian nor a Peruvian "road" was possible.

Given the nature of the coalition, most of the programmatic opposition for the Front was either farther left or more populist in nature. The constraints under which such opposition operated during most of the Front period permitted and probably encouraged the government to leave aside certain problems it might otherwise have been forced to address. Of particular interest is whether policy would have been more socially oriented had the government been more vulnerable to the threat of opposition takeover. Neither Rojas nor the Movimiento Revolucionario Liberal (MRL) of Alfonso López M. appeared to be serious threats to the system prior to 1970. After the critical 1970 election, almost won by Rojas, the government reacted in a number of ways; one was a wide dispersion of infrastructural investments (roads, bridges, etc.) in a rather unplanned way—open to the interpretation that its overriding purpose was to assure a more favorable result in the 1972 elections. This exemplifies the complex and sometimes accidental relation between the nature of political opposition and its ultimate effects. Irresponsible or ill-conceived opposition may be damaging, as when it plays on public misunderstanding (e.g. to make devaluations more difficult, or to oppose all tax increases, etc.); even responsible opposition can lead the administration to defend itself in socially unproductive ways, such as the cited post-1970 reaction. On the general question of poverty redressal, there was both serious (with real program content) and misleading (no program content) opposition. Criticisms and claims by ANAPO often fell in the latter category (e.g., Rojas' pledge to bring the price of *plátanos* back to where it had been under his administration or to put a car in every garage); those of the MRL tended to be serious. Inducement of policies with significant positive effects on distribution is a tall order for any political opposition. Except for the fairly straightforward effects of policies like the progressive tax system and provision of public services for low income groups the distributional impact of economic policies remains a hazy area for technicians as well as for politicians. In any case the National Front government continued and/or instituted many policies that probably had negative distributional impacts—import substitution in capital intensive industries, exemptions for business investment, a monetary system heavily oriented toward those with much capital, and so on.[113] Serious technical consideration of the non-fiscal ways to improve distribution is a very recent thing.[114]

Whatever the effects of the bipartisan character of the government and the weak opposition, a number of steps were taken during the Front which reflected a high technical quality of policy making. Colombia's performance in the area of export inducement compares favorably with that of other countries. Here the issues were mainly technical, and the Front's bipartisan arrangement was not averse to "technical" solutions.[115] In fact, it could be argued that because of its intent to reduce partisanship, the coalition arrangement was conducive to legitimization of technical, as opposed to "political," policies. While these technical steps or improvements were not often "spectacular," some were important.

The National Front period was characterized both by a relatively weak political opposition and by a degree of built-in continuity. It is difficult to judge whether and in what senses continuity of policy was particularly characteristic of the period, partly because rapid shifts of major elements of policy have never been a major difficulty. In this period, as in others, shifting policy was probably a much less important problem than bad policy on some issues.

National Front governments obviously left much to be desired. But overall they seem to compare favorably to most governments in countries at similar income levels, and facing somewhat similar problems. Colombia grew at a reasonable, and lately a quite impressive rate, was freed from the violence of early years and did not undergo the political crises of so many countries. The technical input to its economic policy rose notably, and now appears superior to that of most Latin American nations. With respect to income distribution, the area of major shortcoming, Colombia does not seem to have been atypically tardy in introducing its improvement as a general goal of government. Notably better performances have been limited, for the most part, to revolutionary governments of one stripe or another.

NOTES

1. The comparable figures for the U.S. (1925-1970) are 4.4 percent and 3.2 percent.
2. Miguel Urrutia and Albert Berry, *Income Distribution in Colombia* (New Haven, 1976). Comparable figures for the United States in 1965 were 28 percent, 24 percent and 4 percent. (See U.S. Department of Commerce, *Statistical Abstract of the United States, 1972*, p. 324.)
3. Urrutia estimated a Gini coefficient of 0.57 for the distribution of personal income in 1964. (See Urrutia and Berry, ch. 3.) This coefficient has been estimated at 0.55 in Puerto Rico (1960), 0.49 in Argentina (1961), 0.46 in Chile (1968, families), 0.35 in the U.S. (1964, families). In countries noted for the relative equality of distribution (e.g., Scandinavia) this coefficient may get down to 0.25 or thereabouts.
4. Output and income per member of the labor force grew even faster, at 2.75 and 3.75 respectively; as population growth accelerated and the population became younger, the share of the population in the labor force fell.
5. Schultz' econometric study of migration generated the estimate that for every person killed in a muncipality during the violence period, 40 migrated out. T.P. Schultz, *Population Growth and Internal Migration in Colombia* (Santa Monica, California, 1969). Given the indirect methodology used and the data problems, this could be a misleading figure; and it must be remembered that Schultz estimated all emigration due to violence and his approach did not indicate where the emigrants went—a good proportion doubtless were rural-rural. Most interview-based studies of rural to urban migration have found violence infrequently mentioned as the major cause of the move; but most of these studies focused on immigrants to the large cities. (For a review see A. Berry, "On the Efficiency of the Migration Process in Colombia," Mimeo, 1972, Table 10). I am inclined to believe that the violence did push many people from rural areas to small towns and cities, and that it had some impact on the rate of urbanization, though certainly not a dominant one.
6. We do not have figures for precisely these years; but during the 1938-1964 period these cities grew at 6.5 percent.
7. Housing projects undertaken were beneficial to the middle class but not to the poor people; the rapid increase in real wages of blue collar workers in manufacturing was not evidently a result of any of Rojas's policies, but rather of the general economic expansion facilitated by the high coffee prices. Perhaps the major distribution improving activity of the period was the rapid expansion of the primary school system. The share of the primary school age cohort enrolled rose rapidly from less than 50 percent in 1950 to around 60 percent in 1956, and more slowly thereafter. While enrollment at the other levels was also increasing rapidly in percentage terms, their bases were still quite small; this period is perhaps the one in which the net effect of educational expansion on distribution is most likely to have been positive. Later the expansion of primary slowed down and that of the others remained high. But by and large income distribution considerations had not entered public policy in any general way.
8. A rise in the price of a country's exports constitutes a windfall increase in income, i.e. without any increase in the economy's productivity, income can rise. At the same time such an increase makes output growth easier in developing countries such as Colombia which must import most of the capital equipment

which permits expansion of capacity; the high export price permits more such capital goods imports.

9. Petroleum was the second most important export, but its supply could not be easily or quickly expanded.
10. Robert H. Dix, *Colombia: The Political Dimensions of Change* (New Haven, 1967), p. 131. Dix notes that Rojas' semi-revolutionary stance came quite late in his administration and was essentially a last ditch attempt to gain support in his struggle with the elite; more generally, he was interested in creating a third power or force, but his main objective and that of his followers seems simply to have been a continuation of his own government, rather than specific goals of social change. The relative disinterest of the regime in specific economic policies, despite the several reforms it did undertake, is interpretable in this light. Whether and in what proportions the traditional elites were afraid of the onset of an anarchy or the loss of their own privilege and power will never be clear; but the latter must have been an important objective.
11. Dix, *The Political Dimensions of Change*, pp. 130-131.
12. Political rhetoric in most countries tends to give the appearance of concern with income distribution, so it is necessary, at least in part, to judge intentions and goals by steps taken to improve it. Dix on page 131 cites the description of the Front as the political expression of a great national enterprise of development; by setting aside ancient political hatreds, it would permit the country to move toward the goals of greater social justice, real national independence, and an enhanced measure of political participation for the majority of Colombians. Particular complexities arise in connection with policies which *could* have been adopted with distributional goals in mind but which would not really improve distribution. Many economists would put strong wage legislation in this category. Is the politician who pushes it interested in distribution and naive, or is he uninterested but aware of the political value of the concept. Reviewing most policy steps allegedly taken to improve distribution, one would be tempted to conclude that either politicians tend not to predict the effects of policies well *or* they are systematically misleading in their presentation of the issues.
13. Dix, p. 148.
14. As interpreted by James Payne in *Patterns of Conflict in Colombia* (New Haven, 1968) the degree of violence that has periodically characterized the Colombian political system—reaching its peak in the *violencia* of the late 1940's and early 1950's—was related to the intensity with which each of the political parties desired to exercise control over the government; this intensity was determined by the payoffs, partly direct economic gains from the spoils' system, and partly status, a status that is sought for its own sake but that virtually everyone finds financially rewarding in his later private life.
15. While some corruption obviously characterizes certain stages of the tax and expenditure side of the government and other of its activities, it would take a very in-depth study to ascertain where Colombia falls in relation to other countries. Few observers describe the system so unidimensionally as does Payne.
16. A comparison of the Rojas years with either previous or subsequent ones is complicated by their special character, the very high coffee prices and the associated rapid growth of incomes. Such desirable phenomena as the rapid increase in blue-collar wages in factory manufacturing and the substantial increase in agricultural wage rates during this period cannot be attributed to Rojas' policies. A better indicator could be tax and expenditure policies, social legislation, educational policy, and the like. Fluharty makes many claims in favor of Rojas, but his

discussion is not too persuasive, partly because he takes legislative changes as implying substantive changes around the corner. The emotionalism with which pro-Rojas and anti-Rojas commentators view the issue makes it necessary to rely very heavily on statistics in judging performance.

17. Vernon L. Fluharty, *Dance of the Millions* (Pittsburgh, 1957).
18. Different people support the objective of development for different reasons. The poor presumably desire it for its own sake; for the powerful and the decision makers, it may be sought for its own sake, or as a defence against social unrest and upheaval; for a few reformers and others, it may be seen as a phase in an evolution that will eventually overturn or substantially modify the social system. Note Dix's description of the process of change under the National Front as "modernization by an elite". (p. 389)
19. Though any such generalization is very relative. Payne's views that most Colombian politicians are opportunistic relative to their American counterparts may be partially inconsistent with such a conclusion. (*Patterns of Conflict in Colombia*.)
20. Plans tend to be descriptive rather than analytical; even when good analysis underlies decisions of investment allocation, it tends not to get into the plan. And major areas of policy (especially foreign exchange and monetary), not being the direct responsibility of the Planning Commission, are not discussed. One could argue that foreign exchange policy was the most important policy area during the National Front. This notwithstanding, the increasing technical skills underlying the planning process come through clearly in the higher sophistication of the later plans as opposed to the earlier ones.
21. A detailed discussion of economic trends and economic policy during the National Front is found in Diego Sandoval P., *El Manejo Electoral de la Política Económica Durante el Frente Nacional* (Bogotá, CEDE, Documento No. 019, 1975). See also Germán Puerta, *El ciclo Económico en Colombia: 1950-1972* (unpublished B.A. thesis, 1974); R. Nelson, T.P. Schultz and R. Slighton, *Structural Change in a Developing Economy: Colombia's Problems and Prospects* (Princeton, 1971). Nelson *et al*. see considerable evidence of an economic democracy à la Downs in Colombia's political economy, on pp. 235-44. See Anthony Downs, *An Economic Theory of Democracy* (New York, 1957).
22. For a detailed discussion of the mechanisms involved, see H. Dunkerly, "Exchange Rate Systems in Conditions of Continuing Inflation: Lessons from the Colombian Experience" in Gustav Papanek (editor), *Development Policy: Theory and Practice* (Cambridge, Mass., 1968).
23. Miguel Urrutia M. and Luis Castellanos Ch., *Estudio Económico Social de la Población de Bogotá,* (Bogotá, CAR, 1962).
24. For statistical purposes factories are defined as establishments with five or more workers, or with output above a certain level. Most employment in Colombia (about 55 percent as of 1970) was in smaller units which may be conveniently designated as cottage-shop.
25. More precisely, a period from some time in the mid-1950s to some time in the mid-1960s. See Miguel Urrutia and Albert Berry, *Income Distribution in Colombia*, Ch. 4.
26. The trend of international terms of trade was more favorable than in the previous period so total income growth accelerated a little (but not much) faster. Labor force growth may have speeded up a little. In any case income per worker and per capita grew at a very successful rate of over 3 percent a year.
27. Rapid inflation in Colombia seems to result primarily from excessive demand for

goods and services. During the Pastrana administration this was fueled by substantial budget deficits (sometimes hidden by tricks of definition), by rapid expansion of credit to the private sector and by building up of foreign exchange reserves (rather than using them for imports). When inflation is moderate (say 5-10%), it may be argued that cost factors play a relatively large role. But the acceleration to 20% or more seems unlikely to be attributable to such factors.

28. Persons not working at all on the day (or week, depending on the definitions used) of the unemployment survey. To be distinguished from disguised unemployment (persons working but with little social productivity, or not seeking jobs because they feel it is not worthwhile) which is often argued to be the more serious of the two phenomena. Open unemployment may reflect relative well-being. (See my "Open Unemployment as a Social Problem in Urban Colombia: Myth and Reality", *Economic Development and Cultural Change*, Vol 23, No. 2, January, 1975.)
29. This conclusion is open to question though, since only for Bogotá have systematic samples been taken since 1962. In 1970 DANE took over the task from CEDE and came up with a much higher figure for that year creating some ambiguity.
30. Real wages of unskilled construction workers in Bogotá seem to have fallen while agricultural wages rose only slowly. (See A. Berry, "Changing Income Distribution Under Development: Colombia), *Review of Income and Wealth*, Income and Wealth Series 20, No. 3, September 1974.
31. The impact of inflation on distribution is not generally known. Inflation was higher during 1958-66 than during 1966-70 but distribution moved more favorably in the first period, it seems. It may be, though that a burst of rapid inflation after stability does worsen distribution even though a more chronic inflation would not.
32. For a discussion and history of planning in Colombia see Augusto Cano M., *El Proceso de la Planeación en Colombia*, (Bogotá, Fedesarrollo, 1972).
33. International Bank for Reconstruction and Development, *The Basis of a Development Plan for Colombia*, (Baltimore, The Johns Hopkins Press, 1950).
34. On this point see Guillermo Perry, *Introducción al Estudio de los Planes de Desarrollo Para Colombia*, (Fedesarrollo, Bogotá, 1972), p. 7.
35. Carlos Lleras, who wrote the original draft of the bill, recognized the need for a Council made up of ministers and other important decision makers, but this draft was subsequently modified in Congress. See Cano, *La Planeación*, p. 5.
36. Preparation of the Ten-Year Plan (heavily influenced by the participating ECLA group) was important in setting a tone even though the analysis was not up to current standards. It was an important document in that it brought together much relevant and useful information. A relatively limited amount of economic analysis was undertaken; the Plan tended to be more of a consistency and forecasting analysis than an in depth appraisal of policy alternatives, which in any case could not be undertaken in a short period of time and on such skimpy bases of information and previous work as were at that time available.
37. Cano, *La Planeación*, p. 7.
38. Ibid., p. 40.
39. Ibid., p. 20.
40. Ibid., p. 23.
41. Cano, p. 8 notes that despite the clarification of Planeación's role in the public investment process (by Decree 1675 of 1964), the efficiency of this process was not immediately improved. This was partly because most of the agencies con-

cerned, including Planeación, still lacked the technical and administrative ability to really do it well, and partly through the disinterest of the Valencia government, which left Planeación without a chief at all for nearly a year.

42. In a persuasive discussion on p. 69 of *La Planeación* Cano describes the first task of the Commission under Lleras Restrepo as identifying the "obvious" projects. He might have added "and blocking the obviously bad ones." Certainly, there was no reason, at that time, to expect macro analysis to contribute much, partly because the fine tuned administration required for it to contribute to monetary, fiscal, and trade policy was not (and for the most part, is not) present, and partly because the Commission lacked the human resources to analyze such questions quickly and in depth.
43. Pastrana arrived at the Presidency, it appears, with less firm ideas as to what he wanted to do than had Lleras; hence his relatively greater openness to and dependence on others' policy suggestions. While Planeación was involved, under Lleras, in the deliberations on such strategic issues as Colombia's participation in the Andean Group, the increased attention to agriculture, and the shift to a floating exchange rate, it appears that all these steps would have been taken by Lleras anyway.
44. Based on estimates by the author and on Héctor Tamayo, "La Reforma Agraria en Colombia" in DANE, *Debate Agrario: Documentos* (Bogotá, 1971). For a more detailed discussion of land reform under the National Front, see chapter 12.
45. It is particularly difficult and not very rewarding to estimate INCORA's efficiency, given its funding and mandate, since those "givens" already foreordained its limited impact.
46. The most complete discussion of the evolution of land reform in its early years is Ernest A. Duff, *Agrarian Reform in Colombia* (New York, 1968). An optimistic view from even earlier is given by Albert O. Hirschman in his *Journeys Toward Progress* (New York, 1963).
47. See for example, Francisco Ortega, "Moneda y Crédito", in *Lecturas Sobre la Economía Colombiana* (Bogotá, 1974).
48. Had the Banco not been rather conservative in its money management (at least by Latin American standards), its position of control might have been challenged earlier.
49. In 1957-1958, in the midst of rigorous austerity, the Coffee Federation was the only major recipient of new credit. (See Sandoval, *El Manejo Electoral*, p. 106.)
50. Some countries, like the U.S., give power to an independent monetary authority, partly on the presumption that it will be more "responsible" (i.e., restrained) in money creation than would many governments.
51. In other words, depreciation vis-à-vis the dollar was greater than the differential between the rate of internal inflation and the rate of inflation in the U.S.. More recently this pattern has been reversed, causing some doubts as to whether the export boom will continue if the real exchange rate is as important a determinant of exports as many economists believe.
52. For a detailed discussion, See Carlos Díaz Alejandro, "Minor Colombian Merchandise Exports" (Yale Economic Growth Center, July 1972).
53. In Colombia as in most countries, devaluation has traditionally been politically hazardous, due to popular misunderstanding of its beneficial function and the manipulation of these fears by some politicians, and to the real danger of inflation.
54. Under free markets and monetary neutrality (no change in the supply of money) a

devaluation would not be inflationary unless the supply of imports were simultaneously reduced (in which case that fact would be the real source of inflation). But many prices are administered in Colombia; this and self-fulfilling expectations that devaluation is inflationary seem to be the cause of the relationship in cases such as that of Colombia.

55. The increase in inflation in developed countries has worked in the other direction and has been one, but probably not the main, factor in the rampant inflation currently afflicting Colombia.
56. A. Berry, *The Development of the Agricultural Sector in Colombia* (forthcoming), chapter 3.
57. It rose rapidly from about 5 percent in the early forties.
58. Figures for 1973 and those for 1960 and 1966 are not fully comparable due to the use of different sources—U.N., *Direction of International Trade* for 1973 and DANE, *Boletín Mensual de Estadística* for 1960 and 1966. But the broad trend is adequately indicated.
59. Excluding Venezuela, to facilitate comparison with earlier years.
60. Figures from International Monetary Fund, *Direction of International Trade*, various issues.
61. Some of the increases might have occurred anyway.
62. A union like the Andean Common market is often defended in terms of benefits from a large market. But more evidence suggests that the industries initiated as a result are not competitive with world price and therefore lower the income of the participating countries. Their development benefits capital and labor in those industries, of course. For an individual country where trade with the others shows a surplus (Colombia's situation in the Andean Group), short run gains are more likely, but the nature of the political bargaining process makes it doubtful that the sale of high priced items by one country to the buyers of other member countries can be far out of line with its own purchases of high priced items from those countries.
63. Cano, *La Planeación*, p. 17.
64. See Hoskin's article in this book. Interestingly, the planned role of Congress in the Front was an important one. But the two thirds rule reduced its potential for action (or reaction) especially as, during the course of the Front, it became more heterogenous in socio-economic character as reflected in the rise of the M.R.L. and ANAPO.
65. The legislative role of the Congress has in no case been a major one. The objective of the Constitutional Reform was to further weaken its influence on spending patterns (where its tendency has naturally been to a wide dispersion of funds across projects and regions) and its power to delay or block.
66. Lauchlin Currie, *Accelerating Development: The Necessity and the Means* (New York, 1966), and *Operación Colombia*, Second Edition (Barranquilla, 1965).
67. The economic theory underlying the strategy is internally consistent and rather well articulated; some of the relationships (or parameters) on which the success of the policy was to depend were not well known, creating a wide range of opinions as to its probable effects.
68. For a more detailed discussion of industrial development during the Frente, see chapter 11 in this volume.
69. See Chapter 11 in this volume.
70. For a detailed history see *Colombia—A Case History of U.S. AID* (Washington, D.C., 1969).

71. Data from I.M.F., *Balance of Payments Yearbook*.
72. This figure does not measure the long run contribution of the inflow since (a) the gains accrue over time and depend on how the funds are used, and (b) the loans must eventually be repaid (most of the inflow was loans rather than grants). If the rate of return to this capital were 10 percent to 15 percent and the average cost of these funds 4 percent, a crude estimate would put the gain to Colombia, expressed in present value terms, at 60-100 percent of the actual inflow (assuming a 10 percent social discount rate and an average length of loan of 30 years). Only if the capital was used in very productive ways would the benefits reach say 3 to 4 percent of the national income.
73. Several recent studies have suggested that an inflow of foreign capital may lower domestic savings (e.g. T.E. Weisskopf, "The impact of Foreign Capital Inflow on Domestic Savings in Underdeveloped Countries," *Journal of International Economics*, Vol. 2, No. 1, (February 1972). This is not a bad thing per se, since it means that the present generation—which after all is poorer than future ones will be—can consume more. It would be bad if the reduction of savings was done by the wealthy whose current consumption is not a matter of much interest, or if bad savings habits created now somehow became irreversible.
74. Until economic decision making became more sophisticated, the outside influence of the World Bank, the IMF, and AID was probably beneficial. In retrospect, some of the criteria applied by government and international agencies alike were not well founded. All seemed insufficiently aware of the potential problems associated with the concentration of too many resources on a relatively small, capital intensive, modern sector; all were slow to come to the realization that good distributional policies can coexist with and are often the same as good growth policies. In short, while the international agencies could provide technical advice of value in the 1950s and 1960s, the quality of that advice or those criteria should not be overestimated. It now appears that they often set technical standards well above those which would have been optimal, contributed to bad projects, and so on. They were quite human.

    The terms under which foreign aid is conceded vary with the agency. On average, the real interest rate (i.e. the nominal rate minus the rate of inflation) has been fairly low, creating a presumption that the country does gain from the arrangement in the long as well as the short run.
75. In 1950 it accounted for 58 percent of U.S. capital in Colombia; manufacturing represented 13 percent. In 1963 it was 53 percent of U.S. capital, and manufacturing represented 26 percent. Although data on foreign capital are not good, one study indicated that the U.S. had about 71 percent of capital recorded as having entered before decree 444 of 1967 and about 56 percent of that entering over 1967-1970. These latter figures, however, evidently excluded the petroleum sector, which was still accounting for the majority of U.S. investment over this period. (See Miguel Angel Betancur, et. al., "Inversión Extranjera en Colombia," in DANE, *Boletín Mensual de Estadística # 239*, (Junio 1971), p. 53-90. Lumping petroleum and gas with the above figures suggests that in both 1966 and 1970 U.S. investment constituted 70 percent of foreign capital. And in 1966, the petroleum sector accounted for 43.3 percent of all foreign capital; in 1970 the figure was in the same range. In 1950 and in 1963 the petroleum share was probably 50 to 60 percent of the total.
76. My estimate for 1969 was that about 15 percent of the capital stock in factory manufacturing was foreign owned, See A. Berry, "A Descriptive History of

Colombian Industrial Development in the Twentieth Century'' in A. Berry (editor) *Essays on Colombian Industrialization* (forthcoming), Table 23.

77. Including, in principle, unremitted profits.
78. For a discussion of the government's reasoning in this regard see Fernando Cepeda U. and Mauricio Solaún, ''Direct Private Foreign Investment in Colombia: A Socio-Political Perspective'' *Sonderdruck Aus Vierteljahres Berichte*, Nr. 49 (Sept. 1972). Cepeda and Solaún emphasize the dominance of the balance of payments in the administration's thinking about and attitude to foreign investment at this time. Export oriented firms were welcomed, for example. Decree Law 444 of March 1967, which established regulations for foreign investment (as well as all other balance of payments transactions), was enacted at a time of balance of payments crisis and a famous confrontation between the Lleras Restrepo administration and the International Monetary Fund, the latter pushing Colombia to devalue and Lleras resisting.
79. Under the traditional neoclassical (i.e. perfect competitive market) assumptions of much economic analysis, foreign capital raises the income of the host country; it also raises wages and lowers the return to local capital (by competing with it), thereby improving the income distribution. Since foreign capital almost never enters competitive industries, these results are not directly relevant, and serious analysis becomes highly complicated.
80. Berry, ''A Descriptive History.''
81. Carlos Díaz A., ''Trade and the Import Control System in Colombia; Some Quantifiable Features'' (mimeo, 1974).
82. Preliminary figures for 1972 indicate a lower share of taxes out of GDP than in 1970.
83. Whereby a tax payer could declare himself liable for a given tax payment, however understated, and unless the tax office challenged this within two years it became his actual tax liability. The procedure increased the incentive for tax payers to bribe tax officials. It also increased the incentive not to pay for two years, which under rapid inflation tends to lower the real tax take.
84. Working through this same mechanism (raising the demand for capital) is all government intervention which favors the use of capital rather than labor; the same negative income distribution effect is therefore to be expected from exemptions on capital investment for firms setting up in specific regions or specific industries. Parenthetically, it should be noted that there is little evidence that such incentives are important in encouraging industry to grow. See R.E. Bilsborrow and R.C. Porter, ''The Effects of Tax Exemption on Investment by Industrial Firms in Colombia,'' *Weltwirtschaftliches Archiv*. Vol. 108, #3, (Kiel, 1972).

    If inefficiency kept profits in such industries from being high, or if union or other pressure led to a sharing of high rents with labor their growth would not necessarily worsen distribution. But the labor shares in such industries are in fact below the average for manufacturing. In 1967, when the average labour share was 34%, those in chemicals and petroleum products were 27% and 16% respectively; the average blue collar labor share was 21% while those in chemicals and petroleum products were 11% and 8% respectively.
85. See the discussion in Albert Berry and Carlos Díaz Alejandro, ''Trade Policies and Income Distribution in Developing Countries: Some Necessary Complications and Some Preliminary Soundings in Colombia,'' mimeo 1975.
86. I have roughly estimated this growth at 3.4 percent per year over 1958-66 and

3.6 percent over 1966-70. See A. Berry (editor), *Essays on Colombian Industrialization* (forthcoming), ch. 2. Official statistics are unsatisfactory and have been adjusted to make these estimates.

87. Over 1962-67, chemicals and petrochemicals received 40 percent of total new fixed investment; as of 1967 they accounted for about 7 to 8 percent of the labor force. These figures highlight the fact that import substitution (supported by the government) was moving into some quite capital intensive areas where the income distribution impact of growth was almost sure to be negative.
88. For a detailed discussion see Bruce Bagley and Mathew Edel, "Popular Mobilization Programs," in this volume.
89. Bagley and Edel, p. 271.
90. Bagley and Edel, p. 272. This figure may contain "marginal" members; but there seems little question that recruitment was on a large scale.
91. A detailed discussion of development in education under the National Front is presented by Robert Arnove in this volume.
92. Human capital refers to that part of an individual's productive potential which is learned through practice and/or study; the rest of his productive potential is that related to his basic physical strength. Education is a major source of human capital.
93. According to estimates by the author, this share of national income rose from between 29 and 31 percent in 1958 to between 34 and 37 percent in 1969. (A. Berry, "Changing Income Distribution Under Development: Colombia."
94. Note that this figure is somewhat misleading since the lowest income group usually consumes considerably more than it earns; it includes many people whose long run average income is above that of the survey year.
95. Jean Pierre Jallade, *Public Expenditures on Education and Income Distribution in Colombia*, World Bank Staff Occasional Papers #18 (Baltimore, 1974); (see pages 27/8 and 40). At the same time, in urban areas at least, subsidies per child were twice as high in middle income groups as for low income ones. (*Ibid*. p. 26).

    In terms of central government transfers to the departments, initiated on a substantial scale after 1961 when the former took on the responsibility for paying primary teachers, Jallade finds that these improve the regional distribution of income.(*Ibid*, p. 69).
96. In 1958 probably 15 percent of all children (almost all of them in rural areas) did not enter primary and the ratio "children enrolled/population 6-10" was about 60 to 65 percent; in 1970, these figures were probably about 5 percent and 75 percent respectively. Most non-attendees are in rural areas.
97. A rough calculation suggests that the top quarter of families might have received about half of the educational subsidies in 1958 and a little more in 1970. But their share of income is much higher than this, so the subsidies effect a greater percentage increase in incomes of poorer families than of the rich ones.

    In 1958 we estimated that 61 percent of the public expenditures which could be distributed by educational level went to primary (including all pre-secondary), 15 percent went to the secondary level and 24 percent to higher. In 1970 these percentages were 49, 27 and 24 respectively. (Jallade, *Public Expenditures*, p. 72).
98. Who left office prematurely in 1945.
99. See Jorge Restrepo Hoyos, *Aspectos Económicos de la Seguridad Social en Colombia* (Bogotá, 1960), p. 217.

100. Instituto Colombiano de Seguros Sociales, *Informe Estadístico 1970*, p. 27. Persons protected (including families of affiliates) were about 16 percent of the population.
101. I.e., above the levels which would have resulted from the interaction of demand and supply under a competitive market.
102. When a considerable share of labor force is not covered by wage legislation (unions), the indeterminateness alluded to arises. In Colombia as of 1965 Urrutia concluded that the total number of union members was on the order of 700,000; *The Development of the Colombian Labor Movement* (New Haven, 1968), p. 270. This constituted about 23 percent of the wage and salaried labor force; perhaps a higher share of the blue collar workers were unionized. A sample undertaken by Urrutia in 1965 suggested that three quarters of the workers in manufacturing establishments of 20 or more workers were in union firms. Ibid., p. 262. If no other workers were in unionized firms, this would constitute a little under 40 percent of the paid workers in manufacturing. A plausible guess at the share of all paid manufacturing workers in unions in 1965 would thus be 40 to 50 percent. It has presumably increased since that time.
103. See, however, ibid. Urrutia felt that unions did have a positive impact on wages; he used two types of evidence. First, he compared union and non-union wages, finding the former higher even with firm size "held constant." Ibid. p. 264. Second, he noted that during the period of collective bargaining activity (since the mid-fifties) real wages in manufacturing have risen rapidly whereas before, in the period of "political bargaining" by the unions, wages did not rise. Ibid, p. 253. Subsequent work on the wage statistics suggests that wages also rose rapidly over at least from 1944 to 1955. See A. Berry "Real Wage Trends in Colombian Manufacturing and Construction During the Twentieth Century", University of Western Ontario, Department of Economics Research Report # 7403; and M. Urrutia "Los Salarios Reales en Bogotá", in CEDE, *Empleo y Desempleo en Colombia* (Bogotá, 1968). And Urrutia's union/non union wage analysis may have used plant size categories which were too wide. In short, the issue remains in substantial doubt.

    Urrutia's overall judgement on the issue was that, even if unions had raised wages of members and lowered those of nonmembers, their importance as a political institution could not be underestimated; their absence "may have political repurcussions which will make planning and economic development more difficult." Ibid., p. 251.
104. The income tax is in principle progressive over the full income range. In fact it may have been regressive or neutral within the middle and upper income groups comprising paid employees and owners of capital, since the latter are harder to tax than the former. But in the more important question of redistribution between the poor, who do not pay taxes, and the better off who do, this tax is clearly positive. Note, however that it is rather artificial to consider taxes separately from expenditures; treating the whole system, Urrutia concludes that positive redistribution occurs; although the tax system as a whole has little impact on distribution, the expenditure side raises the incomes of the poor relatively more than the rich; local expenditure, especially on education and health, is key. See Berry and Urrutia, Chapter 7.
105. Ibid., Chapter 7.
106. Although subsidized prices for these services may not.
107. As discussed above, Jallade's calculations show that public education subsidies

constitute a much higher share of the income of the poor than of the rich. At the same time, several authors have found a high payoff (both private and social) to such expenditures. See, for example, Marcelo Selowsky, *The Effect of Unemployment and Growth on the Rate of Return to Education: The Case of Colombia* (Cambridge, Mass., 1968).

108. See data on the income of families getting ICT housing in Departamento Nacional de Planeación, *La Actividad Constructora Popular: Análisis General y Elementos Para Una Política de Apoyo*, Políticas de Desarrollo Urbano y Vivienda, Doc. II, Documento de Trabajo, (April 1972).

   ICT type housing programs would improve distribution only if there existed a substantial trickle down effect, whereby the increase in supply of houses at this quality level would lower their price and make them accessible to lower income people.

109. Another perspective on the relationship between politics and economic policy under the National Front is presented in Sandoval, *El Manejo*. Sandoval tests the hypothesis that the government's desire to win votes generates a different set of economic policies before elections than at other times; he focuses on balance of payments policy, monetary policy and fiscal policy, and finds clear evidence of the use of these policies to further the National Front's electoral fortunes.

110. Which, it should be noted, has never occurred in Colombia's history. A return to the situation of violent political conflict between the two parties was also a possibility but little amenable to such comparisons as those made here.

111. See Robert Dix, "Political Oppositions Under the Colombian National Front," (this volume).

112. For a detailed discussion of the opposition under the National Front see Robert Dix, ibid.

113. For a discussion see Berry and Urrutia, *Income Distribution*, Ch. 10. The performance of Colombia's government was probably not atypical in these respects—apparently not as bad, for example, as that of Brazil.

114. Individual efforts in this direction do go back farther, of course; Alfonso López's social legislation and Land Law in 1936, and the Agrarian Reform Law of 1961 are examples. But such initiatives either were restricted in application by the weight of political opposition (the two agrarian laws) or were simply incapable of affecting distribution much (the social legislation).

115. Making the most of international trade was one of Carlos Lleras' particular interests, though the adoption of a floating exchange rate was not his original intent, but rather a position adopted in the context of a complicated political dispute with the IMF. One could hardly say that it was in any sense a logical result of the National Front type of government.

Chapter 11

Industrial Development Policies During the National Front Years

Francisco E. Thoumi

This chapter discusses the development of the manufacturing industry in Colombia during the National Front governments, and the main issues and economic policies that affected industrial growth during that period.[1] The level of industrial development at the beginning of the period, and the factors that had influenced it are discussed first, followed by an analysis of industrial performance during the National Front years, and then by a study of government policies affecting that performance. The chapter concludes with speculations about current policy and development alternatives.

INDUSTRIAL DEVELOPMENT AT THE BEGINNING OF THE NATIONAL FRONT

Industrial growth in Colombia has followed the ups and downs of the primary goods which are Colombia's exports. In times of high prices for traditional exports, national income rises and so does the demand for industrial consumer goods, inducing some industrial development. In hard times for those traditional exports, the terms of trade turn in favor of industry and against agriculture, producing a different type of industrial stimulus.[2]

Extreme instability in the prices of primary exports has caused serious fluctuations in the economic welfare of Colombia and other Latin American countries. In order to improve this situation, Latin American governments after World War II attempted to broaden the base of their economies and to encourage diversification into nonagrarian industry. This policy was expressed in heavily protectionist policies which favored industry vis-à-vis the agricultural sector.[3]

It is important to point out that protectionism in Latin America was aimed at decreasing the impact of export price fluctuations; autarky was not a goal in itself. Import-substituting industrialization was a reaction against an external condition rather than the product of an autarkical ideology. Thus, it did not follow a single coordinated plan, but was the spontaneous result of individual policy measures, many of which did not have the specific goal of protecting a particular industry—although this was frequently the result.[4] Less thought was originally given to the whys of the economic policies than to their hows, i.e. limiting imports was more important than explaining why this was necessary or why alternative policies would not be adequate.

Tariffs, quantitative import restrictions, and other international trade policy measures were the heart of the protective action—although they were supplemented by such measures as tax exemptions, subsidies, and cheap capital loans. The protective tariff structure fixed high nominal duties on industrial goods which were or could be produced in the country and low duties on the raw materials and capital equipment required to produce those goods. Tariff policies were complemented by an import licensing system involving a "free" list of the commodities that could be imported without a license, a "prior license" list of the goods that could be imported with a license, and a "prohibited" list of the goods whose import was not allowed. These protective barriers had (and still have) notable loopholes: neither the imports of the state nor those of the Catholic church were subject to tariffs or to licensing.[5]

During the year or so immediately preceding the National Front, the protectionist policies had been strengthened in reaction to the catastrophic fall in the world coffee price at the end of 1956. The licensing system had been tightened and the prohibited imports list expanded. Virtually no imports of consumer goods were allowed.

Industry had also been favored by cheap capital loans; most interest rates on industrial loans were not far above the inflation rate, so the real cost of fixed capital for many firms was actually close to zero and in some years even negative.[6] Credit was rationed in favor of the "directly productive sectors," namely agriculture and nonluxury-producing industry, and against the "nondirectly-productive sectors," which included trade, services, and luxury-producing industry.[7]

Over time the combination of high protection and low interest rates favored the development of inward-looking industries which tended to be more capital

Table 1
Structure of Manufacturing Production in Colombia

Year	Value added in manufacturing of consumer goods* as percentage of total manufacturing value added.	Value added in manufacturing of capital goods† as percentage of total manufacturing value added.	Value added in manufacturing of intermediate goods‡ as percentage of total manufacturing value added.
1945	70.71	6.89	22.40
1958	66.00	7.41	26.59
1962	60.13	8.46	31.41
1966	56.92	8.58	34.50
1969	56.04	10.32	33.64

Notes:
*Includes: Food, beverages, tobacco, textiles, clothing, shoes, printed materials, furniture, and miscellaneous industries.
†Includes: Basic metals, electric and nonelectric machinery, and transport equipment.
‡Includes: Pulp and paper, wood, chemicals, rubber products, nonmetallic minerals.
Sources: 1945 data: Dirección Nacional de Estadística, *Primer censo industrial de Colombia, 1945*. Bogotá.
1958, 1962, and 1966 data: Thoumi, F., "Evolución de la industria manufacturera fabril 1958-1967" *Boletín Mensual de Estadística*, Dane, N. 236, p. 69.
1969 data: Dane, *Industria Manufacturera Nacional, 1969* Bogotá.

intensive than the older ones. Protectionism also fostered industrial diversification by providing a myriad of small product markets which promised high profits and security for investors.

In the 1950s, the structure of Colombian industry was changing with more emphasis on consumer durable, intermediate, and capital goods than on nondurable consumer goods (see Table 1). By the beginning of the National Front, almost all the domestic consumption of light industrial products such as clothes, textiles, shoes, furniture, processed foods, cosmetics, etc. was supplied by domestic sources, and some heavy industries also existed. The reasons for the establishment of the latter varied considerably: tire production, for example, had begun when tires could not be imported because of the Second World War embargo; cement production had been set up under the protective umbrella provided by high transportation costs and was already flourishing; tariff protection had fostered the development of a glass industry, and explicit government action had been instrumental in creating the Paz del Río steel mill in the late 1950s.[8] Thus, the National Front governments inherited a growing industrial sector and a changing industrial structure. Industrial value added in 1958 was 13.5 percent of gross national product, up from 10.2 percent in 1945.

Table 2
Change in Manufacturing Importance in Production

Years	Manufacturing value added as percentage of GNP	Gross manufacturing output as percentage of total supply
1945	10.2	31.8
1958	13.5	37.3
1962	16.8	40.5
1966	16.3	40.0
1972	18.2*	43.4*

Notes:
*Preliminary
Sources: 1945 data: Dirección Nacional de Estadística; *Primer Censo industrial de Colombia, 1945*, Bogotá; and Banco de la República, *Cuentas Nacionales*.
1958, 1962, and 1966 data: F. Thoumi "Evolución de la industria manufacturera fabril 1958-1967" *Boletín Mensual de Estadística*, DANE, No. 236, p. 69.
1972 data: unpublished preliminary DANE data and Banco de la República, *Cuentas Nacionales*.

INDUSTRIAL PERFORMANCE DURING THE NATIONAL FRONT GOVERNMENTS

Industrial development during the National Front was characterized by a growth rate above that of the economy as a whole, as well as by output diversification, uneven employment generation, and the development of industrial exports.

Gross industrial output during the National Front increased from 37.3 percent of the total supply of goods and services in 1958 to 43.4 percent in 1972. Simultaneously, value added as a percentage of GNP increased from 13.5 in 1958 to 18.2 in 1972. However, this growth was not continuous (see Table 2). Industrial output expanded more rapidly than GNP during the early National Front years (1958-62), grew at a rate similar to that of GNP during the middle years (1963-67), and at a faster rate again at the end of the period (1968-73).

Employment generation in the manufacturing sector was not spectacular although it was significant. Berry estimates a rate of employment growth in manufacturing of 3.7 percent or higher for the period 1953-62, followed by a decline to 2.5 percent between 1962 and 1968 and a similar increase in more recent years.[9]

One of the most striking features of industrial development during the National Front was the continuing change in the structure of output. Specifically, the production of so-called nondurable consumer goods declined as a percentage of industrial output while the production of intermediate consumer durables and capital goods increased as percentages of industrial output. Impressionistic evidence indicates that this change was accompanied by a great increase in the variety of goods produced—many intermediate and capital goods not previously produced were manufactured, and a variety of new consumer goods appeared in the market.

In 1958, Colombian industrial exports were limited to a few agriculturally-based items such as sugar, to which the natural resources gave a comparative advantage. From 1967 on, industrial exports grew quickly both in value and diversity; from a level of $55.6 million in 1967,[10] they rose to $253.0 million in 1972,[11] or 21 percent of total exports. These changes in industrial structure and performance were significantly influenced by the industrial policy mix that was followed by the Colombian governments, policies that changed greatly during the National Front years.

INDUSTRIAL POLICY MIX OF THE NATIONAL FRONT GOVERNMENTS

The first National Front administrations continued the industrial policies of their predecessors. Import-substituting industrialization was seen as the way to independence from the uncertainties of the international economy, and accordingly pursued vigorously. The first National Front government, however, enjoyed internal political peace that allowed it to focus on economic issues in a more direct and effective way than had been possible earlier. It not only formalized and reinforced the import substitution strategy of the previous governments; it also attempted to plan the economic growth of the country in a more deliberate fashion. The dependence on the foreign sector and its sharp price fluctuations as well as discrediting any export-oriented development policy, had also generated much criticism of the free market process in general, and strong support for economic planning capable of controlling the marketplace. However, the difficult balance of payments conditions and more frequent labor strikes allowed by the more stable political situation were to present a troublesome situation for any industrial policy.

The first National Front administration of Alberto Lleras thus focused on creating an explicitly protectionist long-run policy of industrial development whose means and goals were internally consistent. It proceeded to change the tariff structure, prepare a national development plan, and increase the government's financial and entrepreneurial role in industry.

By May 1959, the new tariff structure had been established.[12] Explicitly protectionist, its purpose was to shield domestic production and capital from foreign competition and to foster the creation of new industries, preferably those producing capital goods. The reforms also established a new set of lists for import licensing purposes, allowing the government better control over the supply of foreign goods. In reading the text of the law, one is struck by the frequency with which the defensive function of the tariff structure is mentioned: it should defend domestic production, defend the domestic markets, defend the economy from outside changes, etc.[13]

Toward the end of 1960 the government presented a ten-year development plan in which import-substituting industrialization received first priority.[14] The plan was elaborated by the Planning Commission (*Departmento Administrativo de Planeación y Servicos Técnicos*), an institution which had been dormant during the preceding governments and which was to gain great importance during the National Front period. The plan called for the development of the intermediate and capital goods sectors in order to take advantage of backward linkages in industrial development, and to free the economy from the effects of the international trade fluctuations. An industrial growth output rate of 8.6 percent per annum was projected for the decade 1960-70, compared with the 6.8 percent achieved during the previous decade.[15] The proposed output growth rate was broken down as follows: 14.1 percent in chemical products, 14.3 percent in basic metals, 13.6 percent in manufactured metals, 12.8 percent in pulp and paper, and 14.6 percent in wood and furniture. These were the high expected growth sectors; the growth of textiles was planned at only 3.6 percent.[16]

It is clear from these growth rates that the plan was pervaded by industrial export pessimism. The only industrial exports anticipated by the plan were wood products, chemical products, fuel oil, cement, steel sheets, and some fabricated metals.[17] These are products for which Colombia would be internationally competitive because of abundant mineral or land resources, or those capital intensive industries where export sales priced marginally above variable costs (dumping) would be more profitable than cutting production if domestic demand were to decline. No labor intensive industrial exports were contemplated.

The plan required a substantial increase in industrial investment; the necessary annual average for the period 1961-65 was estimated at more than double the level of 1957-59, although this was only 43 percent more than the investment level during the high coffee price years 1953-56.[18] This substantial increase in industrial investment called for a large increase in government and direct foreign investment. The government was expected to provide 36 percent of the total financing, mainly through the public industrial finance corporation (Instituto de Fomento Industrial or IFI); direct foreign investment would account for another 33 percent concentrated in pulp and paper, basic chemical products, and fertilizers; while only 31 percent of the net industrial investment was expected to come from the domestic private sector.[19]

The plan thus called for active government involvement in the industrial

Table 3
IFI's 1969 Industrial Portfolio

Oils and Fats	8.6%
Transportation Equipment	15.7%
Jute Packing	2.3%
Manufactured Metals	2.8%
Forges	16.4%
Fertilizers	1.0%
Petro-chemicals	30.2%
Industrial Chemicals	23.0%
	100.0%

Source: IFI, 1969 *Informe del Gerente*

sector. IFI was to play the central role by developing industrial projects and putting them into operation. IFI was founded in 1941 to undertake investments in industries whose large magnitude or high risk prevented the private sector from undertaking them, although they were considered necessary for the development of the country. Successful IFI undertakings were to be sold to the private sector after they were in operation. IFI wholly owns some factories and has also invested in joint projects with the private sector.

As of December 1958, IFI's total assets were 34.7 million pesos, which snowballed to 5,935 million pesos by December 1972. After taking inflation into account this is a forty-five-fold increase in assets, a clear reflection of the importance of IFI policies in the structure of industrial investment in Colombia. In 1958, IFI's investments were limited to partial ownership of Paz del Río (steel), a cement plant, and a pulp and paper plant, as well as full ownership of a metallic cable factory, a coal mine, a basic chemicals plant, and some commercial institutions such as the Corporation of Fairs and Expositions. By 1969, its expanded operations were concentrated in petrochemicals and industrial chemicals, which accounted for over 53 percent of the total IFI investments (see Table 3). Another 22.3 percent of its portfolio was in a large metal working forge and in the automotive industry. IFI's economic philosophy was clearly stated in the manager's report (*Informe del gerente*) of 1969, which reads: "it is well known in economics that the great income differentials between developed and less developed countries are due to differences in the volume and variety of production. The developed countries have a diversified and industrialized economic structure while the low income countries are producers of agricultural goods." Accordingly, IFI's policy was to foster industrialization and diversification. Its 1969 investment plans included a long list of capital intensive industrial products such as pulp and paper, caustic soda, antibiotics, magnesium derivatives, phosphoric acid, synthetic fibers, telephones, industrial colorants, synthetic rubber, glass, heavy trucks, and tractors. A few of these projects have been implemented, but most have been discarded.

IFI was not immune to political pressures, and the locations selected for some of its projects seem to have been the result of such pressures. Not unexpectedly, some of these investments are among those whose economic viability is most questionable, for example, Forjas de Colombia, a metal-working plant located in Bucaramanga; or the split in the auto industry with the assembly plant near Medellín and the projected engine factory in Boyacá.

IFI and other development finance corporations provided long-term industrial credit at real interest rates that were not far above zero. The average rate for their peso loans was about 16 or 17 percent when average devaluation was about 10 percent and world inflation was 2 to 4 percent. Thus, the peso value of any capital equipment imported by a company would increase to only 2 to 3 percent less than the interest rate paid on money borrowed to purchase the equipment. Under these conditions, investment in capital intensive industry was profitable, even when many of the production lines were technically inefficient by international standards as their size was often significantly lower than the minimum efficient size required by the existing technology.[20]

The above import substitution policies were complemented by the Basic Industries Law, which granted income tax exemptions to factories using steel produced by the Paz del Río complex.

In summary, the early National Front policy basically continued in a more coordinated manner the previous approach of import-substituting industrialization. The political stability provided by the National Front which allowed this coordination and the magnitude of the new investments needed during this import-substituting phase increased the role of the government in determining the allocation of investment and in managing new industries. The momentum generated by long-run investment plans carried import substitution into the 1970s even after the government, or at least an important faction within it, had emphasized a different industrialization strategy.

Import substituting industrialization had its successes in Colombia; in some branches a substantial learning-by-doing process lowered costs significantly.[21] Yet the results were disappointing, in that a large share of investment was concentrated in very capital intensive industries, which not only cost a great deal for production, but generated very few jobs. Furthermore, recurrent balance of payments difficulties indicated that Colombian dependence on the foreign sector was not declining. Import substitution had instead actually limited the government's alternatives when balance of payment difficulties arose. Because a larger share of foreign exchange was required to keep import-substituting industry running, any decrease in the imports of intermediate goods led directly to a decrease in employment.

During the National Front years, Colombia had two main balance of payments crises; that of 1962, which led to the devaluation of early 1963; and that of 1966, which led to the reforms of 1967 and Decree 444.[22] From 1958 to 1967, the National Front governments followed the fixed exchange rate policies of the previous governments. These years were characterized by occasional large devaluations, which followed periods during which internal inflation made imports cheaper than domestically produced goods. These devaluations (sometimes of over 30 or 40 percent), followed by periods of exchange rate stability but high domestic inflation, created an environment inhospitable to the development of export industry.[23] It was thus biased in favor of import substitution.

By 1967 the government was disillusioned with the system of fixed exchange rates and periodic devaluations which clearly had not solved the chronic balance of payments problem. With a radical change in policy, it initiated a crawling-peg system of small frequent devaluations. Simultaneously, an export tax credit (CAT) of 15 percent of the value of nontraditional exports was granted.[24] The tariff drawback system for imports to be used in the production of exports was made more flexible, and improved financing was made available to export industries. The new policies were aimed at keeping export markets attractive in the presence of internal inflation and at avoiding the recurrent shocks that large devaluations had on the economy. The results of this policy mix have been quite satisfactory; both exports and industrial employment have grown at accelerated rates. During the first three years after the policy change, most of the increase in nontraditional exports was in agricultural and agroindustrial products; from 1970 on, however, a varied array of industrial products entered the export category.

The 1967 reforms also included stronger government control of foreign investment and transference of technology; limits were set on profit remittances, and a committee was created to approve royalty payments and technology contracts.

In 1969 Colombia became a charter member of the Andean Common Market. One of the Market's main goals is import substituting industrialization at the regional level. Import substitution in the Andean countries had reached a stage at which domestic production was already satisfying the demand for most consumer goods; further import substitution into the production of intermediate and capital goods would be very expensive at the national level because the small size of the market limits the possibilities of plant specialization and economies of scale. The Common Market offers the possibility of furthering import substitution at lower costs than those feasible for individual countries. Following this philosophy, the Common Market places strong emphasis on programs that attempt to give each country a reasonable share of new import-substituting industries. The impact of these programs has yet to be felt as they were only being approved in late 1975, but they may become an important factor in the industrial development of these countries.

The lowering of trade barriers within the Andean Common Market has expanded the market of many Colombian industries; by the end of the National Front, Colombia was exporting approximately 200 million dollars a year (13.5 percent of the 1974 exports) to the Andean countries. Many of these exports are reported to be industrial goods.

The Andean group agreement considered the need for harmonization of policies among the Andean countries. The first step in this direction was the approval of the "Statute of Capitals" in 1970, which was aimed at regulating direct foreign investment in the area. The statute has two parts, one emphasizing control of foreign investment, the other outlining requirements for increased domestic (Andean group) ownership of the foreign firms that benefit from the enlarged Andean market. The first part was patterned on Colombia's Decree 444. Its main control measures are limitations on profit remittances and royalties allowed. The second part requires the gradual purchase of up to 51 percent of the stock of many industrial firms; it may force Colombia to follow a policy she would not necessarily choose on her own. However, the statute has substantial loopholes; for example, it is not clear whether a foreign-owned firm can be prevented from exporting through a small subsidiary of which 51 percent is domestically owned. Recent changes in the political composition of the Andean group governments are likely to result in a loose interpretation of the statute, and thus eliminate some of Colombia's original objections to it.

The policies discussed so far were directed mainly at the development of large-scale, or fairly large-scale industry. A complementary policy developed by the third National Front government was an attempt to foster small-scale industries through the creation of the Corporación Financiera Popular, and Ficitec.[25] While both these institutions seem to have been successful, their impact on the overall industrial development is still difficult to determine.

The last National Front government made important changes in economic policy. It applied a leading sector model of development in which the construction sector (mostly housing) was to play the main role, although the export sector continued to be important.[26] This new policy had important effects on industrial development:

1. Credit was diverted from various sectors of the economy toward the housing sector with the result that the cost of long-term capital for industry increased.
2. The growth in housing production increased the demand for many industrial goods required in construction, and thus fostered activity in some industrial sectors.
3. The housing boom also increased employment of low-skilled workers in the cities, thereby increasing the demand for other industrial products such as processed food, clothes, and shoes.
4. The continued creeping devaluation and export credit expansion allowed industrial exports to expand.

During this last period, industrial development differed greatly from that of the recent past, as labor intensive sectors that had been dormant for some time emerged as leaders of industrial growth due to the increased internal demand and the expansion of exports. Construction-related industries grew at fast rates; the import-substitution industries, which had registered the fastest growth during the 1960s, slowed down.

To summarize, the governments of the National Front followed distinct economic policies, which can be classified into three stages or periods: the 1958-67 period characterized by import-substitution policies; the 1967-70 period when an export promotion drive was superimposed on the import substitution policies; and the 1970-74 period in which the guidelines were set by the so-called Operación Colombia with its heavy emphasis on the construction sector, and secondary emphasis on industrial exports. The momentum of each policy carried it forward into the next period because the policy infrastructure did not completely disappear at the end of any period. Therefore, import substitution was still taking place at the end of the National Front years.

The various policies appear to have benefited different social groups and thus have had different political support. Explicitly, the import-substitution policies have tended to be particularly elitist, producing capital intensive industries and technology, which in turn was inclined to increase the share of the capitalists in value added and simultaneously to raise the wages of the employed workers—although generating few new jobs. Inasmuch as industrial export incentives have fostered the development of labor intensive industries, the 1967 change in industrial policy has had the opposite effect, i.e., it has benefited industries in which, while wages are relatively low, they constitute a large proportion of value added, and employment is easily expanded.[27] The Operación Colombia policies, with their emphasis on construction, have also contributed to the employment of low-skilled workers. Within this framework, one can easily understand why the import substitution "lobby" has continued after the policy changes of the last two National Front governments, as these changes clearly affected well-established interest groups.

CURRENT POLICY DILEMMA

Colombia is now facing new world economic conditions (the recession) which might lead some observers to believe that the export successes of 1972-74 were short-lived, and that more generally, export-oriented industrialization cannot succeed. Further import substitution appears unpromising because it would require the development of capital intensive processes involving such large economies of scale that it would again necessitate achievement of economically efficient production levels. In principle, the Andean group could provide the outlet necessary for the production of such new efficient import-substitution industries; but this alternative could be very difficult to attain as Colombia's participation in the Andean group's industrial programming is likely to be in the automotive industry and in some manufactured metals and basic chemical industries, where either the product variety or the small size of the Andean group total market makes reaching efficient output levels difficult.

These external limitations create a policy dilemma. Should Colombia gamble on the future demand in developed countries for the industrial products of less-developed countries, and follow a clearly export-oriented policy which, if it succeeds, is likely to produce fast industrial growth and abundant low paid employment; or should Colombia follow a more predictable path of further import substitution, thereby creating a smaller number of better paid jobs and probably leading to a lower rate of growth and a more difficult balance of payments situation.

NOTES

1. Thanks are due R. Albert Berry for his useful comments and to Inés García for her research assistance.
2. D.Chu, "The Great Depression and Industrialization in Colombia," in Albert Berry, ed., *Essays on Industrialization in Colombia* (forthcoming), gives an excellent analysis of these two sources of growth in his comparison of the industrial growth of the 1920s and 1930s.
3. For a detailed analysis of these policies in Latin America, see S. Macario, "Protectionism and industrialization in Latin America," *Economic Bulletin for Latin America* (March 1964), pp. 61-102.
4. Ibid.
5. Data on exempted imports are hard to find. However, L.J. Garay, M. Martínez, J. Giordanelli, R. Villaveces, and Y. Castro in "Análisis de la estructura de control a las importaciones en Colombia" (Bogotá, August 1974), estimated that in 1973 the public sector tariff exonerated imports rose over 166 million dollars, which accounted for approximately 16 percent of the "*importaciones reembolsables*," those imports that were paid for with foreign exchange sold by the central bank.
6. The total cost of bank loans exceeds the officially posted rates, since minimum balances, "points," etc. are required to get a loan. However, in a country where an interest rate of 2 and 3 percent per month was frequent in the outside bank market and where inflation during the last twenty years has averaged about 11 percent, an annual rate of 12 percent plus points, minimum balances, etc. is unquestionably cheap.
7. This credit discrimination was stronger against commerce and other services than against "luxury" industrial products. Since most plants have diversified product lines including both luxuries and nonluxuries, it is difficult, if not impossible, for the government to control luxury production through special credit limitations.
8. An excellent history of industrial Colombian development in this century is in Berry's "A Descriptive History of Colombian Industrial Development in the Twentieth Century," in R. Albert Berry, ed., *Essays on Industrialization*.
9. Ibid. Berry's estimates are higher than the increases shown by DANE's data, which underestimates employment due to poor coverage of small manufacturing units in the noncensus years.

10. World Bank, *Economic Growth of Colombia* (Baltimore, 1972), p. 103.
11. *Coyuntura Económica*, vol. 3, No.1 (Bogotá, April 1973).
12. See the Decrees No. 1345 and 1346 of May 10, 1959 in Ministerio de Hacienda y Crédito Público, *Arancel de Aduanas y Régimen Legal de Importaciones* (Bogotá, 1959).
13. See Consejo Nacional de Política Económica y Planeación, Departamento Administrativo de Planeación y Servicios Técnicos, *Colombia: Plan General de Desarrollo Económico y Social,* vol. 1 (Bogotá, 1962), p. ix.
14. Ibid., vol. 2.
15. Ibid., p. 106.
16. Ibid.
17. Ibid., p. 99.
18. Ibid., p. 117.
19. Ibid., p. 124.
20. See D. Morawetz, "Sustitución de importaciones, creación de empleo y generación de divisas en Colombia: Pocas perspectivas para la industria petroquímica" (Bogotá, November 1973).
21. L. Dudley, "The Effects of Learning on Employment and Labor Productivity in the Colombian Metal Products Sector," in Berry, ed. *Essays*.
22. An excellent and extensive discussion of the international trade policy of Colombia during this time is the recent work C.F. Díaz-Alejandro, *Foreign Trade Regimes and Economic Development: Colombia*, National Bureau of Economic Research (New York, 1975).
23. Any long-run export plan requires some stability of the long-run profit margin, especially when it is time-consuming and expensive to break into foreign markets. Individual devaluations could make it profitable to export some industrial goods in the short run. However, with a fixed exchange rate and the expectation of internal inflation, decreasing, and even negative, profit margins in the export markets became likely. Thus, plants were not interested in breaking into export markets, especially since they had the opportunity to produce for the domestic market, where inflation helped to keep profit margins at a more stable and often high level.
24. The CAT, a certificate granted to the exporter-producer, could be used in payment of taxes in the amount of 15 percent of the value of his exports. All exports except coffee, oil, and bananas, were covered, and since CATs were transferable, a very active market in them developed quickly. The CAT itself was not taxable, which made it more valuable to exporters in higher marginal income tax brackets than to those in lower brackets.
25. A technical assistance institution providing mostly managerial and marketing services to small industries.
26. For explicit definitions of this development policy, see two works by the Departamento Nacional de Planeación: *Las cuatro Estrategias* (Bogotá, 1972); and "Guías para una nueva estrategia del desarrollo" in *Revista de Planeación y Desarrollo*, vol. 3, no. 4 (December 1971), pp. 5-96.
27. Díaz-Alejandro in his recent work, *Foreign Trade Regimes*, has shown that the so-called minor exports which benefited from the CAT seem to fall into one or another of the following three categories: (1) resource based industries, (2) capital intensive industries, and (3) labor intensive industries. The resource intensive industries export because of a resource based advantage; the capital intensive industries export because of excess capacity in processes which are uneconomical to operate below capacity, or because of preferences within the Andean Group. Thus, although these industries benefit from the export incentives, their exports

are hardly the result of the subsidies. Thus the impact of the subsidies is expected to affect mainly the labor intensive industries, where subsidies do make a substantial difference to the profitability of exporting.

Chapter 12

Agrarian Reform and the National Front: A Class Analysis

A. Eugene Havens
William L. Flinn
Susana Lastarría Cornhill

Crockcroft states that "Colombia's agrarian reform is generally recognized as a fraud."[1] Even more conservative observers agree that the emphasis of the National Front has been on land distribution (i.e., colonization, titling, extension of new technology) and not on redistribution.[2] When reform is thought of in the more inclusive sense involving also improvements in credit, technical assistance, and marketing for smaller farmers, it still appears that the National Front's efforts have been unimpressive.

In order to understand why this is the case, a historical class analysis of the antecedents of the National Front is useful.[3] The direct economic interest of the dominant class is against land redistribution and heavy public expenditure on small farmers. While some view such steps as necessary to avoid serious political problems, this group has been in the minority. While both direct economic interest and stated views vary somewhat between political parties, the differences are not dramatic. The leaders of the major political parties are from the dominant class, and usually it makes little difference for public policy which party is in power.

The first section of this chapter presents a brief review of some key events in Colombia's political development and their effects on the structure of Colombian agriculture. The second section briefly describes how much land reform has been done under the National Front.[4] In the third section we take a detailed look at small farmers in three communities during the period 1963 to 1970 of the National Front, partly to illustrate the type of situation which generates the call for land reform and partly to look at the consequences of land reform and more generally, of government agricultural policy. These communities are offered as representatives of three types of Colombian agriculture: (1) traditional subsistence peasant farming, (2) small to medium commercial family farms, and (3) large estate (*latifundio*) export-oriented agriculture.[5] The traditional subsistence peasant community's benefits from agricultural policy were restricted mainly to the provision of credit. The small family farm community was affected mainly by credit and the introduction of a new green revolution coffee variety. The third community did have a land distribution project and although none of the small farmers in our sample were in it, this community provides an opportunity to examine possible multiplier effects of the project. Our findings in the three communities show that incomes of some peasants were higher in 1970 than in 1963, but that both land and income were more concentrated; there is a distinct possibility that numerous families became worse off.

Whether and how much worse the situation in these three communities and in rural Colombia in general would have been without the government activities under discussion is difficult to evaluate. The combination of action and lack of action by the National Front has, however, increased peasant consciousness and organization.[6] The last section briefly reviews our overall conclusions.

A CLASS ANALYSIS

Our study of agrarian reform activities by the National Front governments of Colombia will not repeat the excellent descriptions of the agrarian reform process already available.[7] Instead it will try to present in broad outline the class basis of the National Front governments and the ways in which the dominant interests have determined an agrarian reform policy that does little for Colombia's vast peasantry.

Historically, there are three great watersheds in Colombia's attempt to develop along capitalistic lines. The first is the 1850 reforms, which largely centered around "freeing" land, labor, and capital. The social organization of the colonial *latifundio* increasingly conflicted with merchant and other capitalist interests because of the immobility that it imposed upon the factors of economic production—land (because of the *censos* and the church monopoly,)[8] labor (because of *resguardos* [Indian reservations][9] and slavery), and capital (because of protectionism and the taxation system) and because of the relationship between capital and the specific organization of land and labor. At stake was the creation of a cheap source of labor for agricultural production.

The second great watershed was state consolidation in 1902. This consolidation grew out of the War of a Thousand Days, the last in a series of civil wars that highlighted the nineteenth-century history. In these conflicts, factions of the dominant class recruited peasants to fight their battles to gain or maintain power at national and departmental levels. The War of a Thousand Days ended the regional separatist movements. The emerging capitalist class increasingly understood the state's potential for guaranteeing one class's privilege of economic power over the majority of the population.

The third great watershed was the establishment of the National Front. The violence (La Violencia) that preceded the National Front period eventually posed a threat to the interests of the dominant class. Although La Violencia was initially the result of political conflict among elements of the dominant class, resulting in physical violence between Liberals and Conservatives in the rural areas, its spread produced a new phenomenon: peasants turned against "exploiters" (usually landlords, but also merchants) regardless of political affiliation, in order to gain access to land. The dominant class responded to the dangers created by or reflected in the violence with a new political form to control class struggle, the National Front.

In the pages that follow, we will sketch out the historical developments leading to these three watersheds in Colombia'a capitalist development with emphasis on the place of agrarian reforms in the effort of the dominant class to maintain its hegemony and to further capitalist expansion.

Struggle Against the Colonial Economy

Colonial Colombia had an internal economy of subsistence consumption based on a combination of semifeudal and slave institutions,[10] and an external economy based on the extraction of precious metals. Spain's emphasis on mining meant that agricultural and industrial production, as well as the growth of communication lines, were ignored or impeded. Colonial economics were simple—precious metals such as gold and silver were exported, and commodities produced in England and Holland were imported via Spain.[11]

Although the nation had won independence from Spain in 1819, Colombia's social and economic structures continued in the colonial mode until midcentury, when certain commercial-political factions attempted to move the economy toward an independent capitalist structure. The colonial mode of production—extensive territorial property (*latifundios*), collective village economy (*resguardos*), state monopolies (such as tobacco), and many many taxes—presented oppressive obstacles to a number of emerging economic groups. These were the merchants, the artisan producers, incipient manufacturers, and small tobacco cultivators. The Indian *resguardos* and slavery prevented the formation of a wage labor force, necessary as labor for the manufacturers and tobacco cultivators and desirable as a commodity market for the merchants, artisans, and manufacturers. Colonial taxes on commerce and manufacture would not permit an accelerated growth of manufacturing which, in turn, further limited the expansion of commerce. The state monopoly on the cultivation and export of agricultural products, including tobacco, barricaded the free expansion of tobacco cultivation and its export at a competitive price. The merchants particularly disliked the protectionist policy that precluded free trade of commodities—a fundamental condition for the expansion of commerce.

The incipient commercial bourgeoisie, straining for expansion, had led the independence movement in Colombia. This group was assisted by England, which was interested in the separation of Spain from her colonies and more open trade with the latter.[12] While Colombia gained political independence from Spain, the function of its political economy remained the same, except that it traded directly with England instead of through Spain.

The commercial bourgeoisie sought to change this system and to implant new forms of production; but traditional large landowners, who controlled the government, opposed reforms which appeared to threaten the existing system on which they depended. Not until 1850 were new economic groups able to gain control of the government and implement selective reforms.

Reforms of 1850

The new radical government of 1850 believed that its liberal reforms (e.g., freedom to trade, free wage labor) would bring the industrial revolution to Colombia. One of their important steps in the agricultural sector was abolition of the *censo*, a type of mortgage on land. When a landowner borrowed from a merchant or, more typically, from the church at a fixed rate of annual interest, he was obliged to pay the stipulated interest for an undefined number of years. Since the *censo* was attached to the land and was thus transferred to new owners, it hindered free circulation of property. Both large landowners and small agricultural cultivators stood to gain from removal of the *diezmo* and the *censo*. Merchants could also gain in that land would become a free commodity again, breaking the hold the church exercised over capital and land. Consequently, neither faction of the dominant class opposed the reform.

Another "reform" with far-reaching consequences was abolition of the Indian *resguardos*. The *resguardo*, a communal type of agricultural production and ownership of land, involved mainly production for immediate consumption and thereby restricted the purchasing power of the Indians; it also kept them out of the wage labor force and their land out of the market. Such communal ownership of land was incompatible with the capitalist concept of land as a commodity, a transferable piece of private property. The demise of the *resguardo* resulted in commercialization of the *resguardo* land, introduction of the Indians to a monetary economy, expansion of the supply of labor to the large landholdings in the form of *peones*, sharecroppers, and renters (and for the tobacco growers in the form of wage laborers), and territorial expansion of the large estates.[13]

Another significant step taken in 1850 was elimination of the state monopoly on tobacco cultivation and export. This colonial restriction had been designed to prevent competition with Spain or with other colonies and to provide tax revenue, and was preserved after independence because it was one of the biggest sources of revenue. The reform caused an increase in tobacco production, and exports doubled between 1850 and 1852.[14] The production gain stabilized steam transport on the Magdalena River, one of the main arteries of communication and transport in Colombia, and fostered the economic advance of Barranquilla on the Caribbean coast. Other consequences included a rise in the values of territorial property and the wages of workers in the tobacco-growing regions and neighboring areas. However, the higher wages also pushed up production costs for manufacturing in the Oriente, according to Nieto Arteta, and the products of this region became even less competitive with English commodities.[15] As a result of the free trade policy, incipient manufacture was crippled and Colombia became increasingly dependent on the importation of industrial products.

The social revolution of 1850 expanded agriculture and commerce but failed to create an industrial revolution or to generate rapid sustained economic development. Neither the capital to induce industrialization nor a bourgeois class to give the process political support existed in Colombia at the time. Struggle against the colonial structure was not a matter of bourgeois interests against landed interests; it was rather a struggle of the proponents of capitalist advance in whatever sector against the traditional colonial economy. Specific ends of the various participant groups meshed in a desire to destroy an outmoded social and economic structure. There was no pressure to diminish the power of landed interests per se, as for example by making land distribution more equitable.

Land Tenure and Labor in the Nineteenth Century

One continuing characteristic of the land tenure system, through both the independence movement and the reforms of 1850, was the concentration of land. In the early 1800s, regional situations differed somewhat. Santander,

Cundinamarca, and Boyacá had moderate to large numbers of small holders; elsewhere, the concentration of land among relatively few owners was more striking.[16] After independence, the landowners who had supported Spain lost their holdings, but these lands were appropriated by important members of the winning side, with the net effect of increasing land concentration. The abolition of the *resguardos* had a similar effect. An 1861 law ostensibly designed to diminish land concentration called for the expropriation of all property held by either secular or ecclesiastical corporations. Its prime objective was to break up the extensive landed property held by the church and church organizations, but in fact it simply transferred land from the church to other large holders.

During the colonial period, most labor had come from two sources: slaves and semi-enslaved Indians. When the reforms of 1850 abolished slavery and the *resguardos*, a significant number of free laborers were released into the labor market. The agricultural sector found some use for wage workers primarily in the production of export crops. Western regions being colonized could accommodate other wage laborers as well as sharecroppers and subsistence *minifundistas* (small holders). In the warmer regions where extensive cattle raising was practiced, little labor was required. Throughout Colombia, there were many peasants bonded to the land through debts to the large landowners and working as sharecroppers, renters, and laborers.[17]

Until 1850, gold was almost the only product that Colombia exported, but soon after the state monopoly on tobacco was abolished in 1850, production of tobacco increased tremendously. Henceforth, Colombia's exports were mainly agricultural products. All of these—tobacco, quinine, indigo, and later coffee—were produced in the hot or temperate climates rather than the cold highland regions where the great bulk of Colombia's population was concentrated in 1850. Tobacco expansion coincided with the abandonment of the *resguardos* and induced migration down to the warmer lowlands where tobacco was grown. Coffee was responsible for much greater population movements later in the century.

Production of tobacco, quinine, etc. was tied to the world market and dependent on world price and demand fluctuations which tended to be sharp. Only in the late nineteenth and the twentieth centuries would a relatively stable commercial crop—coffee—permit Colombia to integrate itself successfully into the world market, yet already the foundation for coffee production and the associated land tenure arrangements were being laid on the mountain slopes of Santander and Antioquia.

The colonization of Santander during the late colonial epoch had given it a type of development different from that of the other colonial regions in Colombia. The indigenous population had been decimated by disease and overwork, which made the establishment of the *encomienda* (a system whereby colonizers had the right to exact tribute in kind, money, and services from the native peasants, without directly taking over the land) and the *latifundio* impossible. Consequently, the land was distributed relatively equitably.[18] Small scale manufacturing flourished, creating numerous colonial towns with strong local economies. Later, however, the free trade policy of the merchant faction (1850 and on) and the import of foreign products took over much of Santander's markets and destroyed the only budding manufacturing in Colombia. Agriculture became once again the main activity, with emphasis on coffee; because of land tenure history, it was extensively produced by independent peasants as well as *latifundios*.

The settlement of Antioquia during the colonial period was begun by small-scale miners. Later, colonization of Antioquia was spurred during the second half of the 1800s by the availability of land suitable for coffee production. A relative predominance of small and medium sized holdings resulted, partly because of the extremely difficult terrain and the implicit problems of control by large owners from distant Medellín (and later Manizales). Labor needs were supplied by the family and large families were common. When the land could no longer absorb all the family labor, the sons would move on and extend the colonized area. The need to transport coffee beans for export stimulated road and railway construction to connect the whole region with the coast on the west and the Magdalena River on the east.[19] Most important, perhaps, this coffee economy established several conditions favoring the emergence and growth of industry in Antioquia: the exports contributed to accumulation of capital by coffee merchants, to growth of the commodity market, and to the greater efficiency of the transportation system already cited.

By the end of the nineteenth century, the tenure-labor pattern was set. Its main tendencies have persisted to the present. Although some *latifundios* have turned to mechanized production of commercial crops for export, the extensively cultivated *latifundio*, the subsistence *minifundio*, and the small to medium commercial coffee farm are still major agricultural institutions.

Social Basis of Agrarian Reform Law

When industrial development finally came to Colombia in the early twentieth century, it had diverse effects on the agricultural sector.[20] Landowners saw their property grow in value and the demand for and price of agricultural products increased. However, the demand for wage laborers in public works and industry caused a shift of some labor from the rural sector and a rise in wages.[21] Alarmed largeholders denounced industrial development, maintaining that the Colombian economy should remain agricultural, that attempts at industrialization should be abandoned, and that the proletarianized peasants should return to the land. Meanwhile, industry stimulated production of such imputs from agriculture as animal fats and cotton.[22]

In summarizing Colombian agricultural problems during the 1920s García

TABLE 1
Twentieth-Century Peasant Upheavals in Colombia

Year	Province	Type of Economy	Type of Peasants	Peasant Org.	Type of Demand	Type of Action	Government Response
1917-18	Magdalena	plantations (banana)	workers	union	raise in wages, better living conditions	strike	repression
1917-18	Cundinamarca (Viotá)	plantations (coffee)	share-croppers		raise in wages, better living conditions	strike, burning of public buildings	repression
1925	Cundinamarca (Bogotá Valley, Sumapaz)	plantations (coffee)	share croppers		right to plant coffee on their own parcels	strike	
1926-28	Cundinamarca (Sumapaz)	latifundia	''*colonos*''	''Sumapaz Agrarian Movement''	land	land invasions	evictions
1928	Valle (Roldanillo, Buga)	latifundia	''*colonos*''		land	land invasions	evictions
1928	Magdalena	plantations (banana)	workers	union	better wages, cheap food	strike	repression
1930-31	Cundinamarca (Viotá, Anolaima, El Colegio)	plantations (coffee)	peons and share-croppers	union	better wages, right to plant coffee on their own parcels	strike	
1930-31	Cundinmarca (Sumapaz) Santander (low lands)	latifundia	''*colonos*''	league	land	struggle against ''baldío'' owners, land invasions	evictions
1930-31	Tolima (south) Cauca (north) Huila (North)	haciendas	Indians	communal	recuperation of old communal lands	land invasions	evictions

1932-34	Santander Boyacá	minifundia	small tenants		reaction against political repression	guerrillas	"pacification"; diversion of attention with war against Peru
1933	Cundinamarca	plantations (coffee)	sharecropers		right to plant coffee on their own parcels	planted coffee without owner's consent	
1933	Cundinamarca (Fusagasuga)	haciendas and coffee plantations	surrounding minifundistas		land	land invasions	evictions
1933	Cundinamarca (Viotá)	haciendas and coffee plantations	small renters		lower rents	refusal to pay rents	
1933	Sinú (low lands)	cattle ranches	small rice growers		land	land invasions	evictions
1934	Tolima	one hacienda	peons		better wages		repression
1934	Cundinamarca	plantations (coffee)	peons		better conditions	strike at harvest time	
1936-37	all around the country	haciendas & coffee plantations in Cundinamarca	sharecroppers "*colonos*"				evictions
1938	Boyacá (Paipa)	one hacienda	peons		better wages	strike	
1938	Tolima	two haciendas	Indians	communal	land	land invasions	
1938	Cundinamarca (Fusagasugá)	one coffee plantation	peons		land	land invasions	

Source: Tabulated from narrative descriptions in Gilhodes, Pierre, *Las luchas agrarias en Colombia* (Bogotá: Ediciones El Tigre de Papel, 1972).

noted, among other things, (1) the lack of an entrepreneurial class able to impose a capitalist system of production to replace the old seigneurial landlord system characterized by economic waste, (2) the speculative purposes of many land transactions, (3) the servile condition of the peasants, (4) sharecropping's function as a primitive method for paying rent in kind or in work, not as a capitalist rent system.[23] During the 1920s, rapid growth based on an influx of foreign capital led to a rapid increase in the internal demand for foodstuffs, and colonization schemes were seen as a way to raise output. This strategy was reflected in a 1926 Supreme Court decision which declared that in title conflicts, any claimant must show documentary proof that the land had left the public domain. If such proof could not be produced, then the land was ruled public and could be entitled to whoever had worked it for the five preceding years. As urban employment opportunities fell off in 1929-31, many urban dwellers turned once more to the land in search of a livelihood, and the fight to gain title to land by occupying and cultivating it was reinforced by Law 74 of 1926.

Concurrently, peasant conflicts proliferated during the late 1920s and early 1930s (see Table 1). Hirschman describes the form and basis of such turmoil:

> They [peons] were given a plot on which to live and grow subsistence crops and in lieu of paying rent they worked regularly on the [large coffee] plantations. Conflicts arose in the twenties over the seemingly trivial demand of these peons to be allowed to plant coffee trees on their plots in addition to the traditional corn, beans, yucca, plantain, etc. This demand was strongly opposed by the plantation owners, who sensed that once the peons owned coffee trees they would cease to be peons. With a cash income of their own they might turn into a less reliable labor force. As owners of the coffee trees, they could be fired and dislodged only after they were reimbursed for the value of the trees. In general, their bargaining power and status would vastly increase.[24]

The land issue generated one of the most persistent internal conflicts among segments of the dominant class. Interests of the large landowners tend to center on secure property rights to their lands and an abundant source of cheap labor, while the more urban-based merchant industrialists seek a source of staples for the urban workers. Since large landowners have tended to produce livestock (not a wage good) and export crops, the basic source of the staple foods consumed internally by the laboring class has traditionally been the surplus produced by peasants. Such struggles between factions of the dominant class have characteristically determined how agrarian laws were drafted and how they were implemented.

When the landowners refused the peasants' demands, leagues were organized to press for better contracts and sometimes to invade land.[25] With the advent of the international economic crisis in 1929 and the termination of public works policy, some urban workers returned to the villages and the struggle for land intensified. Invasions multiplied as did evictions of peasants from their land, strikes, and protests against evictions; the peasant leagues grew. The government felt compelled to act. It stepped in to resolve the conflicts and save the large landowners by paying them for the invaded land and granting property deeds to the invaders, or by evicting the invaders.[26] Tacit agrarian reform—or at least a recognition of the need for it—was underway.

Law 200 of 1936 was the first major agrarian reform legislation, and it sharpened the cleavage within the dominant class. It was a product of López's first presidency, an administration clearly aligned with the industrial and financial bourgeoisie, as well as with the most dynamic groups in external commerce. The common concern was to quell labor unrest by allowing liberal labor reforms and unionization and to provide a greater flow of foodstuffs to the urban sectors. Thus, agrarian reform meant redistribution of private ownership of land to groups that would produce for the national market. Verbal attacks on *latifundios* almost always pointed out their lack of productivity while couching the need for reform in terms of social justice and reduction of poverty. What was being called for was not a radical reform, but an amelioration of aberrations within the existing system which were impeding further capitalistic expansion. To dispel any doubts on this point, López spoke plainly in his address to Congress:

> Technically, then, we are faced with the juridical alternatives of turning the nation to a socialist orientation or of revalidating the deeds to private property by purifying them of their imperfections. The Government has chosen the second course. The project of the land law has no purposes other than to strengthen property rights, organizing them on the basis of principles of justice, and of resolving the conflicts which have grown out of the vagueness of existing titles . . . . Property should be guaranteed in its use—not in its abuse . . . . The government wants the law to define how, when, and for what reasons one is a landowner, so as to prevent property being held by usurpers and so as to establish the validity of the titles of the large landowner who is putting his holdings to use and also to clarify those of the *colono* who, with tremendous energy, wrests from the jungle a plot of land on which to build his home and raise a family.[27]

The law provided for:

1. A presumption of private ownership over lands economically exploited (Article 1);
2. A presumption that lands *not* economically exploited were in the public domain (Article 2);

3. Stricter requirements for evicting *colonos* (Article 4; Articles 17 to 22);
4. A five year prescription period for *colonos* who entered into and cultivated privately owned lands under the good faith assumption that they were in the public domain (Article 12);
5. Reversion of title to the state, without any compensation, of those lands not economically exploited for a continuous period of ten years (Article 6);
6. Creation of a body of traveling "land judges" to have jurisdiction over all actions arising from Law 200 (Article 25).

While observers differ on the ultimate consequences of Law 200, most agree that it brought a short run abeyance of rural unrest.[28] The peasants developed a wait-and-see attitude hoping that after ten years they would be given titles.[29] In addition, the new criteria for determining land ownership diminished the uncertainty and endless litigation over titles. Once the immediate problems subsided, however, succeeding administrations, more conservative in nature, ignored or softened the most important provisions of Law 200. Law 4 of 1943, for example, did away with the controversial land judges and returned jurisdiction to the local civil courts (which generally favor the vested interests in their community). The reversion of title provisions was never exercised until the enactment of Law 135 of 1961.

Attempts to evaluate the redistributive effects of Law 200 have ranged from the proposition that it did break up certain large estates and plantations to the reverse assertion that it reinforced land concentration.[30] In terms of the present analysis one implication is clear—the law did reflect the existence of important conflicts of economic interests among factions of the dominant class. In any event, Law 100 of 1944 largely negated Law 200 by removing or weakening the reversion and prescription principles. The more conservative segment, whose basic economic interests were tied to land, still generated more political power than the liberal groups of industrial and financial bourgeoisie. Further, the possibility that the unwillingness of large landowners to hire sharecroppers would restrain output became increasingly evident. Within the prevailing structure of crop production, "the only way to increase output was to increase the number of labor-tenants (thereby increasing the number of acres under cultivation) and, therefore, it was necessary to counteract the reluctance of *hacendados* to engage them."[31] This is precisely what Law 100 of 1944 accomplished.

The Violencia that raged from 1948 to 1958 was to a significant degree within the tradition of the Colombian republic—the resolution of conflicts between factions of the dominant class through civil war in which peasants fought under the banner of party solidarity. But it also owed some of its distinct features to Colombia's level of economic and political development. On the economic side, Colombia was already integrated into the world economy; the state was formed and played an important role in national, social and economic life; urbanization and industrialization were fairly well along, an important infrastructural and industrial base existed, and the differentiation of social groups had reached a fairly advanced stage. The level of political development is reflected in the fact that the populist Gaitán could gain leadership of the Liberal party; his assassination in 1948 was one of the sparks leading to the violence. The framework was thus different from those of the "traditional" civil wars of the nineteenth century; once the violence began it could no longer be channeled exclusively along the traditional paths. What began as a "known" form of settling struggles for political and economic supremacy soon roared out of the usual political control from above, and took on aspects of a potential social revolution.[32]

It was this lack of control by traditional means which ushered in the National Front. While coalitions of dominant class factions have been repeated many times in the history of the republic,[33] the National Front coalition is unusual in the degree to which it reflects a concern with the potential power of the disenfranchised; accordingly, it may well represent the first major attempt at a political restructuring designed to consolidate the position of the dominant class at a political as well as an economic level.

The National Front Agrarian Reform Laws

The National Front, coalescing dominant class interests, was born with Alberto Lleras Camargo as president. His major concern was to pacify the general populace and soften the division within the dominant class. Violence remained serious in some regions of the country. Toward the end of this first administration, Carlos Lleras Restrepo, the leader of the Liberal party, and with a political base essentially of industrial and financial groups, took advantage of concerns over growing rural unrest to forge a new agrarian reform law.

The design of the law and subsequent debate reflected both the underlying divisions within the dominant class and the lack of political voice on the part of the peasants. Support for a significant though by no means radical reform came from liberals concerned with the political and economic dangers of rural violence and breakdown for the continued development of Colombia along capitalistic lines. They were supported by many agricultural technicians. Peasants played almost no direct role in the whole process, and little role of any kind. Events proved the large landowners could generate significant political response in the Congress. Table 2 summarizes Hirschman's discussion of the terms of the Lleras Restrepo proposal, their modification in committee and ultimate provisions approved by Congress,[34] and indicates how ably large landowning interests mustered support to protect their property rights. These interests were soon to dictate the course of change in land tenure systems

Table 2
The Bargaining Process on Terms of Payment for Expropriated Lands

<table>
<tr><th></th><th>Original C. Lleras Proposal</th><th>Committee Project</th><th>Law 135</th></tr>
<tr><td>Uncultivated Land</td><td>30-year, 2% bonds; no amortization for 5 years.</td><td>25-year, 2% bonds</td><td>25-year, 2% bonds</td></tr>
<tr><td>Inadequately cultivated land</td><td>20-year, 3% bonds; no amortization for 2 years</td><td rowspan="2">50,000 pesos cash; remainder in 15-year, 7% bonds</td><td rowspan="2">20% of value of property in cash; but not more than 100,000 pesos and not less than 75,000 pesos; remainder in 8 equal annual installments (non-negotiable) with 4% interest.</td></tr>
<tr><td>Adequately cultivated land but through tenants and sharecroppers</td><td>15-year, 6% bonds</td></tr>
<tr><td>Other adequately cultivated land</td><td>15-year, 6% bonds</td><td>200,000 pesos cash; next 500,000 pesos in 15-year, 7% bonds computed at market value; remainder in same bonds computed at nominal value.</td><td>20% of value of property in cash but not more than 300,000 pesos and not less than 150,000; remainder in 5 equal annual installments (non-negotiable) with 6% interest. Expropriation permissible only in specifically enumerated situations.</td></tr>
</table>

Source: Hirschman 1963: 147.

during the National Front. Law 135 of 1961 set forth six propositions to correct the monopolization of land resources. They were designed:

1. To eliminate and prevent the inequitable concentration of land or its subdivision into uneconomic units; to reconstitute adequate units of cultivation in the zones of *minifundio*, and to provide lands to those who lacked them, giving preference to those who would work on the land personally.
2. To promote the adequate economic use of unused or deficiently used lands, by means of programs designed to secure their well-balanced distribution and rational utilization.
3. To increase the productivity of farms by the application of appropriate techniques; and to endeavor to have the land used in the way best suited to their locations and characteristics.
4. To give the small tenants and sharecroppers greater guarantees of security of tenure and to make it easier for them and for wage laborers to gain ownership of land.
5. To elevate the level of living of the rural population, partly through the measures already indicated and partly through the coordination and promotion of services for technical assistance, agricultural credit, housing, the organization of markets, health and social security, the storage and preservation of products, and the promotion of cooperatives.
6. To insure the conservation, defense, improvement, and adequate utilization of the natural resources.

To implement Law 135, an agrarian reform institute (INCORA) was organized with a large staff of relatively young lawyers, economists, and sociologists. Most of them were seriously interested in changing the land tenure structure, but soon found that the legislation was inadequate to effect any basic alteration in the agrarian structure. The same was true of one more piece of legislation and two decrees (Law 1 of 1968, Decree 755 of 1967 and Decree 703 of 1968) which were promulgated during the National Front.

After becoming president in 1966, Lleras Restrepo, a central figure in the agrarian legislation of 1961, named a committee to study the possibility of creating a new peasant organization. Based on the committee's report, Decree 755 of May 1967 was enacted and established the National Campaign for Peasant Organization. The decree defined as *usuario* every peasant who had received, was receiving, or expected to receive a public agricultural service. Thus, every peasant had the possibility of becoming a member of a local association. The objective of the peasant organization was said to be the integration of the peasants *into* national life *within* the countryside with one result being a decrease in the rate of rural-urban migration to a level consistent with the pace of industrial development.[35]

There is considerable disagreement about the extent of radicalization of *usuarios*; we believe that radicalization and peasant unrest in general received a significant impulse from the enactment of Law 1 of 1968, which made privately held lands worked by sharecroppers and renters subject to expropriation. The law contained other provisions (the protection of agricultural investments and greater governmental support for agrarian reform programs), but the provision for expropriating land worked by sharecroppers and renters resulted in a series of conflicts which eclipsed the effects of those other items. Newspapers helped to raise the peasants expectations, but also helped to induce large landowners to take counteraction.[36]

When Decree 703 of May, 1968 was enacted, it defined sharecroppers and small renters as farmers who operated less than fifteen hectares and who made rental payments in cash or part of the crop. It excluded small sharecroppers and renters on land where the landlord was a "co-entrepreneur" in the cultivation; this had the effect of excluding the entire coffee region from the effects of Law 1 of 1968. In coffee production, every landlord could claim to be a partner and a "co-entrepreneur." The fact that the Coffee Growers Federation is one of the strongest associations in the country helps to explain why Law 1 of 1968 could be rendered practically irrelevant in the coffee-producing areas.

In the north coastal departments, where land concentration is highest, Law 1 produced tensions and invasions of land. Although no empirical data exist, some documents from *campesino* groups and large landowners' organizations claim that its effects were similar to those often alleged for Law 200 of 1936, i.e. numerous evictions of sharecroppers and renters.[37]

The agrarian reform legislation of the National Front reflected the changing interests of the large landowners and the related decline in the importance of the traditional extensive *latifundios* vis-à-vis the more modern capitalist farmer. Land was viewed less and less as an end in itself and increasingly as a source of output and income. Property rights were still to be protected; their rationale was expressed more and more in terms of the intensive exploitation of the land. In this context, it is not surprising to find that the cumulative impact of these laws did little to reduce the concentration of land.

LAND REDISTRIBUTION UNDER THE NATIONAL FRONT

A critical appraisal of the legislation approved by Congress described it as "anti-land-reform legislation," which constituted "a true reflection of the existing economic and political structure . . . fully mirrored in parliament."[38] For instance, the progressive objectives in the first article of Law 135 of 1961 were frustrated by subsequent items of the same law, as well as by complementary decrees, especially those related to the acquisition of private lands for redistribution. In application, the lack of redistribution has been due less to any administrative or technical deficiencies in the public agencies than to their inability to cope with the power of the dominant class. Thus, of 115 expropriation cases initiated by INCORA lawyers up to 1969 and relating to the expropriation of lands previously designated as inadequately used, 23 were won, 13 were lost and the rest were blocked or withdrawn in favor of "friendly settlements."[39] Friendly settlements are bargains made with owners in which the government often pays more than appraised price for the land.

Public acquisition of private land for distribution to peasants has been minimal in absolute terms as well. A major thrust of INCORA's program has been directed instead toward the titling of public lands. As Delgado points out, titling in essence formalizes existing relationships, and together with colonization, constitutes not redistribution but distribution.[40] Felstehausen states: "By July 1, 1969 the Colombian government had titled 88,200 farm parcels comprising 2.8 million hectares of land. Nearly 96 percent of the land and 96 percent of the titles were assigned to settlers who were already living on or had recently moved onto public land."[41] Schwinden and Feaster show higher figures for titling as of the end of 1969—some 100,000 adjudications covering a giant 5.2 million hectares.[42] Most of this was due to titling 84,500 families and 2,709,796 hectares. Wilkie estimates that by September 1969, 91,937 families had benefited from expropriation or titling, which affected 2,832,312 hectares.[43] This represented perhaps 6 percent of the families engaged mainly in agriculture in 1964 along with 10.4 percent of the land area recorded in the 1960 agricultural census. Meanwhile, as Delgado indicates, fewer than 200,000 hectares were acquired by INCORA for redistribution, about one-third of these (64,333 hectares) by expropriation and the rest by voluntary acquisition (negotiated purchase).[44] The number of peasant families settled on these expropriated lands amounted to only 5,347 or about .36 percent of the families engaged in agriculture in 1964. In comparison, Chile incorporated as "social property" 2.4 million hectares in one year under Allende, and Peru expropriated about one million hectares in one year.[45]

Another feature of Colombia's reform program has been supervised credit; it is designed to aid and foster family farm units. Small farms and those in the process of receiving parcels under land reform are eligible. As of 1970, 45,000 families had participated, only an estimated 10 percent of those qualified for INCORA credit.[46] Critics have registered other concerns as well. For example, the credit program, seeking to move the farmer up the rungs of a development ladder, directed the largest amount of credit to mechanized farms, with smaller amounts flowing to highland *minifundio* farmers.[47] Whether it is wise from an efficiency point of view or not, this approach has worrisome distribution implications. High administrative cost per peso loaned raises another question. In 1964 the administrative cost per borrowing family was U.S. $290 while the average loan size was U.S. $1,080. By 1970 the administration cost had dropped to U.S. $80, while the average loan size was U.S. $1,855.

By 1969, INCORA's engineering division had invested 307 million pesos

Table 3
Changes in the Distribution of Land in Colombia by Number and Size of Farms, 1960 to 1970-71.

Size of Farms in Hectares	1960 Agricultural Census				1970 Agricultural Census			
	Number of Farms	%	Area in Hectares	%	Number of Farms	%	Area In Hectares	%
Under 1.0	298,071	24.64	131,933	.48	268,705	22.83	126,691	.41
1.0 to 1.9	191,347	15.82	270,308	.99	177,828	15.11	238,694	.77
2.0 to 2.9	117,002	9.68	275,656	1.01	112,519	9.56	259,665	.84
3.0 to 3.9	92,001	7.61	309,165	1.13	84,745	7.20	279,285	.90
4.0 to 4.9	58,181	4.81	251,854	.92	56,428	4.79	241,610	.78
5.0 to 9.9	169,149	13.98	1,164,749	4.26	159,659	13.57	1,088,338	3.51
10.0 to 19.9	114,231	9.44	1,572,076	5.75	117,863	10.02	1,598,668	5.16
20.0 to 29.9	44,049	3.64	1,043,554	3.82	48,854	4.15	1,138,525	3.68
30.0 to 39.9	26,500	2.19	890,100	3.26	30,486	2.59	1,019,394	3.29
40.0 to 49.9	16,240	1.34	705,047	2.58	20,670	1.76	896,569	2.89
50.0 to 99.9	39,990	3.31	2,680.471	9.81	47,763	4.06	3,197,665	10.32
100.0 to 199.9	22,317	1.85	2,996,152	10.96	26,553	2.26	3,552,052	11.46
200.0 to 499.9	13,693	1.13	3,994,319	14.61	16,344	1.39	4,700,980	15.16
500.0 to 999.9	4,141	.34	2,730,764	9.99	4,927	.42	3,229,461	10.42
1000.0 to 2499.9	1,975	.16	2,808,210	10.27	2,363	.20	3,394,725	10.95
Over 2,500	786	.06	5,513,409	20.17	1,104	.09	6,030,868	19.46
Total	1,209,672	100.00	27,337,827	100.00	1,176,811	100.00	30,993,190	100.00

Source: Adapted from Table 1, page 35, Departamento Administrativo Nacional de Estadística (DANE), ''Censo Nacional Agropecuario 1970-71,'' *Boletín mensual de estadística*, Nos. 274-275, May-June 1974.

in land improvement and 87 million in road building. Felstenhausen notes that 40 percent of the funds budgeted in the mid-1960s were for costly irrigation and drainage projects, while only four percent was spent on land purchases and expropriations.[48] Both the provisions of the law and the other political problems in expropriating made this the easier route to take.

Barraclough and Domike believe that a reasonable agrarian reform program should benefit one-half of the group made up of landless laborers, operators of *minifundios*, and small farmers with highly uncertain tenure arrangements.[49] To attain this goal in a decade benefits would have to be extended annually to approximately five percent of the peasant families plus those coming into existence over the decade, or about 62,000 families annually in the Colombian case. Wilke, however, indicates that only an average of 10,215 families benefited from titling or expropriation.[50]

Using the broader definition of reform, DeRoux estimates that the number of peasants actually helped by Colombian reform during 1961-70 was only 129,600 (4,200 in colonization projects, 30,000 in credit programs, 5,400 on expropriated lands and 90,000 on titled land) which is considerably below the 558,000 necessary benefactors using Barraclough's and Domike's criteria.[51] The majority of these recipients secured a title, a decrease in insecurity rather than an increase in resources. The facts and figures on the nation's land reform program are often of questionable quality, but such problems do not affect the general conclusion that little land has been expropriated and redistributed to peasants and that what limited success there has been was in the title security and credit programs—distributive efforts. As of 1973, national policy priorities were clearly focused on land distribution, not redistribution, and INCORA was planning to deemphasize its credit program.[52]

Data from the agricultural censuses confirm the conclusion that INCORA's activities had little impact on the distribution of land. Table 3 presents a comparison of land distribution among operators in 1960, the year before the agrarian reform law, and in 1970, the year the reform essentially stopped. In both years, less than five percent of total land was occupied by about 60 percent of the farms. Conversely, less than five percent of the farms comprised two-thirds of the land area at both ends of the decade. The agricultural census data reveal a decline in the number of farms during this decade. While the overall concentration of land remained nearly the same over the decade, the number of farms decreased in all size categories under 10 hectares,[53] suggesting either an expulsion of peasants engaged in subsistence agriculture or the acquisition of more land by subsistence farmers who then shifted in status to small family farmers. At the opposite extreme, the number of farms for each of the large farm categories (100 hectares or more) increased. Tentative evidence from the 1973 population census suggests a marked increase in the share of the labor force working for a wage, suggesting that the share of agricultural families which was landless—approximately 23 percent of all families in agriculture in 1960[54]—also rose. This cursory analysis indicates that after nine years of operation, the Colombian agrarian reform did not lead to any equalization in the distribution of land; if anything that distribution worsened.[55]

THE RURAL POOR IN THREE COMMUNITIES

The bare statistical outlines of inadequacy in the Colombian reform program do not, of course, speak to the urgency of the task, nor do they give any hints as to whether the conditions of rural life are ameliorating or worsening over time. A number of studies have noted three prominent aspects in the current organization of Colombian agriculture:[56] (1) a recent trend on large properties toward more intensive production for export markets, using wage labor instead of sharecroppers and peons;[57] (2) the habit on small to medium sized farm units, worked largely with family labor, of supplementing income by wage labor during harvest in the coffee-growing regions of Antioquia and Caldas; and (3) a persistence of traditional peasant subsistence agriculture, estimated to exist on 80 percent of the farms in the Departments of Nariño, Cundinamarca, and Boyacá. These and other aspects are exemplified and detailed in the case studies of three communities which follow. Each represents one of these predominant patterns. Cereté, a county in the north coastal plain exemplifies what may happen to small farm owners and day laborers when *latifundios* turn to more intensive production. Támesis, located in the mountainous area, provides a case study of small to medium sized farms in a mountainous coffee region. Contadero, also a mountainous region, is characterized by traditional subsistence peasant farming.

Examination of these three typical areas employed a panel design (before and after interviews with the same people) which covered an eight year period (1963-70). This time span blankets the most active agrarian reform period under the National Front. The types of families included in the sample were: (1) owners of small or medium farms; (2) landless agricultural workers who had usufruct rights to land, or worked as wage laborers; (3) those who neither owned land nor cultivated any land, but rather worked in private or public employ. In other words, the sample was drawn from all rural families within the community except the large landowners. The actual size of large, medium and small farms differs in each community since the type of cultivation, type of crop, and land characteristics of each also vary. Areawise, a small cattle farm in Cereté would be a large coffee farm in Támesis.

In 1963 a total of 293 families in the three communities (92 Contadero, 101 Cereté, and 100 Támesis) were randomly interviewed. A total of 237 families were reinterviewed in 1970 and are the main point of reference for this

Table 4
Changes in the Distribution of Land in Nariño, Colombia by Size of Farms 1960 to 1970 and Contadero, Nariño*, 1970 (percentages)

	Department of Nariño				Contadero, Nariño	
Size of Farms in Hectares	**Number of Farms 1960 (N=90,285)**	**Area in Hectares 1960 (692,777)**	**Number of Farms 1970 (N=77,387)**	**Area in Hectares 1970 (N=862,503)**	**Number of Farms 1970 (N=789)**	**Area in Hectares 1970 (N=3,127)**
Under 1	18.7	1.1	16.7	.8	18.1	2.2
1.00 to 4.9	41.8	11.2	39.8	7.0	55.5	29.0
5.0 to 9.9	23.0	18.2	22.7	12.2	15.7	25.1
10.0 to 49.9	14.5	35.6	17.4	30.9	10.6	42.1
50.0 to 99.9	1.2	10.1	2.3	13.4	.1	1.6
100.0 to 499.9	.7	15.6	1.1	17.5	.0	.0
Over 500.00	.1	8.2	.1	18.2	.0	.0
Total	100.0	100.0	100.0	100.0	100.0	100.0

Source: 1960 and 1970 Agricultural Censuses of Colombia.
*Distribution by farm size and land area were not available at the *municipio* level in 1960.

Table 5
Changes in Amount of Land Owned by Sample Families in Ceretė, Támesis, and Contadero, Colombia from 1963 to 1970*

Ceretė 1963		Size of Landholding, 1970			
Size of Holding	Number of Landowners	Landless	.01-.20	.21-4.9	5.0 or more
Landless	23	15	2	2	4
.01- .20	20	13	1	—	6
.21-4.9	21	15	3	1	2
5.0 or more	20	6	3	1	10
Total	84	49	9	4	22

Támesis 1963		Size of Landholding, 1970		
Size of Holding	Number of Landowners	Landless	.01-2.00	2.01 or more
Landless	28	21	4	3
.01-2.00	29	4	20	5
2.01 or more	27	2	4	21
Total	84	27	28	29

Contadero 1963		Size of Landholding, 1970			
Size of Holding	Number of Landowners	0-.50	.50-2.49	2.50-4.50	4.51 or more
0.0- .50	17	15	2	—	—
.50-2.49	18	6	8	4	—
2.50-4.50	17	6	6	2	3
4.51 or more	17	1	4	6	6
Total	69	28	20	12	9

*The actual size of large, medium and small farms is different for each community since type of cultivation, type of crop and land characteristics of each community are different. Thus, we divided the 1963 samples in each community into quartiles or terciles to observe the overall changes in categories.

analysis. Of those family units not reinterviewed in 1970, forty had migrated, eleven family heads had died, another five could not be relocated or refused to be interviewed. They represent 4.3 percent of all rural families in these communities.

Contadero—a Peasant Community

Contadero is a 17.3 square-mile county located in the state of Nariño. Along with the states of Cundinamarca and Boyacá, Nariño contained 80 percent of the Colombian farms smaller than thirteen acres in 1960. Much of the land has a slope of forty-five degrees or more, making erosion a serious problem and precluding heavy mechanization.

Surplus farm production which is not consumed is taken to the local market or the neighboring town of Ipiales (population 23,320), or sold to a middleman. Lacking storage facilities or good transportation (only one unpaved road cuts through this mountainous community), 57 percent of the peasant families who produced a marketable surplus in 1963 had to sell to middlemen. These middlemen pay one-half to one-third the price being paid in the urban markets.

In order to earn more money, most household heads—80 percent of the 1963 sample—have secondary occupations. In addition, many women engage in cottage industry production of woolen garments and rugs. The small plots cannot, in most cases, absorb all the family's labor, but local wages are only a fraction of the national average.

In 1964, 88 percent of the residents of Contadero had been born in the county, and nearly all the rest had been born in another county in the same state. Population totals for the county have remained relatively stable. In 1951, Contadero had a population of 4,387 (775 living in the county seat and 3,612 in the rest of the county). By 1973 it had increased to 4,966 with 959 in the county seat and 4,007 outside. Even this relatively small increase may be serious where population density is already high and land is relatively scarce.

The Committee for Inter-American Agrarian Development (CIDA) has estimated that a peasant must operate 5 hectares or more (12.3 acres) to absorb family labor in areas such as Contadero.[58] In 1970 approximately 56 percent of the farms in Nariño were smaller than 5 hectares while in Contadero about 74 percent were that small and occupied only 31 percent of the land (see Table 4). Our 1963 sample of the community's peasant farmers found that the average amount of land owned was 11.5 acres, usually fragmented into an average of 2.6 plots of land located in various parts of the community. Among sample families still remaining in the community in 1970, the average amount of land owned was only 5.75, with an accompanying reduction in number of parcels to approximately 2.0.[59] The amount of land rented by respondents doubled during the study period from .29 to .68 hectares. Between 1963 and 1970, thirty-one families (almost 50 percent) remained in the same size class, twenty-nine families (42 percent) moved to a lower class and only nine moved to a higher class. Some families who gained or lost land would remain in the same class, but the above figures present an approximate picture of trends. The data suggests that landownership may have become more concentrated during the period. Table 4 shows that the number of farms (operated units) in the department of Nariño decreased between 1960 and 1970, and that the share of land in large farms of more than fifty hectares increased substantially.

The Colombian Institute of Agrarian Reform has suggested that in 1970 about 14,700 pesos (U.S. $770) were required to provide the minimum necessary food, clothing, and shelter for a rural family.[60] By this standard, only 15 percent of the sampled families were above the poverty level. Of more interest to us here are the trends over 1963-70. Obviously, income has always been low; a bad growing season during 1970 complicates the picture and our data on income and consumption patterns are hard to reconcile with each other, suggesting possibly serious data problems. Among peasant families who stayed in the community between 1963 and 1970, mean reported monetary income per family increased from 2,780 pesos (U.S. $278) to 3,955 pesos (U.S. $395).[61] The distribution of monetary income became more skewed, however, as the median monetary family income rose very little, from 1,912 pesos (U.S. $191) in 1963 to 2,080 pesos (U.S. $208) in 1970. Trends in total income (including home consumption of goods produced on the farm) may have been much less positive; at any rate, our less reliable data on consumption indicate a decrease. Between 1963 and 1970, mean reported food expenditures declined from 3,076 pesos (U.S. $308) to 2,100 pesos (U.S. $210) annually. Weekly consumption of beef and pork per family declined from 4.6 to 3.6 pounds. Other family expenditures, such as clothing and medicine also decreased from 920 pesos (U.S. $92) to 690 (U.S. $69). These data suggest that the peasant families have reduced their caloric intake to the most basic items of food and cut purchases in the outside market to a few essential items.

A quick addition of the average expenditures in 1963 gives a total of 3,976 pesos, far larger than the average monetary income of 2,780 pesos. The difference could be accounted for by consumption of home-produced items. In 1970, however, there was a large discrepancy in the other direction, with an average monetary income (by definition less than average total income) of 3,955 pesos and an average consumption of 2,790 pesos, suggesting either that one or more of the figures is wrong or that average savings had risen rapidly while income distribution worsened markedly. This latter interpretation would imply that a higher share of output was sold in 1970, and that total income was lower for most families so that they were forced to curtail consumption. The bad growing season in 1970 may have encouraged families to allocate more of their time to off-farm or nonagricultural activities. Consistent with this is the fact that about half of the 1963-70 increase in monetary income was earned by family members working as day laborers or in handicrafts. In 1963 they earned an average of 1,006 pesos (U.S. $101) per family; by 1970 this had increased to 1,595 pesos (U.S. $159).

Between 1963 and 1970, mean monetary income of household heads increased from 1,741 pesos (U.S. $174) to 2,314 pesos (U.S. $231), but the median declined from 1,000 pesos (U.S. $100) to 780 pesos (U.S. $78). A small group of peasants increased their incomes substantially while the majority suffered decreases (see Table 6).

Table 6
Changes in Monetary Income of Household Head in Ceretė, Támesis, Contadero, Colombia from 1963 to 1970.*

Ceretė 1963 Income of Household Head In Pesos	Number of Household Heads	Income of Household Head, 1970 No Income	1-1,600	1,601-2,470	2,471 or more
No Income	23	12	—	7	4
1-1,600	22	4	9	4	5
1,601-2,470	20	3	4	8	5
2,471 or more	19	2	4	3	10
Total	84	21	17	22	24

Támesis 1963 Income Household Head In Pesos	Number of Household Heads	Income of Household Head, 1970 0-1,999	2,000-2,600	2,601-4,200	4,201 or more
0-1,999	20	11	2	5	2
2,000-2,600	22	7	5	8	2
2,601-4,200	21	6	4	7	4
4,201 or more	21	1	3	5	12
Total	84	25	14	25	20

Contadero 1963 Income of Household Head In Pesos	Number of Household Heads	Income of Household Head, 1970 0-650	650-1,000	1,001-2,450	2,451 or more
0- 650	18	7	4	4	3
651-1,000	18	9	1	4	4
1,001-2,450	17	9	2	3	3
2,451 or more	16	6	0	2	8
Total	69	31	7	13	18

*Pesos of 1963. The 1963 samples in each community are divided as nearly as possible into quartiles.

For some farmers, the lower incomes of 1970 were associated with reduced use of modern agricultural inputs and techniques. A scale containing six items (chemical fertilizers, weed killers, rental tractors, new seed varieties, pasture improvement, and animal feed concentrates) was used to measure adoption of innovations and registered less use of the six items in 1970 than in 1963, indicating discontinuance of some practices already adopted.

Though the above data on income, consumption and technology have many weaknesses and are not in themselves conclusive, our observation in this

Table 7
Change in the Distribution of Operated Land in Córdoba, Colombia by Size of Farms, 1960 to 1970, and Cereté, Córdoba, 1970 (in Percentages)

	Department of Córdoba				Cereté, Córdoba*	
Size of Farms In Hectares	Number of Farms 1960	Area in Hectares 1960	Number of Farms 1970	Area in Hectares 1970	Number of Farms 1970	Area In Hectares 1970
Under 1	31.7	.3	39.6	.3	65.2	.9
1.0 to 4.9	23.9	1.4	18.7	1.0	18.0	2.7
5.0 to 9.9	12.0	2.2	10.8	1.8	4.8	2.2
10.0 to 49.9	18.8	13.4	17.4	10.8	6.5	9.9
50.0 to 99.9	6.4	13.3	5.9	10.8	2.6	11.3
100.0 to 499.0	6.2	35.0	6.3	33.3	2.4	30.3
Over 500.0	1.0	34.4	1.3	42.0	.5	42.7
Total	100.0	100.0	100.0	100.0	100.0	100.0
(N=)	(48,393)	(1,621,736.6	(50,711)	(1,915,477.05)	(2,676)	(39,043)

Source: 1960 and 1970 Agricultural Censuses of Colombia.

Note: *Distribution by farm size and land area are not available at the *municipio* level in 1960.

municipio led us to believe that underlying economic conditions had worsened for many farm families, perhaps for most.

One contribution of public policy toward offseting income losses in the short run was credit. Almost all institutional credit in Contadero is provided by the nation's Agricultural Development Bank, and approximately 40 percent of sample peasant households received credit from the bank in 1970. The average loan to all families in the sample in 1964 (whether they received credit or not), was 1,781 pesos (U.S. $178); among those families who remained in the community, the average amount of institutional monies loaned in 1970 was 2,758 pesos (U.S. $276). The latter figure represents more than the median monetary family income for that year (2,080 pesos). Interest rates for bank loans are very reasonable, whereas credit from private individuals often carries rates of three to five percent per month. For some families, these small loans are in effect subsistence subsidies for a community impoverished in all its productive resources except labor. The poorest peasants may also pay for services (such as housing) from another peasant farmer by providing labor. Some of the "larger" farms have shacks in which laborers live in exchange for three days of work a week. Under such conditions, it is not surprising that in 1972 a land invasion by fifty-four landless families took approximately eleven acres. One of the invaders summed up the situation: "We don't have to keep on giving away our labor when we could have the freedom (if we have a house) to earn our wages in money."[62]

Another way out of a declining economic situation is migration. The annual out-migration rate of 3 percent for Contadero between 1963 and 1970 is considered high by demographers. Although migration can be due to good opportunities elsewhere, there seems a good chance that in this case it is mainly the result of impoverishment in Contadero.

Cereté

The *municipio* (county) of Cereté is located in the state of Córdoba, in northwestern Colombia's Caribbean coast. It encompasses some 229 square miles and had a population of 29,666 in 1964, about 40 percent (11,849) of whom lived in the county seat of Cereté, the remainder (17,817) inhabiting the rural portions. By 1973 the total population was 37,026 with 18,786 living in the county seat and 18,240 in the rural areas.

Although Córdoba as a whole is a large farm area, the farms considered here are small subsistence units. Adams and Schulman characterize Cereté as a dependent type of small farm area, with the bulk of family income coming from off-farm employment, usually labor on nearby large farms.[63] Table 7 indicates that land is highly concentrated in both the Department of Córdoba and in Cereté.

In 1963 in the state as a whole cattle was the object of greatest agricultural attention. Maize, rice, cotton, plantain and yucca were, in descending importance, the major crops. Between 1959-60 and 1965, area planted in crops in the coastal departments increased by 159 percent.[64] Area planted to cotton, however, increased by over 235 percent. In the rural Cereté study area, the subsistence farms concentrated on pigs and chickens, rice and maize, plantain, and yucca. In 1970 the average size of such subsistence farms was about 3.0 hectares, double the comparable figure for the state as a whole.

Colombia's 1970 agricultural census indicates that 2.9 percent of the farms in Cereté contained 73 percent of the land, while 83.2 percent of the farms had only 3.6 percent of the land (see Table 7). In response to this pressure on the land, INCORA executed one of its two Córdoba drainage projects in Cereté; 20,845 hectares have been distributed (titled and/or adjudicated among 1,622 families). Since few families were living in the area prior to drainage, none of our original sample came from the project area. Nor did the project seem to have any indirect benefits to our sample farmers, as the landless proportion of the group expanded from one quarter in 1963 to more than one half in 1971 (see Table 5). Twenty-seven sample families (32 percent) remained in the same landownership size class, 16 families (19 percent) moved to a higher class and 41 (nearly 50 percent) to a lower one.

The average amount of land "owned" (in the sense that the peasants had some rights to the land) in 1963 (5.6 hectares) had dropped to about 3 hectares in 1970. Whereas in the Andean areas two-thirds of the smallest farmers were title secure owner-operated units, only 48 percent of the small scale coastal peasants have this form of security. The labor exchange system provides the peasant with a small plot of land on which he can build a hut (if there is none) and grow subsistence crops. In exchange, he agrees to work a certain number of days for the landlord. In the *colono*-tenant form of tenancy, the peasant receives permission from an owner to work a fixed amount of land for a fixed number of years. He must clear the land of brush and is permitted to plant subsistence crops. In return he agrees to plant grasses and vacate the property after the stipulated time period.

The large number of sample families who lost land is the result of two factors: the potential threat from agrarian reform legislation to convert workers and small scale renters into owners, and the introduction of mechanized large scale production of cotton. The cotton boom meant prosperity for the large landowners, but its effects on the displaced tenants were naturally less favorable (if not negative). Employment in cotton was seasonal.[65]

The 1961 agrarian reform legislation with its provision for converting tenants to owners could in principle have provided a defense for these families. In actuality, however, the process was a difficult one; the number of documents required for "proof of tenancy" was simply impossible for a poorly educated peasant to provide. For example, the following legal documents were required:

1. Written contracts of the rental agreement;
2. Receipts of rental payments;
3. Written recognition of the tenants and their rights by the owners;
4. Copies of two court summons served upon the owner;
5. Original copy of expulsion order written by the owner;
6. Certificate from bank that the owner had co-signed loans for the tenant.

The land reform agency (INCORA) did take action to try to regain land from which some *colono*-tenants had been evicted. Soles provides an eye witness account of what happened in one case.

> Official inspectors and lawyers of INCORA were simply met at the gate of the hacienda by armed administrators and told that INCORA "had no land there." Further court actions were stopped when lawyers for the proprietress presented certificates attesting to her excellent character signed by an ex-president, ex-governor of the department, a minister of the government, the present governor, and the present mayor of the capital city. That she also owned the building which housed the INCORA offices had nothing to do with the case, as the tenant INCORA officials stated that their relationship with the owner had always been most formally correct. As a conciliatory measure to the remaining two "bull-headed-troublemakers" who would not give up their suit—and who could no longer be classified as tenants since no legal proof of their tenancy existed (and the other ex-tenants had moved away)—the proprietress offered 15 hectares of dry land covered with brush and woods. At last word the new INCORA lawyers were trying to persuade the two ex-tenant widowers to accept the offer of the dry land located a half day's journey from the nearest neighbors.[66]

How did loss of land affect the incomes of our sample families? Between 1963 and 1970, mean monetary family income increased from 3,817 pesos (U.S. $381) to 5,504 pesos (U.S. $550). A considerable share was contributed by members other than household heads whose earnings were 1,543 pesos (U.S. $154) in 1963 and 2,166 pesos (U.S.$216) in 1970. We have no data on total income (including home consumption items); our data indicated that mean family expenditures rose from 2,700 pesos to 3,170 pesos. Median annual food expenditures increased from 2,299 to 2,704 pesos but pounds of beef and pork consumed weekly per family declined from 8.1 to 5.4. Other median annual real expenditures, such as clothing and medicine, increased from 400 pesos (U.S. $40) to 468 pesos (U.S. $47). The typical family seems

Table 8
Changes in the Distribution of Operated Land in Antioquia, Colombia by Size of Farms, 1960 to 1970, and Támesis, Antioquia, 1970
(In Percentages.)

	Department of Antioquia				Támesis, Antioquia*	
Size of Farms In Hectares	**Number of Farms 1960**	**Area in Hectares 1960**	**Number of Farms 1970**	**Area in Hectares 1970**	**Number of Farms 1970**	**Area in Hectares 1970**
Under 1	38.7	1.0	26.9	.4	39.2	1.2
1.0 to 4.9	28.2	3.7	29.5	2.4	33.4	6.2
5.0 to 9.9	14.2	5.6	16.6	3.9	11.1	6.1
10.0 to 49.9	13.0	17.5	17.8	14.9	12.1	19.1
50.0 to 99.9	3.0	12.8	4.4	11.1	1.5	9.0
100.0 to 499.9	2.5	30.6	4.0	29.7	2.5	36.5
Over 500.0	.4	28.8	.8	37.6	.2	21.9
Total	100.0	100.0	100.0	100.0	100.0	100.0
(N=)	(169,299)	(2,759,575.1)	(142,048)	(3,754,398.8)	(2,075)	(26,611)

Source: 1960 and 1970 Agricultural Censuses of Colombia.

Note: *Distribution by farm size and land area are not available at the *municipio* level in 1960.

therefore to have gained in terms of income. This may reflect only a movement of people from largely nonmonetary or subsistence farming to being rural wage earners. It seems probable that displacement from land has harmed a significant proportion. The household heads of families who left the community indicate that they moved because of lack of employment opportunities and/or lack of land.

To summarize, there have been two diverse trends in Cereté. INCORA gave some peasants land reclaimed from drainage projects. Other peasants were expelled from the private land due to a change in type of agriculture and the agrarian reform law. They were usually unable to exercise their legal rights. Some received credit, but few evolved into the small commercial farmers which INCORA had expected. Average incomes appear to have risen. While the new developments may have seriously disrupted the lives of many peasant families, there were important offsetting income sources, so that overall it could be argued that the trends were more encouraging than those of Contadero.

Támesis

The county of Támesis sits on the eastern slopes of the western range of the Colombian Andes, approximately forty air miles southwest of Medellín. In 1964 the total population of the county was 20,484 with 5,247 in the county seat and 15,237 in the rural areas. By 1973 the total population was 20,225—the countyseat had grown to 7,053 and the rural population had fallen to 13,172, a loss probably related to the introduction of labor-saving green revolution technology.

From an agricultural and economic viewpoint, Támesis can be summed up in one word: coffee. The major production changes over the sample years have centered around the introduction of fertilizers and a new coffee variety, Caturra, that does not require shade. More trees can be planted per hectare and each tree produces more than the traditional varieties. Consequently, local coffee production has increased. However, the very small farmer (less than two hectares) has generally not shifted to the new variety because he lacks capital or credit.[67]

The coffee growing areas are part of Colombia's commercial small farm sector. Large farm units to produce coffee abound, however, and they largely control prices and markets. Approximately 72 percent of the farms in Támesis occupy a little more than seven percent of the land, while less than three percent of the farms account for approximately 59 percent of the land (see Table 8). In comparison with other communities studied, Támesis was characterized by stability of the land ownership over 1963-70. However, a third panel study conducted in 1972 showed increase land sales and out-migration.[68] This is probably related to the introduction of the new coffee varieties.

Total monetary income increased substantially from an average of 4,510 pesos (U.S. $451) in 1963 to 6,684 pesos (U.S. $668) in 1970 but the distribution became more skewed and the median monetary family income rose much less—from 4,080 pesos (U.S. $408) in 1963 to 4,420 pesos (U.S. $442) in 1970. Mean monetary income earned by sample household heads increased from 3,269 pesos (U.S. $327) to 4,077 pesos (U.S. $408), while median monetary income rose from 2,631 pesos (U.S. $263) to 2,871 pesos (U.S. $287). Thirty-five household heads (42 percent) remained in the same income class, twenty-three (27 percent) moved to a higher class, and twenty-six (31 percent) moved to a lower class (see Table 6).

Expenditures per family rose slightly, with mean expenditures on food remaining about the same (as did pounds of beef and pork consumed weekly per family). Other expenditures on items such as clothing and medicine increased from 474 pesos (U.S. $47) in 1963 to 652 pesos (U.S. $65) in 1970. The number of recipients of credit from institutional sources increased from twenty families in 1963 to thirty-five families in 1970.

The share of income taking the form of home produced consumption items is probably lower in this commercial zone than in the other two *muncipios*, so the data on monetary income may be reasonably indicative of what happened to total income. Perhaps because of a satisfactory economic situation Támesis exhibits the lowest out-migration rate (2 percent over 1963-70) among the three communities studied.

Supply of credit may be particularly important during periods of technological innovation. In 1970, 40 percent of the household heads had some form of institutional credit. In 1963, sixty-four sample families had control over land, either as renters and/or owners.[69] During the study period, four day laborers in our sample became owners through either inheritance or purchase of small plots. In 1970, fifty-six of these sixty-eight were either owners or tenants. We omitted from our analysis three farmers who owned over 200 acres of coffee land because we were mainly interested in the small farm coffee producers (less than twenty hectares). Thus, our 1970 analysis will concern sixty-five families. Of the remaining sixty-five families, fifty-three still had control over land in 1970 and three were day laborers who lost land but remained in the community. Of the nine who were no longer owners or renters in the community, eight migrated from the community and one died. The major part of our analysis deals with fifty-six families who were in the 1963 sample and remained in the community and were interviewed in 1970. Of these, seventeen adopted the new green revolution coffee variety and thirty-nine did not. By 1972, fourteen of the thirty-nine nonadopters had lost control of their land and were employed as day laborers. Families gaining more land by 1970 were generally among those who used an adequate package of new varieties and a heavier rate of fertilizer, a group which tended to have greater access to institutional credit resources.

To recapitulate, our three communities fared differently over 1963-70. Contadero seemed to stagnate while Cereté and Támesis underwent substantial change. Even though monetary incomes rose in the latter two cases, many families lost land and income (true also in Contadero) so there is a serious possibility that the process of change was a traumatic one for many. Agrarian policy seemed mainly to be a holding action in Contadero (subsistence consumption loans from the Caja Agraria); the failure to protect displaced tenants was notable in Cereté; in Támesis credit contributed to the adoption of a new technological package, though not for some of the smallest farmers who lost their land at this time. More than 70 percent of the respondents in all three communities saw their situation as worse in 1970 than in 1963.

NATIONAL FRONT AGRARIAN REFORM AND CLASS STRUCTURE

Earlier analysis at a national level demonstrated that the agrarian reform efforts of the National Front have not significantly altered the land ownership pattern in Colombia. The three case studies just discussed illustrate the poor economic conditions still characteristic of the various agrarian structures and raise the possibility that in some rural areas real incomes are falling for many families. These particular case studies were not prejudicially selected. They are intended to represent three major types of agricultural organization; subsistence peasant production (as in Contadero), commercial coffee farming typified by a mixture of capitalistic and precapitalistic relations (Támesis), and large farm units which produce cattle and crops such as cotton and sugar, frequently for export (Cereté). Significantly, this last tendency toward large scale capital intensive farming was strong during the National Front.

The consolidation of the dominant class at a political level (in the National Front) and its continued monopolization of the bulk of the gains from agricultural production would seem to create a basis for class consciousness among the disparate rural population. Part of the basis for this *potential* class consciousness was enhanced by later modifications of agrarian reform law under the National Front, especially during the Carlos Lleras Restrepo administration. Apparently Lleras was trying to gain peasant support for a limited reform that might underpin—or at least not undermine—further industrial development. Such a restricted reform, it was thought, would integrate the peasants into national life within the countryside, thereby decreasing cityward migration to a level suitable for industrialization. His aim was the development of capitalism in Colombia, not a popular revolution.[70] In general, the elites manipulated cultural symbols (an agrarian reform law) with a view to legitimizing their domination and maintaining traditional political control.[71] By about 1970, however, the failure of ten years of agrarian reform to substantially improve rural conditions helped to convince many peasant leaders of the intransigence of the ruling groups, and of the strength of the barriers to basic change. These failures to reform the agrarian sector along with the continued attempt to manipulate peasants may have begun a process of class differentiation and radicalization.[72] For example, in 1971 the board of directors of the National Campaign for Peasant Organization rejected Lleras style reformism oriented to gaining voters in the countryside, attacked both traditional parties as representatives of interests of the dominant class, and described the National Front as a union of the ruling class against peasant interests.[73]

Some members of the dominant class have understood this result, and consider direct reform dangerous politically and harmful economically. As a Colombian politician and businessman noted, "the tragedy of Latin American countries is that we have already chosen direct reform by administrative action of the state. This system is inefficient, bureaucratic, and creates land tenure insecurity. In addition, as it has been applied in Chile, and I fear is being applied in Colombia, it produces peasant radicalization."[74] A good example of this process (noted earlier) was Law 1 of 1968, which made privately held lands worked by sharecroppers and renters in plots of no more than fifteen hectares subject to expropriation. While the spirit of the law may have intended to give title security to peasants, its real consequence was a counterattack by large landowners—one that Lleras could not control. No increase in titling (let alone redistribution) occurred; many feel that the law led to substantial eviction of sharecroppers and may thus have worsened the distribution of land.

The unwillingness of the dominant class to relinquish even small plots of land created a reaction among many peasants and their leaders, and doubtless helped the more radical to rise to power in the *usuarios*.[75] This group refused the imposed organization of the movement, expelled government officials from their ranks and organized around their own interests. The Pastrana government abandoned any attempt at appeasement. When peasant groups organized at the local and national level and placed demands on the State by coordinating simultaneous invasion of private lands in several parts of Colombia, the response was police and military repression. The hardening of class lines became clear in the final agrarian reform law of the National Front, Law 5 of 1973. That law plainly ignored peasant demands for land and reinforced the commercialization of the large farm sector. For example, one of its principal aspects created an Agriculture Finance Fund with the avowed purpose to "accelerate further agricultural production to generate new exportable agricultural surpluses other than coffee." Who can produce for such nontraditional export markets? The peasant encountered in the case studies?

The tax incentive section of the law further elucidates the beneficiaries it is meant to serve. Both for property and income, the law declares a five to ten year tax holiday for land in which large investments are made in cattle or in crops, particularly trees such as palm, rubber, fruit, olive, timber and others. Few peasants have these investment capabilities. The peasant organization National Directorate denounced Law 5 of 1973 as a clear reinforcement of the large farms.

The National Front's agrarian policy has not altered ownership patterns but has rather reflected its class basis and the interests it represents. These interests center, increasingly, around capitalist expansion which will tend to concentrate land ownership. Such a trend may eventually foment open class struggle, particularly if the peasants' incomes drop below subsistence levels. The exact shape of class changes and conflicts will depend upon the degree to which the multiple segments of the peasant class coalesce, their relationship to other underprivileged classes, the extent to which urban growth creates job opportunities there, and the reaction of the dominant class. At present, even though an increasing number of peasants seem to be thinking in class terms, there is little commitment to action. Less than 10 percent of the peasants in our study communities saw force as a plausible means of securing land.[76]

NOTES

The data presented herein were gathered under a Ford Foundation Grant to the University of Wisconsin entitled Rural Modernization in Latin America and USAID contract cds2863. The views presented herein are those of the authors and do not necessarily reflect those of the granting agencies.

1. James D. Crockcroft, "Last Rites for the Reformist Model in Latin America," in James D. Crockcroft, Andre Gunder Frank, and Dale L. Johnson, eds. *Dependence and Underdevelopment: Latin America's Political Economy* (New York, 1972), p. 134.
2. James Schwinden and Gerald Feaster, "The INCORA Supervised Credit Program," AID Spring Review of Small Farmer Credit (Washington, D.C., 1973), p. 21.
3. For another and more detailed class analysis of the agrarian structure see Pierre Gilhodes, "Agrarian Struggles in Colombia" in Rodolfo Stavenhagen, ed. *Agrarian Problems and Peasant Movements in Latin America* (New York, 1970). For a class analysis of the entire society see José F. Ocampo, "The Present Stage of the Colombian Revolution," *Latin American Perspectives*, 2, (1975): 5-18.
4. This study employs the broad definition of agrarian reform in order to evaluate all possible benefits; however, we agree with the criticism of this definition by Edmundo Flores, "The Economics of Land Reform," in Rodolfo Stavenhagen, ed. *Agrarian Problems and Peasant Movements in Latin America* (New York, 1970).
5. For a discussion of their representativeness see, Robert L. Whittenbarger, "Socio-Economic Change in Three Colombian Small Farm Communities: A Panel Study," unpublished Ph. D. dissertation (Wisconsin, 1974).

6. See Humberto Rojas, "Peasant Consciousness in Three Rural Communities," unpublished Ph. D. dissertation (Madison, Wisconsin, 1974).
7. See, for example, Albert O. Hirschman, *Journeys Toward Progress* (New York, 1963); T. Lynn Smith, *Colombia: Social Structure and the Process of Development* (Gainesville, Florida, 1967); Herman Felstehausen, "Agrarian Reform: Colombia," in Peter Dorner, ed. *Land Reform in Latin America: Issues and Cases*, a monograph (Madison, 1971); Ernest Feder, "Counter Reform," in Rodolfo Stavenhagen, ed. *Agrarian Probems and Peasants Movements in Latin America* (New York, 1970); and Food and Agricultural Organization (FAO) Rapport du Comité Special de la Reforme Agraire (Rome, 1971).
8. The *censo* was a type of mortgage on land usually incurred by large landowners when attempting to secure credit. The usual source of credit was from merchants or from the church at a fixed rate of annual interest; however, the landowner was obliged to pay the stipulated interest for an undefined number of years. The *censo* was attached to the land and was sold. This hindered free transfer of land and was a means by which the church acquired land when owners defaulted on payments.
9. The *resguardo* was instituted by the Spanish crown in an attempt to protect the Indians and to give them an inalienable economic base. Royal law designated an area as communal Indian property to be worked communally. This *resguardo* land could not be sold or transferred by an individual or the community.
10. Luis Eduardo Nieto Arteta, *Economía y cultura en la historia de Colombia* (Bogotá, 1962), p. 293.
11. Ibid., pp. 309-10.
12. Alvaro Tirado Mejía, *Introducción a la historia económica de Colombia* (Bogotá, 1972), pp. 100-1.
13. Nieto Arteta, pp. 160-63; and Tirado Mejía, p. 134.
14. William Paul McGreevey, *An Economic History of Colombia 1845-1930* (Cambridge, Massachusetts, 1971), p. 112.
15. Nieto Arteta, pp. 242-64. McGreevey's data on page 174 show that no more than five percent of the labor force or 35,000 workers were employed in the export sector at its peak in 1875. This number was not high enough to push up production costs in other sectors. He attributes the loss of 100,000 artisans to the loss of income that would have been generated if the products had been purchased at home instead of imported. This depressed incomes throughout society, and the first to feel the pinch was the artisan group, who lost markets to imported cloth, etc.
16. Tirado Mejía, pp. 129-30.
17. Ibid., p. 161.
18. Nieto Arteta, p. 322.
19. Tirado Mejía, pp. 176-177.
20. Luis Ospina Vásquez, *Industria y protección en Colombia 1810-1930* (Bogotá, 1955).
21. Tirado Mejía, pp. 252-53 and Nieto Arteta, pp. 326-27.
22. Nieto Arteta, pp. 327-28.
23. Antonio García, *Gaitán y el problema de la revolución Colombiana* (Bogotá, 1955), pp. 239-41.
24. Albert O. Hirschman, *Journeys Toward Progress* (New York, 1963), p. 102.
25. Tirado Mejía, p. 253.
26. Tirado Mejía, pp. 259-62.
27. Carlos Silva Martínez, *Por qué caen los partidos políticos* (Bogotá, 1934), pp. 13-14 (emphasis added).

28. For several opinions, see Hirschman, 1963; Smith, 1967; and Gustavo I. De Roux, "The Social Basis of Peasant Unrest: A Theoretical Framework with Special Reference to the Colombia Case," unpublished Ph. D. dissertation (Madison, Wisconsin, 1974), p. 249. There are many opposing arguments; many feel that the law led to numerous evictions of sharecroppers and *colonos*. Most agree, however, that it established the social function of land.
29. Gilhodes, p. 421.
30. Hirschman, p. 157.
31. De Roux, p. 268.
32. Eric Hobsbawm, "The Revolutionary Situation in Colombia," *The World Today* (June, 1963): 248-58.
33. Francisco Leal Buitrago, "Social Classes, International Trade and Foreign Capital in Colombia: An Attempt at Historical Interpretation of the Formation of the State, 1819-1935," unpublished Ph. D. dissertation (Madison, Wisconsin, 1974).
34. Hirschman, p. 147.
35. See Germán Vargas, "La Organización Campesina Freno a la Inmigración," *Carta Agraria*, July 1970.
36. For a detailed description, see De Roux, p. 325.
37. Ibid., p. 329.
38. Ernest Feder, "Counter Reform," in Stavenhagen, Rodolfo, ed., *Agrarian Problems and Peasant Movements in Latin America*, (New York, 1970), p. 178.
39. Felstehausen, p. 167.
40. Oscar Delgado, "La Reforma Agraria Ineficaz y Regresiva," *Flash* (September, 1970).
41. Felstehausen, p. 167.
42. Schwinden and Feaster, p. 11.
43. James W. Wilkie, *Measuring Land Reform: Supplement to the Statistical Abstract of Latin America* (UCLA Latin American Center, 1974).
44. Delgado, p. 12.
45. Enrique Santos Calderón, "Un INCORA millionario, un campesino en ruinas," *El Espectador* (March 5, 1974).
46. Schwinden and Feaster, p. 29. Even if one accepts the distributive definition of land reform, all of the small farmer credit programs in Colombia are reaching only about 450,000 of the estimated 1.2 million small farmers in need of credit (Roger Sandage, "Small Farmer Credit Activities of the Colombian Agricultural Bank," in AID Spring Review of Small Farmer Credit in Colombia (Washington, D.C., February, 1973) pp. 1-4.
47. Dana Dalrymple, "A Supplement to the INCORA Supervised Credit Program by James Schwinden and Gerald Feaster." In AID Spring Review of Small Farmer Credit in Colombia (Washington, D.C. February 1973), pp. 1-13.
48. Felstehausen, p. 193.
49. Barraclough and Domike, "Agrarian Structure," p. 419.
50. Wilkie, p. 7.
51. De Roux, p. 322.
52. Schwinden and Feaster, p. 21.
53. Changes in farm size do not tell the whole story. The census data also indicate an increase between 1960 and 1970 of at least 25 percent in pasture lands by farms under 20 hectares, a decrease in the number of hectares in annual crops of at least 15 percent. This was probably due to the availability of credit for cattle production and the lack of credit for intensive agricultural crops.
54. Solon Barraclough and Arthur Domike, "Agrarian Structure in Seven Latin

American Countries,'' *Land Economics* (November, 1966): 391-424. Note that this figure includes some families who operated land on a rental basis. The share of families who earned all of their income as wage laborers was substantially smaller.

55. Instituto Colombiano Agropecuario, *Proyecto integrado de desarrollo rural de la cordillera nororiental de Colombia*, vol. I (January, 1974).
56. See, for example, Leal, Whittenbarger, Canak, ''Capitalist Penetration and Uneven Development in Two Colombian Communities,'' unpublished M.S. thesis (Madison, Wisconsin, 1974).
57. Many argue that this shift from extensive to intensive agriculture was produced by the threat of expropriation and was thus a benefit of the agrarian reform program. Others, however, contend that the threat of expropriation has caused large owners to reduce investments in intensive agriculture because of the risk of losing their lands.
58. Comité Interamericano de Desarrollo Agrario (CIDA), *Tenencia de Tierra en Colombia* (Washington, 1966).
59. A panel study is only representative of the population in the first wave. Thus, land may be ''lost'' to the sample through sale or inheritance to families not included in the sample population, but not lost to the community as a whole.
60. The exchange rate of U.S. dollars for Colombian pesos in 1970 was U.S $1 = 19.09 pesos.
61. As used here, net monetary income means money earned net of the current paid out costs of production. No attempt was made to measure home consumption of items produced on the farm. To calculate income change, 1970 annual income was converted to constant pesos with base year 1963 using the national consumer price index. An index of prices in Contadero would have been more appropriate.
62. Rojas, p. 110.
63. Dale W. Adams and Sam Schulman, ''Minifundia in Agrarian Reform: A Colombian Example,'' *Land Economics* 44 (August): 274-83.
64. Roger E. Soles, ''Rural Land Invasions in Colombia: A Study of the Macro and Micro Conditions and Forces Leading to Peasant Unrest,'' unpublished Ph. D. dissertation (Madison, Wisconsin, 1972), p. 151.
65. Soles, 1972, p. 156.
66. Soles, 1972, pp. 133-34.
67. A. Eugene Havens and William L. Flinn, ''Green Revolution Technology and Community Development: The Limits of Action Programs,'' *Economic Development and Cultural Change* (April 1975).
68. Michael T. Aiken, A. Eugene Havens and William L. Flinn, ''The Adoption of Innovations: The Neglected Role of Institutional Constraints,'' unpublished paper, 1974.
69. These data deal with owners and renters and differ from Table 5.
70. It is, of course, impossible to know exactly what Lleras wanted to accomplish. Many believe he was trying to accomplish something similar to that tried by Alfonso López with Law 200—develop capitalism but not a revolution, build a base of support in the peasantry but not share power with them.
71. Barbara Chasin and Gerald Chasin, *Power and Ideology* (Cambridge, Massachusetts, 1974).
72. One must be careful not to read into the peasants' thinking the wishes of the outside observer in suggesting that the reforms' failure helped to convince peasants of the intransigence of the ruling class. Peasants have probably always been

unwilling to believe anything the politicians have told them. Rojas, however, found that the majority of the households in our three study sites perceived a two class division in their community. In addition, more than 70 percent of the respondents in all three communities saw their situation as worsening in 1970, which indicates a basis for class consciousness.

73. National Campaign for Peasant Organization (ANUC), *Conclusiones de la IV Junta Directiva* (Fúquene, August 1971).
74. Hernán Echavarría Olózoga, *La Verdadera Reforma Agraria* (Bogotá: Editorial Andec, 1971), p. 1.
75. See the discussion by Bagley and Edel in this volume.
76. Rojas, op. cit.

Chapter 13

Education Policies of the National Front[1]

Robert F. Arnove

In 1958, at the commencement of the National Front, education was a social institution serving the interests of the dominant elite and middle class groups. It was by no means an agency promoting social mobility for children of the rural and urban poor, nor was it an instrument of development integrally related to economic and social plans for preparing skilled human resources and participant citizens. On the contrary, the educational situation in 1958 was one of neglect of the most disadvantaged sectors, notably the rural area, and one of privilege for the economically powerful and politically articulate groups, who used education to certify their status and to guarantee the access to the modern sector of the economy.

The preceding government of the armed forces, led by General Gustavo Rojas Pinilla, had manifested some concern with the archaic state of education. International missions were invited to the country to diagnose the ills of the educational system. A national educational planning office was established in Bogotá, and a comprehensive five-year educational plan was drawn up. Institutions aimed at educating the work force were set in operation. By the end of the Rojas administration, however, over fifty percent of the youth in the country remained outside the school system; and the educational expansion that had occurred between 1953 and 1957 was largely in the private sector and at the secondary school level.

To what extent did the arrival of the National Front signify a marked change in the structure and functioning of the educational system in Colombia? During the period 1958-74, there was a notable expansion of all levels of the education system. Increasing amounts of money were spent on education, as the national government assumed a commanding role in the financing and directing of schools. Educational administrative reforms were instituted. New structures were proposed to open educational opportunity to neglected groups. Out-of-school programs were undertaken to reach illiterate adults and further upgrade the level of knowledge and skills of the work force. Research and planning activities were promoted. Substantial amounts of foreign aid were received, and a number of international technical assistance agencies (UNESCO, the United Nations Development Program, the World Bank and US/AID) selected Colombia as a ''show case'' country of educational innovation.

What were the results sixteen years later? The inequities of the fifties—the gap between rural and urban education, between public and private education, between elite education and basic schooling for the majority—remained unchanged. Greater numbers of children from the lower strata of society were able to take advantage of the education system and to move up in the social hierarchy, but the class-based nature of the school system remained essentially the same. The social origins of the students determined how much education they received and what chances in life were available. Innovations and reforms were largely of an incremental nature. The structure of the outmoded school system was made to work more efficiently. At the same time, the country became increasingly dependent on outside sources of funds and ideas, which shaped the direction and substance of the school system. In essence, the school system continued to reflect the stratification system of Colombian society and its cultural-economic dependency on the United States and Western Europe.

The following discussion will first describe the expansion of schooling during the National Front in relation to the distribution issue of who gets how much of what type of education. Then, the impact of different reforms undertaken by the National Front will be examined. The growing influence of foreign technical assistance will be described; and the conclusion will be an overall assessment of the nation's educational policy.

EXPANSION AND DISTRIBUTION OF EDUCATION

The number of students attending school increased dramatically between 1958 and 1974. In 1958, there were approximately 1,700,000 students enrolled at all levels of the school system. In 1974, there were more than 5,000,000 students enrolled in 38,000 schools, staffed by nearly 200,000 teachers. Primary education enrollment more than doubled from 1,493,128 to 3,844,128. Secondary education increased sixfold from 192,079 to 1,338,876. Higher education expanded from 20,000 to 138,000 students.[2]

Table 1
Distribution of Man Years of Schooling—Colombia, 1964
(In Percentages)

	Age Groups							
	20-24 (1,417,375)		30-34 (1,030,298)		40-49 (1,310,902)		60 or more (864.220)	
	% reaching each grade level	Distribution of man years*	% reaching each grade level	Distribution of man years	% reaching each grade level	Distribution of man years	% reaching each grade level	Distribution of man years
100% =	1,074,898	4,476,839	714,031	2,753,370	877,051	3,473,950	430,467	1,602,530
Primary:								
Grade 1 (1 year)	8.8	2.11	14.31	3.71	11.97	3.02	16.34	4.39
Grade 2 (2 years)	20.0	9.57	22.42	11.63	19.45	9.82	19.77	10.62
Grade 3 (3 years)	21.6	13.67	20.90	16.25	20.09	15.21	18.50	14.91
Grade 4 (4 years)	15.8	15.16	14.58	15.13	15.67	15.82	15.18	16.31
Grade 5 (5 years)	16.0	19.20	14.14	14.44	18.73	23.65	18.70	25.09
Total primary	82.2	61.61	83.35	61.16	85.91	67.53	88.49	71.32
Secondary:								
Grade 1 (6 years)	3.4	4.90	3.07	4.78	2.19	3.32	1.40	2.25
Grade 2 (7 years)	3.2	5.39	3.50	6.35	2.78	4.89	2.03	3.82
Grade 3 (8 years)	2.6	4.98	2.77	5.75	2.48	5.00	1.90	4.06
Grade 4 (9 years)	2.2	4.87	2.09	4.90	1.97	4.48	1.86	4.50
Grade 5 (10 years)	1.2	3.05	.093	2.40	1.05	2.64	1.10	3.00
Grade 6 (11 years)	2.8	7.27	2.16	6.15	1.91	5.31	2.02	6.00
Total secondary	16.4	30.46	14.52	30.33	12.38	25.64	10.31	23.63
Universitary								
Year 1 (12 years)	0.61	1.77	0.17	0.52	0.09	0.27	0.07	0.23
Year 2 (13 years)	0.61	1.91	0.20	0.70	0.10	0.33	0.08	0.27
Year 3 (14 years)	0.49	1.63	0.21	0.77	0.11	0.37	0.08	0.32
Year 4 (15 years)	0.37	1.33	0.28	1.08	0.18	0.70	0.15	0.60
Year 5 (16 years)	0.20	0.79	0.61	2.54	0.63	2.57	0.30	1.27
Year 6 (17 years)	0.12	0.50	0.66	2.90	0.60	2.60	0.52	2.36
Total universitary	2.40	7.93	2.13	8.51	1.71	6.84	1.20	5.05

*This column is computed by multiplying population who have reached each grade level by the total number of years of schooling they have received.

Who Gets What Across Generations?

Education can be examined as a good (like money and land) that is distributed. In this case, it is possible to ask what percentage of the population receives what proportion of the total number of school years distributed. The data in Table I, taken from a study by Rama and Goldsen, indicate the distribution of schooling by different age groups in the 1964 census.[3]

The table shows that although more years of schooling have been made available in recent times, the actual distribution has continued to be inequitable over generations. For example, those people who have attended only primary education (whether complete or incomplete) generally have received less than their fair share. Among the 20 to 24 year olds, they represent 82 percent of all students, but they received only 62 percent of the available total number of years of schooling. Among the oldest population, 60 years or more, these people represented 88 percent, but received only 71 percent of the take. At the primary school level, the ratio of population to take has consistently been between 8:6 and 8:7.

At the secondary level, the ratio reverses. A smaller percentage of people gets approximately twice the amount of schooling they would receive according to an equitable distribution. In 1964, the youngest group who had studied at the secondary education level represented 15 percent of all students, but they received 30 percent of the man years of schooling. Among the oldest group 10 percent received 24 percent. So at this level, the ratio has been 1:2.

At the higher education level, a very small percentage of the population—1 to 2 percent of the students—has received between 5 and 8 percent of the take. The ratio over generations has been 1:3 to 1:4.

Rama and Goldsen conclude that the way in which education has been distributed over the generations has not manifested a notable improvement:

> If we think in terms of relative deprivation rather than absolute gains, then—to the man looking up the educational pyramid from the bottom—things haven't changed very much over the generations. The age group 60 or older was born at the turn of the century. Less education was distributed at that time. But whatever education was distributed got spread around *at least* as equitably as today—or at least the inequities suffered by that generation born at the turn of the century have not been substantially altered for the generation born 1940-44.[4]

The consequences of this inequitable distribution of schooling are reflected in the earning potentials of people with different levels of schooling. An example is Marcelo Selowsky's estimate that for the work force of Bogotá, between 1963 and 1966, the average hourly salary for a person with no schooling was $0.16; for a person with five years of schooling, $0.34; for a

Table 2
Percent of Illiteracy for Population 15 years +

	1938	1951	1964
Urban	25	21	15
Rural	53	50	41

person with eleven years, \$1.34; and for a person with sixteen or seventeen years, \$2.12.[5] An additional year or two of schooling may lead to a disproportionate gain in income. The average hourly wage for a person with six years of secondary education was \$1.34 pesos, nearly double that for a person with three or four years of secondary who earned on the average \$0.69. Six years are required to complete an academic secondary education.

Rural-Urban Inequities

Literacy A continuous history of neglect of the rural areas is manifest in literacy figures and other statistics concerning educational penetration. According to the 1964 census, the illiteracy rate of adults fifteen years and above in Colombia was 27 percent. But 41 percent of the rural population was illiterate, compared with 15 percent of the urban population. An examination of the illiteracy figures for 1938, 1951, and 1964 reveals that the gap between the rural and urban populations remained basically unchanged.[6]

Data from the 1970 household survey, covering the population ten years of age and older, show a similar discrepancy. Fifty percent illiteracy in the rural areas, compared with 30 percent for urban areas. Examining illiteracy rates among the youngest two sets of populations—ages ten to nineteen, and twenty to twenty-nine—provides insight into educational opportunities available to rural and urban youth over the 1958-70 period. Among the youngest group, we find an illiteracy rate of 15 percent in the urban area, and a figure more than twice as high for the rural area—33 percent. Among the twenty-year-olds, we find approximately the same percentage spread—10 percent compared with 29 percent for rural youth.[7]

In 1964, the average amount of schooling completed by the adult rural population was less than two years, compared with slightly more than five years for the urban population. In the early 1970s, this figure for the rural population was essentially the same. As of 1970, 40 percent of the rural children, ages seven to eleven, were not attending school (as against 22 percent for urban children).[8]

Dropout Rates Dropout rates are high over all, but they are disproportionately high for the rural area. Between 1960 and 1964, only 3 percent of students entering the first grade of rural schools completed primary education; the figure for urban schools was 46 percent. Ten years later the situation had not changed appreciably: only 10 percent of rural students reached the fifth grade of primary education, as compared with 52 percent of urban students.[9]

Completion rates are lower for rural areas for a variety of nonschool and school-related reasons. Socioeconomic conditions in rural areas prevent many children from attending school for protracted periods of time. Migration in search of land and work, geographical isolation, and the seasonal need for children to be working in the field—all these factors influence the prospect of rural children completing basic education. Also of critical importance are government policies to extend educational opportunity to the least advantaged sectors of the population. In this respect, the policies of National Front governments have been remiss. Children often do not complete even three years of education because schools do not exist and teachers are not available. Under these conditions, students do not "drop out" but are "pushed out" of the school system. In 1970, only 9 percent of the rural schools offered five full years of primary education, as compared with 72 percent of urban schools. In fact, approximately two-thirds of the rural schools offer only the first two years of elementary education. This situation has remained unchanged for three decades. In 1940, for example, out of 5,723 rural public schools, 3,667 offered only the first two years of education; in 1967, there were 16,548 rural public schools of which 9,852 offered no more than two years of schooling. The numbers had grown, but the proportions had not changed.[10] In a 1970-71 study of six departments by the Office of Primary Education in the Ministry of Education, the percentage of incomplete schools (offering fewer than five years of the complete introductory cycle of education) follows: Tolima, 94 percent; Cauca, 89 percent; Atlántico, 70 percent; Risaralda, 67 percent; Meta, 62 percent; and North Santander, 99 percent. Out of 3,163 incomplete schools studied, less than a fifth had up to the fourth grade of instruction. Out of the 140,228 children in the schools studied, 120,318 were in the first two grades.[11]

These figures make a mockery out of the legislation passed in 1963 to extend five years of elementary education to both the urban and rural populations. Prior to that year, rural education consisted of a diluted curriculum and only four formal years of instruction, compared with five for the urban areas.[12] In 1967, emergency legislation was also passed to extend the educational coverage of rural schools by instituting double sessions and one-room schools with one teacher in charge of several grades at the same time. Governmental building programs and provision of funds and personnel for the rural areas, however, have not been consistent with the declared aims of the legislation.

Another factor contributing to high dropout rates is the national examination system. Colombia has a national curriculum with a concomitant centralized system of supervision and grading. Under this system, students are given the same national examinations, whether they attend poorly endowed schools with unqualified teachers or resource rich schools with highly qualified instructors. Invariably many students fail to pass these examinations and either drop out of school or are required to repeat the same grade. This is particularly the case with rural schools, where over 25 percent of first-grade students and 20 percent of second-grade pupils fail these tests.[13]

In 1974, the last year of the National Front, legislation was passed stipulating that national examinations were no longer to be used for the purpose of determining promotion, but were to serve diagnostic purposes in assisting students with learning problems. The effectiveness of this new policy is yet to be determined. To date, it has been difficult to implement because of teacher resistance to the additional work involved in this new evaluation system.

Physical Conditions Physical conditions of most rural schools are deplorable: dilapidated buildings, overcrowding, lack of educational materials. A study done by a team of sociologists in 1970-71 at the Pedagogical and Technological University in Tunja examined rural schools in Boyacá, one of the least urbanized departments in Colombia.[14] The team found that more than three-fourths of the schools had only one classroom. With few exceptions, schools were without electricity, running water, or sanitary services. One typical school studied by the researchers consisted of one room, a dirt floor, and forty-seven students in three grades studying at the same time. Teacher efforts were aimed mostly at getting students to go through several routine assignments, while maintaining some semblance of order. Another school, in better condition and with a television set, consisted of two teachers, four grades, and fifty-five students. Little learning was observed taking place; instead, misinformation was being transmitted by the teachers.

Even within the relatively unurbanized state of Boyacá, noticeable differences appeared between teaching-learning conditions for children attending schools in the countryside and those studying in the municipal centers or *cabeceras*. Forty-three percent of the teachers were assigned to the rural areas, which had 78 percent of the students. Fifty-seven percent of the teachers worked in the cities with 22 percent of the children. Forty-five percent of urban instructional personnel were in the highest category of the teacher salary and promotional schedule, as against 14 percent of the rural teachers.

Teacher Qualifications Statistics from the Boyacá study concerning teacher preparation do not diverge from those for the nation. According to the Planning Office of the Ministry of Education, in 1970, 78 percent of the urban teachers were in the top two categories of the schedule, while only 30 percent of the rural teachers were. Rural teachers represented 41 percent of the teacher force and 72 percent of the unqualified personnel.[15]

The Boyacá study suggests that about half of the rural teachers change their jobs yearly. Generally, the government has not made living conditions and salaries attractive enough for rural teachers. In 1971, the monetary incentive for teaching in isolated rural areas was only some $25 per annum above that for the cities.

Provision of Funds, Schools and Teachers Budgetary allocations provide a good indication of the relative importance of the rural sector. Out of an education budget of nearly $125 million in 1970-71, the rural areas received less than $12 million.[16] At that time, rural children represented approximately 43 percent of the 3,118,300 children (ages seven to eleven) attending primary schools, but they were receiving less than 10 percent of the education budget.[17]

A good indicator of efforts to improve education was governmental initiative in constructing rural schools. In analyzing the impact of public policy on educational opportunity, Lebot notes that "school matriculation in the rural areas has closely paralleled construction of educational facilities."[18] He provides data on government building programs between 1952 and 1955 (2,000 new places) and from 1958 to 1964 (when almost 5,000 new schools were created). When school construction stopped in 1965, due to lack of external financing from foreign aid programs, the rate of school enrollment slackened, particularly in the rural areas. Urban schools generally have expanded at a more constant rate as shown by Lebot.[19]

These data reveal that teacher positions have been created at a faster pace in urban areas. Between 1960 and 1967, 13,212 new positions opened in the urban areas, and only 7,563 in the rural areas.[20] In addition, expansion for students in the urban sector during the first ten years of the National Front was from 913,253 places to 1,743,663, an increase of 90 percent. The growth rate was lower for the rural sector; only 72 percent from 579,870 to 998,769.[21] It is clear that school construction and creation of new teacher places is not sufficient to keep up with the pace of enrollment in either the urban or rural areas. It is also clear, however, that government bias has been decidedly in favor of the urban sectors in allocating funds and material and personnel resources to education.

Absence of Higher Levels of Education For the small minority of rural children who complete primary education, the next step on the educational ladder will probably take them to the cities. Over 90 percent of the secondary schools are located in urban areas; and, according to former Minister of

Table 3
Indices of Number of Schools, Students, and Teachers
Base: 1951 = 100

	Urban Zone			Rural Zone		
	Schools	Students	Teachers	Schools	Students	Teachers
1955	97	138	137	126	126	130
1958	107	180	170	138	139	143
1961	122	225	219	162	159	177
1964	137	287	294	191	192	232
1967	151	355	345	192	206	247

Education Galán, 80 percent of all education facilities in 1971 were located in three urban areas: Bogotá, Medellín, and Cali.[22] Of the 733,257 students enrolled in secondary education in that year, less than 2 percent were attending schools in rural areas.

Private-Public Inequities

Secondary education is the gateway to the universities and to the modern sector of the economy. As well as being an urban phenomenon, it was mainly private throughout the 1960s. In 1970, more than half (53 percent) of all secondary education students were enrolled in privately owned institutions. The slight decline from the 1958 figure of 60 percent reflects government efforts to expand opportunity at this level.

In the major cities, private control of secondary education was overwhelming during the period of the National Front. In Bogotá, for example, approximately 85 percent of the secondary students attended church-related or private lay schools. According to a World Bank mission report, only about 10 percent of the population can afford to pay the private school fees.[23] Therefore, in Bogotá, some 90 percent of the youth were competing for about 15 percent of the high school places—those in the public schools. The private lay schools in Bogotá, according to Rodríguez, charge on the average about $12 a month.[24] By contrast, enrollment and book fees in the putatively free public primary schools are less than $5 per annum, and in the public secondary schools are generally under $20. As the minister of education observed in 1971, "Secondary education for the most part is reserved for those classes who can afford private education."[25]

The traditional domination of secondary education by the private sector has, however, been gradually eroded. By 1974, there were 666,618 pupils in public secondary schools compared with 674,258 in private schools. Public secondary education expanded fairly fast throughout the 1960s and early

1970s. Moreover, this rate is likely to continue because of an ambitious program of building comprehensive high schools, designated by the acronym INEM (*Institutos de Educación Media Diversificada*). The government of Lleras Restrepo passed Decree 1962 of 1969, establishing the legal and conceptual basis for the creation of nineteen INEMs. The World Bank provided loans to cover 50 percent of the initial building costs of roughly U.S. $29 million. Initially, these high schools will accommodate 40,000 students, and they are expected to reach an enrollment of 80,000 students in double sessions. The comprehensive high schools are designed to provide for both general academic preparation and technical-vocational training, which will enable students to be gainfully employed upon completion of secondary education, or entitled to continue with advanced studies in universities.[26] During the first two years of studies, students are required to explore a wide range of vocational interests; the third and fourth years of study they narrow their focus to a more specific academic or vocational area; and in the last two years, they specialize in the chosen area. By comparison with most public secondary schools, the INEM are well endowed with science laboratories and technical shops, staffed with academic and vocational counselors, and offer a variety of elective subjects and extracurricular activities. The Ministry of Education is using these high schools as a model for desired reforms in secondary education.[27]

At the university level, public education has not kept up with the expansion rate of the private sector. By 1974, there were roughly the same number of students in private and public universities: 69,338 and 69,023 respectively.[28] By comparison, 59 percent of university students were enrolled in public institutions in 1960, and 72 percent in 1950. In 1974, there were thirty-five private universities and twenty-three public universities. Two-thirds of the higher education institutions established during the National Front were private.

The growth of higher education is largely a response to the social demands of the urban middle class, rather than a result of public policy geared to development needs. This is the general pattern in Latin America, where governments have tended to subsidize the middle classes by providing low cost public education. Colombia, however, differs from most Latin American countries in the extensiveness of private higher education. One apparent reason for the rapid growth of private universities was the political turmoil in the public universities. Students were in the forefront of opposition to the policies of the National Front and on numerous occasions effectively disrupted public order through seizure of university buildings and violent street demonstrations. The government's response has been to limit the size and importance of the public universities. By doing this, the National Front in effect further discriminated against lower class students. Low-income students who do not pass the highly competitive examinations to enter the national and departmental universities are unlikely to have the financial resources to pay tuition in the private institutions. The cost could run as high as $200 to $250 a semester in the private institutions, compared with $30 or less in the public institutions. Of the students who apply to the public universities, less than a third are admitted.[29]

At the primary education level, the private sector has consistently represented approximately 15 percent of total enrollments. In 1972, 540,000 out of 3,730,434 primary students were in private schools, which were usually affiliated with the Catholic church.[30] Many people send their children to religiously-run schools at the primary and secondary levels because they prefer religious instruction in terms of doctrine and discipline, also because these institution generally have a higher social prestige.

The National Front never developed a consistent or coherent policy toward private education, despite its extensive coverage and importance. The vacillations of the Front on the issue of private education in part reflect a long tradition of conflict between Conservatives and Liberals over church and state control of education.[31] Private education, moreover, has an extremely powerful constituency of middle-and upper-class groups supporting it. Ministry attempts to diminish the influence wielded by the church and the lay private sector were effectively resisted from 1958 to 1974.[32] Among the instances where public policies did not succeed were a 1959 decree to freeze tuition costs in private establishments, and subsequent government efforts to establish boards to oversee and regulate fees. In 1965, as another example, the Council of State—the highest court in public administrative matters—annulled a decree by which the government sought to control textbooks used in all educational institutions in the country. Private schools consistently have resisted the imposition of a single text throughout the country. The issue here is an ideological one of who will control the content of instruction and thereby the values transmitted in the curriculum, rather than a narrowly pedagogical issue of schools choosing their own textbooks to improve the quality of instruction. In 1971, the private sector helped defeat farsweeping reform measures proposed by the minister of education for all educational institutions (public and private) to provide fellowships for poor children of up to 10 percent of total enrollments. The reforms also included: the creation of parent-teacher associations in private as well as public institutions; compulsory social service for all Colombian youth; the fostering of a cooperative school movement; the full utilization of empty urban lots and of all classrooms in public and private schools for educational purposes; and compulsory educational insurance to guarantee basic education for the children of parents who died.[33]

The strength of the private sector is manifest not only in the defeat of policies detrimental to its economic and social interests, but in its ability to pressure government to undertake policies favorable to its continued growth. In the first five-year plan of education of 1957-62, the chapter on secondary education reads: "The State should assume responsibility for the orientation (of education) and offer those services which cannot be provided by the private sector."[34] The 1971 Draft Law of Education, prepared in the Colombian Institute of Pedagogy (ICOLPE), similarly discusses the benefits accruing to the nation from private education and the need to protect this sector, while integrating its efforts with those of the national educational system.[35]

It is questionable whether the private sector would be as vital and expansive as it is today without substantial government support. Indeed, government allocations to private education during the National Front represented roughly 10 percent of the budget for elementary and secondary education. Private schools, moreover, received substantial financial aid through a national scholarship program created by Decree 185 of 1971, and administered through ICETEX (Colombian Institute for Educational Credit and Foreign Technical Studies). During the first two years of the program, approximately 47 percent of the more than U.S. $5 million made available by the Ministry of Education and UNICEF went to government-supported private schools—over one-third of them were located in Bogotá.[36]

It may be argued that permitting the private sector to operate and expand helps free funds for education of lower income people in the public primary and secondary schools. In the absence of an ideal situation where the state has the means to educate all children in public schools, this is the next best strategy. This argument must be balanced against the negative effects of a dual educational system (with an elite private sector and a nonprestigious public sector), which helps perpetuate the existing stratification system in the society.

Support for Different Levels of the Education System

Government priorities in spending for different education levels also have contributed to strengthening the hold of the middle and upper income groups on education. While the National Front allocated a greater percentage of the education budget to the primary school level, secondary and higher education continued to receive a disproportionate share of funds. It has already been suggested that children of the well-to-do constitute the overwhelming majority of students in secondary (particularly the last two years of this level, grades ten and eleven) and higher education. After attending private secondary schools with higher promotion rates and an emphasis on college preparation, they may then opt to attend publicly-financed institutions of higher education, where tuition costs are low. In effect, the children of the middle and upper classes are being subsidized by the government to attend universities and thereby further confirm their higher social status.

In 1970 more public funds in absolute terms were being spent on the 23,000 students attending the national universities than on the 1,352,000 primary and secondary schoolage children in rural areas.[37] Again it should be noted that although more money is spent on primary education than on higher education, less than 10 percent of the primary school budget went to rural areas. In per capita terms, the government was spending roughly $25 per pupil in primary education, $60 for secondary education (academic track), and more than $225 per student in higher education. Jallade estimates that the public education expenditures in 1970 were distributed as follows: 24 percent went to universities, 15 percent to secondary schools, and 61 percent to the preprimary and primary level; in 1958, at the initiation of the National Front, the corresponding figures were twenty-four, twenty-seven, and forty-nine.[38] This suggests a tendency to strengthen the primary level. Nevertheless, higher education, with 3 percent of the total number of students, continued to command a disproportionate share of resources from the government, while primary education with the vast bulk of students (78 percent) received disproportionately less.

As R. Albert Berry notes in this book, "education is increasingly an important factor in distribution as the share of national income going as payment to special skills rises.... Funds allocated to higher education will normally have a tendency to worsen income distribution and those allocated to primary, especially rural primary will tend to improve it." Between 1958 and 1970, the percentage of children in rural primary school increased. They thereby gained access to public benefits, but as Berry indicates, "the share of public benefits going to the top quarter of families may also have increased."

Cost-benefit calculations for different levels of education indicate that the most profitable investment is made in primary education. It is followed by secondary, and higher education is last. In this type of analysis benefits are measured by comparing lifetime earnings of people in different age categories with one level of educational attainment against people with the next lower level of education. The costs that are deducted from the benefits may include, according to Hansen, (1) school costs incurred by society—that is, teachers' salaries, supplies, interest and depreciation on capital; (2) opportunity costs incurred by individuals—namely, income foregone during school attendance, and (3) incidental school-related costs incurred by individuals—for example, books and travel.[39] "The internal rate of return is then estimated by finding that rate of discount that equates the present value of the cost outlays with the present value of the additional income flows."[40] Studies done in Colombia by M. Selowsky, T.P. Schultz, and C.P.S. Dougherty indicate that the average rate of return is about 21 percent for primary, 20 percent for secondary, and 7 percent for university education.[41]

The rapid growth of higher education (14 percent per annum) corresponds neither to informed government policy nor to considerations concerning its economic benefits. At the higher education level, the areas of fastest growth were in the humanities, fine arts, social sciences, and education—rather than in technical and scientific fields.[42] At the secondary level, the college-preparatory academic track, the *bachillerato*, also grew substantially. By 1970 it accounted for 70 percent of all secondary students, as against 56 percent in 1958. Thus the nontechnical areas of secondary and higher education expanded quickly, despite the government's commitments to establishing polytechnical and more development-oriented higher education institutions, and to establish comprehensive high schools that would orient students toward technical and subprofessional careers.

Higher education in Colombia has expanded according to the demands of the urban and middle sector who use the education system to secure an advantaged status for their offspring. Students graduating from secondary education and attending the public universities are mainly from the upper social strata. Cataño, after reviewing pertinent sociological studies on education in Bogotá, concludes that at most 8 percent of students graduating from the *bachillerato* are from the lower classes; approximately 80 percent are from the middle class, and 12 percent are from the upper class.[43] Rama reports similar results and notes that the students of the National University—a reputedly popular, nonelitist institution—"are the descendents of grandfathers and fathers with a relatively high level of education, compared with the national average."[44] Data on this university and on the two Bogotá elite private universities—the Andes and Javeriana—support this contention. Whereas only 1.7 percent of the national male population 40-59 years old had attended a university, 18.8 percent, 42.5 percent and 38 percent of the students in these institutions had fathers that had been university students.[45] It is interesting to note the emphasis that these relatively successful groups of parents place on obtaining a university education for their children, although a majority of them had not themselves achieved any university education.

ATTEMPTED REFORMS

The previously discussed inequities notwithstanding, some reformist attempts were made during the National Front. In 1968, the government of Carlos Lleras Restrepo passed a number of educational bills designed to make the operations of the Ministry of Education more efficient. Decentralized institutions of education were established as was a program of revenue sharing with the departmental secretariats of education. The major purpose of this legislation was to concentrate policy making and overall supervision of educational activities in the ministry, while leaving implementation of policy and routine administration of the school system to local educational authorities.[46] In line with these new thrusts was the strengthening of educational planning mechanisms, notably the National Planning Department (DNP) with its Human Resources Division; the creation of a national educational research institute (ICOLPE); and the initiation of reforms to democratize education, particularly at the secondary school level.

When Misael Pastrana became president, his administration was increasingly responsive to swelling popular demand for educational programs not only for school-age youth but for school dropouts and adults as well. In 1971, Minister of Education Luis Carlos Galán introduced a highly controversial educational reform package aimed at expanding educational opportunity for both the rural and urban poor.[47] The congressional debate on the proposed reforms highlighted the inadequacies of the educational system, which the minister himself termed an "instrument of discrimination and privilege."[48] General Rojas' ANAPO opposed the legislation on the private education sector and this opposition plus growing concern within the National Front over the escalating criticism of its past educational policies, led to the defeat of these reform measures and the eventual ouster of the Minister. The pattern is fairly typical of unsuccessful reforms proposed during the National Front. Politically ambitious cabinet ministers articulated reforms that had not been proposed by any specific interest group or social movement. The few existing interest groups opposed the proposed changes because their economic interests were directly affected. Anti-National Front political groups, such as ANAPO took a similar stance. The government was incapable of rallying the broad political support required to make the reform, a condition exacerbated by the coalition nature of the Front which required bipartisan support. Solaún et al. document this pattern for the urban reform.

After Galán's educational reform failed, attention shifted to programs with less dramatic short-run impact. Emphasis was placed on restructuring the national school system toward training human resources and relating it to a parallel system of social services and education for adults. The new concept of the education system consisted of two major cycles. The first cycle was composed of nine years of basic education, divided into five different stages, with integrated studies and automatic promotion during the lower stages, and with increasing attention to vocational exploration at the upper stages. The second cycle comprises upper secondary and higher education with different exit points leading to work.

An important element in this projected reform program was the creation of Rural Development Centers. These provide the basic education for grades six through nine as well as various health, nutritional, agricultural extension, credit, and adult education programs. Urban counterparts to these rural centers would serve as educational resource centers containing facilities and materials too expensive for neighborhood schools. The comprehensive high schools also are viewed as resource centers, that open options at the secondary education level and help guide technical education programs in satellite schools. At the higher education level, emphasis is placed on regional planning and the integration of academic programs so that the strengths of certain institutions can be used while unnecessary duplication is avoided. Moreover, cooperative training programs are envisioned between the INEM and higher education institutions with the national occupational training institute, SENA (*Servicio Nacional de Aprendizaje*). It is important to note that as of 1974, the government was proceeding very slowly in implementing these proposed reforms.

The difficulties that beset educational reforms and the limited outcomes of such reforms are described in the following sections on: the Regional Educational Funds (FER), national funding of education, adult education, and educational planning and research.

The Regional Educational Funds (FER)[49]

In 1968 there was a general administrative reform tied to the constitutional reform. The education side of this general reform, Decree 3157, was designed to strengthen the policy-making, supervisory, and financial role of the national Ministry of Education in relation to the department or province secretariats of education. The provision of central government funds was contingent upon the government of each department signing a contract containing a number of constraining clauses.[50] As detailed by Hanson, the principal provisions of these contracts required each department to:

1. Increase annual appropriations for education consistent with the growth of the total department budget.
2. Hire only teachers who met the qualification standards established by the Ministry, and select them by special examination.
3. Replace all nonqualified teachers (primary and secondary) within a period of two years.
4. Create positions for supervisors at the ratio of one for every 200 teachers.
5. Reorganize the department offices of education according to Ministry recommendations.
6. Manage the wage-scale and personnel promotions according to Ministry policy and national law.
7. Permit the Ministry to supervise the department expenditures in education.
8. Demonstrate the availability of funds before hiring additional teachers.
9. Accept the presence of a Ministry official (a *delegado*) who was authorized to supervise all matters mentioned in the contract as well as to investigate irregularities found in other segments of the department educational system.[51]

The outcomes of these polcies were to have been a more unified national program of education, with higher quality instruction resulting from more adequate funds and better qualified personnel.

Evaluating the outcomes of the FER program as of January 1973, Hanson observed that of the "23 programs at least 8 were functioning well and collaborating with FER, 5 were functioning well and not collaborating, and 10 were not collaborating and in various stages of disorganization."[52] Cases of abuse of contractual provisions were rife. The 1970 study by the Colombian Pedagogical Institute of the FER details the violations in one department:

1. Of the 2,100 primary school teachers in the department, 1,131 do not meet minimum standards.
2. In March 1970, 420 new teachers were appointed for political reasons although there were no funds in the budget to pay them.
3. It is not possible to remove the unqualified teachers because the political pressures placed on the secretary of education will not permit it.
4. The department uses educational funds for other purposes.
5. The central government agent or *delegado* is not permitted to approve expenditures for the FER fund.
6. When the principal of a school is changed, everyone down to the janitors is changed.[53]

In no case were sanctions applied against a department for failure to comply with the contract with the central government.

It is difficult to assess the impact of the National Front on these administrative practices. Ostensibly the Front was an attempt to eliminate bureaucratic abuse and corruption resulting from traditional party partisanship or *sectarismo*, as it is called in Colombia. The Front's bipartisan principle of parity in hiring personnel "down to the janitor"—the need for everyone nominally to be a member of either the Conservative or Liberal parties and to be employed in equal proportions—certainly maintained a political dimension in the education system. Nevertheless, it is clear from the data that the regime did not result in a modern and efficient education bureaucracy. The difficulties in applying sanctions are revealed in this interview with one of the ministry's *delegados*: "When the department would not comply with the contract, the Minister would often get mad and talk about suspending the monthly payment to the department, but he never did. You must remember that he is a politician too, and he must work with the governors who are also politicians. The Minister is subject to the same political pressures from the governors that he can use on them."[54] The factors which work against an effective national educational policy included: the historical independence of the departments in educational matters; the absence of regional education planning and pooling of resources to overcome the disparities among individual departments in their finances and their level of educational development; the multiplicity of different power centers at the national level (several autonomous government agencies formulate and implement educational policy); and the power of the private sector in education, which is relatively independent of national government control. The overlapping and conflicting jurisdictions of the nation, departments, and municipalities over education as well as between the public and private sectors all impeded the emergence of a uniform national policy in education.[55]

National Funding of Education

The growing importance of the central government in financing education formed an integral part of the strategy to centralize decision-making in the Ministry of Education. In 1957, before the initiation of the National Front, the Ministry's expenditures represented only 37 percent of total educational expenditures, compared with 50 percent for the departments, and 13 percent for the municipalities.[56] By 1961, the central government had assumed major responsibility for the wages of primary school teachers—the lion's share of educational expenditures. By 1973, approximately 60 percent of those salaries were being paid by national monies, 25 percent by state and municipal funds, and the rest by other agencies.[57] The importance of national funds is attested to by the fact that in 1970, the total amount of national support to the departments (700 million pesos), exceeded their education funds.[58]

During the 1960s, the Ministry of Education also increasingly shifted its budgetary allocations towards capital expenditures (school construction, teacher training, and educational innovations) as against operating expenditures. In 1960, operating costs (salaries, materials, administrative costs) accounted for 91 percent of the budget. By 1971, such costs accounted for 75 percent; 25 percent was going into investments or capital expenditures.[59] The most noticeable shift away from operating expenditures occurred in the period from 1968 on, and the greatest amount of capital funds went to new programs in secondary and higher education. It is questionable if much of this capital investment in educational expansion and innovation would have occurred without massive amounts of foreign capital in loans and grants.

While the national government spent increasing amounts of money on education, it is not at all certain that the allocations kept pace with the growth of the economy, or with the number of school-age children. In 1957, the year preceding the National Front, allocations to the Ministry of Education accounted for 6.22 percent of the national budget; in 1958, expenditures were 8.47 percent; by 1971, they were 14.77 percent.[60] For the most part throughout the 1960s, education represented only 13 percent of the national budget. As a percentage of the GNP, educational expenditures were 1.51 percent in 1958 and 2.24 percent in 1965; by 1970, they had declined to 1.5 percent.[61] As far back as 1965, when Colombia should have been spending 4 percent of its GNP on education (according to the recommendations of the 1954 Conference of Santiago de Chile), the Minister of Education commented, "Colombia is not making the necessary effort that the national dignity demands."[62] (The Santiago de Chile Conference of Latin American Ministers of Education, sponsored by UNESCO and the Organization of American States, established priorities for the expansion and improvement of primary education.) According to projections of the Planning Office of the Ministry of Education in the same year, 1965 allocations to education should have steadily risen to 25 percent of the national budget by 1975, in order to meet the educational needs of the country. Allocating 25 percent of the budget to education, however, might have negative consequences. Less money would be available for investment in alternative areas that possess a relatively high potential for generating employment and improving income distribution—one such area being rural development. Moreover, to assist the lower income groups a larger share of educational funds would have to be spent on the primary schools—an investment that has both a high economic payoff and a positive effect on income distribution.

Article 2 of the 1957 plebiscite—the basis for the National Front itself—established that the nation should commit 10 percent of its budget to education. As Lebot notes, the meaning of this article in the Plebiscite is ambiguous, but if monies spent by the central government's decentralized public institutions are taken into account, in addition to the funds of the ministries, then the government has barely met its obligations.[63] In the three years, 1967 through 1969, combined expenditures by governmental agencies and decentralized institutions actually fell below 10 percent; and by 1971, the combined expenditures in education represented only 10.16 percent of the total central government expenditures. In that year, the decentralized institutes were spending only 8.52 percent of their budgets on education.[64]

Adult Education

As noted earlier, one of the most serious educational problems confronting the successive National Front governments was the high level of adult illiteracy—probably between one-fourth and one-third of the population was unable to read and write simple texts related to everyday life. If more exacting standards are applied as to what constitutes literacy—for example, the UNESCO criterion of 4 years of formal schooling—then, as the Minister of Education noted in 1971, perhaps as many as two-thirds of the adult population is "functionally illiterate."[65]

National Front governments, (and the private sector as well), undertook a variety of adult education programs to provide literacy and the opportunity to obtain the equivalent of primary and secondary school diplomas. In 1969, the government commemorated the one hundred and fiftieth anniversary of Colombia's victory in the War of Independence against Spain by inaugurating a national campaign of "liberation through literacy." A Division of Adult Education was created within the Ministry of Education. A five year plan was drawn up to provide functional literacy for 900,000 and primary education for 600,000 adults (fifteen years and over). More than 400 adult education centers were established. According to Decree 378 of 1970, primary education for adults consists of five cycles of ninety-three class days of four hours a day during which the following areas are covered: language, mathematics, social studies, natural sciences, and religion.

Unfortunately, the level of funding provided by the national government for adult education belies the seriousness with which these efforts were undertaken and lowers the probability of their success. The lofty goal for adult education was "to train adults over fourteen years of age to participate actively in the socioeconomic development of the country."[66] However, in 1970-71, the Ministry allocated to adult education only 1.19 percent of its budget. It is not surprising therefore that at the end of the first year of the literacy campaign only some 24,000 adults had been made literate through efforts of the Ministry, while 54,464 were listed as completing the equivalent of a primary school diploma.[67] These figures were more than 100,000 short of the target for that year.

Given this low level of funding, the government has relied heavily on the private sector efforts in adult education, in particular Popular Cultural Action (ACPO), popularly known as Radio Sutatenza. Radio Sutatenza, which began operation in 1949, combines extensive radio broadcasts (it has the most powerful transmission network in the hemisphere) with discussion groups, a weekly newspaper, and a set of basic readers. The program has helped teach approximately half-a-million Colombians to read and write. Thirty-nine percent of the Ministry's Division of Adult Education's budget went to ACPO in 1969, and over 27 percent in 1970.[68]

In 1969, the government of Lleras Restrepo inaugurated the open-field broadcasts of Capacitación Popular, a program of adult education for urban areas. Television, instead of radio, was used to beam basic education programs (reading, writing, mathematics, civics, and religion) into community reception centers, using volunteer monitors from the communities as instructors in conjunction with the broadcasts. The emphasis was on education in relation to community efforts at self-improvement. This innovative approach was supposed to lead to massive, accelerated, and inexpensive adult education.[69] During its first years of operation, however, the program was limited in scope and very costly. With a budget of approximately $800,000 in 1970, the program was reaching fewer than 4,000 adults in organized viewing centers, and fewer than fifty adults were completing the introductory cycle of nine months of instruction. Moreover, an evaluation of the outcome of this program, which stressed civic responsibilities and community action, showed that over 40 percent of those participating and completing the first course in low income neighborhoods of Bogotá, could not even name the country they lived in.[70] The Capacitación Popular adult education program was unsuccessful for many reasons: an irrelevant and unrealistic curriculum; mediocre television programs; poorly trained and often unmotivated monitors; an unrealistically long schedule of classes lasting nine months; and, most importantly, the low probability of the participants improving their economic and social situation on the basis of completing the program.

Colombia's program of apprenticeship and on-the-job training through the National Apprenticeship Service (SENA) represents another innovative approach to adult education.[71] Established by the Military Junta in 1957, the year prior to the National Front, SENA is an autonomous public corporation attached to the Ministry of Labor. The Governing Board of SENA consists of the Ministries of Labor and Education, the Director of the National Planning Department, and representatives of the Catholic Church, private industry, and labor. The institution's activities are financed by a 2 percent payroll tax on all companies with capital assets over $2,500 or employing ten or more people, plus a 0.5 percent tax on government payrolls. From its inception until 1969, the organization trained 390,050 workers.[72] In the mid-1960s, it accelerated its educational programs. From 1958 to 1965 it trained 135,341 workers (14,254 in agriculture; 60,272 in industry; and 60,815 in commerce and services). In 1968 alone it trained 105,770 (37,320 in agriculture; 32,316 in industry; and 36,134 in commerce and services).[73] In 1970, during the presidential election campaign, the government initiated its program of "popular professional promotion for the rural areas." Using mobile vans and other means of reaching the countryside, the program was intended to provide necessary skills and information to peasant youths and adults who normally would not qualify for the SENA program. (These qualifications are a primary school diploma or equivalent knowledge, and a contract with a sponsoring firm). Critics of this rural program saw it as a political ploy; it was dismantled in 1972.[74]

According to the International Labor Organization 1970 study, *Toward Full Employment*, SENA was satisfying the quantitative and qualitative manpower needs of industry, particularly at the intermediate level.[75] But it is clear that the organization has not contributed adequately to the occupational training of the vast majority of Colombians, who are entering the job market faster than educational programs can prepare or assist them. SENA's programs are serving a relatively small and select group of people. According to a 1972 study by Puryear, who examined graduates of a three-year SENA industrial apprenticeship program in Bogotá, apprentices tended to come from urban areas and have fathers employed in large, private firms. Twenty-one percent of the SENA graduates in the study had either relatives or friends working in the firms that sponsored them.[76] According to the standards applied this percentage may be considered strikingly low for an underdeveloped, family-oriented society; or it may be viewed as a substantial number of people taking advantage of family and personal influence in a supposedly meritocratic institution.

Because SENA apprentices are paid attractive stipends and guaranteed entry into fairly well paying jobs, they are able to accumulate funds to enter secondary education programs. Puryear observes:

> Indeed, when we consider the rather large proportion of SENA graduates (45 percent) who have gone on to continue formal secondary education, there emerges the strong possibility that SENA is operating as a capital market, providing educational investment funds for students who might otherwise find post-primary schooling too expensive. By virtue of their wages in skilled, technical positions, SENA graduates are able to finance additional academic secondary schooling, most probably at night. They thus have access to cheap educational investment capital in a country where capital is scarce and costly.[77]

The apprenticeship programs represent a good investment for these individuals who use it as a springboard to better paying jobs and higher social status. From an investment point of view, the apprenticeship programs are economically sound. Puryear estimates social rates of return for SENA graduates to be 32 percent to 36 percent higher than the return for individuals with comparable levels of formal schooling but no apprenticeship training. Correcting for family background and motivation factors, the social rate of return continues to be relatively high—from 13 percent to 19 percent.[78] The question, however, remains whether alternative investments by SENA might not have benefited more individuals for the same costs. The per capita expenditures in the programs studied by Puryear ranged from a high estimate of $1,300 to a low estimate of $820 to get an apprentice through a three-year program. From a distributional point of view, large sums of money are being invested in relatively few individuals.

Employers, on the other hand, may be reluctant to support apprenticeship programs, because of the costs involved during the training period and the probable loss of trainees at a later date. To maximize profits, employers opt for mechanization and automation, rather than labor-intensive production techniques.[79]Umaña Luna further notes that employers use SENA more for upgrading their employees than for apprenticeship training, preferring to employ minors illegally at substandard wages.[80]

Educational Planning and Research

The relationship between education and the economy was a continuing concern of the National Front, which undertook a number of studies on human resources and planning—often in conjunction with international agencies.[81] Prior to 1968, the initiative in planning resided in the Ministry of Education. The Planning Office of the ministry, established in 1956 (the oldest such office in South America) formulated a five-year plan (1957-62) and forty-three other plans and programs up to 1967. The failure to implement the majority of these plans is reviewed in a 1968 evaluation by a UNESCO specialist, Sánchez Araya, and the partial nature of most of the education plans is critically analyzed in a 1968 study by Cuervo de Correal.[82]

The government of Lleras Restrepo promoted and relied on the technical expertise of the National Planning Department (DNP). In accordance with this policy, a Human Resources Unit was established within the department by 1962. Over the next six years the unit assumed a prominent role in the formulation of educational strategies and policies to integrate different levels and areas of the education system with one another and with national social and economic development plans.

The Human Resources Unit sponsored and conducted a number of excellent studies on the education system, examining its cost-effectiveness, its internal functioning (issues of retention and dropout), and its relation to employment.[83] During the period 1970-71, when the ministry focused national attention on inequities in access to education, DNP's Human Resources Unit developed and disseminated a new concept of the education system. (Its main elements are discussed later in this section.) The theoretical framework elaborated in the 1970-73 education plan set forth an agenda of action that continued beyond 1974.

During the National Front, the nature of educational planning thus changed from the more traditional forecasting and projection techniques of determining the number of classrooms and teachers, and the funds required for specified periods of time, to a broader decision-making approach best described by Benveniste.[84] With the new approach, educational planners formulate different images of the future (alternative ways of organizing the education system), design strategies to implement those images, and form coalitions of decision-makers to implement a plan and pass decisions down to different levels of the education system. The National Planning Department projected a twofold image of the future education system; a national capital-intensive sector where educational innovations would be adopted, tested, and diffused (i.e., the comprehensive high schools and Rural and Urban Development Centers); and a local grassroots level where educational experimentation and production of materials also would take place. In 1971, the Human Resources

Unit served as a hub for the formation and coordination of work teams to study the stage by stage implementation of reforms like the Rural Development Centers and the regional integration of university facilities. These working groups consisted of representatives from different divisions of the Ministry of Education, the National Planning Department, the Colombian Pedagogical Institute (ICOLPE), the Colombian Institute for the Development of Higher Education (ICFES), and the Colombian Educational Construction Institute (ICCE).

Nevertheless, the obstacles to effective coordination of efforts and implementation of these plans are considerable. The Rural Development Centers are a case in point. Human Resources recognized that in the early stages of this innovation, coordination of school construction with rural electrification and building programs would be a substantial accomplishment.[85]

These centers also illustrate the extent to which political factors override technical, planning considerations in so-called "educational reforms." While the National Planning Department carefully designed the geographic placement and coordination of services in the Rural Development Centers, the government on grounds of political expediency went ahead and opened a number of them without prior notice and adequate preparation. Similarly, comprehensive high schools were hurriedly inaugurated without the necessary teachers and equipment.

Throughout the period of the National Front, education reforms were initiated and terminated not according to a strategy of planned educational change—but primarily for political reasons. The chief consideration appears to have been whether or not an educational project would help strengthen the popularity of the National Front with broad sectors of the society. The failure of many reforms can not be attributed to the lack of an adequate administrative bureaucratic structure to implement decisions or to the lack of highly trained technical personnel in the different national educational agencies. The reforms failed because a fundamental change would have challenged the dominance of the existing elites in Colombia, and therefore was never intended. Within the political framework of the National Front, planning and research activities provided mechanisms for understanding the operations of the education system and making it work more efficiently.

INTERNATIONAL TECHNICAL ASSISTANCE AND EDUCATIONAL REFORM

The relative stability of the National Front provided a propitious climate for investments by international technical assistance agencies. They selected Colombia as a leading country for testing their melioristic approaches to educational change and national development. The magnitude of aid provided the donor agencies with sufficient leverage to influence substantially the direction and pace of educational reform. In many cases, the innovations supported by the international agencies were inappropriate for the educational problems of Colombia. There is, however, no evidence that, in the absence of such aid, the National Front would have devised an alternative education system suited to the needs of the majority of its people.

Among Latin American countries, Colombia has been a major recipient of foreign assistance. It is presently the "show case" country for a $13 million United Nations Development Program—UNESCO program of integral development which covers technical assistance in education, science, culture, and communication.[86] Between 1969 and 1972, it received more than $65 million in loans from US/AID.[87] And the World Bank provided more than $10 million in loans for the construction of comprehensive high schools during the same period.

An example of the influence technical assistance agencies wield in the education sector is the 1971 US/AID sector loan of $15 million—it represented roughly half the capital investment in education in the country for that year. US/AID required matching peso funds and determined the amount it considered adequate; it thus partially directed the use of Colombian funds in the education system. The National Planning Department, for example, proposed that loan funds be used to support the construction of public libraries in small cities. AID decided that cultural activities were not the same as educational activities, and therefore no provisions were made for public library development in the loan. According to one of the AID officials who drew up the loan, "The whole point of the sector loan is to induce Colombians to apply their own monies to areas which we think are priorities."

Throughout most of the 1960s, international technical assistance agencies had as their priority the expansion and improvement of higher education.[88] More than $25 million went to this elite level of the education system. By the late 1960s, emphasis had shifted to diversifying secondary education. Nineteen extremely costly comprehensive high schools were built patterned after the United States model. By the 1970s, funds shifted to rural development centers, teacher training, educational planning and research, and educational data management.

In an attempt to control foreign determination of Colombian priorities, the government in 1972 decreed that foreign assistance (officially designated as "international cooperation") had to accord with the national plan for public investment and form part of the regular budget. Authority over the use of foreign funds was centralized in the planning office and ministry of each sector. Prior to this governmental decree, international agencies had negotiated with individual institutions. As of 1972, the Human Resources Unit of the National Planning Department (DNP) assumed responsibility for negotiating with foreign aid donors on behalf of the entire education sector.

While the DNP has responsibility for directing the use of foreign funds, it also is dependent on them for its existence. The determination of where and how these funds will be used lends tremendous significance to the National Planning Department, increasing its leverage vis-à-vis other Colombian institutions which in the past attempted to circumvent its authority. According to the DNP officials, "they would be out of business if it weren't for the sector loans."

The overall effect of international loans and assistance has been to bolster the existing inequitable system. The external aid alleviated pressure on the National Front to develop an education system that was in line with the economic resources of the country and responsive to the pressing problems of its most disadvantaged groups. Instead, the National Front preferred to borrow foreign models requiring massive amounts of foreign money to sustain them in inhospitable soil.

CONCLUSIONS

What difference did the National Front make to the educational system of Colombia? In effect, the political structure of the Front was a coalition of two elitist dominated parties that made a pact in order to maintain political order and promote conditions favorable to the ruling class of Colombia. In this setting, education represented a power resource, along with economic dominion and control of the mass media, for strengthening elite rule.[89] As Dix notes in *Colombia: The Political Dimensions of Change*:

> In general, the effective denial of even a secondary education to the vast majority of Colombians has been one of the important underpinnings of a social and political system founded on a relatively closed elite .... Such denial of education restricts access to both prestige and skills, including those necessary for politics at the departmental or national levels. The availability of education to the upper class, on the other hand, provides it with the intellectual tools and cultural attributes to complement its reliance on land and *abolengo* [ancestry].[90]

The history of education in Colombia is a story of neglect of the poor and powerless. The government of Rojas Pinilla, which preceded the National Front, continued this tradition. The expansion in private and secondary education during the Rojas administration benefited primarily the most advantaged groups. During the National Front, the education system expanded rapidly. There was a flurry of activity and a proliferation of experimental educational programs. Educational innovations and technologies were imported from the advanced industrialized countries with alacrity. At the end of the sixteen-year period of coalitional rule, substantial inequities in access to education continued. As in the past, the rural areas and the low income groups were effectively excluded from the upper levels of the education system and from types of educational programs that would help them advance socially.

One of the ironies of the National Front is that the continuity and lack of uncertainty in the political structure had little beneficial impact on the orderliness and efficiency of educational planning and administration. The educational scene was characterized by a disarray of efforts; by enactment of educational policies that were often inconsistent; by the introduction of reforms that were seldom implemented. The lack of coherence in educational policies during this period is a reflection of the fact that education was essentially a secondary concern of the political leadership of the National Front. Basically there was no unity of purpose, no systematic effort to give priority to education, no sustained commitment to allocate adequate resources to develop the competencies of most Colombians—who then might possess the skills to question and attempt to change the existing social order.

In contrast with other Third World and Latin American countries, Colombia has not expended comparable resources and efforts to provide a basic education to the majority of its youth. Berry, in analyzing the educational performance of twenty-three countries in the mid-1960s, noted that although Colombia ranked ninth in income per capita, it ranked twenty-first in percentage of children between the ages of five and nine enrolled in primary and secondary school.[91] Two-thirds of the Colombian population receive only minimal education. At the same time, the children of the elite and middle class successfully use the education system to maintain their social status and gain entry to the most attractive jobs in the economy and decision-making roles in the public bureaucracies.

The nature and social functioning of the education system changed very little during the period between 1958 and 1974. The education system not only reflected, but helped perpetuate the stratification system in society. What can be said is that the National Front was remarkably adept at creating the image of change and of a benevolent government promoting social development through extension of educational benefits. At the end of the National Front the existing elitist educational and social systems were not only intact but strengthened, thus confirming the French adage:

> The more things change,
> The more they remain the same.

NOTES

1. Research for this study was supported by travel and study grants from Latin

American Studies and the President's Council on Social Science Research at Indiana University. Data were collected in Bogotá, in the summer of 1974. Although the chapter studies the period 1958-1974 generally, the most complete and reliable statistical information available covered the activities of the National Front up to 1971.
2. MEN, *La Educación Ante el Congreso* (Bogotá: Ministerio de Educación Nacional, 1973), preface.
3. Germán W. Rama and Rose K. Goldsen, "A Statistical Overview of Education in Colombia," mimeo (Bogotá, November, 1968), p. 11.
4. Ibid.
5. Marcelo Selowsky, "El Efecto del Desempleo y el Crecimiento Sobre la Rentabilidad de la Inversión Educacional," *Revista de Planeación y Desarrollo* (July 1969), Table XIX-A; for the period 1963-1966, pesos converted to dollars at the rate of 12 pesos to $1.00.
6. For a summary of National Census data for 1938, 1951, 1964, see Ivon Lebot, "Elementos para la Historia de la Educación en Colombia en el Siglo XX," *Boletín Mensual de Estadística*, Departamento Administrativo Nacional de Estadística (DANE), No. 249 (April 1972), p. 141.
7. DANE, *Encuesta de Hogares, 1970* (Bogotá, 1971), Table 5A; also see Lebot, "Historia Educación," p. 168. A significant change is found in the literacy statistics for men and women. For the first time, illiteracy among the youngest population was higher among males than females.
8. MEN, *Educación Congreso*, p. 52.
9. MEN, *Estadísticas Educativas* (Bogotá, July 1975).
10. Lebot, "Historia Educación," p. 144. The percentage figures are 64 and 59.5 respectively.
11. See Guillermo García Niño, *Sociología de la Educación en Colombia* (Bogotá, 1973), p. 29.
12. Lebot, "Historia Educación," p. 132.
13. García Niño, *Sociología Educación*, p. 100.
14. Gonzalo Cataño, Elvia Caro, and Fidel Salazar, *La Educación Rural en Boyacá* (Tunja, 1971).
15. Cited in García Niño, *Sociología Educación*, p. 32.
16. MEN, *Educación Congreso*, p. 55.
17. The fact that over 90 percent of secondary and higher education institutions are located in urban areas further explains the disproportionately lower share of the national education budget allocated to the rural areas.
18. Lebot, "Historia Educación," p. 144.
19. Ibid., p. 145.
20. Ibid., p. 144.
21. Ibid., Table F6, p. 167.
22. Educación Congreso, p. 335.
23. IBRD, "Country Report," mimeo (Bogotá, 1970), p. 26.
24. Jaime Rodríguez Forero, "Características Socioeconómicas del Bachillerato Colombiano," in Gonzalo Cataño, ed. *Educación y Sociedad en Colombia*, (Bogotá, 1973), pp. 178-79.
25. MEN, *Educación Congreso*, p. 178.
26. Under the traditional system of secondary instruction the university-preparatory schools and the technical-vocational schools were rigidly separated. In most cases students from the latter programs were not entitled to continue with their studies in universities.

27. For further discussion of the comprehensive high school program, see, for example, Eduardo Umaña Luna, *Los Derechos Humanos en Colombia* (Bogotá, 1974), pp. 322-323; and Rodolfo Low Maus, *Compendio del Sistema Educativo Colombiano* (Bogotá, 1971), pp. 61-63.
28. ICFES, *Estadísticas Universitarias: Población Estudiantil* (Bogotá, May 1974), p. 1.
29. Ibid.
30. MEN, *Estadísticas Educativas 1972: Primaria Oficial* (Bogotá, March 1974), p. 48.
31. For further discussion of the doctrinaire positions taken by Conservatives and Liberals on the issue of the role of the Catholic Church in education, see Robert H. Dix, *Colombia: The Political Dimensions of Change* (New Haven, Conn., 1967), pp. 233 and 235.
32. Ivon Lebot, "Organización y Funcionamiento del Sistema Educativo Colombiano," DANE, *Boletín Mensual de Estadística*, no. 243 (October 1971), pp. 113-15.
33. For a synopsis of reforms see Rodolfo Low Maus, *Compendio Educativo*, pp. 115-22.
34. Cited in Lebot, "Organización y Funcionamiento," p. 113.
35. ICOLPE, *Anteproyecto de la Ley General de Educación* (Bogotá, 1971), p. xvii.
36. ICETEX, *Informe Labores 1970-1973* (Bogotá, 1974), pp. 42-49.
37. MEN, *Educación Congreso*, p. 55.
38. Jean Pierre Jallade, *Public Expenditures on Education and Income Distribution in Colombia* (Baltimore, Maryland, 1974) pp. 27-28, 40.
39. W. Lee Hansen, "Rates of Return to Investment in Schooling in the United States," in *Economics of Education*, volume I, ed. Mark Blaug (Middlesex, England, 1971), p. 141.
40. Ibid., p. 139.
41. See M. Selowsky, *The Effect of Unemployment and Growth on the Rate of Return to Education: The Case of Colombia*, (Cambridge, Mass., 1969); T.P. Schultz, *Returns to Education in Bogota, Colombia* (Santa Monica, Cal., 1968); and C.R.S. Dougherty, "El Futuro de la Educación Colombiana: Proyecciones y Prioridades," *Revista de Planeación y Desarrollo*, 3 (March 1971), pp. 1-49. The average rates of return are cited from IBRD, "Country Report," p. 32.
42. ICFES, *Carreras Tecnológicas* (Bogotá, 1974), Table 3, p. xxv in appendices.
43. Cataño, "Escolaridad y Movilidad," p. 189; it should be noted that Cataño does not estimate what percentage of the general public belongs to the lower, middle, and upper classes.
44. Germán W. Rama, "Origen Social de la Población Universitaria," in Gonzalo Cataño, ed. *Educación y Sociedad en Colombia* (Bogotá, 1972), p. 215; the article first appeared in Universidad Nacional de Colombia, *Revista de la Dirección Cultural* III (April-August 1966), pp. 141-65.
45. Ibid., p. 213.
46. Among the decentralized institutions created or redefined by 1968 Presidential Decrees are ICFES (Colombian Institute for the Development of Higher Education), ICOLPE (Colombian Pedagogical Institute), ICETEX (Colombian Institute for Educational Credit and Technical Studies Abroad), ICCE (Colombian Educational Construction Institute), and institutions in the related areas of sports (COLDEPORTES), culture (COLCULTURA), and sciences (COLCIENCIAS). See Low Maus, *Compendio Educativo*, pp. 132-33, for a list of enabling legislation.
47. At approximately the same time, in response to widespread university student

unrest, legislation was introduced to reform the system of governance in the public universities. The legislation in large part was designed to diminish the presence of representatives of the public sector, the clergy, and the business sector on the University Councils, and increase the representation by constituent members of the universities.

48. *El Espacio*, (Bogotá, September 18, 1971), p. 4; cited in MEN, *Educación Congreso*, p. 2.
49. FER, *Fondos Educativos Regionales*.
50. Mark Hanson, "Reform and Governance in the Ministry of Education: The Case of Colombia," *International Review of Education* 20 (1970):161.
51. MEN, *La Reforma de la Organización Educativa*, Serie: Transformación Educativa No. 3 (Bogotá, 1969), p. 7; cited in Hanson, "Reform and Governance," p. 162.
52. Hanson, "Reform and Governance," p. 164.
53. ICOLPE, "Reunión de Secretarios de Educación de la Costa Atlántica" (Bogota, November 15, 1970), p. 6; cited in Hanson, ibid., p. 165.
54. Hanson, "Reform and Governance," p. 166.
55. Lebot, "Organización y Funcionamiento," p. 79.
56. Ibid., p. 129.
57. USAID Mission to Colombia, *Colombia: Education Sector Assessment* (Bogotá, May 1973), p. 104; cited in Hanson, "Reform and Governance," p. 160.
58. Lebot, "Organización y Funcionamiento," p. 85.
59. Lebot, ibid., p. 130 for 1960 data; and UNESCO, *Yearbook of Statistics* (Paris, 1973), pp. 418-19 for 1971 data.
60. Lebot, ibid., p. 128 for 1957 and 1958 data; and UNESCO, ibid., for 1971 data.
61. Lebot, ibid., p. 130 for 1958 and 1965 data; and UNESCO, ibid., for 1970 data.
62. Daniel Arango, *Informe del Ministro de Educación al Congreso Nacional* (Bogotá, July 1966), p. 16; cited in Lebot, "Organización y Funcionamiento," p. 86.
63. Lebot, "Organización y Funcionamiento," p. 87.
64. Ibid., p. 88.
65. It should be noted that the UNESCO criterion for literacy of four years of formal schooling is not empirically established.
66. *Presupuesto Nacional* 1970, p. 210; cited in Rodolfo Low Maus, *Compendio Educativo*, pp. 95 and 128.
67. Oficina de Planeamiento Educativo, *La Educación en Colombia 1960-1968*, (Bogotá, October 1972), pp. 182-83. (*Anexo*).
68. Ibid., p. 186.
69. Umaña Luna, *Derechos Humanos*, pp. 325-26.
70. In 1971, Capacitación Popular turned its attention toward providing a degree from secondary school through a combination of correspondence materials, radio and television broadcasts, and meetings with instructors in community education centers.
71. SENA, *Servicio Nacional de Aprendizaje*; parallel institutions in other Latin American countries include SENAI (Brazil), SENATI (Peru), INCAP (Chile), INCE (Venezuela), and INA (Costa Rica).
72. Oficina de Planeamiento Educativo, *Educación Colombia*, p. 211.
73. Lebot, "Historia Educación," p. 139.
74. Umaña Luna, *Derechos Humanos*, p. 333.
75. Dudley Seers, *Hacia El Pleno Empleo* (Bogotá, 1970), p. 258.

76. Jeffrey M. Puryear, "A Cost-Benefit Analysis of the SENA Industrial Apprenticeship Program," p. 28; paper read to the Annual Meeting of the Comparative and International Education Society, San Francisco, March 27, 1975. [Also see his "Comparative Systems of Occupational Training in Colombia: The National Apprenticeship Service" (unpublished Ph.D. dissertation, University of Chicago, 1973).]
77. Puryear, "Cost-Benefit Analysis," p. 27.
78. Ibid., p. 30.
79. See testimony of the representative of the Armed Forces before the evaluation committee of the International Labor Organization; discussed in Umaña Luna, *Derechos Humanos*, p. 334.
80. Ibid., p. 333.
81. For a list of these studies, see Lebot, "Organización y Funcionamiento," p. 93. It is worthy of note that a number of important studies were conducted in conjunction with visiting researchers from the Harvard University Development Advisory Service. Among these researchers were M. Selowsky and C.R.S. Dougherty.
82. R. Sánchez Araya, *Colombia—Planeamiento de la Educación* (Paris, 1967); and Rosa Amalia Cuervo de Correal, *Análisis Estructural del Sistema Educativo Colombiano y Bases para su Planeación Integral* (Bogotá, 1968).
83. For a bibliography of studies by the National Planning Department, see Lebot, "Organización y Funcionamiento," p. 152.
84. Guy Benveniste, *Bureaucracy and National Planning: A Sociological Study in Mexico* (New York, 1970).
85. The Ministry of Education also took the initiative in establishing a National Council for Rural Social Development consisting of representatives from the Ministries of Agriculture, Health, and Government (Community Action Programs). The council is responsible for integration of policies and programs for the rural area; see Departmento Nacional de Planeación, *Fundamentos y Objetivos de la Política Educativa* (Bogotá, 1973), p. 27.
86. MEN, *Plan de Desarrollo para el Sector Educativo, Programa Colombia*—PNUD-UNESCO (Bogotá, 1974), pp. 73-78.
87. The loans are paid back at 2 percent per annum during the first ten years, and 3 percent thereafter for a period up to forty years.
88. According to the IBRD, *Country Report*, p. 29, between 1960 and 1966 the principal assistance donors were US/AID—$8.4 million, the Ford, Rockefeller, and Kellog Foundations—$18 million, the Inter-American Development Bank—$15.6 million, the United Nations Development Program and related agencies—$5.5 million.
89. Robert Dix, *Colombia*, p. 389.
90. Ibid., p. 48.
91. Albert Berry, "Some Implications of Elitist Rule for Economic Development in Colombia," in Gustav Ranis, ed. *Government and Economic Development*, (New Haven, 1971), p. 18.

Chapter 14

Population Policy under the National Front

William Paul McGreevey

This chapter explores the performance of the National Front governments in dealing with a specific policy issue during its accession. That issue had many ramifications and brought into play a number of special interests and political forces which might not have received the attention of the public sector under a different form of political organization.

Population policy, when broadly defined, refers to those government actions (or inactions) affecting the rate of growth and physical distribution of the governed population. Such actions may directly affect fertility, mortality, and migration; indirectly they may affect the age composition, dependency status, and labor force participation of the population. Population policy should not be so narrowly defined as simply a plan of fertility reduction by means of publicly-subsidized family planning programs. Nor should it be so broadly construed as to be confused with all government actions that affect the process of economic development and the accumulation of human capital. Because of the interaction of fertility policy and migration policy during the National Front, population policy cannot be reduced to fertility concerns alone. A government's population policy may be deduced from its allocation of the resources that influence the growth and distribution of population. These resources should be conceived to include the moral suasion of political leaders, whose public statements may influence social behavior. A public statement in favor of slower population growth may imply no direct costs of government programs, but it does make use of a political leader's most fundamental resource—the support and goodwill of the electorate. Thus both moral attitudes and the more conventional financial resources provide the measurable index of a population policy.

Under the leadership of National Front President Carlos Lleras Restrepo, Colombia moved decisively to deal with problems of rapid population growth. The succeeding government of Misael Pastrana Borrero continued the policy and intensified attention to the problems of migration and urban growth.

However, after the National Front ended in August 1974, the government of Alfonso López Michelsen said nothing on the population policy issue. Some observers have suggested that failure to state a policy, represents a reversal of the active policy of the National Front. It is perhaps too early to predict any implications for population policy and population growth. However, the stance of the first post-National Front government supports the hypothesis that the political arrangement between Liberals and Conservatives under the National Front made an openly stated policy easier to sustain than would have been possible under terms of political competition. In that respect at least the National Front made a big difference in policy formulation and implementation on a major issue. Had it not been for the National Front arrangement, the government of Colombia might have moved no further in the population policy arena than have the governments of Venezuela, Ecuador, Chile, and Peru—countries marked by widely different political styles, but which nonetheless have shied away from confronting population growth and rapid urbanization. Noting that prior to the National Front, Colombian parties were prone to give paramount importance to religious issues in their confrontations, it is likely that under competitive conditions, substantial dissension might have arisen over some aspects of population policy.

NATIONAL PLANNING

Some idea of the progress in policy-making under the National Front may be gained from a comparison of where the nation stood in 1958 on the eve of the Front and where it stood in mid-1974 at the end of the sixteen-year arrangement.

Until 1958, the government of Colombia had yet to produce a coherent development plan. Beginning that year, however, a trickle of planning documents began; and it turned into a torrent under Lleras Restrepo and Pastrana Borrero. From Cepal-inspired global programming that touched only public-sector investment activities, the plan documents evolved into complex tools of economic management and strategy. The Plan Cuatrienal de Inversiones Públicas Nacionales, 1961-1964, which carries a cover date of December 1960, was the first fruit of Law 19 of 1958, which established the Consejo Nacional de Política Económica y Planeación and the Departamento Administrativo de Planeación y Servicios Técnicos. (This document would perhaps not have been published except for the requirement in the Charter of Punta del Este that all countries seeking to participate in the Alliance for Progress should prepare ten-year plans for development.) The four-year investment plan was expanded to cover a decade and served as the basis for the first country review under the Alliance for Progress (Consejo Nacional, 1962). It also provided the written document necessary to bolster Colombia's position at that time as showcase of the Alliance.

That original document, prepared under the leadership of Edgar Gutiérrez Castro, who headed the planning office under both Lleras presidencies, was a good work for its time. Subsequent works published by the Departamento Nacional de Planeación (DNP) naturally grew more sophisticated methodologically, more comprehensive, and more practically oriented toward policy decisions.

In his review of Colombian planning documents, Guillermo Perry points out that policies aimed at long-run effects—those concerned with population and the conservation of natural resources—did not have a central role in the early planning documents that influenced the first two presidencies of the National Front.[1] More specifically:

> A population policy does not appear in the first planning documents. The study conducted by Father Lebret, as noted previously, considers rapid population growth to be a positive factor. The 1950 World Bank study limits itself to pointing out that population growth is the major development problem. Operation Colombia simply indicates that application of the recommended actions would facilitate the execution of a population policy . . . . The Ten-Year Plan points out the need for such a policy, but one appears—and then only vaguely delineated—in the plans of 1969, the International Labor Organization's report, *Towards Full Employment*, the 1970 plan, and in *Guidelines for a New Strategy* (1971).[2]

Long term planning evolved under the National Front only after the planning office had begun dealing effectively with short term considerations, an ordering of priorities consistent with Keynes's stricture that in the long run we are all dead.

In the mid-1960s, the middle period of the National Front, universities and private research groups began to produce analytical studies of considerable importance in setting out the intellectual justification for the formulation of a population policy.[3] Because of the interaction between these private research groups and the planning apparatus of the government, the work of these private scholars gradually filtered into the planning process of the public sector.

In January 1969 the DNP began publishing a scientific quarterly *Revista de Planeación y Desarrollo*, which disseminates DNP staff study findings on the development process. Among the important articles that appeared in this journal is "La población en Colombia: Diagnóstico y política."[4] That article and a theoretical piece in the same number prepared by Alvaro López Toro contributed to the scientific basis for a population policy.[5] Such a report was possible because DNP and the private research community had gained high levels of professional competence. The evolution of plan documents continued through *Las cuatro estrategias*, published in 1972 and prepared while Dr. Roberto Arenas Bonilla directed the DNP. The 127 pages of the principal section (*criterios generales*) contain not a single table! There may not be another plan document quite like *Las cuatro estrategias*. Whatever its critics may say, it represents a higher level of planning maturity than its predecessors. It also evinces the awareness of a need for an explicit population policy concerning fertility, mortality, and migration.

The special characteristics of Colombian geography, particularly the fact that most people still live at high altitudes rather than near the sea coast, has led to the growth of a number of urban centers and a less intensive concentration in a single city than one finds in the rest of Latin America. Nonetheless, the four largest cities have in recent decades been gaining on the intermediate cities. In 1918 the four largest cities accounted for 56 percent of the population of the nineteen largest *municipios*. Largely as a result of intensive migration into those large cities, their share rose to 62 percent of the large-city population by 1964.[6] The 1973 census, soon to be available, will reveal still greater concentration in the largest cities. In 1958 there was little recognition of the increasing concentration of the population in the major cities; hence few considered a policy of decentralization to be necessary. As late as 1965 interviews with government officials revealed that no explicit policy of urban and regional development had yet been devised.[7] The Instituto de Crédito Territorial (ICT), which holds major responsibility for public housing, did not appear to take into account the influence of its actions on population distribution. During the Lleras Restrepo government, however, a concerted effort was developed to plot the trajectory of future urban and regional growth and to see whether some policy was needed to influence that trajectory. The elaborate, multivolumed *modelo de regionalización* was developed within DNP by the Unit for Urban and Regional Development with inputs by other units. Sixteen volumes of studies were circulated internally as part of the model. Many aspects of the intermediate-cities strategy—a plan for the development of some thirty cities other than Bogotá, Medellín, Cali, and Barranquilla—were developed in conjunction with the model.[8] In the early 1970s, much external financial support, particularly from AID, was channeled through the intermediate-cities effort. A unique program of *comisiones volantes* or flying commissions was devised during the incumbency of Dr. Roberto Arenas Bonilla as director of the DNP. Professional staff members of the DNP in Bogotá would fly as a group to designated intermediate cities, conduct a rapid evaluation of local bottlenecks to development and assist local officials in the preparation of project proposals for financial assistance. This technical work helped overcome the shortage of professional skills in many of the intermediate cities.[9]

From a situation of no policy at all, Colombia thus moved to a fairly comprehensive urban and regional policy by the close of the National Front period.

POPULATION GROWTH AND POPULATION POLICY

The beginning of a population policy may be seen as a public response to long term structural features of Colombian population dynamics. These had been imbalanced by the impact of external technology—in this case, public health technology that reduced some major health hazards. Malaria-eradication programs, measures to reduce infant mortality, and potable water programs tended to reduce somewhat the incidence of dysentery and other infectious diseases. From its inception, Colombian society must traditionally have been pronatalist, i.e., it encouraged high fertility to compensate for brutally high death rates. However, adjustments to national census data, beginning with the 1890 census, indicate that from the beginning of this century up to the 1960s, the birth rate has been rising. Collver's (1965) estimates indicate that the standardized birth rate per thousand population rose from 40.9 in the intercensal period 1912-18 to 45.4 in the intercensal period 1951-64.[10] Over the same period, the average life expectancy increased from 30.5 years (1910) to 48.5 years (1950); the most intensive improvement in life expectancy was made after 1940.[11] These diverging trends of birth and death rate caused an acceleration in the rate of population growth that lasted well into the middle of the National Front period.

In 1958 rapid population growth would probably not have been listed on any Colombian policy-maker's agenda for action. No one knew for certain how fast the population was growing. As late as 1962, a United Nations review, *Some Aspects of Population Growth in Colombia*, estimated the rate of population growth to be about 2.5 percent per annum.[12] That is a rapid rate of population growth, to be sure, but well below the 3 percent per annum which in fact prevailed in the 1951-64 intercensal period.[13]

Some more recent data on fertility trends in the 1960s indicate a decline of the total fertility rate (roughly translated as the number of children a woman will have throughout her complete fertile period) of 14.3 percent or about one less live birth per woman in the years 1960 through 1968.[14] Until the mid-1960s, the rate of population growth was increasing; since then, it has fallen off so that by the close of the National Front epoch, the increase was estimated to be in the range of 2.7 to 2.9 percent per annum.[15] Private decisions thus seem to have been already inclining toward slower population growth; nonetheless, population policy was still a public issue: should the government of Colombia state publicly its population policy and undertake action favoring smaller families and slower population growth?

No government did so in the first half of the National Front. However, Alberto Lleras Camargo agreed after his incumbency to address an international meeting on population held at Cali, Colombia, in August 1965. On that occasion he risked the wrath of the ecclesiastical hierarchy by stating publicly that the government (of which he was no longer an official member) should foster a slower rate of population growth.

His views gradually worked their way into the Liberal part of the National Front consortium. During the presidency of Carlos Lleras Restrepo (1966-1970) the National Front did express itself in favor of slower population growth. Lleras Restrepo was the only Latin American president to sign the United Nations Declaration on Population on Human Rights Day, December 10, 1966. Four months earlier the Ministry of Health had signed a contract with ASCOFAME (Colombian Association of Medical Faculties) for a program of training and research that included family planning as an important component in addition to maternal and child health.[16] The last National Front government, headed by Pastrana Borrero, a Conservative, continued support for a population policy. *Las cuatro estrategias*, the 1972 plan document that gives detail to Pastrana Borrero's Frente Social, expresses clearly the government's population policy.

Colombia is the only country on the continent of South America to make an explicit commitment to slow the rate of population growth.[17] In contrast, Brazil remains pronatalist, perhaps because of its military government's hegemonic ambitions. Argentina recently expressed a desire for a more rapid population growth via higher birth rate and immigration.[18] Oral contraceptive pills are to be available in Argentina only on the basis of a prescription signed by three medical authorities. The age-old rivalry between these two South American powers may explain their population policies. However, the fact that the National Front could have behaved in a manner so different from neighboring governments is remarkable and worthy of study.

In 1958 there were no officially-sponsored family planning programs in Colombia. As late as 1963, when my own son was born in Bogotá and my

Table 1
Maternal and Child Health and Fertility-Related Programs by Executing Agency, Source and Amount of Financing, US Dollars and Colombian Pesos, 1972

Executing Agency	Source of Funds	US Dollars (millions)	Pesos (millions)
Ministry of Health*	National Government		15.0
	WHO and PAHO		19.4
ASCOFAME	Population Council	1.6	
	Ford Foundation	0.1	
	Milbank Memorial Fund	0.1	
	Rockefeller Foundation	———	
Sub-total		1.9	37.7
Population Reference Bureau (PRB)	Ford Foundation	0.2	
	Population Council	———	
	Rockefeller Foundation	———	
Sub-total		0.3	5.2
Profamilia*			21.0
Universidad del Valle	Rockefeller Foundation	0.2	
	Population Council	———	
	Milbank Memorial Fund	———	
Sub-total		0.2	3.5
Universidad de los Andes	Population Council	0.2	3.2
Universidad de Antioquia*	Population Council		5.0
DANE (Proyecto CIMED)	AID		4.5
	National Government		0.3
United Nations, Magdalena Project			1.3
Swedish International Development Agency			1.2
TOTAL†			117.7

Notes:
———less than US $50,000. Total and subtotals do not add, as per source.
*Data for the Ministry of Health, Profamilia and the Universidad de Antioquia refer to 1971.
†Total does not include FEPAFEM, the Pan American Federation of Faculties of Medicine.

Source: Departamento Nacional de Planeación, *Las cuatro estrategias* (1972: 199-200).

wife wished to have access to family planning devices with the objective of child spacing, the then-available technology was available only through upper-class doctors. Only in the past several years have such services reached significant numbers of women. In 1967 about 35,000 women accepted family planning services from one or another of the private clinics supported in large

Table 2
External Population Assistance to Colombia, 1965-72

Donor	Middle Man	Executing Agency	Purpose	US dollars ($ millions)
AID	University of North Carolina	DANE	T & R	
AID	IPPF	Profamilia	Programs	1.4
AID	Population Council	ASCOFAME	T & R	1.4
	Population Council	PAFAMS	T & R	0.45
AID		PAFAMS	T & R	0.3
AID	Pathfinder	Profamilia	Programs	0.3
AID	Pan American Health Organ.	Min. Health	M C H	1.4
AID			E I C	0.6
AID	Celade		T & R	0.4
Ford Fdn.		U del Valle	T & R	0.025
Ford Fdn.		ASCOFAME	T & R	0.812
Rocke-feller		U del Valle	T & R	0.144
SIDA			Commodities	0.082
IDRC		ASCOFAME	T & R	0.013
AID	None	Unstated	Programs	7.45
Total, Estimated, All Donors, 1965-72				14.776

Source: AID Office of Population, Population Program Assistance (1972: 146-48). For estimating procedure, see text.

Notes:
T & R - Training and Research
DANE - Departamento Administrativo Nacional de Estadística
IPPF - International Planned Parenthood Federation
PAFAMS - Pan American Federation of Medical Schools
ASCOFAME - Colombian Association of Faculties of Medicine
Celade - Latin American Demographic Center
SIDA - Swedish International Development Agency
IDRC - International Development Research Centre (Ottawa, Canada)
EIC - Education, Information and Communication
MCH - Maternal and Child Health

part by external donors. That number had grown to about 164,000 by 1972, but it still constituted only about three to four percent of the total number of Colombian women in the fertile age groups.[19] About half the married women interviewed in Bogotá in mid-1973 were practicing some form of contraception—quite a change in a decade.[20] Like other social innovations, however, modern technology of fertility control moved but slowly into rural and small-town areas of Colombia.[21] There is a clear tendency for more educated and more urbanized women to accept family planning services and to have lower fertility.[22] Despite the outcry of genocide and the purported desire of the rich to cut down on the numbers of the poor, there is every indication that family planning programs are used by all social strata in Colombia.

Foreign financial aid to family planning may be estimated by examining two tables detailing external support in the population field. Table 1, taken from *Las cuatro estrategias*, shows total contributions for 1972 both from external sources and from the Ministry of Health. (A note to the table indicates that data for certain entities apply to 1971).Total support for reduction of infant and child mortality and for "*servicios en aspectos de fecundidad*" was nearly 118 million pesos or about US $5.9 million, with the bulk of support coming from external sources.

A World Bank study has estimated net public capital movements into Colombia in 1970 to have totaled US $320 million.[23] Population assistance therefore may have constituted only about 2 percent of total external assistance.

In Table 2, estimates appear of external assistance in the population field over the period 1965-72. Prior to 1965, assistance was relatively unimportant; at most, a few conferences and a little research were sponsored by international donors. Since 1965 AID has provided assistance through middleman donors to a variety of recipients in Colombia. This assistance is the hardest to trace. Estimates depend on the assumption that assistance by some middlemen (University of North Carolina, IPPF, Population Council and Pathfinder) is equal to a quarter of their total Latin American regional programs as identified in AID (1971, 1972). The estimates also include a lump sum equal to one-fourth of the country programs listed in the source mentioned. Other donor programs are then added on as reported in the 1971 AID report.

The total indicated in Table 2 for population assistance from 1965 to 1972 comes to nearly U.S. $15 million. This figure may constitute an overestimate as one-fourth of all Latin American assistance that could not be made country-specific was allocated to Colombia—a proportion that may be too high. Thus, assistance would appear to be *at the most* U.S. $15 million or only about U.S. $2 million annually over the period considered. If total external support in 1972 was U.S. $5 million (as may be estimated from Table 1), then external support must have been growing substantially in the late 1960s and early 1970s. Such a pattern is consistent with total AID support in Latin America to population activities; in fiscal year 1968 total Latin American support was U.S. $7.9 million, rising to US $15.2 million in fiscal year 1971.[24] The distribution of external support by recipient is sufficiently similar in the two tables to conclude that these two independent sources are in basic agreement about the size and extent of the population program and the level of external support.

Family planning and broader population programs are small potatoes in the overall picture of external development assistance. By 1972, in a country of

23 million people, 40 physicians were working full-time for the provision of family planning services. They were assisted by another 660 doctors working part-time, and 1,150 paramedics plus 2,300 rural health promoters. A total of 573 health facilities of all types included family planning among the services offered.[25] Significant progress had been made since the inception of the National Front.

TWO MODELS OF POPULATION POLICY DEVELOPMENT

Without doing too much damage to reality one can distinguish two avenues by which population policy developed in Colombia. One depends on the influence of physicians on policy, the other on social scientists and *técnicos*. Both groups had significant roles to play in the formulation of Colombian population policy. However, their intellectual origins and forms of attack on the population problem are different enough to deserve separate discussion.

Members of the medical profession have direct contact with the problems associated with unwanted pregnancies. They observe in their daily practice high incidence of induced abortion, often with serious negative health consequences for mother and child alike. Through their contact with and administration of hospital systems, they become aware of the high costs of dealing with ill-performed abortions outside the circle of professional medical practice since often the victims of unskilled abortionists must come to the hospital for lifesaving help. It was not always so, however. As J. Mayone Stycos has pointed out in his general review of attitudes about population growth in Colombia, both physicians and technicians traditionally ignored population: "Thus, while the economists were busy saying that birth control was not related to economic development, the physicians were busily adding that it was not related to health either. Only when they began to see it as a medical and social problem did they begin to change. The change occurred largely because of the increasing evidence that induced abortion, clearly a medical problem, was becoming of epidemic proportions—an incidence not only taxing hospital facilities but demonstrating a demand on the part of the lower classes for fertility control."[26]

One eminent Colombian specialist on population, Dr. Juan B. Londoño, when on temporary assignment in El Salvador, conducted a cost-effectiveness analysis of the alternatives of providing family planning service as against caring for unwanted pregnancies and tending to misperformed abortions.[27] His analysis demonstrated an awareness in the medical profession of the costs and benefits of high fertility.[28] Members of the medical profession are also aware of the serious economic difficulties that a family with many children can have. Thus they see the necessity of providing modern means of fertility control to prevent such strain.

In Colombia, ASCOFAME and such leaders of the medical profession as Hernán Mendoza Hoyos, Ramiro Delgado, and Guillermo López Escobar played a major role in bringing the population problem to the attention of government officials. They operated through the leading medical institutions and universities to build support for a population policy. Their efforts were in turn supported by external entities such as International Planned Parenthood Federation (IPPF), Pathfinder, and the Population Council, which have concerned themselves with the provision of family planning services on a voluntary basis.

Other professionals such as economists, sociologists, demographers, and urban planners were becoming aware of the problems associated with rapid population growth. In contrast to the medical doctors, who became aware of the problem through direct person-to-person contact with their patients, these professionals became aware of other problems: the burgeoning costs of supplying public services in major cities; the reality of unemployment and underemployment; the failure of the agrarian reform program to provide a solution to poverty and landlessness in the countryside; and the interrelationship between rural and urban problems that manifests itself in rapid rural-to-urban migration. Their perceptions were of aggregate national, regional and municipal problems associated with rapid population growth. Some critical figures among the social scientist/*técnicos* were Alvaro López Toro, Colombia's most eminent economist-demographer; Ramiro Cardona, director of migration studies for ASCOFAME and for a time of the Unit for Urban and Regional Development of the DNP; and Germán Bravo, head of the Socio-Demographic Division of DNP and also secretary for the Colombian Population Council. But no individual was more central to the formulation of population policy in Colombia than was Lauchlin Currie.

Currie headed the first World Bank mission to Colombia in 1949. The report of that mission observed that "population is completely out of balance with other factors in Colombia. If it were merely a question of utilizing existing resources, including land, more efficiently and increasing capital equipment, especially power-generating facilities, the problem would be relatively simple. The difficulty arises from the fact that while these other things are being done, population itself continues to increase."[29] Thus Currie himself was among the earliest of the professionals to call attention to rapid population growth.

However, he was at that time an outsider sent by an international organization. His liking for the country led him to settle in Colombia. Building on a distinguished career as a key advisor to the Roosevelt government in the United States, he played an advisory role with each of the Colombian Governments from the early 1950s onward, with but few exceptions. His initial emphasis in the World Bank report had been on the need for expansion of infrastructure—hydroelectric power and internal transportation. Huge investments in these two utilities were completed and brought into service throughout the 1950s and 1960s because of the World Bank's report and subsequent studies of specific projects. One result was the acceleration of internal migration and increased concentration of population in the four largest cities that were served by improved transport and power supply.[30]

Currie perceived the impact of the growing availability of infrastructure on the spatial pattern of growth. However, his Operation Colombia, originally prepared as a government memorandum in 1960,[31] called for still more rapid migration into the cities than was occurring at the beginning of the National Front. He favored massive urban housing construction as a way to create jobs as well as shelter for the new urban arrivals. Operation Colombia would have relocated many women from rural areas where they have high fertility to urban areas where fertility is much lower.[32] The overall plan was to move Colombia quickly to an economic structure that was urbanized, industrialized, and highly efficient in agriculture.

The concentration of activities generated by World Bank loans would then have been complemented by the Currie plan—Operation Colombia, which was not implemented by the Lleras Camargo government. But even without Operation Colombia, urban populations grew at a dizzying rate. The population of Bogotá more than doubled in the sixteen years of the National Front. The same was true of most other cities. It was perhaps appropriate that Currie, the World Bank consultant who in the 1950s started the rush to the cities with cheap power and transport, should be the government of Colombia consultant who in the 1970s called for a slowdown in the rate of growth of Bogotá and helped to develop a strategy for more balanced urban growth. He served as a board member overseeing the Bogotá Study done by Llewelyn, Davis and Company in 1973; the study advised limiting private automobiles to no more than 13 percent of families, a critical decision that could limit the city's future growth. A financial plan he helped develop in DNP marshalled private savings to increase private, middle-class housing in the cities. The specific effects of this vast expansion on population distribution are not yet clear.

Both the medical and the *técnico* approach were necessary elements to bring the population problem to the attention of policy-makers. In the preparation for each electoral campaign the presidential candidates formed advisory groups of specialists who prepared policy papers on major issues. These *comités operativos* in which several physicians participated set the stage for the formulation of Carlos Lleras Restrepo's population policy.[33] The committees were of equal importance during Misael Pastrana Borrero's campaign for the presidency. In both cases medical specialists were able to bring the weight of their community prestige and their knowledge of the conditions that would require an explicit population policy in order to achieve the government's development objectives. To a large extent the medical leaders brought the social scientist/*técnico* community around to a perception of the population problem and secured their participation in the formulation and execution of a population policy. The *técnicos* had the signal advantage of direct participation in the planning process by means of their occupational activities and their interaction with the DNP, which developed the necessary policy documents. There are numerous instances of faculty and staff of major universities who took positions in the DNP, and of DNP staffers who, on completion of a term of government service, returned to the universities and research institutions. This continuing interaction established personal confidence in the policy relevance of applied research done by the universities and research institutions on population problems.[34]

Whatever the views of special interest groups, even those that believe they have a clear vision of national problems, they always face the problem of bringing policy-makers to agree with them on the diagnosis and prescription for action. Perhaps the only successful way to persuade the policy-makers to formulate a policy, particularly in an area so potentially sensitive as population, is to demonstrate to them that it is in their own interest to do so, and that inaction will be more costly than action. In this regard the *técnicos* were probably more important than the physicians.

CONVINCING THE POLITICIANS

During the years of the National Front the coalition of Liberal and Conservative parties had a quasi-monopoly on public offices. No one could be elected to office except from the list of candidates put up by the two traditional parties. With the outcome of elections virtually decided by the National Front monopoly, voter participation dropped to a low level as detailed in Losada's paper elsewhere in this volume. Abstention was particularly evident in the elections held in the early 1960s.[35] Later in the decade a third party, ANAPO (National Popular Alliance), headed by former dictator General Gustavo Rojas Pinilla, managed to place its candidates on both Liberal and Conservative lists, thus gaining access to public office.

In the elections of 1970, Rojas, as the ANAPO candidate for president, came close to defeating the National Front candidate, Misael Pastrana Borrero. Rojas Pinilla's electoral showing was most impressive in the largest cities, many of which he won by sizable margins over Pastrana Borrero. Even before the 1970 elections, it must have been apparent to many National Front politicians that the Front was weak in the cities. But the ANAPO challenge surely played a substantial role in Pastrana Borrero's decision to develop the Frente Social, a broad statement of policy objectives aimed at offering a more equitable distribution of the benefits of economic development. If the

Figure 1
Colombian Newspaper Articles on Population and Family Planning, per Month, 1965-67

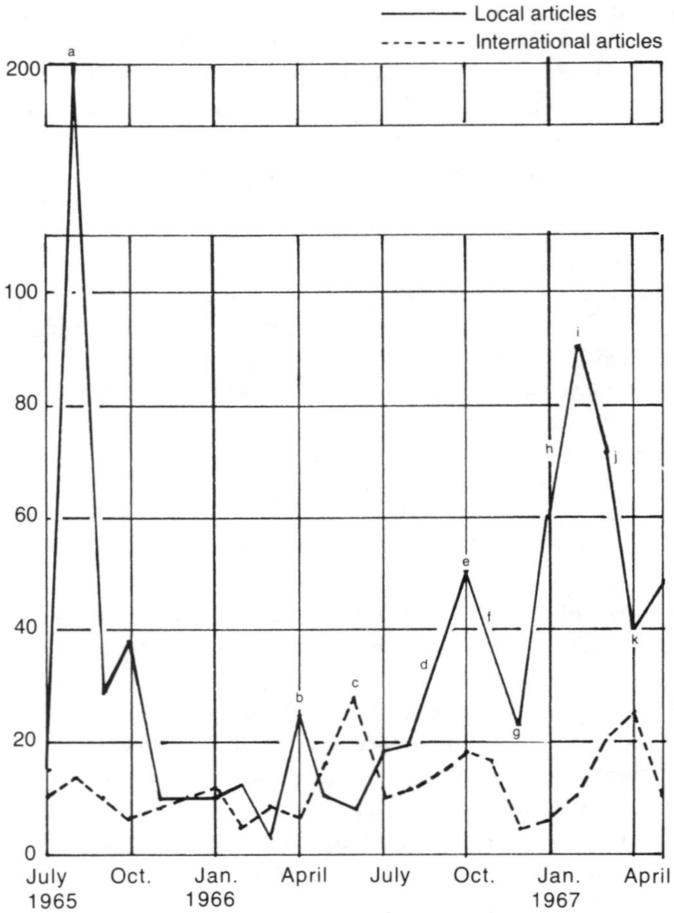

Notes:
(a) Pan-American Assembly Conference.
(b) Bishop of Cali attacks.
(c) Papal Commission.
(d) National Academy of Medicine *pro*, Cardinal Concha *con*.
(e) Population program established in ASCOFAME.
(f) Population Reference Bureau established.
(g) Lleras Restrepo signs world leaders' statement.
(h) *El Catolicismo* attacks.
(i) Senate debate.
(j) Cardinal and archbishop of Medellin attack.
(k) Provincial courses on family planning announced.

Source: Stycos, p. 148, figure 2.

Table 3
Editorials and Features of Five Colombian Newspapers, August 1965-April 1967

	Editorials		Features		
Newspaper	**Fav.**	**Unfav.**	**Fav.**	**Unfav.**	**Total**
El Tiempo	20	1	20	10	51
El Espectador	13	0	10	9	32
El Siglo	0	7	7	10	24
Occidente	5	7	9	17	38
La República	0	1	8	10	19

Source: Stycos, p. 151.

ANAPO challenge helped inspire the Frente Social, it could also have inspired the specific inclusion of population policy.

A major objective of the Frente Social was to correct regional disequilibria, i.e., to pull backward regions up to levels of development enjoyed by the advanced regions. It was generally those backward regions which offered support to the Conservative party side of the National Front government. The Frente Social also concentrated a good deal of its moral resources and AID's external financial assistance in promoting the development of secondary cities where the Conservative party enjoys somewhat more political support than it does in the four largest cities. No explicit statements were made concerning the desirability of limiting or damping the growth of Bogotá, but that certainly would be the effect of a concerted effort to improve conditions in secondary cities. The intermediate-cities strategy, one plank in the population policy platform, would yield a future urban pattern with fewer voters in the places that voted against the National Front and particularly against the Conservative party. The urban and regional development policy of the last National Front government was consistent with the political interests of the Conservative party.

It is not so obvious that adoption of an antinatalist policy (as part of a population policy) was equally in the interest of the Conservative party or of the National Front. Such a policy would have no immediate effect on numbers of voters. Moreover, the centrist Liberals, from the time of the Lleras Camargo Cali speech in 1965, accepted the necessity of reducing the rate of population growth.

The intensity of public reaction to Lleras Camargo's speech is indicated in the accompanying Figure 1. It shows the monthly number of newspaper articles published on population and family planning between 1965 and 1967. The notes indicate some key events which energized the press at the time. Pro-Liberal newspaper opinion as expressed on editorial pages was strongly favorable to population policy and family planning (see Table 3). Virtually all the editorials of *El Tiempo* and *El Espectador*, the leading Liberal dailies were favorable. In contrast *El Siglo*, which normally represents the views of the Gómez wing of the Conservative party, was unfavorable toward population and family planning. During that formative period for population policy, the role of leadership exercised by Alberto Lleras Camargo must have been central in bringing about the formulation of a policy. He was certainly influential with the opinion leaders who in turn operated the major newspapers.

Once the subject of population was fully addressed the *médicos* and *técnicos* played important roles in defending their opinions. Stycos argues that the Senate debate of early 1967 provided a signal opportunity for the proponents of a population policy. They were ready with sophisticated and compelling arguments (facts and figures, as the saying goes) to refute those who wished to maintain a pronatalist public policy. As Stycos observes:

> Even the nation's President felt compelled to speak out, and in February 1967 he told the conference of bishops that there was no foreign compulsion in the family planning program, and that it is the inalienable right of parents to decide the number of their children. That the net effect of the verbal storm was in favor of family planning is also seen from the conclusions of the congressional inquiry, which were finally made public in October 1969. They amounted to a resounding vote of confidence in the family planning program and supported "the conduct which the government has assumed in this important matter," expressing the hope "that the respective plans increase as a first procedure to better the conditions of Colombian society."[36]

The centrist Liberals may simply have believed that a population policy was a necessary element in the drive to achieve various goals of economic and social development. The Conservatives, on the other hand, did not appear equally convinced in the 1965-67 period. However, by the time the Pastrana Borrero government came to power in 1970, the Conservative leadership was prepared to keep population policy as part of national development planning. In this regard the work of the medical and technical specialists may have been of paramount importance. Among other things, the technical group was able to assist in neutralizing Catholic church opposition to population policy and family planning.

The Catholic church is not opposed to responsible parenthood or small families; official opposition has centered on the use of mechanical and chemical devices to limit fertility. Thus a basis could be found for obviating church opposition; that work was facilitated by the efforts of Dr. Germán Bravo of DNP who held seminars with the hierarchy of the Catholic church for many months in 1969 and 1970 to find grounds for a government population policy that the hierarchy would not openly oppose. The National Population Council, which included representation of the Episcopate, then offered a forum in which the government could determine the nature and extent of church opinion (adverse or otherwise) and hence could offer a public declaration that would not arouse church ire. The church supported the National Front (particularly the Conservative party within the Front); it did not wish to break with the government on this issue. Moreover, the population policy emphasizes the right and duty of each family to decide for itself the number of children which it can successfully bear and raise, thus deemphasizing any social duty of the state to control overall fertility.[37]

Surely religious leaders were an important element suggesting caution to the policy-makers. But on the other side—and more powerful with the policy-makers than was the church hierarchy—was the international donor community: AID, the Inter-American Development Bank (IDB) and the World Bank. IDB had and has virtually no interest in the population question. AID has vigorously pressed for fertility-reducing population policies since the Johnson administration; not surprisingly, the World Bank position on population matters developed under a Johnson lieutenant, Robert McNamara. The first overt sign that population growth mattered to the World Bank came in McNamara's speech to the Joint Bank/Fund Meeting in 1968. AID and the World Bank have been major sources of financial support to Colombia since the 1950s. Policy-makers could not turn a deaf ear to the stated concerns of those agencies.

The national government *cum* institution was caught in a dilemma between two major supranational forces: the Roman church which opposed mechanical birth control, and the international donor agencies which offer family planning services, i.e., the mechanical and chemical devices opposed by the church. The policy-makers thus had no easy choice. Since the two forces balanced each other the policy-makers have been led to do what they are supposed to do anyway: come to a decision based on an assessment of what is best for Colombia and Colombians. In the long run that decision may also have been to the advantage of the policy-makers as well.

CONCLUSION

Can one say with any assurance that the Colombian population policy owed its existence to the National Front? Categorical statements of conditionals do not admit of proof. The statement, "If there had not been a National Front government, then there would not have been a population policy," is an empirical statement that cannot be verified or rejected. At best one can offer circumstantial evidence to support such a statement. Such circumstantial evidence includes the following:

1. No other South American country has adopted an antinatalist policy; Colombia was the only nation in the area with a coalition regime during the studied time period.
2. Prior to the Front, the radicalization of the Colombian parties endemically involved religious issues; the spirit of compromise that prevailed among the two parties during the Front was consonant with the discrete population policy that was followed, while inhibiting the articulation of extremist positions within the ruling group, the ecclesiastical hierarchy included.
3. The Front possibly facilitated the impact of the international donor community on two grounds: (1) as a civilian "democratic" regime replacing an authoritarian one the Front was consonant with the manifest political objectives of the Alliance for Progress, Colombia becoming an attractive recipient of aid; (2) the limited interparty competition prescribed by the Front facilitated the receptiveness of Colombians to international, "nonpartisan," technical initiatives.
4. The only other Hispanic nation to adopt a population policy is the Dominican Republic; it shares with Colombia considerable dependence on the international donor agencies, and hence could also have been subjected to external pressures to formulate a policy.
5. The openness of the National Front system, as compared to some military regimes in other Latin American countries, permitted a continuous flow of people and ideas between major national institutions—universities, private research organizations, and government planning entities. Without that flow of people and ideas, population policy might not have been successfully conceptualized as a Colombian policy and therefore might have been rejected by the politicians.
6. The alternation of technical personnel between government service and private research institutions that characterized the Front's technological development gave government officials the opportunity to step back from the details of shortterm planning to consider the long run implications of rapid population growth; alternation was a key feature of the National Front that may have delivered many unexpected benefits.
7. Social scientists who worked on questions of migration, rural development, urbanization, and employment easily made the shift of concern from population distribution to population growth inasmuch as the variables are intimately interrelated; the institutional structure (DNP, the universities, ASCOFAME) encouraged the rapid communication of research results to policy-makers.

None of these points in itself proves that matters would have proceeded very differently under another system of government. Together, however, they do tend to support the view that the formulation of population policy in Colombia owes much to the sixteen-year National Front.

NOTES

1. Guillermo E. Perry, (1974) "Introducción al estudio de los planes de desarrollo en Colombia," *Lecturas sobre desarrollo económico colombiano* (Bogotá, 1974), p. 287.
2. Perry, p. 289, footnote 33, my translation. The reports referred to are: Comité Nacional de Planeación (1958); the study headed by Lebret, World Bank (1950); Currie, 1965, first published earlier; Consejo Nacional de Política Económica y

Planeación (1962); Departamento Nacional de Planeación (1969); Organización Internacional de Trabajo (1970); and Departamento Nacional de Planeación (1972).

3. It would not be possible to cite all the important works during these years. Thanks to Dr. Guillermo López Escobar, some major citations can be listed. Several works done at the Centro de Estudios sobre Desarrollo Económico (CEDE) of the Universidad de los Andes may be mentioned: *Análisis de la encuesta de fecun-didad de CELADE, Informe preliminar*, 1968, included some commentary by Francisco Ortega, an outstanding economic demographer, on data requirements for a population policy; R. Albert Berry's *Breve estudio de los determinantes de crecimiento de la población*, 1965, presented data on the correlates of fertility and migration that improved understanding of population dynamics; projections of population by Enrique Pérez Sanín offered a picture of future population problems. Studies by the Asociación Colombiana de Facultades de Medicina (ASCOFAME) began in 1965 to detail some aspects of the problems of rapid population growth. Dr. López Escobar also calls attention to Sam Schulman's *An Analytical Technique for the Determination of Population Pressure in Latin America*, a pamphlet published in Bogotá, which I have not seen. The work of the Comité Universitario de Investigaciones sobre Población (CUIP) at the Universidad del Valle del Cauca, was important during that epoch.
4. Departamento Nacional de Planeación, "La población en Colombia: diagnóstico y política," *Revista de Planeación y Desarrollo* 1 (December): 19-82.
5. Ibid. pp. 3-18.
6. William Paul McGreevey, "Urban Growth in Colombia" *Journal of Interamerican Studies and World Affairs* 16 (November 1974): 387-408.
7. William Paul McGreevey, "Causas de la migración interna en Colombia." In *Empleo y desempleo en Colombia* (Bogotá).
8. Departamento Nacional de Planeación, "Plan de desarrollo económico y social 1970-1973," mimeo, Bogotá, 1970.
9. I am indebted to Dr. Ramiro Cardona for some background on the *comisiones volantes* for which he was in part responsible during his tenure as Jefe, Unidad de Desarrollo Regional y Urbano, DNP.
10. Andrew Collver, *Birth Rates In Latin America* (Berkeley, 1965), p. 90.
11. Eduardo E. Arriaga, *New Life Tables for Latin American Populations in the Nineteenth and Twentieth Centuries* (Berkeley, 1968), p. 2.
12. United Nations Economic Commission for Latin America, "Some Aspects of Population Growth in Colombia," mimeo (Santiago, Chile, 1962), p. 6.
13. Alvaro López Toro, *Análisis demográfico de los censos colombianos: 1951 y 1964* (Bogotá, 1968), p. 65.
14. Henry C. Elkins, "Cambio de fecundidad en Colombia," Rodolfo Heredia B. and Elena Prada S., ed., *La fecundidad en Colombia: Encuesta Nacional de Fecundidad* (1973), p. 32.
15. In a personal communication from Dr. Guillermo López Escobar, 1975.
16. Germán A. Bravo, "Population Policy Determinants in Colombia," mimeo (Chapel Hill, North Carolina, 1974), p. 18.
17. Dorothy Nortman, "Population and Family Planning Programs: A Fact Book," *Reports on Population/Family Planning* 2 (New York 1973).
18. *New York Times*, March 17, 1974, p. 4.
19. Nortman, p. 57.
20. Asociación Colombiana de Estudios de Población (ACEP), quoted in AID Population Project, (Colombia, 1974), p. 21.

21. Alan B. Simmons and Ramiro Cardona, *Family Planning in Colombia* (Ottawa, Canada, 1973).
22. Elkins, p. 39.
23. World Bank, "Economic Growth of Colombia: Problems and Prospects," (mimeo). Special Study No. 1. (Washington, 1970), Table 3.
24. Agency for International Development (AID), Office of Population, *Population Program Assistance* (Washington, 1974), pp. 264-66.
25. Nortman, p. 45.
26. Mayone J. Stycos, *Ideology, Faith and Family Planning in Latin America: Studies in Public and Private Opinion on Fertility Control* (New York, 1971), p. 67.
27. Juan B. Londoño, "A Cost Effect Analysis of a Family Planning Program in El Salvador," *Studies in Family Planning* (1973).
28. Dr. Londoño is not himself a medical doctor but rather was trained as an economist. However, much of his professional work has been in the field of population economics closely associated with medical professionals.
29. World Bank, *The Basis of a Development Program for Colombia* (Baltimore, 1950), p. 358.
30. Alan Gilbert, *La concentración industrial y su impacto sobre el crecimiento de las ciudades colombianas* (Bogotá, 1973), p. 10.
31. Lauchlin L. Currie, *Operación Colombia* (Barranquilla, 1965).
32. Elkins, p. 31.
33. I am indebted to Dr. Guillermo López Escobar for background information on the role of medical specialists in this critical stage of providing policy advice to presidential hopefuls.
34. This vision of the importance of *técnicos* and their circulation among public and private institutions may be biased by the fact that these are the people I personally know best in Colombia. The role of the medical profession may be just as significant in this respect, but I am not familiar with it. Either way, this phenomenon of circulation among institutions would seem to deserve careful study.
35. Kenneth F. Johnson, "Political Radicalism in Colombia: Electoral Dynamics of 1962 and 1964," *Journal of Inter-American Studies* 7 (January 1975):15-26.
36. Stycos, p. 154.
37. Departamento Nacional de Planeación, *Las cuatro estrategias* (Bogotá, 1972), pp. 195-197.

Part IV
Conclusions

Chapter 15

Notes Toward an Interpretation of the National Front

R. Albert Berry
Mauricio Solaún

The preceding chapters of this book have probed various aspects of Colombia's evolution during the National Front years. Inevitably, some important problems and trends have not been dealt with. Notwithstanding these shortcomings, we attempt here a summary picture based on the previous essays, on what we have learned from discussions with the contributing colleagues, and on our own, at times, conjectural interpretations of the sixteen-year period and its meaning for Colombia's development. For more detailed expositions of specific issues and defense of specific propositions, the reader is referred to the earlier chapters.

Strictly speaking, the Front was a political phenomenon: the superimposition of a coalition constitutional structure onto the traditional, pre-Violencia presidential regime. An elite-dominated, bipartisan "hegemonic" regime replaced the traditional system of elite-dominated party hegemonies.[1] The Front was formally hegemonic in that the constitution limited political competition for office to the two traditional parties, establishing the rule that the presidency alternate every four years between these two parties and that governmental offices be shared exclusively and equally between them. Interparty competition for the control of government had led to La Violencia and political breakdown. Each of the parties had supported different constitutional structures. The Frente proposed to solve the first problem by guaranteeing an equal division of the state between the two historical rivals. Dissension over the constitutional system was solved in the preamble of the new constitutional order wherein both parties agreed to recognize the Roman Catholic Church as the official religion "in order to guarantee national unity" and to abrogate all post-1947 Conservative-inspired constitutional innovations. Most of the obviously special features of the Front period (relative either to other periods of Colombian history or to other countries without presidential coalition regimes) lie in the realm of political development. Naturally, many of the developments or trends in economic and social structures were partially or perhaps wholly independent of the existence of a coalition regime; this chapter is particularly concerned with the ones that were affected by it.

In the eyes of its proponents from the civilian elite, the National Front was a transitory political arrangement which they hoped would bring political stability to Colombia under restored civilian control. More than an agreement over approaches to modernization, the Front was a formula to minimize mass mobilization along traditional partisan lines, that is, interparty competition for power. The civilian elite had ruled Colombia for almost all of the twentieth century and had served itself well enough. By mid-century, however, the extreme competition between Conservatives and Liberals for control of the government had led to the Violencia, and the party system was no longer capable of maintaining order. With support from the parties, General Rojas Pinilla, the head of the armed forces, took power in a 1953 coup d'état. Though military rule did serve the purpose of bringing the violence increasingly under control, Rojas soon manifested political ambitions which challenged the civilian elite. He tried to organize a Third Force (a political movement separate from the traditional parties and their largely upper-class elites) in the guise of a populist authoritarian regime à la Perón, and he attempted to build the army into a durable personal political base. By the mid-1950s, the role of the military was growing, and its political orientations appeared to be increasingly to the left of the civilian elite. This plus General Rojas's manipulations to remain personally in power, and the residues of *violencia* with its associated chaos were threats to the traditionally powerful groups in the society. The dangers paved the way for an agreement between the two old parties in the form of the National Front arrangement. Many of the influential members of both parties felt that a form of truce with a sharing of power and benefits was the best option open to them.

Less tangible than a military, middle- and lower-class-based antiparty regime had been the threat of social revolution. Outbursts of class conflict had dotted 20th-century Colombian history (for instance, the strikes of the banana workers in 1928, land invasions of the 1930s), and Gaitán's forceful reentrance on the political stage in the mid-1940s introduced the class element more saliently into Colombian politics. Nevertheless, the lack of a strong direct instrument of lower class interests in the political system (e.g., a working-class party) was notable. Gaitán had posed a challenge from within one of the traditional parties; that challenge died with him. Rojas also dueled with the civilian elite from the left, and represented a threat both as a military man and as a middle-class "populist." As Colombia urbanized rapidly, education spread and the pressures for lower class organization were reasserted; reasonable foresight suggested that further challenges would emerge from the popular sectors in the future. Although not a formal oligarchy or timocracy, the National Front regime structure promised to protect the civilian elite from this threat too, as it constrained all voting competition into the multiclass framework of the two traditional parties that had been dominated by the elite. The continued absence of well-established institutions to elect the party leadership competitively assured oligarchic dominance within the parties.

In synthesis, the political stability sought by the founders of the Front was synonymous with protecting the central role of the civilian party elites in the management of Colombia's destinies.[2] This presumed a return to the closely constrained role of the military in Colombian politics. The founders sought to move toward a system within which the Liberals and Conservatives could share in the benefits from governing, and thus limit the violence-prone party competition. By sharing and alternating the various offices of the regime, it presumed such management of the polity and the economy as would avoid damaging confrontations or even loss of power to groups whose interests would differ substantially from those of the elite. The interparty consensus required to maintain the coalition system assured middle-of-the-Colombian-road policies. Stability also implied the need for continued support from the lower classes or, better, the weakness of active organized hostility from counterelite led masses. Of course, for many, the coalition regime meant the continued strength of a very traditional, hierarchical, and rigid social structure, the continued political control of old leaders and traditional vested interests, the continued strength of conservative-controlled institutions such as the Catholic church, etc.

In the view of many of the elite, for the National Front to be successful, considerable economic growth was necessary to create more jobs and higher incomes, and to permit better education, health, and other social services. The promised land toward which it was hoped the National Front would point Colombia was thus one in which: (1) Liberals and Conservatives could coexist peacefully with minimum competition, the total fruits of government would be large, and the military would have no excuse to interpose themselves on the political process; (2) the military would not constitute a strong and independent politicized power that would threaten continued two-party or civilian rule; (3) any threat from emergent civilian counterelites would be overcome, since the fairly traditional and modest aspirations of the lower class could be satisfied from the expanding economic base and neutralized through "minor" programs whose costs would not dislocate the class structure; (4) the continuation of traditional party identification and loyalties would be sufficient to enable the combined party elites to overcome emergent forces in elections. It is against this picture that the National Front must be partly evaluated.

The Front was designed to smooth hostilities and to set in motion a process of working together between the two traditional parties. In this respect the success was considerable, even though tensions did not entirely vanish. One basic problem was partly traceable to the very broad coalition aspect of the system, which spilled over from the regime, (i.e., the formation and maintenance of coalition governments) to include the sphere of party politics. Specifically, the tendency was to select an "official" presidential candidate, identified with the party entitled to the office but supported by both parties. This implied both intra- and interparty agreements. Since there was no solid tradition of party primary elections and legitimized single party conventions, and there was a tradition of party factionalism, the process of selecting the candidate was cumbersome. Ultimately, the "official" candidate was selected by the extralegal, informal ruling body of the Front—a bipartisan "inner club" dominated by some expresidents and national party leaders, who were themselves "viable" presidential aspirants, a group that clustered around the parties' national newspapers and that we could call the Informal Council of the National Front. Indeed, oligarchic political modes of domination continued to prevail during the National Front and were reinforced by the relative impotence of convention politics up to 1974.

However, the selection process of the candidate was full of uncertainties (e.g., the coup-prone crises surrounding the Lleras Restrepo candidacy), and the best man or the aspirant with greatest party support was not necessarily selected (e.g., Valencia and Pastrana, respectively). Throughout the Frente, party factions or interparty coalitions sought to employ the electoral road to dismantle the constitutional coalition regime itself. Therefore, an aura of crisis often presided over candidate selection, reflecting the danger that factionalism would prevail and the antiregime candidate win, as was nearly the case in 1970. (There were allegations of an anti-Rojas Pinilla electoral fraud in this unusual four candidate race.) In short, instability was brought about by (1) the excessively broad scope of the coalition (e.g., the felt need for an "official" bipartisan presidential candidate); (2) the absence of formal-legal or other well-established mechanisms to assure a popular, oligarchical or bureaucratic selection of the coalition candidate, the second mode de facto prevailing but not without challenges; (3) the existence of antiregime forces that were not entirely electorally outlawed or repressed. The implicit illegalities of some modes of opposition (e.g., the 1962 Liberal dissident challenge to the Conservative right to occupy the presidency) coupled with attacks on the constitutional structure helped to create recurrent states of perceived "normlessness." They also contributed toward concern that the Informal Council would not prevail and the government structure would collapse.

Interparty (and interfaction) suspicions did not disappear entirely and their existence inhibited the development of policies that threatened to strengthen one party (or faction) at the expense of others. Coalition maintenance in government limited the capacity of the government to mobilize the population. The bipartisan nature of the Front required that any such efforts be "apolitical" but the transitory nature of the regime prompted the question—which party will benefit most from any expansive major mobilization. This was partly the case when the Lleras Restrepo administration tried to organize the peasantry into associations of government credit recipients or *usuarios*. Under government auspices, other "apolitical" grass roots organizations were formed, such as the Acción Comunal (community development associations). Both types of organizations were to become controversial because of their links with political forces other than the two traditional parties. Government-sponsored organizations had to be nonpartisan, yet they tended to become politicized. In order to avoid this, the government opted for "bureaucratizing" some of them, transforming the grassroots organizations into quasi-public legal entities which could be more readily controlled.[3] Thus, during the Front, grassroot organizations formed independently of the elites, and especially of the government, continued to be weak. In contrast to some periods of the past (e.g., the Liberal government sponsored unionization of the 1930s and 1940s), Frente governments were for obvious reasons less prone to mobilize new groups. Nevertheless, as in the past, governments monitored and partially repressed grassroot organizational development, lest anti-system organizations grow beyond "acceptable" boundaries.

There were other problems. Initiation and sustained implementation of *major* social reforms, those perceived to alter significantly the institution of private property (e.g., the agrarian and urban reform statutes and bills), required the top level interparty support of the Informal Council. This was evidenced by the relatively greater success of the former; in the absence of Council backing, the latter was not even enacted. The required support guaranteed that only relatively mild reforms would be enacted, for the top party leadership continued to express (toned-down) ideological differences—Conservatives remained relatively more conservative.[4] The constraints that the consociational regime structure posed on reform were also present in Congress. Prior to the 1968 constitutional changes, the requirement of a two-thirds majority to enact legislation gave veto power to any minority. The Front seemed to increase traditional congressional ineffectiveness by further factionalizing it.[5] The initial rule that each party was entitled to half the parliamentary seats encouraged factionalism; the autonomy and multiplicity of *regional* party factions with multiple lists of candidates led to a Congress that represented local factions; the weakness of party discipline in a polity with low partisan mobilization further contributed to factionalism. Recurrently Congress appeared to be a "veto" organ that had to be prompted to legislate by the "aggregating" action of the top elite. The low level of traditional party activism appeared to weaken the two-party system and promote periodic perceptions of increased social class unrest.

Overall, however, available evidence indicates that interparty relations were substantially smoothed during the Front. Overt interparty hostility almost disappeared, as did the traditional accusations that one or the other political party had appropriated (or fused with) the regime structure or offices. Although the moderating impact of the recentness of the escalated violence and the existence of the coalition regime itself complicate an adequate evaluation, it is widely felt that Colombia is now too civilized politically to revert to the character of the Violencia period. The church's retreat from political partisanship, a trend reinforced by post-Vatican II foreign ecumenical developments, strengthens the hopes for continued interparty peace.[6] So do, perhaps, the increases in education and urbanization that have been experienced. Most significant are the facts that the National Front survived the planned period, that a more limited coalition institution remained in effect at the cabinet level beyond the sixteen year period, and that the first post-Front election transpired roughly along the lines originally conceived by its framers. Changes from Conservative-led to Liberal-led administrations and vice versa during the Front were not associated with violence, and violence did not appear in the 1974 free interparty presidential contest. These events encourage the belief that certain chronic historical problems have been overcome. The smoothness of the 1974 election suggests that the maintenance of some, although limited, coalition institutions in the regime might be a fruitful future option rather than a full return to the traditional regime. In this respect, Colombian institution builders may wish to study Western European democratic consociational experiences. It is surprising how isolated the Frente Nacional experiment was from somewhat comparable foreign experiments, as evidenced by the lack of comparative analysis on the subject.

Although Liberal-Conservative relations were softened by the coalition, serious electoral and military challenges appeared during these years, so the passage was not entirely smooth. There was, not surprisingly, considerable disaffection with the Front, but is hard to judge how close it was to premature demise, and even harder to judge what changes would have occurred had one of the challenges been successful. Nor is the nature of the popular disaffection fully clear. The Rojas vote of 1970 may be presumed to reflect several attitudes: a preference for a substantial swing to the left, resentment against the technocratic oriented reforms of the Lleras Restrepo administration, and/or a general unhappiness with "oligarchical" rule, but not necessarily with civilian rule. Rojista strength, however, does not appear to have gone beyond the status of a substantial minority group incapable of predominating among the intelligentsia and middle classes. The large electoral abstention experienced during the Front could reflect many things; perhaps the majority of those most estranged from the Frente participated the least.

In any case, in terms of past Colombian electoral and civil rights history, the National Front cannot be considered to have been unduly restrictive; it was a liberalizing departure from post-1949 developments. In the past the basic political dilemma involved the alternatives of high competitive participation with *violencia* or peace with low participation.[7] Under the traditional system, the out-party only intermittently challenged the in-party in elections. During the Frente, electoral challenges to the regime were constant; little violence was associated with them, presumably because they could not be and were not made by an entire out-party. The Front commanded the bipartisan support of the majority of the professional politicians; it never experienced the disruptive and destructive dissent of the Violencia period.

Central to the question of the coalition regime's effects on socioeconomic development are some of the structural and dynamic characteristics of the system as they affected the articulation and implementation of public policies. This chapter has noted the limiting impact on political mobilization, the impossibility of making drastic socioeconomic structural changes under the consociational regime structure, and the need for interparty agreements at the top leadership level for any major structural change. This was particularly the case for major changes requiring legislation from a factionalized Congress.

Congress was the realm of the politician—*el país político*.[8] It had a high turnover of personnel and a low task (e.g., legislative) orientation and tradition. The latter was dramatically evident during its heyday of power early in La Violencia, when convulsive "parliamentary" activities (the delivery of radical populistic speeches, etc.) prevailed. The decentralized nature of congressional selection, evidenced by the multiplicity of regional lists of candidates and the practice of "automatic inclusion" of the winners to form loose confederations of politically successful middle-level elites, provided this body with a significant measure of autonomy from both the national party leadership and the president himself. Hence, the difficulties of mobilizing congressional action for reform should not be underemphasized, especially when the vested interests of these provincial elites are also taken into account.

There is nothing unusual in conservative tendencies having strength in a parliament. On the other hand, although interparty ideological differences were diluted during the National Front, there remained significant differences among the major national factions. As voiced by their organs—roughly, the Bogotá newspapers—Conservative *El Siglo* consistently favored the role of private enterprise in development, while Liberal *El Espectador* was more favorable to an active governmental role in redistributing wealth and "social" development. Conservative *La República* and Liberal *El Tiempo* usually followed positions between these two poles. Thus the Front meandered about the middle-left in the symbolic realm, between "capitalistic" formal positions (e.g., Brazil) and "socialistic" ones (e.g., Peru), never pretending to adopt any extreme solution.

Beyond this, resources, in terms of property, income, and access to higher education, continued to be highly concentrated, placing the popular sectors in a situation of dependency. During the Frente, working class organizations remained incapable of sustaining a strong bargaining position vis-à-vis the government. As in the early stages of La Violencia, albeit with less militancy on both sides, there were strikes with political revolutionary implications (e.g., the call for a general strike in late 1964 related to the Ruiz Novoa military challenge)[9] and other "political" strikes with less dramatic implications. However, social unrest was ultimately quelled by a compliant military, the executive very often employing extraordinary constitutional powers: the state of siege.

The two pivotal political institutions of the National Front were the Informal Council and the chief executive, who had virtually dictatorial formal-legal powers.[10] These collaborated to produce the periodic rotation of the presidency and the distribution of the top executive positions between the two parties and to prevail against anti-Frente forces. The concentration of powerful political resources held by the Informal Council—e.g., the control of the national press and of the mechanisms to appoint the "official" presidential candidate—and of legal resources controlled by the president, provided the basic integrative mechanism of the system.[11] This mechanism was in turn generally supported or accepted by the largest plurality of pro-Frente politicians and by the majority of the *active* electorate.

The preceding comments do not mean to imply that there was no "reformism" among the politicians during the Front. There were "internal" and "external" reform elements in the regime. National party factions supportive of the regime exemplify the former, while those (and their coalitions) seeking the termination of the coalition regime illustrate the latter. The Frente was besieged by recurrent feelings among the middle and upper classes that there was social class alienation—by perceptions that the regime would collapse. These feelings were, of course, reinforced by the spotty signs of working class, military, and guerrilla unrest, as well as by the antiregime electoral activities of politicians, some of which were important enough to have a measure of credibility. There was no *strong* political or social revolutionary movement really organized for violent regime overthrow, and the antiregime politicians were correspondingly reluctant to go beyond verbal revolutionary threats. Nevertheless, the problems of regime support that lingered from the past (although now with a lesser magnitude in the coalition context of low overall mobilization) had an effect on the *país político*.

In a polity subject to these recurrent problems of regime support, rhetorical reformism had a place. Periodic interparty agreements on reformist platforms could be expected to materialize in order to neutralize the opposition, and in fact, reformist development programs tended to be periodically agreed upon by the interparty coalitions supporting the "official" presidential candidates. It often appeared that the elite itself was articulating socioeconomic reformist programs that had not been articulated or demanded by any social group, for the feelings of discontent were sensed by and centered among the elites and middle classes themselves, and the recurrent social alienation was relatively diffuse. For instance, no single major social force demanded or actively supported an agrarian reform in Colombia, which was proposed (in the initial National Front administration) and widely discussed in the press. As in the past, although with much less virulence and momentum, opposition groups adopted a vague "ideological" approach which stigmatized the ruling groups with the label of "collective immorality" and challenged the regime, without emphasizing their demands for the adoption of specific reform policies. In this context, naturally, it was difficult to make compromises, and reformist policies were less likely to be adopted. Nevertheless, the reformist rhetoric that permeated "officialist" sectors of the *país político* during the Front did serve as a mechanism of adaptation and system-maintenance; for it guided the initiatives of the ruling political group, producing an air of responsiveness while not excessively threatening any key social group.

Intraparty factionalism of pro-Frente groups also contributed to the espousal of socioeconomic reforms. Some national factions seeking identity, legitimacy and support emphasized programs involving a variety of reforms. Even some members of the "inner club" wanted to modernize the society. And some of the younger members of government circles (at times technicians seeking political prominence, perhaps to become viable future presidential candidates), desired to claim credit for reforms made while they were holding a cabinet post or other important administrative position. However, efforts from within the government were limited by: (1) the constraints placed on the political mobilization of social groups (particularly the lower classes) in support of their actions; (2) intrabureaucratic and factional rivalries; (3) the rudimentary character of most reform techniques (e.g., inadequate liaisons with congress and/or interest groups); (4) the search, at times, for political status or notoriety over and above a viable project; and (5) the need for Informal Council backing proportional to the impact of the reform on the vested interests themselves. Ultimately, successful reforms had to be of a limited nature, at least approved by the "center" of the political spectrum, and had to contend with interest group activities, which had proliferated in Colombia since the 1930s as state intervention increased.

These groups tended to respond only to those reform issues that affected their sectoral interest. With the exception of occasional intervention in support of the regime itself and of effective government policies when there were increasing feelings of alienation from government and the traditional party leadership (e.g., the mid-Valencia administration), these groups did not behave as a single, unified power block. Usually, their stance included recognition of the need for some type of reform, together with a demand for a major role in its formulation and implementation. Naturally, they placed emphasis on the importance of the private sector (e.g., profit making) in carrying out Colombia's modernization; they often presented specific counter-proposals for reform; and they engaged in publicity campaigns and in lobbying with the administration and Congress to protect their interest. Of course, upper class interest groups were better organized and staffed than lower class ones.

The outlined limits to reforms—defined on the one hand by the need to maintain a coalition government and on the other by the felt need to promise some changes to maintain a claim to popular support—in a situation in which there was factionalism and real competition with the opposition was not explicitly foreclosed,[12] define the structure for the National Front's liberal rhetoric, a rhetoric which went well beyond actual accomplishments. This is not to say that no reforms were enacted. For instance, prompted by the Alliance for Progress which roughly coincided with the Front, the bulk of the "inner club" was successfully mobilized into obtaining non-cash compensation agrarian reform legislation from Congress. Midway during the Frente there was the strong technocratic oriented Lleras Restrepo administration that successfully pressured Congress for constitutional-administrative changes deemed necessary to modernize and strengthen the regime and the executive branch. Lleras Restrepo also raised tax collections and modified the system regulating the foreign sector, foreign direct private investment included.[13] Under his administration an effort was made to sponsor the development of peasant class organizations partly tied to the Agrarian Reform. The limited scope of the latter policy[14] underscores the difficulties encountered by any major redistributive public measures—those perceived to worsen the income or economic resources of a sector to directly benefit others. As in the past under López Pumarejo—the Liberal reformer (1934-38 and 1942-45), reform implementation was divisive during the National Front, ultimately weakening the ruling group itself. López's innovations, mainly in labor relations, had led to an increased social mobilization of the urban working class along traditional party lines, and ultimately had divided the Liberal party and opened the door to a Conservative regime in 1946. Under Lleras Restrepo, partisanship and mobilization were much lower, due to the National Front constraints, but reform was almost followed by the dismantling of the regime via a Rojista electoral victory in 1970. Implementation of reforms without significantly challenging the existing regime—i.e., the constitutional structure—remained very difficult. These challenges cannot be treated lightly as leading to an evolutionary "democratization" of the system; this was not the result in the 1940s, and in the 1950s Rojas had been an authoritarian ruler. In the more recent case, the less disruptive nature of changes carried out without substantial mobilization and under a bipartisan protective banner suggests that the Front's limiting consociational institutions acted as a buffer.

Other important dimensions of policy-making should be noted. Within the discussed boundaries, presidents in Colombia had a degree of autonomy in the selection of high level administrative personnel and could carry out some policies more or less independently of party and congressional control. These patterns were less clear in the first two administrations of the Front. Under Lleras Camargo, the problem of factionalism was solved by staffing the cabinet partly in response to congressional electoral results; Valencia followed the less responsive policy of an "automatic" equal division of the cabinet among existing pro-Frente national factions, regardless of electoral outcomes. (There was some tendency to factionalism in the party not holding the presidency, in anticipation of the selection of the next "official" presidential candidate. Ultimately, national factionalism reflected the presidential aspirations of viable candidates).[15] However, despite this tendency to reflect the power alignments of factions in the cabinet, National Front presidents often recurred to emergency powers to regulate the economy, thus bypassing Congress. Further, the latter often gave the executive broad statutory authority to legislate in various important areas. In many ways Congress, the regime's epitome of the *país político*, was a weak and ineffective formal organization during this period. And the courts were fairly consistent in backing executive action in major policy decisions.

Along with, and often complementary to, the president's power, the executive branch had a relatively autonomous sphere of administrative-bureaucratic decision-making. This allowed the technocrats to maximize their contribution, since major political agreements were not required as long as central institutions such as private property were not challenged. For instance, during the last administration of the Front, the executive branch reorganized the financial system to establish protection for savings and investments in the construction sector. Although this implied for *future* borrowers the periodic upward adjustment of the mortgage payments of part of the middle class, and also a preferential channeling of funds into the construction sector, Congress was not consulted. Soon after its initiation, the new UPAC (Unidad de Poder

Adquisitivo Constante) system created by the executive was capturing a substantial flow of funds. In another area, the foreign-backed birth control policies, carried out bureaucratically and outside the political limelight, were fairly uncontroversial and successful.[16] There was surely an element of selectivity about the reform channels that were employed. To the extent that the issues and policies were placed in the political arena by the reformists *themselves*, they were more likely to be contested. Needless to say, the nature of the policies carried with them risks and limitations, as indicated by the agrarian reform.

It was via the executive-bureaucratic level of the polity that what could be called the Alliance for Progress "syndrome,"—involving international technocratic input (and in many instances financing) from public foreign, national and multinational agencies—had its greatest impact. These agencies generally tended to support what were, in the early Front years, quite incipient technocratic trends in Colombia, and to promote "precautionary" modernizing policies to avoid social revolution under the "reform or revolution" banner. Agrarian reform, tax reform, changes in the regulation of foreign direct private investment, and other redistribution policies fall in this latter category. Reformism in Colombia was perhaps especially linked to U.S. government foreign policy.[17] The impact of the foreign agencies in orienting economic and social policy appears to have been substantial, particularly during the early years of the Front when there was still a great scarcity of Colombian social scientists capable of articulating development policy, and the economy suffered from chronic foreign exchange shortages. Yet not all administrations were equally responsive to or capable of implementing the foreign technocratic inputs. Agencies with available resources like the World Bank were particularly capable of inducing governments to follow what *they* considered to be priority investment patterns,[18] and priorities shifted.

Central planning itself received an impetus from the Alliance for Progress. Throughout Latin America, either planning ministries or special offices attached to the presidency were created in response to the conditions for aid established by the Alliance. The latter was the Colombian case. Some broad development plans elaborated by foreign missions became controversial within the *país político* (e.g., the Sears International Labor Office recommendations). However, to a considerable extent, the articulation and implementation of actual investment plans was bureaucratic and deliberately segregated from the political arena proper, where technical expertise was scarce. Despite a much propagandized need for government "planning," no major effort was made to establish a centralized system of overall planning. Reinforced by the multiplicity and specialized priorities of the foreign agencies, the Front witnessed the creation and strenthening of a system of "depoliticized," technocratically oriented, decentralized government agencies.

Although formally under presidential or ministry control, these "autonomous" agencies developed into a complex bureaucratic system difficult to control and coordinate. During the Front Colombia experienced a redistribution of power away from the traditional, largely regional-based political class toward an increasingly complex, differentiated and technologically-oriented national bureaucracy. This strengthening of the public sector received a major ideological and financial impetus from abroad.

It is difficult to assess the contribution of the existing coalition regime to these technocratic developments and their consequences. It is noteworthy that they were linked to a substantial increase in Colombia's foreign debt.[19] Surely, the anti-partisan climate of the coalition system favored them, and there were probably ideological implications to the Frente's existence. In contrast to the pre-1964 Brazilian experience, for instance, the issue of planning itself was not part of any rancorous public debate in Colombia. Apparently the coalition nature of the regime facilitated a workable intra-elite consensus on this issue. In addition, in the context of the coalition, governments adopted a technocratically-based "development ideology" that transcended the more traditional and conflictive ideological labels and stereotypes, such as the "left," "falangism," etc., so dysfunctional during La Violencia. Noting the different ideological impact of these Alliance for Progress inspired technocratic developments throughout Latin America (for instance, the results in Brazil as opposed to those in Colombia) it is apparent that the uses given to them depended significantly upon the political structure and dynamics of the receiving country. However, the often pretended ideological "neutrality" of the technocracy (its formulas for obtaining commonly accepted goals, such as "economic development," "social progress," etc.) was well suited to a coalition regime; these technologically-based slogans were widely used by the ruling coalition. Yet as we have noted, the technocratic developments produced some resentment among both vested economic interests and pro-regime politicians.

The growing technocratic presence in the national bureaucracy probably led to less personalistic modes of decision making. Increasingly, interest groups had to deal with government on a more technical basis. The technocrats' expertise in specific areas gives them a certain independence from pressure groups. It seems not implausible that the autonomy associated with technological professionalism could also serve in the long run or on the average to mitigate political conflict in the society. To the extent that technical arguments prevail in the political arena, conflict tends to center, not on ideology, but on specific optimum ways to implement what are increasingly seen as commonly desired values or goals. In sum, although it is too early to assess these developments in any quantitative way, it seems plausible to presume that a continued interdisciplinary technocratic impetus has a potential through its objective style for secularizing and modernizing the political culture. At least during the Front years technological inputs contributed to articulate the adaptive reformism that, in our opinion, reduced the overall level of conflict in the polity, thus leading to system-maintenance.[20]

These trends, however, were concentrated at the national bureaucratic level, not the legislative one, nor in the area of opposition politics. Grass roots political organizations remained weak. Municipal governments managed resources on a significant scale only in the cities, and there the councils probably reflected more clientelistic relationships than grass roots interests. Despite some (foreign reinforced) government interest in developing new grass roots, apolitical, participatory organizations for civic action and community development, such as Acción Comunal, they were unable to attain much in the way of resources or power. There were fears that they might develop into anti-Frente agencies.

THE NATIONAL FRONT AND SOCIOECONOMIC DEVELOPMENT

There is much interest in analyzing the degree to which the National Front contributed to the economic and social welfare of Colombians. It is reasonable to assume that welfare depends on the character of the society and the income levels, which are in turn reflected in people's satisfaction with the political system. The Front period witnessed a measure of economic and social change away from traditional modes toward more modern ones. The economy grew in real per capita terms; the weight of industry and services in the economy rose markedly. Urbanization proceeded apace, with the three largest cities growing at an average annual rate of 6.5 percent and the share of population residing in urban areas (centers of 1,500 people or more) rising from 32-33 to 44 percent; the urban economy came to outweigh the rural one. Export diversification helped to make the economy less vulnerable to world market fluctuations and to overcome what appeared to be chronically permanent balance of payments deficits.[21] The occupational structure evolved so that the share of the labor force in relatively prestigious white collar occupations rose, and female participation in the labor force grew rapidly. Income levels rose for both rich and poor, as nearly as can be judged. Educational levels rose notably, and life expectancy lengthened. Attitudes toward the society appeared to be modernizing; the extremely rigid class attitudes eroded somewhat, and a generation with little experience of the Violencia gradually emerged.

Though Front governments had to place initial priority on problems of interparty relations,[22] by the 1960s traditional party policy-makers were becoming more conscious of poverty and maldistribution of income as possible sources of social conflict. The increasingly urban character of poverty doubtless helped to make it more visible and threatening. Moreover, the rhetoric of distribution had become the worldwide fashion by the 1960s.

However, despite serious consideration of the distributional impact of public policy by a few National Front policy-makers, no articulated overall strategy was launched. The actual impact of public policy on distribution was largely unplanned, and distribution was probably about as bad in 1974 as in 1958, improving under some governments and worsening under others, especially during years of accelerated economic growth. Concern with the problem was mounting, but the combined hurdles of political constraints on redistribution posed by the coalition system of government and the need for high quality analysis to correctly predict how various policies would affect the poor had still to be conquered. Economic policy had thus not contributed to such long-run political stability as might have been encouraged by a more equal distribution of income. The consociational regime only led to economic progress within the existing and quite unequal structure of distribution.

This is not to say that public policy did nothing for the poor but rather that, as expected from our political analysis, the combined impact of the pattern of public policy and of economic growth was to leave distribution roughly unchanged. Lower income groups did benefit from a broadening of primary education, especially in rural areas; the less needy middle income groups were helped by public housing, educational expansion in cities, the expansion of social security, and other measures. Were dissatisfaction of lower income groups related mainly to absolute income levels, it might have been expected to fall during the Front years.To the extent that relative income (vis-à-vis other groups) and rising expectations played important roles, the opposite might have been true.

Policy areas discussed earlier in this volume exemplify the varied nature of public action and of its distributional impact. Agrarian reform ultimately ran aground on the natural opposition of the threatened interests; the only politically feasible general programs focused on colonization of public lands, land titling of already occupied land, irrigation projects and the like.[23] Although the rural population was blessed with a further reduction of violence during the Front and with expanded educational facilities, the four administrations together made only a dent in the problems of rural poverty. When the *Usuarios campesino* organizations threatened to get out of hand in the early 1970s, the government responded vigorously to maintain the status quo.[24]

Industrial policy, while less often and less easily judged in terms of its social impact than is agrarian reform or agricultural policy in general, may have been one of the least socially oriented.[25] Various policy tools such as foreign exchange and import controls, credit rationing, and direct public sector involvement in industry through IFI (the government's industrial investment bank) contributed to a capital intensive sector which created little employment, especially of lower skilled workers, while eating up large amounts of scarce capital and creating significant differences in wage levels. Most urban employment was created in the service sector, where public policy was less directly involved, and thus had less effect on the way labor and capital were combined and on the relative success of different types of firms.

Educational policy had mixed effects on distribution, but one aspect of it—rapid expansion of primary schooling—was an undoubted plus. Overall, the old patterns of different access for the rich and the poor, rural and urban, etc. were only modestly altered; the government continued to subsidize disproportionately the higher social classes via its expenditures on the higher levels of education.[26] Indeed, in some areas (such as education and public housing) the Front continued the traditional pattern of state support for relatively well-off groups. Under the guise of alleviating the welfare problems of the needy, scarce government resources were employed for the benefit of what were in fact economically privileged middle- and working-class groups.

One area where clear-cut progress was made was that of population policy. From a potentially politically explosive issue in the pre-Frente theocratic context of partisanship, it became an area in which Colombia moved ahead of many developing countries.[27] While the macro effects of population policy (e.g., on the rate of growth of income per capita) may not have been earth shaking to date, in the long run, they will presumably raise the incomes of poorer persons by making labor scarcer. At the same time the direct benefits to many women have probably already been substantial.

The interests of lower income groups may be represented by interest groups such as labor organizations and peasant leagues and/or by one or more political parties; in a system such as Colombia's, with no party representing mainly the interests of such groups, the government may take account of their concerns in light of their voting power and any threat of hostile action they may make. Neither the role of unions (not discussed in the preceding essays) nor their membership appears to have experienced any major expansion during the Front period. Membership continued to consist mainly of the better-off workers. Prior to the breakdown of the traditional regime in 1949 with the emergence of party dictatorship, unions were closely linked to the traditional party system and its conflicts. In the absence of any strong working class party the labor movement had divided into two poles. At one end was the CTC, a secular, marxist-influenced organization; at the other end was the Catholic UTC, founded as a counterweight to the CTC and the character of its influence on workers. Although the CTC and the Liberal governments clashed on occasion during the 1930s and 1940s, the CTC was expanded with government support, as part of the political and reformist strategy of the ruling Liberal elite.[28] The CTC provided support for the second López administration during an aborted military rebellion, and during the early Violencia, it was an active instrument in the Liberal attempts to impede the consolidation of a Conservative regime. However, the political weaknesses of a small movement in a relatively unindustrialized society became apparent with the collapse of pro-Liberal revolutionary labor and the failure of its solidarity and general strikes during the Gaitanista period. Under Conservative government sponsorship, the UTC ultimately surpassed the CTC in membership.

The Frente did witness a progressive differentiation between labor and the traditional party system, as well as periodic labor activism. Ironically, it was the UTC in particular which became involved in political initiatives: it provided support to General Ruiz Novoa's protocoup activities and also attempted unsuccessfully to form a new political party. The differentiation between labor and the traditional parties was a response to the search for interparty balance and consociational regime maintenance. Governments sought to avoid any active linkage that would mobilize labor, lest a severe disequilibrium materialize between the two labor forces and affect interparty balance. Occasional labor-management conflicts, although involving less violence than during the early Violencia, did escalate to the point of being defined and suppressed by the government as "subversive." In other words, the propensity to politicize labor activities persisted; some of these activities continued to be part of a syndrome of attacks against the regime itself. With the large income gains experienced by members,[29] however, it is not surprising that union activities were largely concentrated on preventing the erosion of their favored position within the labor market and on pushing for a higher share of income vis-à-vis capital. All of this occurred within a system in which government often intervened—a system of bargaining with "political involvement," as opposed to pure collective bargaining—in the settlement of labor contracts. Labor was too weak economically to sustain long strikes prior to new contracts, and the unions were threatened by high levels of unemployment. Surely, these facts, coupled with the recurrent legitimacy problems facing governments and the regime itself, continued to favor a certain amount of courting of labor by government in the form of intervention in the labor market, not to expand labor organization (as earlier) but to "adapt-neutralize" a force that was needed for system-maintenance.

Peasant organization presented some similar issues and dilemmas. In contrast to the urban-based labor, however, the peasantry had not been organized along class lines by either of the traditional parties prior to the Front; their political allegiances continued to be based on party identification and clientelism, mediated by the local elites. Nevertheless, from the early 1930s through La Violencia, some Marxist territorial enclaves developed, and the 1950s witnessed substantial *bandolerismo*. The National Front experienced the development of foreign-induced, Castro-inspired revolutionary guerrillas and the continuation of substantial rural *bandolerismo*. Some efforts were made to organize peasant leagues, the activities of the Catholic FANAL, a spinoff of the UTC, being noteworthy. Although most of Colombia's rural population seems still to be conservative in attitude, land invasions and unrest increased during the National Front. During the Lleras Restrepo administration, some impetus was given by government to peasant organization in conjunction with the agrarian reform, the *usuarios*—government credit users—movement in particular. As with labor, some peasant organizations came under the leadership of radical factions (e.g., the ANUC in 1970) that encouraged the occupation of privately owned lands and other direct "revolutionary" changes. Government repression succeeded in containing such "subversive" developments; no strong rural-based revolutionary movement materialized, since peasant class organization was still in a formative stage. However, the gradual radicalization of part of the agricultural labor force may occur in any case, if, as is suggested by partial and preliminary results from the 1973 population census, the share of the labor force who are farmers has decreased, and the share who are employees has increased correspondingly. If the number of employees on relatively large farms rose substantially, the costs and difficulties of further organization would be much lower.

CHALLENGES TO THE NATIONAL FRONT

The more credible challenges to the National Front were not posed by working class or peasant unrest, the student movement, or the small middle class-student led bands of social revolutionaries. They came, rather, from within the regime itself, from the military and anti-Front electoral coalitions of varying scope. One diagnosis prevalent during the Frente years claimed that the political problems were created by the destitute masses. Actually, however, the dynamics for system stress and regime change came from the middle and even upper class (e.g., López Michelsen's MRL). Within the ruling elite, a measure of stress and dynamics for change was also provided to the system by: (1) party factions that did not oppose the coalition per se, but whose desire to prevail in the selection of the coalition presidential candidate made them willing to oppose the government and withdraw support from the ruling coalition, despite the risk that anti-coalition regime forces would prevail; (2) the articulation and implementation of reform policies by the elite under the guise of making social justice and/or preventing a social upheaval; these policies had a foreign component, had not been articulated by the beneficiaries themselves, and created a recurrent malaise among wealthy elite sectors; and (3) the temporary nature of the National Front and lack of clarity as to the ultimate constitutional formula that would succeed it.

Thus during the Front there was a variable but chronic crisis of legitimacy involving the basic constitutional structure of the regime. This was not entirely new in Colombian history,[30] nor was the associated "crisis of participation" that characterized the Front—the abrupt fluctuatons in electoral participation[31] that were interpreted by many as evidence of lack of support for the constitutional system or the form of government.

Colombian twentieth-century history had been characterized by civilian elite political control, notwithstanding sporadic rumors of military unrest and even aborted rebellions. The Violencia did bring a brief period of military rule that ended, not without civil-military friction, in the initiation of the National Front. Mediating intervention in interparty violence by "third" forces was not without precedent (e.g., the Reyes post-Mil Días civil war regime that moved to create a more professional-bureaucratic army). But such antiparty political initiatives were ultimately incapable of substituting a personal dictatorship for oligarchical, civilian party system rule, as evidenced by the short duration of the military-bureaucracy based regime of Rojas Pinilla.

Still, the evolution of the military-civilian relationship during the Front was by no means without incident. The position of the military remained salient enough through the period to make its relations with the civilian government a matter of continuing interest and delicacy. Every Front administration experienced not only rumors of imminent coups d'état but also potential or actually sensitive removals of military personnel by the executive. Meanwhile, the Colombian military experienced a substantial U.S.-supported expansion under new professional orientations which emphasized counterinsurgency priorities rather than conventional warfare. The increase in material resources that was associated with this modernization of the Armed Forces[32] should be viewed as contributing to military satisfaction and compliance with the regime. On the other hand, the change from conventional warfare to the emphasis on counter-insurgency has been seen as favoring politicization and interventionism. As the armed forces shifted their attention from external enemies to internal ones, they tended to become preoccupied with the socio-economic problems that underlie internal revolt. This development culminated in 1965 when the Joint Chiefs of Staff removed the Minister of Defense, General Ruiz Novoa, amidst a rapidly crystallizing coup situation. Military discipline and compliance ultimately prevailed. The Armed Forces subsequently shifted toward a more conservative, anti-communist orientation and away from the coup-prone social reformism. The move away from politicization was justified by the military in terms of maintaining the integrity of their "professionalism." Similarly, in other sensitive conflicts over military leadership during the National Front the professional ethos served to legitimize military compliance and discipline.[33]

The National Front experiences contribute interesting evidence toward a theory of military intervention. Any attempt to predict a coup and the emergence of a military regime must take into account several general factors known to have had such effects.[34] Their specification and evaluation must be placed in the historical context of the concrete society; the society's past coup propensity also is an important conditioner; the availability of a proven mechanism to change the executive reduces the likelihood that a coup will occur. Coups d'état are probable when: (1) interclass conflict escalates—the basic economic and social interests of the better off citizens (and their foreign allies) are threatened by hegemony-seeking governments or other groups likely to gain power; (2) there are threats to the military corporate interests; (3) there is escalated civilian violence; (4) under economic crises, especially when accompanied by social unrest; (5) presidential *continuismo*; (6) electoral fraud. During the National Front neither of the first two conditions was present; guerrillas never achieved a sustained revolutionary impetus since civilian violence was relatively under control; no major economic or social crises occurred, there was economic growth without extraordinarily high inflation rates; there was no presidential *continuismo*, the coalition seeing to it that the executive was changed periodically through electoral mechanisms; while in one instance (1970) there was suspicion of an electoral fraud, the victimized group had only plurality support in the election.

This possible electoral manipulation was not only "minor" in terms of the share of votes miscounted, but was probably viewed as *protecting* military corporate interest, as defined by the military hierarchy. General Rojas had been ousted in 1957 by the military leadership, and a lingering resentment and distrust prevailed in his group. The relationship between ANAPO and low ranking ex-military personnel was disquieting to the military elite, who feared changes in personnel or even purges upon an ANAPO victory. The delicate position of the military elite was reinforced by the recentness of intramilitary conflicts about Rojas' *continuismo* and the dismantling of the military regime in 1957.

In sum, although foreign-induced military developments during the Front may have increased the long run potential for independent military intervention and action, no military regime materialized because the factors that usually trigger coups d'état in Latin America were absent or neutralized. In the Colombian historical situation the less risky policy of a well-fed military was nonintervention.

The most developed challenge to the National Front regime was posed by Rojas Pinilla's Alianza Nacional Popular, ANAPO.[35] Front governments, as opposed to the regime itself, had been subjected to the vagaries of factionalism. These were at times destabilizing in that they seemed to jeopardize the broad coalition nature of the regime, i.e., they appeared to run counter to expected party behavior within what was a broadly defined bipartisan consociational framework. But these patterns never constituted a full-blown opposition even to the existing governments. The regime itself—i.e., the consociational constitutional-political structure—was also attacked by single traditional party factions. This was the case of the Movimiento Revolucionario Liberal, MRL—the López Michelsen Liberal faction. To some extent, the MRL was an unsuccessful reincarnation of the traditional Liberal leftist dissidence; it had some similarities with Gaitán's movement. The MRL sought a majority-rule regime in a country where Conservatives had been an electoral minority at least since the mid-1940s. It thus appealed to traditional Liberal "hegemonic" sentiments surely present in the rural periphery. In addition, as in the past, there were marxist elements in this leftist faction; it appealed to some of the lower classes and had a measure of success among members of the nonclerical-oriented intelligentsia, as well as among students and the less traditional urban segments. It was not a social revolutionary movement—it did not seek to destroy any social class nor did it eschew the electoral road in favour of revolutionary violence. Moreover, it was led by ex-President López's son, himself a member in full standing in Bogota's society circles. Like other Latin American "revolutionary" (notice the second word in the MRL title) reformist opposition parties, however, its anti-regime platform projected an image of a certain illegality or lack of due process, thus making it disproportionately threatening to vested interests. Because these antiregime parties appear capable of unilaterally altering the constitutional structure, they seem to demand more than changes in personnel and policy; there is an ambiguous *political* revolutionary dimension to them that spills a bit into the social realm. Hence, they are not "reformist" in the sense applicable to the phenomenon in stable democracies. In any case, by the mid-1960s ANAPO had surpassed the MRL in electoral support, and the latter returned to the Liberal party fold by participating in the Lleras Restrepo administration.

There were, of course, a number of similarities between ANAPO and the MRL, including their anti-regime character. However, in contrast to the latter, ANAPO grew as an interparty coalition of factions (although Conservatives predominated), was led by an expresident, and had ramifications in the armed forces. These characteristics added strength to it. ANAPO signaled a substantial departure from the norms of Colombia's traditional politics in other ways too. For one thing, it broke the tradition of *civilian* party leadership that had usually been oligarchical in the past.[36] ANAPO crystallized around General Rojas and his family, a middle-class family with life-styles conspicuously different from those of Bogotá's upper class. Around them materialized a heterogeneous entourage involving military related individuals; Catholic-influenced proto-Falangist, corporatist ideologues; marginal, maverick Liberals, a few with socialistic or marxist background and ideology; and marginal elites seeking fuller access to the material and status rewards of power. Second, the mainstay of its orientation was the "*mi General*" symbol. There was a Bonapartist element in ANAPO—a general directly representing the people—that post-French Revolution "democratic" authoritarianism that revived Caesarism. In Colombia this symbolism included a messianic populistic and anarchic element by which victory implied the immediate improvement of lower class living standards through such things as lower prices of food, better housing, etc. As is not uncommon for out of power groups, there was little or no discussion of how such objectives were to be reached. This helped to make ANAPO's "reformism" appear anti-technocratic and its economic management questionable. Possibly there was a Poujadist-like lower-middle-class appeal in the movement.

While populistic economic symbolism was not an innovation, ANAPO's middle-class Bonapartism was outside Colombia's civilian aristocratic tradition and closer to the militaristic authoritarian traditions of other Latin American polities. There were, however, elements in its appeal that were consonant with Colombian tradition, such as the moralistic radical message characteristic of earlier Colombian populist movements.[37] While ANAPO was a "reformist" movement—it sought vaguely defined social institutional changes with a bearing on the class structure—it also catered to some traditional forces, e.g., its stance against the agrarian reform. It appeared to have an element of provincial traditionalism against the centers of metropolitan power, capable in Wallace-like fashion of appealing to some politicians at the margin of the Front's bureaucratic "developmentalist" modernization. In the absence of survey data and multivariate analysis all these interpretations must remain impressionistic. Available evidence suggests, however, that ANAPO's voting support was strongest among (1) urban dwellers; (2) lower-middle to lower class segments; (3) the young; (4) nonidentifiers with the traditional parties and previous electoral abstainers; (5) provincial Conservative strongholds; and (6) groups with a highly religious orientation.

Most striking about ANAPO was its electoral collapse after its controversial possible plurality showing in 1970 and its formal transformation into a third party in 1971. Essentially the movement waned as the health of General Rojas deteriorated. Other factors probably playing a role in the demise of this "flash" protest party were: (1) the incapacity of the movement to obtain sufficient respectability via substantial intelligentsia and middle class support; (2) the termination of the broader coalition aspects of the Front, indicating a resumption of a greater measure of inter-traditional-party competition; (3) the accession to leadership of a woman in the context of a male-dominated society; (4) demoralizing beliefs that the ruling groups would not allow an ANAPO victory, the General having followed fairly adaptive policies vis-à-vis the alleged 1970 electoral fraud; (5) disappointment with ANAPO performance in local governments; (6) weakening of the anti-political "establishment" sentiments that Lleras Restrepo's technocratic reformism had aroused among the rich and the politicians.

What is of particular significance is that once again, despite the lull in traditional party partisanship during the Front, another third force had been defeated. ANAPO's substantial strength must be interpreted as evidence that the polity continued to have features inimical to the development of a stable political democracy. Albeit with new modalities, there remained wide segments in Colombia with a propensity toward (paraphrasing Comte) "metaphysical" politics, by which the political institutions of the regime itself, its symbols and basic constitutional formal-legal structure, were contested; there was not widespread consensus about a stable constitutional normative order *within* which discrete, although significant, political and socioeconomic reforms could be implemented. In sum, there remained a tendency toward a diffuse ideologizing of conflict and toward the pursuit through political channels of parareligious messianic-millenarian goals that were "ideologized," not "technologized."

This collection of essays has inquired into some of the ways by which the National Front affected Colombian history. Of particular interest are its possible contributions to the evolution toward a modern society, with high consumption levels, an egalitarian concept of class, adequate political participation, and reasonable standards of justice. The Front established a political-legal framework for evolutionary change with definite socioeconomic structural constraints. During the period, repressive extremism did not prevail in this remaining South American democracy. The Front was a welcomed departure from the violence and crude authoritarianism of the immediate past. Its quiet transformation into less elaborate and rigid forms of interparty cooperation geared to impede any future rancorous or violent polarization of Colombia's political forces boded well for the future. Economic progress under the Front was good, and was shared by most groups, although current (and still only partial) evidence suggests that some better off groups benefited more than proportionally, i.e. that income distribution worsened during the last two Front administrations. Certainly, substantial poverty remained as the Front ended, and there remained a number of political innovations that could be made within a democratic consociational regime framework to insure a greater and more just participation. It is up to the readers to match the discussed accomplishments and limitations with their own values and preferences. The editors would be satisfied if this book furthers the rational discussion of Colombia's political and socioeconomic problems and its alternatives for the future.

NOTES

In this chapter, following David Easton, the term regime usually signifies the basic governmental constitutional structure, its values and principles.

1. Chapter 1 discusses the nature of the traditional type of party hegemonies as a case of "protodemocratic" or partially democratic rule.
2. As noted by Kline in chapter 2, the Front elite vocalized the notion of the existence and responsibility of a ruling class (*clase dirigente*). Yet any open expression of extreme oligarchical views was absent. Examples of what the Colombian elite would consider extreme views are provided by John Stuart Mill: "the lot of the poor . . . should be regulated for them, not by them . . . It is the duty of the higher classes to think for them . . . The rich should be in *loco parentis* to the poor, guiding and restraining them like children"; John Stuart Mill, *Principles of Political Economy* (Boston, 1848), 2, pp. 319-20.
3. See the Bagley and Edel discussion in Chapter 9 which concludes that these measures reduced the dynamism and effectiveness of Acción Comunal.
4. See Mauricio Solaún, Fernando Cepeda, and Bruce Bagley, "Urban Reform in Colombia: The Impact of the 'Politics of Games' on Public Policy," in *Latin American Urban Research*, 3, Francine F. Rabinovitz and Felicity M. Trueblood, eds. (Beverly Hills, Calif. 1973), pp. 97-130.
5. The Colombian Congress had been characterized by a traditional weakness in the area of major legislative initiative and by frequent delegations of its legislative authority to the President. See Carlos Restrepo Piedrahita, *Las Facultades Extraordinarias, Pequeña Historia De Una Transfiguración* (Bogotá, 1973).
6. For a description of these developments see Wilde's discussion in chapter 7.
7. See Losada's comments in chapter 3.
8. See Hoskin's analysis in chapter 4.
9. For details, see Ruhl's historical description in chapter 6.
10. The president, with the support of his cabinet, can unilaterally declare a state of siege in cases of public disturbances. Under the state of siege, the executive assumes full legislative powers, including the right to suspend any prior legislation (article 121, 1968 constitutional codification). Judicial constitutional control of emergency decrees has consistently supported presidential authority, not addressing itself to the right of the president to legislate in the specific circumstances but to the substantive constitutionality of his decree-laws, standards that have been met in any executive action to maintain the "social fabric." While the president's authority to suspend legislation is limited to the emergency period, the noted congressional factionalism makes the executive legislation likely to prevail beyond this period. Article 122 assures that in the absence of an explicit congressional repeal, socioeconomic legislation by the executive will continue in full force after the emergency. See Jaime Vidal Perdomo, *Historia de la Reforma Constitucional de 1968 y Sus Alcances Jurídicos* (Bogotá, 1970) and Jaime Castro, *Orden Público Económico* (Bogotá, 1976).
11. It is possible to trace the roots of this system to some aspects of the colonial patrimonial bureaucratic system with the exception, of course, of the "sovereign" powers of the Informal Council, the executive rotation and other electoral features of the system, and the low legal corporatist profile.
12. As noted by Losada in this volume, in every presidential election the "official" bipartisanly supported Frente candidate was opposed by another candidate. Only the 1962 anti-Front candidacy of Liberal Alfonso López Michelsen was declared illegal; his votes were counted "void" because the constitution prescribed that a Conservative be president for the 1962-1966 term. The strongest anti-Front electoral challenge was posed by General Rojas' bipartisan supported 1970 candidacy. As confirmed by this experience, the continued implication that an opposition

victory would lead to a unilateral constitutional change by the winners—e.g., the dismantling of the Frente regime itself—contributed to perceptions that illegal methods might be used to prevent such a victory. Periodically, rumors circulated that electoral irregularities and even a preventive coup d'état might be employed to block an opposition victory. Yet an anti-Front electoral victory was not entirely foreclosed; there was ambiguity in the matter. We have noted in chapter 1 that this ambiguity is a general characteristic of protodemocracies.

13. A dramatic change during the Lleras Restrepo administration was the substantial modernization of Bogotá in the form of infrastructure building and urban growth; the basis for a megalopolis was established then.
14. For a discussion of the agrarian reform, see the Havens, Flinn, and Lastarría-Cornhill, and the Bagley and Edel contributions in this volume.
15. For an analysis of opposition patterns during the Front, see Dix's chapter in this volume.
16. See McGreevey's discussion in chapter 14.
17. The nationalistic provisions regulating foreign private direct investment show that not all the recommendations of foreign technical missions represented what the foreign private business community considered in their best interests. For the nature and origin of these regulations see Mauricio Solaún and Fernando Cepeda, "Political and Legal Challenges to Foreign Direct Private Investment in Colombia," *Journal of Inter-American Studies and World Affairs* 15 (1973): 77-101.
18. As noted by Cepeda and Mitchell in Chapter 8 the capacity of the foreign agencies to influence policy was not uniform; the wealthier agencies were more successful in the foreign exchange thirsty inflationary economy of the early years.
19. On January 1, 1958, Colombia's public external debt was U.S. 456 million; at the end of 1972 it was 2227 million (of which 1,490 million had been disbursed). At this latter date 1916 million were owed to US and international agencies. The above figures exclude debt instruments of less than one year's duration, and IMF drawings.
20. The reader familiar with the historical arguments in chapter 1 might note that we are suggesting for this post-Violencia period an adaptive function to the technocratic orientation that finds parallels in its effects to the post-Mil Días *cultura* orientation of refined self-restraint.
21. These developments are detailed in chapter 10.
22. As noted, during the early years, presidents were quite sensitive toward finding formulas for an adequate bipartisan representation in the cabinet, initially linking faction representation to electoral results. Increasingly, as the executive was strengthened, cabinet formation became less dependent on the vagaries of factional politics.
23. As of March 1969, only about 5,700 families had received, ceded, or expropriated land on which they had not previously been working. Most of the 75,000 families who received title to land which was previously owned by the government had previously been working on it. These two figures correspond to less than 0.5 percent and perhaps 6 percent respectively of all agricultural families in 1970. (See A. Berry, *The Development of the Agricultural Sector in Colombia*, forthcoming.)
24. As of 1972, when the Usuarios (ANUC) was split into the Armenia and Sincelejo groups, the latter (the radical wing) claimed 750-800 thousand active members. An observer put the estimate at 300,000, suggesting that 500,000 had dropped from the organization at the time of the split. Some government officials had much

lower estimates (see Chapter 9). In any case it is clear that its membership was large relative to the total farming population, and it was viewed as a threat by the Pastrana government.

25. See Thoumi's discussion in chapter 11.
26. Arnove analyzes these questions in chapter 13.
27. While it was only one of many factors, population policy did presumably contribute to the rapid decline in Colombian fertility since the early 1960s. A Bogotá survey revealed that in 1964 27.1 percent of women 20 to 50 years of age were practicing contraception and a 1974 survey showed that 50 percent were. The prevalence of contraception would be lower in smaller cities and in rural areas, but it probably increased considerably over these years. (See Joseph E. Potter, Myriam Ordóñez G. and Anthony R. Measham, "The Rapid Decline in Colombian Fertility," *Population and Development Review* 2 (Sept./Dec. 1976): 523-24.)
28. For a detailed discussion see Miguel Urrutia, *The Development of the Colombian Labor Movement* (New Haven, 1969).
29. During most of the Front years, at least up till about 1970 and especially during the 1960s, blue collar workers in industry saw their real wages rise significantly; for example, they rose by about 50 percent over 1958-70. (See Albert Berry and Miguel Urrutia, *Income Distribution in Colombia*, New Haven, Yale University Press, 1976, p. 91).
30. See the discussion in Chapter 1.
31. Losada analyzes this problem in this volume.
32. See the data and discussion in Ruhl's chapter.
33. Two polar interpretations about the role of "professionalism" characterize the literature on the military: (1) that it contributes to civilian rule; (2) that it promotes military regimes (especially, if professional training concentrates on counterinsurgency, as opposed to conventional warefare); Alfred Stepan, "The New Professionalism of Internal Warfare and Military Role Expansion," in Stepan (1973), pp. 47-65. The Colombian data show that regardless of the nature of the training, "professionalism" as a military ideology can serve to justify nonintervention, not government overthrow or a military regime. Up to the 1973 coup d'état a similar pattern prevailed in Chile. Quite simply, military coup activity is the result of complex forces. Witness the coup propensity present in Latin America prior to the emergence of this new professionalism of internal warfare.
34. For a catalogue of Latin American coup precipitants as they cluster to constitute various coup types see Solaún and Quinn (1973). We deal here only with those pertinent to our discussion.
35. See Dix's treatment of ANAPO in his chapter in this volume.
36. One can find exceptions to this pattern—e.g., Gaitán's brief period of domination (1947-48) in the Liberal party. Gaitán rebelled against a party leadership that had previously appointed him a cabinet post member and mayor of Bogotá.
37. See the discussion in chapter 1.

Contributors

Robert F. Arnove is Associate Professor of Comparative and International Education at Indiana University, Bloomington. He was educational advisor to the Ford Foundation in Bogotá, Colombia between 1969 and 1972. He has written extensively on the role of education and development in Latin America. His books include: *Student Alienation: A Venezuelan Study; Educational Television: A Policy Critique and Guide for Developing Countries*; and the forthcoming *Philanthropy and Cultural Imperialism*. Professor Arnove received his Ph.D. from Stanford University in 1969.

Bruce Bagley is Assistant Professor of Latin American Studies at the School of Advanced International Studies of Johns Hopkins University in Washington, D.C. From 1973 to 1975, Bagley was a Foreign Area Dissertation Fellow in Colombia. From 1975 to 1977, he was a Visiting Professor of Political Science in the Departamento de Ciencias Políticas of the Universidad de Los Andes in Bogotá, Colombia. He is presently working on a book titled *Political Power and Public Policy in Colombia: Case Studies of the Urban and Agrarian Reforms during the Frente Nacional, 1958-1974*.

R. Albert Berry is a Professor of Political Economy at the University of Toronto. Berry is a graduate of the University of Western Ontario (B.A., Economics, 1959) and Princeton University (Ph. D., 1963). He was a member of the Economic Growth Center and the economics department of Yale University, 1962-72. He has also been program advisor in economics for the Ford Foundation in Bogotá, 1968-69, and Economic Advisor to the Colombian Planning Commission, 1971-73. During 1974-75, Berry served as Economist for the Rural and Employment Division in the Development Economics Department of the World Bank. He is the coauthor with Miguel Urrutia of *Income Distribution in Colombia* and author of articles and reviews on various economic issues, especially topics related to the Colombian economy.

Robert H. Dix is Professor of Political Science at Rice University, where he has taught for the past ten years. He has a Ph.D from Harvard University and previously taught at Yale University. From 1957 to 1960, he served in the U.S. Foreign Service, assigned to the embassy in Bogotá, Colombia. Dix is the author of *Colombia: The Political Dimensions of Change* (Yale University Press, 1967), and is a contributor to *Regimes and Oppositions*, edited by Robert A. Dahl (Yale University Press, 1973).

Matthew Edel is Associate Professor of Urban Studies at Queens College, City University of New York. He received his doctorate in economics from Yale University, and previously taught at MIT. Edel held a Foreign Area Fellowship in Colombia from 1966 to 1967, teaching at the Universidad Javeriana in Bogotá as Fulbright-Hays Lecturer in 1974. He is the author of *Food Supply and Inflation in Latin America* (Praeger, 1969) and *Economics and the Environment* (Prentice Hall, 1973).

William L. Flinn is Professor of Sociology and Associate Chairman of Agricultural Economics and Rural Sociology at Ohio State University. He worked in Colombia with the Land Tenure Center of the University of Wisconsin in the 1960s and 1970s. He was Fulbright Lecturer at the Faculty of Sociology at National University in Bogotá in 1964. He is author and coauthor of a number of articles and books on Colombia, including *Internal Colonialism and Structural Change in Colombia and Metodología y desarrollo en las Ciencias Sociales: Efectos del Crecimiento dependiente sobre la estructura social Colombiana*.

A. Eugene Havens is Professor of Rural Sociology at the University of Wisconsin-Madison. He was a Visiting Professor at Catholic University in Lima, Peru and a consultant with the Ford Foundation from 1976-77. His experience in Colombia dates from the early 1960s when he was a Fulbright Lecturer at the Faculty of Sociology at National University in Bogotá. He was Director of the Land Tenure Center office in Bogotá from 1962 to 1964 and Director of the University of Wisconsin Ford Foundation Rural Modernization Project in Colombia from 1970 to 1972. He is the author and coauthor of many articles and books on Colombia which include: *Internal Colonialism and Structural Change in Colombia; Támesis: Estructura y Cambio; Ceretè: un Area de Latifundio;* and *Barrancabermeja*.

Ronald G. Hellman is Director of Public Affairs at the Center for Inter-American Relations and General Editor of *Latin American International Affairs*. From 1970 to 1972, he was a Visiting Professor at the Institute of Political Science at the Catholic University of Chile. He also served in 1971 as a Social Science Consultant to the Ford Foundation office in Santiago de Chile and held a National Institute of Mental Health fellowship during his graduate studies in political science at New York University. He was a staff member of the Commission on United States-Latin American Relations (Linowitz Commission) and is coeditor of *Latin America: The Search for a New International Role* (Sage-Halsted, 1975) and *Terms of Conflict: Ideology in Latin American Politics* (ISHI Press, 1977).

Gary Hoskin received his Ph. D from the Unviersity of Illinois, Champaign-Urbana, in 1967. From 1973 to 1975 he served as Visiting Professor of Political Science at Los Andes University in Bogotá, Colombia. He has written numerous articles on Colombian and Venezuelan politics. Hoskin's research on the Colombian legislature in 1968-70 was sponsored by a grant from the Rockefeller Foundation, and in 1973-74, by a grant from Colciencias. In 1974, Hoskin worked with Fernando Cepeda in a project related to Colombian parties and elections under the Collaborative Research Training Grant of the Foreign Area Fellowship Program.

Harvey Kline is a graduate of the University of North Carolina (B.A., 1966) and the University of Texas (Ph.D., 1970). From 1968-70 he served as Professor of Political Science at the University of Los Andes, Bogotá. He is the author of many articles, both in Spanish and English, on the problems of the Colombian National Front, as well as coauthor of *El Comportamiento Legislativo en Colombia*. Kline is currently Associate Professor of Political Science at the University of Massachusetts, Amherst.

Susana Lastarría-Cornhill received her M.A. in Sociology from the University of Wisconsin-Madison, where she currently is a doctoral candidate for the Ph.D. in Development. She has also studied at St. Louis University and taught at the Catholic University in Lima, Peru.

Rodrigo Losada is a native Colombian from Bogotá. He has been a professor at the University of Los Andes and is currently a full-time researcher for FEDESARROLLO (Foundation for Higher Education and Development), Bogotá. Losada has been involved in research on the nature of the Colombian electorate. His doctoral work at Georgetown University dealt with this subject, and was supported by a Ford Foundation scholarship for dissertation research. He is the author of several articles on Colombian politics.

William Paul McGreevey whose Ph.D thesis (MIT, 1964) was on the "Economic Development of Colombia," has been Director of Battelle Memorial Institute's Population and Development Policy Program since 1977. McGreevey is the author of *An Economic History of Colombia, 1845-1930* (Cambridge University Press, 1971; Spanish edition, *Historia Económica de Colombia*, Bogotá, 1975), as well as articles on the urban growth of Colombia, the infrastructural development of Colombia (1835-1962), and the causes of Colombian internal migrations. He has also authored articles on Latin

American development and economic history, in addition to his ongoing studies on questions of population growth and distribution.

Christopher Mitchell is Associate Professor of Politics at New York University. He is a graduate of Harvard University (B.A., 1966; Ph.D, 1971). Mitchell has conducted research on Bolivian, Chilean, and Peruvian political parties and revolutionary mobilization under a Foreign Area Fellowship during 1968-69. From 1974-75, Mitchell spent eleven months in Colombia and the Dominican Republic researching the political role of United States economic aid. He is the author of *The Legacy of Populism in Bolivia* (Praeger, 1977), and of articles on U.S.-Latin American policy, and Latin American economic integration.

J. Mark Ruhl is Assistant Professor of Political Science and Coordinator of the Latin American Studies Program at Dickinson College in Carlisle, Pennsylvania. His research deals with the political consequences of modernization in Latin America. Recent articles by Ruhl have appeared in *Latin American Research Review, Inter-American Economic Affairs*, and in *Patterns of Civil-Military Relations in Latin America*—a collection edited by Jorge Heine. Ruhl received his Ph.D. from Syracuse University in 1975.

Mauricio Solaún was U.S. Ambassador to Nicaragua. He has a Ph.D. in Sociology from the University of Chicago, an M.A. in Economics from Yale University, and a Doctor of Law, Universidad de Villanueva (Cuba). Solaún has held several fellowships, including Fulbright-Hays and Foreign Area Fellowship Program awards, and has been a consultant for the United Nations Development Programme and several public and private organizations in Latin America. His main publications are *Sociología de los Golpes de Estado Latinoamericanos; Sinners and Heretics: The Politics of Military Intervention in Latin America* (with Michael Quinn), and *Discrimination Without Violence: Miscegenation and Racial Conflict in Latin America* (with Sidney Kronus). His current research is mostly concerned with the problems of political integration in the Third World, with an emphasis on the role of law.

Francisco E. Thoumi received his degrees from Universidad de Los Andes (Economista, 1964) and the University of Minnesota (Ph.D. 1973). He has worked at the National Planning Office of Colombia, the World Bank, the Universidad Nacional de Colombia and George Washington University. Thoumi is currently the head of the Social Studies Section of the Inter-American Development Bank. He is the author of various articles on Colombia's industrialization and international trade.

Fernando Cepeda Ulloa is former Vice-Rector of the Universidad de los Andes, Bogotá. A graduate of Colombia's Universidad Nacional, he founded the Department of Political Science at Universidad de los Andes, where he helped direct studies of Colombian electoral and Congressional behavior. He was recently codirector of an SSRC graduate training project, examining results of Colombia's 1974 election. Among previous publications is "Direct Private Foreign Investment in Colombia: A Socio-Political Perspective," co-authored with Mauricio Solaún.

Alexander Wilde is Research Associate of the Latin American Program, Woodrow Wilson International Center for Scholars, Washington, D.C. His research in Colombia in 1968-69, 1972, and 1974, resulted in two forthcoming books, *Politics and the Church in Colombia* (Duke University Press), and *Conversaciones de caballeros: quiebra de la democracia oligárquica en Colombia* (Universidad de los Andes). He also has written more broadly on the Latin American church for *Commonweal, Christianity and Crisis*, and other magazines.

Index